MANAGEMENT

MANAGEMENT

ELEVENTH CANADIAN EDITION

STEPHEN P. ROBBINS
SAN DIEGO STATE UNIVERSITY

MARY COULTER
MISSOURI STATE UNIVERSITY

ED LEACH
DALHOUSIE UNIVERSITY

MARY KILFOIL
DALHOUSIE UNIVERSITY

PEARSON

Toronto

Editor-in-Chief: Claudine O'Donnell
Acquisitions Editor: Carolin Sweig
Marketing Manager: Jessica Saso
Program Manager: Karen Townsend
Project Manager: Jessica Hellen
Developmental Editor: Suzanne Schaan
Media Editor: Nicole Mellow
Media Producer: Kelli Cadet
Production Services: Cenveo® Publisher Services
Permissions Project Manager: Joanne Tang
Photo Permissions Research: Krystyna Borgen, PMG
Text Permissions Research: James Fortney, PMG
Cover and Interior Designer: Anthony Leung
Cover Image: Ken Redding/Corbis images

10 9 8 7 6 5 4 3 2 1 [CKV]

Library and Archives Canada Cataloguing in Publication

Robbins, Stephen P., 1943-, author
      Management / Stephen P. Robbins, San Diego State University,
Mary Coulter, Missouri State University, Ed Leach, Dalhousie University,
Mary Kilfoil, Dalhousie University.—Eleventh Canadian edition.

Revision of: Management / Stephen P. Robbins ... [et al.].—10th
      Canadian ed.—Toronto : Pearson, [2011], ©2012.
Includes bibliographical references and index.
ISBN 978-0-13-335727-1 (bound)

      1. Management–Textbooks. 2. Management—Canada—Textbooks.
I. Coulter, Mary, author II. Leach, Ed (Professor of management), author
III. Kilfoil, Mary, 1956-, author IV. Title.

HD31.R5647 2015   658.4   C2014-904803-3

ISBN 978-0-13-335727-1

Contents

PART ONE
Defining the Manager's Terrain

CHAPTER 1
Introduction to Management and Organizations **1**

CHAPTER 2
Organizational Culture and the Organizational Environment **35**

CHAPTER 3
Managing in a Global Environment **62**

PART TWO
Planning

CHAPTER 7
Decision Making **162**

CHAPTER 8
Foundations of Planning 188

CHAPTER 9
Managing Strategically 207

Module 2: Planning and Control Techniques 233

PART THREE
Organizing

CHAPTER 10
Organizational Design 249

CHAPTER 11
Managers and Communication **275**

CHAPTER 12
Managing Human Resources **302**

PART FOUR
Leading

Chapter 13
Leadership **332**

CHAPTER 14
Motivating Employees **359**

CHAPTER 15
Managing Groups and Teams **387**

PART FIVE

Controlling

Chapter 16
Managerial Controls: Evidence-Based Decision Making **412**

Preface

This course and this book are about management and managers. Managers are the one thing that all organizations—no matter the size, kind, or location—need. And there's no doubt that the world that managers face has changed, is changing, and will continue to change. The dynamic nature of today's organizations means both rewards and challenges for the individuals who will be managing those organizations. Management is a dynamic subject, and a textbook on it should reflect those changes to help prepare you to manage under the current conditions. Thus, we've written this eleventh Canadian edition of *Management* to provide you with the best possible understanding of what it means to be a manager confronting change.

General Content and Approach

The underlying philosophy of our textbook is that "Management Is for Everyone." Students who are not managers, or do not envision themselves as managers, do not always understand why studying management is important or relevant. We use examples from a variety of settings and provide several different end-of-chapter applications, such as *Learning to Be a Manager*, to help you understand the relevance of studying management for your day-to-day life. We have once again expanded the discussion of ethics and social responsibility to reflect the commitment of today's students to making the world a better place.

We have broadened the discussion of adaptability across all chapters—the need for managers to continuously scan for new opportunities and then act strategically to take advantage of them. Design thinking is an emerging and important trend in management that is also considered.

In this edition, we have continued to make enhancements that add to both learning and instruction:

- The chapter on change and innovation (previously Chapter 13) has been moved to Part One: Defining the Manager's Terrain and retitled "Innovation and Adaptability" to reflect its new focus on actual innovation rather than change management.

- Two chapters have been turned into briefer modules with fewer features. The previous Chapter 9 has become Module 2, "Planning and Control Techniques" (following Chapter 9). The previous Chapter 18 has become Module 3, "Managing Operations" (following Chapter 16).

- A new *Datapoints* feature has been added in most chapters (Chapters 1, 2, 3, 5, 7, 8, 9, 10, 11, 12, 13, 14, 15).

- End-of-chapter elements have been streamlined, and each chapter now features two *Case Applications* with discussion questions, rather than only one.

- A new part closer features *A Manager's Dilemma*, which outlines a realistic dilemma for students to resolve, and *Global Sense*, which includes additional information on global issues for students to research and discuss.

Chapter Pedagogical Features

This new edition of *Management* continues to offer a rich variety of pedagogical features, including the following:

- Numbered learning outcomes at the opening of each chapter guide student learning. These are repeated in the margin at the start of each major chapter section to reinforce the learning outcome.

- A vignette opens each chapter and is threaded throughout the chapter to help students apply a story to the concepts they are learning.

- *Think About It* questions follow the vignette, as well as the return to the opening story throughout the chapter, giving students a chance to put themselves into the shoes of managers in various situations.

- *Management Reflections* are longer examples designed to enhance student learning. Some address general managerial issues, while others focus on international issues, ethics, or innovation.

- *Summary and Implications* are organized around the learning outcomes introduced at the beginning of each chapter.

Our end-of-chapter features provide students with a variety of opportunities to apply the material right now, even if they are not managers:

- *Reading and Discussion Questions.* Students can review their understanding of the chapter content and see the application of theory to management situations.

- *Ethical Dilemma.* This exercise gives students an opportunity to consider ethical issues that relate to chapter material, including values-led management and sustainability.

- *Skills Exercise.* To reflect the importance being placed on skills, each chapter has this skills-based feature that encompasses the four management functions. The feature includes lessons about a particular skill, steps in developing the skill, a practice assignment to use the skill (often a mini-case), and a set of reinforcement assignments to further work on accomplishing the skill.

- *Working Together: Team Exercise.* Students get a chance to work together in groups to solve a management challenge.

- *Learning to Be a Manager.* Students can apply chapter material to their daily lives, helping them see that planning, leading, organizing, and controlling are useful in one's day-to-day life too. This feature is suggests activities and actions students can do right now to help them in preparing to become a manager.

- *Case Applications.* Each chapter has two decision-focused cases that ask students to determine what they would do if they were in the situation described.

New to the Eleventh Canadian Edition

Content and examples throughout the text have been revised and updated. Key content changes include the following:

Chapter 1: Introduction to Management and Organizations includes new coverage of social media and sustainability, as well as an enhanced discussion of innovation and creativity as contributors to building an adaptable organization.

Module 1: Management History has updated exhibits and examples.

Chapter 2: Organizational Culture and the Organizational Environment explores new trends in organizational culture, including new examples.

Chapter 3: Managing in a Global Environment has updated information on international trade alliances and agreements as well as a new discussion of cultural intelligence and global mindset. A new vignette on Ford in the global marketplace runs throughout the chapter.

Chapter 4: Managing Entrepreneurially offers new coverage of start-ups and a discussion of how existing companies can apply the entrepreneurial approach to developing new products (drawing on lean methodologies). A new vignette on Futurepreneur Canada runs throughout the chapter.

Chapter 5: Managing Responsibly and Ethically includes updated information on and examples of sustainability and ethical management.

Chapter 6: Innovation and Adaptability has an enhanced focus on innovation to induce change and a reduced focus on managing change, and also introduces design thinking. A new vignette on Blackberry and its fall from grace runs throughout the chapter.

Chapter 7: Decision Making has new discussion of evidence-based management and design thinking and decision making. A new vignette based on the disruptions that airlines faced in the winter of 2013–2014 because of adverse weather patterns runs throughout the chapter.

Chapter 8: Foundations of Planning has a new discussion of stated goals and real goals.

Chapter 9: Managing Strategically now includes a separate learning outcome on competitive advantage and a new discussion of design thinking.

Module 2: Planning and Control Techniques, formerly a separate chapter, is now a module and has updated exhibits and examples.

Chapter 10: Organizational Design has expanded coverage of chain of command, including new figures, as well as a revised discussion of contemporary organizational designs.

Chapter 11: Managers and Communication has an enhanced focus on social media and technology, and new coverage of the impact of workplace design on communication. A new vignette looks at the use of Twitter by organizations.

Chapter 12: Managing Human Resources has a new discussion of the impact of downsizing.

Chapter 13: Leadership includes Leader–Member Exchange Theory (LMX) and has a reduced emphasis on the early theories of leadership and motivation.

Chapter 14: Motivating Employees has expanded material on the job characteristics model and job redesign. The section on current issues has been revised to include tough economic circumstances, open-book management, and new information on cross-cultural challenges.

Chapter 15: Managing Groups and Teams includes new material on team-building skills.

Chapter 16: Managerial Controls: Evidence-Based Decision Making has a revised approach, using the frame of evidence-based decision making. New material includes controlling customer interactions and the use of dashboards to manage information for decision makers.

Module 3: Managing Operations, formerly a separate chapter, is now a module and has new coverage of lean organizations.

Supplements

MyManagementLab

With this eleventh Canadian edition of *Management*, we continue to offer MyManagementLab, which provides students with an assortment of tools to help enrich and expedite learning. MyManagementLab is an online study tool for students and an online homework and assessment tool for faculty. MyManagementLab lets students assess their understanding through auto-graded tests and assignments, develop a personalized study plan to address areas of weakness, and practise a variety of learning tools to master management principles. New and updated MyManagementLab resources include the following:

- **Personal Inventory Assessment (PIA):** Students learn better when they can connect what they are learning to their personal experience. PIA is a collection of online exercises designed to promote self-reflection and engagement in students, enhancing their ability to connect with concepts taught in principles of management, organizational behaviour, and human resource management classes. Assessments are assignable by instructors, who can then track students' completions. Student results include a written explanation along with a graphic display that shows how their results compare to the class as a whole. Instructors will also have access to this graphic representation of results to promote classroom discussion.

- **NEW Personalized Study Plan.** As students work through MyManagementLab's new Study Plan, they can clearly see which topics they have mastered—and, more importantly, which they need to work on. Each question has been carefully written to match the concepts, language, and focus of the text, so students can get an accurate sense of how well they've understood the chapter content.

- **NEW Business Today Videos.** *Business Today* is a dynamic and expanding database of videos covering the disciplines of management, business, marketing, and more. Instructors will find new videos posted monthly, which makes *Business Today* the ideal resource for up-to-date video examples that are perfect for classroom use.

- **NEW Learning Catalytics.** Learning Catalytics is a "bring your own device" student engagement, assessment, and classroom intelligence system. It allows instructors to engage students in class with a variety of question types designed to gauge student understanding.

- **Assignable Mini-Cases and Video Cases.** Instructors have access to a variety of case-based assessment material that can be assigned to students, with multiple-choice quizzes or written-response format in MyManagementLab's new Writing Space.

- **eText.** Students can study without leaving the online environment. They can access the eText online, including videos and simulations. The interactive eText allows students to highlight sections, bookmark pages, or take notes electronically just as they might do with a traditional text. Instructors can also add their own notes to the text and then share them with their students.

- **Glossary Flashcards.** This study aid is useful for students' review of key concepts.

- **BizSkill and Decision-Making Mini-Simulations.** The BizSkill and Decision-Making mini-simulations help students analyze and make decisions in common business situations; the simulations assess student choices and include reinforcement quizzes, outlines, and glossaries.

- **Careers in Management.** These documents outline professional management associations in Canada and describe some key management positions and the skills students need to pursue specific careers.

Additional Instructor Resources

Management is accompanied by a complete set of instructor resources. Some of these items are available for download from a password-protected section of Pearson Canada's online catalogue (www.pearsoncanada.ca/highered). Navigate to your book's catalogue page to view a list of those supplements that are available. See your local sales representative for details and access.

Instructor's Resource Manual: This manual includes detailed lecture outlines, answers, and teaching suggestions for the end-of-chapter questions and activities, and video teaching notes.

PowerPoint Slides: These chapter-by-chapter presentations cover key points and exhibits, are correlated to the learning objectives, and provide detailed speaking notes.

TestGen: The new edition of *Management* comes with TestGen, a computerized test bank that enables instructors to view and edit the existing questions, add questions, generate tests, and print the tests in a variety of formats. Powerful search and sort functions make it easy to locate questions and arrange them in any order desired. TestGen also enables instructors to administer tests on a local area network, have the tests graded electronically, and have the results prepared in electronic or printed reports. The TestGen for the eleventh Canadian edition includes over 2500 questions in true/false, multiple-choice, and short-answer formats.

Test Item File: All the questions from the TestGen test bank are also available in Microsoft Word format.

Video Guide: This guide provides a synopsis and questions for the *Business Today* videos available on MyManagementLab.

Image Library: All exhibits from the text are provided in electronic format for instructor use.

CourseSmart: CourseSmart goes beyond traditional expectations—providing instant, online access to the textbooks and course materials you need at a lower cost for students. And even as students save money, you can save time and hassle with a digital eTextbook that allows you to search for the most relevant content at the very moment you need it. Whether it's evaluating textbooks or creating lecture notes to help students with difficult concepts, CourseSmart can make life a little easier. See how when you visit www.coursesmart.com/instructors.

Learning Solutions Managers: Pearson's Learning Solutions managers work with faculty and campus course designers to ensure that Pearson technology products, assessment tools, and online course materials are tailored to meet your specific needs. This highly qualified team is dedicated to helping schools take full advantage of a wide range of educational resources, by assisting in the integration of a variety of instructional materials and media formats. Your local Pearson Education sales representative can provide you with more details on this service program.

Pearson Custom Library: For enrollments of at least 25 students, you can create your own textbook by choosing the chapters that best suit your own course needs. To begin building your custom text, visit www.pearsoncustomlibrary.com. You may also work with a dedicated Pearson Custom editor to create your ideal text—publishing your own original content or mixing and matching Pearson content. Contact your local Pearson Representative to get started.

Acknowledgments

We want to thank Colin Conrad, a Masters of Electronic Commerce student, who helped edit the manuscript. His background in economics and philosophy and his fearless nature assisted us in more clearly conveying the material for the reader. Thank you, Colin!

We want to acknowledge the many reviewers of this textbook for their detailed and helpful comments. The following reviewers, plus others who choose to remain anonymous, provided feedback on the tenth Canadian edition and/or the manuscript for the eleventh Canadian edition:

Mahfooz A. Ansari, University of Lethbridge

Matt Archibald, University of Ottawa

Bruce Bennett, College of New Caledonia

Tabea K. Berg, NAIT

Kerry D. Couet, Grant MacEwan University

Claude J. Dupuis, Athabasca University

Jai Goolsarran, Centennial College

James Hebert, Red River College

Sarah Holding, Vancouver Island University

Michelle Inness, University of Alberta

Angela Karwal, University of Alberta

Horatio Morgan, Ryerson University

Lyndsay Passmore, Kwantlen Polytechnic University

Rhonda Reich, Grant MacEwan University

Carol Ann Samhaber, Algonquin College

Bryan Webber, Vancouver Island University

Steve Robbins would like to thank his wife, Laura, for her encouragement and support. Mary Coulter would like to thank her husband and family for being supportive and understanding and for patiently enduring her many hours at the computer! And Mary would like to acknowledge her Wednesday night Bible study class … you ladies have been so supportive of me and you continue to be an important part of my life. Thank you!

Ed Leach and Mary Kilfoil dedicate this book to their parents, Charles and Florence Leach and Gerald and Joan Kilfoil, who have taught them so much. In addition, they would like to thank their students, who have been the inspiration for this edition. Thank you all for keeping it so interesting!

About the Authors

Stephen P. Robbins (Ph.D., University of Arizona) is professor emeritus of management at San Diego State University and the world's best-selling textbook author in the areas of both management and organizational behavior. His books have sold more than 5 million copies and have been translated into 20 languages. His books are currently used at more than 1500 U.S. colleges and universities as well as hundreds of schools throughout Canada, Latin America, Australia, New Zealand, Asia, and Europe. Dr. Robbins is also the author of the best-selling *The Truth About Managing People*, 2nd ed. (Financial Times/Prentice Hall, 2008) and *Decide & Conquer* (Financial Times/Prentice Hall, 2004).

Dr. Robbins actively participates in masters' track competitions. Since turning 50 in 1993, he's won 23 national championships and 14 world titles. He was inducted into the U.S. Masters' Track & Field Hall of Fame in 2005 and is currently the world record holder at 100m (12.37) and 200m (25.20) for men 65 and over.

Mary Coulter (Ph.D., University of Arkansas) is professor emeritus of management at Missouri State University. Dr. Coulter has published other books with Prentice Hall, including *Strategic Management in Action*, now in its sixth edition, and *Entrepreneurship in Action*, which is in its second edition. When she's not busy writing, Dr. Coulter enjoys puttering around in her flower garden, trying new recipes on family members (usually successful!), reading a variety of books, and enjoying many different activities with family: Ron, Sarah and James, Katie and Matt, granddaughter, Brooklynn, and grandson, Blake. Love my sweet babies!

Ed Leach received his Ph.D. in computing technology in education from Nova Southeastern University in Ft. Lauderdale and an MBA from the University of Western Ontario. Prior to completing his graduate work, Dr. Leach was an entrepreneur who also taught in the professional programs of the Society of Management Accountants and the Purchasing Management Association of Canada. His interest in working with entrepreneurs has continued since joining Dalhousie University, where Dr. Leach has mentored lead entrepreneurs during the start-up phase of their technology businesses, including two IPOs. Dr. Leach is an award-winning professor who developed the introductory management course at Dalhousie and has taught it since its inception in 1999. His research interests lie in the field of entrepreneurship and specifically the role of creativity in triggering innovation. Dr. Leach is the director of the Norman Newman Centre for Entrepreneurship, in the School of Business, Dalhousie University, and is a past president of the Canadian Council for Small Business and Entrepreneurship (CCSBE), 2006. When he is not busy teaching, he enjoys cooking and spending time with family, especially his and Mary's four grandchildren.

Mary Kilfoil received her Ph.D. from Dalhousie University and her master's degree from Carleton University, in economics. Dr. Kilfoil is the academic lead for the Starting Lean initiative and in 2014 was named national educator of the year by Startup Canada. Mary has taught the introductory management course in the Faculty of Management as well as courses in economics, program evaluation, and research methods at Dalhousie University. She has developed course curricula for the MBA Financial Services Program and the Executive Masters of Public Administration (MPA-M) Program offered to government employees across Canada. Dr. Kilfoil has more than 20 years' experience as a manager in the private sector and holds the position of senior economist and partner at Gardner Pinfold Consultants, one of Canada's leading firms specializing in economic analysis. She has extensive experience as a researcher, analyst, and report writer in the field of environmental and natural resource economics, economic impact analysis, and climate change policy, with some 75 major reports to her credit. She is also the co-director for the Dalhousie Shad Valley Program, a residential academic program for gifted youth. When she is not busy working, Mary enjoys spending time with family, gardening, outdoor recreational activities, and travelling.

Introduction to Management and Organizations

In this chapter, we'll introduce you to who managers are and what they do. One thing you'll discover is that the work managers do is vitally important to organizations. But you'll also see that being a manager—a good manager—isn't easy. The best companies and organizations are more flexible, more efficient, and more adaptable. After reading and studying this chapter, you will achieve the following learning outcomes.

Learning Outcomes

1. Explain why managers are important to an organization.

2. Tell who managers are and where they work.

3. Describe the characteristics of an organization.

4. Describe the factors that are reshaping and redefining the manager's job.

5. Explain the value of studying management.

▶ ▶ ▶ The celebration in 1984 of the 450th anniversary of explorer Jacques Cartier's arrival in Canada saw a small troupe of street performers put together a circus.[1] Who could have imagined at the time that this ragtag bunch of French-Canadian hippies would become the Cirque du Soleil ("circus of the sun") that we know today? Thirty years later, Cirque du Soleil's big-budget, animal-free circuses are Canada's largest cultural export, pulling in an estimated $1 billion a year in revenue. The dynamic between CEO Daniel Lamarre and company founder Guy Laliberté is an interesting one as the pragmatic (Lamarre) meets the creative (Laliberté). As Lamarre puts it, "I'm very lucky because we are so complementary. What Guy likes to do, I don't and what I like to do, he doesn't." Laliberté rather likes people with stratospheric ambitions. At a time when most businesses have reasonably modest expectations, Carmen Ruest, one of the original Cirque pioneers and now the company's director of creation, has been known to say, "The word *impossible* does not exist here."

Guy Laliberté created the ONE DROP Foundation in 2007 to fight global poverty by providing sustainable access to safe water. The ideals of the foundation reflect the values that have always been at the heart of Cirque du Soleil: the belief that life gives back what you have given and even the smallest gesture will make a difference. When Guy Laliberté became the first Canadian private space explorer, he dedicated his mission to raising awareness of water issues on Earth. As part of the first Poetic Social Mission in space, Laliberté hosted *Moving Stars and Earth for Water* from the International Space Station, a webcast concert featuring various artistic performances unfolding in 14 cities around the world.

NASA Images

Think About It

What kinds of skills do managers need? Put yourself in Guy Laliberté's shoes. What kinds of leadership skills would you need to manage 4000 employees in 40 countries? Is managing in a creative and artistic organization different from managing in any other organization? Do other organizations share Laliberté's belief that "life gives back what you have given"?

This text is about the important managerial work that managers do. The reality facing today's managers—and that might include you in the near future—is that the world is changing. In workplaces of all types—offices, retail stores, restaurants, factories, and the like—managers deal with changing expectations and new ways of managing employees and organizing work.

In this chapter, we explain why managers are important to organizations, who managers are, where they work, and what managers do. Finally, we wrap up the chapter by looking at the factors redefining the manager's job and discussing why it's important to study management.

Who Are Managers and Why Are They Important?

❶ Explain why managers are important to an organization.

". . . A great boss can change your life, inspiring you to new heights both professionally and personally, and energizing you and your team to together overcome new challenges bigger than any one of you could tackle alone."[2] If you've worked with a manager like this, consider yourself lucky. Such a manager can make a job a lot more enjoyable and productive. However, even managers who don't live up to such lofty ideals and expectations are important to organizations. Let's look at three reasons why.

The first reason managers are important is because organizations need their managerial skills and abilities more than ever in uncertain, complex, and chaotic times. As organizations deal with today's challenges—the worldwide economic climate, changing technology, ever-increasing globalization, and so forth—managers play an important role in identifying critical issues and crafting responses. For example, John Zapp, general manager of several car dealerships in Oklahoma City, struggled to keep his businesses afloat and profitable in the difficult economic environment, just as many other car dealers did. However, after four decades in the car business, Zapp understands that he's the one calling the shots and his "call" was to focus on selling more used cars. How? By keeping inventory moving and by keeping his salespeople engaged through small cash payment rewards for hitting sales goals. His skills and abilities as a manager have been crucial in guiding his organization.

Secondly, *managers do matter* to organizations! How do we know that? The Gallup Organization, which has polled millions of employees and tens of thousands of managers, has found that the single most important variable in employee productivity and loyalty isn't pay or benefits or workplace environment—it's the quality of the relationship between employees and their direct supervisors.[3] In addition, a KPMG/Ipsos Reid study of Canadian companies found that those that made the top 10 list for great human resource practices also scored high on financial performance and investment value. Six of the "Most Respected Corporations for Human Resources Management" placed in the top 10 on both financial measures, and nine scored in the top 10 of at least one of the financial measures.[4] So, as you can see, managers can and do have an impact—positive and negative. Finally, one more study of organizational performance recently found that managerial ability was important in creating organizational value.[5] Here's what we can conclude from such reports: Managers are important—and they *do* matter!

Finally, Guy Laliberté is a good example of what today's successful managers are like and the skills they must have to deal with the problems and challenges of managing in the twenty-first century. These managers may not be who or what you might expect. They range in age from under 18 to over 80. They run large corporations, as well as entrepreneurial start-ups. They are found in government departments, hospitals, small businesses, not-for-profit agencies, museums, schools, and even such nontraditional organizations as political campaigns and consumer cooperatives—in every country on the globe.

Who Is a Manager?

It used to be fairly simple to define who managers were: They were the organizational members who told others what to do and how to do it. It was easy to differentiate *managers* from *nonmanagerial employees*. But it isn't quite so simple anymore. In many organizations, the changing nature of work has blurred the distinction between managers and nonmanagerial employees. Many nonmanagerial jobs now include managerial activities.[6] At General Cable Corporation's facility in Moose Jaw, Saskatchewan, for example, managerial responsibilities are shared by managers and team members. Most of the employees are cross-trained and multiskilled. Within a single shift, an employee may be a team leader, an equipment operator, a maintenance technician, a quality inspector, and an improvement planner.[7] Or consider an organization like Morning Star Company, the world's largest tomato processor, where no employees are called managers—just 400 full-time employees who do what needs to be done and who "manage" issues such as job responsibilities, compensation decisions, and budget decisions.[8] Sounds crazy, doesn't it? But it works—for this organization.

Today, how do we define who managers are? A **manager** is someone who works with and through other people by coordinating their work activities in order to accomplish organizational goals. A manager's job is not about *personal* achievement—it's about helping *others* do their work and achieve. That may mean coordinating the work of a departmental group, or it might mean supervising a single person. It could involve coordinating the work activities of a team composed of people from several different departments or even people outside the organization, such as temporary employees or employees who work for the organization's suppliers. Keep in mind, also, that managers may have other work duties not related to coordinating and integrating the work of others. For example, an insurance claims supervisor may process claims in addition to coordinating the work activities of other claims clerks.

Types of Managers

Is there some way to classify managers in organizations? In traditionally structured organizations (often pictured as being shaped like a pyramid where the number of employees is greater at the bottom than at the top), managers are often described as first-line, middle, or top (see Exhibit 1-1). Identifying exactly who the managers are in these organizations isn't difficult, although they may have a variety of titles. **First-line managers** are at the lowest level of management and manage the work of nonmanagerial employees who are directly or indirectly involved with the production or creation of the organization's products. They are often called *supervisors* but may also be called shift managers, district managers, department managers, office managers, or even foremen. **Middle managers** include all levels of management between the first-line level and the top level of the organization. These managers manage the work of first-line managers and may have titles such as regional manager, project leader, plant manager, or division manager. At or near the top of the organization are the **top managers** who are responsible for making organization-wide decisions and establishing the plans and goals that affect the entire organization. These individuals typically have titles such as executive vice-president, president, managing director, chief operating officer, chief executive officer, or chair of the board. In the chapter-opening case, Guy Laliberté is the founder and driving creative force of Cirque du

manager Someone who coordinates and oversees the work of other people so organizational goals can be accomplished

first-line managers Managers at the lowest level of the organization who manage the work of nonmanagerial employees who are directly or indirectly involved with the production or creation of the organization's products.

middle managers Managers between the first-line level and the top level of the organization who manage the work of first-line managers.

top managers Managers at or near the top level of the organization who are responsible for making organization-wide decisions and establishing the plans and goals that affect the entire organization.

Exhibit 1-1

Managerial Levels

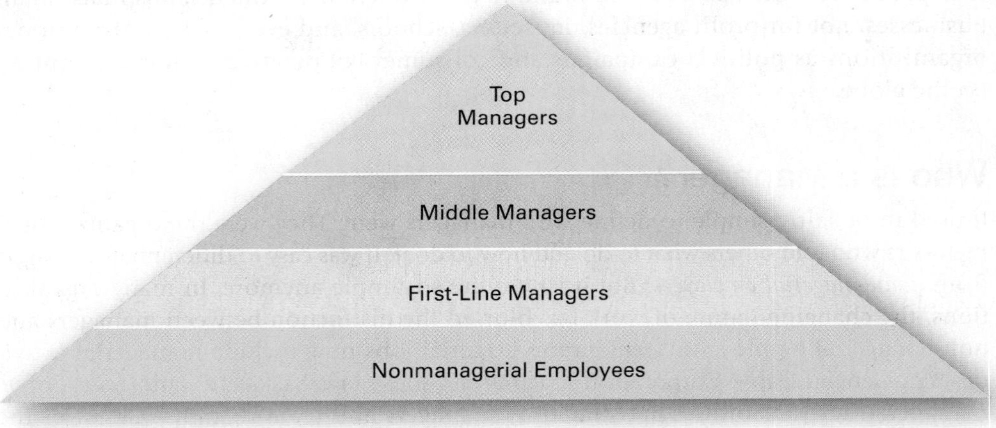

Top Managers

Middle Managers

First-Line Managers

Nonmanagerial Employees

Soleil. He is involved in creating and implementing broad and comprehensive changes that affect the entire organization.

Not all organizations get work done using this traditional pyramidal form, however. Some organizations are more flexible and loosely structured with work being done by ever-changing teams of employees who move from one project to another as work demands arise. Although it's not as easy to tell who the managers are in these organizations, we do know that someone must fulfill that role—that is, there must be someone who works with and through other people by coordinating their work to accomplish organizational goals. This holds true even if that "someone" changes as work tasks or projects change or that "someone" doesn't necessarily have the title of manager.

What Is Management and What Do Managers Do?

② Tell who managers are and where they work.

▶ ▶ ▶ Managers plan, lead, organize, and control, and Daniel Lamarre, as chief executive officer of Cirque du Soleil, certainly carries out all these tasks. He has to coordinate the work activities of the entire company efficiently and effectively. But just as important to Lamarre is the creative side of Cirque—in fact, he sees his mission as finding work for artists. With operations in 40 countries, it might be tempting for Lamarre to try to arrive at consensus on issues, but at Cirque it is all about the power of the idea. Lamarre feels that the best ideas are lost if everyone has to compromise. So although it can be uncomfortable for some, debating ideas has become embedded in the company culture. "That is what we do," says Lamarre, "we are debating all of the time."[10]

Think About It

As a manager, Daniel Lamarre needs to plan, lead, organize, and control, and he needs to be efficient and effective. How might Lamarre balance the needs of efficiency and effectiveness with the creative and artistic mandate of his role as CEO of Cirque du Soleil? What skills are needed for him to plan, lead, organize, and control effectively? What challenges does he face performing these functions while running an international business?

Simply speaking, management is what managers do. But that simple statement does not tell us much, does it? A more thorough explanation is that **management** is coordinating work activities with and through other people so that the activities are completed *efficiently* and *effectively*. Management researchers have developed three specific categorization schemes to describe what managers do: functions, roles, and skills. In this section, we consider the challenges of balancing efficiency and effectiveness, and then examine the approaches that look at what managers do. In reviewing these categorizations, it might be helpful to understand that management is something that is a learned talent, rather than something that comes "naturally." Many people do not know how to be a manager when they first are appointed to that role.

management Coordinating work activities with and through other people so the activities are completed efficiently and effectively.

Efficiency and Effectiveness

Efficiency refers to getting the most output from the least amount of inputs, or as management expert Peter Drucker explained, "doing things right."[11] Because managers deal with scarce inputs—including resources such as people, money, and equipment—they are concerned with the efficient use of those resources by getting things done at the least cost.

It's not enough just to be efficient, however. Management is also concerned with being effective, completing activities so that organizational goals are achieved. **Effectiveness** is often described as "doing the right things"—that is, those work activities that will help the organization reach its goals. For instance, hospitals may try to be efficient by reducing the number of days that patients stay in hospital. This may not be effective, however, if patients get sick at home shortly after being released from hospital.

Whereas efficiency is concerned with the means of getting things done, effectiveness is concerned with the ends, or attainment of organizational goals (see Exhibit 1-2). Management is concerned, then, not only with getting activities completed and meeting organizational goals (effectiveness) but also with doing so as efficiently as possible. In successful organizations, high efficiency and high effectiveness typically go hand in hand. Poor management is most often due to both inefficiency and ineffectiveness or to effectiveness achieved despite inefficiency.

◄●┤Simulate on **MyManagementLab**

Improving a Business

efficiency Getting the most output from the least amount of inputs; referred to as "doing things right."

effectiveness Completing activities so that organizational goals are achieved; referred to as "doing the right things."

Management Functions

According to the functions approach, managers perform certain activities or duties as they efficiently and effectively coordinate the work of others. What are these activities or functions? In the early part of the twentieth century, a French industrialist named Henri Fayol first proposed that all managers perform five functions: planning, organizing, commanding, coordinating, and controlling.[12] Today, most management textbooks

Exhibit 1-2

Efficiency and Effectiveness in Management

Exhibit 1-3

Management Functions

Planning	Organizing	Leading	Controlling	
Defining goals, establishing strategy, and developing subplans to coordinate activities	Determining what needs to be done, how it will be done, and who is to do it	Directing and motivating all involved parties and resolving conflicts	Monitoring activities to ensure that they are accomplished as planned	*Lead to* Achieving the organization's stated purpose

---

management functions Planning, organizing, leading, and controlling.

(including this one) are organized around the **management functions**: planning, organizing, leading, and controlling (see Exhibit 1-3). But you do not have to be a manager in order to have a need to plan, organize, lead, and control, so understanding these processes is important for everyone. Let's briefly define what each of these functions encompasses.

Planning

planning A management function that involves defining goals, establishing a strategy for achieving those goals, and developing plans to integrate and coordinate activities.

If you have no particular destination in mind, then you can take any road. However, if you have some place in particular you want to go, you have to plan the best way to get there. Because organizations exist to achieve some particular purpose, someone must clearly define that purpose and the means for its achievement. Managers performing the **planning** function define goals, establish an overall strategy for achieving those goals, and develop plans to integrate and coordinate activities. This can be done by the CEO and senior management team for the overall organization. Middle-level managers often have a planning role within their units. First-line managers have a more limited role in the planning process, but may need to use planning to adequately schedule work and employees. Planning, by the way, is not just for managers. For instance, as a student, you need to plan for exams and your financial needs.

Organizing

organizing A management function that involves determining what tasks are to be done, who is to do them, how the tasks are to be grouped, who reports to whom, and where decisions are to be made.

Managers are also responsible for arranging work to accomplish the organization's goals. We call this function **organizing**. When managers organize, they determine what tasks are to be done, who is to do them, how the tasks are to be grouped, who reports to whom (that is, they define authority relationships), and where decisions are to be made. When you work in a student group, you engage in some of these same organizing activities—deciding on a division of labour and what tasks will be carried out to get an assignment completed.

Leading

leading A management function that involves motivating subordinates, directing the work of individuals or teams, selecting the most effective communication channels, and resolving employee behaviour issues.

Every organization includes people, and a manager's job is to work with and through people to accomplish organizational goals. This is the **leading** function. When managers motivate subordinates, direct the work of individuals or teams, select the most effective communication channel, or resolve employee behaviour issues, they are leading. Knowing how to manage and lead effectively is an important, and sometimes difficult, skill as it requires the ability to successfully communicate. Leading is not just for managers, however. As a student, you might want to practise leadership skills when working in groups or club activities. You might also want to evaluate whether you need to improve your leadership skills in anticipation of the needs of future jobs.

Controlling

The final management function is **controlling**. After the goals are set (planning); the plans formulated (planning); the structural arrangements determined (organizing); and the people hired, trained, and motivated (leading); there has to be some evaluation of whether things are going as planned (controlling). To ensure that work is going as it should, managers must monitor and evaluate the performance of employees, technology, and systems. Actual performance must be compared with the previously set goals. If performance of individuals or units does not match the goals set, it's management's job to get performance back on track. This process of monitoring, comparing, and correcting is what we mean by the controlling function. Students, whether working in groups or alone, also face the responsibility of controlling; that is, they make sure the goals and actions are achieved and take corrective action when necessary.

Just how well does the functions approach describe what managers do? Do managers always plan, organize, lead, and then control? In reality, what a manager does may not always happen in this logical and sequential order. But that does not negate the importance of the basic functions that managers perform. Regardless of the order in which the functions are performed, the fact is that managers do plan, organize, lead, and control as they manage.

The continued popularity of the functions approach to describe what managers do is a tribute to its clarity and simplicity. But some have argued that this approach isn't appropriate or relevant.[13] So let's look at another perspective.

controlling A management function that involves monitoring actual performance, comparing actual performance to a standard, and taking corrective action when necessary.

Management Roles

Henry Mintzberg, a prominent management researcher at McGill University in Montreal, studied actual managers at work. He says that what managers do can best be described by looking at the roles they play at work. His studies allowed him to conclude that managers perform 10 different but highly interrelated management roles.[14] The term **management roles** refers to specific categories of managerial behaviour. (Think of the different roles you play and the different behaviours you are expected to perform in these roles as a student, a sibling, an employee, a volunteer, and so forth.) As shown in Exhibit 1-4, Mintzberg's 10 management roles are grouped around interpersonal relationships, the transfer of information, and decision making. Note that, since first proposed in 1973, email and social media have enriched the way in which communication takes place.

The **interpersonal roles** involve working with people (subordinates and persons outside the organization) or performing duties that are ceremonial and symbolic in nature. The three interpersonal roles include being a figurehead, leader, and liaison. The **informational roles** involve receiving, collecting, and disseminating information. The three informational roles include monitor, disseminator, and spokesperson. Finally, the **decisional roles** involve making significant choices that affect the organization. The four decisional roles include entrepreneur, disturbance handler, resource allocator, and negotiator.

A number of follow-up studies have tested the validity of Mintzberg's role categories among different types of organizations and at different levels within given organizations.[15] The evidence generally supports the idea that managers—regardless of the type of organization or level in the organization—perform similar roles. However, the emphasis that managers give to the various roles seems to change with their organizational level.[16] Specifically, the roles of disseminator, figurehead, negotiator, liaison, and spokesperson are more important at the higher levels of the organization, while the leader role (as Mintzberg defined it) is more important for lower-level managers than it is for either middle- or top-level managers.

management roles Specific categories of managerial behaviour.

interpersonal roles Management roles that involve working with people or performing duties that are ceremonial and symbolic in nature.

informational roles Management roles that involve receiving, collecting, and disseminating information.

decisional roles Management roles that involve making significant choices that affect the organization.

Functions vs. Roles

So which approach to describing what managers do is better—functions or roles? Each has merit. However, the functions approach still represents the most useful way of conceptualizing the manager's job. "The classical functions provide clear and discrete methods of

Exhibit 1-4

Mintzberg's Management Roles

Interpersonal Roles

- Figurehead
- Leader
- Liaison

Informational Roles

- Monitor
- Disseminator
- Spokesperson

Decisional Roles

- Entrepreneur
- Disturbance handler
- Resource allocator
- Negotiator

classifying the thousands of activities that managers carry out and the techniques they use in terms of the functions they perform for the achievement of goals."[17] Many of Mintzberg's roles align well with one or more of the functions. For instance, resource allocation is part of planning, as is the entrepreneurial role, and all three of the interpersonal roles are part of the leading function. Although most of the other roles fit into one or more of the four functions, not all of them do. The difference can be explained by the fact that all managers do some work that isn't purely managerial.[18]

Management Skills

Dell Inc. is one company that understands the importance of management skills.[19] It started an intensive five-day offsite skills-training program for first-line managers augmented by online tools from Harvard as well as in-house tools such as MentorConnect, as a way to improve its operations. One of Dell's directors of learning and development thought this was the best way to develop "leaders who can build that strong relationship with their front-line employees." What did the supervisors learn from the skills training? Some things they mentioned were how to communicate more effectively and how to refrain from jumping to conclusions when discussing a problem with a worker.

Managers need certain skills to perform the duties and activities associated with being a manager. What types of skills does a manager need? Research by Robert L. Katz found that managers needed three essential skills: technical skills, human skills, and conceptual skills.[20]

Technical skills include knowledge of and expertise in a certain specialized field, such as engineering, computers, accounting, or manufacturing. These skills are more important

technical skills Knowledge of and expertise in a specialized field.

Exhibit 1-5

Skills Needed at Different Management Levels

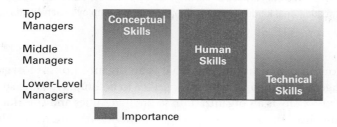

at lower levels of management since these managers are dealing directly with employees doing the organization's work.

Human skills involve the ability to work well with other people, both individually and in a group. Because managers deal directly with people, this skill is crucial for managers at all levels! Managers with good human skills are able to get the best out of their people. They know how to communicate, motivate, lead, and inspire enthusiasm and trust. These skills are equally important at all levels of management. Management professor Jin Nam Choi, of McGill University, reports that research shows that 40 percent of managers either leave or stop performing within 18 months of starting at an organization "because they have failed to develop relationships with bosses, colleagues or subordinates."[21] Choi's comment underscores the importance of developing human skills.

Finally, **conceptual skills** involve the mental ability to analyze and generate ideas about abstract and complex situations. These skills help managers see the organization as a whole, understand the relationships among various subunits, and visualize how the organization fits into its broader environment. These skills are most important at the top management levels.

Exhibit 1-5 shows the relationship of the three skills to each level of management. Note that the three skills are important to more than one function. Additionally, in very flat organizations with little hierarchy, human, technical, and conceptual skills would be needed throughout the organization.

As you study the management functions in more depth, the skills exercises found at the end of most chapters will give you the opportunity to practise some of the key skills that are part of doing what a manager does. We feel that understanding and developing management skills is so important that we've included a skills feature in MyManagementLab. There, you'll find material on skill building as well as several interactive skills exercises. As you study the four management functions throughout the rest of the book, you'll be able to practise some key management skills. Although a simple skill-building exercise won't make you an instant expert, it can provide an introductory understanding of some of the skills you'll need to master in order to be an effective manager.

human skills The ability to work well with other people, both individually and in a group.

conceptual skills The mental ability to analyze and generate ideas about abstract and complex situations.

What Is an Organization?

▶ ▶ ▶ Cirque du Soleil has grown from 73 employees in 1984 to more than 5000 employees worldwide with almost 2000 working at the international headquarters in Montreal. Today there are more than 1000 different occupations at Cirque du Soleil! In the process of expanding the reach of the company internationally, Cirque has dealt with many different kinds of organizations including government, quasi-government, large corporations, and independent contractors. Cirque has also established a number of charitable initiatives that required the formation of independent foundations as well as soliciting support from other foundations.

❸ Describe the characteristics of an organization.

◄⊙ Simulate on **MyManagementLab**

What is Management

organization A deliberate arrangement of people who act together to accomplish some specific purpose.

Managers work in organizations. But what is an organization? An **organization** is a deliberate arrangement of people who act together to accomplish some specific purpose. Your college or university is an organization; so are fraternities and sororities, government departments, churches, Amazon.ca, your neighbourhood video store, the United Way, the Toronto Raptors basketball team, your local co-op, and Canadian Tire. These are all organizations because they have three common characteristics, as shown in Exhibit 1-6:

1. *Distinct purpose.* This purpose is typically expressed in terms of a goal or a set of goals that the organization hopes to accomplish.

2. *Composed of people.* One person working alone is not an organization, and it takes people to perform the work that is necessary for the organization to achieve its goals.

3. *Deliberate structure.* Whether that structure is open and flexible or traditional and clearly defined, the structure defines members' work relationships.

In summary, the term *organization* refers to an entity that has a distinct purpose, includes people or members, and has some type of deliberate structure.

Although these three characteristics are important to our definition of *what* an organization is, the concept of an organization is changing. It's no longer appropriate to assume that all organizations are going to be structured like Air Canada, Suncor Energy, or General Motors, with clearly identifiable divisions, departments, and work units. Just how is the concept of an organization changing? Exhibit 1-7 lists some differences between traditional organizations and new organizations. As these lists show, today's organizations are becoming more open, flexible, and responsive to changes.[22]

Why are organizations changing? Because the world around them has changed and continues to change. Societal, economic, political, global, and technological changes have created an environment in which successful organizations (those that consistently attain their goals) must embrace new ways of getting work done. As we stated earlier, even though the concept of organizations may be changing, managers and management continue to be important to organizations.

Exhibit 1-6

Characteristics of Organizations

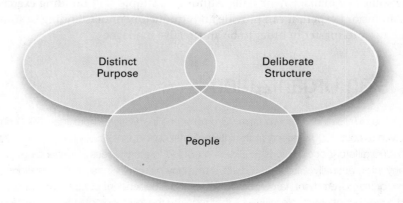

Exhibit 1-7

The Changing Organization

Traditional Organization	New Organization
• Stable	• Dynamic
• Inflexible	• Flexible
• Job-focused	• Skills-focused
• Work is defined by job positions	• Work is defined in terms of tasks to be done
• Individual-oriented	• Team-oriented
• Permanent jobs	• Temporary jobs
• Command-oriented	• Involvement-oriented
• Managers always make decisions	• Employees participate in decision making
• Rule-oriented	• Customer-oriented
• Relatively homogeneous workforce	• Diverse workforce
• Workdays defined as 9 to 5	• Workdays have no time boundaries
• Hierarchical relationships	• Lateral and networked relationships
• Work at organizational facility during specific hours	• Work anywhere, anytime

The Size of Organizations

Managers don't just manage in large organizations, which represent only about 2 percent of organizations in Canada. Small businesses (those that employ fewer than 100 individuals) represent 98 percent of all Canadian companies. These businesses employ almost half of all Canadian workers. Small businesses also contribute significantly to the economy. Businesses employing 50 or fewer individuals generated about 29 percent of total GDP in 2008.[23] Organizations of every size need managers. Moreover, in 2010, about 16 percent of the labour force was self-employed, meaning that these people were managing themselves.[24]

Managers are also not confined to manufacturing work, as only 12 percent of Canadians work in manufacturing organizations. Twenty-one percent work in public sector jobs (those in the local, provincial, or federal government), while most Canadians (around 78 percent) work in the service sector of the economy.[25] The government is a large employer in Canada. For instance, Public Service Canada employs 263 000 while Canada Post, a Crown corporation employs 68 000. [26]

The Types of Organizations

Managers work in a variety of situations, and thus the people to whom they are held accountable vary considerably. Large organizations in the **private sector** are often **publicly held**, which means that their shares are available on the stock exchange for public trading. Managers of these companies report to a board of directors that is responsible to shareholders (also known as stockholders). There are also numerous **privately held organizations** (whose shares are not available on the stock market), both large and small. Privately held organizations can be individually owned, family owned, or owned by some other group of individuals. A number of managers work in the **not-for-profit sector** (or nonprofit sector), where the emphasis is on providing charity or services rather than on making a profit. Examples of such organizations include the SPCA (Society for the Prevention of Cruelty to Animals), the Royal Ontario Museum, and Vancouver's Bard on the Beach Festival. Other organizational forms such as **NGOs** (nongovernmental organizations), partnerships, and cooperatives also require managers.

private sector The part of the economy run by organizations that are free from direct government control; organizations in this sector operate to make a profit.

publicly held organization A company whose shares are available on the stock exchange for public trading.

privately held organization A company whose shares are not available on the stock exchange but are privately held.

not-for-profit sector The part of the economy run by organizations that operate for purposes other than making a profit (that is, providing charity or services).

NGO An organization that is independent from government control and whose primary focus is on humanitarian, development, and environmental sustainability activities.

public sector The part of the economy that is controlled by government.

civil servant A person who works in a local, provincial, or federal government department.

Crown corporation A commercial company owned by the government but independently managed.

Many managers work in the **public sector** as **civil servants** for the provincial, federal, and local governments. The challenges of managing within government departments can be quite different from the challenges of managing in publicly held organizations. Critics argue that it is less demanding to work for governments because there are few measurable performance objectives, allowing employees to feel less accountable for their actions.

Some managers and employees work for **Crown corporations** such as Canada Post, the CBC, and the Business Development Bank of Canada. Crown corporations are structured like private sector corporations and have boards of directors, CEOs, and so on, but are owned by governments rather than shareholders. Employees in Crown corporations are not civil servants, and managers in Crown corporations are more independent than the senior bureaucrats who manage government departments.

Many of Canada's larger organizations are actually subsidiaries of American parent organizations (for example, Sears, Safeway, General Motors, and Ford Motor Company). These managers often report to American top managers and are not always free to set their own goals and targets. Conflicts can arise between how Canadian managers and the American managers to whom they report think things should be done.

How Is the Manager's Job Changing?

4 Describe the factors that are reshaping and redefining the manager's job.

▶ ▶ ▶ As CEO of Cirque du Soleil, Daniel Lamarre manages 4000 employees in 40 countries and also must manage his relationship with company founder Guy Laliberté, who is quite the character. "The reality is that Guy understands business and he understands that that is what he wants to do in life. . . . The first thing that you have to do when you work with someone like that, you have to like and love artists because Guy is an artist. If you are not able to work with an artist, you are in the wrong place."[27]

Think About It

Managing is far more complicated today than it ever was. Daniel Lamarre, like many managers, must deal with multicultural challenges, technological challenges, and the demand for more accountability from customers and clients. In the fall of 2008, Cirque and organizations around the world also had to deal with the global economic crisis. But unlike many other businesses, Cirque expected to maintain its profitability. How might managers in other organizations mimic the success of Cirque du Soleil in facing these challenges and create an adaptive organization that can react to the unexpected?

Managers have always had to deal with changes taking place inside and outside their organizations. In today's world, where managers everywhere are dealing with corporate ethics scandals, demands to be more socially responsible, challenges of managing a diverse workforce, and globalization, change is constant. We briefly describe these challenges below, and then throughout this textbook we discuss their impact on the way managers plan, organize, lead, and control.

Importance of Customers to the Manager's Job

John Chambers, CEO of Cisco Systems, likes to listen to voice mails forwarded to him from dissatisfied customers. He says, "E-mail would be more efficient, but I want to hear the emotion, I want to hear the frustration, I want to hear the caller's level of comfort with the strategy we're employing. I can't get that through e-mail."[28] This manager understands the importance of customers. You need customers. Without them, most organizations would cease to exist. Yet, focusing on the customer has long been thought to be the responsibility of marketing types. "Let the marketers worry about the customers" is how many managers felt. We're discovering, however, that employee attitudes and behaviours play a big role in customer satisfaction. For instance, passengers of Qantas Airways were asked to rate their "essential needs" in air travel. Almost every factor listed was one directly influenced by the actions of company employees—from prompt baggage delivery, to courteous and efficient cabin crews, to assistance with connections, to quick and friendly check-ins.[29]

Today, the majority of employees in developed countries work in service jobs. For instance, almost 72 percent of the Canadian labour force is employed in service industries, in the USA 77%, in Australia, 70 percent, and in the United Kingdom, Germany, and Japan, the percentages are 78, 74, and 75, respectively. Even in developing countries like India, Russia, and China, we find 56 percent, 59 percent, and 43 percent of the labour force employed in service jobs.[30] Examples of service jobs include technical support representatives, food servers or fast-food counter workers, sales clerks, teachers, nurses, computer repair technicians, front desk clerks, consultants, purchasing agents, credit representatives, financial planners, and bank tellers. The odds are pretty good that when you graduate, you'll go to work for a company that's in a service industry, not in manufacturing or agriculture.

Managers are recognizing that delivering consistent, high-quality customer service is essential for survival and success in today's competitive environment and that employees are an important part of that equation.[31] The implication is clear—managers must create a customer-responsive organization where employees are friendly and courteous, accessible, knowledgeable, prompt in responding to customer needs and willing to do what's necessary to please the customer.[32] We'll look at customer service management in several chapters. Before we leave this topic, though, we want to share one more story that illustrates why it's important for today's managers (all managers, not just those in marketing) to understand what it takes to serve customers. During a broadcasted Stanley Cup playoff game, Comcast subscribers suddenly found themselves staring at a blank screen. Many of those customers got on Twitter to find out why. And it was there, not on a phone system, that they discovered a lightning strike in Atlanta had caused the power outage and that transmission would be restored as quickly as possible. Managers at Comcast understood how to exploit popular communications technology, and the company's smart use of Twitter "underscores what is becoming a staple in modern-day customer service . . . beefing up communications with customers through social-media tools."[33]

Importance of Social Media to the Manager's Job

You probably can't imagine a time when employees did their work without e-mail or internet access. Yet, 15 years ago, as these communication tools were becoming more common in workplaces, managers struggled with the challenges of providing guidelines for using the internet and e-mail in their organizations. Today, the new frontier is **social media**, forms of electronic communication through which users create online communities to share ideas, information, personal messages, and other content. "More than a billion people use social platforms such as Facebook, Twitter, YouTube, LinkedIn, and others."[34] Employees don't just use these on their personal time, but also for work purposes. That's why managers need to understand and manage the power and peril of social media. For instance, at grocery chain SuperValu, managers realized that keeping 135 000 plus employees connected and engaged was imperative to continued success.[35] They decided to adopt an internal social media tool to foster cooperation and collaboration among its 10 distinct store brands operating in 44 states. And they're not alone. More and more businesses are turning to social media not just as a way to connect with customers but also as a way to manage their human resources and tap into their innovation and talent. That's the potential power of social media. But the potential peril is in how it's used. When the social media platform becomes a way for boastful employees to brag about their accomplishments, for managers to publish one-way messages to employees, or for employees to argue or gripe about something or someone they don't like at work, then it's lost its usefulness. To avoid this, managers need to remember that social media is a tool that needs to be managed to be beneficial. At SuperValu, about 9000 store managers and assistant managers use the social media system. Although sources say it's too early to draw any conclusions, it appears that managers who actively make use of the system are having better store sales revenues than those who don't. In the remainder of the book,

social media Forms of electronic communication through which users create online communities to share ideas, information, personal messages, and other content.

This young woman in Switzerland competing in a worldwide paper airplane event created by Red Bull Media House illustrates the importance of innovation for Red Bull, the Austrian-based energy-drink firm. Rather than just sponsoring an event or developing an ad campaign to promote its brand, Red Bull launched its own global media company that produces, publishes, and distributes print, multimedia, and audiovisual material in the fields of sports, culture, and entertainment. The innovative marketing approach with its core message of "Gives You Wings" has created a strong bond between Red Bull and its young target audience and has helped the company capture close to half of the energy-drink market.

Maurin Bisig/ZUMA Press/Newscom

we'll look at how social media is impacting how managers manage, especially in the areas of human resource management, communication, teams, and strategy.

Importance of Innovation to the Manager's Job

"Nothing is more risky than not innovating."[36] Innovation means doing things differently, exploring new territory, and taking risks. And innovation isn't just for high-tech or other technologically sophisticated organizations. Innovative efforts can be found in all types of organizations. For instance, the manager of the Best Buy store in Manchester, Connecticut, clearly understood the importance of getting employees to be innovative, a task made particularly challenging because the average Best Buy store is often staffed by young adults in their first or second jobs. "The complexity of the products demands a high level of training, but the many distractions that tempt college-aged employees keep the turnover potential high." However, the store manager tackled the problem by getting employees to suggest new ideas. One idea—a "team close," in which employees scheduled to work at the store's closing time, closed the store together and walked out together as a team—has had a remarkable impact on employee attitudes and commitment.[37] As you'll see throughout the book, innovation is critical throughout all levels and parts of an organization. For example, the top manager of India's Tata Group, chairman Ratan Tata, told his employees during the global economic downturn to "Cut costs. Think out of the box. Even if the world around you is collapsing, be bold, be daring, think big."[38] And his employees obviously got the message. The company's $2000 minicar, the Nano, was the talk of the global automotive industry. As these stories illustrate, innovation is critical. It's so critical to today's organizations and managers that we also address this topic in several later chapters.

Importance of Adaptability to the Manager's Job

Earlier in the chapter, we distinguished between effectiveness and efficiency, but there is another point of view worthy of discussion. As early as 1972 it was suggested that the best companies in any field outshine their competitors in three areas: They are more flexible, more efficient, and more adaptable (see Exhibit 1-8).[39] Being flexible means reacting to events, while being adaptable means being proactive. An adaptable organization creates a set of skills, processes, and a culture that enable it to continuously look for new problems and offer solutions before the clients even realize they have a need.[40]

Importance of Sustainability to the Manager's Job

It's the world's largest retailer with nearly $447 billion in annual sales, 2.2 million employees, and 8,00 stores. Yes, we're talking about Walmart. And Walmart is probably the last company that you'd think about in a section describing sustainability. However,

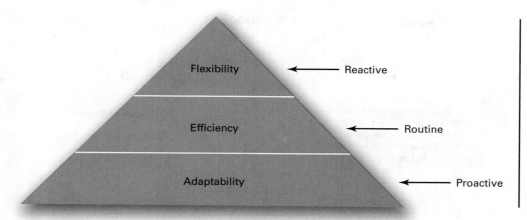

Exhibit 1-8

Characteristics of Effective Organizations

Flexibility ← Reactive

Efficiency ← Routine

Adaptability ← Proactive

Flexibility = Organizing to cope with the unexpected

Efficiency = Organizing for the expected

Adaptability = Organizing to anticipate new problems, trends, and opportunities

Source: Basadur Applied Creativity, Presentation March 18 and 19, 2010, Halifax, Nova Scotia.

Walmart announced at the beginning of this decade that it would "cut some 20 million metric tons of greenhouse gas emissions from its supply chain by the end of 2015—the equivalent of removing more than 3.8 million cars from the road for a year."[41] Walmart achieved this goal in 2011 and, among other things, have moved 21 percent of their energy consumption to renewables, have improved fleet energy by 80 percent, and now reuses or recycles more than 80 percent of the waste produced in its domestic stores and in other U.S. operations.[42] This corporate action affirms that sustainability and green management have become mainstream issues for managers.

What's emerging in the twenty-first century is the concept of managing in a sustainable way, which has had the effect of widening corporate responsibility not only to managing in an efficient and effective way, but also to responding strategically to a wide range of environmental and societal challenges.[43] Although "sustainability" means different things to different people, in essence, according to the World Business Council for Sustainable Development (2005), it is concerned with "meeting the needs of people today without compromising the ability of future generations to meet their own needs." From a business perspective, **sustainability** has been defined as a company's ability to achieve its business goals and increase long-term shareholder value by integrating economic, environmental, and social opportunities into its business strategies.[44] Sustainability issues are now moving up the agenda of business leaders and the boards of thousands of companies. Like the managers at Walmart are discovering, running an organization in a more sustainable way will mean that managers have to make informed business decisions based on thorough communication with various stakeholders; understanding their requirements; and starting to factor economic, environmental, and social aspects into how they pursue their business goals. We'll examine managing for sustainability and its importance to planning, organizing, leading, and controlling in other places throughout the book.

sustainability A company's ability to achieve its business goals and increase long-term shareholder value by integrating economic, environmental, and social opportunities into its business strategies.

Why Study Management?

You may be wondering why you need to study management. If you are an accounting major, marketing major, or any major other than management, you may not understand how studying management is going to help you in your career. We can explain the value of studying management by looking at the universality of management, the reality of work, and how management applies to anyone wanting to be self-employed.

5 Explain the value of studying management.

Exhibit 1-9

Universal Need for Management

The Universality of Management

Just how universal is the need for management in organizations? We can say with absolute certainty that management is needed in all types and sizes of organizations, at all organizational levels, in all organizational work areas, and in all organizations, no matter what countries they are located in. This is known as the **universality of management** (see Exhibit 1-9). Managers in all these settings will plan, organize, lead, and control. However, this is not to say that management is done the same way in all settings. The differences in what a supervisor in a software applications testing facility at Microsoft does compared with what the CEO of Microsoft does are a matter of degree and emphasis, not of function. Because both are managers, both will plan, organize, lead, and control, but how they do so will differ.

Since management is universally needed in all organizations, we have a vested interest in improving the way organizations are managed. Why? We interact with organizations every single day of our lives. Are you irritated when none of the salespeople in a department store seems interested in helping you? Do you get annoyed when you call a technical help desk because your software application is no longer working, go through seven voice menus, and then get put on hold for 15 minutes? These are all examples of problems created by poor management. Organizations that are well managed—and we share many examples of these throughout the text—develop a loyal customer base, grow, and prosper. Those that are poorly managed find themselves with a declining customer base and reduced revenues. By studying management, you will be able to recognize poor management and work to get it corrected. In addition, you will be able to recognize good management and encourage it, whether it's in an organization with which you are simply interacting or whether it's in an organization in which you are employed.

The Reality of Work

Another reason for studying management is the reality that most of you, once you graduate and begin your career, will either manage or be managed. For those who plan on management careers, an understanding of the management process forms the foundation upon

universality of management The reality that management is needed in all types and sizes of organizations, at all organizational levels, in all organizational work areas, and in organizations in all countries around the globe.

which to build your management skills. For those of you who don't see yourselves in management positions, you are still likely to have to work with managers. Also, assuming that you will have to work for a living and recognizing that you are very likely to work in an organization, you will probably have some managerial responsibilities even if you are not managers. Our experience tells us that you can gain a great deal of insight into the way your manager behaves and the internal workings of organizations by studying management. Our point is that you don't have to aspire to be a manager to gain something valuable from a course in management.

Self-Employment

You may decide that you want to run your own business rather than work for someone else. This will require that you manage yourself, and may involve managing other people as well. Thus, an understanding of management is equally important whether you are a manager in someone else's business or running your own business.

CHAPTER 1

SUMMARY AND IMPLICATIONS

1. Explain why managers are important to an organization. Managers are important to organizations for three reasons. First, organizations need their managerial skills and abilities in uncertain, complex, and chaotic times. Second, managers are critical to getting things done in organizations. Finally, managers contribute to employee productivity and loyalty; the way employees are managed can affect the organization's financial performance; and managerial ability has been shown to be important in creating organizational value. Management is not about *personal* achievement—it's about helping *others* to achieve for the benefit of the organization as a whole.

▶ ▶ ▶ We saw that Guy Laliberté is both a visionary who guides the company and, together with Daniel Lamarre, a cheerleader who helps everyone in the organization do a better job.

2. Tell who managers are and where they work. Managers coordinate and oversee the work of other people so that organizational goals can be accomplished. Nonmanagerial employees work directly on a job or task and have no one reporting to them. In traditionally structured organizations, managers can be first-line, middle, or top. In other more loosely configured organizations, the managers may not be as readily identifiable, although someone must fulfill that role.

Management is coordinating work activities so that they are done efficiently and effectively. *Efficiency* means "doing things right" and getting things done at the least cost.

Effectiveness means "doing the right things" and refers to completing activities that will help achieve the organization's goals. To do their jobs, managers plan, organize, lead, and control. This means they set goals and plan how to achieve those goals; they figure out what tasks need to be done, and who should do them; they motivate individuals to achieve goals, and communicate effectively with others; and they put accountability measures into place to make sure that goals are achieved efficiently and effectively.

Mintzberg's managerial roles include interpersonal, which involve people and other ceremonial/symbolic duties (figurehead, leader, and liaison); informational, which involve collecting, receiving, and disseminating information (monitor, disseminator, and spokesperson); and decisional, which involve making choices (entrepreneur, disturbance handler, resource allocator, and negotiator). Mintzberg's newest description proposes that managing is about influencing action by managing actions directly, by managing people who take action, and by managing information that impels people to take action. Katz's managerial skills include technical (job-specific knowledge and techniques), human (ability to work well with people), and conceptual (ability to think and express ideas). Technical skills are most important for lower-level managers while conceptual skills are most important for top managers. Human skills are equally important for all managers.

▶▶▶ In Daniel Lamarre's role as CEO of Cirque du Soleil, he manages the relationship with founder Guy Laliberté and, with managers in the rest of Cirque du Soleil, and sets the goals for the overall organization.

3. Describe the characteristics of an organization. Managers work in an organization, which is a deliberate arrangement of people to accomplish some specific purpose. Organizations have three characteristics: a distinctive purpose, composed of people, and a deliberate structure. Many of today's organizations are structured to be more open, flexible, and responsive to changes. Managers work in a variety of organizations, both large and small, in a variety of industries including manufacturing and the service sector. The organizations they work for can be publicly held, privately held, public sector, or not-for-profit.

▶▶▶ As Cirque du Soleil has grown since its founding in 1984, the purpose of the organization has changed and the forms of organization employed to achieve this purpose have grown in number.

4. Describe the factors that are reshaping and redefining the manager's job. The changes impacting managers' jobs include global economic and political uncertainties, changing workplaces, ethical issues, security threats, and changing technology. Managers must be concerned with customer service because employee attitudes and behaviours play a big role in customer satisfaction. Managers must be concerned with social media because these forms of communication are becoming important and valuable tools in managing. Managers must also be concerned with innovation because it is important for organizations to be competitive. And finally, managers must be concerned with sustainability as business goals are developed.

▶▶▶ With the establishment of the ONE DROP Foundation, Guy Laliberté, like many others, expanded his sense of responsibility beyond the company and its employees to the global community. The foundation works to fight poverty around the world by providing sustainable access to safe water.

5. Explain the value of studying management. There are many reasons students end up in management courses. Some of you are already managers, and are hoping to learn more about the subject. Some of you hope to be managers someday. And some of you might not have ever thought about being managers. Career aspirations are only one reason to study management, however. Any organization you encounter will have managers, and it is often useful to understand their responsibilities, challenges, and experience. Understanding management also helps us improve organizations.

▶▶▶ When Guy Laliberté launched Cirque du Soleil, management style could be best described as "management by clowning around" but this swiftly changed as the company grew. Management and the principles discussed in this chapter provided the underpinnings that allowed Cirque du Soleil to thrive and grow, illustrating that management principles can be applied successfully in diverse settings.

MyManagementLab Study, practise, and explore real management situations with these helpful resources:
- **Interactive Lesson Presentations:** Work through interactive presentations and assessments to test your knowledge of management concepts.
- **PIA (Personal Inventory Assessments):** Enhance your ability to connect with key concepts through these engaging, self-reflection assessments.
- **Study Plan:** Check your understanding of chapter concepts with self-study quizzes.
- **Simulations:** Practise decision-making in simulated management environments.

PIA PERSONAL INVENTORY ASSESSMENT

REVIEW AND DISCUSSION QUESTIONS

1. How do managers differ from nonmanagerial employees? Is your course instructor a manager? Discuss in terms of managerial functions, managerial roles, and skills.

2. In today's economic environment, which is more important to organizations—efficiency, effectiveness, or adaptability? Explain your choice.

3. What are the four functions of management? Briefly describe each of them.

4. What are the three categories of management roles proposed by Mintzberg? Provide an example of each.

5. "The manager's most basic responsibility is to focus people toward performance of work activities to achieve desired outcomes." What is your interpretation of this statement? Do you agree with it? Why or why not?

6. What is an organization? Why are managers important to an organization's success?

7. Why is an understanding of management important even if you don't plan to be a manager?

8. How could an organization build an adaptive culture?

ETHICS DILEMMA

Moving to a management position isn't easy and organizations often provide little help in making the transition. Would it surprise you to learn that 26 percent of new managers feel they are unprepared to transition into management roles, 58 percent of new managers don't receive any training to help them make the transition, and 50 percent of first-time managers fail in that transition?[45]

Does an organization have an ethical responsibility to assist its new managers in their new positions? Why or why not? What could organizations do to make this transition easier? Suppose you were a new manager; what support would you expect from your organization? From your manager?

SKILLS EXERCISE

Mentoring—About the Skill

A mentor is someone in the organization, usually older, more experienced, and in a higher-level position, who sponsors or supports another employee (a protégé) who is in a lower-level position in the organization. A mentor can teach, guide, and encourage. Some organizations have formal mentoring programs, but even if your organization does not, mentoring should be an important skill for you to develop.

Steps in Developing the Skill

You can be more effective at mentoring if you use the following six suggestions as you mentor another person:[46]

1. **Communicate honestly and openly with your protégé.** If your protégé is going to learn from you and benefit from your experience and knowledge, you are going to have to be open and honest as you talk about what you have done. Bring up the failures as well as the successes. Remember that mentoring is a learning process, and in order for learning to take place you are going to have to be open and honest in "telling it like it is."

2. **Encourage honest and open communication from your protégé.** You need to know as the mentor what your protégé hopes to gain from this relationship. You should encourage the protégé to ask for information and be specific about what he or she wants to gain.

3. **Treat the relationship with the protégé as a learning opportunity.** Don't pretend to have all the answers and all the knowledge, but do share what you have learned through your experiences. In your conversations and interactions with your protégé, you may be able to learn as much from that person as he or she does from you. So be open to listening to what your protégé is saying.

4. **Take the time to get to know your protégé.** As a mentor, you should be willing to take the time to get to know your protégé and his or her interests. If you are not willing to spend that extra time, you should probably not embark on a mentoring relationship.

5. **Remind your protégé that there is no substitute for effective work performance.** In any job, effective work performance is absolutely essential for success. It does not matter how much information you provide as a mentor if the protégé is not willing to strive for effective work performance.

6. **Know when it's time to let go.** Successful mentors know when it's time to let the protégé begin standing on his or her own. If the mentoring relationship has been effective, the protégé will be comfortable and confident in handling new and increasing work responsibilities. Just because the mentoring relationship is over does not mean that you never have contact with your protégé. It just means that the relationship becomes one of equals, not one of teacher and student.

Practising the Skill

Read the following scenario. Write some notes about how you would handle the situation described. Be sure to refer to the six suggestions for mentoring.

Scenario

Lora Slovinsky has worked for your department in a software design firm longer than any other of your employees. You value her skills and commitment, and you frequently ask for her judgment on difficult issues. Very often, her ideas have been better than yours and you have let her know through both praise and pay increases how much you appreciate her contributions. Recently, though, you have begun to question Lora's judgment. The fundamental problem is in the distinct difference in the ways you both approach your work. Your strengths lie in getting things done on time and under budget.

Although Lora is aware of these constraints, her creativity and perfectionism sometimes make her prolong projects, continually looking for the best approaches. On her most recent assignment, Lora seemed more intent than ever on doing things her way. Despite what you felt were clear guidelines, she was two weeks late in meeting an important customer deadline. While her product quality was high, as always, the software design was far more elaborate than what was needed at this stage of development. Looking over her work in your office, you feel more than a little frustrated and certain that you need to address matters with Lora. What will you say?

Reinforcing the Skill

The following activities will help you practise and reinforce the skills associated with mentoring:

1. If there are individuals on your campus who act as mentors (or advisers) to first-time students, make an appointment to talk to one of these mentors. They may be upper-division students, professors, or staff employees. Ask them about their roles as mentors and the skills they think it takes to be an effective mentor. How do the skills they mention relate to the behaviours described here?

2. Athletic coaches often act as mentors to their younger assistant coaches. Interview a coach about her or his role as a mentor. What types of things do coaches do to instruct, teach, advise, and encourage their assistant coaches? Could any of these activities be transferred to an organizational setting? Explain.

WORKING TOGETHER: TEAM EXERCISE

A New Beginning

By this time in your life, all of you have had to work with individuals in managerial positions (or maybe you were the manager), either through work experiences or through other organizational experiences (social, hobby/interest, religious, and so forth). What do you think makes some managers better than others? Are there certain characteristics that distinguish good managers? Form groups of three or four individuals. Discuss your experiences with managers—good and bad. Draw up a list of the characteristics of those individuals you felt were good managers. For each characteristic, indicate which management function (planning, organizing, leading, and controlling) you think it falls under. Also identify which of Mintzberg's 10 roles the good managers seemed to fill. Were any of the roles missing from your list of characteristics? What explanation can you give for this? As a group, be prepared to explain the functions and roles that good managers are most likely to fill.

LEARNING TO BE A MANAGER

- Think about where you hope to be in your life five years from now (that is, your major goal). What is your competitive advantage for achieving your goal? What do you need to plan, organize, lead, and control to make sure that you reach your goal?
- Looking over Mintzberg's management roles (see Exhibit 1-4, on page xx), which roles seem comfortable for you? What areas need improvement?
- Keep up with the current business news.
- Read books about good and bad examples of managing.
- Observe managers and how they handle people and situations.

- Talk to actual managers about their experiences—good and bad.
- In other classes you take, see what ideas and concepts potentially relate to being a good manager.
- Get experience in managing by taking on leadership roles in student organizations.
- Start thinking about whether or not you would enjoy being a manager.
- Stay informed about the current trends and issues facing managers.

CASE APPLICATION 1

Building a Better Boss

Google doesn't do anything halfway. So when it decided to "build a better boss," it did what it does best—look at data.[47] Using data from performance reviews, feedback surveys, and supporting papers turned in for individuals nominated for top-manager awards, Google correlated "phrases, words, praise, and complaints" trying to find what makes for a great boss. The project, dubbed Project Oxygen, examined some 100 variables and ultimately identified eight characteristics or habits of Google's most effective managers. Here are the "big eight":

- Have a clear vision and strategy for the team
- Help your employees with career development
- Express interest in your team members' success and well-being

- Have technical skills so you can advise the team
- Be a good communicator and listen to your team
- Be a good coach
- Be productive and results-oriented
- Empower your team and don't micromanage

At first glance, you're probably thinking these eight attributes seem pretty simplistic and obvious, and you may be wondering why Google spent all this time and effort to uncover these. Even Google's vice president for people operations, Laszlo Bock, said, "My first reaction was, 'that's it?'" Another writer described it as "reading like a whiteboard gag from an episode of *The Office.*" But, as the old saying goes, there *was* more to this list than meets the eye.

When Bock and his team began looking closer and rank ordering the eight items by importance, Project Oxygen got interesting—a lot more interesting! And to understand this, you have to understand something about Google's approach to management since its founding in 1999. Plain and simple, managers were encouraged to "leave people alone. Let the engineers do their stuff. If they become stuck, they'll ask their bosses, whose deep technical expertise propelled them to management in the first place." It's not hard to see what Google wanted its managers to be—outstanding technical specialists. Mr. Bock explains, "In the Google context, we'd always believed that to be a manager, particularly on the engineering side, you need to be as deep or deeper a technical expert than the people who work for you." However, Project Oxygen revealed that technical expertise was ranked number eight (very last) on the list. So, here's the complete list from most important to least important, along with what each characteristic entails:

- *Be a good coach* (provide specific feedback and have regular one-on-one meetings with employees; offer solutions tailored to each employee's strengths)
- *Empower your team and don't micromanage* (give employees space to tackle problems themselves, but be available to offer advice)
- *Be interested in your team members' successes and well-being* (make new team members feel welcome and get to know your employees as people)
- *Be productive and results-oriented* (focus on helping the team achieve its goals by prioritizing work and getting rid of obstacles)
- *Be a good communicator and listen to your team* (learn to listen and to share information; encourage open dialogue and pay attention to the team's concerns)

- *Help your employees with career development* (notice employees' efforts so they can see how their hard work is furthering their careers; appreciate employees' efforts and make that appreciation known)
- *Have a clear vision and strategy for the team* (lead the team, but keep everyone involved in developing and working toward the team's vision)
- *Have technical skills so you can advise the team* (understand the challenges facing the team and be able to help team members solve problems)

Now, managers at Google aren't just encouraged to be great managers—they know what being a great manager involves. And the company is doing its part, as well. Using the list, Google started training managers as well as providing individual coaching and performance review sessions. You can say that Project Oxygen breathed new life into Google's managers. Bock says the company's efforts paid off quickly. "We were able to have a statistically significant improvement in manager quality for 75 percent of our worst-performing managers."

DISCUSSION QUESTIONS

1. Describe the findings of Project Oxygen using the functions approach, Mintzberg's roles approach, and the skills approach.
2. Are you surprised at what Google found out about "building a better boss?" Explain your answer.
3. What's the difference between encouraging managers to be great managers and knowing what being a great manager involves?
4. What could other companies learn from Google's experiences?
5. Would you want to work for a company like Google? Why or why not?

CASE APPLICATION 2

Lipschultz Levin & Gray

You might be surprised to find a passionate emphasis placed on people at an accounting firm. Yet at Lipschultz Levin & Gray (**www.thethinkers.com**), self-described "head bean counter" Steven P. Siegel recognizes that his people make the organization. He describes his primary responsibility as ensuring that LLG's clients have the best professionals working for them. And the best way to do this, Siegel feels, is by developing the creativity, talent, and diversity of its staff so that new knowledge can be acquired and shared without getting hung up on formal organizational relationships or having employees shut away in corner offices.

Siegel's commitment to his people starts with the company's mission:

LLG's goal is to be the pre-eminent provider of the highest quality accounting, tax and consulting services. We seek to accomplish this goal by leaving no stone unturned in exploring new and superior alternatives of supplying our services, and developing such methods on a global basis. Our environment promotes creativity, individual development, group interchange, diversity, good humour, family and community, all for the purpose of assisting in our clients' growth.

To further demonstrate that commitment, Siegel has implemented several significant changes at LLG. Because he is convinced that people do their best intellectual work in nontraditional settings, every telltale sign of what most people consider boring, dull accounting work has been eliminated. None of the firm's employees or partners has an office or desk to call his or her own. Instead, everyone is part of a nomadic arrangement where stuff (files, phones, laptops) is wheeled to a new spot every day. Everywhere you look in the company's office, you see versatility, comfort, and individuality. For instance, a miniature golf course is located in the middle of everything. The motivation behind this open office design is to create opportunities for professionals to gather—on purpose or by accident—without walls, cubicles, or offices to get in the way.

Visitors to LLG realize that the firm is different as soon as they walk in the door. A giant, wall-mounted abacus (remember the image of bean counters) decorates the interior. And visitors are greeted by a "Welcome Wall" with a big-screen television that flashes a continuous slide show of one-liners about business, life, and innovation. The setting may be fun and lighthearted, but the LLG team is seriously committed to serving its clients. So serious, in fact that they state:

> We have one goal. To "Delight" you. Good, even great, is not enough anymore. We will "Dazzle" you and we will guarantee it; We will deliver our service with integrity, honesty and openness in everything we do for you and with you; We will absolutely respect the confidentiality of our working relationship; We will return your phone calls, facsimiles and e-mails within 24 hours; We will always provide exceptional service, designed to help you add significant value to your business; We will meet the deadlines we set together with you; We will communicate with you frequently, building a win-win relationship with you; and You will always know in advance our fee arrangement for any service.

Yesterday, one of Siegel's new employees complained in an email to him that the work environment is too informal, and that employees need their own desks. This employee has done well in her first few months on the job. Siegel is meeting with her in an hour. What should he say to her?

DISCUSSION QUESTIONS

1. Describe the culture at the Lipshultz firm.
2. What is your sense of how committed Siegel is to the culture?
3. How comfortable/uncomfortable would you be working in this environment?
4. Would should Siegel say to the employees? Why?

Management History

▶ ▶ ▶ Henry Ford once said, "History is more or less bunk." Well, he was wrong! History is important because it can put current activities in perspective. In this module, we're going to take a trip back in time to see how the field of study called management has evolved. What you're going to see is that today's managers still use many elements of the historical approaches to management.

3000 BC–1776	1911–1947	Late 1700s–1950s	1940s–1950s	1960s–present
Early Management	**Classical Approach**	**Behavioural Approach**	**Quantitative Approach**	**Contemporary Approaches**

Early Management

Management has been practised a long time. Organized endeavours directed by people responsible for planning, organizing, leading, and controlling activities have existed for thousands of years. Let's look at some of the most interesting examples.

The Egyptian pyramids and the Great Wall of China are proof that projects of tremendous scope, employing tens of thousands of people, were completed in ancient times.[1] It took more than 100 000 workers some 20 years to construct a single pyramid. Who told each worker what to do? Who ensured there would be enough stones at the site to keep workers busy? The answer is *managers*. Someone had to plan what was to be done, organize people and materials to do it, make sure those workers got the work done, and impose some controls to ensure that everything was done as planned.

Another example of early management can be found in the city of Venice, which was a major economic and trade centre in the 1400s. The Venetians developed an early form of business enterprise and engaged in many activities common to today's organizations. For instance, at the arsenal of Venice, warships were floated along the canals, and at each stop, materials and riggings were added to the ship.[2] Sounds a lot like a car "floating" along an assembly line, doesn't it? In addition, the Venetians used warehouse and inventory systems to keep track of materials, human resource management functions to manage the labour force (including wine breaks), and an accounting system to keep track of revenues and costs.

division of labour (job specialization) The breakdown of jobs into narrow and repetitive tasks.

In 1776, Adam Smith published *The Wealth of Nations*, in which he argued the economic advantages that organizations and society would gain from the **division of labour** (or **job specialization**)—that is, breaking down jobs into narrow and repetitive tasks. Using the pin industry as an example, Smith claimed that 10 individuals, each doing a specialized task, could produce about 48,000 pins a day among them. However, if each person worked alone performing each task separately, it would be quite an accomplishment to produce even 10 pins a day! Smith concluded that division of labour increased productivity by increasing each worker's skill and dexterity, saving time lost in changing tasks, and creating labour-saving inventions and machinery. Job specialization continues to be popular. For example, think of the specialized tasks performed by members of a hospital surgery team, meal preparation tasks done by workers in restaurant kitchens, or positions played by players on a football team.

industrial revolution A period during the late eighteenth century when machine power was substituted for human power, making it more economical to manufacture goods in factories than at home.

Starting in the late eighteenth century when machine power was substituted for human power, a point in history known as the **industrial revolution**, it became more economical to manufacture goods in factories rather than at home. These large efficient factories needed someone to forecast demand, ensure that enough material was on hand to make products, assign tasks to people, direct daily activities, and so forth. That "someone" was

Exhibit MH-1

Major Approaches to Management

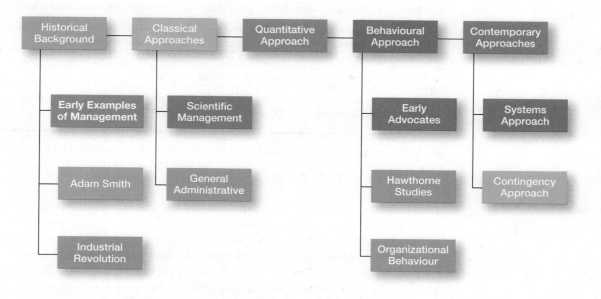

---

a manager: These managers would need formal theories to guide them in running these large organizations. It wasn't until the early 1900s, however, that the first steps toward developing such theories were taken.

In this module, we'll look at four major approaches to management theory: classical, behavioural, quantitative, and contemporary. (See Exhibit MH-1.) Keep in mind that each approach is concerned with trying to explain management from the perspective of what was important at that time in history and the backgrounds and interests of the researchers. Each of the four approaches contributes to our overall understanding of management, but each is also a limited view of what it is and how to best practise it.

3000 BC–1776	1911–1947	Late 1700s–1950s	1940s–1950s	1960s–present
Early Management	Classical Approach	Behavioural Approach	Quantitative Approach	Contemporary Approaches

Classical Approach

Although we've seen how management has been used in organized efforts since early history, the formal study of management didn't begin until early in the twentieth century. These first studies of management, often called the **classical approach**, emphasized rationality and making organizations and workers as efficient as possible. Two major theories make up the classical approach: scientific management and general administrative theory. The two most important contributors to scientific management theory were Frederick W. Taylor and the husband-wife team of Frank and Lillian Gilbreth. The two most important contributors to general administrative theory were Henri Fayol and Max Weber. Let's take a look at each of these important figures in management history.

classical approach First studies of management, which emphasized rationality and making organizations and workers as efficient as possible.

Scientific Management

If you had to pinpoint when modern management theory was born, 1911 might be a good choice. That was when Frederick Winslow Taylor's *Principles of Scientific Management* was published. Its contents were widely embraced by managers around the world. Taylor's book

Exhibit MH-2

Taylor's Scientific Management Principles

1. Develop a science for each element of an individual's work to replace the old rule-of-thumb method.

2. Scientifically select and then train, teach, and develop the worker.

3. Heartily cooperate with the workers to ensure that all work is done in accordance with the principles of the science that has been developed.

4. Divide work and responsibility almost equally between management and workers. Management does all work for which it is better suited than the workers.

Source: The Principles of Scientific Management by Frederick Winslow Taylor. Published 1911.

scientific management An approach that involves using the scientific method to find the "one best way" for a job to be done.

described the theory of **scientific management**: the use of scientific methods to define the "one best way" for a job to be done.

Taylor worked at the Midvale and Bethlehem Steel Companies in Pennsylvania. As a mechanical engineer with a Quaker and Puritan background, he was continually appalled by workers' inefficiencies. Employees used vastly different techniques to do the same job. They often "took it easy" on the job, and Taylor believed that worker output was only about one-third of what was possible. Virtually no work standards existed, and workers were placed in jobs with little or no concern for matching their abilities and aptitudes with the tasks they were required to do. Taylor set out to remedy that by applying the scientific method to shop-floor jobs. He spent more than two decades passionately pursuing the "one best way" for such jobs to be done.

Taylor's experiences at Midvale led him to define clear guidelines for improving production efficiency. He argued that these four principles of management (Exhibit MH-2) would result in prosperity for both workers and managers.[3] How did these scientific principles really work? Let's look at an example.

Probably the best known example of Taylor's scientific management efforts was the pig iron experiment. Workers loaded "pigs" of iron (each weighing 92 lbs.) onto rail cars. Their daily average output was 12.5 tons. However, Taylor believed that by scientifically analyzing the job to determine the "one best way" to load pig iron, output could be increased to 47 or 48 tons per day. After scientifically applying different combinations of procedures, techniques, and tools, Taylor succeeded in getting that level of productivity. How? By putting the right person on the job with the correct tools and equipment, having the worker follow his instructions exactly, and motivating the worker with an economic incentive of a significantly higher daily wage. Using similar approaches for other jobs, Taylor was able to define the "one best way" for doing each job. Overall, Taylor achieved consistent productivity improvements in the range of 200 percent or more. Based on his groundbreaking studies of manual work using scientific principles, Taylor became known as the "father" of scientific management. His ideas spread in the United States and to other countries and inspired others to study and develop methods of scientific management. His most prominent followers were Frank and Lillian Gilbreth.

A construction contractor by trade, Frank Gilbreth gave up that career to study scientific management after hearing Taylor speak at a professional meeting. Frank and his wife, Lillian, a psychologist, studied work to eliminate inefficient hand-and-body motions. The Gilbreths also experimented with the design and use of the proper tools and equipment for optimizing work performance.[4] Also, as parents of 12 children, the Gilbreths ran their household using scientific management principles and techniques. In fact, two of their children wrote a book, *Cheaper by the Dozen*, which described life with the two masters of efficiency.

Frank is probably best known for his bricklaying experiments. By carefully analyzing the bricklayer's job, he reduced the number of motions in laying exterior brick from 18 to about 5, and in laying interior brick from 18 to 2. Using Gilbreth's techniques, a bricklayer was more productive and less fatigued at the end of the day.

The Gilbreths invented a device called a microchronometer that recorded a worker's hand-and-body motions and the amount of time spent doing each motion. Wasted motions missed by the naked eye could be identified and eliminated. The Gilbreths also devised a classification scheme to label 17 basic hand motions (such as search, grasp, hold), which they called **therbligs** (Gilbreth spelled backward with the *th* transposed). This scheme gave the Gilbreths a more precise way of analyzing a worker's exact hand movements.

therbligs A classification scheme for labelling basic hand motions.

How today's managers use scientific management

Many of the guidelines and techniques Taylor and the Gilbreths devised for improving production efficiency are still used in organizations today. When managers analyze the basic work tasks that must be performed, use time-and-motion study to eliminate wasted motions, hire the best-qualified workers for a job, or design incentive systems based on output, they're using the principles of scientific management.

General Administrative Theory

General administrative theory focused more on what managers do and what constituted good management practice. We introduced Henri Fayol in Chapter 1 because he first identified five functions that managers perform: planning, organizing, commanding, coordinating, and controlling.[5]

general administrative theory An approach to management that focuses on describing what managers do and what constitutes good management practice.

Fayol wrote during the same time period as Taylor. While Taylor was concerned with first-line managers and the scientific method, Fayol's attention was directed at the activities of *all* managers. He wrote from his personal experience as the managing director of a large French coal-mining firm.

Fayol described the practice of management as something distinct from accounting, finance, production, distribution, and other typical business functions. His belief that management was an activity common to all business endeavours, government, and even the home led him to develop 14 **principles of management**—fundamental rules of management that could be applied to all organizational situations and taught in schools. These principles are shown in Exhibit MH-3.

principles of management Fundamental rules of management that could be applied in all organizational situations and taught in schools.

Exhibit MH-3

Fayol's 14 Principles of Management

1. **Division of work.** Specialization increases output by making employees more efficient.
2. **Authority.** Managers must be able to give orders, and authority gives them this right.
3. **Discipline.** Employees must obey and respect the rules that govern the organization.
4. **Unity of command.** Every employee should receive orders from only one superior.
5. **Unity of direction.** The organization should have a single plan of action to guide managers and workers.
6. **Subordination of individual interests to the general interest.** The interests of any one employee or group of employees should not take precedence over the interests of the organization as a whole.
7. **Remuneration.** Workers must be paid a fair wage for their services.
8. **Centralization.** This term refers to the degree to which subordinates are involved in decision making.
9. **Scalar chain.** The line of authority from top management to the lowest ranks is the scalar chain.
10. **Order.** People and materials should be in the right place at the right time.
11. **Equity.** Managers should be kind and fair to their subordinates.
12. **Stability of tenure of personnel.** Management should provide orderly personnel planning and ensure that replacements are available to fill vacancies.
13. **Initiative.** Employees allowed to originate and carry out plans will exert high levels of effort.
14. **Esprit de corps.** Promoting team spirit will build harmony and unity within the organization.

Exhibit MH-4

Characteristics of Weber's Bureaucracy

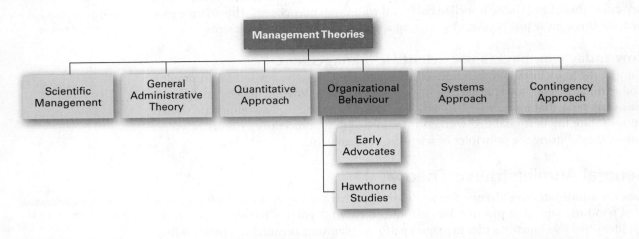

bureaucracy A form of organization characterized by division of labour, a clearly defined hierarchy, detailed rules and regulations, and impersonal relationships.

Weber (pronounced VAY-ber) was a German sociologist who studied organizations.[6] Writing in the early 1900s, he developed a theory of authority structures and relations based on an ideal type of organization he called a **bureaucracy**—a form of organization characterized by division of labour, a clearly defined hierarchy, detailed rules and regulations, and impersonal relationships. (See Exhibit MH-4.) Weber recognized that this "ideal bureaucracy" didn't exist in reality. Instead, he intended it as a basis for theorizing about how work could be done in large groups. His theory became the structural design for many of today's large organizations.

Bureaucracy, as described by Weber, is a lot like scientific management in its ideology. Both emphasized rationality, predictability, impersonality, technical competence, and authoritarianism. Although Weber's ideas were less practical than Taylor's, the fact that his "ideal type" still describes many contemporary organizations attests to their importance.

How today's managers use general administrative theory

Several of our current management ideas and practices can be directly traced to the contributions of general administrative theory. For instance, the functional view of the manager's job can be attributed to Fayol. In addition, his 14 principles serve as a frame of reference from which many current management concepts—such as managerial authority, centralized decision making, reporting to only one boss, and so forth—have evolved.

Weber's bureaucracy was an attempt to formulate an ideal prototype for organizations. Although many characteristics of Weber's bureaucracy are still evident in large organizations, his model isn't as popular today as it was in the twentieth century. Many managers feel that a bureaucratic structure hinders individual employees' creativity and limits an organization's ability to respond quickly to an increasingly dynamic environment. However, even in flexible organizations of creative professionals—such as Google, Samsung, General Electric, or Cisco Systems—bureaucratic mechanisms are necessary to ensure that resources are used efficiently and effectively.

3000 BC–1776	1911–1947	Late 1700s–1950s	1940s–1950s	1960s–present
Early Management	Classical Approach	Behavioural Approach	Quantitative Approach	Contemporary Approaches

Behavioural Approach

As we know, managers get things done by working with people. This explains why some writers have chosen to look at management by focusing on the organization's people. The field of study that researches the actions (behaviour) of people at work is called **organizational behaviour (OB)**. Much of what managers do today when managing people—motivating, leading, building trust, working with a team, managing conflict, and so forth—has come out of OB research.

Although a number of individuals in the early twentieth century recognized the importance of people to an organization's success, four stand out as early advocates of the OB approach: Robert Owen, Hugo Munsterberg, Mary Parker Follett, and Chester Barnard. Their contributions were varied and distinct, yet all believed that people were the most important asset of the organization and should be managed accordingly. Their ideas provided the foundation for such management practices as employee selection procedures, motivation programs, and work teams. Exhibit MH-5 summarizes each individual's most important ideas.

Without question, the most important contribution to the OB field came out of the **Hawthorne Studies**, a series of studies conducted at the Western Electric Company Works in Cicero, Illinois. These studies, which started in 1924, were initially designed by Western Electric industrial engineers as a scientific management experiment. They wanted to examine the effect of various lighting levels on worker productivity. Like any good scientific experiment, control and experimental groups were set up with the experimental group exposed to various lighting intensities, and the control group working under a constant intensity. If you were the industrial engineers in charge of this experiment, what would

organizational behaviour (OB) The study of the actions of people at work.

Hawthorne Studies A series of studies during the 1920s and 1930s that provided new insights into individual and group behaviour.

Exhibit MH-5

Early Advocates of Organizational Behaviour

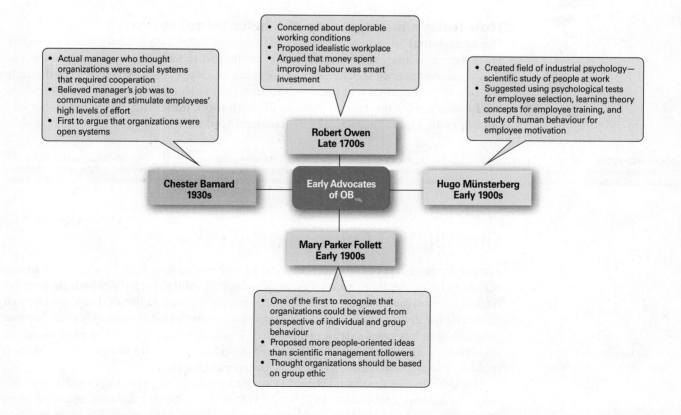

you have expected to happen? It's logical to think that individual output in the experimental group would be directly related to the intensity of the light. However, they found that as the level of light was increased in the experimental group, output for both groups increased. Then, much to the surprise of the engineers, as the light level was decreased in the experimental group, productivity continued to increase in both groups. In fact, a productivity decrease was observed in the experimental group *only* when the level of light was reduced to that of a moonlit night. What would explain these unexpected results? The engineers weren't sure, but concluded that lighting intensity was not directly related to group productivity and that something else must have contributed to the results. They weren't able to pinpoint what that "something else" was, though.

In 1927, the Western Electric engineers asked Harvard professor Elton Mayo and his associates to join the study as consultants. Thus began a relationship that would last through 1932 and encompass numerous experiments in the redesign of jobs, changes in workday and workweek length, introduction of rest periods, and individual versus group wage plans.[7] For example, one experiment was designed to evaluate the effect of a group piecework incentive pay system on group productivity. The results indicated that the incentive plan had less effect on a worker's output than group pressure, acceptance, and security. The researchers concluded that social norms or group standards were the key determinants of individual work behaviour.

Scholars generally agree that the Hawthorne Studies had a game-changing impact on management beliefs about the role of people in organizations. Mayo concluded that people's behaviour and attitudes are closely related, that group factors significantly affect individual behaviour, that group standards establish individual worker output, and that money is less a factor in determining output than group standards, group attitudes, and security. These conclusions led to a new emphasis on the human behaviour factor in the management of organizations.

Although critics attacked the research procedures, analyses of findings, and conclusions, it's of little importance from a historical perspective whether the Hawthorne Studies were academically sound or their conclusions justified.[8] What *is* important is that they stimulated an interest in human behaviour in organizations.

How today's managers use the behavioural approach

The behavioural approach has largely shaped how today's organizations are managed. From the way managers design jobs to the way they work with employee teams to the way they communicate, we see elements of the behavioural approach. Much of what the early OB advocates proposed and the conclusions from the Hawthorne studies have provided the foundation for our current theories of motivation, leadership, group behaviour and development, and numerous other behavioural approaches.

3000 BC–1776	1911–1947	Late 1700s–1950s	1940s–1950s	1960s–present
Early Management	Classical Approach	Behavioural Approach	Quantitative Approach	Contemporary Approaches

Quantitative Approach

Although passengers bumping into each other when trying to find their seats on an airplane can be a mild annoyance for them, it's a bigger problem for airlines because lines get backed up, slowing down how quickly the plane can get back in the air. Based on research in space-time geometry, one airline innovated a unique boarding process called "reverse pyramid" that has saved at least two minutes in boarding time.[9] This is an example of the **quantitative approach**, which is the use of quantitative techniques to improve decision making. This approach also is known as *management science*.

The quantitative approach evolved from mathematical and statistical solutions developed for military problems during World War II. After the war was over, many of these techniques used for military problems were applied to businesses. For example, one

quantitative approach The use of quantitative techniques to improve decision making.

group of military officers, nicknamed the Whiz Kids, joined Ford Motor Company in the mid-1940s and immediately began using statistical methods and quantitative models to improve decision making.

What exactly does the quantitative approach do? It involves applying statistics, optimization models, information models, computer simulations, and other quantitative techniques to management activities. Linear programming, for instance, is a technique that managers use to improve resource allocation decisions. Work scheduling can be more efficient as a result of critical-path scheduling analysis. The economic order quantity model helps managers determine optimum inventory levels. Each of these is an example of quantitative techniques being applied to improve managerial decision making. Another area where quantitative techniques are used frequently is in total quality management.

A quality revolution swept through both the business and public sectors in the 1980s and 1990s.[10] It was inspired by a small group of quality experts; the most famous was W. Edwards Deming and Joseph M. Juran. The ideas and techniques they advocated in the 1950s had few supporters in the United States but were enthusiastically embraced by Japanese organizations. As Japanese manufacturers began beating U.S. competitors in quality comparisons, however, Western managers soon took a more serious look at Deming's and Juran's ideas, which became the basis for today's quality management programs.

Total quality management, or **TQM**, is a management philosophy devoted to continual improvement and responding to customer needs and expectations. (See Exhibit MH-6.) The term *customer* includes anyone who interacts with the organization's product or services, internally or externally. It encompasses employees and suppliers as well as the people who purchase the organization's goods or services. *Continual improvement* isn't possible without accurate measurements, which require statistical techniques that measure every critical variable in the organization's work processes. These measurements are compared against standards to identify and correct problems.

total quality management (TQM) A philosophy of management that is driven by continuous improvement and responsiveness to customer needs and expectations.

How today's managers use the quantitative approach

No one likes long lines, especially people waiting in line to do their banking. Customers are often guided into serpentine single lines that feed into numerous teller stations resulting in wait times that are shorter than expected.[11] The science of keeping lines moving is known as queue management. For Canadian banks, this quantitative technique translated into less frustration and better customer service.

Exhibit MH-6

What Is Quality Management?

1. **Intense focus on the customer.** The customer includes outsiders who buy the organization's products or services and internal customers who interact with and serve others in the organization.

2. **Concern for continual improvement.** Quality management is a commitment to never being satisfied. "Very good" is not good enough. Quality can always be improved.

3. **Process focused.** Quality management focuses on work processes as the quality of goods and services is continually improved.

4. **Improvement in the quality of everything the organization does.** This relates to the final product, how the organization handles deliveries, how rapidly it responds to complaints, how politely the phones are answered, and the like.

5. **Accurate measurement.** Quality management uses statistical techniques to measure every critical variable in the organization's operations. These are compared against standards to identify problems, trace them to their roots, and eliminate their causes.

6. **Empowerment of employees.** Quality management involves the people on the line in the improvement process. Teams are widely used in quality management programs as empowerment vehicles for finding and solving problems.

The quantitative approach contributes directly to management decision making in the areas of planning and control. For instance, when managers make budgeting, queuing, scheduling, quality control, and similar decisions, they typically rely on quantitative techniques. Specialized software has made the use of these techniques less intimidating for managers, although many still feel anxious about using them.

3000 BC–1776	1911–1947	Late 1700s–1950s	1940s–1950s	1960s–present
Early Management	Classical Approach	Behavioural Approach	Quantitative Approach	Contemporary Approaches

Contemporary Approaches

As we've seen, many elements of the earlier approaches to management theory continue to influence how managers manage. Most of these earlier approaches focused on managers' concerns *inside* the organization. Starting in the 1960s, management researchers began to look at what was happening in the external environment *outside* the boundaries of the organization. Two contemporary management perspectives—systems and contingency—are part of this approach. Systems theory is a basic theory in the physical sciences, but had never been applied to organized human efforts. In 1938, Chester Barnard, a telephone company executive, first wrote in his book, *The Functions of an Executive,* that an organization functioned as a cooperative system. However, it wasn't until the 1960s that management researchers began to look more carefully at systems theory and how it related to organizations.

A **system** is a set of interrelated and interdependent parts arranged in a manner that produces a unified whole. The two basic types of systems are closed and open. **Closed systems** are not influenced by and do not interact with their environment. In contrast, **open systems** are influenced by and do interact with their environment. Today, when we describe organizations as systems, we mean open systems. Exhibit MH-7 shows a diagram of an organization from an open systems perspective. As you can see, an organization takes in inputs (resources) from the environment and transforms or processes these resources into outputs that are distributed into the environment. The organization is "open" to and interacts with its environment.

system A set of interrelated and interdependent parts arranged in a manner that produces a unified whole.

closed systems Systems that are not influenced by and do not interact with their environment.

open systems Systems that interact with their environment.

Exhibit MH-7

The Organization as an Open System

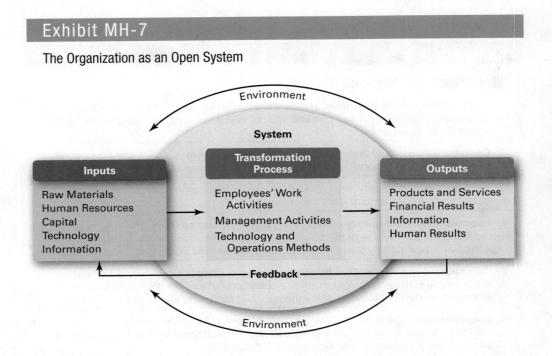

How does the systems approach contribute to our understanding of management?

Researchers envisioned an organization as made up of "interdependent factors, including individuals, groups, attitudes, motives, formal structure, interactions, goals, status, and authority."[12] What this means is that as managers coordinate work activities in the various parts of the organization, they ensure that all these parts are working together so the organization's goals can be achieved. For example, the systems approach recognizes that, no matter how efficient the production department, the marketing department must anticipate changes in customer tastes and work with the product development department in creating products customers want—or the organization's overall performance will suffer.

In addition, the systems approach implies that decisions and actions in one organizational area will affect other areas. For example, if the purchasing department doesn't acquire the right quantity and quality of inputs, the production department won't be able to do its job.

Finally, the systems approach recognizes that organizations are not self-contained. They rely on their environment for essential inputs and as outlets to absorb their outputs. No organization can survive for long if it ignores government regulations, supplier relations, or the varied external constituencies on which it depends.

How relevant is the systems approach to management? Quite relevant. Consider, for example, a shift manager at a Starbucks restaurant who must coordinate the work of employees filling customer orders at the front counter and the drive-through windows, direct the delivery and unloading of food supplies, and address any customer concerns that come up. This manager "manages" all parts of the "system" so that the restaurant meets its daily sales goals.

The early management theorists came up with management principles they generally assumed to be universally applicable. Later research found exceptions to many of these principles. For example, division of labour is valuable and widely used, but jobs can become *too* specialized. Bureaucracy is desirable in many situations, but in other circumstances, other structural designs are *more* effective. Management is not (and should not be) based on simplistic principles to be applied in all situations. Different and changing situations require managers to use different approaches and techniques. The **contingency approach** (sometimes called the *situational approach*) says that organizations are different, face different situations (contingencies), and require different ways of managing.

A good way to describe contingency is "if, then." *If* this is the way my situation is, *then* this is the best way for me to manage in this situation. It is intuitively logical because organizations and even units within the same organization differ—in size, goals, work activities, and the like. It would be surprising to find universally applicable management rules that would work in *all* situations. But, of course, it's one thing to say that the way to manage "depends on the situation" and another to say what the situation is. Management researchers continue working to identify these situational variables. Exhibit MH-8 describes

contingency approach A management approach that recognizes organizations as different, which means they face different situations (contingencies) and require different ways of managing.

Exhibit MH-8

Popular Contingency Variables

Organization Size. As size increases, so do the problems of coordination. For instance, the type of organization structure appropriate for an organization of 50 000 employees is likely to be inefficient for an organization of 50 employees.

Routineness of Task Technology. To achieve its purpose, an organization uses technology. Routine technologies require organizational structures, leadership styles, and control systems that differ from those required by customized or nonroutine technologies.

Environmental Uncertainty. The degree of uncertainty caused by environmental changes influences the management process. What works best in a stable and predictable environment may be totally inappropriate in a rapidly changing and unpredictable environment.

Individual Differences. Individuals differ in terms of their desire for growth, autonomy, tolerance of ambiguity, and expectations. These and other individual differences are particularly important when managers select motivation techniques, leadership styles, and job designs.

four popular contingency variables. Although the list is by no means comprehensive—more than 100 different variables have been identified—it represents those most widely used and gives you an idea of what we mean by the term *contingency variable.* The primary value of the contingency approach is that it stresses there are no simplistic or universal rules for managers to follow.

So what do managers face today when managing? Although the dawn of the information age is said to have begun with Samuel Morse's telegraph in 1837, dramatic changes in information technology that occurred in the latter part of the twentieth century and continue through today directly affect the manager's job. Managers now may manage employees who are working from home or working halfway around the world. An organization's computing resources used to be mainframe computers locked away in temperature-controlled rooms and accessed only by the experts. Now, practically everyone in an organization is connected—wired or wireless—with devices no larger than the palm of the hand. Just like the impact of the Industrial Revolution in the 1700s on the emergence of management, the information age has brought dramatic changes that continue to influence the way organizations are managed.

REVIEW AND DISCUSSION QUESTIONS

1. Explain why studying management history is important.
2. What early evidence of management practice can you describe?
3. Describe the important contributions made by the classical theorists.
4. What did the early advocates of OB contribute to our understanding of management?
5. Why were the Hawthorne Studies so critical to management history?
6. What kind of workplace would Henri Fayol create? How about Mary Parker Follett? How about Frederick W. Taylor?
7. Explain what the quantitative approach has contributed to the field of management.
8. Describe total quality management.
9. How do systems theory and the contingency approach make managers better at what they do?
10. How do societal trends influence the practice of management? What are the implications for someone studying management?

Organizational Culture and the Organizational Environment

Are managers free to do whatever they want? In this chapter, we'll look at the factors that define the discretion managers have in doing their jobs. These factors are both internal (the organization's culture) and external (the organizational environment). After reading and studying this chapter, you will achieve the following learning outcomes.

Learning Outcomes

1 Compare and contrast the actions of managers according to the omnipotent and symbolic views.

2 Discuss the characteristics and importance of organizational culture.

3 Describe what kinds of cultures managers can create.

4 Describe the features of the specific and general organizational environments.

▶ ▶ ▶ Technical workers at 3M spend up to 15 percent of their time working on projects of their own choosing.[1] This is openly encouraged by 3M as long as the project has the potential to become an important breakthrough for the company. The "15 percent rule" has been a central part of 3M's overall culture of innovation since being introduced by company president William McKnight in 1948. The innovative culture is further encouraged by the "30 percent rule" that requires each division to produce 30 percent of its annual revenue from products that did not exist five years ago.

3M clearly prizes delegation and initiative, and has a strong tolerance for failure. Managers are directed to "hire the right people, and then get out of the way." The company culture emphasizes that a failure can turn into a success; there is no punishment for a product failing in the market. The human resources team also plays a pivotal role in reinforcing a stronger, customer-oriented culture through regular training programs that focus on the acronym $E = MC^2$ (Engagement = More Customer Connect).

Implementation of these practices has built a company with over 76 000 employees and annual revenue of \$23 billion, and has placed 3M at the forefront of innovative companies globally. After the bursting of the dot-com bubble in 2001, however, there was a shift in thinking at the company. James McNerney was hired from General Electric as president to deal with what was felt to be too great a focus on innovation and creativity. He was asked to make the company more efficient using the Six Sigma discipline (a quality control philosophy) and to "whip the company into shape." McNerney left in 2005 to run Boeing, and the new CEO and president, George Buckley, was left with the task of rebuilding 3M's traditional innovative culture, which many felt had suffered as a result of the emphasis on process improvement. Buckley was succeeded as president of 3M by Inge Thulin in 2012.

> **Think About It**
>
> What would it be like to work at 3M? How would you feel about having 15 percent of your time to work on projects that meet your personal agenda? What kinds of resistance might James McNerney have encountered when he tried to establish a new culture of efficiency in the face of the established culture of innovation? What challenges might George Buckley have encountered when he became CEO in 2005? How does the 3M culture differ from the work cultures you have experienced?

The Manager: Omnipotent or Symbolic?

❶ Compare and contrast the actions of managers according to the omnipotent and symbolic views.

omnipotent view of management The view that managers are directly responsible for an organization's success or failure.

symbolic view of management The view that much of an organization's success or failure is due to external forces outside managers' control.

How much difference does a manager make in how an organization performs? The dominant view in management theory and society in general is that managers are directly responsible for an organization's success or failure. We will call this perspective the **omnipotent view of management**. In contrast, some observers have argued that much of an organization's success or failure is due to external forces outside managers' control. This perspective has been labelled the **symbolic view of management**. Let's look more closely at each of these perspectives so that we can try to clarify just how much credit or blame managers should receive for their organizations' performance.

The Omnipotent View

In Chapter 1 we discussed the importance of managers to organizations. This view reflects a dominant assumption in management theory: The quality of an organization's managers determines the quality of the organization itself. It's assumed that differences in an organization's effectiveness or efficiency are due to the decisions and actions of its managers. Good managers anticipate change, exploit opportunities, correct poor performance, and lead their organizations toward their goals, which may be changed if necessary. When profits are up, managers take the credit and reward themselves with bonuses, stock options, and the like—even if they had little to do with the positive outcomes. When profits are down, top managers are often fired in the belief that "new blood" will bring improved results. The buck stops here! Following the oil spill in the Gulf of Mexico in April 2010, people were enraged when BP CEO Tony Hayward attended a weekend sailing event in which his yacht *Bob* was competing. The following Monday, Hayward was removed from direct responsibility for the cleanup. By early July 2010, there was speculation that the leadership at BP would be cleared out, including Hayward as well as Carl-Henric Svanberg, the Swedish chairman who in his apology to those affected by the spill referred to the "small people."[2] Though Svanberg ultimately remained chairman, BP later agreed to a $4.5 billion settlement with the U.S. Department of Justice, while three BP employees were later indicted with criminal charges.

The view of managers as omnipotent is consistent with the stereotypical picture of the take-charge business executive who can overcome any obstacle in carrying out the organization's goals. This omnipotent view, of course, is not limited to business organizations. We can also use it to help explain the high turnover among college and professional sports coaches, who can be considered the "managers" of their teams. Coaches who lose more games than they win are seen as ineffective. They are fired and replaced by new coaches who, it is hoped, will correct the inadequate performance.

In the omnipotent view, when organizations perform poorly, someone has to be held accountable regardless of the reasons, and in our society, that "someone" is the manager. Of course, when things go well, we need someone to praise. So managers also get the credit—even if they had little to do with achieving positive outcomes.

The Symbolic View

When tunnelling for the Canada Line transit system started tearing up Vancouver's Cambie Street, a busy shopping area, customers stopped coming to the stores and restaurants. The street was noisy, there was no parking, and the area was a traffic nightmare. Facing a

Don Healy/Leader Post

When both Home Hardware and Army and Navy closed their stores in downtown Regina, Blue Mantle, a thrift store in the same area, faced a loss of customer traffic and sales. As a result, Dave Barrett, the store's manager at the time, closed Blue Mantle soon after. He explained his decision: "When Home Hardware closed, and department store Army and Navy closed, that cut away a lot of our traffic to the store. We used to have lots of seniors that would swing over to our place." He also noted that the state of the economy was a factor in the store closing.[3] The Roman Catholic Archdiocese of Regina eventually re-opened Blue Mantle after receiving numerous requests from customers, and now runs the store with volunteers.

significant drop in customers, Christian Gaudreault, owner of Tomato Fresh Food Café, moved his restaurant elsewhere. Giriaj Gautam, who runs the Cambie General Store, found his sales down 25 percent and hoped he could hang on until construction finished up in the area, more than a year after it started. Was the declining revenue the result of decisions and actions by Gaudreault and Gautam, or was it the result of factors beyond their control? Similarly, when a massive power outage hit Ontario, mad cow disease struck in Alberta, and the avian flu killed chickens in British Columbia, were these the result of managerial actions or circumstances outside managers' control? The symbolic view would suggest the latter.

The symbolic view says that a manager's ability to affect outcomes is influenced and constrained by external factors.[4] According to this view, it's unreasonable to expect managers to significantly affect an organization's performance. Instead, an organization's results are influenced by factors managers do not control, such as the economy, customers, government policies, competitors' actions, industry conditions, control over proprietary technology, and decisions made by previous managers.

According to the symbolic view, managers merely symbolize control and influence.[5] How? They create meaning out of randomness, confusion, and ambiguity or try to innovate and adapt. Because managers have a limited effect on organizational outcomes, their actions involve developing plans, making decisions, and engaging in other managerial activities for the benefit of shareholders, customers, employees, and the public. However, the part that managers actually play in organizational success or failure is minimal.

Reality Suggests a Synthesis

In reality, managers are neither helpless nor all powerful. Internal and external constraints that restrict a manager's decision options exist within every organization. Internal constraints arise from the organization's culture, and external constraints come from the organization's environment.

As Exhibit 2-1 shows, managers operate within the limits imposed by the organization's culture and environment. Yet, despite these constraints, managers are not powerless. They can still influence an organization's performance. In the remainder of this chapter, we discuss how an organization's culture and environment impose limits on managers. However, as we will see in other chapters, these constraints don't mean that a manager's hands are tied. As George Buckley of 3M recognized, managers can and do influence their culture and environment.

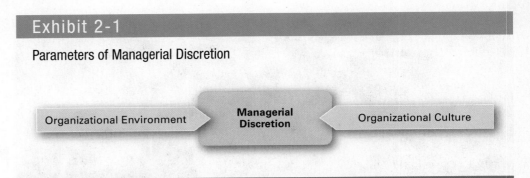

Exhibit 2-1

Parameters of Managerial Discretion

② Discuss the characteristics and importance of organizational culture.

The Organization's Culture

▶ ▶ ▶ Every organization has a culture, a way that those in the organization interact with each other and with their clients or customers. When George Buckley was appointed president and CEO of 3M following the departure of James McNerney, he faced a crisis of confidence in what really mattered at 3M—either innovation or efficiency. McNerney had brought a passion for efficiency with him from GE, and the remnants of this new culture were still in place even as 3M declared a return to the focus on innovation.[6]

> **Think About It**
>
> **What is organizational culture, and how did it affect both James McNerney's and George Buckley's ability to manage? Is the impact of culture different if the organization is a not-for-profit rather than a business organization?**

We know that every person has a unique personality—a set of relatively permanent and stable traits that influence the way we act and interact with others. When we describe someone as warm, open, relaxed, shy, or aggressive, we are describing personality traits. An organization, too, has a personality, which we call its *culture*. It is that culture that influences the way employees act and interact with others.

What Is Organizational Culture?

In September 2013, Hudson's Bay Company announced the appointment of Marigay McKee as the new president for the recently acquired Saks Fifth Avenue.[7] As chief merchant of Harrods, McKee had overseen the planning and implementation of the merchandising and creative strategies since 2011. HBC, founded in 1670, is North America's longest continually operated company. In Canada, HBC operates Hudson's Bay, Canada's largest department store with 90 locations, Home Outfitters with 69 locations and in the United States, HBC operates Lord & Taylor, a department store with 48 full-line store locations throughout the northeastern United States. Hudson's Bay Company operating units provide stylish, quality merchandise at great value, with a dedicated focus on service excellence. Saks Fifth Avenue, one of the world's pre-eminent specialty retailers, is renowned for its superlative American and international designer collections. Saks operates 41 full-line stores in 20 states, and five international licensed stores. Given the long-established traditions in place at HBC and Saks and the different targeted markets, what challenges are likely to arise as the two company cultures are merged?

organizational culture The shared values, principles, traditions, and ways of doing things that influence the way organizational members act and that distinguish the organization from other organizations.

What is **organizational culture**? It's a system of shared meaning and beliefs held by organizational members that determines, in large degree, how they act toward each other and outsiders. It represents a common perception held by an organization's members that influences how they behave. In every organization, there are values, symbols, rituals, myths, and practices that have evolved over time.[8] These shared values and experiences determine, in large degree, what employees perceive and how they respond to their world.[9] When faced with problems or issues, the organizational culture—the "way we do things around here"—influences what employees can do and how they conceptualize, define, analyze, and resolve issues. When considering different job offers, it makes sense to evaluate whether you can fit into the organization's culture.

Our definition of organizational culture implies three things:

- Culture is a *perception*. It's not something that can be physically touched or seen, but employees perceive it on the basis of what they experience within the organization.

- Culture is a *descriptive* term. It's concerned with how members perceive the organization, not with whether they like it.

- Culture is *shared*. Even though individuals may have different backgrounds or work at different organizational levels, they tend to describe the organization's culture in similar terms. That's the *shared* aspect of culture.

Research suggests that seven dimensions capture the essence of an organization's culture.[10] These dimensions are described in Exhibit 2-2. Each dimension ranges from low (it's not very typical of the culture) to high (it's very typical of the culture). Describing an organization using these seven dimensions gives a composite picture of the organization's culture. In many organizations, one of these cultural dimensions often is emphasized more than the others and essentially shapes the organization's personality and the way organizational members work. For instance, at Sony Corporation the focus

Exhibit 2-2

Dimensions of Organizational Culture

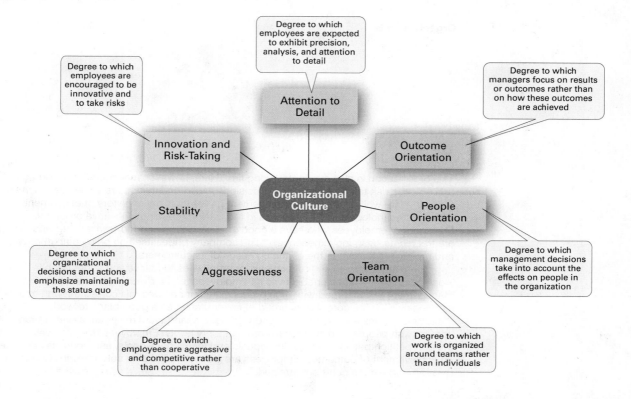

is on product innovation. The company "lives and breathes" new-product development (outcome orientation), and employees' work decisions, behaviours, and actions support that goal. In contrast, WestJet Airlines has made its employees a central part of its culture (people orientation). Exhibit 2-3 describes how the dimensions can be combined to create significantly different organizations.

Exhibit 2-3

Contrasting Organizational Cultures

Organization A

 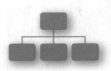

This organization is a manufacturing firm. Managers are expected to fully document all decisions, and "good managers" are those who can provide detailed data to support their recommendations. Creative decisions that incur significant change or risk are not encouraged. Because managers of failed projects are openly criticized and penalized, managers try not to implement ideas that deviate much from the status quo. One lower-level manager quoted an often-used phrase in the company: "If it ain't broke, don't fix it."

Employees are required to follow extensive rules and regulations in this firm. Managers supervise employees closely to ensure there are no deviations. Management is concerned with high productivity, regardless of the impact on employee morale or turnover.

Work activities are designed around individuals. There are distinct departments and lines of authority, and employees are expected to minimize formal contact with other employees outside their functional area or line of command. Performance evaluations and rewards emphasize individual effort, although seniority tends to be the primary factor in the determination of pay raises and promotions.

Organization B

This organization is also a manufacturing firm. Here, however, management encourages and rewards risk taking and change. Decisions based on intuition are valued as much as those that are well rationalized. Management prides itself on its history of experimenting with new technologies and its success in regularly introducing innovative products. Managers or employees who have a good idea are encouraged to "run with it," and failures are treated as "learning experiences." The company prides itself on being market driven and rapidly responsive to the changing needs of its customers.

There are few rules and regulations for employees to follow, and supervision is loose because management believes its employees are hardworking and trustworthy. Management is concerned with high productivity but believes this comes through treating its people right. The company is proud of its reputation as a good place to work.

Job activities are designed around work teams, and team members are encouraged to interact with people across functions and authority levels. Employees talk positively about the competition between teams. Individuals and teams have goals, and bonuses are based on achievement of outcomes. Employees are given considerable autonomy in choosing the means by which the goals are attained.

◄⊙ Simulate on MyManagementLab

Organizational Structure

Exhibit 2-4

Strong versus Weak Cultures

Strong Cultures	Weak Cultures
Values widely shared	Values limited to a few people—usually top management
Culture conveys consistent messages about what's important	Culture sends contradictory messages about what's important
Most employees can tell stories about company history or heroes	Employees have little knowledge of company history or heroes
Employees strongly identify with culture	Employees have little identification with culture
Strong connection between shared values and behaviours	Little connection between shared values and behaviours

Strong Cultures

All organizations have cultures, but not all cultures equally influence employees' behaviours and actions. **Strong cultures**—those in which the key values are deeply held and widely shared—have a greater influence on employees than weaker cultures. (Exhibit 2-4 contrasts strong and weak cultures.) At 3M, the 15 percent rule and the 30 percent rule make the cultural commitment to innovation crystal clear. Yet some organizations do not make clear what is important and what is not, and this lack of clarity is a characteristic of weak cultures. In such organizations, culture is unlikely to greatly influence managers. Most organizations, however, have moderate to strong cultures. There is relatively high agreement on what is important, what defines "good" employee behaviour, what it takes to get ahead, and so forth.

The more employees accept the organization's key values and the greater their commitment to those values, the stronger the culture. Most organizations have moderate to strong cultures, that is, there is relatively high agreement on what's important, what defines "good" employee behaviour, what it takes to get ahead, and so forth. The stronger a culture becomes, the more it affects the way managers plan, organize, lead, and control.[11]

Why is having a strong culture important? For one thing, in organizations with strong cultures, employees are more loyal than employees in organizations with weak cultures.[12] Research also suggests that strong cultures are associated with high organizational performance, and it's easy to understand why.[13] After all, if values are clear and widely accepted, employees know what they're supposed to do and what's expected of them, so they can act quickly to take care of problems. However, the drawback is that a strong culture also might prevent employees from trying new approaches, especially when conditions change rapidly.[14]

Subcultures

Organizations do not necessarily have one uniform culture. In fact, most large organizations have a dominant culture and numerous sets of subcultures.[15]

When we talk about an organization's culture, we are referring to its *dominant* culture. A **dominant culture** expresses the core values that are shared by the majority of an organization's members. It's this macro view of culture that gives an organization its distinct personality.[16] **Subcultures** tend to develop in large organizations to reflect the common problems, situations, or experiences that members face. The existence of subcultures in an organization suggests that individual managers play a role in moulding a common culture in their own units. By conveying and then reinforcing core values, managers can influence the common culture of the employees in their unit.

Subcultures are likely to be defined by department designations and geographical separation. An organization's marketing department, for example, can have a subculture

strong cultures Organizational cultures in which the key values are intensely held and widely shared.

dominant culture A system of shared meanings that expresses the core values of a majority of the organization's members; it gives the organization its distinct personality.

subcultures Minicultures within an organization, typically defined by department designations and geographical separation.

Exhibit 2-5

How an Organization's Culture Is Established and Maintained

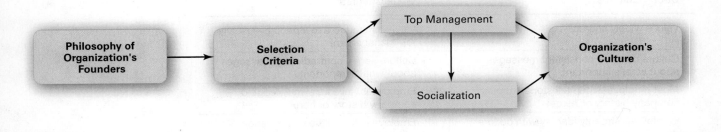

core values The primary, or
dominant, values that are accepted
throughout the organization.

that is uniquely shared by members of that department. It will include the **core values** of
the dominant culture, plus additional values unique to members of the marketing department. Similarly, offices or units of the organization that are physically separated from the
organization's main operations may take on a different personality. Again, the core values
are essentially retained but modified to reflect the separated unit's distinct situation.

Where Culture Comes From and How It Continues

Exhibit 2-5 illustrates how an organization's culture is established and maintained. The
original source of an organization's culture usually reflects the vision or mission of the
organization's founders. They are not constrained by previous customs or approaches. And
the small size of most new organizations helps the founders instill their vision in all organizational members. Frank Stronach had a strong impact on the culture of the organization
he founded, Magna International. Stronach still has a profound effect on Magna's culture,
even though he is no longer CEO.[17] Magna's Corporate Constitution and the Employee's
Charter provide the roadmap for the company's Fair Enterprise culture, first introduced by
Stronach. Stronach's policies of profit-sharing and empowerment have created a workforce
that has made Magna one of the largest and most profitable companies in the country.

Once the culture is in place, however, certain organizational practices help maintain
it. For instance, during the employee selection process, managers typically judge job candidates not only on the job requirements, but also on how well they might fit into the
organization. At the same time, job candidates find out information about the organization and determine whether they are comfortable with what they see.

The actions of top managers also have a major impact on the organization's culture. For
instance, at Best Buy, the company's chief marketing officer would take groups of employees
for "regular tours of what the company called its retail hospital." Wearing white lab coats,
employees would walk into a room with a row of real hospital beds and patient charts
describing the ills affecting each of the company's major competitors. As each of those competitors "succumbed to terminal illness" and was no longer in business, the room would
be darkened. Just think of the powerful message such a display would have on employees
and their work.[18] Through what they say and how they behave, top managers establish
norms that filter down through the organization and can have a positive effect on employees' behaviours. For instance, former IBM CEO Sam Palmisano wanted employees to value
teamwork, so he chose to take several million dollars from his yearly bonus and give it to
his top executives based on their teamwork. He said, "If you say you're about a team, you
have to be a team. You've got to walk the talk, right?"[19] However, as we've seen in numerous
corporate ethics scandals, the actions of top managers also can lead to undesirable outcomes.

socialization The process that
helps employees adapt to the
organization's culture.

Finally, organizations help employees adapt to the culture through **socialization**, a process that helps new employees learn the organization's way of doing things. For instance,
new employees at Starbucks stores go through 24 hours of intensive training that helps
turn them into brewing consultants (baristas). They learn company philosophy, company

jargon, and even how to assist customers with decisions about beans, grind, and espresso machines. One benefit of socialization is that employees understand the culture and are enthusiastic and knowledgeable with customers.[20] Another benefit is that it minimizes the chance that new employees who are unfamiliar with the organization's culture might disrupt current beliefs and customs.

How Employees Learn Culture

Employees "learn" an organization's culture in a number of ways. The most common are stories, rituals, material symbols, and language.

Stories

Organizational "stories" typically contain a narrative of significant events or people, including such things as the organization's founders, rule breaking, reactions to past mistakes, and so forth.[21] Managers at Southwest Airlines tell stories celebrating employees who perform heroically for customers.[22] Such stories help convey what's important and provide examples that people can learn from. At 3M Company, the product innovation stories are legendary. There's the story about the 3M scientist who spilled chemicals on her tennis shoe and came up with Scotchgard. Then, there's the story about Art Fry, a 3M researcher, who wanted a better way to mark the pages of his church hymnal and invented the Post-It Note. These stories reflect what made 3M great and what it will take to continue that success.[23] To help employees learn the culture, organizational stories anchor the present in the past, provide explanations and legitimacy for current practices, exemplify what is important to the organization, and provide compelling pictures of an organization's goals.[24]

Rituals

In the early days of Facebook, founder Mark Zuckerberg had an artist paint a mural at company headquarters showing children taking over the world with laptops. Also, he would end employee meetings by pumping his fist in the air and leading employees in a chant of "domination." Although the cheering ritual was intended to be something simply fun, other company executives suggested he drop it because it made him seem silly, and they feared that competitors might cite it as evidence of monopolistic goals.[25] That's the power that rituals can have in shaping what employees believe is important. Corporate rituals are repetitive sequences of activities that express and reinforce the important values and goals of the organization. One of the best-known corporate rituals is Mary Kay Cosmetics' annual awards ceremony for its sales representatives. The company spends more than $50 million annually on rewards and prize incentives. Looking like a cross between a circus and a Miss America pageant, the ceremony takes place in a large auditorium, on a stage in front of a large, cheering audience, with all the participants dressed in glamorous evening clothes. Salespeople are rewarded for sales goal achievements with an array of expensive gifts, including big-screen televisions, diamond rings, trips, and pink Cadillacs. This "show" acts as a motivator by publicly acknowledging outstanding sales performance. In addition, the ritual aspect reinforces late founder Mary Kay's determination and optimism, which enabled her to overcome personal hardships, start her own company, and achieve material success. It conveys to her salespeople that reaching their sales goals is important and through hard work and encouragement, they too can achieve success. The contagious enthusiasm and excitement of Mary Kay sales representatives make it obvious that this annual "ritual" plays a significant role in establishing desired levels of motivation and behavioural expectations, which is, after all, what management hopes an organization's culture does.

German automaker BMW helps employees learn its company's culture by repeating the "story of 1959." New employees learn that 1959 was a pivotal year for BMW because it almost went bankrupt after badly misjudging the market by producing a large expensive car few people could afford and a tiny two-seater that was too small to be practical. Management devised a turnaround plan for BMW that focused on producing a new class of sporty sedans and made a pact with employees that would help keep the company afloat. The "story of 1959" reflects the importance of employees in turning around BMW and steering it on the road to success. This photo shows BMW employees signing a new car model they helped produce, signifying the powerful role they continue to play in the company's performance.

Andreas Gebert/EPA/Newscom

One area where organizational culture influences employee behaviour is how employees dress for work. Look at what each of these four individuals is wearing. At what kinds of organizations do you think each of these styles is appropriate work wear? What do you think the cultures might be like at the organizations where each person works?

Ken Hurst/Shutterstock   Lisa F. Young/Shutterstock   markos86/Shutterstock   Brian Mueller/Shutterstock

Material Artifacts and Symbols

When you walk into different businesses, do you get a "feel" for what type of work environment it is—formal, casual, fun, serious, and so forth? These reactions demonstrate the power of material symbols or artifacts in creating an organization's personality.[26] The layout of an organization's facilities, how employees dress, the types of automobiles provided to top executives, and the availability of corporate aircraft are examples of material symbols. Others include the size of offices, the elegance of furnishings, executive "perks" (extra benefits provided to managers such as health club memberships, use of company-owned facilities, and so forth), employee fitness centres or on-site dining facilities, and reserved parking spaces for certain employees. At WorldNow, a business that helps local media companies develop new online distribution channels and revenue streams, an important material symbol is an old dented drill that the founders purchased for $2 at a thrift store. The drill symbolizes the company's culture of "drilling down to solve problems." When an employee is presented with the drill in recognition of outstanding work, he or she is expected to personalize the drill in some way and devise a new rule for caring for it. One employee installed a Bart Simpson trigger; another made the drill wireless by adding an antenna. The company's "icon" carries on the culture even as the organization evolves and changes.[27]

Material symbols convey to employees who is important and the kinds of behaviour (for example, risk taking, conservative, authoritarian, participative, individualistic, and so forth) that are expected and appropriate.

Language

Many organizations and units within organizations use language as a way to identify and unite members of a culture. By learning this language, members attest to their acceptance of the culture and their willingness to help preserve it. For instance, at Cranium, a Seattle board game company, "chiff" is used to remind employees of the need to be incessantly innovative in everything they do. "Chiff" stands for "clever, high-quality, innovative, friendly, fun."[28] At Build-A-Bear Workshop stores, employees are encouraged to use a sales technique called "Strive for Five," in which they work to sell each customer five items. The simple rhyming slogan is a powerful tool to drive sales.[29]

Over time, organizations often develop unique terms to describe equipment, key personnel, suppliers, customers, processes, or products related to its business. New employees are frequently overwhelmed with acronyms and jargon that, after a short period of time, become a natural part of their language. Once learned, this language acts as a common denominator that bonds members.

How Culture Affects Managers

Because an organization's cultural norms define what its employees can and cannot do, they are particularly relevant to managers even though they are rarely explicitly stated or written down. It's unlikely that they will even be spoken. But they are there, and all managers quickly learn what to do and what not to do in their organization. For instance, you will not find the following values written down anywhere, but each comes from a real organization.

- Look busy even if you are not.
- If you take risks and fail around here, you will pay dearly for it.
- Before you make a decision, run it by your manager so that he or she is never surprised.
- We make our product only as good as the competition forces us to.
- What made us successful in the past will make us successful in the future.
- If you want to get to the top here, you have to be a team player.

The link between values such as these and managerial behaviour is fairly straightforward. If an organization's culture supports the belief that profits can be increased by cost cutting and that the company's best interests are served by achieving slow but steady increases in quarterly earnings, managers are unlikely to pursue programs that are innovative, risky, long term, or expansionary. For organizations that value and encourage workforce diversity, the organizational culture, and thus managers' decisions and actions, will be supportive of diversity efforts. In an organization whose culture conveys a basic distrust of employees, managers are more likely to use an authoritarian leadership style than a democratic one. Why? The culture establishes for managers what is appropriate behaviour.

Current Organizational Culture Issues Facing Managers

▶ ▶ ▶ 3M has consistently ranked in the top five of the Global Innovation 1000 survey yet does not rank in the top 20 R&D spenders. How is this possible? The explanation is in the way 3M uses culture to support a "winning overall business strategy, deep customer insight, great talent and the right set of capabilities to achieve successful execution." In the study, culture was defined as the organization's "self-sustaining patterns of behaving, feeling, thinking and believing." The study pointed out that organizations with unsupportive cultures and poor strategic alignment significantly underperform their competitors.

Think About It

3M has been strategic in building a sustaining innovative culture over the long term. What were some of the steps they took? Could similar steps be taken to support an ethical culture? A customer responsive culture? A culture that supports diversity? An inclusive workplace culture?

Calgary-based WestJet Airlines is renowned for its attention to customers. Nike's innovations in running-shoe technology are legendary. Royal Bank (RBC Financial Group) consistently takes top honours for corporate responsibility and citizenship. How have these organizations achieved such reputations? Their organizational cultures have played a crucial role. Let's look at four current cultural issues managers should consider: creating an ethical culture, creating an innovative culture, creating a customer-responsive culture, and creating a culture that supports diversity.

Creating an Ethical Culture

The content and strength of an organization's culture influences its ethical climate and the ethical behaviour of its members.[31] A strong organizational culture will exert more influence on employees than a weak one. If the culture is strong and supports high ethical standards, it should have a very powerful and positive influence on employee behaviour. Likewise, a strong culture that encourages unethical behaviour will have a powerful influence on employees, as the following *Management Reflection* shows.

---

datapoints[30]

43 percent of workers surveyed would not recommend a job at their workplace to a friend or family member.

70 percent of large companies are likely to begin using digital-game–like reward and competitive tactics to motivate employee performance and encourage friendly competition.

61 percent of employees surveyed in Great Britain felt their boss was unapproachable.

8 percent of executives surveyed said fostering a shared understanding of values was an important capability.

32 percent of workers surveyed said acclimating to a different corporate culture could pose the greatest challenge when reentering the workforce.

67 percent of men surveyed never wear a tie to work.

45 percent of employees surveyed said their companies' ability to innovate was below average when it came to moving quickly from generating ideas to selling products.

45 percent of senior managers surveyed said their company's culture is clear about what motivates employees.

---

❸ Describe what kinds of cultures managers can create.

MANAGEMENT REFLECTION FOCUS ON ETHICS

Let My People Go Surfing

Can a manager encourage individuals to act responsibly? Canadian-born Yvon Chouinard founded the clothing company Patagonia forty years ago. He and his wife are sole owners of Patagonia, a privately held company that brought in $414 million in sales in fiscal 2011 and projected a 30 percent increase in sales for this year. His flex-time policies allow workers to come and go whenever they want—say, when waves are high at the nearby surf point—as long as deadlines are met. There's a yoga room available any time of day (I walked in on the head menswear designer meditating there at around 11 a.m. on a Tuesday.) At the prodding of Chouinard's wife, Malinda, Patagonia was one of the first companies in California to provide on-site, subsidized day care. Even the chief bean counter, COO and CFO Rose Marcario, seems ethcially fulfilled. In previous jobs at other companies, she says, "I might have looked for ways to defer taxes in the Cayman Islands. Here, we are proud to pay our fair share of taxes. It's a different philosophy. My life is more integrated with my work because I'm trying to stay true to the same values in both."[32] ∎

An organizational culture most likely to shape high ethical standards is one that is high in risk tolerance, low to moderate in aggressiveness, and focused on means as well as outcomes. Managers in such a culture are supported for taking risks and innovating, are discouraged from engaging in uncontrolled competition, and will pay attention to *how* goals are achieved as well as to *what* goals are achieved (as in the Patagonia example).

Creating an Innovative Culture

You may not recognize IDEO's name, but you've probably used a number of its products. As a product design firm, it takes the ideas that corporations bring to it and turns them into reality. Some of its creations range from the first commercial mouse (for Apple Computer) to the first stand-up toothpaste tube (for Procter & Gamble) to the handheld personal organizer (for Palm). It's critical that IDEO's culture support creativity and innovation.[33] IDEO has won more *BusinessWeek*/DSA Industrial Design Excellence awards than any other firm. It also has been ranked by *BusinessWeek* in the top 25 most innovative companies and does consulting work for the other 24.[34] The company's emphasis is on simplicity, function, and meeting user needs. IDEO believes that the best ideas for creating or improving products or processes come from keen observation of how users work and play on a daily

As we saw in Chapter 1, organizational culture is what makes Cirque du Soleil so special. Employees focus on solutions rather than blame. Consensus is not a virtue because CEO Daniel Lamarre feels that the best ideas get lost if everyone has to compromise. Lamarre encourages dissent, and tempers fly during discussions, but the results are the creative, dynamic shows that the Cirque produces.

Ian Rutherford/ZUMA Press/Newscom

basis.[35] Another innovative organization is Cirque du Soleil, the Montreal-based creator of circus theatre. Its managers state that the culture is based on involvement, communication, creativity, and diversity, which they see as keys to innovation.[36]

Although these two companies are in industries in which innovation is important (product design and entertainment), the fact is that any successful organization needs a culture that supports innovation. How important is culture to innovation? In a recent survey of senior executives, more than half said that the most important driver of innovation for companies was a supportive corporate culture.[37]

What does an innovative culture look like? According to Swedish researcher Goran Ekvall, it is characterized by the following:

- **Challenge and involvement**—Are employees involved in, motivated by, and committed to long-term goals and success of the organization?

- **Freedom**—Can employees independently define their work, exercise discretion, and take initiative in their day-to-day activities?

- **Trust and openness**—Are employees supportive and respectful to each other?

- **Idea time**—Do individuals have time to elaborate on new ideas before taking action?

- **Playfulness/humour**—Is the workplace spontaneous and fun?

- **Conflict resolution**—Do individuals make decisions and resolve issues based on the good of the organization rather than personal interest?

- **Debates**—Are employees allowed to express opinions and put forth ideas for consideration and review?

- **Risk taking**—Do managers tolerate uncertainty and ambiguity, and are employees rewarded for taking risks?[38]

Creating a Customer-Responsive Culture

Isadore Sharp, chair and CEO of Toronto-based Four Seasons Hotels and Resorts, believes keenly in customer service. Creating a customer-responsive culture starts with employee selection: every candidate faces four or five interviews to ensure they have the right attitude. As part of employee training, all new employees spend one night in the hotel as a guest to help them understand the perspective of the customer. Sharp notes that the hotel chain has "30 000 employees who are always thinking of new ways to make our guest experience more rewarding."[39]

Harrah's Entertainment, the Las Vegas–based national gaming company, is also devoted to customer service, and for good reason. Company research showed that customers who were satisfied with the service they received at a Harrah's casino increased their gaming expenditures by 10 percent, and those who were extremely satisfied increased their gaming expenditures by 24 percent. When customer service translates into these types of results, of course managers would want to create a customer-responsive culture![40]

But what does a customer-responsive culture look like? Research shows that six characteristics are routinely present in successful service-oriented organizations:

- *Outgoing and friendly employees.* Successful service-oriented organizations hire employees who are outgoing and friendly.

- *Few rigid rules, procedures, and regulations.* Service employees need to have the freedom to meet changing customer service requirements.

- *Widespread use of empowerment.* Employees are empowered to decide what is necessary to please the customer.

- *Good listening skills.* Employees in customer-responsive cultures have the ability to listen to and understand messages sent by the customer.

This jubilant customer jumps for joy to celebrate his purchase of an iPad tablet on the first day of its release at an Apple retail store in London. By creating an innovative and customer-responsive culture, Apple has achieved financial success and earned high customer satisfaction ratings and brand loyalty for its products and services. This culture fosters employee creativity, commitment to company goals, trust and openness, and risk taking. It involves hiring friendly and helpful employees and empowering them to make decisions about their jobs and what they can do to satisfy and delight customers.

Carl Court/AFP/Getty Images/Newscom

- *Role clarity.* Service employees act as links between the organization and its customers, which can create considerable ambiguity and conflict. Successful customer-responsive cultures reduce employees' uncertainty about their roles and the best way to perform their jobs.

- *Employees attentive to customer needs.* They are willing to take the initiative, even when it's outside their normal job requirements, to satisfy a customer's needs.[41]

In general, to create any type of culture (and to reinforce the culture), managers need to communicate the elements of the culture, model the appropriate behaviours, train employees to carry out the new actions, and reward desired behaviours while creating negative incentives for straying from the desired behaviour.[42]

Creating a Culture That Supports Diversity

workforce diversity The mix of people in organizations in terms of gender, race, ethnicity, age, and other characteristics that reflect differences.

Today's organizations are characterized by **workforce diversity**, the mix of people in organizations in terms of gender, race, ethnicity, age, and other characteristics that reflect differences. Managers must look long and hard at their culture to see whether the shared meaning and beliefs that were appropriate for a more homogeneous workforce will accept and promote diverse views. Although organizations in the past may have supported diversity to meet federal hiring requirements, organizations today recognize that diversity-supportive cultures are good for business. Among other things, diversity contributes to more creative solutions and enhances employee morale. But how can such a culture be encouraged? The following *Management Reflection* discusses what managers can do.

MANAGEMENT REFLECTION

Creating an Inclusive Workplace Culture

How can managers create a culture that allows diversity to flourish? Creating a workplace culture that supports and encourages the inclusion of diverse individuals and views is a major organizational effort.[43] There are two things managers can do. First, managers must show that they value diversity through their decisions and actions. As they plan, organize, lead, and control, they need to recognize and embrace diverse perspectives. For instance, at the Marriott Marquis Hotel in New York's Times Square, managers take required diversity-training classes, where they learn that the best way to cope with diversity-related conflict is by focusing on performance and not defining problems in terms of gender, culture, race, or disability. At Prudential, the annual planning process includes key diversity performance goals that are measured and tied to managers' compensation. The second thing managers can do is look for ways to reinforce employee behaviours that exemplify inclusiveness. Some suggestions include encouraging individuals to value and defend diverse views, creating traditions and ceremonies that celebrate diversity, rewarding "heroes" and "heroines" who accept and promote inclusiveness, and communicating formally and informally about employees who champion diversity issues. ■

The Organizational Environment

4 Describe the features of the specific and general organizational environments.

▶ ▶ ▶ During the American stock market crash of 1929, the Dow Jones average fell by 54.7 percent.[44] Between October 11, 2007, and March 2, 2009, the market declined 50.2 percent! In the midst of the widespread market chaos during the recent market downturn, 3M reacted by aggressively managing costs and cash, as well as putting in place tighter operational discipline. In the fourth quarter of 2008, more than 2400 jobs were eliminated. Factory workers were temporarily laid off until production volumes returned to normal levels, pay raises were deferred in 2009, the policy of banking vacations was eliminated, and capital expenditures were cut back by 30 percent.[45]

In the Management History module, our discussion of an organization as an open system explained that an organization interacts with its environment as it takes in inputs and distributes outputs. Digital technology has disrupted all types of industries—from financial services to recorded music. One industry in particular, the publishing industry, has been impacted significantly. As e-book sales skyrocketed, competition among e-book reader devices intensified. Amazon introduced the first device, the Kindle, in November 2007. As with any new product, customers had to adjust to the new technology, but once they did, the Kindles were on fire! Two years later, retailer Barnes & Noble introduced the Nook, a cheaper e-book device. Amazon responded by cutting the price of its cheapest Kindle. Three months later in January 2010, Apple introduced its iPad tablet. It was more expensive, but its functionality and options (and the Apple name) made it an instant hit with customers. In response, Barnes & Noble cut the price of its Nook, and Amazon again lowered the price of the Kindle. By September 2011, the basic Kindle's starting price had dropped to $79, and Amazon launched Kindle Fire. Then in November 2011, Barnes & Noble joined the tablet battle with its $249 Nook Tablet. And now Microsoft has invested $300 million in Barnes & Noble (which had been struggling) in an attempt to be more competitive with Amazon. In addition, Toronto-based Kobo Inc has recently gained international attention for doubling its readership in 2013 and capturing 3% of the American e-reader market. Since 2009, Kobo has managed to capture dominant positions in Canada and Japan, and has expanded its selection to include attractive low-cost alternatives. As the popularity of e-books accelerates, the "reader wars" are likely to continue.[46] Anyone who doubts the impact the external environment has on managing just needs to look at what's happened in both the publishing industry and the e-book reader industry during the last few years.

Defining the External Environment

The term **external environment** refers to forces and institutions outside the organization that potentially can affect the organization's performance. The external environment is made up of three components, as shown in Exhibit 2-6: the specific environment, the general environment, and the global environment. We discuss the first two types of external environment in this chapter. Today, globalization is one of the major factors affecting managers of both large and small organizations. We address the global environment in Chapter 3.

external environment Outside forces and institutions that potentially can affect the organization's performance.

The Specific Environment

The **specific environment** includes those external forces that have a direct and immediate impact on managers' decisions and actions and are directly relevant to the achievement of the organization's goals. Each organization's specific environment is unique and changes with conditions. For instance, Timex and Rolex both make watches, but their specific environments differ because they operate in distinctly different market niches. What forces make up the specific environment? The main ones are customers, suppliers, competitors, and pressure groups.

specific environment The part of the external environment that is directly relevant to the achievement of an organization's goals.

Customers   Organizations exist to meet the needs of customers. It's the customer or client who consumes or uses the organization's output. This is true even for government organizations and other not-for-profits.

Customers obviously represent potential uncertainty to an organization. Their tastes can change or they can become dissatisfied with the organization's products or service. Of course, some organizations face considerably more uncertainty as a result of their

Exhibit 2-6

The External Environment

customers than do others. For example, what comes to mind when you think of Club Med? Club Med's image was traditionally one of carefree singles having fun in the sun at exotic locales. Club Med found, however, that as its target customers married and had children, these same individuals were looking for family-oriented vacation resorts where they could bring the kids. Although Club Med responded to the changing demands of its customers by offering different types of vacation experiences, including family-oriented ones, the company found it hard to change its image.

Suppliers   When you think of an organization's suppliers, you typically think in terms of organizations that provide materials and equipment. For Canada's Wonderland, just outside of Toronto, that includes organizations that sell soft drinks, computers, food, flowers and other nursery stock, concrete, and paper products. But the term *suppliers* also includes

When the internet search engine Google decided to accept heavy censorship of its Chinese site in compliance with Communist Party requirements, its founders said the widely criticized compromise was made to allow internet access to a fifth of the world's population. Among those who disagreed with Google's compromise were these members of Students for a Free Tibet. In March of 2010 Google reconsidered its decision and withdrew its services from mainland China in protest of the self-censorship required as the price of doing business in China. [47]

Dino Vournas/AP Photos

providers of financial and labour inputs. Shareholders, banks, insurance companies, pension funds, and other similar organizations are needed to ensure a continuous supply of money. Labour unions, colleges and universities, occupational associations, trade schools, and local labour markets are sources of employees. When the sources of employees dry up, it can impact managers' decisions and actions. For example, a lack of qualified nurses, a serious problem plaguing the health care industry, is making it difficult for health care providers to meet demand and keep service levels high.

Competitors   All organizations have one or more competitors. Even though it is a monopoly, Canada Post competes with FedEx, UPS, and other forms of communication such as the telephone, email, and fax. Nike competes with Reebok, Adidas, and Fila, among others. Coca-Cola competes with Pepsi and other soft drink companies. Not-for-profit organizations such as the Royal Ontario Museum and Girl Guides also compete for dollars, volunteers, and customers. One competitor that many managers ignore when launching new products or services is the status quo—customers tend to keep doing what they have always done unless there is a compelling reason to try something new. With this in mind, some would suggest that entering a new market with a new product is infinitely more risky than entering an established market where you find a compelling way to fulfill a need not served by your competitors.

Public Pressure Groups   Managers must recognize the special-interest groups that attempt to influence the actions of organizations. For instance, both Walmart and Home Depot have had difficulty getting approval to build stores in Vancouver. Neighbourhood activists worry about traffic density brought about by big-box stores, and in the case of both stores there is concern that local businesses will fail if the stores move in. Home Depot's director of real estate called Vancouver City Hall's review process "confusing and unfair" and "unlike anything in [his] experience."[48] Local hardware store owners and resident groups have lobbied against the store to city planners, hoping to keep big-box stores out of the Kitsilano neighbourhood. Though Walmart eventually succeeded in entering the Vancouver market, in nearby Richmond, public pressure delayed Walmart's entry by almost 10 years.

As social and political attitudes change, so too does the power of public pressure groups. For example, through their persistent efforts, groups such as MADD (Mothers Against Drunk Driving) and SADD (Students Against Destructive Decisions) have managed to make changes in the alcoholic beverage and restaurant and bar industries, and have raised public awareness about the problem of drunk drivers.

The General Environment

The **general environment** includes the broad economic, legal–political, socio-cultural, demographic, and technological conditions that *may* affect the organization. Changes in any of these areas usually do not have as large an impact as changes in the specific environment do, but managers must consider them as they plan, organize, lead, and control.

general environment Broad external conditions that may affect the organization.

Economic Conditions   Interest rates, inflation, changes in disposable income, stock market fluctuations, and the stage of the general business cycle are some of the economic factors that can affect management practices in an organization. For example, many specialty retailers such as IKEA, Roots, Birks, and Williams-Sonoma are acutely aware of the impact consumer disposable income has on their sales. When consumers' incomes fall or when their confidence about job security declines, as happened following the subprime mortgage crisis in 2008, they will postpone purchasing anything that isn't a necessity. Even charitable organizations such as the United Way or the Heart and Stroke Foundation feel the impact of economic factors. During economic downturns, not only does the demand for their services increase, but also their contributions typically decrease.

Legal–Political Conditions   Federal, provincial, and local governments influence what organizations can and cannot do. Some federal legislation has significant implications. For example, the Canadian Human Rights Act makes it illegal for any employer or provider of service that falls within federal jurisdiction to discriminate on the following grounds: race, national or ethnic origin, colour, religion, age, sex (including pregnancy and childbirth), marital status, family status, mental or physical disability (including previous or present drug or alcohol dependence), pardoned conviction, or sexual orientation. The act covers federal departments and agencies; Crown corporations; chartered banks; national airlines; interprovincial communications and telephone companies; interprovincial transportation companies; and other federally regulated industries, including certain mining operations.

Canada's Employment Equity Act of 1995 protects several categories of employees with employment barriers: Aboriginal peoples (whether First Nation, Inuit, or Métis); persons with disabilities; members of visible minorities (non-Caucasian in race or non-white in colour); and women. This legislation aims to ensure that members of these four groups are treated equitably. Employers covered by the Canadian Human Rights Act are also covered by the Employment Equity Act.

Many provinces have their own legislation, including employment equity acts, to cover employers in their provinces. Companies sometimes have difficulty complying with equity acts, as recent audits conducted by the Canadian Human Rights Commission show. In an audit of 180 companies, only Status of Women Canada; Elliot Lake, Ontario-based AJ Bus Lines; the National Parole Board; Canadian Transportation Agency; Les Méchins, Quebec-based Verreault Navigation; and Nortel Networks were compliant on their first try.[49]

The Competition Act of 1986 created the Bureau of Competition Policy (now called the Competition Bureau) to maintain and encourage competition in Canada. For example, if two major competing companies consider merging, they come under scrutiny from the bureau.

To protect farmers, the Canadian government has created marketing boards that regulate the pricing and production of such things as milk and eggs. Those who decide that they want to manufacture small amounts of cheese in Canada would have great difficulty doing so because the Canadian government does not open production quotas to new producers very often. Marketing boards restrict imports of some products, but the unintended result is that foreign governments oppose exports from Canada.

Organizations spend a great deal of time and money meeting government regulations, but the effects of these regulations go beyond time and money.[50] They also reduce managerial discretion by limiting the choices available to managers. In a 2004 COMPAS survey of business leaders, most respondents cited interprovincial trade barriers as a significant hurdle to doing business in this country, calling the barriers "bad economics."[51] An article published in May 2007 backed up the views of these Canadian business leaders, arguing that nearly half of the productivity advantage that the United States has over Canada could be accounted for by interprovincial trade barriers.[52]

Other aspects of the legal–political conditions are the political climate, the general stability of a country where an organization operates, and the attitudes that elected government officials hold toward business. This is discussed in more detail in Chapter 3.

Socio-Cultural Conditions

A recent Harris Interactive Poll found that only 10 percent of adults think economic inequality is "not a problem at all." Most survey respondents believed it is either a major problem (57 percent) or a minor problem (23 percent).[53] Perhaps you saw news stories during late 2011 about a grassroots movement of protesters (Occupy) that started on Wall Street and soon spread to other cities in United States, Canada, and around the world. These protests focused on social and economic inequality, greed, corruption, and the undue influence of corporations on government. The protestors' slogan, *We are the 99%*, referred to the growing income and wealth gap between the wealthiest 1 percent and the rest of the population. Why has this issue become so sensitive? After all, those who worked hard and were rewarded because of their hard work or innovativeness have long been admired. And an income gap has always existed. In the North America, that gap between the rich and the rest has been much wider than in other developed nations for decades and is now becoming part of the dialogue that politicians and policy makers are speaking to as exemplified by the Occupy Wall Street movement.[54] As economic growth has languished and sputtered, and as people's belief that anyone could grab hold of an opportunity and have a decent shot at prosperity has wavered, social discontent over growing income gaps has increased. The bottom line is that business leaders need to recognize how societal attitudes in the economic context also may create constraints as they make decisions and manage their businesses.[55]

Demographic Conditions   "You can't understand the future without demographics. The composition of a society … shapes every aspect of civic life, from politics, economics, and culture to the kinds of products, services, and businesses that are likely to succeed or fail. Demographics isn't destiny, but it's close."[56] This quote should make it obvious why it's important to examine demographics.

From technology to work attitudes, the Gen Y age group is making its imprint in the workplace. Gen Y is an important demographic at Facebook, where most employees are under 40. The company values the passion and pioneering spirit of its young employees who enjoy taking on the challenge of building ground-breaking technology and the excitement of working in a fast-paced environment with considerable change and ambiguity. Facebook has created a casual and fun-loving work environment where its young cohorts interact in a creative climate that encourages experimentation and tolerates conflict and risk.

Paul Sakuma/AP Photos

Baby Boomers. Gen Y. Post-Millennials. Maybe you've heard or seen these terms before. Population researchers use these terms to refer to three of the more well-known age groups found in the North American population. Baby Boomers are those individuals born between 1946 and 1964. Much is written and reported about "boomers" because there are so many of them. The sheer number of people in that cohort means they've significantly affected every aspect of the external environment (from the educational system to entertainment/lifestyle choices to the Social Security system and so forth) as they cycle through the various life stages.

Gen Y (or the "Millennials") is typically considered to encompass those individuals born between 1978 and 1994. As the children of the Baby Boomers, this age group is also large in number and making its imprint on external environmental conditions as well. From technology to clothing styles to work attitudes, Gen Y is making its imprint on workplaces.

Then, we have the Post-Millennials—the youngest identified age group— those born between the late 1990s and 2005.[57] This group has also been called the iGeneration, primarily because they've grown up with technology that customizes everything to the individual. Population experts say it's too early to tell whether elementary school-aged children and younger are part of this demographic group or whether the world they live in will be so different that they'll comprise a different demographic cohort.[58]

Demographic age cohorts are important to our study of management because, as we said earlier, large numbers of people at certain stages in the life cycle can constrain decisions and actions taken by businesses, governments, educational institutions, and other organizations. In Canada the proportion of the population older than 65 was 13.7 percent in the latest census[59] and is expected to increase to 26.5 percent by 2051.[60] This aging of the population will result in a labour shortage, and creative ways will need to be found to keep seniors working beyond the age of 65, along with pressure to increase immigration. Another effect will be a mounting fiscal burden, with fewer taxpayers to support each retired person (3.6 in Canada in 1995 and projected to be only 1.6 by 2050). We as a society and our politicians as our voice will be forced to make difficult choices to balance the needs of the aging population (for health care, in particular) and the needs of the general population (for education and social benefits such as welfare and employment insurance) with our capacity to pay for them. The aged will also face significant cultural challenges as they will have fewer children and grandchildren to care for them in family settings.[61]

Technological Conditions   In terms of the general environment, the most rapid changes have occurred in technology. We live in a time of continuous technological change. For instance, advances in genomics and bioinformatics has made it such that and individual's genetic information can be used to create personalized medicines that meet their unique medical needs.[62] Information gadgets are getting smaller and more powerful. We have automated offices, electronic meetings, robotic manufacturing, lasers, integrated circuits, faster and more powerful microprocessors, cloud computing, synthetic fuels, and entirely new models of doing business in an electronic age. It is possible that nano sensors may someday be able to "smell" cancer, allowing physicians to employ a nano device rather than having to do a biopsy.[63] Companies that capitalize on technology, such as Blackberry, eBay, and Google, prosper, and again struggle or change to meet the realities of newer disruptive technologies. In addition, many successful retailers such as Walmart use sophisticated information systems to keep on top of current sales trends. Similarly, hospitals, universities, airports, police departments, and even military organizations that adapt to major technological advances have a competitive edge over those that do not. The whole area of technology is radically changing the fundamental ways that organizations are structured and the way that managers manage.

How the Organizational Environment Affects Managers

Knowing *what* the various components of the organizational environment are is important to managers. However, understanding *how* the organizational environment affects managers is equally important. The organizational environment affects managers through the degree of uncertainty that is present and through the various stakeholder relationships that exist between the organization and its external constituencies.

Assessing Environmental Uncertainty

environmental uncertainty The degree of change and the degree of complexity in an organization's environment.

Not all environments are the same. They differ by what we call their degree of **environmental uncertainty**, which is the degree of change and the degree of complexity in an organization's environment (see Exhibit 2-7).

The first of these dimensions is the degree of change. If the components in an organization's environment change frequently, we call it a *dynamic* environment. If change is minimal, we call it a *stable* one. A stable environment might be one in which there are no new competitors, few technological breakthroughs by current competitors, little activity by pressure groups to influence the organization, and so forth. For instance, Zippo Canada, best known for its Zippo lighters, faces a relatively stable environment. There are few competitors and there is little technological change. Probably the main environmental concern for the company is the declining trend in tobacco smokers, although the company's lighters have other uses and global markets remain attractive.

Exhibit 2-7

Environmental Uncertainty Matrix

		Degree of Change	
		Stable	**Dynamic**
Degree of Complexity	Simple	**Cell 1** Stable and predictable environment Few components in environment Components are somewhat similar and remain basically the same Minimal need for sophisticated knowledge of components	**Cell 2** Dynamic and unpredictable environment Few components in environment Components are somewhat similar but are in continual process of change Minimal need for sophisticated knowledge of components
	Complex	**Cell 3** Stable and predictable environment Many components in environment Components are not similar to one another and remain basically the same High need for sophisticated knowledge of components	**Cell 4** Dynamic and unpredictable environment Many components in environment Components are not similar to one another and are in continual process of change High need for sophisticated knowledge of components

In contrast, the recorded music industry faces a dynamic (highly uncertain and unpredictable) environment. Digital formats and music-downloading sites have turned the industry upside down, while YouTube and streaming services make new internet celebrities every month.. If change is predictable, is that considered dynamic? No. Think of department stores that typically make one-quarter to one-third of their sales in December. The drop-off from December to January is significant. But because the change is predictable, we don't consider the environment to be dynamic. When we talk about degree of change, we mean change that is unpredictable. If change can be accurately anticipated, it's not an uncertainty that managers must confront.

The other dimension of uncertainty describes the degree of **environmental complexity**. The degree of complexity refers to the number of components in an organization's environment and the extent of the knowledge that the organization has about those components. For example, Hasbro, the second-largest toy manufacturer (behind Mattel), has simplified its environment by acquiring many of its competitors, such as Tiger Electronics, Wizards of the Coast, Kenner Toys, Parker Brothers, and Tonka Toys. The fewer competitors, customers, suppliers, government agencies, and so forth that an organization must deal with, the less complexity and therefore the less uncertainty there is in its environment.

environmental complexity The number of components in an organization's environment and the extent of the organization's knowledge about those components.

Complexity is also measured in terms of the knowledge an organization needs to have about its environment. For instance, managers at the online brokerage E*TRADE must know a great deal about their internet service provider's operations if they want to ensure that their website is available, reliable, and secure for their stock-trading customers. On the other hand, managers of grocery stores have a minimal need for sophisticated knowledge about their suppliers.

How does the concept of environmental uncertainty influence managers? Looking again at Exhibit 2-7, each of the four cells represents different combinations of the degree of complexity and the degree of change. Cell 1 (an environment that is stable and simple) represents the lowest level of environmental uncertainty. Cell 4 (an environment that is dynamic and complex) represents the highest. Not surprisingly, managers' influence on organizational outcomes is greatest in cell 1 and least in cell 4.

Because uncertainty is a threat to an organization's effectiveness, managers try to minimize it. Given a choice, managers would prefer to operate in environments such as those in cell 1. However, they rarely have full control over that choice. In addition, most industries today are facing more dynamic changes, making their environments more uncertain. The discipline of managing uncertainty is known as "risk management" and is deployed by managers in both for-profit and not-for-profit organizations.

Managing Stakeholder Relationships

Managers are also affected by the nature of the relationships they have with external stakeholders. The more obvious and secure these relationships become, the more influence managers will have over organizational outcomes.

Who are **stakeholders**? We define them as groups in the organization's external environment that are affected by and/or have an effect on the organization's decisions and actions. These groups have a stake in or are significantly influenced by what the organization does. In turn, these groups can influence the organization. For example, think of the groups that might be affected by the decisions and actions of Starbucks—coffee bean farmers, employees, specialty coffee competitors, local communities, and so forth. Some of these stakeholders also may impact decisions and actions of Starbucks' managers. The idea that organizations have stakeholders is now widely accepted by both management academics and practising managers.[64]

stakeholders Any constituencies in the organization's external environment that are affected by the organization's decisions and actions.

Who are an organization's stakeholders? Exhibit 2-8 identifies some of the most common. Note that these stakeholders include internal and external groups. Why? Because both can affect what an organization does and how it operates. However, we are primarily interested in the external groups and their impact on managers' discretion in planning, organizing, leading, and controlling. This does not mean that the internal stakeholders are not important, but we explain these relationships, primarily with employees, throughout the rest of the book.

Exhibit 2-8

Organizational Stakeholders

Why is stakeholder relationship management important? Why should managers care about managing stakeholder relationships? [65] It can lead to improved predictability of environmental changes, more successful innovations, a greater degree of trust among stakeholders, and greater organizational flexibility to reduce the impact of change. But does it affect organizational performance? The answer is yes! Management researchers who have looked at this issue are finding that managers of high-performing companies tend to consider the interests of all major stakeholder groups as they make decisions.[66]

The more critical the stakeholder and the more uncertain the environment, the more managers need to rely on establishing explicit stakeholder partnerships rather than just acknowledging their existence. An organization depends on these external groups as sources of inputs (resources) and as outlets for outputs (goods and services), and managers should consider the interests of these external groups as they make decisions and take actions. We address this issue in more detail in Chapter 5 as we look at the concepts of managerial ethics and corporate social responsibility.

CHAPTER 2

SUMMARY AND IMPLICATIONS

1. Compare and contrast the actions of managers according to the omnipotent and symbolic views. The omnipotent view of management suggests that managers are directly responsible for an organization's success or failure. While this is the dominant view of managers, there is another perspective. The symbolic view of management argues that much of an organization's success or failure is due to external forces outside managers' control. The reality is probably somewhere in between these two views, with managers often able to exert control, but also facing situations over which they have no control.

▶ ▶ ▶ At 3M, the 15 percent rule allows technical employees to work on projects to which they feel a personal commitment (the omnipotent view). However, when markets collapsed in 2001 (after 9/11 and the dot-com bust) and again in late 2008 (as a result of the subprime mortgage crisis), the company found itself at the mercy of market forces beyond its managers' control (symbolic view).

2. Discuss the characteristics and importance of organizational culture. Culture influences how people act within an organization. A strong culture in which everyone supports the goals of the organization makes it easier for managers to achieve goals. A weak culture, in which people do not feel connected to the organization, can make things more difficult for managers. Managers can also influence culture through how it is conveyed to employees, which employees are hired, and how rewards occur in organizations.

▶ ▶ ▶ The innovation culture at 3M changed when James McNerney moved the cultural pendulum toward efficiency of operation and away from innovation. The pendulum swung back toward innovation with the appointment of George Buckley in 2005.

3. Describe what kinds of cultures managers can create. Managers can create a variety of cultures. In this chapter, we discussed ethical, innovative, customer-responsive, and diversity supportive cultures. By having a culture that is consistent with organizational goals and values, managers can more easily encourage employees to achieve organizational goals and values.

▶ ▶ ▶ At 3M managers not only "talk the talk," they also "walk the talk" in their approach to collaboration and the incentives that support the stated cultural objectives.

4. Describe the features of the specific and general organizational environments. The organizational environment plays a major role in shaping managers' decisions and actions. Managers have to be responsive to customers and suppliers while being aware of competitors and public pressure groups. As well, economic, legal–political, socio-cultural, demographic, and technological conditions affect the issues managers face in doing their job.

▶ ▶ ▶ The 30 percent rule at 3M requiring that 30 percent of the current year's sales must come from products not in existence five years ago forces the company to proactively stay in touch with customers, competitors, and changes in the marketplace.

MyManagementLab   Study, practise, and explore real management situations with these helpful resources:

- **Interactive Lesson Presentations:** Work through interactive presentations and assessments to test your knowledge of management concepts.
- **PIA (Personal Inventory Assessments):** Enhance your ability to connect with key concepts through these engaging, self-reflection assessments.
- **Study Plan:** Check your understanding of chapter concepts with self-study quizzes.
- **Simulations:** Practise decision-making in simulated management environments.

P I A PERSONAL INVENTORY ASSESSMENT

REVIEW AND DISCUSSION QUESTIONS

1. Contrast the actions of managers according to the omnipotent and symbolic views.

2. Classrooms have cultures. Describe your classroom culture using the seven dimensions of organizational culture. Does the culture constrain your instructor? How?

3. What is the impact of a strong culture on organizations and managers? Can a strong culture be a liability to an organization? Explain.

4. What is the source of an organization's culture? How does organizational culture continue?

5. How do employees learn an organization's culture?

6. What are the characteristics of an ethical culture, an innovative culture, an adaptable culture, a customer-responsive culture, and a diversity-supportive culture?

7. What forces influence the specific and the general organizational environments? Describe an effective culture for (a) a relatively stable environment and (b) a dynamic environment. Justify your choices.

8. "Businesses are built on relationships." What do you think this statement means? What are the implications for managing the external organizational environment?

ETHICS DILEMMA

In many ways, technology has made all of us more productive. However, ethical issues do arise in how and when technology is used. Take the sports arena. All kinds of technologically advanced sports equipment (swimsuits, golf clubs, ski suits, etc.) have been developed that can sometimes give competitors/players an edge over their opponents.[67] We saw it in swim meets at the summer Olympics and on the ski slopes at the winter Olympics. What do you think? Is this an ethical use of technology? What if your school (or country) were competing for a championship and couldn't afford to outfit athletes in such equipment and it affected your ability to compete? Would that make a difference? What ethical guidelines might you suggest for such situations?

SKILLS EXERCISE

Developing Your Environmental Scanning Skill—About the Skill

Anticipating and interpreting changes that take place in the environment are important skills that managers need. Information that comes from scanning the environment can be used in making decisions and taking actions. And managers at all levels of an organization need to know how to scan the environment for important information and trends.

Steps in Practising the Skill

You can be more effective at scanning the environment if you use the following suggestions:[68]

1. *Decide which type of environmental information is important to your work.* Perhaps you need to know changes in customers' needs and desires, or perhaps you need to know what your competitors are doing. Once you know the type of information you'd like to have, you can look at the best ways to get that information.

2. *Regularly read and monitor pertinent information.* There is no scarcity of information to scan, but what you need to do is read pertinent information sources. How do you know information sources are pertinent? They're pertinent if they provide you with the information you identified as important.

3. *Incorporate the information you get from your environmental scanning into your decisions and actions.* Unless you use the information you're getting, you're wasting your time getting it. Also, the more you use information

from your environmental scanning, the more likely it is that you'll want to continue to invest time and other resources into gathering it. You'll see that this information is important to your ability to manage effectively and efficiently.

4. *Regularly review your environmental scanning activities.* If you're spending too much time getting nonuseful information, or if you're not using the pertinent information you've gathered, you need to make some adjustments.

5. *Encourage your subordinates to be alert to information that is important.* Your employees can be your "eyes and ears" as well. Emphasize to them the importance of gathering and sharing information that may affect your work unit's performance.

Practising the Skill

The following suggestions are activities you can do to practise and reinforce the behaviours associated with scanning the environment.

1. Select an organization with which you're familiar either as an employee or perhaps as a frequent customer. Assume you're the top manager in this organization. What types of information from environmental scanning do you think would be important to you? Where would you find this information? Now assume you're a first-level manager in this organization. Would the types of information you would get from environmental scanning change? Explain.

2. Assume you're a regional manager for a large bookstore chain. Using the internet, what types of environmental and competitive information are you able to identify? For each source, what information did you find that might help you do your job better?

WORKING TOGETHER: TEAM EXERCISE

Assessing the Organization's Environment

All organizations are informed by the realities of their internal and external environments, yet the forces in their specific and general environments differ. Form a small group with three or four other class members and choose two organizations in different industries. Describe the specific and general environmental forces that affect each organization. How are your descriptions different for the two organizations? How are they similar? Now, using the same two organizations, see if you can identify their important stakeholders. Also, indicate whether these stakeholders are critical for the organization and why they are or are not. As a group, be prepared to share your information with the class and to explain your choices.

LEARNING TO BE A MANAGER

Pick two organizations you interact with frequently (as an employee or as a customer) and assess their cultures by looking at the following aspects:

- *Physical Design* (buildings, furnishings, parking lot, office or store design): Where are they located and why? Where do customers and employees park? What does the office/store layout look like? What activities are encouraged or discouraged by the physical layout? What do these things say about what the organization values?

- *Symbols* (logos, dress codes, slogans, philosophy statements): What values are highlighted? Where are logos displayed? Whose needs are emphasized? What concepts are emphasized? What actions are prohibited? Which are encouraged? Are any artifacts prominently displayed? What do those artifacts symbolize? What do these things say about what the organization values?

- *Words* (stories, language, job titles): What stories are repeated? How are employees addressed? What do job titles say about the organization? Are jokes/anecdotes used in conversation? What do these things say about what the organization values?

- *Policies and Activities* (rituals, ceremonies, financial rewards, policies for how customers or employees are treated; note that you may be able to assess these only if you're an employee or know the organization well): What activities are rewarded? Ignored? What kinds of people succeed? Fail? What rituals are important? Why? What events get commemorated? Why? What do these things say about what the organization values?

CASE APPLICATION 1

Making You Say Wow

When you hear the name Ritz-Carlton Hotels, what words come to mind? Luxurious? Elegant? Formal, or maybe even stodgy? Way beyond my budget constraints? Three words that the company hopes comes to mind are *exemplary customer service*. Ritz-Carlton is committed to treating its guests like royalty. It has one of the most distinctive corporate cultures in the lodging industry, and employees are referred to as "our ladies and gentlemen." Its motto is printed on a card that employees carry with them: "We are Ladies and Gentlemen serving Ladies and Gentlemen." And these ladies and gentlemen of the Ritz have been trained in very precise standards and specifications for treating customers. These standards were established more than a century ago by founders Caesar Ritz and August Escoffier. Ritz employees are continually schooled in company lore and company values. Every day at 15-minute "line-up" sessions at each hotel property, managers reinforce company values and review service techniques. And these values are the basis for all employee training and rewards. Nothing is left to chance when it comes to providing exemplary customer service. Potential hires are tested both for cultural fit and for traits associated with an innate passion to serve. A company executive says, "The smile has to come naturally." Although staff members are expected to be warm and caring, their behaviour toward guests had been extremely detailed and scripted. That's why a new customer service philosophy implemented in mid-2006 was such a radical departure from what the Ritz had been doing.

The company's new approach is to not tell employees how to make guests happy. Employees are now expected to figure it out. This is almost the opposite from what the company had been doing, Says Diana Oreck, vice-president, "We moved away from that heavily prescriptive, scripted approach and toward managing to outcomes." The outcome didn't change, though. The goal is still a happy guest who's wowed by the service received. However, under the new approach, staff member interactions with guests are more natural, relaxed, and authentic rather than sounding like they're recited lines from a manual.[69]

DISCUSSION QUESTIONS

1. What is the culture like at Ritz-Carlton Hotels? Why do you think this type of culture might be important to a luxury hotel? What might be the drawbacks of such a culture?
2. What challenges do you think the company faced in changing the culture? What is Ritz-Carlton doing to maintain this new culture?
3. What kind of person do you think would be happiest and most successful in this culture? How do you think new employees "learn" the culture?
4. What could other organizations learn from Ritz-Carlton about the importance of organizational culture?

CASE APPLICATION 2

A Perfect Response to an Imperfect Storm

Twelve days.[70] That is how long it took for Mississippi Power to restore electrical power to the heavily damaged areas of southern Mississippi after Hurricane Katrina slammed into the Mississippi Gulf Coast on August 29, 2005, with 233 kilometre-per-hour winds and pounding rain. That is remarkable, given the devastation that news photos and television newscasts so graphically displayed. It's something that even the federal and state governments could not accomplish. How bad was the damage company employees dealt with? One hundred percent of the company's customers were without power. Sixty-five percent of its transmission and distribution facilities were destroyed. And yet, this organization of 1250 employees did what it had to do, despite the horrible circumstances

and despite the fact that more than half of its employees suffered substantial damage to their own homes. It speaks volumes about the cultural climate that the managers of Mississippi Power had created.

As a corporate subsidiary of utility holding company Southern Company, Mississippi Power provides electrical services to more than 190 000 customers in the Magnolia State. When Hurricane Katrina turned toward Mississippi, managers at Mississippi Power swung into action with a swift and ambitious disaster plan. After Katrina's landfall, Mississippi Power's management team responded "with a style designed for speed and flexibility, for getting things done amid confusion and chaos." David Ratcliffe, senior executive of Southern Company, said, "I could not be prouder of our response."

What factors led to the company's ability to respond as efficiently and effectively as it did?

One key element is the company's can-do organizational culture, which is evidenced by the important values inscribed on employees' identification tags: "Unquestionable Trust, Superior Performance, Total Commitment." Because the values were visible daily, employees knew their importance. They knew what was expected of them in a disaster response or in just doing their everyday work. In addition, through employee training and managerial example, the organization had "steeped its culture" in Stephen Covey's book *The 7 Habits of Highly Effective People.* (The company's training building—the Covey Center—flooded during the storm.) These ingrained habits—be proactive; begin with the end in mind; put first things first; think win–win; seek first to understand, then to be understood; synergize; and sharpen the saw—also guided employee decisions and actions.

Another important element in the company's successful post-storm response was the clear lines of responsibility of the 20 "storm directors," who had clear responsibility and authority for whatever task they had been assigned. These directors had the power to do what needed to be done, backed by unquestionable trust from their bosses. Said one, "I don't have to ask permission."

Finally, the company's decentralized decision-making approach contributed to the way in which employees were able to accomplish what they did. The old approach of responding to a disaster with top-down decision making had been replaced by decision making being pushed further down to the electrical substation level, a distribution point that serves some 5000 people. Crews working to restore power reported to these substations and had a simple mission—get the power back on. "Even out-of-state line crews, hired on contract and working unsupervised, were empowered to engineer their own solutions." What the crews often did to "get the power back on" was quite innovative and entrepreneurial. For instance, one crew "stripped a generator off an ice machine to get a substation working." Mississippi Power's president, Anthony Topazi, said, "This structure made things happen faster than we expected. People were getting more done."

All in all, employees at Mississippi Power, working in difficult, treacherous, and often dangerous situations, did what they had to do. They got the job done. In recognition of the company's outstanding efforts to restore power in the wake of Hurricane Katrina, Mississippi Power was honoured with an "Emergency Response Award" by the Edison Electric Institute in January 2006. It's an award that all the company's employees can be proud of.

DISCUSSION QUESTIONS

1. Using Exhibit 2-2 on page xx, describe the culture at Mississippi Power. Why do you think this type of culture might be important to an electric power company? On the other hand, what might be the drawbacks of such a culture?

2. Describe how you think new employees at Mississippi Power "learn" the company's culture.

3. What stakeholders might be important to Mississippi Power? What concerns might each of these stakeholders have? Would these stakeholders change if there was a disaster to which the company had to respond?

4. What could other organizations learn from Mississippi Power about the importance of organizational culture?

Managing in a Global Environment

Learning Outcomes

Every organization is affected in some way by the global environment. In this chapter, we'll look at what managers need to know about managing in a global environment, including regional trading alliances, how organizations go international, and cross-cultural differences. After reading and studying this chapter, you will achieve the following learning outcomes.

① Compare and contrast the ethno-centric, polycentric, and geocentric attitudes toward global business.

② Discuss the importance of regional trading alliances and global trade mechanisms that affect trade relations among countries in the world.

③ Describe the structures and techniques organizations use as they become global.

④ Explain the relevance of the legal–political, economic, and cultural environments to global business.

▶ ▶ ▶ "In a global market, success flows from having ONE TEAM working on ONE PLAN with ONE GOAL in mind."[1] Alan Mulally, CEO and president of Ford Motor Company (Ford), long realized the importance of managing globally and stated so in the company's 2012 Outlook. Mulally joined Ford Motor in September 2006 from Boeing, where he led a successful turnaround effort. Although he recognized the massive problems facing Ford in being globally competitive and profitable, he was determined to take the dramatic, painful steps and to "plow through gut-wrenching change" to transform the company and return it to global prominence. Guiding his efforts was the Way Forward plan first announced in January 2006.

This comprehensive plan addressed seven areas where organizational changes would be focused: bold leadership; customer focus; strong brands; bold, innovative products; great quality; clear pricing; and competitive costs and capacity. In addition to the Way Forward plan, Mulally fashioned a strategic effort dubbed ONE FORD in an attempt to "fully leverage the tremendous worldwide resources of Ford." In his remarks at an annual shareholders meeting, Mulally said: "We operate in a fiercely competitive global industry. To achieve profitable growth we have to make the best use of our human resources and take advantage of every potential economy of scale and best practice we can find. That means operating as one team around the world, with one plan and one goal . . . ONE FORD . . . profitable growth for all."

In early 2011, Ford introduced a worldwide line of compact cars under the Ford Focus name. Ford called the Focus its first truly global product—that is, designed to share as many parts as possible wherever it is built or sold. The company also introduced a new SUV, the 2012 Escape, which showcases the company's world car strategy. The car is made from a common set of parts and components that Ford will use to make its Focus compact car, two future minivans, and at least six other models. But the company is making its biggest global bet yet—in China, investing some $5 billion "in what it calls its largest industrial expansion in at least 50 years."

ChinaFotoPress/ZUMAPRESS/Newscom

Ford has been late to the game in China, and its sales and production capacity have lagged behind other auto manufacturers in this market. Now, with plans to double production capacity and sales outlets by 2015, Ford is expanding. When its expansion is complete, the company will be able to build 1.2 million passenger cars a year in China—a number that rivals what it built in North America in 2011. Ford's Asia chief, Joe Hinrichs, says, "Should we have done this five years ago? Sure. But we can't change that. We can only change the future."

Think About It

Despite Ford's late push into the Chinese market, it anticipates bolstering its global sales. Despite their vast experience in global markets, what challenges might managers at Ford's US operations still face as they enter new markets? What issues might local managers face as production ramps up at the company's newest facilities in China?

Going global is something that most organizations want to do. As illustrated by the Ford example, the global marketplace presents both opportunities and challenges for managers. With the entire world as a market and national borders becoming increasingly irrelevant, the potential for organizations to grow expands dramatically. However, even large, successful organizations with talented managers face challenges managing in the global environment. Managers must deal with cultural, economic, and political differences. New competitors can suddenly appear at any time from any place on the globe. Managers who don't closely monitor changes in their global environment or who don't take the specific characteristics of their location into consideration as they plan, organize, lead, and control are likely to find limited global success. In this chapter, we discuss the issues managers face in managing in a global environment.

◄•Simulate on **MyManagementLab**

Managing in a Global Environment

What's Your Global Perspective?

It's not unusual for Germans, Italians, or Indonesians to speak three or four languages. Japanese schoolchildren begin studying English in elementary school.[2] "More than half of all primary school children in China now learn English and the number of English speakers in India and China—500 million—now exceeds the total number of mother-tongue English speakers elsewhere in the world." On the other hand, even though we are officially a bilingual country, many Canadians tend to think of English as the only international business language and don't see a need to study other languages. This could lead to future problems as a major research report commissioned by the British Council says that the competitiveness of a country can be undermined by only speaking English.[3]

❶ Compare and contrast the ethnocentric, polycentric, and geocentric attitudes toward global business.

Successful global management requires enhanced sensitivity to differences in national customs and practices. Management practices that work in Vancouver might not be appropriate in Bangkok or Berlin. However, not everyone recognizes that others have different ways of living and working, particularly those who suffer from **parochialism**, which is viewing the world narrowly through one's own perspective.[4] Monolingualism is just one of the ways that people can be unfamiliar with the cultures of others and is a sign that a nation suffers from parochialism. Parochialism is a significant obstacle for managers working in a global business world. If managers fall into the trap of ignoring others' values and customs and rigidly applying an attitude of "ours is better than theirs" to foreign cultures, they will find it difficult to compete with other managers and organizations around the world. This type of narrow, restricted attitude is one approach that managers might take, but isn't the only one.[5] In fact, there are three possible global attitudes. Let's look at each more closely.

parochialism Viewing the world solely through your own perspective, leading to an inability to recognize differences among people.

Exhibit 3-1 summarizes the key points about three possible global attitudes.

First, an **ethnocentric attitude** is the belief that the best work approaches and practices are those of the *home* country (the country in which the company's headquarters are

ethnocentric attitude The belief that the best work approaches and practices are those of the home country.

Exhibit 3-1

Key Information About Three Global Attitudes

Orientation	Ethnocentric Home Country	Polycentric Host Country	Geocentric World
Advantages	Simpler structure	Extensive knowledge of foreign market and workplace	Extensive understanding of global issues
	More tightly controlled	More support from host government	Balance between local and global objectives
		Committed local managers with high morale	Best people and work approaches used regardless of origin
Drawbacks	More ineffective management	Duplication of work	Difficult to achieve
	Inflexibility	Reduced efficiency	Managers must have both local and global knowledge
	Social and political backlash	Difficult to maintain global objectives because of intense focus on local traditions	

located). Managers with an ethnocentric attitude believe that people in foreign countries do not have the skills, expertise, knowledge, or experience that people in the home country do. They would not trust foreign employees with key decisions or technology. While managers with a parochial outlook have a lack of knowledge about other cultures, managers who are ethnocentric believe that their home culture is better than any other.[6]

Next, a **polycentric attitude** is the view that the managers in the *host country* (the foreign country in which the organization is doing business) know the best work approaches and practices for running their businesses. Managers with a polycentric attitude view every foreign operation as different and hard to understand. Thus, these managers are likely to leave their foreign facilities alone and let foreign employees figure out how best to do things.

The final type of global attitude that managers might have is a **geocentric attitude**, which is a *world-oriented* view that focuses on using the best approaches and people from around the globe. Managers with this type of attitude have a global view and look for the best approaches and people regardless of origin. For instance, Carlos Ghosn, CEO of Nissan and Renault, was born in Brazil to Lebanese parents, educated in France, and speaks four languages fluently. He could very well be the "model of the modern major corporate

polycentric attitude The view that the managers in the host country know the best work approaches and practices for running their businesses.

geocentric attitude A world-oriented view that focuses on using the best approaches and people from around the globe.

Reto Wittwer is the president and CEO of Kempinski Hotels. Born in Switzerland and educated in Catholic schools in France, he became a Buddhist when he fell in love with and married a Vietnamese woman after living in Asia for many years. Wittwer is a good example of a geocentric manager: in addition to German, French, Italian, and a Latin-based gypsy language called Rhaeto-Romanish, he speaks eight other languages.

Cabrera Georges/Kempinski Hotels

leader in a globalized world bestraddled by multinational companies."[7] Ghosn's background and perspective have given him a much broader understanding of what it takes to manage in a global environment—something characteristic of the geocentric attitude. A geocentric attitude requires eliminating parochial attitudes and developing an understanding of cross-cultural differences. That's the type of approach successful managers need in today's global environment.

Later in this chapter and throughout the rest of the book, you will see how a geocentric attitude toward managing requires eliminating parochial attitudes and carefully developing an understanding of cultural differences between countries. It is important to realize that, while in some organizations all managers may express the same perspective toward the world (perhaps because the company has a strong culture), different views can also be held by individual managers; thus, the company does not necessarily present a unified front when dealing with people from another culture. However, the way that a company chooses to go global may indicate an overall perspective on the best way to do business in other countries.

Understanding the Global Environment

◉ **Watch** on **MyManagementLab**
MINI: Globalization

2 Discuss the importance of regional trading alliances and global trade mechanisms that affect trade relations among countries in the world.

▶ ▶ ▶ Many companies such as Ford expand into global markets and operate in multiple countries in an effort to capture significant opportunities for sales growth and higher profitability. However, there are many challenges facing companies operating in global environment that can vary considerably by location, including differences in inspection regulations, labelling, legal requirements, and labour standards, to name a few. There are also important socioeconomic differences to consider. A failure to consider these location-specific characteristics as they expand into global markets will greatly impede a company's global success.

Think About It

As we discussed in Chapter 1, management is no longer constrained by national borders. Managers in all sizes and types of organizations are faced with the opportunities and challenges of managing in a global environment. Can you think of other organizations who succeeded in making the global transition? Which organizations failed?

What is the global environment like? An important feature of today's global environment is global trade—which is not new. Countries and organizations have been trading with each other for centuries. "Trade is central to human health, prosperity, and social welfare."[8] When trade is allowed to flow freely, countries benefit from economic growth and productivity gains because they specialize in producing the goods they are best at and importing goods that are more efficiently produced elsewhere. Global trade is shaped by two forces: regional trading alliances and trade mechanisms that ensure that global trade can happen.

Regional Trading Alliances

Just a few years ago, global competition was best described in terms of country against country—the United States vs. Japan, France vs. Germany, Mexico vs. Canada. Now, global competition has been reshaped by the creation of regional trading alliances, such as the European Union (EU), the North American Free Trade Agreement (NAFTA), the Association of Southeast Asian Nations (ASEAN), and others.

The European Union

The **European Union (EU)** is an economic and political partnership of 27 democratic European countries. (See Exhibit 3-1.) Eight countries (Croatia, the former Yugoslav Republic of Macedonia, Turkey, Albania, Bosnia-Herzegovina, Iceland, Montenegro, and

European Union (EU) A union of 27 European countries that forms an economic and political entity.

Exhibit 3-2

European Union Countries

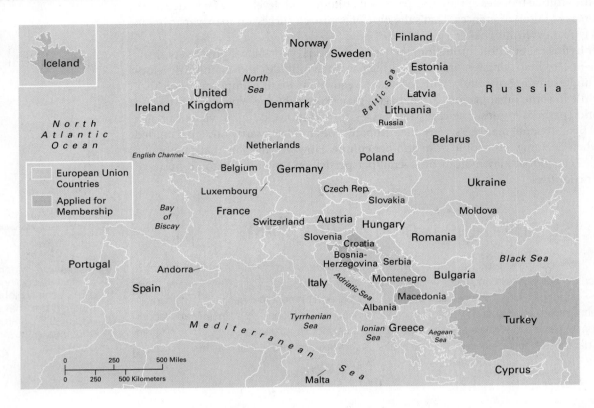

Serbia) are candidates to join the EU.[9] Before being allowed to join, however, the countries must meet the criteria which include democracy, rule of law, a market economy, and adherence to the EU's goals of political and economic union. When the 12 original members formed the EU in 1992, the primary motivation was to reassert the region's economic position against the United States and Japan. Previously, each European nation had border controls, taxes, and subsidies; nationalistic policies; and protected industries. These barriers to travel, employment, investment, and trade prevented European companies from developing economic efficiencies. Now, with these barriers removed, the economic power represented by the EU is considerable. Its current membership covers a population base of more than half a billion people (7 percent of the world population) and accounts for approximately 31 percent of the world's total economic output.[10] (See Exhibit 3-2.)

Another step toward full unification occurred when the common European currency, the **euro**, was adopted. The euro is currently in use in 17 of the 27 member states, and all new member countries must adopt the euro. Only Denmark, the United Kingdom, and Sweden have been allowed to opt out of using the euro.[11] Another push in unification has been attempts to develop a unified European constitution. EU leaders struggled for nearly a decade to enact a treaty designed to strengthen the EU and give it a full-time president. The so-called Lisbon Treaty (or Reform Treaty), which was ratified by all 27 member states, provides the EU with a common legal framework and the tools to meet the challenges of a changing world, including climatic and demographic changes, globalization, security, and energy. Supporters feel the new structure will help strengthen the EU's common foreign policy. Many believe that a more unified Europe could have more power and say in the global arena. As the former Italian prime minister and European Commission president said, "Europe has lost and lost and lost weight in the world."[12]

euro A single common European currency.

The last few years have been difficult economically for the EU and its members, like it was for many global regions. "The traditional concept of 'solidarity' is being undermined by protectionist pressures in some member countries and the rigors of maintaining a common currency for a region that has diverse economic needs."[13] Some analysts believe that the EU is at a pivotal point. "They can spur growth across the region by following through on long-overdue pledges to trim benefits and free up labour markets. Or they can face a decade of economic stagnation."[14] The European Commission—the executive body for the European union—faced with major economic issues of the 17 euro zone members, including the massive debt crisis in Greece, severe economic uncertainties in Spain and Italy, and bank uncertainties, has been given new powers to monitor national budgets.[15] Although European leaders came together and bridged sharp philosophical divides and joined forces with the International Monetary Fund to forge an agreement to bail out Greece when its debt troubles intensified, the region's economic crisis has worsened and the member disputes have intensified as much of Europe appears to be sliding into a new recession.[16]

The euro zone is a larger economic unit than the United States or China and is a major source of world demand for goods and services. As the economic crisis in the region intensifies, "a growing number of companies in the United States are warning investors that sales are slowing and could get much worse."[17] Therefore, the importance of this regional trading alliance will continue to evolve as EU members work together to resolve the region's economic issues and once again assert their economic power with successful European businesses continuing to play a crucial role in the global economy.

North American Free Trade Agreement (NAFTA) An agreement among the Canadian, American, and Mexican governments in which barriers to free trade were reduced.

North American Free Trade Agreement and Other Latin American Agreements

When agreements in key issues covered by the **North American Free Trade Agreement (NAFTA)** were reached by the Canadian, US, and Mexican governments in August 1992, a vast economic bloc was created where barriers to free trade were reduced. As of 2012, it is the second-largest trade bloc in the world in terms of combined GDP of its members.[18] Between 1994, when NAFTA went into effect, and 2007, merchandise trade among the United States, Canada, and Mexico more than tripled with some $2.6 billion exchanged on a daily basis among NAFTA partners.[19] Bilateral investment stock between Canada and the United States totalled almost $616 billion in 2012, a development which has largely been attributed to NAFTA. Canada's exports to Mexico have also quadrupled since the NAFTA agreement was signed, and its foreign investments in Mexico increased by a factor of five.[20] Westcoast Energy, Scotiabank, and BCE are just a few Canadian companies that have expanded their operations to Mexico. Despite early criticisms of the trade agreement, the North American trading bloc has proven to be a powerful force in today's global economy.

Other Latin American nations have also become part of free-trade blocs. Colombia, Mexico, and Venezuela led the way when all three signed an economic pact in 1994 eliminating import duties and tariffs. Another agreement, the US–Central America Free Trade Agreement (CAFTA), promotes trade liberalization between the United States and five Central American countries: Costa Rica, El Salvador, Guatemala, Honduras, and Nicaragua. However, only El Salvador and Costa Rica have joined. The other countries have yet to change laws to be in line with the agreement.[21] The United States also signed a trade deal with Colombia that is said to be the "largest Washington has concluded with a Latin American country since signing" NAFTA.[22] Also, negotiators from 34 countries in the western hemisphere continue work on a Free Trade Area of the Americas (FTAA) agreement, which was to have been operational no later than 2005, a missed targeted deadline.

Since NAFTA went into effect in 1994, the lifting of trade barriers has made it easier for Canadian-based aircraft maker Bombardier to operate across Canadian, US, and Mexican borders. And because of NAFTA, Bombardier is boosting Mexico's aerospace industry by adding the country to its global manufacturing network. At its plant in Queretaro, Mexico, Bombardier employs more than 2000 workers to produce electrical harnesses, fuselages (shown in this photo), and flight controls for all Bombardier aircraft in production. The plants in Mexico help Bombardier reduce production costs and put the company closer to the growing demand for its aircraft in the Latin American markets.

Bloomberg/Getty Images

Leaders of these nations have yet to reach any agreement, leaving the future of the FTAA up in the air.[23] However, another free trade bloc of 10 South American countries known as the Southern Common Market or Mercosur already exists. Some South Americans see Mercosur as an effective way to combine resources to better compete against other global economic powers, especially the EU and NAFTA. With the future of FTAA highly doubtful, this regional alliance could take on new importance.

Canada has also recently begun expanding free trade beyond the Americas. In late 2013, the Canadian Prime Minister and President of the EU Trade Commission signed a political agreement for the Canada-EU Trade Agreement (CETA), promising to remove over 99% of tariffs between the two countries. Though the technical details remain to be negotiated, the treaty is estimated to increase bilateral trade in goods and services by 23%, worth over €26 billion annually.[24] The Canadian government has also been invited to negotiate its place in a Trans-Pacific Partnership (TPP), a trade agreement between 12 nations in the Americas, East Asia, and Australasia. Though the TPP currently remains in the negotiation phase, if implemented, the treaty would represent a market of 792 million people, and a combined GDP of $28.1 trillion, among the largest trade agreements in the world.[25]

Association of Southeast Asian Nations

Association of Southeast Asian Nations (ASEAN) A trading alliance of 10 Southeast Asian countries.

The **Association of Southeast Asian Nations (ASEAN)** is a trading alliance of 10 Southeast Asian nations (see Exhibit 3-3). The ASEAN region has a population of more than 592 million with a combined gross domestic product of $1.5 trillion (US).[26] In addition to these 10 nations, leaders from a group dubbed ASEAN+3, which includes China, Japan, and South Korea, have met to discuss trade issues. Also, leaders from India, Australia, and New Zealand have participated in trade talks with ASEAN+3 as well. The main issue with creating a trade bloc of all 16 nations has been the lack of any push toward regional integration. Despite the Asian culture's emphasis on consensus building, "ASEAN's biggest problem is that individual members haven't been willing to sacrifice for the common good."[27] Although Southeast Asian leaders agree that closer regional integration would help economic growth, the large differences in wealth among ASEAN members have made it "difficult to create common standards because national standards remain so far apart."[28]

Exhibit 3-3

ASEAN Members

Source: Based on J. McClenahen and T. Clark, "ASEAN at Work," *IndustryWeek*, May 19, 1997, p. 42.

However, the challenges brought on by the 2008–09 worldwide recession, which adversely affected many countries in this region, triggered greater interest in pushing for integration. On January 1, 2010, China and ASEAN launched an ambitious free-trade agreement, making it the world's third largest trade bloc.[29] In addition to these free trade alliances, it's hoped that by 2015 an established ASEAN economic community will allow goods, skilled workers, and capital to move freely among member countries. This fast-growing region means ASEAN will be an increasingly important regional economic and political alliance.

Other Trade Alliances

Other regions around the world have also developed regional trading alliances. For instance, the 53-nation African Union (AU), which came into existence in 2002, has the vision of "building an integrated, prosperous and peaceful Africa."[30] Members of this alliance have created an economic development plan to achieve greater unity among Africa's nations. Like members of other trade alliances, these countries hope to gain economic, social, cultural, and trade benefits from their association. Such cooperation couldn't be more important as Africa's economic output is booming like never before. GDP growth rates have been averaging 4.8 percent, the highest rate outside Asia, with most of that growth coming domestically. In addition, Africa has been experiencing a "virtually unprecedented period of political stability with governments steadily deregulating industries and developing infrastructure."[31]

Five east African nations—Burundi, Kenya, Rwanda, Tanzania, and Uganda—have formed a common market called the East African Community (EAC).[32] Under this agreement, goods can be sold across borders without tariffs. The next step for the EAC will be monetary union, although that will take time to implement.

Finally, the South Asian Association for Regional Cooperation (SAARC), composed of eight member states (India, Pakistan, Sri Lanka, Bangladesh, Bhutan, Nepal, the Maldives, and Afghanistan), began eliminating tariffs in 2006.[33] Its aim, like all the other regional trading alliances, is to allow free flow of goods and services.

The preceding discussion indicates that global trade is alive and well. Regional trade alliances continue to be developed in areas where member countries believe it's in their best interest economically and globally to band together and strengthen their economic position.

Global Trade Mechanisms

Global trade among nations doesn't just happen on its own. As trade issues arise, global trade systems ensure that trade continues efficiently and effectively. Indeed, one of the realities of globalization is the interdependence of countries—that is, what happens in one can impact others, good or bad. For example, the financial crisis that started in the United States in 2008 threw the global economy into a tailspin. Although things spiralled precariously out of control, it didn't completely collapse. Why? Because governmental interventions and trade and financial mechanisms helped avert a potential crisis. We're going to look at four important global trade mechanisms: the World Trade Organization, the International Monetary Fund, the World Bank Group, and the Organisation for Economic Cooperation and Development.

The World Trade Organization

One of the most important of these mechanisms is the multilateral trading system called the **World Trade Organization (WTO)**.[35] The WTO was formed in 1995 and evolved from the General Agreement on Tariffs and Trade (GATT), an agreement that had been in effect from the end of World War II until 1994. Today, the WTO is the only *global* organization dealing with the rules of trade among nations. Its membership consists of 155 member countries and 29 observer governments (which have a specific time frame within which they must apply to become members). At its core are the various trade agreements negotiated and ratified by the vast majority of the world's trading nations. The goal of the WTO is to help businesses conduct trade (importing and exporting) among countries

datapoints[34]

75 percent of U.S. labour productivity growth has been attributed to MNCs.

61 percent of HR professionals say there will be a greater need for cross-cultural understanding and savvy in business settings.

17.5 percent of Canadians report being able to conduct a conversation in both English and French.

82 percent of global executives say they are willing to relocate to another region, province or country.

58 percent of high-performing companies have some type of global leadership program in place.

44 percent of Canadian primary or secondary school students outside of Quebec are enrolled in a French as a Second Language program.

32 percent of post-secondary graduates see themselves using a language other than their first language at work.

70 percent of Americans aged 18 to 24 have not travelled outside the United States in the last three years.

54 percent of business travellers say they're more successful in their career because of global business travel experience.

World Trade Organization (WTO) A global organization of 155 countries that deals with the rules of trade among nations.

without undesired side effects. Although a number of vocal critics have staged visible protests and criticized the WTO, claiming that it destroys jobs and the natural environment, the WTO appears to play an important role in monitoring and promoting global trade.

For instance, the WTO played a pivotal role in keeping global trade active during the 2008–09 global economic crisis. WTO Director-General Pascal Lamy said, "During these difficult times, the multilateral trading system has once again proven its value. WTO rules and principles have assisted governments in keeping markets open and they now provide a platform from which trade can grow as the global economy improves."[36] The WTO has played an important role in promoting and protecting global trade.

International Monetary Fund and World Bank Group

International Monetary Fund (IMF) An organization of 188 countries that promotes international monetary cooperation and provides advice, loans, and technical assistance.

Two other important and necessary global trade mechanisms include the International Monetary Fund and the World Bank Group. The **International Monetary Fund (IMF)** is an organization of 188 countries that promotes international monetary cooperation and provides member countries with policy advice, temporary loans, and technical assistance to establish and maintain financial stability and to strengthen economies.[37] During the global financial turmoil of the last few years, the IMF has been on the forefront of advising countries and governments in getting through the difficulties.[38] The **World Bank Group** is a group of five closely associated institutions, all owned by its member countries, that provides vital financial and technical assistance to developing countries around the world. The goal of the World Bank Group is to promote long-term economic development and poverty reduction by providing members with technical and financial support.[39] For instance, during the recent global recession, financial commitments by the World Bank Group reached $100 billion as it helped nations respond to and recover from the economic downturn.[40] Both entities have an important role in supporting and promoting global business.

World Bank Group A group of five closely associated institutions that provides financial and technical assistance to developing countries.

Organisation for Economic Co-operation and Development (OECD)

Organisation for Economic Co-operation and Development (OECD) An international economic organization that helps its 30 member countries achieve sustainable economic growth and employment.

The forerunner of the OECD, the Organisation for European Economic Co-operation, was formed in 1947 to administer Canadian and American aid under the Marshall Plan for the reconstruction of Europe after World War II. Today, the **Organisation for Economic Co-operation and Development (OECD)** is a Paris-based international economic organization whose mission is to help its 34 member countries achieve sustainable economic growth and employment and raise the standard of living in member countries while maintaining financial stability in order to contribute to the development of the world economy.[41] When needed, the OECD gets involved in negotiations with OECD countries so they can agree on "rules of the game" for international cooperation. One current focus is combating small-scale bribery in overseas commerce. The OECD says such "so-called facilitation payments are corrosive . . . particularly on sustainable economic development and the rule of law."[42] With a long history of facilitating economic growth around the globe, the OECD now shares its expertise and accumulated experiences with more than 70 developing and emerging market economies.

Doing Business Globally

❸ Describe the structures and techniques organizations use as they become global.

▶ ▶ ▶ The Ford Motor Company (known as simply "Ford") is the second-largest U.S.-based automaker and the fifth-largest in the world based on 2012 vehicle sales.[43] In 2011, Ford produced 5.595 million automobiles and employed about 164 000 employees at around 70 plants and facilities worldwide.[44] To tailor its product to regional needs in Asia Pacific, Africa, and South America, Ford produces a global Ranger pickup and a compact sport utility EcoSport. These new vehicles, offer a product line in markets that prefer smaller-sized vehicles and are designed to reflect the needs of these markets.

Daimler, Nissan Motor, and Renault are part of a strategic partnership that shares small-car technology and power trains—an arrangement that all three automakers say will allow them to better compete in an environment where cutting costs is crucial. Procter & Gamble Company relocated the top executives from its global skin, cosmetics, and personal-care unit from its Cincinnati headquarters to Singapore. Reckitt Benckiser, the U.K.-based maker of consumer products (Lysol, Woolite, and French's mustard are just a few of its products), has operations in more than 60 countries, and its top 400 managers represent 53 different nationalities. As these examples show, organizations in different industries and from different countries do business globally. But *how* do they do so?

> ### Think About It
> **How is Ford structured to do business globally? Would it make sense for Ford to form a strategic alliance or a joint venture in a country that produces the raw materials Ford needs or that distributes its vehicles? How might it choose partners to do so, if that strategy were chosen?**

Organizations in different industries *and* from different countries are pursuing global opportunities. In this section, we look at different types of international organizations and how they do business in the global marketplace.

Different Types of International Organizations

Multinational Corporations

Organizations doing business globally are not anything new. Ford Motor Company set up its first overseas sales branch in France in 1908. By the 1920s, other companies, including Fiat, Unilever, and Royal Dutch Petroleum Company/Shell had gone international. But it was not until the mid-1960s that international companies became commonplace. Today, there are very few companies that do not have some type of international dealings. However, in spite of the fact that doing business internationally is so widespread, there is no one generally accepted approach to describing the different types of international companies—they are called different things by different authors. We use the terms *multinational, multidomestic, global,* and *transnational* to describe the various types of international organizations.[45] A **multinational corporation (MNC)** is a broad term usually used to refer to any and all types of international companies that maintain operations in multiple countries.

multinational corporations (MNCs) A broad term that refers to any and all types of international companies that maintain operations in multiple countries.

Multidomestic Corporations

One type of MNC is a **multidomestic corporation,** which maintains significant operations in more than one country but decentralizes management to the local country. This type of globalization reflects the polycentric attitude. A multidomestic corporation does not attempt to manage foreign operations from its home country. Instead, local employees typically are hired to manage the business, and marketing strategies are tailored to that country's unique characteristics. This type of global organization reflects the polycentric attitude (see page xx). For example, Switzerland-based Nestlé can be described as a multidomestic corporation. With operations in almost every country on the globe, its managers match the company's products to its consumers. In parts of Europe, Nestlé sells products that are not available in North America or Latin America. Another example of a multidomestic corporation is Frito-Lay, a division of PepsiCo, which markets a Doritos chip in the British market that differs in both taste and texture from the Canadian and US versions. Many consumer product companies organize their global businesses using this approach because they must adapt their products and services to meet the needs of the local markets.

multidomestic corporation An MNC that decentralizes management and other decisions to the local country.

Global Companies

global company An MNC that centralizes management and other decisions in the home country.

Another type of MNC is a **global company,** which centralizes its management and other decisions in the home country. This approach to globalization reflects the ethnocentric attitude. Global companies treat the world market as an integrated whole and focus on the need for global efficiency and cost savings. Although these companies may have considerable global holdings, management decisions with company-wide implications are made from headquarters in the home country. Some examples of companies that can be considered global companies include Montreal-based transport manufacturer Bombardier, Montreal-based aluminum producer Rio Tinto Alcan, Tokyo-based consumer electronics firm Sony, Frankfurt-based Deutsche Bank AG, and New York City–based financial services provider Merrill Lynch.

Transnational or Borderless Organizations

transnational or borderless organization An MNC in which artificial geographical barriers are eliminated.

Other companies use an arrangement that eliminates artificial geographical barriers. This type of MNC is often called a **transnational or borderless organization**. The transnational or borderless organization approaches global business with a geocentric attitude.[46] For example, Ford Motor Company is pursuing its One Ford concept as it integrates its operations around the world. IBM dropped its organizational structure based on country and reorganized into industry groups such as business solutions, software, IT services, and financing. Bristol-Myers Squibb changed its consumer business to become more aggressive in international sales and created a management position responsible for worldwide consumer medicines such as Bufferin and Excedrin. And Spain's Telefónica eliminated the geographic divisions between Madrid headquarters and its widespread phone companies. Borderless management is an attempt by organizations to increase efficiency and effectiveness in a competitive global marketplace.[47]

Born Globals

born global An international company that chooses to go global from inception.

Our classification of different types of international organizations tends to describe large international businesses. However, there is an increasing number of businesses called **born globals** that choose to go global from inception.[48] These companies (also known as *international new ventures,* or *INVs*) commit resources (material, people, financing) upfront to doing business in more than one country and are likely to continue to play an increasingly important role in international business.

How Organizations Go International

When organizations do go international, they often use different approaches (see Exhibit 3-4). Managers who want to get into a global market with minimal investment may start with **global sourcing** (also called *global outsourcing*), which is purchasing materials or labour

global sourcing Purchasing materials or labour from around the world wherever it is cheapest.

◄●─Simulate on MyManagementLab

Going Global

Exhibit 3-4

How Organizations Go International

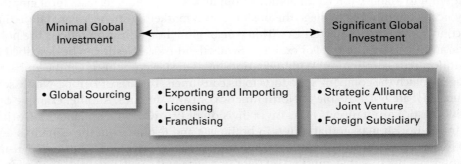

from around the world wherever it is cheapest. The goal: Take advantage of lower costs in order to be more competitive. For instance, in fall 2006, Montreal-based Bell Canada contracted with Sitel India and two other Indian companies to provide technical support and customer care to Canadian customers.[49] Although global sourcing is often the first step to going international, many organizations continue to use this approach even as they become more international because of the competitive advantages it offers. Each successive stage of going international beyond global sourcing, however, requires more investment and thus entails more risk for the organization.

Importing and Exporting

An organization can go international by **exporting** its products to other countries—that is, by making products at home and selling them overseas. In addition, an organization can go international by **importing** products—that is, by selling products at home that are made abroad. Both exporting and importing are small steps toward being a global business and usually involve minimal investment and minimal risk. Many, especially small businesses, continue with exporting and importing as the way they do business globally. For instance, Haribhai's Spice Emporium, a small business in Durban, South Africa, exports spices and rice to customers all over Africa, Europe, and the United States. However, other organizations have built multimillion-dollar businesses by importing or exporting; that is what Montreal-based Mega Brands (formerly Mega Bloks) has done. Mega Brands is Canada's largest toy company, with sales in over 100 countries.[50] The company operates in 14 countries, with more than 1300 employees. Mega Brands is only one example of Canada's increasing reliance on export business. Transportation equipment manufacturing, primary metal manufacturing, and paper manufacturing account for the largest volume of Canadian exports.

exporting An approach to going global that involves making products at home and selling them abroad.

importing An approach to going global that involves acquiring products made abroad and selling them at home.

Licensing and Franchising

Managers also might use *licensing* or *franchising*, which are similar approaches involving one organization giving another organization the right to use its brand name, technology, or product specifications in return for a lump sum payment or a fee usually based on sales. The only difference is that **licensing** is primarily used by manufacturing organizations that make or sell another company's products, and **franchising** is primarily used by service organizations that want to use another company's name and operating methods. For example, Russian consumers can enjoy McDonald's hamburgers because McDonald's Canada opened the first Russian franchise in Moscow. Franchises have also made it possible for Mexicans to dine on Richmond, BC-based Boston Pizza and Koreans to consume frozen yogourt from Markham, Ontario-based Coolbrands' Yogen Früz. Anheuser-Busch licenses the right to brew and market Budweiser beer to other brewers, such as Labatt in Canada, Modelo in Mexico, and Kirin in Japan. Licensing and franchising involve more investment and risk than exporting and importing because the company's brand is more at stake.

licensing An approach to going global in which a manufacturer gives another organization the right to use its brand name, technology, or product specifications.

franchising An approach to going global in which a service organization gives a person or group the right to sell a product, using specific business methods and practices that are standardized.

Strategic Alliances

When an organization has been doing business internationally for a while and has gained experience in international markets, managers may decide to make a more direct investment. One way to increase investment is through a **strategic alliance**, which is a partnership between a domestic organization and a foreign company in which both share resources and knowledge in developing new products or building production facilities. The partners also share the risks and rewards of this alliance. For example, Honda Motor and General Electric teamed up to produce a new jet engine. A specific type of strategic alliance in which the partners form a separate, independent organization for some business purpose is called a **joint venture**. For example, Hewlett-Packard has had numerous joint ventures with various suppliers around the globe to develop different components for its computer equipment. These partnerships provide a relatively easy way for companies to compete globally.

strategic alliance An approach to going global that involves a partnership between a domestic and a foreign company in which both share resources and knowledge in developing new products or building production facilities.

joint venture An approach to going global in which the partners agree to form a separate, independent organization for some business purpose; it is a type of strategic alliance.

Fast-food giant KFC, like many big franchise firms, is opening more new outlets overseas. Along the way, the company is making appropriate changes in its menu offerings, such as substituting juice and fruit for Coke and fries. This Shanghai promotion features new egg tarts.

FEATURECHINA/ZHU GANG/
FEATURECHINA/Newscom

foreign subsidiary An approach to going global that involves a direct investment in a foreign country by setting up a separate and independent production facility or office.

Foreign Subsidiaries

Finally, managers may choose to directly invest in a foreign country by setting up a **foreign subsidiary**, a separate and independent production facility or office. This subsidiary can be managed as a multidomestic organization (local control), a global organization (centralized control), or a transnational/borderless organization (global control). As you can probably guess, this arrangement involves the greatest commitment of resources and poses the greatest amount of risk. Many of the larger companies operating in Canada are actually subsidiaries of US corporations, including GM Canada, Procter & Gamble Canada, and McDonald's Canada. Canadian subsidiaries manage their operations and set their own targets and goals, but they also report to head office in the United States. Canada has been a good investment opportunity for American firms. The low Canadian dollar from the early 1990s until 2003 resulted in lower costs and higher productivity. Employers in Canada have long paid far less for health premiums for their employees than they would in the United States because of Canada's health care system. Prior to the collapse of the automobile industry in late 2008 and the subsequent bankruptcy of General Motors, the company agreed to a settlement with the United Auto Workers (UAW) in 2007 that brought into question whether Canada's health care advantage would continue. The American car manufacturer and the UAW agreed that the union would be responsible for paying its retired workers' health care costs going forward. This lowered GM's labour and benefits costs and put GM's costs closer to Japan's labour costs.[51]

Managing in a Global Environment

4 Explain the relevance of the legal–political, economic, and cultural environments to global business.

▶ ▶ ▶ As Ford expands into global markets, its managers must consider all areas of the general environment—the broad economic, legal–political, socio-cultural, demographic, and technological conditions—that may affect the organization. For example, labour laws in other countries are often significantly different. Canadian or US companies expanding production to Europe discover that in some countries, by law, they must offer 36 days' holiday (vacation) pay to local workers who worked more than a 35-hour week. This is different from vacation time awarded to Canadian or U.S. workers where the maximum is often four weeks—and this is for the company's chief executive.

> **Think About It**
> How have the global legal–political and economic environments affected Ford's ability to produce its product? What could Ford do to protect itself from importing raw materials from countries that have lower quality standards and fewer regulations than Canada or the United States?

Assume for a moment that you are a manager going to work for a branch of a global organization in a foreign country. You know that your environment will differ from the one at home, but how? What should you be looking for?

Any manager who finds himself or herself in a foreign country faces new challenges in the general environment that will impact their organizational decision making. In this section, we'll look at some of these challenges. Although our discussion is presented through the eyes of a Canadian manager, our analytical framework could be used by any manager who has to manage in a foreign environment, regardless of national origin.

The Legal–Political Environment

Canadian managers are accustomed to stable legal and political systems. Changes are slow, and legal and political procedures are well established. Elections are held at regular intervals, and even when the political party in power changes after an election, it's unlikely that anything too radical will happen. The stability of laws governing the actions of individuals and institutions allows for accurate predictions. However, this certainly isn't true for all countries. Managers in a global organization must stay informed of the specific laws in countries where they do business. Recent examples of differences in the legal–political environment include president of Zimbabwe pushing ahead with plans to force foreign companies to sell majority stakes to locals.[52] Such a law represents a major barrier to foreign business investment. In China, foreign businesses are finding a less-than-welcoming climate as government policies are making it more difficult to do business there.[53] And Swedish retailer Ikea halted further investment in Russia because of continual governmental red tape delays. Per Kaufmann, Ikea's Russia country manager, said the decision was "due to the unpredictability of the administrative processes in some regions."[54]

Also, some countries have risky political climates. Managers of businesses in these countries face dramatically greater uncertainty as a result of political instability. For example, during BP's long involvement in Russia, the company "had so many police run-ins that its stock price nudged up or down in response to raids or the arrests of employees." Recently, not long after Exxon formed a strategic alliance with Russia's state-owned oil company, armed commandos raided BP's offices in "one of the ritual armed searches of white-collar premises that are common here."[55] Also, some countries have risky political climates. Chicago-based Aon Corporation does an annual political risk assessment, and its 2012 report found that businesses faced the highest level of risk in the following countries: Afghanistan, Belarus, Bissau, Democratic Republic of Congo, Iran, Iraq, North Korea, Pakistan, Somalia, South Sudan, Sudan, Syria, Venezuela, Yemen, and Zimbabwe. Company analysts said that political and financial instability remained a feature of the business landscape as a result of the global recession. They also said that "significant risks are shown for exchange transfer, sovereign non-payment, political interference, supply chain disruption, legal and regulatory risk, and political violence."[56] Managers of businesses in countries with higher risk levels face dramatically greater uncertainty. In addition, political interference is a fact of life in some regions, especially in some Asian countries such as China.[57]

Keep in mind that a country's legal–political environment does not have to be unstable or revolutionary to be a concern to managers. Just the fact that a country's laws and political system differ from those of Canada is important. Managers must recognize these differences to understand the constraints under which they operate and the opportunities that exist.

The Economic Environment

Strange as it may sound, 17 000 tons of Parmesan cheese, with an estimated value of $187 million, were held in the vaults of Italian bank Credito Emiliano. The cheese is collateral from Italian cheese makers struggling through the recession.[58] Such an example of an economic factor of business may seem peculiar for those of us in Canada, but it's not all that unusual for Italian businesses. A global manager must be aware of economic issues when doing business in other countries. First, it's important to understand a country's type of economic system. The two major types are a free market economy and a planned economy. A **free market economy** is one in which resources are primarily owned and

free market economy An economic system in which resources are primarily owned and controlled by the private sector.

planned economy An economic system in which economic decisions are planned by a central government.

controlled by the private sector. A **planned economy** is one in which economic decisions are planned by a central government. In actuality, no economy is purely market or command. For instance, Canada and the United States are two countries at the market end of the spectrum, but their governments do have some control over economic activities. The economies of Vietnam and North Korea, however, would be more planned. China's economy was once planned, but is moving toward a more free–market-based economy. Why would managers need to know about a country's economic system? Because it has the potential to constrain decisions and actions. Other economic issues a manager might need to understand include currency exchange rates, inflation rates, and diverse tax policies.

An MNC's profits can vary dramatically, depending on the strength of its home currency and the currencies of the countries in which it operates. For instance, prior to the overall global economic slowdown, the rising value of the euro against both the dollar and the yen had contributed to strong profits for German companies.[59] Any currency exchange revaluations can affect managers' decisions and the level of a company's profits.

Inflation means that prices for products and services are increasing, but it also affects interest rates, exchange rates, the cost of living, and the general confidence in a country's political and economic system. Country inflation rates can, and do, vary widely. The *World Factbook* states rates ranging from a negative 0.80 percent in the Northern Mariana Islands to a positive 57.4 percent in Belarus.[60] Managers need to monitor inflation trends so they can anticipate possible changes in a country's monetary policies and make good business decisions regarding purchasing and pricing.

Finally, tax policies can be a major economic worry. Some countries' tax laws are more restrictive than those in an MNC's home country. Others are more lenient. About the only certainty is that they differ from country to country. Managers need accurate information on tax rules in countries in which they operate to minimize their business's overall tax obligation.

The Cultural Environment

For five weeks in June and July of 2011, the entire senior leadership team at Starwood Hotels relocated to Shanghai, China. Why? Because clearly China is a huge growth market and "working closely with people from a different culture helps you to see pitfalls and opportunities in a very different way."[61]

Managing today's talented global workforce can be a challenge![62] A large global oil company found that employee productivity in one of its Mexican plants was off 20 percent and sent a US manager to find out why. After talking to several employees, the manager discovered that the company used to have a monthly fiesta in the parking lot for all the employees and their families. Another US manager had cancelled the fiestas, saying they were a waste of time

National culture influences many aspects of competing abroad. India now has about 350 000 engineering graduates each year; the United States has 70 000. Organizations that need employees with engineering skills in order to be competitive are going to have to understand national cultures, such as that of India. Indra Nooyi, ceo of PepsiCo, knows the importance of understanding global markets and cultures from the ground up, as you will see in the *Management Reflection*.

Goodshoot/Thinkstock/Getty Images

MANAGEMENT REFLECTION

Leadership at Pepsi

How can gaining an understanding of global cultures improve a manager's ability to succeed in today's global environment? She has been on the Most Powerful Woman in Business list by *Fortune* magazine for more than five years and was named one of the 100 most powerful women in the world by Forbes magazine.[66] "She" is Indra Nooyi, CEO of PepsiCo. Born in India, Ms. Nooyi joined PepsiCo as head of corporate strategy in 1994 and moved quickly up the ladder to become chief executive officer and chairman of PepsiCo's board of directors. As the ceo of a large American company, Nooyi recognizes the importance of her company's global business operations. On a recent trip to China, a critical market for PepsiCo, Nooyi didn't take the usual "ceo tour" of conference rooms, but spent 10 days immersing herself in China. She says, "I wanted to look at how people live, how they eat, what the growth possibilities are." Here's a leader who knows what it will take to succeed in today's global environment. What can you learn from this leader who made a difference? ■

and money. The message employees were getting was that the company did not care about their families anymore. When the fiestas were reinstated, productivity and employee morale soared. At Hewlett-Packard, a cross-global team of American and French engineers were assigned to work together on a software project. The American engineers sent long, detailed emails to their counterparts in France. The French engineers viewed the lengthy emails as patronizing and replied with quick, concise emails. This made the American engineers think that their French colleagues were hiding something from them. The situation spiralled out of control and negatively affected output until team members went through cultural training.[63]

As we know from Chapter 2, organizations have different cultures. Countries have cultures too. **National culture** is the values and attitudes shared by individuals from a specific country that shape their behaviour and beliefs about what is important.[64]

Which is more important to a manager—national culture or organizational culture? For example, is an IBM facility in Germany more likely to reflect German culture or IBM's corporate culture? Research indicates that national culture has a greater effect on employees than does their organization's culture.[65] German employees at an IBM facility in Munich will be influenced more by German culture than by IBM's culture.

Legal, political, and economic differences among countries are fairly obvious. The Japanese manager who works in Canada or his or her Canadian counterpart in Japan can get information about a country's laws or tax policies without too much difficulty. Getting information about a country's cultural differences isn't quite that easy! The primary reason is that it's hard for natives to explain their country's unique cultural characteristics to someone else. For instance, if you are a Canadian raised in Canada, how would you characterize Canadian culture? In other words, what are Canadians like?

national culture The values and attitudes shared by individuals from a specific country that shape their behaviour and beliefs about what is important.

Hofstede's Framework for Assessing Cultures

Geert Hofstede developed one of the most widely referenced approaches to helping managers better understand differences between national cultures. His research found that managers and employees vary on five dimensions of national culture, which are as follows:

- *Individualism vs. collectivism.* Individualism is the degree to which people in a country prefer to act as individuals rather than as members of groups. In an individualistic society, people are supposed to look after their own interests and those of their immediate family and do so because of the large amount of freedom that an individualistic society allows its citizens. The opposite is collectivism, which is characterized by a social framework in which people prefer to act as members of groups and expect others in groups of which they are a part (such as a family or an organization) to look after them and to protect them.

- *Power distance.* Hofstede used the term *power distance* as a measure of the extent to which a society accepts the fact that power in institutions and organizations is distributed unequally. A high power distance society accepts wide differences in power in organizations. Employees show a great deal of respect for those in authority. Titles, rank, and status carry a lot of weight. In contrast, a low power distance society plays down inequalities as much as possible. Superiors still have authority, but employees are not afraid of or in awe of the boss.

- *Uncertainty avoidance.* Uncertainty avoidance describes the degree to which people tolerate risk and prefer structured over unstructured situations. People in low uncertainty avoidance societies are relatively comfortable with risks. They are also relatively tolerant of behaviour and opinions that differ from their own because they don't feel threatened by them. On the other hand, people in a society that is high in uncertainty avoidance feel threatened by uncertainty and ambiguity and experience high levels of anxiety in such situations, which manifests itself in nervousness, high stress, and aggressiveness.

- *Achievement vs. nurturing.* The fourth cultural dimension, like individualism/collectivism, is a dichotomy. Achievement reflects the degree to which values such as assertiveness, the acquisition of money and material goods, and competition prevail. Nurturing is a national cultural attribute that emphasizes relationships and concern for others.[67]

- *Long-term and short-term orientations.* This cultural attribute looks at a country's orientation toward life and work. People in cultures with long-term orientation look to the future and value thrift and persistence. Also, in these cultures, leisure time is not so important, and it is believed that the most important events in life will occur in the future. A short-term orientation values the past and present and emphasizes respect for tradition and fulfilling social obligations. Leisure time is important, and it is believed that the most important events in life happen in the past and in the present.

We provide 12 examples of the first four variables in Exhibit 3-5. The long-term orientation variable isn't included in this table because scores for some of the countries were

Exhibit 3-5

Examples of Hofstede's Cultural Dimensions

Country	Individualism/ Collectivism	Power Distance	Uncertainty Avoidance	Achievement/ Nurturing*
Australia	Individual	Small	Moderate	Strong
Canada	Individual	Moderate	Low	Moderate
England	Individual	Small	Moderate	Strong
France	Individual	Large	High	Weak
Greece	Collective	Large	High	Moderate
Italy	Individual	Moderate	High	Strong
Japan	Collective	Moderate	High	Strong
Mexico	Collective	Large	High	Strong
Singapore	Collective	Large	Low	Moderate
Sweden	Individual	Small	Low	Weak
United States	Individual	Small	Low	Strong
Venezuela	Collective	Large	High	Strong

* A weak achievement score is equivalent to high nurturing.

Source: Based on G. Hofstede, "Motivation, Leadership, and Organization: Do American Theories Apply Abroad?" *Organizational Dynamics,* Summer 1980, pp. 42–63.

not reported. The top five countries with higher long-term orientation (LTO) scores are China, Hong Kong, Taiwan, Japan, and South Korea. Countries such as Sweden, Germany, Australia, United States, United Kingdom, and Canada had lower LTO scores, which reflect a more short-term orientation.[68]

The GLOBE Framework for Assessing Cultures

The **Global Leadership and Organizational Behavior Effectiveness (GLOBE)** is an ongoing research program that extended Hofstede's work by investigating cross-cultural leadership behaviours and giving managers additional information to help them identify and manage cultural differences. Using data from more than 18 000 managers in 62 countries, the GLOBE research team (led by Robert House) identified nine dimensions on which national cultures differ.[69] Two dimensions (power distance and uncertainty avoidance) fit directly with Hofstede's. Four are similar to Hofstede's (assertiveness, which is similar to achievement–nurturing; humane orientation, which is similar to the nurturing dimension; future orientation, which is similar to long-term and short-term orientations; and institutional collectivism, which is similar to individualism–collectivism). The remaining three (gender differentiation, in-group collectivism, and performance orientation) offer additional insights into a country's culture. Here are descriptions of these nine dimensions. For each of these dimensions, we have indicated which countries rated high, which rated moderate, and which rated low.

- *Power distance.* The extent to which a society accepts that power in institutions and organizations is distributed unequally. (*High:* Russia, Spain, and Thailand. *Moderate:* England, France, and Brazil. *Low:* Denmark, the Netherlands, and South Africa.)

- *Uncertainty avoidance.* A society's reliance on social norms and procedures to alleviate the unpredictability of future events. (*High:* Austria, Denmark, and Germany. *Moderate:* Israel, United States, and Mexico. *Low:* Russia, Hungary, and Bolivia.)

- *Assertiveness.* The extent to which a society encourages people to be tough, confrontational, assertive, and competitive rather than modest and tender. (*High:* Spain, United States, and Greece. *Moderate:* Egypt, Ireland, and Philippines. *Low:* Sweden, New Zealand, and Switzerland.)

- *Humane orientation.* The degree to which a society encourages and rewards individuals for being fair, altruistic, generous, caring, and kind to others. (*High:* Indonesia, Egypt, and Malaysia. *Moderate:* Hong Kong, Sweden, and Taiwan. *Low:* Germany, Spain, and France.)

- *Future orientation.* The extent to which a society encourages and rewards future-oriented behaviours such as planning, investing in the future, and delaying gratification. (*High:* Denmark, Canada, and the Netherlands. *Moderate:* Slovenia, Egypt, and Ireland. *Low:* Russia, Argentina, and Poland.)

- *Institutional collectivism.* The degree to which individuals are encouraged by societal institutions to be integrated into groups within organizations and society. (*High:* Greece, Hungary, and Germany. *Moderate:* Hong Kong, United States, and Egypt. *Low:* Denmark, Singapore, and Japan.)

- *Gender differentiation.* The extent to which a society maximizes gender role differences as measured by how much status and decision-making responsibilities women have. (*High:* South Korea, Egypt, and Morocco. *Moderate:* Italy, Brazil, and Argentina. *Low:* Sweden, Denmark, and Slovenia.)

- *In-group collectivism.* The extent to which members of a society take pride in membership in small groups, such as their family and circle of close friends, and the organizations in which they're employed. (*High:* Egypt, China, and Morocco. *Moderate:* Japan, Israel, and Qatar. *Low:* Denmark, Sweden, and New Zealand.)

Global Leadership and Organizational Behavior Effectiveness (GLOBE) program The research program that studies cross-cultural leadership behaviours.

- *Performance orientation.* The degree to which a society encourages and rewards group members for performance improvement and excellence. (*High:* United States, Taiwan, and New Zealand. *Moderate:* Sweden, Israel, and Spain. *Low:* Russia, Argentina, and Greece.)

The GLOBE studies confirm that Hofstede's dimensions are still valid and extend his research rather than replace it. GLOBE's added dimensions provide an expanded and updated measure of countries' cultural differences. It's likely that cross-cultural studies of human behaviour and organizational practices will increasingly use the GLOBE dimensions to assess differences among countries. [70]

Global Management in Today's World

Doing business globally today isn't easy! As we look at managing in today's global environment, we want to focus on two important issues. The first issue involves the challenges associated with globalization, especially in relation to the openness that's part of being global. The second issue revolves around the challenges of managing a global workforce.

The challenge of openness   The push to go global has been widespread. Advocates praise the economic and social benefits that come from globalization, but globalization also creates challenges because of the openness that's necessary for it to work. One challenge is the increased threat of terrorism by a truly global terror network. Globalization is meant to open up trade and to break down the geographical barriers separating countries. Yet, opening up means just that—being open to the bad as well as the good. In a wide range of countries, from the Philippines and the United Kingdom to Israel and Pakistan, organizations and employees face the risk of terrorist attacks. Another challenge from openness is the economic interdependence of trading countries. As we saw over the last few years, the faltering of one country's economy can have a domino effect on other countries with which it does business. So far, however, the world economy has proved to be resilient. And as we discussed earlier, structures that are currently in place, such as the World Trade Organization and the International Monetary Fund, help to isolate and address potential problems.

Challenges of Managing a Global Workforce

- "As more Canadians go to mainland China to take jobs, more Chinese and Canadians are working side by side. These cross-cultural partnerships, while beneficial in many ways, are also highlighting tensions that expose differences in work experience, pay levels, and communication."[71]

- Global companies with multicultural work teams are faced with the challenge of managing the cultural differences in work-family relationships. The work-family practices and programs appropriate and effective for employees in one country may not be the best solution for employees in other locations.[72]

These examples indicate challenges associated with managing a global workforce. As globalization continues to be important for businesses, it's obvious that managers need to understand how to best manage that global workforce. Some researchers have suggested that managers need **cultural intelligence** or cultural awareness and sensitivity skills.[73] Cultural intelligence encompasses three main dimensions: (1) knowledge of culture as a concept—how cultures vary and how they affect behaviour; (2) mindfulness—the ability to pay attention to signals and reactions in different cross-cultural situations; and (3) behavioural skills—using one's knowledge and mindfulness to choose appropriate behaviours in those situations.

Other researchers have said that what effective global leaders need is a **global mind-set,** attributes that allow a leader to be effective in cross-cultural environments.[74] Those attributes have three components as shown in Exhibit 3-6.

cultural intelligence Cultural awareness and sensitivity skills.

global mind-set Attributes that allow a leader to be effective in cross-cultural environments.

Exhibit 3-6

A Global Mind-Set

Intellectual capital:	Knowledge of international business and the capacity to understand how business works on a global scale	nmarques74/Forolia
Psychological capital:	Openness to new ideas and experiences	Alex White/Fotolia
Social capital:	Ability to form connections and build trusting relationships with people who are different from you	tang90246/Fotolia

Source: Based on "Making It Overseas," by M. Javidan, M. Teagarden, and D. Bowen, from *Harvard Business Review,* April 2010; and "Testing Managers' Global IQ," by J. McGregor (ed.), from *Bloomberg BusinessWeek,* September 28, 2009.

Leaders who possess such cross-cultural skills and abilities—whether cultural intelligence or a global mind-set—will be important assets to global organizations. Successfully managing in today's global environment will require incredible sensitivity and understanding. Managers from any country will need to be aware of how their decisions and actions will be viewed, not only by those who may agree, but more importantly, by those who may disagree. They will need to adjust their leadership styles and management approaches to accommodate these diverse views, and at the same time be as efficient and effective as possible in reaching the organization's goals.

SUMMARY AND IMPLICATIONS

1. Compare and contrast the ethnocentric, polycentric and geocentric attitudes toward global business. We can view global differences from ethnocentric, polycentric, and geocentric perspectives. An ethnocentric attitude is the belief that the best work approaches and practices are those of the *home* country (the country in which the company's headquarters are located). The polycentric attitude is the view that the managers in the *host* country (the foreign country in which the organization is doing business) know the best work approaches and practices for running their businesses. The geocentric attitude, which is a *world-oriented* view, focuses on using the best approaches and people from around the globe.

▶ ▶ ▶ Ford likely understood the best practices for doing business in the United States and Canada, but would have had to undertake substantive research to understand the socio-economic, legal, political, and economic environment in China in order to successfully expand its operations into that country.

2. Discuss the importance of regional trading alliances and global trade mechanisms that affect trade relations among countries in the world. Global trade is affected by two forces: regional trading alliances and the agreements negotiated through the World Trade Organization (WTO). Regional trading alliances include the European Union (EU), the North American Free Trade Agreement (NAFTA), the Association of Southeast Asian Nations (ASEAN), and others. These regional alliances specify how trade is conducted among countries. The goal of the WTO, which consists of 153 member countries and 30 observer governments, is to help businesses (importers and exporters) conduct their business through the various trade agreements negotiated and ratified by the vast majority of the world's trading nations.

▶ ▶ ▶ As the Ford Motor Company expanded into global markets, it had to consider not only the trading alliances and mechanisms, but also consider the economic, political, legal, cultural, and social differences compared to those in North America. Recently, Ford announced that it expects a loss of about $2 billion for Ford Europe for the fiscal year 2013.[75] Ford will continue to monitor the situation in Europe and take further action as necessary. However, the business environment in Europe remains uncertain and Ford's decline in Europe has been deeper than the company originally thought. The challenges in the European market is largely out of Ford's control, and based largely on the problems in Greece and Spain and continued sluggishness in Britain.

3. Describe the structures and techniques organizations use as they become global. Organizations can take on a variety of structures when they go global, including multinational corporations, multidomestic corporations, global companies, and transnational or borderless organizations. An organization can take lower-risk and lower-investment strategies for going global through importing or exporting, hiring foreign representation, or contracting with foreign manufacturers. It can also increase its presence in another country by joining with another business to form a strategic alliance or joint venture. Or it can set up a foreign subsidiary in order to have a full presence in the foreign country.

▶ ▶ ▶ When the Ford Motor Company first began to expand its production operations into global markets, the company originally had a business strategy of diversification with different operations for different markets with different standards and specifications. This strategy caused them heavy costs in terms of high parts costs, separate R&D for different markets and models, inefficient production cycles, and no knowledge sharing among business units, resulting in silos instead of synergies, which in turn caused net revenue losses. In response, Ford launched its globalization 2000 plan that paved a way forward for them to become profitable as market leader and adopted a strategy of standardization to reduce the cost of R&D and gain production efficiencies. A successful merger with Volvo, Aston Martin, and Jaguar, and the integration of suppliers, distributors, and a global workforce enabled Ford to share knowledge and make their production more cost efficient by adopting each other's best practices.

4. Explain the relevance of the legal–political, economic, and cultural environments to global business. When managers do business in other countries, they will be affected by the global legal–political and economic environments of those countries. Differing laws and political systems can create constraints as well as opportunities for managers. The type of economic system in some countries can place restrictions on how foreign companies are able to conduct business. In addition, managers must be aware of the culture of the countries in which they do business to understand *how* business is done and what customers expect.

▶ ▶ ▶ As the Ford Motor Company expanded into global markets it needed to adopt a global business strategy to remain competitive internationally and to ensure success at home in the United States. Ford needed to consider the cultural and economic environment as well as the legal and political constraints when designing a worldwide line of smaller (compact) cars under the Ford Focus name that would allow the company to expand into global markets.

MyManagementLab   Study, practise, and explore real management situations with these helpful resources:
- **Interactive Lesson Presentations:** Work through interactive presentations and assessments to test your knowledge of management concepts.
- **PIA (Personal Inventory Assessments):** Enhance your ability to connect with key concepts through these engaging, self-reflection assessments.   PERSONAL INVENTORY ASSESSMENT
- **Study Plan:** Check your understanding of chapter concepts with self-study quizzes.
- **Simulations:** Practise decision-making in simulated management environments.

REVIEW AND DISCUSSION QUESTIONS

1. Contrast ethnocentric, polycentric, and geocentric attitudes toward global business.

2. Describe the current status of each of the various international and regional trading alliances.

3. Contrast multinational, multidomestic, global, and transnational organizations.

4. What are the managerial implications of a borderless organization?

5. Describe the different ways organizations can go international.

6. Can the GLOBE framework presented in this chapter be used to guide managers in a Russian hospital or a government agency in Egypt? Explain.

7. What challenges might confront a Mexican manager transferred to Canada to manage a manufacturing plant in Winnipeg, Manitoba? Will these issues be the same for a Canadian manager transferred to Guadalajara? Explain.

8. How might the cultural differences in the GLOBE dimensions affect how managers (a) use work groups, (b) develop goals/plans, (c) reward outstanding employee performance, and (d) deal with employee conflict?

ETHICS DILEMMA

Workers' rights. It's not something we often think about when we're purchasing the latest tech gadget.[76] However, look at this list of some issues that investigations have uncovered: work shifts lasting up to 60 hours; a factory explosion killing numerous workers that resulted from a build-up of combustible dust; repetitive motion injuries that are so bad workers lose the use of their hands. "According to recent press reports, that's what work is like for assembly workers in China who build Apple's iPhones, iPads, and iPods." In other locations where workers are assembling products for other tech companies, factory workers have committed suicide because of the pressure and stress.

What do you think? Whose responsibility is it to ensure that workplaces are safe, especially when work is outsourced?

Should managers even consider such issues as they navigate the global market? Why or why not? One analyst said, "It's a tricky dance between first-world brands and third-world production." What do you think this statement means? What are the implications for managers?

SKILLS EXERCISE

Developing Your Collaboration Skill

Collaboration is the teamwork, synergy, and cooperation used by individuals when they seek a common goal. In many cross-cultural settings, the ability to collaborate is crucial. When all partners must work together to achieve goals, collaboration is critically important to the process.

Steps in Practising the Skill

1. *Look for common points of interest.* The best way to start working together in a collaborative fashion is to seek commonalities that exist among the parties. Common points of interest enable communications to be more effective.

2. *Listen to others.* Collaboration is a team effort. Everyone has valid points to offer, and each individual should have an opportunity to express his or her ideas.

3. *Check for understanding.* Make sure you understand what the other person is saying. Use feedback when necessary.

4. *Accept diversity.* Not everything in a collaborative effort will "go your way." Be willing to accept different ideas and different ways of doing things. Be open to these ideas and the creativity that surrounds them.

5. *Seek additional information.* Ask individuals to provide additional information. Encourage others to talk and more fully explain suggestions. This brainstorming opportunity can assist in finding creative solutions.

6. *Don't become defensive.* Collaboration requires open communications. Discussions may focus on things you and others may not be doing or need to do better. Don't take the constructive feedback as personal criticism. Focus on the topic being discussed, not on the person delivering the message. Recognize that you cannot always be right!

Practising the Skill

Interview managers from three different organizations about how they collaborate with others. What specific tips have they discovered for effectively collaborating with others? What problems have they encountered when collaborating? How have they dealt with these problems?

WORKING TOGETHER: TEAM EXERCISE

Assessing Your Global Perspective

You are part of a multicultural team of eight students, two from each of Canada, China, South Africa, and Germany. You are trying to put together a business plan for a small business that could be operated in your community. This is a course assignment, but winning proposals have the opportunity to be funded up to $10 000. Your team is struggling to come up with a workable idea, and cannot even agree on a potential course of action to get the project completed. What might be some of the multicultural differences that could be getting in your way? What could you do to smooth over some of these differences? How might each student's global perspective be affecting team performance?

LEARNING TO BE A MANAGER

- Find two current examples of each of the ways that organizations go international. Write a short paper describing what these companies are doing.

- The U.K.-based company Kwintessential has several cultural knowledge "quizzes" on its website [www.kwintessential.co.uk/resources/culture-tests.html]. Go to the website and try two or three of them.

Were you surprised at your score? What does your score tell you about your cultural awareness?

- On this website, you'll also find Country Etiquette Guides. Pick two countries to study (from different regions), and compare them. How are they the same? Different? How would this information help a manager?

- Interview two or three professors or students at your school who are from other countries. Ask them to describe what the business world is like in their country. Write a short paper describing what you found out.

- Take advantage of opportunities you might have to travel to other countries, either on personal trips or on school-sponsored trips.

- Create a timeline illustrating the history of the European Union and a timeline illustrating the history of NAFTA.

- Suppose you were sent on an overseas assignment to another country (you decide which one). Research that country's economic, legal–political, and cultural environments. Write a report summarizing your findings.

- If you don't have your passport yet, go through the process to get one.

- If you want to better prepare yourself for working in an international setting, take additional classes in international management and international business.

- You've been put in charge of designing a program to prepare your company's managers to go on an overseas assignment. What should (and would) this program include? Be specific. Be thorough. Be creative.

- In your own words, write down three things you learned in this chapter about being a good manager.

CASE APPLICATION 1

Global Employees Required

Moving to a foreign country isn't easy, no matter how many times you have done it or how receptive you are to new experiences. Successful global organizations are able to identify the best candidates for global assignments, and one of the ways they do this is through individual assessments prior to assigning people to global facilities. Form groups of three to five individuals. Your newly formed team, the Global Assignment Task Force, has been given the responsibility for developing a global aptitude assessment form for Zara, the successful European clothing retailer.[77] The company is starting to become well known in North America, and Zara's managers have positioned the company for continued global success. That success is based on a simple principle—in fashion, nothing is as important as time to market.

Zara's store managers (more than 600 worldwide) offer suggestions every day on cuts, fabrics, and even new lines. After reviewing the ideas, a team at headquarters in A Coruña, Spain, decides what to make. Designers draw up the ideas and send them over the company's intranet to nearby factories. Within days, the cutting, dyeing, sewing, and assembling starts. In three weeks, the clothes will be in stores from Barcelona to Berlin to Bangkok. That is 12 times faster than its

rivals. Zara has a twice-a-week delivery schedule that restocks old styles and brings in new designs. Rivals tend to get new designs once or twice a season.

Because Zara is expanding its global operations significantly, it wants to make sure that it is sending the best possible people to the various global locations. Your team's assignment is to come up with a rough draft of a form to assess people's global aptitudes. Think about the characteristics, skills, attitudes, and so on that you think a successful global employee would need. Your team's draft should be at least half a page but no longer than one page. Be prepared to present your ideas to your classmates and instructor.

DISCUSSION QUESTIONS

1. What characteristics, skills, and attitudes do you think a successful global employee would need?

2. What additional information might the firms need to know to assess potential global employees? What life experiences or activities might be good indicators of a suitable global employee? Explain why you think these indicators are important.

CASE APPLICATION 2

Walking a Mile in Someone Else's Basketball Shoes

Using an exceptionally well-executed game plan, the National Basketball Association (NBA) is trying to emerge as a truly global sports league appealing to fans around the world with players being drawn from a variety of countries.[78] The game was invented in 1891 by James Naismith, from Almonte, Ontario, and the Toronto Raptors and Vancouver

Grizzlies were the first non-US cities in the modern era to join the league, during the 1995–1996 season.

The desire to transform the once-faltering domestic sport into a global commercial success reflects a keen understanding of managing in a global environment. And much of the credit should go to NBA commissioner David

Stern, who has been consciously building the NBA into a global brand.

Professional basketball sparked the interest of fans and players around the globe in the mid-1990s, and the NBA cashed in on the game's universal appeal. At one time, if you had asked someone in China what the most popular basketball team was, the answer would have been the "Red Oxen" from Chicago (the Bulls). More recently, the NBA's centre of attention comes from China. Yao Ming, the 2.2-metre-tall centrepiece of the Houston Rockets, has a personality that appeals to fans around the world. But he is not the only global player in the league. Others include the Dallas Mavericks' Dirk Nowitzki from Germany; Pau Gasol of the Memphis Grizzlies, a native of Spain; San Antonio Spurs' guard Tony Parker from France; Denver Nuggets' forward Nenê Hilario from Brazil; and Utah Jazz guard Gordan Giricek from Croatia. The Raptors' first-round draft pick in 2004, Rafael Araujo, is from Brazil. What started as a trickle in the 1980s with occasional non-US stars like Hakeem Olajuwon (Nigeria) and the late Dražen Petrovic (Croatia), has turned into a flood. A total of 60 players from 28 countries and territories outside the United States were playing in the NBA as of July 2007. These included Canadian players Jamaal Magloire of the Portland Trail Blazers and Steve Nash of the Phoenix Suns. Nineteen Canadian basketball players have played in the NBA over the years. The NBA wants to prove that the game can be played globally also.

DISCUSSION QUESTIONS

1. What strategies can Stern take to increase consumer familiarity with basketball both domestically and globally? How can he develop a greater basketball presence in Canada?

2. What activities could help NBA players from around world become familiar with social and cultural norms in North America, keeping in mind their busy schedules? Explain.

3. Pick one of the countries mentioned in the case and do some cultural research on it. What did you find out about the culture of that country? How might this information affect the way an NBA manager could help a player from that country adjust to North American culture?

Managing Entrepreneurially

In this chapter, we're going to look at the activities of entrepreneurs. We'll start by looking at how the opportunity focus of entrepreneurs enables organizations to build cultures that are flexible, nimble, and innovative. We will then look at the difference between searching for a viable business model and executing against the business model once it is validated. After reading and studying this chapter, you will achieve the following learning outcomes.

Learning Outcomes

1. Embrace the capacity of entrepreneurial thinking and practices to add value in both new and existing organizations.

2. Identify opportunities and build the business case for launching an entrepreneurial/intrapreneurial venture.

3. Choose appropriate organizational structures to support an entrepreneurial culture.

4. Make appropriate choices in leading an entrepreneurial venture.

5. Deploy appropriate control structures to respond to the unique challenges faced by entrepreneurial ventures.

▶ ▶ ▶ Julia Deans joined Futurepreneur Canada (formerly known as the Canadian Youth Business Foundation — CYBF), as Chief Executive Officer in January 2013 with a track record of success in the corporate, entrepreneurial, not-for-profit, and public service sectors. Futurepreneur Canada is a national not-for-profit organization "dedicated to growing Canada's economy one young entrepreneur at a time" and "launching thriving Canadian entrepreneurs who are changing their communities and the world."[1] The mission is to champion and mobilize young and emerging Canadian entrepreneurs by providing the guidance, investment, community and a voice to drive the success and Canada's economic growth. [2]

Each year Futurepreneur Canada helps more than 700 young Canadians launch businesses in all sectors and industries. The flagship Start-up Program offers young entrepreneurs the expertise, financing, mentoring, and resources to be successful. Futurepreneur Canada also offers specialized programs to assist entrepreneurs with unique needs. The Newcomer Program offers enhanced services that include tailored mentoring and insight into Canadian business and cultural customs for new Canadians. The Spin Master Innovation Fund supports cohorts of highly innovative young Canadians. The MoMENTum Program offers mentoring to those who do not require or qualify for financing. Finally, the Prince's Operation Entrepreneur, a program of the Prince's Charities Canada, helps veterans transition from service to entrepreneurship

Futurpreneur Canada

by supporting the veterans with business coaching, financing, and mentoring. Futurepreneur Canada also helps young entrepreneurs gain access to international markets and perspectives.

In the past four years, Futurepreneur Canada has engaged 66 young entrepreneurs to be G20 Young Entrepreneur's Alliance Canadian delegates, where they advance global youth entrepreneurship as a key driver of global and domestic job creation, innovation, and economic growth. Futurepreneur Canada also hosts Global Entrepreneurship week in Canada, engaging 29 190 Canadians and 400 partners, supporters, and sponsors in 515 events and activities across Canada.

> **Think About It**
> Why is Futurepreneur Canada focusing on young entrepreneurs? What challenges might arise for Julia Deans and Futurepreneur Canada in working with young entrepreneurs? What support programs would be most effective?

The Context of Entrepreneurship

 1 Embrace the capacity of entrepreneurial thinking and practices to add value in both new and existing organizations.

It may seem odd that we have included a chapter on managing entrepreneurially in a section called *Defining the Manager's Terrain.* But, when you think about it, all organizations had a starting point, and if they were successful, they grew and had to go through the process of passing from the hands of the founders to the next generation of family or professional management. As we examine the natural cycle of organizational formation, we will learn some general lessons that can provide context for the discussion in later chapters on planning, organizing, leading, and controlling. In looking at the behaviour of entrepreneurs, we can build a stronger understanding of the role that managers play in building an innovative culture, such as those at Cirque du Soleil (discussed in Chapter 1) and at 3M (discussed in Chapter 2). More importantly, the management lens of an entrepreneur, with its focus on opportunity, has a particularly valuable contribution to make to our understanding of what it takes to build an adaptive organization, as defined in Chapter 1.[3]

What Is Entrepreneurship?

entrepreneurship The process of starting new organizations, generally in response to opportunities.

social enterprises/ ventures Organizations that are started in response to needs within the community.

Entrepreneurship is the process of starting new organizations, generally in response to opportunities. These new organizations may be for traditional for-profit purposes, but more and more often they are being started in response to needs within the community and are known as **social enterprises/ventures**. Entrepreneurs pursue opportunities by changing, revolutionizing, transforming, or introducing new products or services. When used as an adjective, *entrepreneurial* applies to individuals who embrace one or more of the acquirable and desirable skills identified by Jeffrey Timmons: commitment and determination; leadership; opportunity obsession; tolerance of risk and uncertainty; creativity, self-reliance and ability to adapt; and motivation to excel. For example, when Apple launched the iPhone, Blackberry, Nokia, and the other existing cell phone companies looked at the new entry as a toy and noted that Apple had no market share—why should we worry about that? That is not what they are saying today. [4]

How Entrepreneurial Ventures Add Value to the Economy

creative destruction The process of transformation that accompanies radical innovation, where the way things were done before is "destroyed."

There are two common and yet differing explanations of how entrepreneurs add value to an economy. One view, based on the work of Austrian economist Joseph Schumpeter, proposed that the entrepreneur creates an opportunity through innovation and then takes advantage of it. In the process of transformation that accompanies a radical innovation, the way things were done before is "destroyed." This process became known as **creative destruction**.[5] On the other hand, Israel Kirzner, another leading economist, suggested that entrepreneurs are able to perceive the opportunities for entrepreneurial profits by being sensitive to signals in the marketplace—they are **entrepreneurially alert**. The entrepreneur's role is to constantly look for imbalances in what people need and what is available (opportunities) and then take advantage of them.[6]

When Jim Balsillie and Mike Lazaridis introduced the BlackBerry, they created a disruptive technology that changed the rules of the game for everybody, under Schumpeter's theory. The person who buys goods from yard sales on the weekend and then posts them on eBay for sale at a higher price fits Kirzner's entrepreneurially alert model, which states that successful entrepreneurs have an uncanny ability to spot opportunities. Which of these two explanations is the best one? The answer is that they both explain how entrepreneurs create value.

The Nature of Opportunities and the Role of Entrepreneurial Managers

Because pursuing opportunity lies at the heart of our definition of entrepreneurship, it is important to better understand the nature of opportunity and strategies for identifying and commercializing it. How you best find an opportunity depends on the type of opportunity. Opportunities can be recognized, discovered, or enacted. A recognition strategy works best when both supply and demand are known. Using Kirzner's concept of entrepreneurial alertness, entrepreneurs *recognize* opportunities when they are alert to information in the environment. But if only supply or only demand is known, simply being alert will not help in finding opportunities. In this case, the entrepreneur relies on his or her experience and actively employs sophisticated search techniques to *discover* the opportunity. The assumption is that the opportunity exists—we just have to find it![7]An example could be a mining company that employs geologists and seismic data to discover new deposits. The third type of opportunity occurs when neither supply nor demand is known and the entrepreneur creates something new, or *enacts* an opportunity. As the entrepreneur takes the idea to market, it may change as more information is gained. The entrepreneur begins to imagine (rather than recognize or actively search for) future opportunities. Why predict the future when you can create it![8]

Many people think that entrepreneurial ventures and small businesses are one and the same, but they're not. There are some key differences between the two. Entrepreneurs and intrapreneurs (those who act entrepreneurially within an existing organization) create **entrepreneurial ventures**—organizations that pursue opportunities, that are characterized by innovative practices, and that have growth and profitability as their main goals. They also pursue opportunities and create social ventures where the objective is to maximize social return on investment (SROI) rather than traditional return on investment (ROI). It should be noted that radical innovation of and by itself does not create the most value for an entrepreneur. Innovations in an existing marketplace well populated by competitors are often higher-value and lower-risk opportunities.

On the other hand, a **small business** is a business that is independently owned, operated, and financed; has fewer than 100 employees; doesn't necessarily engage in any new or innovative practices; and has relatively little impact on its industry.[9] A small business isn't necessarily entrepreneurial just because it's small. The entrepreneurial business must be innovative and constantly seek out new opportunities. Even though entrepreneurial ventures may start small, they pursue growth. Some new small firms may grow, but many remain small businesses, by choice or by default.

Why Is Entrepreneurship Important?

Entrepreneurship and innovation are seen to be the cornerstones of a competitive national economy by governments. Because both are associated with "doing something new," in most countries entrepreneurship policies are closely tied to innovation policies. The entrepreneurial process introduces innovative products, processes, and organizational structures across an economy.[10] Its importance can be shown in three areas—innovation, number of new start-ups, and jobs created through global entrepreneurship efforts.

entrepreneurially alert The ability to perceive opportunities for entrepreneurial profits by being sensitive to signals in the marketplace.

entrepreneurial ventures Organizations that are pursuing opportunities, are characterized by innovative practices, and have growth and financial viability as their main goals.

small business An organization that is independently owned, operated, and financed; has fewer than 100 employees; doesn't necessarily engage in any new or innovative practices; and has relatively little impact on its industry.

Innovation

Innovation is a process of changing, experimenting, transforming, and revolutionizing, and it's a key aspect of entrepreneurial activity. The "creative destruction" process that characterizes innovation leads to technological changes and employment growth. Entrepreneurial firms act as "agents of change" by providing an essential source of new and unique ideas that may otherwise go untapped.[11] Statistics back this up. New small organizations generate 24 times more innovations per research and development dollar spent than do *Fortune* 500 organizations, and they account for more than 95 percent of new and "radical" product developments.[12] In the United States, small entrepreneurial firms produce 13 to 14 times more patents per employee than large patenting firms.[13]

Number of New Start-Ups

Because all businesses—whether they fit the definition of entrepreneurial ventures or not—were new start-ups at one point in time, the most suitable measure we have of the important role of entrepreneurship is to look at the number of new firms over a period of time. As of December 2012 there were almost 1.2 million small businesses in Canada and between 2002 and 2007 an average of 104 000 new small businesses were created annually in Canada.[14]

Job Creation

Businesses with fewer than 100 employees represent 98.2 percent of the total business establishments in Canada. These small businesses employ 7.7 million employees, or 69 percent of the Canadian private workforce, and were responsible for creating 77.7 percent of all private jobs from 2002 to 2012.[15] Job creation is important to the overall long-term economic health of communities, regions, and nations. Small organizations have been creating jobs at a fast pace, even as many of the world's largest and well-known global corporations have continued to downsize. These facts reflect the importance of entrepreneurial firms as job creators.

Global Entrepreneurship

What about entrepreneurial activity outside Canada and the United States? What kind of impact has it had? An annual assessment of global entrepreneurship called the Global Entrepreneurship Monitor (GEM) studies the impact of entrepreneurial activity on economic growth in various countries. The 2013 GEM report covered 70 economies and surveyed 197 000 adults and estimated that "nearly half the world's entrepreneurs are between the ages of 25 and 45 while in all geographic regions 25–34 year olds showed the highest rates of entrepreneurial activity."[16]

What Do Entrepreneurs Do?

Small Business and the Entrepreneur

Describing what entrepreneurs do isn't an easy or simple task. No two entrepreneurs' work activities are exactly alike. In a general sense, entrepreneurs create something new, something different. They search for change, respond to it, and exploit it.[17]

Initially, an entrepreneur is engaged in assessing the potential for the entrepreneurial venture and then dealing with start-up issues. In exploring the entrepreneurial context, an entrepreneur gathers information, identifies potential opportunities, and pinpoints possible competitive advantage(s). Then, armed with that information, the entrepreneur researches the venture's feasibility—uncovering business ideas, looking at competitors, and exploring financing options.

After looking at the potential of a proposed venture and assessing the likelihood of pursuing it successfully, an entrepreneur proceeds to plan the venture. This includes such activities as developing a viable organizational mission, exploring organizational culture issues, and creating a well-thought-out business plan. When these planning issues have been resolved, the entrepreneur must look at organizing the venture, which involves choosing a legal form of business organization, addressing other legal issues such as patent or copyright searches, and coming up with an appropriate organizational design for structuring how work is going to be done.

Only after these start-up activities have been completed is the entrepreneur ready to actually launch the venture. This involves setting goals and strategies, as well as establishing the technology operations methods, marketing plans, information systems, financial accounting systems, and cash-flow-management systems.

When the entrepreneurial venture is up and running, the entrepreneur's attention switches to managing it. An important activity of managing the entrepreneurial venture is managing the various processes that are part of every business: making decisions, establishing action plans, analyzing external and internal environments, measuring and evaluating performance, and making needed changes. Also, the entrepreneur must perform activities associated with managing people, including selecting and hiring, appraising and training, motivating, managing conflict, delegating tasks, and being an effective leader. Finally, the entrepreneur must manage the venture's growth, including such activities as developing and designing growth strategies, dealing with crises, exploring various avenues for financing growth, placing a value on the venture, and perhaps even eventually exiting the venture.

Jeffrey Timmons, a professor at Babson College in Wellesley, Massachusetts, developed a model to explain the elements needed for entrepreneurial success (Exhibit 4-1). The Timmons model of entrepreneurship considers opportunities, teams, and resources as the three critical factors available to an entrepreneur and holds that success depends on the ability of the entrepreneur to balance these critical factors.

Exhibit 4-1

The Timmons Model of the Entrepreneurial Process

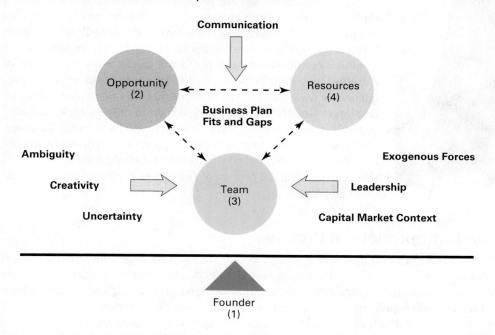

1. The Timmons Model bases itself on the founder (entrepreneur). Success of the venture depends on the ability of the founder to balance the critical factors of opportunity, team, and resources. The founder also has a commitment to sustainability for the environment, community, and society.

2. Unlike conventional entrepreneurship models that start with a business plan, the Timmons Model starts with a market opportunity and with the capacity of the founder to distinguish the difference between an idea and an opportunity.

3. Once the founder identifies an opportunity, he or she works to start a business by putting together the team. The founder's ability to build an effective team is a major factor in the success of the founder's vision in spite of the challenges to be faced.

4. The Timmons Model discounts the popular notion that extensive resources reduce the risk of starting a venture and encourages *bootstrapping* or starting with the bare minimal requirements as a way to attain competitive advantages. The founder works to "minimize and control" rather than "maximize and own."

Source: Based on the work of Jeffery Timmons in J. Timmons, S. Spinelli, and P. Ensign, *New Venture Creation*, 1st Canadian ed. (Toronto: McGraw-Hill Ryerson, 2009).

Social Responsibility and Ethical Issues Facing Entrepreneurs

As they launch and manage their ventures, entrepreneurs are faced with the often difficult issues of social responsibility and ethics. Just how important are these issues to entrepreneurs? The International Standards Organization has developed standards for sustainability and for social responsibility.[18] There are some entrepreneurs who take their social responsibilities seriously. For example, Jeff Skoll is a Canadian-born engineer who was the first employee and first president of eBay and owner of Participant Media, a producer of socially conscious movies such as *An Inconvenient Truth* and *Syriana*. Skoll donated over $1 billion of his eBay stock to found the Skoll Foundation in 1999. The foundation's mission is to drive large-scale change by investing in, connecting, and celebrating social entrepreneurs and other innovators dedicated to solving the world's most pressing problems. He defines social entrepreneurs as "society's change agents; creators of innovations that disrupt the status quo and transform our world for the better."[19]

Other entrepreneurs have pursued opportunities with products and services that protect the global environment. For example, Corporate Knights is an independent Canadian-based media company that works to prompt and reinforce sustainable development in Canada. Included in its "Cleantech 10" list are Westport Innovations of Vancouver, a leading developer of environmental technologies that enable vehicles to operate on clean-burning alternative fuels, as well as Carmanah Technologies Corp. of Victoria, a solar LED lighting company.[20]

Ethical considerations also play a role in decisions and actions of entrepreneurs. Entrepreneurs need to be aware of the ethical consequences of what they do. The example they set—particularly for other employees—can be profoundly significant in influencing behaviour.

If ethics are important, how do entrepreneurs stack up? Unfortunately, not too well! In a survey of employees from different sizes of businesses who were asked whether they thought their organization was highly ethical, 20 percent of employees at companies with 99 or fewer employees disagreed.[21]

The Giving Pledge project, launched by Warren Buffett and Bill and Melinda Gates, invites the wealthiest individuals to give at least 50 percent of their money to charitable projects of their choosing. As part of his public pledge, Jeff Skoll (pictured here at the Third Metric conference on redefining success) stated, "The world is a vast and complicated place and it needs each of us doing all we can to ensure a brighter tomorrow for future generations. Conrad Hilton said it is the duty of successful people to give back to the society from which their success was derived. I feel privileged to have grown up in Canada and to now live in the US, two countries that value and reward education, hard work and good choices. I feel lucky to have been able to pursue my dreams and I hope that my contributions will in some small way lead to a sustainable world of peace and prosperity."

Jonathon Ziegler/PatrickMcMullan.com/Sipa USA (Sipa via AP Images)

The Entrepreneurial Process

Entrepreneurs must address four key steps as they start and manage their entrepreneurial ventures. The first is *exploring the entrepreneurial context*. The context includes the realities of today's economic, political/legal, social, and work environments. It's important to look at each of these aspects of the entrepreneurial context because they determine the "rules" of the game and which decisions and actions are likely to meet with success.

Also, it's through exploring the context that entrepreneurs confront the next critically important step in the entrepreneurial process—*identifying opportunities and possible competitive advantages*. We know from our definition of entrepreneurship that the pursuit of opportunities is an important aspect.

Once entrepreneurs have explored the entrepreneurial context and identified opportunities and possible competitive advantages, they must look at the issues involved with actually bringing their entrepreneurial venture to life. Therefore, the next step in the entrepreneurial process is *starting the venture*. Included in this phase are researching the feasibility of the venture, planning the venture, organizing the venture, and launching the venture.

Finally, once the entrepreneurial venture is up and running, the last step in the entrepreneurial process is *managing the venture*, which an entrepreneur does by managing processes, managing people, and managing growth. We can explain these important steps in the entrepreneurial process by looking at what it is that entrepreneurs do.

Start-Up and Planning Issues for an Entrepreneurial Venture

▶ ▶ ▶ Steve Blank and Jerry Engle, professors at the Haas School of Business, University of California Berkley, have developed a new way of looking at start-ups. They point out that, for years, we have thought of start-ups as smaller versions of large companies. The reality is that a start-up is a temporary organization designed to search for a repeatable (the ability to do the same thing more than once and achieve the same result) and **scalable** (the ability to generate revenues faster than the rate you are incurring costs) business model. Within this definition, a start-up can be a new venture, or it may be a new division or business unit in an existing company. A business model describes how a company creates, delivers, and captures value (drives revenue to itself). The primary objective of a start-up is to validate its business model hypotheses/guesses until it finds a model that is repeatable and scalable and continues to iterate and pivot (look for a different business model) until it does. Then it moves into execution mode. It is at this point the business needs an operating plan, financial forecasts, and other well-understood management tools.

As shown in Exhibit 4-2, Blank and Engle separate the search process (customer discovery and customer validation) from the execution process (customer creation and company building).[22]

The steps:

- *Customer discovery* first captures the founders' vision and turns it into a series of business model hypotheses. Then it develops a plan to test customer reactions to those hypotheses and turn them into facts.

- *Customer validation* tests whether the resulting business model is repeatable and scalable. If not, you return to customer discovery.

- *Customer creation* is the start of execution. It builds end-user demand and drives it into the sales channel to scale the business.

- *Company-building* transitions the organization from a start-up to a company focused on executing a validated model.

❷ Identify opportunities and build the business case for launching an entrepreneurial/ intrapreneurial venture.

scalable The ability to generate revenues faster than the rate you are incurring costs.

Think About It

The 2013 GEM study found that, globally, 25- to 34-year-olds showed the highest rates of entrepreneurial activity. What kinds of opportunities do you think they are identifying? How are they turning the opportunities they identify into startups?

Exhibit 4-2

A Model for Company Building

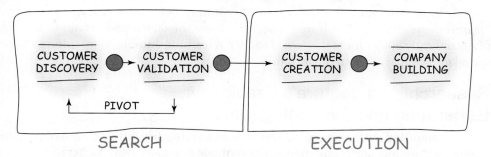

Source: Steven Blank & Jerry Engle, *The Lean LaunchPad Educators Teaching Handbook*, July 2012

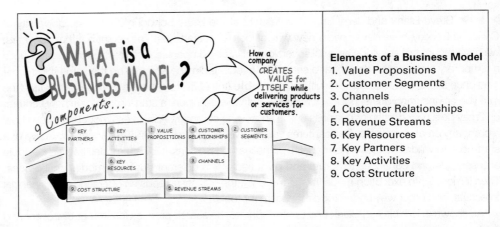

Exhibit 4-3

The Elements of a Business Model

Source: Steven Blank & Jerry Engle, *The Lean LaunchPad Educators Teaching Handbook*, July 2012

If your business model is unknown (Exhibit 4-3)—that is, just a set of untested hypotheses—you are a start-up searching for a repeatable business model. Once your business model is known, you will be executing it. Search versus execution is what differentiates a new venture from an existing business unit.

Embracing Failure as Learning

Search embraces failure as a natural part of the start-up process. Existing companies often fire executives when they fail to match a plan, while start-ups need to keep the founders and change the model. Once a company has found a business model (it knows its market, customers, product/service, channel, pricing, etc.), the organization moves from search to execution.

Searching for a business model requires a different organizational structure than the one used to execute a plan. Searching requires the company to be organized around a customer development team led by the founders. It's only the founders who can make the strategic decisions to iterate and/or pivot the business model, and to do that they need to hear customer feedback directly. In contrast, execution (which follows search) assumes that the job specifications for each of the senior roles in the company can be tightly defined, often resulting in a "fear-of-failure culture." In a fear-of-failure culture managers are hesitant to try new things in case they might fail, leading to a stagnant organization. Alternatively, start-ups need customer development teams that have a "learning-and-discovery" culture for search, where the teams understand that failing often and early allows them to succeed sooner. A learning-and-discovery culture enables the adaptive capacity of an organization.

Researching a Venture's Feasibility: Generating and Evaluating Ideas

It's important for entrepreneurs to research a venture's feasibility by generating and evaluating business ideas. Entrepreneurial ventures thrive on ideas. Generating ideas is an innovative, creative process. It's also one that takes time, not only in the beginning stages of the entrepreneurial venture but throughout the life of the business. Where do ideas come from?

Exhibit 4-4

Evaluating Potential Ideas

Personal Consideration	Marketplace Consideration
Do you have the capabilities to do what you've selected?	Have you educated yourself about financing issues?
Are you ready to be an entrepreneur?	Are you willing and prepared to do continual financial and other types of analyses?
Are you prepared emotionally to deal with the stresses and challenges of being an entrepreneur?	Who are the potential customers for your idea: who, where, how many?
Are you prepared to deal with rejection and failure?	What similar or unique product features does your proposed idea have compared to what's currently on the market?
Are you ready to work hard?	How and where will potential customers purchase your product?
Do you have a realistic picture of the venture's potential?	Have you considered pricing issues and whether the price you'll be able to charge will allow your venture to survive and prosper?
	Have you considered how you will need to promote and advertise your proposed entrepreneurial venture?

Generating Ideas

Studies of entrepreneurs have shown that the sources of their ideas are unique and varied. One survey found that only 33.2 percent of business founders engaged in a deliberate search for a business idea, while 55.9 percent of founders attributed their business idea to experience in a specific industry or market).[23] The same survey indicated that 70.9 percent of entrepreneurs indicated that their business opportunity "unfolded over time" and could not be attributed to a one-time insight.

What should entrepreneurs look for as they explore the sources of ideas? They should look for limitations of what is currently available, new and different approaches, advances and breakthroughs, unfilled niches, or trends and changes.

Evaluating Ideas

Evaluating entrepreneurial ideas involves personal and marketplace considerations. Each of these assessments will provide an entrepreneur with key information about the idea's potential. Exhibit 4-4 describes some questions that entrepreneurs might ask as they evaluate potential ideas.

A more structured evaluation approach that an entrepreneur might want to use is a **feasibility study**—an analysis of the various aspects of a proposed entrepreneurial venture, designed to determine its feasibility. Not only is a well-prepared feasibility study an effective evaluation tool to determine whether an entrepreneurial idea is a potentially successful one, but it can also serve as a basis for the all-important business plan.

A feasibility study should give descriptions of the most important elements of the entrepreneurial venture and the entrepreneur's analysis of the viability of these elements.

feasibility study An analysis of the various aspects of a proposed entrepreneurial venture that is designed to determine the feasibility of the venture.

Researching a Venture's Feasibility: Researching Competitors

Part of researching a venture's feasibility is looking at the competitors. What would entrepreneurs like to know about their potential competitors? Exhibit 4-5 lists some possible questions to ask when evaluating potential competitors.

When an entrepreneur has information about competitors, he or she should assess how the proposed entrepreneurial venture is going to fit into its competitive arena. Will the

Exhibit 4-5

Evaluating Potential Competitors

What types of products or services are competitors offering?

What are the major characteristics of these products or services?

What are the strengths and weaknesses of competitors' products?

How do competitors handle marketing, pricing, and distributing?

What do competitors attempt to do differently from other companies?

Do they appear to be successful at it? Why or why not?

What are they good at?

What competitive advantage(s) do they appear to have?

What are they not so good at?

What competitive disadvantage(s) do they appear to have?

How large and profitable are these competitors?

value proposition An analysis of the benefits, costs, and value that an organization can deliver to customers and other groups within and outside of the organization.

entrepreneurial venture be able to compete successfully? In doing the analysis, remember that often the biggest competitors are the status quo (customers have no need to make a change) and substitutes (customers can use something else to satisfy their need). At the heart of every successful venture is the articulation of a compelling **value proposition**—an analysis of the benefits, costs, and value to the target customer and other groups within and outside of the organization.[24] This type of competitor analysis becomes an important part of the feasibility study and the business plan. If, after all this analysis, the situation looks promising, the final part of researching the venture's feasibility is to look at the various financing options. This isn't the final determination of how much funding the venture will need or where this funding will come from, but is simply the gathering of information about various financing alternatives.

Researching a Venture's Feasibility: Researching Financing

Getting financing isn't always easy. For instance, when William Carey first proposed building a liquor distributor business in Poland, more than 20 investment banking houses in New York passed on funding his idea. Carey recalls, "They didn't know Poland, and the business was small. We were ready to give up." Then a New York investment banking boutique agreed to fund the venture. Today, Carey's company, CEDC (Central European Distribution), has more than 3000 employees and sales revenues of more than $1.1 billion (US).[25]

Planning a Venture: Developing a Business Plan

Planning is important to entrepreneurial ventures. Once a venture's feasibility has been thoroughly researched, the entrepreneur must look at planning the venture. The most important thing that an entrepreneur does in planning a venture is develop a **business plan**—a written document that summarizes a business opportunity and defines and articulates how the identified opportunity is to be seized and exploited.

business plan A written document that summarizes a business opportunity and defines and articulates how the identified opportunity is to be seized and exploited.

For many would-be entrepreneurs, developing and writing a business plan seems like a daunting task. However, a good business plan is valuable. It pulls together all the elements of the entrepreneur's vision into a single coherent document. The business plan requires careful planning and creative thinking. If done well, it can be a convincing document that serves many functions. It serves as a blueprint and road map for operating the business. And the business plan is a "living" document that guides organizational decisions and actions throughout the life of the business, not just in the start-up stage.

Issues in Organizing an Entrepreneurial Venture

▶ ▶ ▶ As Futurepreneur Canada scaled from its founding in 1996 as CYBF to the organization it is today, staff was added, partners were appointed in key regions, and programming was expanded.

③ Choose appropriate organizational structures to support an entrepreneurial culture.

> ### Think About It
>
> **What organizational issues might Futurepreneur Canada have needed to address as they made the transition from start-up to scaling to an operating as an established organization while experiencing rapid growth?**

Once the start-up and planning issues for an entrepreneurial venture have been addressed, the entrepreneur is ready to begin organizing the entrepreneurial venture. There are four organizing issues an entrepreneur must address: organizational design and structure, human resource management, how to stimulate and make changes, and the continuing importance of innovation.

Organizational Design and Structure

The choice of an appropriate organizational structure is an important decision when organizing an entrepreneurial venture. At some point, successful entrepreneurs find that they can't do everything alone. More people are needed. The entrepreneur must then decide on the most appropriate structural arrangement for effectively and efficiently carrying out the organization's activities. Without some suitable type of organizational structure, the entrepreneurial venture may soon find itself in a chaotic situation.

In many small firms, the organizational structure tends to evolve with very little intentional and deliberate planning by the entrepreneur. For the most part, the structure may be very simple—one person does whatever is needed. As the entrepreneurial venture grows and the entrepreneur finds it increasingly difficult to go it alone, employees are brought on board to perform certain functions or duties that the entrepreneur can't handle. These individuals tend to perform those same functions as the company grows. As the entrepreneurial venture continues to grow, each of these functional areas may require managers and employees.

With the evolution to a more deliberate structure, an entrepreneur faces a whole new set of challenges. All of a sudden, he or she must share decision making and operating responsibilities. This is typically one of the most difficult things for an entrepreneur to do—let go and allow someone else to make decisions. *After all,* he or she reasons, *how can anyone know this business as well as I do?* Also, what might have been a fairly informal, loose, and flexible atmosphere that worked well when the organization was small may no longer be effective. But having a structured organization doesn't necessarily mean giving up flexibility, adaptability, and freedom. In fact, the structural design may be as fluid as the entrepreneur feels comfortable with and yet still have the rigidity it needs to operate efficiently.

When pursuing opportunities within an existing organization, it is important to note the structure of the parent organization may impose rigidities that make innovation close to impossible in the new division and that a different, more creative structure will be needed to support a startup culture.

Human Resource Management

As an entrepreneurial venture grows, additional employees will need to be hired to perform the increased workload. As employees are brought on board, an entrepreneur faces certain human resource management (HRM) issues. Two HRM issues of particular importance to entrepreneurs are employee recruitment and employee retention.

Employee Recruitment

Entrepreneurs, particularly, are looking for high-potential people who can perform multiple roles during various stages of venture growth. They look for individuals who buy into the venture's entrepreneurial culture—individuals who have a passion for the business.[26] They look for people who are exceptionally capable and self-motivated, flexible, and multiskilled and who can help grow the entrepreneurial venture. Entrepreneurial managers are more concerned with matching characteristics of the person to the values and culture of the organization; that is, they focus on matching the person to the organization.[27]

Employee Retention

Getting competent and qualified people into a venture is just the first step in effectively managing the human resources. An entrepreneur wants to keep the people he or she has hired and trained. Many entrepreneurs understand the importance of having good people on board and keeping them. In the rough-and-tumble, intensely competitive world they operate in, entrepreneurs realize that the loss of talented employees can harm client services. To combat this, they often offer employees a wide array of desirable benefits, such as raises each year, profit sharing, trust funds for employees' children, paid sabbaticals, personal development funds, and so forth. This approach has the potential to keep employees loyal and productive.

How to Stimulate and Make Changes

We know that entrepreneurs face dynamic change. Entrepreneurs need to be alert to problems and opportunities that may create the need for change. In fact, of the many hats an entrepreneur wears, that of change agent may be one of the most important.[28] If changes are needed in an entrepreneurial venture, often it is the entrepreneur who first recognizes the need for change and acts as the catalyst, coach, cheerleader, and chief change consultant. Even if a person is comfortable with taking risks—as entrepreneurs usually are—change can be difficult. That's why it's important for an entrepreneur to recognize the critical roles he or she plays in stimulating and implementing change.

Because organizational change of any type can be disruptive and scary, an entrepreneur must explain and communicate the benefits of a change to employees and encourage change efforts by supporting employees, getting them excited about the change, building them up, and motivating them to put forth their best efforts. Finally, an entrepreneur may have to guide the actual change process as changes in strategy, technology, products, structure, or people are implemented. In this role, the entrepreneur answers questions, makes suggestions, gets needed resources, facilitates conflict resolution, and does whatever else is necessary to get the change(s) implemented. Further information on managing change can be found in Chapter 6, Innovation and Adaptability.

The Continuing Importance of Innovation

In today's dynamically chaotic world of global competition, organizations must continually innovate new products and services if they want to compete successfully. Innovation is a key characteristic of entrepreneurial ventures and, in fact, is what makes an entrepreneurial venture "entrepreneurial." If you were a fly on the wall at a research-intensive organization, you would likely see innovation taking place in several different forms:

- **Curiosity-driven research**—Also referred to as basic research, this is research that is directed toward acquiring new knowledge rather than toward some more practical objective. The Perimeter Institute of Applied Physics in Waterloo, Ontario, was

curiosity-driven research Research directed toward acquiring new knowledge rather than toward some more practical objective (also referred to as basic research).

MANAGEMENT REFLECTION   FOCUS ON INNOVATION

Finding Opportunity with Creativity

Can organizations use creativity to gain a competitive edge? Min Basadur is professor of innovation in the Michael G. DeGroote School of Business at McMaster University, in Hamilton, Ontario, and founder of Basadur Applied Creativity.[29] Basadur is recognized as a world leader in the field of applied creativity, with years of experience in building creative thinking, innovation, and problem-solving capabilities across organizations, including many *Fortune* 500 companies like PepsiCo, Procter & Gamble, and Pfizer.

Basadur's Simplex model asks participants to

- Use divergent thinking and brainstorming to come up with as many alternatives as possible
- Defer judgment while brainstorming alternatives to allow the group to build on wild and crazy ideas, as well as the more practical ones
- Use convergent and evaluative thinking to choose the alternative that fits best

We all have a preferred way of solving problems, and Basadur maps out four problem-solving styles: generators, conceptualizers, optimizers, and implementers. Innovative organizations require a culture where all four approaches are represented on the problem-solving team. ■

founded in 1999 based on a $100 million donation from Michael Lazaridis.[30] Researchers at this facility are dedicated to exploring the world around them without regard to solving problems that have commercial application. They are generating new knowledge in its purest form.

- **Applied research**—Applied research accesses, rather than generates, new knowledge and applies it to a practical or commercial purpose.
- **Research and development (R&D)**—This includes investigative activities that an organization conducts to lead to discoveries that will help develop new products or procedures.[31]

applied research Research that accesses, rather than generates, new knowledge and applies it to a practical or commercial purpose.

research and development (R&D) Investigative activities that an organization conducts to lead to discoveries that will help develop new products or procedures.

Is there a systematic approach that an entrepreneurial venture can take to be more innovative? The *Management Reflection—Finding Opportunity with Creativity* (above) describes one approach.

Why are some companies able to consistently conceive of, create, and bring to market innovative and profitable new products and services while so many others struggle? It isn't the amount of money they spend on research and development. After all, the annual Global Innovation 1000 study, conducted by management consulting firm Booz & Company, has shown that there is no statistically significant relationship between financial performance and innovation spending—in terms of either total R&D dollars or R&D as a percentage of revenues.[32] As part of the research, a survey was conducted to explore the relationship between innovation capabilities, corporate strategy, and financial performance. More than 450 innovation leaders in over 400 companies and 10 industries were asked to name the three companies they considered to be the most innovative in the world. Apple captured 79 percent of the vote, followed by Google with 49 percent and 3M with 20 percent of the vote. Exhibit 4-6 provides the full list of the 10 most innovative firms. [33] Research conducted by Booz Allen Hamilton suggests that companies often underperform at the commercialization stage. At this stage there are three customer- and market-oriented capabilities that matter most: gathering customer insights during the idea-generating stage, assessing market potential during the selection stage, and engaging with customers during the development stage.

Exhibit 4-6

Global Innovation 1000: The 10 Most Innovative Firms

| | Company | R&D Spending | | |
		2013 US$ (billions)	Rank	As % of Revenue
1	Apple	$3.4	43	2.2%
2	Google	$6.8	12	13.5%
3	Samsung	$10.4	2	5.8%
4	Amazon	$4.6	30	7.5%
5	3M	$1.6	85	5.5%
6	GE	$4.5	31	3.1%
7	Microsoft	$9.8	5	13.3%
8	IBM	$6.3	16	6.0%
9	Tesla Motors	$0.3	377	66.3%
10	Facebook	$1.4	101	27.5%

Source: Bloomberg data, Capital IQ, Booz & Company

What matters more than R&D is the particular combination of talent, knowledge, team structures, tools, and processes—the capabilities—that successful companies put together to enable innovation and create products and services they can successfully take to market. This means that companies must first choose the capabilities that matter most to their particular innovation strategy and then execute them well.

Issues in Leading an Entrepreneurial Venture

4 Make appropriate choices in leading an entrepreneurial venture.

▶ ▶ ▶ Innovative companies invest in both applied research, often by putting resources toward R&D, and curiosity-driven research. The company also fosters a culture that supports innovation. Innovation is about creating economic and social prosperity, and leadership and management are as essential to the process as science and technology. Management innovation is "about the skills managers have in applying knowledge, judgment, and the ability to adapt and fashion new tools to solve problems."[34]

The role of a leader changes as a start-up begins to execute its business model and scales to becoming a larger organization. When Futurepreneur Canada was founded in 1996, it was modelled on the Prince's Youth Business Trust, and by 1997 had already assisted 115 young entrepreneurs. In the early days there were few staff, and the organization chose to scale by building local community partnerships in provinces across Canada. At this point the leader needed to be an evangelist who was able to engage delivery partners as well as funding partners. As Futurepreneur Canada grew, the complexity and needs of the stakeholders changed and increased in sophsitcation.

Think About It

What organizational issues might Futurepreneur Canada have needed to address as they made the transition from start-up to operating as an established organization, while experiencing rapid growth?

The 2010 movie *The Social Network* told the story of Mark Zuckerberg and the founding years of Facebook. As the company grew, enormous strains were put on personal relationships, the architecture needed to support the Facebook platform, and the financial and human resources of the company.

Robert Galbraith/Reuters/Landov

The Entrepreneur as Leader

Leading is an important function of entrepreneurs. As an entrepreneurial venture grows and people are brought on board, an entrepreneur takes on a new role—that of a leader. In this role, the entrepreneur has certain leadership responsibilities in leading the venture.

Today's successful entrepreneur must be like the leader of a jazz ensemble known for its improvisation, innovation, and creativity. Max DePree, former head of Herman Miller, Inc., a leading office furniture manufacturer known for its innovative leadership approaches, said it best in his book *Leadership Jazz:* "Jazz band leaders must choose the music, find the right musicians, and perform—in public. But the effect of the performance depends on so many things—the environment, the volunteers playing in the band, the need for everybody to perform as individuals and as a group, the absolute dependence of the leader on the members of the band, the need for the followers to play well . . . The leader of the jazz band has the beautiful opportunity to draw the best out of the other musicians. We have much to learn from jazz band leaders, for jazz, like leadership, combines the unpredictability of the future with the gifts of individuals."[35]

The way an entrepreneur leads the venture should be much like the jazz band leader's job—drawing the best out of other individuals, even given the unpredictability of the situation. One way an entrepreneur does this is through the vision he or she creates for the organization. In fact, the driving force through the early stages of the entrepreneurial venture is often the visionary leadership of the entrepreneur. The entrepreneur's ability to articulate a coherent, inspiring, and attractive vision of the future is a key test of his or her leadership. But if an entrepreneur can do this, the results can be worthwhile. A study contrasting visionary and nonvisionary companies showed that visionary companies outperformed the nonvisionary ones 6 times over on standard financial criteria, and their stocks outperformed the general market 15 times over.[36]

Issues in Controlling an Entrepreneurial Venture

▶ ▶ ▶ "Speed Kills!" is a mantra often used to encourage safe driving habits. The same is often true for rapidly growing companies that are unable to manage the stresses and strains caused by growth, such as the need for cash injections, a growing workforce, and the need to figure out the logistics of invoicing customers and getting paid. The Futurepreneur Canada Board includes

⑤ Deploy appropriate control structures to respond to the unique challenges faced by entrepreneurial ventures.

entrepreneurs like John Risley, chair of Futurepreneur Canada and also chair of Clearwater Fine Foods; David Aisestat, president and CEO of the Keg Steakhouse and Bar; and Ronnen Harary, chair and co-CEO of Spinmaster Ltd. All of these entrepreneurs have experienced the stresses imposed by rapid growth.

In the previous vignette we looked at the impact of rapid growth on Futurepreneur Canada and the leadership challenges that arose as Futurepreneur Canada grew. This phenomenon was not only occurring internally but was also being experienced by the clients that Futurepreneur Canada served. In many cases the Futurepreneur Canada clients had strong sales numbers but were being forced to close because they had run out of cash. Evidence of financial literacy skills, especially cash flow forecasting and adequate and timely record keeping, became core criteria in approving loan applications.

Think About It

What challenges does a rapidly growing company face? How might the managers at Futurepreneur Canada have dealt with these challenges internally and externally with clients? How is it possible for a company to have profits but run out of cash?

Entrepreneurs must look at controlling the venture's operations in order to survive and prosper in both the short run and the long run. The unique control issues facing entrepreneurs include managing growth, managing downturns, and exiting the venture.

Managing Growth

Growth is a natural and desirable outcome for entrepreneurial ventures. Growth is what distinguishes an entrepreneurial venture. Entrepreneurial ventures pursue growth.[37] Growing slowly can be successful, but so can rapid growth. Growing successfully doesn't occur randomly or by luck. Successfully pursuing growth typically requires an entrepreneur to manage all the challenges associated with growing.

The best growth strategy is a well-planned one.[38] Ideally, the decision to grow doesn't come about spontaneously but instead is part of a venture's overall business goals and plan. Rapid growth without planning can be disastrous. Entrepreneurs need to address growth strategies as part of their business planning but shouldn't be overly rigid in that planning. The key challenges for an entrepreneur in organizing for growth include finding capital, finding people, and strengthening the organizational culture. John Baker is the founder of Desire2Learn, an e-learning company based out of Kitchener, Ontario, that has grown from 350 to 750 employees over the course of two years. As the company grows, Baker is facing new organizational challenges.[39]

Having enough capital is a major challenge facing growing entrepreneurial ventures. The money issue never seems to go away, does it? Simply put, if you grow rapidly you will need to raise cash—rapid growth makes it almost impossible to fund the growth from annual profits. It takes capital to expand. The processes of finding capital to fund growth are much like those used for the initial financing of the venture. Hopefully, at this time the venture has a successful track record to back up the request. If it doesn't, it may be extremely difficult to acquire the necessary capital. That's why we said earlier that the best growth strategy is a planned one.

Another challenge that growing entrepreneurial ventures face is reinforcing already established organizational controls. Maintaining good financial records and financial controls over cash flow, inventory, customer data, sales orders, receivables, payables, and costs should be a priority of every entrepreneur—whether pursuing growth or not. However, it's particularly important to reinforce these controls when the entrepreneurial venture is expanding. It's all too easy to let things "get away" or to put them off when there's an unrelenting urgency to get things done. It's particularly important to have established procedures, protocols, and processes and to use them. Even though mistakes and inefficiencies can never be eliminated entirely, an entrepreneur should at least ensure that every effort is being made to achieve high levels of productivity and organizational effectiveness.

Managing Downturns

Although an entrepreneur hopes to never have to deal with organizational downturns, declines, or crises, there may come a time when he or she must do just that. After all, nobody likes to think about things going badly or taking a turn for the worse. But that's exactly what the entrepreneur should do—think about it *before* it happens by designing the control system to signal this early in the game.[40] It's important to have an up-to-date **contingency plan**, or Plan B, for dealing with a worst-case situation or crisis, just as you map exit routes from your home in case of a fire. An entrepreneur wants to be prepared before an emergency hits. This plan should focus on providing specific details for controlling the most fundamental and critical aspects of running the venture—cash flow, accounts receivable, costs, and debt. Beyond having a plan for controlling the venture's critical inflows and outflows, other actions would involve identifying specific strategies for cutting costs and restructuring the venture.

contingency plan A plan for dealing with a worst-case situation or crisis (often referred to as a Plan B).

Exiting the Venture

Exiting a venture is not something only entrepreneurs have to deal with. It is an issue that almost all organizations must face. When is the best time to plan your exit from the business? The answer may surprise you. The best time to plan an exit strategy is at the time you enter. Getting out of an entrepreneurial venture may seem to be a strange thing for entrepreneurs to do. However, there may come a point when the entrepreneur decides it's time to move on. That decision may be based on the fact that the entrepreneur hopes to capitalize financially on the investment in the venture—called **harvesting**—or on the fact that the entrepreneur is facing serious organizational performance problems and wants to get out, or even on the entrepreneur's desire to focus on other pursuits (personal or business). The issues involved with exiting the venture include choosing a proper business valuation method and knowing what's involved in the process of selling a business.

harvesting Exiting a venture when an entrepreneur hopes to capitalize financially on the investment in the venture.

Setting a value on a business can be a little tricky. In many cases, the entrepreneur has sacrificed much for the business and sees it as his or her "baby." Calculating the value of the baby based on objective standards such as cash flow or some multiple of net profits can sometimes be a shock. That's why it's important for an entrepreneur who wishes to exit a venture to get a comprehensive business valuation prepared by professionals. Remember that if the value of the venture depends solely on the part the entrepreneur plays in the venture, it will have little value to prospective purchasers. A wise entrepreneur will build a venture whose value will persist after his or her departure.

Although the hardest part of preparing to exit a venture is valuing it, other factors should also be considered.[41] These include being prepared, deciding who will sell the business, considering the tax implications, screening potential buyers, and deciding whether to tell employees before or after the sale. The process of exiting an entrepreneurial venture should be approached as carefully as the process of launching it.

CHAPTER 4

SUMMARY AND IMPLICATIONS

1. Embrace the capacity of entrepreneurial thinking and practices to add value in both new and existing organizations. Entrepreneurship is the process of starting new organizations or ventures, generally in response to opportunities. Entrepreneurs pursue opportunities by changing, revolutionizing, transforming, or introducing new products or services. Today, job growth and innovation are driven by entrepreneurial firms.

▶ ▶ ▶ Most of the innovation in society takes place in smaller firms like those founded by the recipients of Futurepreneur Canada funding and support programs. Innovation may lead to creative destruction, changing the way things were done before. Other innovation builds on existing technology.

2. Identify opportunities and build the business case for launching an entrepreneurial/intrapreneurial venture. For years, we have thought of start-ups as smaller versions of large companies. The reality is that a start-up is a temporary organization designed to search for a repeatable (the ability to do the same thing more than once and achieve the same result) and scalable (the ability to generate revenues faster than its cost base) business model. The next steps are to research the feasibility of the venture; develop a formal business plan; organize the financial, physical, and human resources; and then launch the venture.

▶ ▶ ▶ Lisa von Sturmer (a recipient of Futurepreneur Canada funding) was inspired to go into the business of composting after spending a week at a cabin on Desolation Sound, where composting is mandatory. After seeing how much organic waste ended up in office trash, Lisa saw an opportunity to create a business and help the planet at the same time.

3. Choose appropriate organizational structures to support an entrepreneurial culture. Once the start-up and planning issues have been dealt with, the entrepreneur is ready to begin organizing the entrepreneurial venture. There are four organizing issues to be addressed: organizational design and structure, human resource management, stimulation and execution of changes, and the continuing importance of innovation.

▶ ▶ ▶ Futurepreneur Canada began operation in 1996 and has grown, expanding geographically and increasing program offerings as it made the transition from start-up to scaling to operating as an established organization while experiencing rapid growth.

Futurepreneur Canada had to plan for a future that was largely unknown and in many ways unpredictable. The design and structure of the organization had to support its ability to be adaptable. At the same time, recruiting and retaining employees and finding partners who would thrive in such an environment was core to Futurepreneur Canada's success. It was vital to build a culture that embraced change and cherished innovation as a core organizational value.

4. Make appropriate choices in leading an entrepreneurial venture. Leading is an important function of entrepreneurs. As an entrepreneurial venture grows and people are brought on board, an entrepreneur takes on a new role—that of a leader. No two entrepreneurs are the same, but they do share some common attributes, such as commitment and determination, strong leadership skills, an obsession with identifying opportunities, tolerance for risk and ambiguity, creativity, willingness to embrace building adaptable organizations, and finally a strong belief that what they do will make a difference (a strong internal locus of control). As the organization grows, it becomes impossible for the founder to be all things to all people and to be in all places at once. Empowering employees and developing effective work teams are effective ways of building management capacity in the entrepreneurial venture.

▶▶▶ As Futurepreneur Canada made the transition from start-up to operating as an established organization they experienced rapid growth. Leadership in this environment was provided by the board and a series of chief operating officers who needed to build a team.

5. Deploy appropriate control structures to respond to the unique challenges faced by entrepreneurial ventures. Entrepreneurs must look at controlling the venture's operations in order to survive and prosper. Control issues that entrepreneurs face include managing growth, maintaining a culture that supports disruptive innovation, managing downturns, and exiting the venture.

▶▶▶ As the loan portfolio grew at Futurepreneur Canada, significant effort had to be put into the procedures for approving loans and then ensuring their repayment. This issue was complicated by the fact that loan approval was frequently done by a panel of local volunteers.

MyManagementLab   Study, practise, and explore real management situations with these helpful resources:

- **Interactive Lesson Presentations:** Work through interactive presentations and assessments to test your knowledge of management concepts.
- **PIA (Personal Inventory Assessments):** Enhance your ability to connect   **P I A**   PERSONAL INVENTORY ASSESSMENT
  with key concepts through these engaging, self-reflection assessments.
- **Study Plan:** Check your understanding of chapter concepts with self-study quizzes.
- **Simulations:** Practise decision-making in simulated management environments.

REVIEW AND DISCUSSION QUESTIONS

1. What is the difference between a small business and an entrepreneurial venture?

2. How do entrepreneurs add value to the economy?

3. How does the concept of social entrepreneurship relate to entrepreneurs and entrepreneurial ventures?

4. Why do you think many entrepreneurs find it difficult to step aside and let others manage their business?

5. What is an entrepreneurial opportunity? How do entrepreneurs locate them?

6. What are the two steps performed in the search process? What are the two steps in the execution process? Why is it important to validate the business model before writing a business plan?

7. What role does innovation play in the success of entrepreneurial ventures? What does an organizational culture that supports innovation look like?

8. How does the role of the entrepreneur change as the venture moves from start-up to operation, to growth, and finally to exit?

9. How does growth impact an entrepreneurial venture? Why do high-growth firms constantly require cash to support their growth?

10. Why do many entrepreneurs have problems creating an appropriate work–life balance?

ETHICS DILEMMA

Since its inception, *Cirque du Soleil* has chosen to become involved in communities, with two initiatives coming to the fore: their work with troubled youth and the ONE DROP Foundation. It fights poverty by providing access to water and sanitation in developing countries. Working together with valued partners, *Cirque du Soleil* is making a difference in nearly 80 communities, in over 20 countries on five continents. *Cirque du Soleil*'s citizenship principles are founded on the conviction that the arts, business, and social initiatives can, together, contribute to making a better world.

Is it possible to run a social venture with the traditional bottom-line mindset? Are seeking to earn profits and the quest for efficiency compatible with doing the right thing?

SKILLS EXERCISE

Interviewing an Entrepreneur—About the Skill

Many students are fearful that they are imposing upon the person they wish to interview. Experience shows otherwise. There is no greater compliment than to acknowledge others' wisdom and ask them to share it. Yes, some people will refuse the interview for a variety of reasons (they're too busy, there may be confidentiality issues, etc.), but you will find most very approachable.

Conducting interviews not only allows you to access the experience and knowledge of others but also helps you to build a network that will support your career. Before conducting your interview, you need to set an objective and identify someone to interview; then conduct the interview and debrief it with your classmates.

Steps in Developing the Skill

Try to find a way to make both yourself and your interviewee comfortable. Be sure to explain who you are, why you are there, and what you expect. Tips include the following:

1. **Avoid closed-ended questions.** These are questions that allow a brief or simple yes or no response. Some examples are listed here:
   a. How old are you?
   b. How many children do you have?
   c. Did your parents have a small business?
   d. How many customers do you have?
   e. Do you have any challenges in your business?

2. **Use as many open-ended questions as possible.** These kinds of responses will be rich in information. Some sample questions are listed here, and you are encouraged to develop your own.
   a. Tell me about a time when . . .
   b. You must have a lot of experience in . . . Which of those experiences had the most impact? Why?
   c. I see from the pictures on your desk that you have several children. How have they affected the way you run the business?
   d. You have stated that your parents also ran a business. How did this influence the way you run yours?
   e. You seem to have a lot of customers. Which do you consider special? Why?

   f. Of the challenges you face in your business, which are the most difficult? Why?

3. **Try to use the laddering technique in your interview wherever possible.** One response will allow you to drill deeper as answers are given to the original questions. The experience of most interviewers is that they have problems getting their subjects to stop talking, not the reverse.

   The confidentiality of the interview must be respected. Do not share any of the matters discussed without the express permission of the interviewee. It is always a good idea to thank the interviewee and, if appropriate, send a summary of what you learned.

Practising the Skill

Find an entrepreneur you respect and ask that person to share his or her experiences with you. Many students interview their parents or other family members. Others interview small business advisers. It is important to conduct the interview face-to-face with your interviewee rather than by phone or email, as the face-to-face setting has a richness of communication that is absent in the other forms. Another best practice is to share the questions with your interviewee prior to the interview to allow for more considered answers.

Reinforcing the Skill

After completing the interview, create a journal that details what you learned in the interview process and how you will be able to apply what you learned the next time you want to gather information from an expert. Remember to distinguish between the expected and the unexpected lessons learned. Many times the unexpected lessons are the most powerful.

- Identify the skills necessary to interview successfully.

- Reflect on the content of the interview to assimilate the knowledge gained. How does it apply or not apply to you?

- Identify what you expected to learn and identify any surprises/unexpected learning.

- Comment on the value of tacit (interviews) versus explicit (databases) techniques for gathering knowledge.

WORKING TOGETHER: TEAM EXERCISE

What Bugs You?

Form groups of three or four individuals and think back over the events of the past 24 hours, including classes, commuting, social interactions, work, and family. Think about all of your interactions, including those with technology and appliances. For the next five minutes, list anything that did not work the way it was supposed to. Pick one of the problems your group has identified, and

for the next 10 minutes, develop a solution that could result in a business opportunity. As a group, present your report to the class, identifying some of the problems from your original list, which problem you chose to develop a solution for, and why and how the solution you chose will add value for those affected by the problem (the value proposition).

LEARNING TO BE A MANAGER

- Identify an entrepreneur you admire, and research his or her background.

- If you have a family member or family friend who is an entrepreneur, ask about his or her experiences.

- Visit a local support agency for small businesses outside of your educational institution. Ask about the services they provide to the entrepreneurial community and why those services are valued.

- If your college/university has an entrepreneurship or small business centre, go visit it.

- Identify seminars on small business and entrepreneurship available in your community and attend one.

- Invite an entrepreneur to lunch and use the opportunity to learn about his or her journey. In particular, explore how that person maintains a work–life balance.

- Take the time to think about what bugs you (what doesn't work as it is supposed to), and keep a journal for a week of everything you find. At the end of the week, pick one problem and come up with a solution that could lead to the creation of a venture.

- Imagine you are working for an entrepreneurial venture shortly after start-up. Describe what your typical day would be like.

CASE APPLICATION 1

Apple

Apple was named the top firm in the 2009 Global Innovation 1000 survey, beating Google, at second place, and 3M, at third, by a wide margin.[42] In the survey, Apple was held up as an example of the idea that innovation success is driven not by the amount of money spent but rather by how and where it is spent. Apple is known for bringing innovative and stylish products to market.[43] Yet the company spends less than half the average percentage of sales on R&D as the rest of the computing and electronics industry, while earning a high return for shareholders. Winners in the innovation game are those who can innovate successfully without breaking the bank. At Apple, this was not always the case. In the 1990s, Apple invested precious human resources and billions of dollars in a succession of failed products, including the Newton PDA (personal digital assistant).[44] Following the return of Steve Jobs as CEO in 1997,[45] Apple has focused on the strengths that allow it to stand out from its competitors, including a deep understanding of end-users, a high-touch consumer experience, intuitive user interfaces, sleek product design, and iconic branding. In spite of Jobs' 2011 resignation

and subsequent death, Apple continues to be ranked among the world's most innovative companies.[46]

The survey of the 2009 Global Innovation 1000 suggested that successful innovators follow one of three strategies. Need seekers build adaptable organizations that look for meaningful customer problems to solve and strive to be the first to market with those new offerings. Market readers invest in market intelligence on customers and competitors, and focus on creating value through incremental change and by capitalizing on proven market trends. Technology drivers invest in R&D to develop leading-edge technology to solve customers' unstated needs. It is interesting to note that no one of these strategies was seen as better than the others.

DISCUSSION QUESTIONS

1. In your opinion, which of these three innovation strategies is Apple using?
2. As a manager at Apple, what would you need to do to keep the firm adaptable in the future?

Second Chance: The Business of Life

The Centre for Entrepreneurship Education and Development (CEED), through its Second Chance Program, gives youth who have been in conflict with the law the chance for a new start.[47] Many young people who break the law possess misdirected entrepreneurial characteristics. Second Chance provides participants between the ages of 15 and 30 with an opportunity to redirect their entrepreneurial energy and develop the life skills they need to become productive citizens—to manage the "business of life." Second Chance intends to break the cycle of criminal behaviour. One participant describes what that cycle is like:

> For most of my life, I've been involved in illegal activities and arrested at least once a month. I wound up on the streets at the early age of six, and had to learn how to fend for myself. Many of the skills I learned along the way kept me alive, but it was a one-sided life. I didn't trust anyone, care for anyone, or even love anyone, including myself. I was cursed to live a life of crime and emotional solitude.

Referrals for candidates for Second Chance are made by corrections officials, parole officers, and former participants. Perpetrators of violent crimes such as rape, murder, and assault with a deadly weapon are excluded. Applications always exceed the number of seats available. In 2009, 40 applications were made and 14 applicants were accepted. The recidivism rate (rate of reoffence) is around 5 percent for Second Chance graduates, compared to 60 percent for other offenders.

Social Return on Investment

It is becoming increasingly important to estimate the economic benefit of social programs such as Second Chance when attempting to secure public sector funding. The director of the Second Chance Program, Ed Matwawana, recently attended a conference where discussion focused on extending the measurement framework to include the social return on investment (SROI).

Ed Matwawana and CEED president and CEO Kathy Murphy make the business case for Second Chance by comparing the annual operating cost of the program ($300 000) with the annual cost of incarceration for a single inmate ($100 000), pointing out that the program breaks even when incarceration is reduced by three years.

DISCUSSION QUESTIONS

Watch the Second Chance stories video at the Centre for Entrepreneurship and Education Development website (www.ceed.ca).

Think about how Ed Matwawana can make the business case for funding based on earning a social return on investment for the participants and the community at large.

1. Is there a dollar value that you can assign to the reduction in community-based crime from the participants? What is the value for others in the community?
2. What other "social" values can you identify? How would you place a dollar value on them?

Managing Responsibly and Ethically

How important is it for organizations and managers to be socially responsible and ethical? In this chapter, we'll look at what it means to be socially responsible and ethical and what role managers play in both. After reading and studying this chapter, you will achieve the following learning outcomes.

Learning Outcomes

1 Understand what it means to be a socially responsible manager.

2 Describe how managing responsibly contributes to organizational performance.

3 Identify sustainable management practices.

4 Understand the principles of values-based management.

5 Discuss current ethics issues.

▶ ▶ ▶ Since its founding in 1973 by Ray Anderson, Interface Inc., a manufacturer of carpet tiles, has grown into a billion-dollar business with 3000 employees.[1] In 1994, after reading Paul Hawken's *The Ecology of Commerce,* Anderson made a drastic change in course for his company. It became his mission to "turn the myth that you could do well in business or do good, but not both, on its head." Anderson believed that the classic "take, make waste" business model had to be replaced by one that respected the earth. Between 1996 and today, Interface reduced its greenhouse gas emissions by 37.5 percent while substantially growing its sales and profits.

Since 2003, Interface has manufactured 83 million yards of its carbon-neutral Cool Carpet—the company invests in renewable energy and sequestration projects to offset the carbon footprint from manufacturing. Interface's dedication to sustainability has evolved into the company's Mission Zero commitment, a promise to eliminate any negative impact Interface has on the environment by 2020. Interface hopes its commitment will inspire other businesses to create their own Mission Zero journey to sustainability.

Deciding how much social responsibility is enough—for instance, looking at when it's better to simply focus on profits—is just one example of the complicated types of ethical and social responsibility issues that managers have to address as they plan, organize, lead, and control. As managers go about their business, social factors can and do influence their actions. In this chapter, we introduce you to the issues surrounding social responsibility and managerial ethics. Our discussion of these topics appears here in the textbook because both corporate social responsibility and ethics are responses to a changing environment and are influenced by organizational culture (Chapter 2); they have an influence on how we do business globally (Chapter 3); and they are important considerations when making decisions (Chapter 7).

Kim Kulish/Corbis

> **Think About It**
>
> What are the elements of corporate responsibility at Interface? What question is Ray Anderson most often asked when he finishes his presentations—by shareholders, advocacy groups, and company employees? What balance between profitability and social responsibility might local Interface managers need to strike? In what ways might Interface's Mission Zero commitment create a competitive advantage?

What Is Meant by Socially Responsible Management?

❶ Understand what it means to be a socially responsible manager.

Large global corporations lower their costs by outsourcing to countries where human rights are not a high priority and justify it by saying they're bringing in jobs and helping strengthen the local economies. Businesses facing a drastically changed industry environment offer employees early retirement and buyout packages. Are these companies being socially responsible? Managers regularly face decisions that have a dimension of social responsibility, such as those involving employee relations, philanthropy, pricing, resource conservation, product quality and safety, and doing business in countries that devalue human rights. What does it mean to be socially responsible?

From Obligations to Responsiveness to Responsibility

The concept of *social responsibility* has been described in different ways. For instance, it has been called "profit making only," "going beyond profit making," "any discretionary corporate activity intended to further social welfare," and "improving social or environmental conditions."[2] We can understand it better if we first compare it to two similar concepts: social obligation and social responsiveness.[3]

The Classical View: Social Obligation

social obligation A firm's engaging in social actions because of its obligation to meet certain economic and legal responsibilities.

classical view The view that management's only social responsibility is to maximize profits.

Social obligation is a firm's engaging in social actions because of its obligation to meet certain economic and legal responsibilities. The organization does what it's obligated to do and nothing more. This idea reflects the **classical view** of social responsibility, which says that management's only social responsibility is to maximize profits. The most outspoken advocate of this approach was economist and Nobel laureate Milton Friedman. He argued that managers' primary responsibility is to operate the business in the best interests of the shareholders, whose primary concerns are financial.[4] He also argued that when managers decide to spend the organization's resources for "social good," they add to the costs of doing business, which have to be passed on to consumers through higher prices or absorbed by shareholders through smaller dividends. You need to understand that Friedman doesn't say that organizations shouldn't be socially responsible. But his interpretation of social responsibility is to maximize profits for shareholders.

Joel Bakan, professor of law at the University of British Columbia, author of *The Corporation*, and co-director of the documentary of the same name, is more critical of organizations than Friedman. He finds that current laws support corporate behaviour that some might find troubling. Bakan suggests that today's corporations have many of the same characteristics as a psychopathic personality (for example, self-interested, lacking empathy, manipulative, and reckless in their disregard of others). Bakan notes that even though companies have a tendency to act psychopathically, this is not why they are fixated on profits. Rather, though they may have social responsibilities, the only legal responsibility corporations have is to maximize organizational profits for shareholders.[5] He suggests that more laws and more restraints need to be put in place if corporations are to behave more socially responsibly, as current laws direct corporations to be responsible to their shareholders, and make little mention of responsibility toward other stakeholders.

The Socio-Economic View:
Social Responsiveness and Social Responsibility

The other two concepts—social responsiveness and social responsibility—reflect the **socio-economic view**, which says that managers' social responsibilities go beyond making profits to include protecting and improving society's welfare. This view is based on the belief that corporations are *not* independent entities responsible only to shareholders. They also have a responsibility to the larger society. Organizations around the world have embraced this view, as shown by a global survey of executives in which 84 percent said that companies must balance obligations to shareholders with obligations to the public good.[6] So how do the concepts of social responsiveness and social responsibility differ?

> **socio-economic view** The view that management's social responsibility goes beyond making profits and includes protecting and improving society's welfare.

Social Responsiveness

Social responsiveness is demonstrated when a company engages in social actions in response to some popular **social need**. Managers are guided by social norms and values and make practical, market-oriented decisions about their actions.[7] For instance, Ford Motor Company became the first automaker to endorse a federal ban on sending text messages while driving. A company spokesperson said: "The most complete and most recent research shows that activity that draws drivers' eyes away from the road for an extended period while driving, such as text messaging, substantially increases the risk of accidents."[8] By supporting this ban, company managers "responded" to what they felt was an important social need. When the disastrous earthquake and tsunami hit Japan in 2011, many tech companies responded with resources and support. For instance, social networking giant Facebook set up a Japan earthquake page for users to find information about disaster relief. After the Haiti earthquake in January 2010, many companies responded to the immense needs in that region. Mississauga, Ontario-based Purolator Courier developed its Tackle Hunger campaign because no major Canadian corporations were tackling this important issue. The program visits Canadian Football League (CFL) cities annually, and fans can have their picture taken with the Grey Cup if they bring a nonperishable food item or make a cash donation. In addition, Purolator donates the quarterback's weight in food to the local food bank whenever he gets sacked in a regular season game.

> **social responsiveness** A firm's engaging in social actions in response to some popular social need.

> **social need** A need of a segment of society caused by factors such as physical and mental disabilities; language barriers; or cultural, social, or geographical isolation.

Social Responsibility

A *socially responsible* organization views things differently. It goes beyond what it's obligated to do and chooses to do so because of some popular social need and does what it can to help improve society because it's the right thing to do. We define **social responsibility** as a business's efforts, beyond its legal and economic obligations, to do the right things and act in ways that are good for society.[9] Our definition assumes that a business obeys the law and cares for its shareholders, *and* it adds an ethical imperative to do those things that make society better and not to do those that make it worse, including environmental degradation. Note that this definition assumes that a firm has to differentiate between right and wrong. As Exhibit 5-1 shows, a socially responsible organization does what is right because it feels it has an ethical responsibility to do so. For example, the Royal Bank of Canada (RBC) has identified water stewardship as an environmental priority. Under the RBC Blue Water Project, the organization has committed $50 million to fresh water initiatives, announced significant grants to three universities for water research and programs, and pledged more than $38 million since 2007 to 650 organizations worldwide that are working to protect watersheds and provide access to clean drinking water.[10]

> **social responsibility** A business's intention, beyond its legal and economic obligations, to do the right things and act in ways that are good for society.

Social responsibility adds an ethical imperative to determine what is right or wrong and to engage in ethical business activities. A socially responsible organization does what is right because it feels it has a responsibility to act that way. For example, Vancouver-based Mountain Equipment Co-op, which makes outdoor sports clothing and gear, has a green building policy. Its Ottawa and Winnipeg stores were the first and second Canadian retail buildings to comply with standards requiring a 50 percent reduction in energy consumption over regular buildings. CEO Peter Robinson says, "The bottom line is that

Exhibit 5-1

Social Responsibility vs. Social Responsiveness

	Social Responsibility	Social Responsiveness
Major consideration	Ethical	Pragmatic
Focus	Ends	Means
Emphasis	Obligation	Responses
Decision framework	Long term	Medium and short terms

Source: Adapted from S. L. Wartick and P. L. Cochran, "The Evolution of the Corporate Social Performance Model," *Academy of Management Review,* October 1985, p. 766.

sustainability is good business: for the ledger books and for the planet."[11] That's the attitude of a socially responsible manager and organization.

In 2013, Vancouver City Savings Credit Union topped *Corporate Knights* magazine's ranking of corporate social responsibility in Canada.[12] The British Columbia-based financial cooperative "Vancity" is an example of an organization that actively promotes sustainability beyond measuring greenhouse gases and related energy use indicators, including encouraging its employees to switch to sustainable transit modes, developing banking products for disadvantaged groups and promoting socially responsible investments.

In 2013, Strandberg Consulting published a study examining companies traded on the Toronto Stock Exchange (TSX) and their commitment to sustainability. The study found that 57 percent of TSX top 60 companies are measuring their progress toward their sustainability targets, and their success in attaining these targets is a criteria in determining compensation plans for their executives. This can be considered as a strong indication of change in Canadian corporate culture that has emerged in recent years.[13] The Bank of Montreal launched its Clear Blue Skies Initiative in 2009 as a company-wide strategy of energy reduction and efficiency; waste management; and sustainable transport, materials, and procurement—all aimed at protecting and improving air quality.[14]

At Charlottetown, PEI-based APM Group, a construction and property development company, (from left) Terry Palmer, APM Group vice-president of finance; Tim Banks, president; Duane Lamont, vice-president of construction; and Pam Mullally, director of accounting, think about the bottom line when they review plans for new subdivisions APM might build. However, they also know that social responsibility is a guiding principle for the company. So they evaluate each project's impact on the environment, focus on design that promotes energy conservation, and strive to create a healthy economic community through the building plan.

APM Construction Services

Social Responsibility vs. Social Responsiveness

How should we view an organization's social actions? A Canadian business that meets federal pollution control standards or that doesn't discriminate against employees over age 40 in job promotion decisions is meeting its social obligation because laws mandate these actions. However, when it provides on-site child care facilities for employees; packages products using recycled paper; or announces that it will not purchase, process, or sell any tuna caught along with dolphins, it's being socially responsive. Why? Working parents and environmentalists have voiced these social concerns and demanded such actions.

For many businesses, their social actions are better viewed as being socially responsive than socially responsible (at least according to our definition). However, such actions are still good for society. For example, Walmart Canada is a leader in the transition toward environmental sustainability in Canada's retail sector. Walmart Canada's green plan includes a $25-million fund to support the restoration of community green space until 2015, hard targets for reductions in its carbon footprint and energy consumption, a commitment to being Canada's largest consumer of renewable energy, and a sustained program to offer environmentally efficient products and educate consumers about their benefits.[15]

The Evolution of Socially Responsible Management

Understanding the various socially responsible management strategies that exist today is easier if we think in terms of differing views about to whom organizations are responsible. Those supporting the socio-economic view would respond that managers should be responsible to any group affected by the organization's decisions and actions—that is, the stakeholders (such as employees and community members).[16] Classicists would say that shareholders, or owners, are the only legitimate concern. Exhibit 5-2 shows a four-stage model of the progression of an organization's social responsibility.[17]

At stage 1, managers are following the classical view of social responsibility and obey all laws and regulations while caring for shareholders' interests. At stage 2, managers expand their responsibilities to another important stakeholder group—employees. Because they want to attract, keep, and motivate good employees, stage 2 managers improve working conditions, expand employee rights, increase job security, and focus on human resource concerns.

At stage 3, managers expand their responsibilities to other stakeholders in the specific environment, primarily customers and suppliers. Socially responsible actions for these stakeholders might include fair prices, high-quality products and services, safe products, good supplier relations, and similar actions. Managers' philosophy is that they can meet their responsibilities to all stakeholders only by meeting the needs of customers and suppliers.

Finally, at stage 4, which characterizes the highest socio-economic commitment, managers feel they have a responsibility to society as a whole. They view their business as a public entity and therefore feel that it's important to advance the public good. The acceptance of such responsibility means that managers actively promote social justice, preserve the environment, and support social and cultural activities. They do these things even if such actions may negatively affect profits.

Exhibit 5-2

To Whom Is Management Responsible?

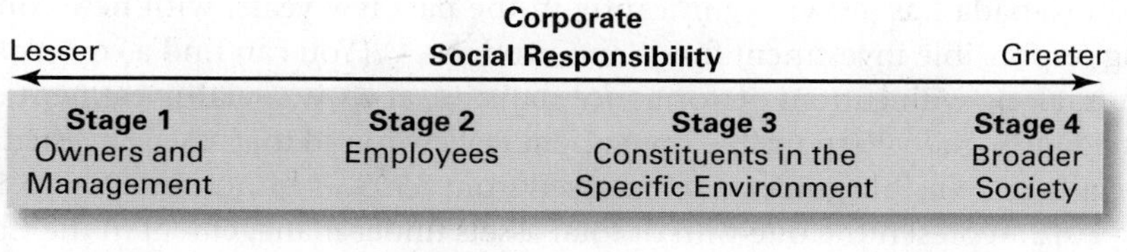

▣ Watch on **MyManagementLab**

Honest Tea: Corporate Social
Responsibility

❷ Describe how managing
responsibly contributes
to organizational
performance.

Corporate Social Responsibility and Economic Performance

▶ ▶ ▶   During his time as founder, CEO, and leader of the Interface journey toward sustainability, Ray Anderson said, "Our costs are down, our profits are up, and our products are the best they've ever been. It has rewarded us with more positive visibility and goodwill among our customers than the slickest, most expensive advertising or marketing campaign could possibly have generated. And a strong environmental ethic has no equal for attracting and motivating good people, galvanizing them around a shared higher purpose, and giving them a powerful reason to join and stay."[18]

Through its dedication to sustainability, Interface has created a working model that since 1996 has reduced greenhouse gas emissions by 37.5 percent and offset 2.8 million gallons of fuel. Interface has also committed to eliminating all negative impacts on the environment by 2020, all while substantially growing sales and share value.

Think About It

Can a company be socially responsible and achieve good financial performance? Put yourself in Ray Anderson's shoes. What advantages does Interface gain through working toward its goal of a zero carbon footprint? Would you like to work for Interface? Why or why not? Is this a values-led organization? Why don't more businesses adopt the Interface model?

In this section, we look at the question: How do socially responsible activities affect a company's economic performance? Findings from a number of research studies can help us answer this question.[19]

The majority of studies show a positive relationship between social involvement and economic performance. However, we cannot generalize these findings because the studies haven't used standardized measures of social responsibility and economic performance.[20] Another concern in these studies has been causation: If a study showed that social involvement and economic performance were positively related, this didn't necessarily mean that social involvement *caused* higher economic performance. It could simply mean that high profits afforded companies the "luxury" of being socially involved.[21] Such methodological concerns can't be taken lightly. In fact, two studies found that if the flawed empirical analyses in these studies were "corrected," social responsibility had a positive impact on financial performance only when it was strategically linked to stakeholder preferences.[22] Another found that participating in sustainability issues was negatively associated with shareholder value, but positively associated with research progress.[23] However, a reanalysis of several studies concluded that managers can afford to be (and should be) socially responsible, while a recent study demonstrates the impact of social responsibility on employee productivity.[24]

Another way to view social involvement and economic performance is by looking at socially responsible investing (SRI) funds, which provide a way for individual investors to support socially responsible companies. Typically, these funds use some type of **social screening**; that is, they apply social and environmental criteria to investment decisions. For instance, SRI funds usually do not invest in companies that are involved in liquor, gambling, tobacco, nuclear power, weapons, price fixing, or fraud or in companies that have poor product safety, employee relations, or environmental track records. The SRI industry in Canada has grown significantly in the past few years, with new companies launching responsible investment funds and products.[25] (You can find a complete list of these funds, along with current performance statistics, at **www.socialinvestment.ca.**) The 2008 Canadian Socially Responsible Investment Review found that assets invested according to socially responsible guidelines increased from $503.61 billion in 2006 to $600.90 billion in 2012, representing one-fifth of total assets under management in the Canadian financial industry.[26]

social screening Applying social criteria (screens) to investment decisions.

We can also examine different ways of measuring business success. B Corps ("Benefit Corporations") that are certified by the nonprofit B Lab are required to meet rigorous standards of accountability, transparency, environmental and social performance.[27] B Corps still try to make as much profit as possible, but do it in a way that has a measurable, positive impact on the world. Efficient B Corps are not just efficient at making profit, they are also efficient at social good, as measured by their score on the B Impact Assessment.

What conclusion can we draw from all of this? The most meaningful one is that there is little evidence to say that a company's social actions hurt its long-term economic performance, if a company's CSR efforts are in line with the stakeholder's goals. Given political and societal pressures on business to be socially involved, managers would be wise to take social goals into consideration as they plan, organize, lead, and control. Jason Mogus, president of Vancouver-based Communicopia, agrees: "The times that we are in right now are tough times for a lot of high-tech firms, and the ones that are thriving are the ones that really did build community connections and have strong customer and employee loyalty." Says Mogus, "If everyone's just there for the stock price and it goes under water, then what you have is a staff of not very motivated workers."[28]

Sustainable Management Practices

▶ ▶ ▶ Interface sees itself as a restorative enterprise.[29] This includes a commitment to eliminate all forms of waste in every area of business, reduce greenhouse gases, and use renewable energy sources. Interface's goal is to ensure that by 2020, all fuels and electricity to operate manufacturing, sales, and office facilities will be from renewable sources, such as solar, wind, and geothermal energy. Products and processes have been redesigned to reduce and simplify the amount of resources used, so that material "waste" is remanufactured into the "nutrients" for the next cycle of production. Since 1995, Interface diverted 260 million pounds of reclaimed carpet and postindustrial scrap from landfill.

At Interface, all nonrenewable energy is also considered waste. In three of its production facilities, the company generates green power on site, and it purchases additional requirements through green power. Interface started a company-wide waste reduction program called QUEST (Quality Utilizing Employee's Suggestions and Teamwork) and in the first three-and-a-half years saved $67 million worldwide. Since 1999, the QUEST program has saved the company $433 million. Interface is also committed to creating a culture that uses sustainability principles to improve the lives and livelihoods of all its stakeholders—employees, partners, suppliers, customers, investors, and communities. This includes a commitment to transport people and products efficiently to eliminate waste and emissions.

③ Identify sustainable management practices.

Think About It

Why has Interface chosen to follow an approach to business that incorporates environmental sustainability? What benefits does managing sustainably provide to a company? What benefits does managing sustainably provide to society?

Rachel Carson's *Silent Spring*, a book about the negative effects of pesticides on the environment that was published in 1962, is often cited as having launched the environmental movement. Until that time, few people (and organizations) paid attention to the environmental consequences of their decisions and actions.[30] Although there were some groups concerned with conserving natural resources, about the only popular reference to saving the environment you would have seen was the ubiquitous printed request "Please Do Not Litter."

Since the publication of Carson's book, a number of highly publicized environmental disasters—the BP oil spill (2010), the Hungary toxic sludge disaster (2010), the Fukushima

Daiichi nuclear disaster (2011), and natural disasters that displace millions of people and cause environmental damage each year—have increased environmental awareness among individuals, groups, and organizations. Increasingly, managers began to confront questions about an organization's impact on the natural environment. The recognition by business of the close link between its decisions and activities and their impact on the natural environment is referred to as **sustainable management**. Let's look at some sustainability issues managers may have to address.

sustainable management The recognition by business of the close link between its decisions and activities and their impact on the natural environment.

Global Environmental Problems

Some of the more serious global environmental problems include global climate change, natural resource depletion, pollution (air, water, and soil), industrial accidents, and toxic wastes. How did these problems occur? Much of the blame can be placed on industrial activities in developed (economically wealthy) countries over the past half-century.[31] Various reports have shown that industrialized societies account for the vast majority of the world's energy and resource consumption and create most of the industrial, toxic, and consumer waste.[32] An equally unsettling picture is that, as the world population continues to grow and as emerging countries become more market-oriented and well off, shortages in resources such as water and other global environmental problems can be expected to worsen.[33] But the good news is that things are changing. Increasingly, managers and organizations around the world have begun to consider the impact of their organizations on the natural environment and have embraced their responsibility to respect and protect the earth. For instance, IKEA encourages customers to use fewer bags and has cut the price of its large reusable totes from 99 cents to 59 cents. Tokyo-based Ricoh hires workers to sort through company trash to analyze what might be reused or recycled. And company employees have two cans—one for recycling and one for trash. If a recyclable item is found in a trash bin, it's placed back on the offender's desk for proper removal. These sustainable management practices, also known as green management practices, are increasingly being implemented by organizations.[34] What role can organizations play in addressing global environmental problems? In other words, how can they implement sustainable management practices?

How Organizations Manage Sustainably

Managers and organizations can do many things to protect and preserve the natural environment. Some do no more than what is required by law—that is, they fulfill their social obligation. However, others have made radical changes to make their products and production processes cleaner. For instance, Vancouver-based Teck has reduced its mining operations in areas with at-risk species, and partnered with the government of British Columbia to respond and restore declining white sturgeon populations. UPS, the world's largest package delivery company, has taken numerous environmental actions, such as retrofitting its aircraft with advanced technology and fuel-efficient engines, using alternative fuel to run its trucks, and reducing customers' package waste through its Eco-Responsible Packaging program. There are many more examples of organizations committed to sustainable management. Although these examples are interesting, they don't tell us much about *how* organizations engage in sustainable management. One model of environmental responsibility describes the different approaches that organizations take.[35] (See Exhibit 5-3.)

The first approach to sustainable management is the *legal approach*—that is, simply doing what is required legally. Organizations that follow this approach exhibit little environmental sensitivity. They obey laws, rules, and regulations willingly and without legal challenge and may even try to use the law to their own advantage, but that is the extent of their implementation of sustainable management practices. For example, many durable product manufacturers have taken the legal approach and comply with the relevant environmental laws and regulations, but go no further. This approach is a good illustration of social obligation—these organizations simply follow the legal requirements to prevent pollution and protect the environment.

As an organization becomes more sensitive to environmental issues, it may adopt the *market approach,* where organizations respond to the environmental preferences of their customers. Whatever customers demand in terms of environmentally friendly products will be what the organization provides. For example, the Chemistry Industry Association of Canada (CIAC) promotes the development of safer and more environmentally friendly products and services by its member companies. Dow Chemicals Canada, one of many members of CIAC, has successfully reduced the nitrogen oxide (NO_x) emissions at its cogeneration plant in Fort Saskatchewan by more than 90 percent.[36] Through the cogeneration process, the company was able to recover energy that would normally be wasted, and use it to produce heat in its manufacturing processes.[37]

Environmental sustainability standards driven by consumers are emerging across all industry sectors, ranging from primary sectors such as fisheries and agriculture to manufacturing sectors. In the case of the fisheries sector, the global export markets for Canada's commercial fisheries are increasingly looking for Marine Stewardship Council (MSC) certification as a prerequisite for market access. The MSC has developed standard principles, criteria, and chain of custody requirements, requiring an independent third-party assessment of a fishery before certification is granted. Once a fishery has been certified, all companies in the supply chain, from fishing boat to the consumer's table, must have MSC certification to ensure that the products can carry the MSC label.

Organizations that follow the *stakeholder approach* work to meet the environmental demands of multiple stakeholders such as employees, suppliers, and the community. For instance, Hewlett-Packard has several corporate environmental programs in place for its supply chain (suppliers), product design and product recycling (customers and society), and work operations (employees and community). Both the market approach and the stakeholder approach are good illustrations of social responsiveness.

Finally, if an organization pursues an *activist approach to sustainable management,* it looks for ways to respect and preserve the earth and its natural resources. Organizations that follow the activist approach exhibit the highest degree of environmental sensitivity. For example, Walmart, the world's largest retailer, has committed to being totally supplied by renewable energy, to creating zero waste, and to selling products that sustain the environment. The company chose to establish an on-line sustainability hub for Walmart suppliers, partners, and associates to collaborate to drive sustainability as part of its commitment to protecting the environment. The activist approach is an illustration of corporate social responsibility that goes beyond the usual definition of responsibility.

Exhibit 5-3

Approaches to Sustainable Management

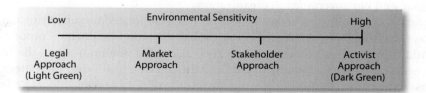

Source: Based on R. E. Freeman, J. Pierce, and R. Dodd, *Shades of Green: Business Ethics and the Environment* (New York: Oxford University Press, 1995).

Richard Kouwenhoven, manager of digital services at Burnaby, BC-based Hemlock Printers, founded by his father, has been one of the leaders in his generation's push to have the company, already known for its responsible management practices, become a leader in sustainable paper use.

Ric Ernst/The Province

Evaluating Sustainable Management

As organizations implement sustainable management practices, we find more and more of them issuing detailed reports on their environmental performance, many of them through the guidelines developed by the Global Reporting Initiative (GRI). Founded in 1997, the GRI is an independent entity that develops and disseminates globally applicable Sustainability Reporting Guidelines, providing one of the world's most prevalent standards for sustainability reporting. Using G3 guidelines (reporting principles, reporting guidance, and standard disclosures) for ecological footprint reporting, environmental social governance (ESG), triple bottom line (TBL), and corporate social responsibility (CSR) reporting, over 1000 organizations around the globe voluntarily report their efforts in promoting environmental sustainability. These reports, which can be found in the database on the GRI website, describe the numerous sustainable management practices these organizations are pursuing.

Another way that organizations can show their commitment to sustainable management practices is by adopting ISO standards. The nongovernmental ISO (International Organization for Standardization) is the world's largest developer of standards. Organizations that want to become ISO 14000 compliant must develop a total environmental management system for meeting environmental challenges. This means that the organization must minimize the effects of its activities on the environment and continually improve its environmental performance. The ISO 26000 social responsibility guidelines were released in November 2010 and represent an international consensus on what social responsibility means and the issues that need to be addressed to implement it, based on broad stakeholder input, including developing countries, business, government, consumers, labour, and nongovernmental organizations.[38]

The final way to evaluate whether a company has incorporated sustainable management practices is by its inclusion in the list of the Global 100 Most Sustainable Corporations in the World, a project that was launched in 2005 as a collaboration between the Toronto-based media company Corporate Knights and the research firm Innovest Strategic Value Advisers. To be named to this list, a company must have displayed an ability to effectively manage environmental and social factors. The companies that make it onto the Global 100 are announced each year at the renowned World Economic Forum in Davos, Switzerland. The companies on the 2014 list of top 50 Canadian corporate citizens include Mountain Equipment Co-op, Vancouver City Savings Credit Union, Bombardier, Tim Hortons, Mouvement des Caisses Desjardins, and Teck Resources.[39]

Values-Based Management

▶ ▶ ▶ Interface practises values-based management. "Interface's values are our guiding principles."[40] As part of its values, the company is committed to sustainable management practices, with a zero carbon footprint as its goal. The company developed its model for sustainable business based on the "Seven Fronts of Mount Sustainability" and put in place a measurement framework, called EcoMetrics, to monitor its progress and provide a framework that other organizations can use. Through its actions and deeds, Interface would like to not only demonstrate sustainable practices in all its dimensions—people, process, product, place, and profits—by 2020, but also become a "restorative" operation by returning more to the environment than it takes. As a first step, the organization strives to attain sustainability and a zero carbon footprint in its own business practices. To meet the higher goal of becoming a restorative business, it will work to help other organizations achieve sustainability. Interface believes that when stakeholders fully understand sustainability and the challenges that lie ahead, they will come together into a community of shared environmental and social goals.

④ Understand the principles of values-based management.

Think About It

Do Interface's sustainable management practices create advantages for other companies? For society as a whole?

Values-based management is an approach to managing in which managers establish and uphold an organization's shared values. An organization's values reflect what it stands for and what it believes in. As we discussed in Chapter 2, the shared organizational values form the organization's culture and serve many purposes.[41]

Vancouver-based Mountain Equipment Co-op (MEC) practises values-based management. MEC passionately pursues environmental preservation. Its strong environmental commitment influences employees' actions and decisions in areas such as product design, manufacturing, marketing, shipping, and store design. For instance, in designing its store in Montreal, the company favoured using recycled building materials.[42] Although contractors quoted cheaper prices for using new material, MEC held out, to be consistent with the company's values.

values-based management An approach to managing in which managers establish and uphold an organization's shared values.

When Mountain Equipment Co-op opened its first Montreal store in 2003, the building was the first in Quebec to meet Natural Resource Canada's C-2000 standard. The store is much more energy efficient than conventional retail buildings. The building was made with reused building materials, and water for toilet flushing and landscape irrigation comes from roof water runoff. MEC has a high commitment to social and environmental responsibility, and its products come from factories that meet high labour, health, and safety standards.

Mountain Equipment Co-Op

Exhibit 5-4

Purposes of Shared Values

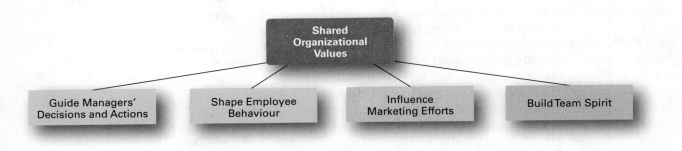

Purposes of Shared Values

Exhibit 5-4 shows the four purposes of shared organizational values. One purpose is to guide managers' decisions and actions.[43] For instance, at Tom's of Maine, a manufacturer of all-natural personal care products, the corporate Statement of Beliefs guides managers as they plan, organize, lead, and control. One of the company's eight beliefs states, "We believe that different people bring different gifts and perspectives to the team and that a strong team is founded on a variety of gifts."[44] This statement expresses to managers the value of diversity—diversity of opinions, diversity of abilities—and serves as a guide for managing teams of people. Another belief states, "We believe in products that are safe, effective, and made of natural ingredients." Again, think how this statement might influence and guide company managers.

A second purpose of shared values is to shape employee behaviour by communicating what the organization expects of its members. Shared values also influence marketing efforts. Finally, shared values are a way to build team spirit in an organization.[45] When employees embrace the stated organizational values, they develop a deeper personal commitment to their work and feel obligated to take responsibility for their actions. Because the shared values influence the way work is done, employees become more enthusiastic about working together as a team to support the values they believe in. At companies such as Bolton, Ontario-based Husky Injection Molding, Vancouver-based Weyerhaeuser, Vancouver-based Vancity, Toronto-based Home Depot Canada, and numerous others, employees know what is expected of them on the job. The shared organizational values not only guide the way they work, but serve to unite them in a common quest. Just how do shared organizational values affect employee actions? They can promote behaviours that mirror the values of the organization, as the following *Management Reflection* shows.

MANAGEMENT REFLECTION FOCUS ON ETHICS

Living an Examined Life

Can shared organization values promote positive employee behaviours? Canadian-born Yvon Chouinard is a self-taught blacksmith who, in 1957, started crafting mountain-climbing pitons he and other climbing enthusiasts used as anchors on risky climbs.[46] His hardware became so popular that he would go on to found the outdoor-clothing company Patagonia. As his company grew, Chouinard embraced the philosophy of leading an examined life. In the process he realized that everything his company did had an effect—mostly negative—on the environment. Today, he defines the company's mission in eco-driven terms: "To use business to inspire and implement solutions to the environmental crisis." Chouinard has put environmental activism at the forefront of his company. Since 1985, Patagonia has donated 1 percent of its annual sales to grassroots environmental groups and has gotten more than 1300 companies to follow its lead as part of its "1% for the Planet" group. He recognizes that "every product, no matter how much thought goes into it, has a destructive impact on Earth." In 2012 he wrote *The Responsible Company: What We've Learned From Patagonia's First 40 Years.* Nonetheless, he keeps doing what he does because "it's the right thing to do." What can you learn from this leader who made a difference? ▪

Thus, an organization's managers do play an important role here. They're responsible for creating an environment that encourages employees to embrace the culture and the desired values as they do their jobs. In fact, research shows that the behaviour of managers is the single most important influence on an individual's decision to act ethically or unethically.[47] People look to see what those in authority are doing and use that as a benchmark for acceptable practices and expectations.

Managerial Ethics

▶ ▶ ▶ Like many companies today, Interface has an ethics policy. The policy affirms the company's intention to act ethically in all its dealings. Employees and associates are expected to

⑤ Discuss current ethics issues.

- Engage in and promote honest and ethical conduct, including the ethical handling of actual or apparent conflicts of interest between personal and professional relationships

- Comply with applicable governmental laws, rules, and regulations

- Be committed to the full, fair, accurate, timely, and understandable disclosure in reports and documents that the company files

- Promptly report any possible violation of this Code to the appropriate person or persons

Among the most common conflicts of interest at Interface are doing business with relatives, misuse of business time, competition with Interface, acceptance of gifts, illegal or improper payments, corporate opportunities, investment in other entities, and misuse of confidential information (insider trading).[48]

Think About It

Managers—at all levels, in all areas, and in all kinds of organizations—will face ethical issues and dilemmas. As managers plan, organize, lead, and control, they must consider ethical dimensions. How might an ethics policy provide guidance to employees, managers, leaders, and stakeholders?

What do we mean by ethics? **Ethics** refers to rules and principles that define right and wrong behaviour.[49] In this section, we examine the ethical dimensions of managerial decisions. Many decisions that managers make require them to consider who may be affected—in terms of the result as well as the process.[50]

ethics Rules and principles that define right and wrong behaviour.

Factors That Affect Employee Ethics

Whether a person acts ethically or unethically when faced with an ethical dilemma is the result of complex interactions between his or her stage of moral development and several moderating variables, including individual characteristics, the organization's structural design, organizational culture, and the intensity of the ethical issue (Exhibit 5-5). People who lack a strong moral sense are much less likely to do the wrong things if they are

Exhibit 5-5

Factors That Affect Ethical and Unethical Behaviour

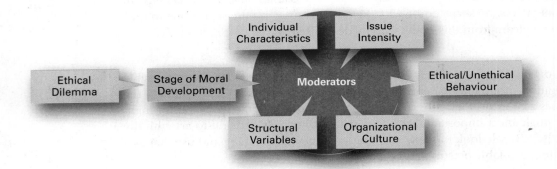

constrained by rules, policies, job descriptions, or strong cultural norms that disapprove of such behaviours. Conversely, intensely moral individuals can be corrupted by an organizational structure and culture that permits or encourages unethical practices. Let's look more closely at the factors that influence whether individuals will behave ethically or unethically.

Stage of Moral Development

Research confirms the existence of three levels of moral development, each composed of two stages.[51] At each successive stage, an individual's moral judgment becomes less and less dependent on outside influences. The three levels and six stages are described in Exhibit 5-6.

The first level is labelled *preconventional*. At this level, a person's choice between right and wrong is based on the personal consequences involved, such as physical punishment, reward, or exchange of favours. Ethical reasoning at the *conventional* level indicates that moral values reside in maintaining expected standards and living up to the expectations of others. At the *principled* level, individuals make a clear effort to define ethical principles apart from the authority of the groups to which they belong or society in general.

We can draw some conclusions from research on the levels and stages of moral development.[52] First, people proceed through the six stages sequentially. They move up the

Exhibit 5-6

Stages of Moral Development

Level	Description of Stage
Principled	6. Following self-chosen ethical principles even if they violate the law
	5. Valuing rights of others and upholding absolute values and rights regardless of the majority's opinion
Conventional	4. Maintaining conventional order by fulfilling obligations to which you have agreed
	3. Living up to what is expected by people close to you
Preconventional	2. Following rules only when doing so is in your immediate interest
	1. Sticking to rules to avoid physical punishment

Source: Based on L. Kohlberg, "Moral Stages and Moralization: The Cognitive-Development Approach," in *Moral Development and Behavior: Theory, Research, and Social Issues,* ed. T. Lickona (New York: Holt, Rinehart & Winston, 1976), pp. 34–35.

moral ladder, stage by stage. Second, there is no guarantee of continued moral development. An individual's moral development can stop at any stage. Third, the majority of adults are at stage 4. They are limited to obeying the rules and will be inclined to behave ethically, although for different reasons. For instance, a manager at stage 3 is likely to make decisions that will receive peer approval; a manager at stage 4 will try to be a "good corporate citizen" by making decisions that respect the organization's rules and procedures; and a stage 5 manager is likely to challenge organizational practices that he or she believes to be wrong.

Individual Characteristics

Every person joining an organization has a relatively entrenched set of **values**. Our values—developed at a young age from parents, teachers, friends, and others—represent basic convictions about what is right and wrong. Thus, managers in the same organization often possess very different personal values.[53] Although *values* and *stage of moral development* may seem similar, they are not. Values are broad and cover a wide range of issues; the stage of moral development is a measure of independence from outside influences.

Two personality variables also have been found to influence an individual's actions according to his or her beliefs about what is right or wrong: ego strength and locus of control. **Ego strength** is a personality measure of the strength of a person's convictions. People who score high on ego strength are likely to resist impulses to act unethically and instead follow their convictions. That is, individuals high in ego strength are more likely to do what they think is right. We would expect employees with high ego strength to be more consistent in their moral judgments and actions than those with low ego strength.

Locus of control is a personality attribute that reflects the degree to which people believe they control their own fate. People with an *internal* locus of control believe that they control their own destinies; those with an *external* locus believe that what happens to them is due to luck or chance. How does this influence a person's decision to act ethically or unethically? Externals are less likely to take personal responsibility for the consequences of their behaviour and are more likely to rely on external forces to guide their actions. Internals, on the other hand, are more likely to take responsibility for consequences and rely on their own internal standards of right and wrong to guide their actions.[54] Also, employees with an internal locus of control are likely to be more consistent in their moral judgments and actions than those with an external locus of control.

Structural Variables

An organization's structural design influences whether employees behave ethically. Some structures provide strong guidance, whereas others create ambiguity and uncertainty. Structural designs that minimize ambiguity and uncertainty through formal rules and regulations and those that continuously remind employees of what is ethical are more likely to result in ethical behaviour.

Other organizational mechanisms that influence ethics include performance appraisal systems and reward allocation procedures. Some organizational performance appraisal systems focus exclusively on outcomes, such as number of sales. Others evaluate means as well as ends, such as how customer-oriented employees are when customers speak with them. When employees are evaluated only on outcomes, they may be pressured to do "whatever is necessary" to look good on the outcome variables and not be concerned with how they got those results. Recent research suggests that "success may serve to excuse unethical behaviors."[55] Just think of the impact of this type of thinking. The danger is that, if managers take a more lenient view of unethical behaviours for successful employees, other employees will model their behaviour on what they see.

Closely associated with the performance appraisal system is the way rewards are allocated. The more that rewards or punishments depend on specific goal outcomes, the more pressure there is on employees to do whatever they must to reach those goals and perhaps compromise their ethical standards. Although these structural factors are important influences on employees, they are not the most important. What *is* the most important?

values Basic convictions about what is right and wrong.

ego strength A personality measure of the strength of a person's convictions.

locus of control A personality attribute that reflects the degree to which people believe they control their own fate.

The Boeing Company's imaginative poster series reinforces the core values of integrity and ethical behaviour for its employees.

Courtesy of Boeing Aircraft Company

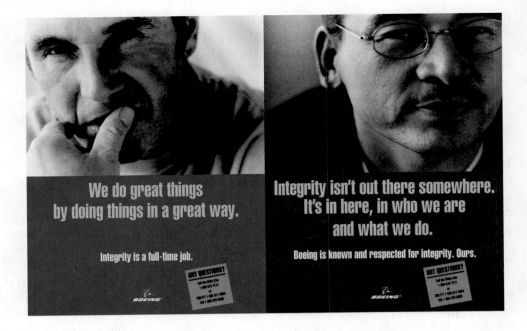

Organizational Culture

The content and strength of an organization's culture also influence ethical behaviour.[56] An organizational culture most likely to encourage high ethical standards is one that is high in risk tolerance, control, and conflict tolerance. Employees in such a culture are encouraged to be aggressive and innovative, are aware that unethical practices will be discovered, and feel free to openly challenge expectations they consider to be unrealistic or personally undesirable.

As we discussed in Chapter 2, a strong culture will exert more influence on employees than a weak one. If the culture is strong and supports high ethical standards, it has a very powerful and positive influence on an employee's decision to act ethically or unethically. The Boeing Company, for example, has a strong culture that has long stressed ethical dealings with customers, employees, the community, and shareholders. To reinforce the importance of ethical behaviours, the company developed a series of serious and thought-provoking posters designed to get employees to recognize that their individual decisions and actions are important to the way the organization is viewed.

Issue Intensity

A student who would never consider breaking into an instructor's office to steal an accounting exam does not think twice about asking a friend who took the same course from the same instructor last semester what questions were on the exam. Similarly, a manager might think nothing about taking home a few office supplies yet be highly concerned about the possible embezzlement of company funds.

These examples illustrate the final factor that affects a manager's ethical behaviour: the intensity of the ethical issue itself.[57] As Exhibit 5-7 shows, six characteristics determine issue intensity: greatness of harm, consensus of wrong, probability of harm, immediacy of consequences, proximity to victim(s), and concentration of effect.[58] These six factors determine how important an ethical issue is to an individual. According to these guidelines, the larger the number of people harmed, the more agreement that the action is wrong, the greater the likelihood that the action will cause harm, the more immediately that the consequences of the action will be felt, the closer the person feels to the victim(s), and the more concentrated the effect of the action on the victim(s), the greater the issue intensity. When an ethical issue is important—that is, the more intense it is—the more we should expect employees to behave ethically.

Exhibit 5-7

Determinants of Issue Intensity

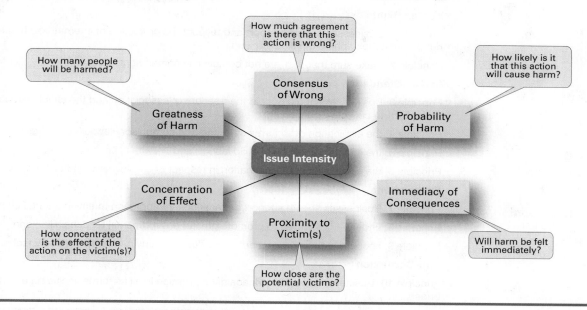

Ethics in an International Context

Are ethical standards universal? Hardly! Social and cultural differences between countries are important factors that determine ethical and unethical behaviour. For example, the manager of a Mexican firm bribes several high-ranking government officials in Mexico City to secure a profitable government contract. Such a practice would be seen as unethical, if not illegal, in Canada, but is standard business practice in Mexico.

Should Canadian companies operating in Saudi Arabia adhere to Canadian ethical standards, or should they follow local standards of acceptable behaviour? If Airbus (a European company) pays a "broker's fee" to a middleman to get a major contract with a Middle Eastern airline, should Montreal-based Bombardier be restricted from doing the same because such practices are considered improper in Canada?

In Canada and many other western countries, engaging in bribery to conduct business in one's home country is considered unethical and often illegal. Bribing foreign public officials is widespread, however. The US government found bribery in more than 400 competitions for international contracts between 1994 and 2001.[60] Another study found that some Asian governments were far more tolerant of corruption than others. Singapore, Japan, and Hong Kong scored relatively low on corruption (0.83, 2.5, and 3.77 out of 10, respectively), while Vietnam, Indonesia, India, the Philippines, and Thailand scored as the most corrupt of the 12 Asian countries surveyed.[61]

Another guide to being ethical in international business is the United Nations Global Compact, which is an initiative created by the United Nations outlining principles for doing business globally in the areas of human rights, labour, the environment, and anti-corruption (Exhibit 5-8). More than 8700 corporate participants and stakeholders from over 130 countries have committed to the UN Global Compact, making it the world's largest voluntary corporate citizenship initiative.[62] The goal of the UN Global Compact is a more sustainable and inclusive global economy. Organizations making this commitment do so because they believe that the world business community plays a significant role in improving economic and social conditions. In addition, the Organisation for Economic Co-operation and Development (OECD) has made fighting bribery and corruption in international business a high priority. The centrepiece of its efforts is the Anti-Bribery Convention (or set of rules and guidelines), which was the first global instrument to combat

datapoints[59]

29 percent of employees said they don't feel guilty calling in sick when they aren't.

22 percent of employees who reported misconduct say they experienced some form of retaliation.

13 percent of employees perceived pressure to compromise standards in order to do their jobs.

42 percent of companies are believed to have weak ethics cultures according to their employees.

45 percent of employees witnessed misconduct at work.

49 percent of employees said, if granted access to a confidential document accidently, they would look at it.

14 percent of employees in an employee engagement survey said their company's leaders are ethical and honest.

Exhibit 5-8

The Ten Principles of the United Nations Global Compact

Human Rights

Principle 1: Businesses should support and respect the protection of international human rights within their sphere of influence; and

Principle 2: make sure that they are not complicit in human rights abuses.

Labour Standards

Principle 3: Businesses should uphold the freedom of association and the effective recognition of the right to collective bargaining;

Principle 4: the elimination of all forms of forced and compulsory labour;

Principle 5: the effective abolition of child labour; and

Principle 6: the elimination of discrimination in respect of employment and occupation.

Environment

Principle 7: Businesses should support a precautionary approach to environmental challenges;

Principle 8: undertake initiatives to promote greater environmental responsibility; and

Principle 9: encourage the development and diffusion of environmentally friendly technologies.

Anti-Corruption

Principle 10: Businesses should work against corruption in all its forms, including extortion and bribery.

Source: United Nations Global Compact website, 2010 guidance documents on anti-corruption at http://www. unglobalcompact.org/ Issues/transparency_anticorruption/Anti-Corruption_Guidance_Material.html (accessed November 11, 2010).

corruption in cross-border business deals. To date, significant gains have been made in fighting corruption in the 38 countries that have ratified it.[63]

Canada's *Corruption of Foreign Public Officials Act* makes it a criminal offence for Canadians to participate in bribery when doing business internationally. In addition, the Organisation for Economic Development (OECD), of which Canada is a member, has committed to take concerted action against corruption. It is important for individual managers working in foreign cultures to recognize the various social, cultural, political, and legal influences on what is appropriate and acceptable behaviour.[64] And global organizations must clarify their ethical guidelines so that employees know what is expected of them while working in a foreign location, which adds another dimension to making ethical judgments.

Encouraging Ethical Behaviour

◄●─Simulate on MyManagementLab

Ethics in the Workplace

Managers can do a number of things if they are serious about reducing unethical behaviour in their organizations. They can seek to hire individuals with high ethical standards, establish codes of ethics and rules for decisions, lead by example, delineate job goals and undertake performance appraisals, provide ethics training, conduct independent social audits, and support individuals facing ethical dilemmas. Taken individually, these actions will probably not have much impact. But when all or most of them are implemented as part of a comprehensive ethics program, they have the potential to significantly improve an organization's ethical climate. The key term here, however, is *potential*. There are no guarantees that a well-designed ethics program will lead to the desired outcome. Sometimes corporate ethics programs can be little more than public relations gestures, having minimal influence on managers and employees. For instance, retailer Sears has a long history of encouraging ethical business practices and, in fact, has a corporate Office of Compliance and Ethics. However, the company's ethics programs did not stop managers from illegally trying to collect payments from bankrupt charge-account holders or from routinely deceiving automotive service centre customers in California into thinking they needed unnecessary repairs.

Employee Selection

Given that individuals are at different stages of moral development and possess different personal value systems and personalities, the selection process—interviews, tests, background checks, and so forth—could be used to eliminate ethically questionable applicants. The selection process should be viewed as an opportunity to learn about an individual's level of moral development, personal values, ego strength, and locus of control.[65] But it isn't easy! Even under the best circumstances, individuals with questionable standards of right and wrong will be hired. However, this should not be a problem if other ethics controls are in place.

Codes of Ethics and Rules for Decisions

Toronto-based Royal Bank of Canada has had a corporate code of conduct for more than 25 years. Christina Donely, the bank's senior adviser on employee relations and policy governance, says that the code "focuses on outlining behaviours that support honesty and integrity . . . and covers environmental [and] social issues."[66] However, that is not the way it is in all organizations. The Canadian Securities Administrators put into effect best corporate governance practices in March 2004 to crack down on business wrongdoing in publicly traded companies.[67] As well, the securities regulators of the 10 provinces and 3 territories have proposed that all public companies adopt written codes of ethics and conduct or explain why they do not have one.[68] But these proposals carry no enforcement requirements or mechanisms.

Ambiguity about what is and is not ethical can be a problem for employees. A **code of ethics**, a formal statement of an organization's primary values and the ethical rules it expects its employees to follow, is a popular choice for reducing that ambiguity. About 60 percent of Canada's 650 largest corporations have some sort of ethics code. Codes of ethics are also becoming more popular globally. A survey of S&P 500 companies found that 92 percent have formally stated ethics standards and codes of ethics.[69]

What should a code of ethics look like? It's been suggested that codes should be specific enough to show employees the spirit in which they are supposed to do things yet loose enough to allow for freedom of judgment.[70] A survey of Canadian companies' codes of ethics found that a code's perceived success was determined by 18 factors, such as whether the code designated an ombudsperson, whether new employees were informed of the code, and whether the code was available to customers and the public.[71]

How well do codes of ethics work? In reality, they are not always effective in encouraging ethical behaviour in organizations. While no comparable Canadian data are available, a survey of employees in US businesses with ethics codes found that 41 percent of those surveyed had observed misconduct. Though this was a decrease from 45 percent in 2011, the same study found that only 63 percent of observed violations were reported, and that in more than one-fifth of cases, whistle-blowers faced retaliation for reporting.[72] The 2009 UN Global Compact report *Reporting Guidance on the 10th Principle Against Corruption* provides businesses and organizations with a practical guideline for whistle-blowing effectively, as public reporting sends a strong signal to employees, investors, and consumers that a company is serious about ethical business practices.[73] Vancouver public employees were concerned enough about whistle-blower protection that it was one of the major stumbling blocks in reaching an agreement for a new collective agreement in summer 2007, leading to a 12-week strike.

Does this mean that codes of ethics shouldn't be developed? No. However, in doing so, managers should use these suggestions:[74]

1. Organizational leaders should model appropriate behaviour and reward those who act ethically.

2. All managers should continually reaffirm the importance of the ethics code and consistently discipline those who break it.

3. The organization's stakeholders (employees, customers, and so forth) should be considered as an ethics code is developed or improved.

code of ethics A formal statement of an organization's primary values and the ethical rules it expects its employees to follow.

4. Managers should communicate and reinforce the ethics code regularly.

5. Managers should use the five-step process (Exhibit 5-8) to guide employees when faced with ethical dilemmas.

Ethical Leadership

Doing business ethically requires a commitment from top managers. Why? Because it's the top managers who uphold the shared values and set the cultural tone. They are role models in terms of both words and actions, although what they *do* is far more important than what they *say*. If top managers, for example, take company resources for their personal use, inflate their expense accounts, or give favoured treatment to friends, they imply that such behaviour is acceptable for all employees. (To learn more about how trust works, see *the skills exercise Building Trust* on pages 133–134.)

Top managers also set the cultural tone by their reward and punishment practices. The choices of who and what are rewarded with pay increases and promotions send a strong signal to employees. As we said earlier, when an employee is rewarded for achieving impressive results in an ethically questionable manner, it indicates to others that those ways are acceptable. When wrongdoing is uncovered, managers who want to emphasize their commitment to doing business ethically must punish the offender and publicize the fact by making the outcome visible to everyone in the organization. This practice sends a message that doing wrong has a price and it's not in employees' best interests to act unethically!

A recent review of survey data from the *National Post Business Magazine* found that of the large Canadian companies with codes of ethics, 98 percent indicated that there were consequences for breaching their codes. Of those respondents, 76.7 percent had their board of directors involved with the development of the code and 91.9 percent saw their ethics codes as having a positive impact on organizational policies.[75]

Job Goals and Performance Appraisal

Employees in three Internal Revenue Service offices (the American equivalent of the Canada Revenue Agency) were found in the washrooms flushing tax returns and other related documents down the toilets. When questioned, they openly admitted doing it but offered an interesting explanation for their behaviour. The employees' supervisors had been putting increasing pressure on them to complete more work in less time. If the piles of tax returns were not processed and moved off their desks more quickly, they were told, their performance reviews and salary raises would be adversely affected. Frustrated by few resources and an overworked computer system, the employees decided to "flush away" the paperwork on their desks. Although these employees knew what they did was wrong, it illustrates the impact of unrealistic goals and performance appraisals on behaviour.[76]

Under the stress of unrealistic job goals, otherwise ethical employees may feel they have no choice but to do whatever is necessary to meet those goals. Exhibit 5-9 provides

Exhibit 5-9

A Process for Addressing Ethical Dilemmas

Step 1: What is the **ethical dilemma**?

Step 2: Who are the **affected stakeholders**?

Step 3: Which **personal**, **organizational**, and **external factors** are important in this decision?

Step 4: What are possible **alternatives**?

Step 5: What is my **decision** and how will I act on it?

Ethical leadership starts with being a good role model. When Michael McCain, CEO of Maple Leaf Foods, learned of a listeriosis outbreak in one of the company's plants, he immediately took personal and organizational responsibility for the problem rather than trying to deflect the responsibility.

Toronto Star/Aaron Harris/CP Images

a process for thinking through ethical dilemmas. Also, goal achievement is usually a key issue in performance appraisal. If performance appraisals focus only on economic goals, ends will begin to justify means. To encourage ethical behaviour, both ends *and* means should be evaluated. For example, a manager's annual review of employees might include a point-by-point evaluation of how their decisions measured up against the company's code of ethics as well as how well goals were met.

Ethics Training

More and more organizations are setting up seminars, workshops, and similar ethics training programs to encourage ethical behaviour. A 2002 ethics survey by KPMG found that 71 percent of Canadian corporations provided ethics training (up from 21 percent in 1997), although most provided fewer than eight hours per year.[77] But these training programs are not without controversy. The primary debate is whether you can actually teach ethics. Critics, for instance, stress that the effort is pointless because people establish their individual value systems when they are young. Proponents, however, note that several studies have found that values can be learned after early childhood. In addition, they cite evidence that shows that teaching ethical problem solving can make an actual difference in ethical behaviours;[78] that training has increased individuals' level of moral development;[79] and that, if it does nothing else, ethics training increases awareness of ethical issues in business.[80]

Ethics training sessions can provide a number of benefits.[81] They reinforce the organization's standards of conduct. They are a reminder that top managers want employees to consider ethical issues in making decisions. They clarify what practices are and are not acceptable. Finally, when employees discuss common concerns among themselves, they get reassurance that they are not alone in facing ethical dilemmas, which can strengthen their confidence when they have to take unpopular but ethically correct stances.

Independent Social Audits

The fear of being caught can be an important deterrent to unethical behaviour. Independent social audits, which evaluate decisions and management practices in terms of the organization's code of ethics, increase that likelihood. Such audits can be regular

Chief Superintendent Fraser Macaulay was one of several RCMP officers who complained to Giuliano Zaccardelli, then RCMP commissioner, about how problems with the RCMP's pension and insurance plans were investigated. Consistent with the way many whistle-blowers are treated, Zaccardelli did not follow up with an investigation, and Macaulay was told that he was "on an island by [him]self."

Reprinted with permission of the CBC.

evaluations or they can occur randomly with no prior announcement. An effective ethics program probably needs both. To maintain integrity, auditors should be responsible to the company's board of directors and present their findings directly to the board. This arrangement gives the auditors clout and lessens the opportunity for retaliation from those being audited. Because in the United States the Sarbanes-Oxley Act holds businesses to more rigorous standards of financial disclosure and corporate governance, more organizations are finding the idea of independent social audits appealing. As the publisher of *Business Ethics* magazine stated, "The debate has shifted from *whether* to be ethical to *how* to be ethical."[82]

Formal Protective Mechanisms

Our last recommendation is for organizations to provide formal mechanisms to protect employees who face ethical dilemmas so that they can do what is right without fear of reprimand. An organization might designate ethics counsellors. When employees face an ethics dilemma, they could go to these advisers for guidance. As a sounding board, the ethics counsellor would let employees openly state their ethics problem, the problem's cause, and their own options. After the options are clear, the adviser might take on the role of advocate who champions the ethically "right" alternatives. Other organizations have appointed ethics officers who design, direct, and modify the organization's ethics programs as needed.

It is important that managers assure employees who raise ethical concerns or issues to others inside or outside the organization that they will face no personal or career risks. These individuals, often called **whistle-blowers**, can be a key part of any company's ethics program because they are willing to step forward and expose unethical behaviour, no matter what the cost, professional or personal. Former prime minister Paul Martin tabled the Public Servants Disclosure Protection Act in March 2004 to protect those who expose government wrongdoings and financial mismanagement. Many critics complained that the act does not go far enough to protect whistle-blowers and hoped Parliament would have tabled a tougher bill.

whistle-blowers Individuals who raise ethical concerns or issues to others inside or outside the organization.

CHAPTER 5

SUMMARY AND IMPLICATIONS

1. Understand what it means to be a socially responsible manager. We define corporate social responsibility as a business's obligation, beyond that required by law and economics, to pursue long-term goals that are good for society. Not everyone would agree that businesses have any responsibility to society. The classical view says that management's only responsibility is to maximize profits; shareholders, or owners, are the only legitimate concern. The socio-economic view says that management's responsibility goes beyond maximizing profits; any group affected by the organization's decisions and actions—that is, its stakeholders—are also its concern.

▶ ▶ ▶ Interface takes a socio-economic view toward corporate social responsibility. The company emphasizes being a good corporate citizen and helping to develop sustainable practices among its employees, suppliers, and competitors.

2. Describe how managing responsibly contributes to organizational performance. Some evidence suggests that socially responsible firms perform better, and they are certainly appreciated by many members of society. There is little evidence to say that a company's social actions hurt its long-term economic performance when those actions align with the goals of the company's stakeholders. Given political and societal pressures on business to be socially involved, managers would be wise to take social goals into consideration as they plan, organize, lead, and control.

▶ ▶ ▶ Interface has been able to be a successful company, even as it supports a socially responsible approach to doing business. "Our costs are down, our profits are up, and our products are the best they've ever been. It has rewarded us with more positive visibility and goodwill among our customers than the slickest, most expensive advertising or marketing campaign could possibly have generated. And a strong environmental ethic has no equal for attracting and motivating good people, galvanizing them around a shared higher purpose, and giving them a powerful reason to join and stay."[83]

3. Identify sustainable management practices. One model of environmental responsibility uses the phrase *shades of green* to describe the different approaches that organizations take to becoming environmentally responsible. Organizations that follow a *legal* (or *light green*) *approach* simply do what is required legally. Organizations that follow a *market approach* respond to the environmental preferences of their customers. Organizations that follow a *stakeholder approach* work to meet the environmental demands of multiple stakeholders such as employees, suppliers, and the community. Organizations that follow an *activist* (also called a *dark green*) *approach* look for ways to respect and preserve the earth and its natural resources.

▶ ▶ ▶ Interface's sustainable practices include a commitment to eliminate all forms of waste in every area of business, reduce and eliminate greenhouse gases, and operate facilities with renewable energy sources. Interface's goal is to ensure that, by 2020, all fuels and electricity to operate manufacturing, sales, and office facilities will be from renewable sources. Products and processes have been redesigned to reduce and simplify the amount of resources used, so that material "waste" is remanufactured into new resources, providing technical "nutrients" for the next cycle of production.

4. Understand the principles of values-based management. An organization's values reflect what it stands for and what it believes in. Thus, an organization's values are reflected in the decisions and actions of employees. Shared values form an organization's culture and serve to (a) guide managers' decisions and actions, (b) shape employee behaviour, (c) influence marketing efforts, and (d) build team spirit.

▶ ▶ ▶ Interface not only talks the talk, it walks the walk. The corporate website provides a rich history of the journey up "Mount Sustainability" and shares the details of the journey with employees, stakeholders, suppliers, and competitors.[84]

5. Discuss current ethics issues. The behaviour of managers is the single most important influence on an individual's decision to act ethically or unethically. Ethics refers to rules and principles that define right and wrong behaviour. Ethical behaviour is encouraged (or discouraged) through organizational culture. A strong culture that supports ethical standards will have a powerful and positive influence on managers and employees. To improve ethical behaviour, managers can hire individuals with high ethical standards, design and implement a code of ethics, lead by example, delineate job goals and undertake performance appraisals, provide ethics training, perform independent social audits, and provide formal protective mechanisms for employees who face ethical dilemmas.

▶ ▶ ▶ Interface, like many companies, has an ethics policy to help guide the decisions and actions of its employees. In addition, Interface has made a commitment to support communities that are committed to the shared journey to sustainability.[85]

MyManagementLab Study, practise, and explore real management situations with these helpful resources:
- **Interactive Lesson Presentations:** Work through interactive presentations and assessments to test your knowledge of management concepts.
- **PIA (Personal Inventory Assessments):** Enhance your ability to connect with key concepts through these engaging, self-reflection assessments.
- **Study Plan:** Check your understanding of chapter concepts with self-study quizzes.
- **Simulations:** Practise decision-making in simulated management environments.

P I A PERSONAL INVENTORY ASSESSMENT

REVIEW AND DISCUSSION QUESTIONS

1. Differentiate among social obligation, social responsiveness, and social responsibility.

2. What does social responsibility mean to you personally? Do *you* think business organizations should be socially responsible? Explain.

3. What factors influence whether a person behaves ethically or unethically? Explain all relevant factors.

4. Do you think values-based management is just a "do-gooder" ploy? Explain your answer.

5. Internet file-sharing programs are popular among college students. These programs work by allowing non-organizational users to access any local network where desired files are located. Because these types of file-sharing programs tend to clog bandwidth, local users'

ability to access and use a local network is reduced. What ethical and social responsibilities does a university have in this situation? To whom do they have a responsibility? What guidelines might you suggest for university decision makers?

6. What are some problems that could be associated with employee whistle-blowing for (a) the whistle-blower and (b) the organization?

7. Describe the characteristics and behaviours of someone you consider to be an ethical person. How could the types of decisions and actions this person engages in be encouraged in a workplace?

8. Explain the ethical and social responsibility issues facing managers today.

ETHICS DILEMMA

Workers' rights. It's not something we often think about when we're purchasing the latest tech gadget. However, look at this list of some issues that investigations have

uncovered: work shifts lasting up to 60 hours; factory explosion killing numerous workers that resulted from a build-up of combustible dust; repetitive motion injuries that are so bad workers lose the use of their hands. "According to recent press reports, that's what work is like for assembly workers in China who build Apple's iPhones, iPads, and iPods." In other locations where workers are assembling products for other tech companies, factory workers have committed suicide because of the pressure and stress.[86] Whose responsibility is it to ensure that workplaces are safe, especially when work is outsourced? "It's a tricky dance between first-world brands and third-world production." What do you think this statement means? Should ethical/corporate responsibility issues be part of the international strategy decision-making process? Why or why not?

SKILLS EXERCISE

Building Trust—About the Skill

When individuals evaluate companies for their social responsibility policies, trust plays an important role in how the company is viewed. Trust is also important in the manager's relationships with his or her employees. Given the importance of trust, managers should actively seek to foster it within their work group.

Steps in Developing the Skill

You can be more effective at building trust among your employees if you use the following eight suggestions:[87]

1. **Practise openness.** Mistrust comes as much from what people don't know as from what they do. Being open with employees leads to trust. Keep people informed. Make clear the criteria you use in making decisions. Explain the rationale for your decisions. Be forthright and candid about problems. Fully disclose all relevant information.

2. **Be fair.** Before making decisions or taking actions, consider how others will perceive them in terms of objectivity and fairness. Give credit where credit is due. Be objective and impartial in performance appraisals. Pay attention to equity perceptions in distributing rewards.

3. **Speak your feelings.** Managers who convey only hard facts come across as cold, distant, and unfeeling. When you share your feelings, others will see that you are real and human. They will know you for who you are, and their respect for you is likely to increase.

4. **Tell the truth.** Being trustworthy means being credible. If honesty is critical to credibility, then you must be perceived as someone who tells the truth. Employees are more tolerant of hearing something "they don't want to hear" than of finding out that their manager lied to them.

5. **Be consistent.** People want predictability. Mistrust comes from not knowing what to expect. Take the time to think about your values and beliefs and let those values and beliefs consistently guide your decisions. When you know what is important to you, your actions will follow, and you will project a consistency that earns people's trust.

6. **Fulfill your promises.** Trust requires that people believe that you are dependable. You need to ensure that you keep your word. Promises made must be promises kept.

7. **Maintain confidences.** You trust those whom you believe to be discreet and those on whom you can rely. If people open up to you and make themselves vulnerable by telling you something in confidence, they need to feel assured you will not discuss it with others or betray that confidence. If people perceive you as someone who leaks personal confidences or someone who cannot be depended on, you have lost their trust.

8. **Demonstrate competence.** Develop the admiration and respect of others by demonstrating technical and professional ability. Pay particular attention to developing and displaying your communication, negotiation, and other interpersonal skills.

Practising the Skill

Read the following scenario. Write some notes about how you would handle the situation described. Bear in mind that the employees feel that they have been betrayed because the vacation that they had come to expect has been taken away from them. In determining what to do, be sure to refer to the eight suggestions for building trust.

Scenario

Donna Romines is the shipping department manager at Tastefully Tempting, a gourmet candy company based in New Brunswick. Orders for the company's candy come from around the world. Your six-member team processes these orders. Needless to say, the two months before Christmas are quite hectic. Everybody counts the days until December 24, when the phones finally stop ringing off the wall, at least for a few days.

When the company was first founded five years ago, after the holiday rush the owners would shut down Tastefully Tempting for two weeks after Christmas. However, as the business has grown and moved into internet sales, that practice has become too costly. There is too much business to be able to afford that luxury. The rush for Valentine's Day starts as orders pour in the week after Christmas. Although the two-week post-holiday company-wide shutdown was phased out formally last year, some departments found it difficult to get employees to gear up once again after the Christmas break. The employees who came to work after Christmas accomplished little. This year, though, things have got to change. You know that the cultural "tradition" will not be easy to overcome, but your shipping team needs to be ready to tackle the orders that have piled up. How will you handle the situation?

Reinforcing the Skill

The following activities will help you practise and reinforce the skills associated with building trust:

1. Keep a one-week log describing ways that your daily decisions and actions encouraged people to trust you or

to not trust you. What things did you do that led to trust? What things did you do that may have led to distrust? How could you have changed your behaviour so that the situations of distrust could have been situations of trust?

2. Review recent issues of a business periodical (for example, *BusinessWeek, Fortune, Forbes, Fast Company, IndustryWeek,* or the *The Wall Street Journal*) for articles where trust (or lack of trust) may have played a role. Find two articles and describe the situation. Explain how the person(s) involved might have used skills in developing trust to handle the situation.

WORKING TOGETHER: TEAM EXERCISE

Ethical Guidelines and Corporate Social Responsibility

In an effort to be (or at least appear to be) socially responsible, many organizations donate money to philanthropic and charitable causes. In addition, many organizations ask their employees to make individual donations to these causes. Suppose you're the manager of a work team, and you know that several of your employees can't afford to pledge money right now because of personal or financial problems. You've also been told by your supervisor that the CEO has been known to check the list of individual contributors to see

who is and is not "supporting these very important causes." Working together in a small group of three or four, answer the following questions:

- How would you handle this situation?
- What ethical guidelines might you suggest for individual and organizational contributions in such a situation?
- Create a company policy statement that expresses your ethical guidelines.

LEARNING TO BE A MANAGER

- Find five different examples of organizational codes of ethics. Using Exhibit 5-7, describe what determinants of issue intensity each contains. Compare and contrast the examples.
- Using the examples of codes of ethics you found, create what you feel would be an appropriate and effective organizational code of ethics. In addition, create your own *personal code of ethics* you can use as a guide to ethical dilemmas.
- Take advantage of volunteer opportunities. Be sure to include these on your résumé. If possible, try to do things in these volunteer positions that will improve your managerial skills in planning, organizing, leading, or controlling.
- Go to the Global Reporting Initiative Web site (www.globalreporting.org) and choose three businesses from the list that have filed reports. Look at those reports and describe/evaluate what's in them. In addition, identify the stakeholders that might be affected and how they might be affected by the company's actions.
- Make a list of what green management things your school is doing. If you're working, make a list of what

green management things your employer is doing. Do some research on being green. Are there additional things your school or employer could be doing? Write a report to each, describing any suggestions. (Look for ways you could use these suggestions to be more "green" in your personal life.)

- Over the course of two weeks, see what ethical "dilemmas" you observe. These could be ones you face personally or they could be ones that others (friends, colleagues, other students talking in the hallway or before class, and so forth) face. Write these dilemmas down and think about what you might do if faced with that dilemma.
- Interview two different managers about how they encourage their employees to be ethical. Write down their comments and discuss how these ideas might help you be a better manager.
- If you have the opportunity, take a class on business or managerial ethics or on social responsibility—often called business and society—or both. Not only will this look good on your résumé, it could help you personally grapple with some of the tough issues managers face in being ethical and responsible.

CASE APPLICATION 1

The Responsible Organization

Lynn Patterson is Director of Corporate Responsibility for the Royal Bank of Canada (RBC), a major Canadian corporation that has embraced "responsibility" as a core value within the framework of corporate citizenship. RBC has more than 15 million clients in 38 countries and employs over 70 000 people globally.[88]

RBC has a fundamental belief that corporate responsibility isn't only about how a company spends its money—it's also about how a company makes its money. According to the company's website, "Our goal is to be a responsible bank, acting with integrity every day and charting a stable course so that we are there for our clients, shareholders, employees and communities, today and tomorrow."

RBC's 2009 Corporate Responsibility Report and Public Accountability Statement identifies the four key elements of its corporate responsibility strategy: (1) generate a positive economic impact, (2) create a workplace of choice, (3) support community causes, and (4) promote environmental sustainability.

Lynn Patterson has a background in communications and is the public face for the bank's responsibility policy for consumers, investors, the press, and the public at large. In her presentations to shareholders and the public, Patterson points out that in 2000, RBC was the first Canadian bank to be named to the Dow Jones Sustainability Index. In 2003, RBC was the first Canadian bank to adopt the equator principles, which assess the social and environmental impacts of large-scale project finance deals, and in 2007, it was the only Canadian bank to be named one of the Global 100 Most Sustainable Corporations in the World.

DISCUSSION QUESTIONS

1. Is RBC a responsible organization?
2. What is your best guess as to the initial reaction to this change in policy from clients, branch managers, the investment community, and activists?
3. Identify both the business case for acting responsibly and the ethical case for acting responsibly.

CASE APPLICATION 2

A Better Tomorrow

It's an incredibly simple but potentially world-changing idea.[89] For each pair of shoes sold, a pair is donated to a child in need. That's the business model followed by TOMS Shoes. During a visit to Argentina in 2006 as a contestant on the CBS reality show *The Amazing Race,* Blake Mycoskie, founder of TOMS, "saw lots of kids with no shoes who were suffering from injuries to their feet." Just think what it would be like to be barefoot, not by choice, but from lack of availability and ability to own a pair. He was so moved by the experience that he wanted to do something. That something is what TOMS does now by blending charity with commerce. (The name TOMS is actually short for "Shoes for a better tomorrow" which eventually became "Tomorrow's Shoes" which then became "Toms.") And a better tomorrow is what Blake wanted to provide to shoeless children around the world. Those shoe donations have been central to the success of the TOMS brand, which is popular among tweens, teens, and twenty-somethings. And TOMS has helped provide more than 1 million shoes to kids in need in the United States and abroad since its founding. Hoping to build on this success, the company recently launched its second one-for-one product—an

eyewear line whose sales will help provide improved vision to those in need.

Building on his success of giving children a better tomorrow by providing them with a pair of shoes, TOMS founder Blake Mycoskie is giving more people a better tomorrow through a new venture that provides prescription eyeglasses, sight-saving surgery, and other medical treatment to people throughout the world who suffer from impaired vision.

DISCUSSION QUESTIONS

1. How can TOMS balance being socially responsible *and* being focused on profits?
2. Would you describe the TOMS approach as social obligation, social responsiveness, or social responsibility? Explain.
3. It's time to think like a manager. TOMS' one-for-one approach is a wonderful idea, but what would be involved with making it work?
4. Do you think consumers are drawn to products with a charitable connection? Why or why not?

Innovation and Adaptability

Change is a constant for organizations and thus for managers. An organization's ability to foster a culture of innovation and adaptability is often closely tied to an organization's change efforts; thus, managers must know how to manage change as well. Because change can't be eliminated, managers must learn not only how to manage change successfully but also how to promote innovation and adaptability within their organizations. The most successful organizations are more flexible, more efficient, and more adaptable. After reading and studying this chapter, you will achieve the following learning outcomes.

▶ ▶ ▶ At BlackBerry Limited, formerly known as Research In Motion (RIM), it was claimed that "innovation knows no boundaries or borders."[1] The company is the designer and manufacturer of the award-winning BlackBerry smartphone, used by millions of people around the world. It has also created applications to provide mobile access to email, applications, media, and the internet through the BlackBerry.

The company was founded in 1984 in Waterloo, Ontario, by 23-year-old Michael Lazaridis and two friends, backed by funds from friends and family. Lazaridis had recently dropped out of the University of Waterloo, where he had been studying electrical engineering. The company's first contract came from General Motors. Moving from contract to contract, the company reached annual sales of $1 million and 12 employees by 1990. Contracts from Ericsson and GE Mobile followed. By 1992 Lazaridis realized that he was better at engineering than running the company, and he hired Jim Balsillie, a chartered accountant and Harvard graduate with an MBA, as co-CEO. RIM's sales soared to $21 million by 1998, with profits of $400 000. In February 1999, the company launched the BlackBerry, marking the beginning of RIM's huge growth in the information and communication technologies market. In subsequent years the company thrived under the combined leadership of Michael Lazaridis and Jim Balsillie and became the world's biggest supplier of mobile devices.

THE CANADIAN PRESS/Nathan Denette

When iPhone and Android phones were released in the late 2000s, Blackberry's fortunes changed. On Sunday January 22, 2012, Jim Balsillie and Mike Lazaridis, the company's co-chief executives, stepped aside and turned the reins over to Thorsten Heins, previously one of two chief operating officers.[2] For months, investors had clamoured for fresh leadership or a sale of the company as it lost market share to Apple's iPhone and Google's Android brands amid operational blunders and a tumbling share price. In 2011, RIM's stock lost about three-quarters of its value, and finally on September 23, 2013, the company was sold for $4.7 billion at roughly $9 US per share.

Simulate on **MyManagementLab**

Market Research Matters

The Context of Innovation and Adaptability

Big companies and small businesses, universities and colleges, and governments at all levels are being forced to significantly change the way they do things. Although change has always been a part of the manager's job, it has become even more important in recent years. In this chapter, we describe why change is important and how managers can manage change and build a culture of innovation and adaptability. Since change is often closely tied to an organization's innovation efforts, we also discuss ways in which managers can stimulate innovation and increase their organization's adaptability. More importantly, understanding why innovation is critical in today's organizations contributes to our understanding of why it is important to build adaptive organizations, as defined in Chapter 1. We then conclude by looking at some current issues in stimulating innovation and adaptability.

1 Understand the importance of building an innovative and adaptable organization.

Why Build an Adaptable Organization?

When Jim Balsillie and Mike Lazaridis introduced the BlackBerry, they created a disruptive technology that changed the rules of the game for everybody. For years, Blackberry helped give birth to the mobile phone industry. Through 2004, things were going well for the company, but then it started to lose its competitive edge.

BlackBerry delayed its response to competition from Apple and Google, and faced a big challenge. In 2007, Google was worth $160 billion (US) on the stock market while BlackBerry's shares were worth only $37 billion (US). Moreover, BlackBerry was facing a hostile takeover from Microsoft in early 2008 for $44.6 billion (US) that was subsequently rejected. In 2011, BlackBerry had market value of $22.4 billion (US) but by September 23, 2013, the company was acquired for $4.7 billion by a consortium led by Fairfax Financial.[3]

BlackBerry began as a dominant player in the smartphone market for both business and government usage, with 43% US market share in 2010. However, the company lost market share in recent years by not recognizing and adapting to the disruptive innovation introduced in the market by Apple's iPhone and Google's Android brands.

As we discussed in Chapter 1, successful organizations are not only efficient and effective. They are adaptable rather than simply flexible. (Recall that being flexible means reacting to events, while being adaptable means being proactive.) They create a culture within their organizations that enables them to continuously recognize new problems, identify the potential impact of these problems, and offer solutions in advance of the impacts on their organizations or to their customers. They create a culture of adaptability through the development of a set of skills and processes that allows their organization to be proactive rather than just reactive. Both external and internal changes require continuous innovation and adaptability.

Innovation

"Now, economic progress depends more than ever on innovation. And the potential for technology innovation to improve lives has never been greater."[4]

—Bill Gates, co-founder of Microsoft

When Apple came up with the Mac, IBM was spending at least 100 times more on R&D. According to Steve Jobs, co-founder of Apple, "It's not about money. It's about the people you have, how you're led, and how much you get it."[5]

In June 2010 the International Task Force on Business Schools and Innovation released its report *Business Schools on an Innovation Mission*. The report emphasized that innovation is about creating economic and social prosperity, and leadership and management are as essential to the process as science and technology. Innovation was seen as the bridge that connects business schools to a broader social purpose. The report observed that management innovation is "about the skills managers have in applying knowledge, judgment, and the ability to adapt and fashion new tools to solve problems."[6]

"Nothing is more risky than not innovating."[7] Innovation means doing things differently, exploring new territory, and taking risks. Innovation isn't just for high-tech and technologically advanced organizations. In today's world, organizational managers—at all levels and in all areas—need to encourage their employees to be on the lookout for new ideas and new approaches, not just in the products or services the organization provides, but in everything that is done. We examine the topic of building adaptable organizations and the role of innovation in accomplishing this objective in future chapters, where we discuss the core management competencies of planning, organizing, and leading.

Adaptability

adaptability Organizing to anticipate new problems, trends, and opportunities.

wicked problem A problem that is impossible to solve because each attempt to create a solution changes the understanding of the problem.

It is becoming increasingly important for managers to build a capacity for **adaptability** within their organizations in light of today's **wicked problems**. The term *wicked problem* was first used in social planning in the 1960s to describe one that is impossible to solve because each attempt to create a solution changes the understanding of the problem.[8] Wicked problems are a continuing work in progress: They cannot be solved step by step because they are complex, and each possible solution may create a new problem. The world faces many wicked problems today, including climate change, poverty, pandemics, the fallout from the 2008 global financial crisis, terrorism, and environmental disasters like the 2010 massive oil spill in the Gulf of Mexico. All of these have an impact on how organizations do their business. A *Harvard Business Review* article suggests that many management strategy issues also are wicked problems as they have no easy solution.[9] How can these seemingly unsolvable problems be addressed, and what will be the impact on future management practice?

Forces for Change

❷ Describe the forces that create the need for change, innovation, and adaptability.

▶ ▶ ▶ At Blackberry Limited, the dedication to both applied and basic research helped propel the company to the global stage.

The company had to plan for a future that was largely unknown and in many ways unpredictable. The design and structure of the organization had to support its ability to be adaptable. At the same time, recruiting and retaining employees who would thrive in such an environment was core to Blackberry's success. It was vital to build a corporate culture that embraced change and cherished innovation and adaptability as core organizational values.

Think About It

What role did innovation played in Blackberry Limited's success? What role did adaptability played in Blackberry Limited's success? Why is it important for an organization such as Blackberry to recruit managers who anticipate change or learn and adapt to changes in a global environment?

If it were not for change, the manager's job would be relatively easy. Planning would be simple because tomorrow would be no different from today. The issue of effective organizational design would also be solved because the environment would be free from uncertainty and there would be no need to adapt. Similarly, decision making would be dramatically streamlined because the outcome of each alternative could be predicted with almost certain accuracy. It would certainly simplify the manager's job if, for example, competitors did not introduce new products or services, if customers did not demand new and improved products, if government regulations were never modified, or if employees' needs never changed. But that is not the way it is. Change is an organizational reality, and managing change is an integral part of every manager's job. Managers who make no attempt to anticipate change or learn and adapt to changes in the global environment end up reacting rather than innovating; their organizations often become uncompetitive and fail. In Chapter 2, we pointed out the external and internal forces that constrain managers. These same forces also bring about the need for change. Let's briefly look at these forces in the context of innovation and adaptability.

External Forces

The external forces that create the need for change, innovation, and adaptability come from various sources. In recent years, the *marketplace* has affected firms such as Blackberry as competition from Apple, Samsung, Google, and Microsoft has intensified. These companies constantly adapt to changing consumer desires as they develop new mobile devices and applications.

Government laws and regulations are a frequent impetus for change. For example, the Canadian Securities Administrators rules, which came into effect in March 2004, require Canadian companies to change the way they disclose financial information and to carry out corporate governance.

Technology also creates the need for change. For example, technological improvements in diagnostic equipment have created significant economies of scale for hospitals. Assembly-line technology in other industries is changing dramatically as organizations replace human labour with robots. Technological change from analogue to digital recording has meant the shift from records and film to digital media. In just 10 years, DVD players went from the test stage to virtually eliminating the videotape rental market. The companies that produced videotapes and the companies that rented them had to develop new strategies or go out of business in the face of companies like Netflix. Netflix began as a subscription-based digital distribution service in 1999 and grew to more than 10 million subscribers by 2009. By April 2013, Netflix became a "streaming TV network service" competing with cable and network television with 44 million subscribers worldwide.[10]

One of the biggest challenges facing both large and small companies and organizations today is a faster pace of technological change. To face the uncertainties resulting from technological change, it is important that companies be nimble, build a culture of innovation, recognize the impact of new technologies, and have the foresight incorporate appropriate innovation in advance of negative impacts resulting from the technological change. In a market of economic uncertainty, successful companies are changing their business strategies in order to adapt for success.

Companies and organizations must deal with the demands of a rapidly changing market. As a result, companies face challenges during their business growth cycle and must tailor comprehensive solutions.

Profound changes taking place in the Chinese economy are creating labour shortages at hundreds of factories, as seen in the many public job postings at this location in Qingdao, China. Companies around the world must now anticipate that wages in China will go up as the middle class continues to grow, which will have an impact on the price of manufacturing goods. Some international companies are already adapting and are considering proactive solutions, including moving to lower-wage countries like Vietnam.

Imaginechina/AP Photos

The convergence of technology and communications is profoundly changing the way business is conducted. For example, a retailer cannot afford not to consider the ways that mobile technologies are changing the how, when, and what of selling. According to Deloitte research, by 2016, smartphones, used as part of a shopping experience, could impact 17–21 percent of retail sales in North America, representing $620 billion to $750 billion. If retail stores are not preparing for that today, they are already behind the curve.[11]

The fluctuation in *labour markets* also forces managers to change. Organizations that need certain kinds of employees must change their human resource management activities to attract and retain skilled employees in the areas of greatest need. For instance, health care organizations facing severe nursing shortages have had to change the way they schedule work hours.

Economic changes, of course, affect almost all organizations. For instance, global recessionary pressures force organizations to become more cost efficient. But even in a strong economy, uncertainties about interest rates, federal budget deficits, and currency exchange rates create conditions that may force organizations to change.

Internal Forces

In addition to the external forces just described, internal forces also create the need for change, innovation, and adaptability. These internal forces tend to originate primarily from the internal operations of the organization or from the impact of external changes.

A redefinition or modification of an organization's *strategy* often introduces a host of changes. For instance, when Steve Bennett took over as CEO of Intuit (Quicken, QuickBooks, and QuickTax are its best-known products), the company was losing money. By orchestrating a series of well-planned and dramatic strategic changes, he was able to build a culture of innovation and adaptability which turned Intuit into a profitable company with extremely committed employees.

Two Views of the Change Process

3 Compare and contrast views of the change process.

▶ ▶ ▶ BlackBerry Limited faced an uncertain and dynamic environment after years of dominating the smart phone industry. BlackBerry operated in an industry that is increasingly defined by rapid technology, information, ideas, and knowledge, and therefore the "white-water rapids" metaphor discussed in this section helps to explain why the company started to lose its competitive edge from 2004 onward.

Think About It

Is change a constant process, or can organizations take breaks from worrying about change, as BlackBerry seems to have done in the past few years? How does innovation and adaptability happen in organizations?

We can use two very different metaphors to describe the change process.[12] One metaphor envisions the organization as a large ship crossing calm waters. The ship's captain and crew know exactly where they are going because they have made the trip many times before. Change comes in the form of an occasional storm, a brief distraction in an otherwise calm and predictable trip. In the other metaphor, the organization is seen as a small raft navigating a raging river with uninterrupted white-water rapids. Aboard the raft are half a dozen people who have never worked together before, who are totally unfamiliar with the river, who are unsure of their eventual destination, and who, as if things were not bad enough, are travelling at night. In the white-water rapids metaphor, change is an expected and natural state, and managing change is a continuous process. These two metaphors present very different approaches to understanding and responding to change. Let's take a closer look at each one.

The Calm Waters Metaphor

Up until the late 1980s, the calm waters metaphor pretty much described the situation that managers faced. It's best illustrated by Kurt Lewin's three-step description of the change process.[13] (See Exhibit 6-1.)

According to Lewin, successful change can be planned and requires *unfreezing* the status quo, *changing* to a new state, and *refreezing* to make the change permanent. The status quo can be considered an equilibrium state. To move from this equilibrium, unfreezing is necessary. Unfreezing can be thought of as taking a proactive approach to identifying the appropriate change, preparing for the needed change, and cultivating an on-going culture of innovation. It can be achieved by increasing the *driving forces*, which are forces that drive change and direct behaviour away from the status quo; decreasing the *restraining forces*, which are forces that resist change, dampen innovation and adaptability, and direct behaviour toward the status quo; or combining the two approaches.

Once unfreezing is done, the required change itself can be implemented. However, merely introducing change does not ensure that the change will take hold. The new

Exhibit 6-1

The Change Process

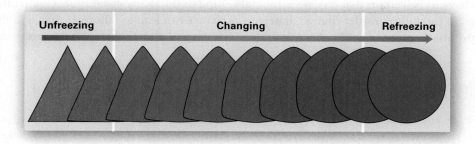

situation needs to be *refrozen* so that it can be sustained over time. Unless this last step is taken, there is a strong chance that the change will be short-lived as employees revert back to the old equilibrium state—that is, the old ways of doing things. The objective of refreezing, then, is to stabilize the new situation by reinforcing the new behaviours.

Note how Lewin's three-step process treats change simply as a break in the organization's equilibrium state. The status quo has been disturbed and change is necessary to establish a new equilibrium state. However, a calm waters environment is not what most managers face today.[14]

The White-Water Rapids Metaphor

The white-water rapids metaphor is consistent with our discussion of uncertain and dynamic environments in previous chapters. It's also consistent with a world that's increasingly dominated by information, ideas, and knowledge.[15] We can see how the metaphor applies to BlackBerry, which faced an uncertain and dynamic environment after dominating the smart phone industry for many years.

To get a feeling of what managing change might be like when you have to continuously manoeuvre in uninterrupted and uncertain rapids, consider attending a college or university that has the following rules: Courses vary in length. Unfortunately, when you sign up, you don't know how long a course will run. It might go for 2 weeks or 30 weeks. Furthermore, the instructor can end a course any time he or she wants, with no prior warning. If that is not bad enough, the length of the class changes each time it meets; sometimes the class lasts 20 minutes, other times it runs for 3 hours. And the time of the next class meeting is set by the instructor during this class. There is one more thing. All exams are unannounced, so you have to be ready for a test at any time. To succeed in this type of environment, you would have to be incredibly flexible and able to respond quickly to changing conditions. Students who are overly structured, "slow" to respond, or uncomfortable with change would not survive.

Growing numbers of managers are coming to accept that their job is much like what a student would face in such a college. The stability and predictability of the calm waters metaphor do not exist. Disruptions in the status quo are not occasional and temporary, and they are not followed by a return to calm waters. Many managers never get out of the rapids. They face constant change, bordering on chaos.

Putting the Two Views in Perspective

Does *every* manager face a world of constant and chaotic change? No, but the number who don't is dwindling. Managers in such businesses as telecommunications, computer software, and women's clothing have long confronted a world of white-water rapids. These managers used to envy their counterparts in industries such as banking, utilities, oil exploration, publishing, and air transportation, where the environment was historically more stable and predictable. However, those days of stability and predictability are long gone!

Today, any organization that treats change as the occasional disturbance in an otherwise calm and stable world runs a great risk. Too much is changing too fast for an organization or its managers to be complacent. Managers must be ready to efficiently and effectively manage the changes facing their organizations or their work areas. Nevertheless, managers have to be certain that change is the right thing to do at any given time. Companies need to carefully consider change strategies, as change can lead to failure. If change is the appropriate course of action, how should it be managed? That's what we'll discuss next.

Managing Organizational Change

④ Classify types of organizational change.

▶ ▶ ▶ In 2012, Jim Balsillie and Mike Lazaridis stepped down as executives and co-chairs of the board for BlackBerry Limited, formerly known as Research In Motion Ltd., the Waterloo-based global smartphone giant. Thorsten Heins became the new chief executive officer (CEO), and Barbara Stymiest replaced Mr. Balsillie and Mr. Lazaridis as chair of the board of directors.

le g

Before these changes, calls for radical change at the company had been mounting. Critics of the company's performance argued that this management change was not enough to promote a culture of innovation and adaptability because Mr. Heins was only moving up the ranks and Ms. Stymiest had been a director since 2007. In addition, Mr. Balsillie and Mr. Lazaridis had been grooming Mr. Heins as a successor for some time and decided to act as the company entered a new phase.

Think About It

What problems might come from promoting an employee from within the company who had been groomed by the previous owners of the company to the position of CEO, to act as a change agent at BlackBerry Limited?

What Is Organizational Change?

Most managers, at one point or another, will have to change some things in their workplace. We classify these changes as **organizational change**, which is any alteration of people, structure, or technology. Organizational changes often need someone to act as a catalyst and assume the responsibility for managing the change process—that is, a **change agent**. For major changes, an organization often hires outside consultants to provide advice and assistance. Because consultants are from the outside, they have an objective perspective that insiders may lack. But outside consultants have a limited understanding of the organization's history, culture, operating procedures, and people. They're also more likely than insiders to initiate drastic change because they don't have to live with the repercussions after the change is implemented. In contrast, internal managers may be more thoughtful but possibly overcautious because they must live with the consequences of their decisions.

organizational change Any alteration of people, structure, or technology in an organization.

change agent Someone who acts as a catalyst and assumes the responsibility for managing the change process.

Types of Change

What *can* a manager change? The manager's options fall into three categories: structure, technology, and people. (See Exhibit 6-2.)

◄●─ Simulate on **MyManagementLab**

Change

Exhibit 6-2

Three Categories of Change

Structure → Work specialization, departmentalization, chain of command, span of control, centralization, formalization, job redesign, or actual structural design

Technology → Work processes, methods, and equipment

People → Attitudes, expectations, perceptions, and behaviour

Changing Structure

Managers' organizing responsibilities include such activities as choosing the organization's formal design, allocating authority, and determining the degree of formalization. Once those structural decisions have been made, however, they are not final. Changing conditions or changing strategies bring about the need to make structural changes. We will discuss organizational structure issues in more detail Chapter 10.

What options does the manager have for changing structure? An organization's structure is defined in terms of work specialization, departmentalization, chain of command, span of control, centralization and decentralization, and formalization. Managers can alter one or more of these *structural elements*. A few examples should make this clearer. For instance, departmental responsibilities could be combined, organizational levels eliminated, or spans of control widened to make the organization flatter and less bureaucratic. Or more rules and procedures could be implemented to increase standardization. An increase in decentralization can be used to make decision making faster. Even downsizing involves changes in structure.

Another option would be to make major changes in the actual *structural design*. For instance, when Hewlett-Packard acquired Compaq, several structural changes were made as product divisions were dropped, merged, or expanded. Or structural design changes might include a shift from a functional to a product structure or the creation of a project structure design. Hamilton, Ontario-based Dofasco became a more profitable steel producer after revamping its traditional functional structure to a new design that arranges work around cross-functional teams. Some government agencies and private organizations are looking to new organizational ventures, forming public–private partnerships to deal with these changes.

Changing Technology

Managers can also change the technology used to convert inputs into outputs. Most early studies in management—such as the work of Taylor and the Gilbreths described in Module 1, Management History—dealt with efforts aimed at technological change. If you recall, scientific management sought to implement changes that would increase production *efficiency* based on time-and-motion studies. Today, major technological changes usually involve the introduction of new equipment, tools, or methods; automation; or computerization.

Competitive factors or new innovations within an industry often require managers to introduce *new equipment, tools*, or *operating methods*. For example, coal mining companies

Computerization has been the engine for all kinds of changes in the business environment, including employee training. Cisco Systems' Internet Learning Solutions Group is charged with developing electronic training programs both for Cisco's own sales force and channel partners and for the company's hundreds of thousands of customers. The team, whose leaders are pictured here, has developed tools ranging from virtual classrooms to video server technology and content development templates. "We really believe that our e-learning programs are a more effective way to grow skills in high volume in a shorter time than in the past," says the group's director.

Robert Houser

in New South Wales, Australia, updated operational methods, installed more efficient coal-handling equipment, and made changes in work practices to be more productive. New innovations do not always inspire organizations to change, however. The Canadian Armed Forces has been criticized in recent years because it has not taken advantage of new technology to update its equipment.[16]

Automation is a technological change that uses machines for tasks previously done by people. Automation has been introduced (and sometimes resisted) in organizations such as Canada Post, where automatic mail sorters are used, and in automobile assembly lines, where robots are programmed to do jobs that blue-collar workers used to perform.

Probably the most visible technological changes in recent years, though, have come through managers' efforts to expand *computerization*. Most organizations have sophisticated information systems. For instance, grocery stores and other retailers use scanners linked to computers that provide instant inventory information. Also, it's very uncommon for an office to not be computerized. At British Petroleum (BP), employees had to learn how to deal with the personal visibility and accountability brought about by the implementation of an enterprise-wide information system. The integrative nature of this system meant that what any employee did on his or her computer automatically affected other computer systems on the internal network.[17] The Benetton Group uses computers to link its manufacturing plants outside Treviso, Italy, with the company's various sales outlets and a highly automated warehouse.[18]

Changing People

Changing people—that is, changing their attitudes, expectations, perceptions, and behaviours—is not easy. Yet, for over 30 years now, academic researchers and actual managers have been interested in finding ways for individuals and groups within organizations to work together more effectively. The term **organizational development (OD)**, though occasionally referring to all types of change, essentially focuses on techniques or programs to change people and the nature and quality of interpersonal work relationships.[19] The most popular OD techniques are described in Exhibit 6-3. The common thread in these techniques is that each seeks to bring about changes in the organization's

organizational development (OD) Techniques or programs to change people and the nature and quality of interpersonal work relationships.

Exhibit 6-3

Organizational Development Techniques

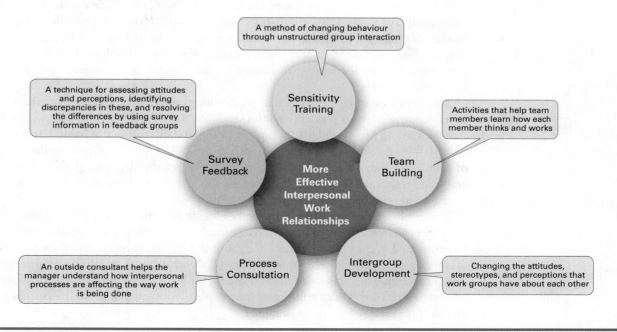

A method of changing behaviour through unstructured group interaction → **Sensitivity Training**

A technique for assessing attitudes and perceptions, identifying discrepancies in these, and resolving the differences by using survey information in feedback groups → **Survey Feedback**

Activities that help team members learn how each member thinks and works → **Team Building**

More Effective Interpersonal Work Relationships

An outside consultant helps the manager understand how interpersonal processes are affecting the way work is being done → **Process Consultation**

Intergroup Development → Changing the attitudes, stereotypes, and perceptions that work groups have about each other

people. For example, executives at Scotiabank, Canada's third-largest bank in terms of market capitalization, knew that the success of a new customer sales and service strategy depended on changing employee attitudes and behaviours. Managers used different OD techniques during the strategic change, including team building, survey feedback, and intergroup development. One indicator of how well these techniques worked in getting people to change was that every branch in Canada implemented the new strategy on or ahead of schedule.[20]

Global Organizational Development

Much of what we know about OD practices has come from North American research. However, managers need to recognize that although there may be some similarities in the types of OD techniques used, some techniques that work for North American organizations may not be appropriate for organizations or organizational divisions based in other countries.[21] For instance, a study of OD interventions showed that "multirater (survey) feedback as practiced in the United States is not embraced in Taiwan" because the cultural value of "saving face is simply more powerful than the value of receiving feedback from subordinates."[22] What is the lesson for managers? Before using the same techniques to implement behavioural changes, especially across different countries, managers need to be sure that they have taken into account cultural characteristics and whether the techniques "make sense for the local culture."

Managing Resistance to Change

Change can be a threat to people in an organization. Organizations can build up inertia that motivates people to resist changing their status quo, even though change might be beneficial. Why do people resist change and what can be done to minimize their resistance?

Why People Resist Change

Resistance to change is well documented.[23] Why *do* people resist change? An individual is likely to resist change for the following reasons: uncertainty, habit, concern over personal loss, and the belief that the change is not in the organization's best interest.[24]

Change replaces the known with ambiguity and uncertainty. When you finish school, you will be leaving an environment where you know what is expected of you to join an organization where things are uncertain. Employees in organizations are faced with similar uncertainty. For example, when quality control methods based on sophisticated statistical models are introduced into manufacturing plants, many quality control inspectors have to learn the new methods. Some inspectors may fear that they will be unable to do so and may, therefore, develop a negative attitude toward the change or behave poorly if required to use the methods.

Another cause of resistance is that we do things out of habit. Every day, when you go to school or work, you probably go the same way. If you are like most people, you find a single route and use it regularly. As human beings, we are creatures of habit. Life is complex enough—we don't want to have to consider the full range of options for the hundreds of decisions we make every day. To cope with this complexity, we rely on habits or programmed responses. But when confronted with change, this tendency to respond in our accustomed ways becomes a source of resistance.

The third cause of resistance is the fear of losing something already possessed. Change threatens the investment you have already made in the status quo. The more that people have invested in the current system, the more they resist change. Why? They fear the loss of status, money, authority, friendships, personal convenience, or other economic benefits that they value. This helps explain why older employees tend to resist change more than younger employees. Older employees have generally invested more in the current system and thus have more to lose by changing.

Exhibit 6-4

Helping Employees Accept Change

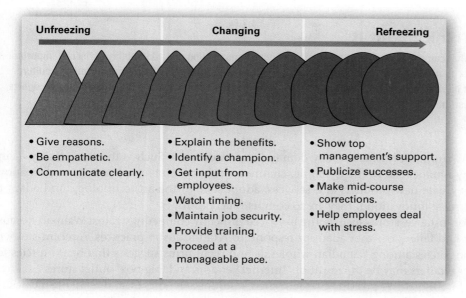

Source: J. Liebowitz and G. J. Iskat, "What to Do When Employees Resist Change," *Supervision* 57, no. 8 (August 1996), pp. 3–5. With permission.

A final cause of resistance is a person's belief that the change is incompatible with the goals and interests of the organization. For instance, an employee who believes that a proposed new job procedure will reduce product quality or productivity can be expected to resist the change.

Techniques for Reducing Resistance

When managers see resistance to change as dysfunctional, they can use a variety of actions to deal with it.[25] Exhibit 6-4 shows how to manage resistance at the unfreezing, changing, and refreezing stages. Actions include communicating the reasons for change, getting input from employees, choosing the timing of change carefully, and showing management support for the change process. Providing support to employees to deal with the stress of the change is also important. Depending on the type and source of the resistance, managers might choose to use any of these. In general, resistance is likely to be lower if managers involve people in the change, offer training where needed, and are open to revisions once the change has been implemented. (For more suggestions on reducing resistance, see the skills exercise *Managing Resistance to Change* on pages 157–158.)

Stimulating Innovation and Adaptability

▶ ▶ ▶ In 2012 BlackBerry entered the battle of its life with its new Z10 smart phone. In order to improve its market performance, BlackBerry needed to launch an innovative product. This wasn't just about a single phone or a single operating system (OS); it was about BlackBerry's fight to stay afloat. The company came back with its new touchscreen smartphone to take on even the most entrenched players in the game. Could the new phone, along with BlackBerry 10, put the company back on track, or was this too little, too late? Customers are fickle in the face of changing technology—and have gone or are going. The company was slow to catch on to the magnitude of the disruptive innovations created by Apple's iPhone and Google's Android systems. The company needed to nurture a culture of innovation and adaptability, where

5 Describe techniques for stimulating innovation and adaptability.

disruptive technologies are recognized and the company is able to identify and implement the necessary changes in a timely fashion to avoid loss in market share in the face of rapid technological change.

> ### Think About It
>
> **What can companies do to stimulate and nurture innovation and adaptability? Why is it important for companies or organizations to recognize disruptive innovation? How can nurturing a culture of innovation and adaptability within an organization or company help the organization recognize disruptive innovation?**

"Winning in business today demands innovation."[26] Such is the stark reality facing today's managers. In the dynamic, chaotic world of global competition, organizations must create new products and services, adopt state-of-the-art technology, and adapt to disruptive innovation if they are to compete successfully.[27]

For instance, stores such as The Bay faced difficulty competing against Walmart because they had failed to either adapt or respond to retail industry practices. A recent study of bankruptcies among Canadian wholesale and retail firms suggests that bankruptcies for older retailers may be the result of "Internet vendors and 'big-box' outlet stores . . . eroding the competitive position of established, traditional wholesale and retail businesses."[28] Meanwhile, fast-food restaurants such as McDonald's appeared to be out of touch when the "low carb" fad swept the diet industry. How do companies keep up in a quickly changing environment?

When you think of companies that have incorporated successful innovation and adaptability strategies, you probably consider companies such as Sony, who makes PlayStations Cyber-Shot digital cameras, and OLED display TV, and 3M. 3M continually encourages its employees to come up with novel variations on its product line. Intel makes continual advances in chip designs. Apple constantly upgrades its operating system for its mobile devices. What is the secret to the success of these innovator champions? What, if anything, can other managers do to make their organizations more innovative and adaptable? In the following pages, we discuss the characteristics of innovative organizations.

Creativity vs. Innovation

Watch on **MyManagementLab**

iRobot: Creativity and Innovation

creativity   The ability to combine ideas in a unique way or to make unusual associations between ideas.

innovation   The process of taking creative ideas and turning them into useful products, services, or work methods.

Creativity refers to the ability to combine ideas in a unique way or to make unusual associations between ideas.[29] An organization that stimulates creativity develops unique ways to work or novel solutions to problems. But creativity by itself is not enough. Creative ideas need to be turned into useful products, services, or work methods; this process is defined as **innovation**. The innovative organization is characterized by its ability to channel creativity into useful outcomes. When managers talk about changing an organization to make it more creative, they usually mean they want to stimulate and nurture innovation. However, creativity and innovation are also not enough to sustain growth. Organizations must also create a culture of adaptability whereby they proactively identify disruptive innovations, new problems, and challenges and actively develop novel approaches and solutions to these challenges before they are impacted by these changes. Adaptability requires forward-thinking leadership within organizations.

In Chapter 4, we pointed out that in today's dynamically chaotic world of global competition, organizations must continually innovate new products and services if they want to compete successfully. Innovation is a key characteristic of entrepreneurial ventures and, in fact, is what makes an entrepreneurial venture "entrepreneurial." In the same chapter, we pointed out that innovation can take place in three forms—curiosity-driven research, applied research, and research and development (R&D).

Sony, 3M, Intel, and Apple are aptly described as both innovative and adaptable because they consistently seek new problems to solve, they are outwardly facing, and they have developed a culture of taking novel ideas and turning them into profitable products and work methods.

Stimulating and Nurturing Innovation and Adaptability

In Chapter 1, we discussed the value proposition for building adaptive organizations where successful organizations differentiate themselves from their competitors in three dimensions: They are more flexible, more efficient, and more adaptable.[30] Tata Sons builds such a culture, as shown in the following *Management Reflection*.

MANAGEMENT REFLECTION FOCUS ON INNOVATION

Building Innovation into the DNA of a Company

How can innovation become a shared organizational value within an organization? Ratan Tata, former chair of Tata Sons, built one of the world's largest conglomerates.[31] When India's long-protected economy was opened in 1981, Tata decided that for his myriad companies to survive and thrive in a global economy, he had to "make innovation a priority and build it into the DNA of the Tata Group so that every employee at every company might think and act like an innovator." One unique way innovation is encouraged at Tata is an internal innovation competition. Teams from units of the Indian conglomerate are presented with a challenge and prepare projects that are presented at the global finals at headquarters in Mumbai. Employee teams register for the competition and the winners get no cash, only awards such as the Tata's Promising Innovation Award or the Dare to Try Award. The real prize for employees is the respect and recognition of Tata's leadership. However, the biggest winner is probably the company itself. What can you learn from this leader who made innovation a shared organizational value embedded in the organizational culture? ∎

Using the systems approach we introduced in Module 1, we can better understand how organizations become more innovative and adaptive.[32] (See Exhibit 6-5.) We see from this model that getting the desired outputs (innovative products) involves both the inputs and the transformation of those inputs. Inputs include creative individuals and groups within the organization. But having creative individuals is not enough. It takes the right environment for the innovation and adaptability processes to take hold and prosper as the inputs are transformed. What does this "right" environment—that is, an environment that stimulates innovation and adaptability —look like? We have identified three sets of

Exhibit 6-5

Systems View of Innovation and Adaptability

Inputs	Transformation	Outputs
Creative individuals, groups, organizations	Creative environment, process, situation	Innovative product(s), work methods

Source: Adapted from R. W. Woodman, J. E. Sawyer, and R. W. Griffin, "Toward a Theory of Organizational Creativity," *Academy of Management Review*, April 1993, p. 309.

Exhibit 6-6

Innovation Variables

Structural Variables
- Organic structures
- Abundant resources
- High inter-unit communication
- Minimal time pressure
- Work and nonwork support

Human Resource Variables
- High commitment to training and development
- High job security
- Creative people

Stimulate Innovation

Cultural Variables
- Acceptance of ambiguity
- Tolerance of the impractical
- Low external controls
- Tolerance of risks
- Tolerance of conflict
- Focus on ends
- Open-system focus
- Positive feedback

variables that have been found to stimulate innovation and adaptability: the organization's structure, culture, and human resource practices. (See Exhibit 6-6.)

Structural Variables

Research into the effect of structural variables on innovation and adaptability shows five things.[33] First, organic structures positively influence innovation and adaptability. Because this type of organization is low in formalization, centralization, and work specialization, organic structures facilitate the flexibility, adaptability, and cross-fertilization. Second, the easy availability of plentiful resources provides a key building block for innovation and adaptability. With an abundance of resources, managers can afford to purchase innovations, can afford the cost of instituting innovations, and can absorb failures and can look for new solutions to emerging challenges. Third, frequent inter-unit communication helps break down barriers to innovation and adaptability.[34] Cross-functional teams, task forces, and other such organizational designs facilitate interaction across departmental lines and are widely used in innovative and adaptive organizations. Fourth, innovative and adaptive organizations try to minimize extreme time pressures on creative activities despite the demands of white-water environments. Although time pressures may spur people to work harder and may make them feel more creative, studies show that it actually causes them to be less creative.[35] Finally, studies show that when an organization's structure provides explicit support for creativity from work and non-work sources, an employee's creative performance is enhanced. What kinds of support are beneficial? Useful support includes encouragement, open communication, readiness to listen, and useful feedback.[36] Toronto-based Labatt Breweries, for instance, gathers employees from across the country to an annual "innovation summit" to allow them to present ideas.[37] At one summit, Don Perron, a power engineer from Labatt's Edmonton brewery, presented an idea to move pumps from the ceiling of the plant to the floor; his idea was accepted. This impressed

Perron, who said, "It gives you a sense of satisfaction." His co-workers have become enthusiastic about developing ideas as a result. "It has taken away some of the monotony [of production-line work]," Perron said. Labatt helps employees develop good ideas by investing time and money in the research and development of new ideas.

Cultural Variables

"Throw the bunny" is part of the lingo used by a project team at toy company Mattel. It refers to a juggling lesson in which team members try to learn to juggle two balls and a stuffed bunny. Most people easily learn to juggle two balls but cannot let go of that third object. Creativity, like juggling, is learning to let go—that is, to "throw the bunny." For Mattel, having a culture in which people are encouraged to "throw the bunny" is important to its continued product innovations.[38]

Innovative and adaptive organizations tend to have similar cultures.[39] They encourage experimentation, reward both successes and failures, and celebrate mistakes. An innovative culture is likely to have the following characteristics:

- *Acceptance of ambiguity.* Too much emphasis on objectivity and specificity constrains creativity.

- *Tolerance of the impractical.* Individuals who offer impractical, even foolish, answers to what-if questions are not stifled. What at first seems impractical might lead to innovative solutions.

- *Low external controls.* Rules, regulations, policies, and similar organizational controls are kept to a minimum.

- *Tolerance of risk.* Employees are encouraged to experiment without fear of consequences should they fail. Mistakes are treated as learning opportunities.

- *Tolerance of conflict.* Diversity of opinions is encouraged. Harmony and agreement between individuals or units are *not* assumed to be evidence of high performance.

- *Focus on ends.* Goals are made clear, and individuals are encouraged to consider alternative routes to meeting the goals. Focusing on ends suggests that there might be several right answers to any given problem.

- *Open-system focus.* Managers closely monitor the environment and respond to changes as they occur.

- *Positive feedback.* Managers provide positive feedback, encouragement, and support so employees feel that their creative ideas will receive attention.

The toy industry is very competitive, and picking the next great toy is not easy. Still, Toronto-based Spin Master is better than most at finding the most innovative new toys. Co-CEOs Anton Rabie and Ronnen Harary and executive vice-president Ben Varadi rely on intuition. They have also created a "culture of ideas" and pick everyone's brains for new ideas, "from inventors and licensing companies to distributors and retailers around the world." They give a prize to one employee each month for the best idea.

THE CANADIAN PRESS/Frank Gunn

Human Resource Variables

In this category, we find that innovative and adaptive organizations actively promote the training and development of their members so their knowledge remains current; offer their employees high job security to reduce the fear of getting fired for making mistakes; and encourage individuals to become "champions" of change. **Idea champions** are individuals who actively and enthusiastically support new ideas, build support, overcome resistance, and ensure that innovations are implemented. Research finds that idea champions have common personality characteristics: extremely high self-confidence, persistence, energy, and a tendency to take risks. Champions also display characteristics associated with dynamic leadership. They inspire and energize others with their vision of the potential of an innovation and through their strong personal conviction in their mission. They are also good at gaining the commitment of others to support their mission. In addition, champions have jobs that provide considerable decision-making discretion. This autonomy helps them introduce and implement innovations in organizations.[40] For instance, *Spirit* and *Opportunity*, the two golf-cart-sized exploration rovers that landed on Mars in 2004 to explore its surface, never would have been built had it not been for an idea champion by the name of Donna L. Shirley. As the head of Mars exploration in the 1990s at NASA's Jet Propulsion Laboratory in Pasadena, California, Shirley had been working since the early 1980s on the idea of putting roving vehicles on Mars. Despite ongoing funding and management support problems, she continued to champion the idea until it was approved in the early 1990s.[41]

Adaptive Organizations

Doing business in an intensely competitive global environment, British retailer Tesco realizes how important it is for its stores to run well behind the scenes.[42] And it does so using a proven "tool" called Tesco in a Box, a self-contained complete IT system and matching set of business processes that provides the model for all of Tesco's international business operations. This approach promotes consistency in operations and is a way to share innovations.[43] Tesco is an example of an adaptive organization, an organization that has developed the capacity to continuously learn, adapt, and change. "Today's managerial challenge is to inspire and enable knowledge workers to solve, day in and day out, problems that cannot be anticipated."[44] In an adaptive organization, employees continually acquire and share new knowledge and apply that knowledge in making decisions or doing their work. Some organizational theorists even go so far as to say that an organization's ability to do this—that is, to learn and to apply that learning—may be the only sustainable source of competitive advantage.[45] What structural characteristics does an adaptable organization need?

Employees throughout the entire organization—across different functional specialties and even at different organizational levels—must share information and collaborate on work activities. Such an environment requires minimal structural and physical barriers, allowing employees to work together in doing the organization's work the best way they can and, in the process, learn from each other. Finally, empowered work teams tend to be an important feature of an adaptive organization's structural design. These teams make decisions about doing whatever work needs to be done or resolving issues. With empowered employees and teams, there's little need for "bosses" to direct and control. Instead, managers serve as facilitators, supporters, and advocates.

Innovation and Design Thinking

A strong connection exists between design thinking and innovation. "Design thinking can do for innovation what Total Quality Management (TQM) did for quality."[46] Just as TQM provides a process for improving quality throughout an organization, design thinking can provide a process for coming up with things that don't exist. When a business approaches innovation with a design thinking mentality, the emphasis is on getting a deeper understanding of what customers need and want. It entails knowing customers as real people with real problems—not just as sales targets or demographic statistics. But it also entails being able to convert those customer insights into real and usable products. For instance, at Intuit, the company behind TurboTax software, founder Scott Cook felt "the company wasn't innovating fast enough."[47] So he decided to apply design thinking. He called the initiative "Design for Delight" and it involved customer field research to understand their "pain points"—that is, what most frustrated them as they worked in the office and at home. Then, Intuit staffers brainstormed (they nicknamed it "painstorm") a "variety of solutions to address the problems and experiment with customers to find the best ones." For example, one pain point uncovered by an Intuit team was how customers could take pictures of tax forms to reduce typing errors. Some younger customers, used to taking photos with their smartphones, were frustrated that they couldn't just complete their taxes on their mobiles. To address this, Intuit developed a mobile app called SnapTax, which the company says has been downloaded more than a million times since it was introduced in 2010. That's how design thinking works in innovation.

Changing Organizational Culture

Today's change issues—changing organizational culture, handling employee stress, and making change happen successfully—are critical concerns for managers. What can managers do to change an organization's culture when that culture no longer supports the organization's mission? How can managers successfully manage the challenges of introducing and implementing change? How can managers successfully promote a culture of innovation and adaptability? These are the topics we look at in this section.

As we saw in Chapter 2, when James McNerney took over as CEO of 3M, he brought with him managerial approaches from his old employer, General Electric. He soon discovered that what was routine at GE was unheard of at 3M. For instance, he was the only one who showed up at meetings without a tie. His blunt, matter-of-fact, and probing style of asking questions caught many 3M managers off guard. McNerney soon realized that he would need to address the cultural issues before tackling any needed organizational changes.[48] The fact that an organization's culture is made up of relatively stable and permanent characteristics tends to make that culture very resistant to change.[49] A culture takes a long time to form, and once established it tends to become entrenched. Strong cultures are particularly resistant to change because employees have become so committed to them.

The explosion of the space shuttle *Columbia* in 2003 highlights how difficult changing an organization's culture can be. An investigation of the explosion found that the causes were remarkably similar to the reasons given for the *Challenger* disaster 20 years earlier.[50] Although foam striking the shuttle was the technical cause, NASA's organizational culture was the real problem. Joseph Grenny, a NASA engineer, noted that "the NASA culture does not accept being wrong." The culture does not accept that "there's no such thing as a stupid question." Instead, "the humiliation factor always runs high."[51] Consequently, people do not speak up. As this example shows, if, over time, a certain culture becomes inappropriate to an organization and a handicap to management, there might be little a manager can do to change it, especially in the short run. Even under favourable conditions, cultural changes have to be viewed in years, not weeks or even months.

Understanding the Situational Factors

What "favourable conditions" might facilitate cultural change? The evidence suggests that cultural change is most likely to take place when most or all of the following conditions exist:

- *A dramatic crisis occurs.* This can be the shock that weakens the status quo and makes people start thinking about the relevance of the current culture. Examples are a surprising financial setback, the loss of a major customer, or a dramatic technological innovation by a competitor.

- *Leadership changes hands.* New top leadership, who can provide an alternative set of key values, may be perceived as more capable of responding to the crisis than the old leaders were. Top leadership includes the organization's chief executive but might include all senior managers.

- *The organization is young and small.* The younger the organization, the less entrenched its culture. Similarly, it's easier for managers to communicate new values in a small organization than in a large one.

- *The culture is weak.* The more widely held the values and the higher the agreement among members on those values, the more difficult it will be to change. Conversely, weak cultures are more receptive to change than are strong ones.[52]

These situational factors help explain why a company such as Yahoo! faces challenges in reshaping its culture. For the most part, employees like the old ways of doing things and don't always see the company's problems as critical. This may also be why Yahoo! was slow to recognize the importance of Facebook and YouTube to the online scene.

How Can Cultural Change Be Accomplished?

Now we ask the question, If conditions are right, how do managers go about changing culture? The challenge is to unfreeze the current culture, implement the new "ways of doing things," and reinforce those new values. No single action is likely to have the impact necessary to change something that is so ingrained and highly valued. Thus, there needs to be a comprehensive and coordinated strategy for managing cultural change.

Organizational members don't quickly let go of values that they understand and that have worked well for them in the past. Managers must, therefore, be patient. Change, if it comes, will be slow. And managers must stay constantly alert to protect against any return to old, familiar practices and traditions.

Making Change Happen Successfully

When changes are needed, who makes them happen? Who manages them? Although you may think that it's the responsibility of top managers, actually managers at *all* organizational levels are involved in the change process.

Even with the involvement of all levels of managers in change efforts, change processes don't always work the way they should. In fact, a global study of organizational change concludes that "hundreds of managers from scores of U.S. and European companies [are] satisfied with their operating prowess . . . [but] dissatisfied with their ability to implement change."[53] One of the reasons that change fails is that managers do not really know how to introduce change in organizations. Professor John Kotter of the Harvard Business School identifies a number of places where managers make mistakes when leading change. These are illustrated in Exhibit 6-7.

How can managers make change happen successfully? Managers can increase the likelihood of making change happen successfully in three ways. First, they should focus on making the organization ready for change. Exhibit 6-8 summarizes the characteristics of organizations that are ready for change.

Second, managers need to understand their own role in the process. They do this by creating a simple, compelling statement of the need for change; communicating the benefits of change throughout the process; getting as much employee participation as possible; respecting employees' apprehension about the change but encouraging them to be flexible; removing those who resist, but only after all possible attempts have been made to get their commitment to the change; aiming for short-term change successes, since large-scale change can be a long time coming; and setting a positive example.[54]

Third, managers need to encourage employees to be change agents—to look for those day-to-day improvements and changes that individuals and teams can make. For instance, a study of organizational change found that 77 percent of changes at the work-group level were reactions to a specific, current problem or to a suggestion from someone outside the work group; 68 percent of those changes occurred in the course of employees' day-to-day work.[55]

Exhibit 6-7

Mistakes Managers Make When Leading Change

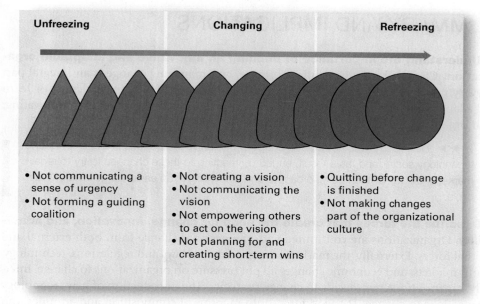

Sources: J. P. Kotter, "Leading Change: Why Transformation Efforts Fail," *Harvard Business Review*, March–April 1995, pp. 56–67; and *Management*, First Canadian Edition by Williams/Kondra/Vibert. © 2004. Reprinted with permission of Nelson, a division of Thomson Learning: www.thomsonrights.com. FAX 800-730-2215.

Exhibit 6-8

Characteristics of Adaptive Organizations

- Link the present and the future. Think of work as more than an extension of the past; think about future opportunities and issues and factor them into today's decisions.

- Make learning a way of life. Change-friendly organizations excel at knowledge sharing and management.

- Actively support and encourage day-to-day improvements and changes. Successful change can come from the small changes as well as the big ones.

- Ensure diverse teams. Diversity ensures that things won't be done the way they are always done.

- Encourage mavericks. Since their ideas and approaches are outside the mainstream, mavericks can help bring about radical change.

- Shelter breakthroughs. Change-friendly organizations have found ways to protect those breakthrough ideas.

- Integrate technology. Use technology to implement changes.

- Build and deepen trust. People are more likely to support changes when the organization's culture is trusting and managers have credibility and integrity.

- Couple permanence with perpetual change. Because change is the only constant, companies need to figure out how to protect their core strengths during times of change.

- Support an entrepreneurial mindset. Many younger employees bring a more entrepreneurial mindset to organizations and can serve as catalysts for radical change.

Source: Based on S. Ante, "Change Is Good—So Get Used to It," *BusinessWeek*, June 22, 2009, pp. 69–70; and P.A. McLagan, "The Change-Capable Organization," *Training & Development*, January 2003, pp. 50–59.

SUMMARY AND IMPLICATIONS

1. Understand the importance of building an innovative and adaptable organization. Change is an organizational reality, and managing change is an integral part of every manager's job. Managers who make no attempt to anticipate change or learn and adapt to changes in the global environment end up reacting rather than innovating; their organizations often become uncompetitive and fail.

▶ ▶ ▶ BlackBerry was not able to adapt to disruptive innovations in the smartphone technology sector and, as a result, ended up reacting to these changes to try to regain market share rather than being proactive and innovating at an earlier stage in its product cycle.

2. Describe the forces that create the need for change, innovation, and adaptability. Organizations are confronted with the need for change from both external and internal forces. Externally, the marketplace, government laws and regulations, technology, labour markets, and economic changes all put pressure on organizations to change. Internally, organizations may decide to change strategies. The introduction of new technology can also lead to change. The workforce, both in terms of composition and attitudes, can also lead to demands for change.

▶ ▶ ▶ BlackBerry faced substantial challenges as a large organization operating in an industry characterized by ever-changing technology, disruptive technology, and aggressive organizations leading to a downturn in growth and a drop in market share.

3. Compare and contrast views of the change process. Until the late 1980s, change was viewed as episodic, something that could be planned and managed readily. In between periods of change, organizations "stayed the course." In more recent years, environments have become more uncertain and dynamic, and this has led to more continuous demands for change.

▶ ▶ ▶ Blackberry has had to respond to various changes in the smartphone industry (even as it introduced technological changes itself). To regain its leadership edge as the company moved forward, it needed to be able to identify new opportunities on an ongoing basis and figure out a way to provide services that its competitors did not.

4. Classify types of organizational change. What *can* a manager change? The manager's options fall into three categories: structure, technology, and people. (See Exhibit 6-2 on page 143.) Changing *structure* includes any alteration in authority relations, coordination mechanisms, employee empowerment, job redesign, or similar structural variables. Changing *technology* encompasses modifications in the way work is performed or the methods and equipment that are used. Changing *people* refers to changes in employee attitudes, expectations, perceptions, and behaviour.

▶ ▶ ▶ BlackBerry Limited replaced Jim Balsillie and Mike Lazaridis as co-chairs of the board in 2012 with the assumption that this change would bring about the change required to generate increased innovation and adaptability for the company. At the same time however, critics of BlackBerry's performance argued that this management change was not enough to create change within the company's corporate structure to generate the culture required for company to become competitive.

5. Describe techniques for stimulating innovation and adaptability. Innovation is the process of taking creative ideas and turning them into useful products, services, or work methods. Organizations that have greater structural flexibility, encourage training and development of employees, and encourage risk-taking and new ideas are more likely to be innovative.

▶ ▶ ▶ At the outset, RIM was a very innovative company, but in recent years its innovations have been more limited, which has allowed Apple and Google to gain substantial market share.

MyManagementLab Study, practise, and explore real management situations with these helpful resources:
- **Interactive Lesson Presentations:** Work through interactive presentations and assessments to test your knowledge of management concepts.
- **PIA (Personal Inventory Assessments):** Enhance your ability to connect with key concepts through these engaging, self-reflection assessments.
- **Study Plan:** Check your understanding of chapter concepts with self-study quizzes.
- **Simulations:** Practise decision-making in simulated management environments.

P I A PERSONAL INVENTORY ASSESSMENT

REVIEW AND DISCUSSION QUESTIONS

1. What is meant by innovative and adaptive organizations?
2. Define *organizational* change.
3. What are the external and internal forces for change?
4. Describe Lewin's three-step change process. How is it different from the change process needed in the white-water rapids metaphor of change?
5. What can be done to promote innovation and adaptability within organizations?

6. Discuss what it takes to make change happen successfully.
7. "Innovation requires allowing people to make mistakes. However, being wrong too many times can be fatal." Do you agree? Why or why not? What are the implications for nurturing innovation?

ETHICS DILEMMA

Think of something that you would like to change in your personal life. It could be your study habits, your fitness and nutrition, the way you interact with others, or anything else that is of interest to you. What values and assumptions have encouraged the behaviour that currently exists (that is, the one you want to change)?

What driving and restraining forces can you address in order to make the desired change?

SKILLS EXERCISE

Managing Resistance to Change—About the Skill

Managers play an important role in organizational change—that is, they often serve as change agents. However, managers may find that change is resisted by employees. After all, change represents ambiguity and uncertainty, or it threatens the status quo. How can this resistance to change be effectively managed?

Steps in Developing the Skill

You can be more effective at managing resistance to change if you use the following three suggestions:[56]

1. **Assess the climate for change.** One major factor why some changes succeed and others fail is the readiness for change. Assessing the climate for change involves

asking several questions. The more affirmative answers you get, the more likely it is that change efforts will succeed.

- Is the sponsor of the change high enough in the hierarchy to have power to effectively deal with resistance?
- Is senior management supportive of the change and committed to it?
- Is there a strong sense of urgency from senior managers about the need for change, and is this feeling shared by others in the organization?
- Do managers have a clear vision of how the future will look after the change?

- Are there objective measures in place to evaluate the change effort, and have reward systems been explicitly designed to reinforce them?
- Is the specific change effort consistent with other changes going on in the organization?
- Are managers willing to sacrifice their personal self-interests for the good of the organization as a whole?
- Do managers pride themselves on closely monitoring changes and actions by competitors?
- Are managers and employees rewarded for taking risks, being innovative, and looking for new and better solutions?
- Is the organizational structure flexible?
- Does communication flow both down and up in the organization?
- Has the organization successfully implemented changes in the recent past?
- Are employee satisfaction with and trust in management high?
- Is there a high degree of interaction and cooperation between organizational work units?
- Are decisions made quickly, and do decisions take into account a wide variety of suggestions?

2. **Choose an appropriate approach for managing the resistance to change.** There are five tactics that have been suggested for dealing with resistance to change. Each is designed to be appropriate for different conditions of resistance. They are *education and communication* (used when resistance comes from lack of information or inaccurate information); *participation* (used when resistance stems from people not having all the information they need or when they have the power to resist); *facilitation and support* (used when those with power will lose out in a change); *manipulation and cooptation* (used when any other tactic will not work or is too expensive); and *coercion* (used when speed is essential and change agents possess considerable power). Which one of these approaches will be most effective depends on the source of the resistance to the change.

3. **During the time the change is being implemented and after the change is completed, communicate with employees regarding what support you may be able to provide.** Your employees need to know that you are there to support them during change efforts. Be prepared to offer the assistance that may be necessary to help your employees enact the change.

Practising the Skill

Read the following scenario. Write some notes about how you would handle the situation described. Be sure

to refer to the three suggestions for managing resistance to change.

Scenario

You are the nursing supervisor at a local hospital that employs both emergency room and floor nurses. Each of these teams of nurses tends to work almost exclusively with others doing the same job. In your professional reading, you have come across the concept of cross-training nursing teams and giving them more varied responsibilities, which in turn has been shown to improve patient care while lowering costs. You call the two team leaders, Sue and Scott, into your office to explain that you want the nursing teams to move to this approach. To your surprise, they are both opposed to the idea. Sue says she and the other emergency room nurses feel they are needed in the ER, where they fill the most vital role in the hospital. They work special hours when needed, do whatever tasks are required, and often work in difficult and stressful circumstances. They think the floor nurses have relatively easy jobs for the pay they receive. Scott, the leader of the floor nurse team, tells you that his group believes the ER nurses lack the special training and extra experience that the floor nurses bring to the hospital. The floor nurses claim they have the heaviest responsibilities and do the most exacting work. Because they have ongoing contact with patients and families, they believe they should not be called away from vital floor duties to help the ER nurses complete their tasks. What should you do about your idea to introduce more cross-training for the nursing teams?

Reinforcing the Skill

The following activities will help you practise and reinforce the skills associated with effectively managing resistance to change.

1. Think about changes (major and minor) that you have dealt with over the past year. Perhaps these changes involved other people and perhaps they were personal. Did you resist the change? Did others resist the change? How did you overcome your resistance or the resistance of others to the change?

2. Interview managers at three different organizations about changes they have implemented. What was their experience in implementing the change? How did they manage resistance to the change?

3. Pay attention to how you handle change. Figure out why you resist certain changes and not others.

4. Practise using different approaches to managing resistance to change at work or in your personal life.

5. Read material that has been written about how to be a more creative person.

6. Find ways to be innovative and creative as you complete class projects or work projects.

WORKING TOGETHER: TEAM EXERCISE

A company's future depends on how well it is able to learn.

Form small groups of three to four individuals. Your team's "job" is to find some current information on learning organizations. You'll probably be able to find numerous articles about the topic, but limit your report to five of what you consider to be the best sources of information on the topic.

Using this information, write a one-page bulleted list discussing your reactions to the statement set in bold at the beginning of this exercise. Be sure to include bibliographic information for your five chosen articles at the end of your one-page bulleted list.

LEARNING TO BE A MANAGER

- Pay attention to how you handle change. Try to figure out why you resist certain changes and not others.
- Pay attention to how others around you handle change. When friends or family resist change, practise using different approaches to managing this resistance to change.
- When you find yourself experiencing dysfunctional stress, write down what's causing the stress, what stress symptoms you're exhibiting, and how you're dealing with the stress. Keep this information in a journal and evaluate how well your stress reducers are working and how you could handle stress better. Your goal is to get to a point where you recognize that you're stressed and can take positive actions to deal with the stress.
- Research information on how to be a more creative person. Write down suggestions in a bulleted-list format and be prepared to present your information in class.

- Is innovation more about (1) stopping something old or (2) starting something new? Prepare arguments supporting or challenging each view.
- Choose two organizations you're familiar with and assess whether these organizations face a calm-waters or white-water rapids environment. Write a short report describing these organizations and your assessment of the change environment each faces. Be sure to explain your choice of change environment.
- Choose an organization with which you're familiar (employer, student organization, family business, etc.). Describe its culture (shared values and beliefs). Select two of those values/beliefs and describe how you would go about changing them. Put this information in a report.
- Take responsibility for your own future career path. Don't depend on your employer to provide you with career development and training opportunities. Right now, sign up for things that will help you enhance your skills—workshops, seminars, continuing education courses, etc.

CASE APPLICATION 1

In Search of the Next Big Thing

It all started with a simple plan to make a superior T-shirt. As special teams captain during the mid-1990s for the University of Maryland football team, Kevin Plank hated having to repeatedly change the cotton T-shirt he wore under his jersey as it became wet and heavy during the course of a game.[57] He knew there had to be a better alternative and set out to make it. After a year of fabric and product testing, Plank introduced the first Under Armour compression product—a synthetic shirt worn like a second skin under a uniform or jersey. And it was an immediate hit! The silky fabric was light and made athletes feel faster and fresher, giving them, according to Plank, an important psychological edge. Today, Under Armour continues to passionately strive to make all athletes better by relentlessly pursuing innovation and design. A telling sign of the company's philosophy is found over the door of its product design studios: "We have not yet built our defining product."

Today, Baltimore-based Under Armour (UA) is a $1.4-billion company. In 16 years, it has grown from a college start-up to a "formidable competitor of the Beaverton, Oregon behemoth" (better known as Nike, a $21-billion company). The company has nearly 3 percent of the fragmented U.S. sports apparel market and sells products from shirts, shorts, and cleats to underwear. In addition, more than 100 universities wear UA uniforms. The company's logo—an interlocking U and A—is becoming almost as recognizable as the Nike swoosh.

Starting out, Plank sold his shirts using the only advantage he had—his athletic connections. "Among his teams from high school, military school, and the University of Maryland, he knew at least 40 NFL players well enough to call and offer them the shirt." He was soon joined by another Maryland player, Kip Fulks, who played lacrosse. Fulks used the same "six-degrees strategy" in the lacrosse world. (Today, Fulks is the company's COO.) The strategy worked. UA sales quickly gained momentum. However, selling products to teams and schools would take a business only so far. That's when Plank began to look at the mass market. In 2000, he made his first deal with a big-box store, Galyan's (which was eventually bought by Dick's Sporting Goods). Today, almost 30 percent of UA's sales come from Dick's and the Sports Authority. But they haven't forgotten where they started, either. The company has all-school deals with 10 Division 1 schools. "Although these deals don't bring in big bucks, they deliver brand visibility...."

Despite their marketing successes, innovation continues to be the name of the game at UA. How important is innovation to the company's heart and soul? Consider what you have to do to enter its new products lab. "Place your hands inside a state-of-the-art scanner that reads—and calculates—the exact pattern of the veins on the back. If it recognizes the pattern, which it does for only 20 out of 5000 employees, you're in. If it doesn't, the vault-like door won't budge." In the unmarked lab at the company's headquarters campus in Baltimore, products being developed include a shirt that can monitor an athlete's heart rate, a running shoe designed like your spine, and a sweatshirt that repels water almost as well as a duck's feathers. There's also work being done on a shirt that may help air condition your body by reading your vital signs.

So what's next for Under Armour? With a motto that refers to protecting this house, innovation will continue to be important. Building a business beyond what it's known for—that is, what athletes wear next to their skin—is going to be challenging. However, Plank is "utterly determined to conquer that next layer, and the layer after that." He says, "There's not a product we can't build."

DISCUSSION QUESTIONS

1. What do you think of UA's approach to innovation? Would you expect to see this type of innovation in an athletic wear company? Explain.
2. What do you think UA's culture might be like in regard to innovation?
3. Could design thinking help UA improve its innovation efforts? Discuss.
4. What's your interpretation of the company's philosophy posted prominently over the door of its design studio? What does it say about innovation?
5. What could other companies learn from the way UA innovates?

CASE APPLICATION 2

The Anti-Hierarchy

A major function of an organization's hierarchy is to increase standardization and control for managers. Using the chain of command, managers can direct the activities of subordinates toward a common purpose. If the right person with a creative vision is in charge of a hierarchy, the results can be phenomenal. For instance, the late Steve Jobs would be an example. At Apple, where he was CEO, there was a strongly top-down creative process in which most major decisions and innovations flowed directly through Jobs and then were delegated to sub-teams as specific assignments to complete. This approach worked well for Apple.

On the other hand, there's "creative deviance," in which individuals create extremely successful products despite being told by senior management to stop working on them.[58] For instance, the electrostatic displays used in more than half of Hewlett-Packard's instruments, the tape slitter that was one of 3M's most important process innovations, and Nichia's development of multi-billion-dollar LED bright lighting technology were all officially rejected by the organizational management hierarchy. In all these examples, an approach like Apple's would have turned away some of the most successful products these companies ever produced. Doing "business as usual" can be so entrenched in a hierarchical organization that new ideas—creative deviance—are seen as threats rather than opportunities for development.

We don't know why top-down decision making works so well for one highly creative company like Apple, and why hierarchy nearly ruined innovations at other organizations. It might be that Apple's structure is actually quite simple, with relatively few layers, and a great deal of responsibility placed on each individual for his or her outcomes. Or it might be that Apple simply had a very unique leader who was able to rise above the conventional boundaries of a CEO to create a culture of constant innovation.

DISCUSSION QUESTIONS

1. Do you think it's possible for an organization to deliberately create an "anti-hierarchy" to encourage employees to engage in acts of creative deviance? What steps might a company take to encourage creative deviance?
2. What are the drawbacks of an approach that encourages creative deviance?
3. Why do you think a company like Apple is able to be creative with a strongly hierarchical structure, while other companies find hierarchy limiting?
4. Do you think Apple's success was entirely dependent on Steve Jobs in his role as head of the hierarchy? What are the potential drawbacks when a company is so strongly connected to the decision making of a single individual?

PART ONE

Management Practice

A Manager's Dilemma

As global health leaders look at statistics on what's killing us, they used to focus on diseases that can spread from person to person—AIDS, tuberculosis, and new and odd flu bugs. To combat these, they've pushed for better vaccines, treatments, and other ways to control germs that could multiply quickly via air travel patterns and start an outbreak anywhere in the world. Now, these experts are looking at a whole new set of culprits that are contributing to an international public health emergency. But this time, it's not germs, but we humans and our bad habits that are the target: bad habits like smoking, overeating, and too little exercise. These habits have been linked to chronic diseases, including cancer, diabetes, and heart and lung disease, which together account for nearly two-thirds of deaths worldwide. The sad part is many of these are preventable. So, global leaders are changing direction. Now, they're looking at ways to get people to change their bad habits.

Based on what you've read in Part 1 of the text, especially when it comes to change,

- What suggestions would you make to these leaders in getting people to change? Be creative!
- What opportunities might be presented to new or existing organizations as a result of these challenges?
- Given the broad social implications posed by these challenges, are they best addressed by the private sector, not for profit sector, or government?

Global Sense

Who holds more managerial positions worldwide: women or men? Statistics tell an interesting story. In the United States, women held 50 percent of all managerial positions, but only 2.4 percent of the Fortune 500 CEO spots. In the United Kingdom, only 1.8 percent of the FTSE 500 companies' top positions are held by women. In Germany, women hold 35.6 percent of all management positions, but only 3 percent of women are executive board members. Asian countries have a much higher percentage of women in CEO positions. In Thailand, 30 percent of female managers hold the title of CEO as do 18 percent in Taiwan. In China, 19 percent of China's female workforce are CEOs. Even in Japan, 8 percent of senior managers are women. A census of Australia's top 200 companies listed on the Australian Stock Exchange showed that 11 percent of company executive managers

were women. Finally, in Arab countries, the percentage of women in management positions is less than 10 percent.

As you can see, companies across the globe have a large gender gap in leadership. Men far outnumber women in senior business leadership positions. These circumstances exist despite efforts and campaigns to improve equality in the workplace. One company—Deutsche Telekom—is tackling the problem head-on. It says it intends to "more than double the number of women who are managers within five years." In addition, it plans to increase the number of women in senior and middle management to 30 percent by the end of 2015. One action the company is taking is to improve and increase the recruiting of female university graduates. The company's goal: at least 30 percent of the places in executive development programs held by women. Other steps taken by the company revolve around the work environment and work-family issues. Deutsche's chief executive René Obermann said, "Taking on more women in management positions is not about the enforcement of misconstrued egalitarianism. Having a greater number of women at the top will quite simply enable us to operate better."

Discuss the following questions in light of what you learned in Part 1:

- What issues might Deutsche Telekom face in recruiting female university graduates?
- How could they address those issues?
- What issues might it face in introducing changes in work-family programs, and how could they address those issues?
- What do you think of Obermann's statement that having a greater number of women at the top will enable the company to operate better?
- What could other organizations around the globe learn from Deutsche Telekom?

Sources: J. Nerenberg, "Nearly 20 percent of Female Chinese Managers Are CEOs," [www.fastcompany.com], March 8, 2011; S. Doughty, "Cracking the Glass Ceiling: Female Staff Have the Same Chance As Men of Reaching the Top, Figures Reveal," [www.dailymail.co.uk], March 4, 2011; G. Toegel, "Disappointing Statistics, Positive Outlook," Forbes.com, February 18, 2011; E. Butler, "Wanted: Female Bosses for Germany," [www.bbc.co.uk], February 10, 2011; S. P. Robbins, M. Coulter, Y. Sidani, and D. Jamali, *Management: Arab World Edition*, (London: Pearson Education Limited), 2011, p. 5; "Proportion of Executive Managers and Board Directors of ASX 200 Companies Who Are Women," Australian Bureau of Statistics [www.abs.gov.au], September 15, 2010; Stevens and J. Espinoza, "Deutsche Telekom Sets Women-Manager Quota," *Wall Street Journal Online*, March 22, 2010; J. Blaue, "Deutsche Telekom Launches Quota for Top Women Managers," www.german-info.com/business_shownews; and N. Clark, "Goal at Deutsche Telekom: More Women as Managers," *New York Times Online*, March 15, 2010.

Decision Making

1. Describe the eight steps in the decision-making process.

2. Explain the four ways managers make decisions.

3. Classify decisions and decision-making conditions.

4. Describe different decision-making styles, and discuss how biases affect decision making.

5. Identify effective decision-making techniques.

Managers make decisions. And they want those decisions to be good decisions. In this chapter, we'll study the steps in the decision-making process. We'll also look at the various things that influence a manager as he or she makes decisions. After reading and studying this chapter, you will achieve the following learning outcomes.

▶ ▶ ▶ It was the end of the Christmas holiday in 2013 and Alexa Reedman, like students across the nation, was planning to return to Dalhousie University in Halifax for the winter term. This was not to be. Massive winter storms across North America in the days leading up to and immediately following New Year's day 2014 led to massive delays for travellers across Canada and North America. Some were stuck in airports for 48 hours and longer, while others had their return to university delayed for up to two weeks.[1] These are the types of days that airline managers and airport managers dread.

The polar vortex, which was at the heart of the cancellations and delays by Alexa Reedman faced as she attempted to return to Dalhousie University, ultimately resulted in the cancellation of 49 000 flights and delays of another 300 000 flights, impacting 30 million passengers during the month of January 2014. It turned out that two regulatory changes exacerbated the problem—one imposing fines for delays of longer of three hours with passengers on the plane and the other related to time that pilots are available to fly. (Time spent on the ground waiting counted against their total amount of available flying time for the month.)[2]

Aaron Harris/Reuters

How do organizations like the major airlines and airport authorities develop policies to develop protocols for making decisions under both routine and unplanned conditions?

Put yourself in the decision maker's shoes. What steps would you take to determine your course of action as the delays unfolded? How could the effectiveness of the decisions be evaluated after they were made?

The Decision-Making Process

Managers at all levels and in all areas of organizations make **decisions**. That is, they make choices. For instance, top-level managers make decisions about their organization's goals, where to locate manufacturing facilities, or what new markets to move into. Middle- and lower-level managers make decisions about production schedules, product quality problems, pay raises, and employee discipline. Making decisions isn't something that just managers do; all organizational members make decisions that affect their jobs and the organization they work for. But our focus is on how *managers* make decisions.

Although decision making is typically described as the act of choosing among alternatives, that view is simplistic. Why? Because decision making is a comprehensive process.[3] Even for something as straightforward as deciding where to go for lunch, you do more than just choose burgers or pizza. You may consider various restaurants, how you will get there, who might go with you. Granted, you may not spend a lot of time contemplating a lunch decision, but you still go through a process when making that decision. What *does* the decision-making process involve?

Exhibit 7-1 shows the eight steps in the **decision-making process** that begins with identifying a problem and decision criteria, and allocating weights to those criteria; moves to developing, analyzing, and selecting an alternative that can resolve the problem; then moves to implementing the alternative; and concludes with evaluating the decision's effectiveness.

This process is as relevant to your personal decision about what movie to see on a Friday night as it is to a corporate action such as a decision to use technology in managing client relationships. Let's take a closer look at the process in order to understand what each step involves. We will use an example—a manager deciding which laptop computers are best to purchase—to illustrate.

Step 1: Identify a Problem

Your team is dysfunctional, your customers are leaving, or your plans are no longer relevant.[4] Every decision starts with a **problem**, a discrepancy between an existing and a desired condition.[5] Amanda is a sales manager whose reps need new laptops because their old ones are outdated and inadequate for doing their job. To make it simple, assume it's not economical to add memory to the old computers and it's the company's policy to purchase, not lease. Now we have a problem—a disparity between the sales reps' current computers (existing condition) and their need to have more efficient ones (desired condition). Amanda has a decision to make.

How do managers identify problems? In the real world, most problems don't come with neon signs flashing "problem." When her reps started complaining about their computers, it was pretty clear to Amanda that something needed to be done, but few problems are that obvious. Managers also have to be cautious not to confuse problems with symptoms of a problem. Is a 5 percent drop in sales a problem? Or are declining sales merely a symptom of the real problem, such as poor-quality products, high prices, or bad advertising? Also, keep in mind that problem identification is subjective. What one manager considers a problem might not be considered a problem by another manager. In addition, a manager who resolves the wrong problem perfectly is likely to perform just as poorly as a manager

---

① Describe the eight steps in the decision-making process.

decision A choice from two or more alternatives.

decision-making process A set of eight steps that includes identifying a problem, selecting an alternative, and evaluating the decision's effectiveness.

problem A discrepancy between an existing and a desired state of affairs.

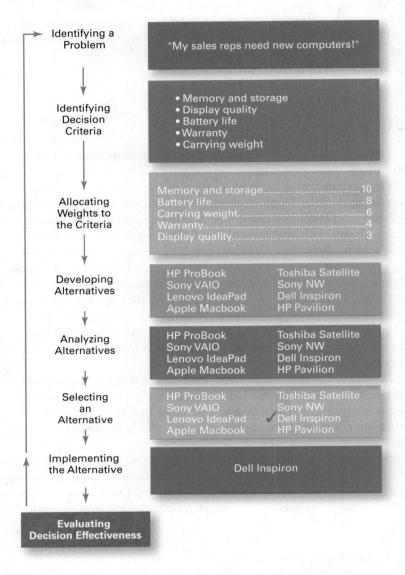

Exhibit 7-1

The Decision-Making Process

| Identifying a Problem | "My sales reps need new computers!" |

Identifying Decision Criteria
- Memory and storage
- Display quality
- Battery life
- Warranty
- Carrying weight

Allocating Weights to the Criteria

Memory and storage	10
Battery life	8
Carrying weight	6
Warranty	4
Display quality	3

Developing Alternatives

HP ProBook	Toshiba Satellite
Sony VAIO	Sony NW
Lenovo IdeaPad	Dell Inspiron
Apple Macbook	HP Pavilion

Analyzing Alternatives

HP ProBook	Toshiba Satellite
Sony VAIO	Sony NW
Lenovo IdeaPad	Dell Inspiron
Apple Macbook	HP Pavilion

Selecting an Alternative

HP ProBook	Toshiba Satellite
Sony VAIO	Sony NW
Lenovo IdeaPad	✓ Dell Inspiron
Apple Macbook	HP Pavilion

Implementing the Alternative

| | Dell Inspiron |

Evaluating Decision Effectiveness

who doesn't even recognize a problem and does nothing. As you can see, effectively identifying problems is important but not easy.[6]

Step 2: Identify Decision Criteria

Once a manager has identified a problem, he or she must identify the **decision criteria** important or relevant to resolving the problem. Every decision maker has criteria guiding his or her decisions even if they're not explicitly stated. In our example, Amanda decides after careful consideration that memory and storage capabilities, display quality, battery life, warranty, and carrying weight are the relevant criteria in her decision.

Step 3: Allocate Weights to Criteria

If the relevant criteria aren't equally important, the decision maker must weight the items in order to give them the correct priority in the decision. How? A simple way is to give the most important criterion a weight of 10 and then assign weights to the rest using that

decision criteria Criteria that define what is relevant in making a decision.

Decision making is an eight-step process that begins with identifying a problem and ends with evaluating the outcome of the decision. After problem identification, managers must determine the decision criteria that are relevant to solving the problem. For a manager looking for new laptops for her sales reps, the decision criteria may include price, display quality, memory and storage capabilities, battery life, and carrying weight. After the manager identifies the criteria, she must assign weights to the criteria if they aren't equally important.

Alex Segre/Alamy

standard. Of course, you could use any number as the highest weight. The weighted criteria for our example are shown in Exhibit 7-2.

Step 4: Develop Alternatives

The fourth step in the decision-making process requires the decision maker to list viable alternatives that could resolve the problem. In this step, a decision maker needs to be creative, and the alternatives are only listed—not evaluated—just yet. Our sales manager, Amanda, identifies eight laptops as possible choices (Exhibit 7-3).

Exhibit 7-2

Criteria and Weights for Laptop Replacement Decision

Criterion	Weight
Memory and storage capacity	10
Battery life	8
Carrying weight	6
Warranty	4
Display quality	3

Exhibit 7-3

Possible Alternatives

	Memory and Storage	Battery Life	Carrying Weight	Warranty	Display Quality
HP ProBook	10	3	10	8	5
Sony VAIO	8	7	7	8	7
Lenovo IdeaPad	8	5	7	10	10
Apple Macbook	8	7	7	8	7
Toshiba Satellite	7	8	7	8	7
Sony NW	8	3	6	10	8
Dell Inspiron	10	7	8	6	7
HP Pavilion	4	10	4	8	10

Exhibit 7-4

Evaluation of Laptop Alternatives Against Weighted Criteria

	Memory and Storage	Battery Life	Carrying Weight	Warranty	Display Quality	Total
HP ProBook	100	24	60	32	15	231
Sony VAIO	80	56	42	32	21	231
Lenovo IdeaPad	80	40	42	40	30	232
Apple Macbook	80	56	42	32	21	231
Toshiba Satellite	70	64	42	32	21	229
Sony NW	80	24	36	40	24	204
Dell Inspiron	100	56	48	24	21	249
HP Pavilion	40	80	24	32	30	206

Step 5: Analyze Alternatives

Once alternatives have been identified, a decision maker must evaluate each one. How? By using the criteria established in Step 2. Exhibit 7-3 shows the assessed values that Amanda gave each alternative after doing some research on them. Keep in mind that these data represent an assessment of the eight alternatives using the decision criteria, but *not* the weighting. When you multiply each alternative by the assigned weight, you get the weighted alternatives as shown in Exhibit 7-4. The total score for each alternative, then, is the sum of its weighted criteria.

Sometimes a decision maker might be able to skip this step. If one alternative scores highest on every criterion, you wouldn't need to consider the weights because that alternative would already be the top choice. Or if the weights were all equal, you could evaluate an alternative merely by summing up the assessed values for each one. (Look again at Exhibit 7-3.) For example, the score for the HP ProBook would be 36, and the score for the Sony NW would be 37.

Step 6: Select an Alternative

The sixth step in the decision-making process is choosing the best alternative or the one that generated the highest total in Step 5. In our example (Exhibit 7-4), Amanda would choose the Dell Inspiron because it scored higher than all other alternatives (249 total).

That said, occasionally, when one gets to this step, the alternative that looks best according to the numbers may not feel like the best solution. (For example, your intuition might suggest some other alternative.) Often the reason is that the individual did not give the correct weight to one or more criteria. (Perhaps because one criterion was actually much more important than the individual realized initially, when assigning weights.) Thus, if the individual finds that the "best alternative" does not seem like the right alternative, the decision maker needs to decide if a review of the criteria is necessary before implementing the alternative.

Step 7: Implement the Alternative

Step 7 is concerned with putting the decision into action. This involves conveying the decision to those affected by it and getting their commitment to it. Managers often fail to get buy-in from those around them before making a decision, even though successful implementation requires participation. One study found that managers used participation in only 20 percent of decisions, even though broad participation in decisions led to successful implementation 80 percent of the time. The same study found that managers most commonly tried to implement decisions through power or persuasion (used in 60 percent of decisions). These tactics were successful in only one of three decisions, however.[7] If the people who must carry out a decision participate in the process, they're more likely to enthusiastically support the outcome than if you just tell them what to do.

Step 8: Evaluate Decision Effectiveness

The last step in the decision-making process involves evaluating the outcome or result of the decision to see if the problem was resolved. If the evaluation showed that the problem still exists, then the manager needs to assess what went wrong. Was the problem incorrectly defined? Were errors made when evaluating alternatives? Was the right alternative selected but poorly implemented? The answers might lead you to redo an earlier step or might even require starting the whole process over.

→◉ Simulate on MyManagementLab

Decision-Making

The Manager as Decision Maker

▶ ▶ ▶ Toronto's Pearson International Airport is Canada's busiest airport, serving more than 36 million passengers[8] and 435 thousand aircraft movements.[9] Decision making is in the hands of managers at all levels of the organization and ranges from routine and recurring events to one-time non-recurring events and, in the case of the January weather story, an event that fell outside the known parameters.

❷ Explain the four ways managers make decisions.

Think About It

Although everyone in an organization makes decisions, decision making is particularly important to managers. As Exhibit 7-5 shows, it's part of all four managerial functions. In fact, that's why we say that decision making is the essence of management.[10] And that's why managers—when they plan, organize, lead, and control—are called *decision makers*. What management decisions are the managers at Pearson International Airport likely to be making in each of the four management areas in Exhibit 7-5?

Exhibit 7-5

Decisions in the Management Functions

Planning
- What are the organization's long-term objectives?
- What strategies will best achieve those objectives?
- What should the organization's short-term objectives be?
- How difficult should individual goals be?

Organizing
- How many employees should I have report directly to me?
- How much centralization should there be in the organization?
- How should jobs be designed?
- When should the organization implement a different structure?

Leading
- How do I handle employees who appear to be low in motivation?
- What is the most effective leadership style in a given situation?
- How will a specific change affect worker productivity?
- When is the right time to stimulate conflict?

Controlling
- What activities in the organization need to be controlled?
- How should those activities be controlled?
- When is a performance deviation significant?
- What type of management information system should the organization have?

Exhibit 7-6

Assumptions of Rationality

- The problem is clear and unambiguous.
- A single, well-defined goal is to be achieved.
- All alternatives and consequences are known.
- Preferences are clear.
- Preferences are constant and stable.
- No time or cost constraints exist.
- Final choice will maximize payoff.

Lead to → **Rational Decision Making**

The fact that almost everything a manager does involves making decisions doesn't mean that decisions are always time-consuming, complex, or evident to an outside observer. Most decision making is routine. Every day of the year, you make a decision about what to eat for dinner. It's no big deal. You've made the decision thousands of times before. It's a pretty simple decision and can usually be handled quickly. It's the type of decision you almost forget *is* a decision. And managers also make dozens of these routine decisions every day—for example, which employee will work what shift next week, what information should be included in a report, or how to resolve a customer's complaint. Keep in mind that even though a decision seems easy or has been faced by a manager a number of times before, it still is a decision. Let's look at four perspectives on how managers make decisions.

The decision-making process described in Exhibit 7-1 suggests that individuals make rational, carefully scripted decisions. But is this the best way to describe the decision-making situation and the person who makes the decisions? We look at those issues in this section.

Making Decisions: Rationality

Our model of the decision-making process, as laid out in Exhibit 7-6, implies that individuals engage in **rational decision making**. By that we mean that people make consistent, value-maximizing choices within specified constraints.[11] What are the underlying assumptions of rationality, and how valid are those assumptions?

Assumptions of Rationality

A rational decision maker would be fully objective and logical. The problem faced would be clear and unambiguous, and the decision maker would have a clear and specific goal and know all possible alternatives and consequences. Finally, making decisions rationally would consistently lead to selecting the alternative that maximizes the likelihood of achieving that goal. These assumptions apply to any decision—personal or managerial. However, for managerial decision making, we need to add one additional assumption: Decisions are made in the best interests of the organization. Most decisions that managers face in the real world don't meet the assumptions of rationality.[12] So how are most decisions in organizations usually made? The concept of bounded rationality can help answer that question.

Making Decisions: Bounded Rationality

Despite the unrealistic assumptions, managers *are* expected to be rational when making decisions.[13] They understand that "good" decision makers are supposed to do certain things and exhibit good decision-making behaviours as they identify problems, consider alternatives, gather information, and act decisively but prudently. When they do so, they show others that they're competent and that their decisions are the result of intelligent deliberation. Most decisions that managers make don't fit the assumptions of perfect

rational decision making
Making decisions that are consistent and value-maximizing within specified constraints.

rationality (where all the steps above are followed, and all alternatives are known and fully understood). Instead, managers make those decisions under assumptions of **bounded rationality**. That is, they make decisions rationally, but are limited (bounded) by their ability to process information.[14] Because they cannot possibly analyze all information on all alternatives, managers **satisfice** rather than maximize. Rather than carefully evaluate each alternative in great detail, managers settle on an alternative that is "good enough"— one that meets an acceptable level of performance. The first alternative that meets the "good enough" criterion ends the search.

Let's look at an example. Suppose that you are a finance major and upon graduation you want a job, preferably as a personal financial planner, with a minimum salary of $50 000 and within 100 kilometres of your hometown. You accept a job offer as a business credit analyst—not exactly a personal financial planner but still in the finance field—at a bank 50 kilometres from home at a starting salary of $55 000. A more comprehensive job search would have revealed a job in personal financial planning at a trust company only 25 kilometres from your hometown and starting at a salary of $57 000. Because the first job offer was satisfactory (or "good enough"), you behaved in a boundedly rational manner by accepting it, although according to the assumptions of perfect rationality, you did not maximize your decision by searching all possible alternatives and then choosing the best.

Most decisions that managers make don't fit the assumptions of perfect rationality, so they satisfice. However, keep in mind that their decision making is also likely influenced by the organization's culture, internal politics, power considerations, and by a phenomenon called **escalation of commitment,** an increased commitment to a previous decision despite evidence that it may have been wrong.[15] The *Challenger* space shuttle disaster is often used as an example of escalation of commitment. Decision makers chose to launch the shuttle even though the decision was questioned by several individuals who believed it was a bad one. Why will decision makers escalate commitment to a bad decision? Because they don't want to admit that their initial decision may have been flawed. Rather than search for new alternatives, they simply increase their commitment to the original solution.

Making Decisions: The Role of Intuition

When managers at stapler maker Swingline saw the company's market share declining, they decided to use a logical scientific approach to help them address the issue. For three years, they exhaustively researched stapler users before deciding what new products to develop.

However, at Accentra Inc., founder Todd Moses used a more intuitive decision approach to come up with his line of unique PaperPro staplers. His stapler sold 1 million units in 6 months in a market that sells only 25 million units in total annually—a pretty good result for a new product.[16]

Like Todd Moses, managers regularly use their intuition, which may actually help improve their decision making.[17] What is **intuitive decision making**? It's making decisions on the basis of experience, feelings, and accumulated judgment. Researchers studying managers' use of intuitive decision making identified five different aspects of intuition, which are described in Exhibit 7-7.[18]

Making a decision on intuition or "gut feeling" does not necessarily happen independently of rational analysis; rather, the two complement each other. A manager who has had experience with a particular, or even similar, type of problem or situation often can act quickly with what appears to be limited information. Such a manager does not rely on a systematic and thorough analysis of the problem or identification and evaluation of alternatives but instead uses his or her experience and judgment to make a decision.

bounded rationality Limitations on a person's ability to interpret, process, and act on information.

satisfice To accept solutions that are "good enough."

escalation of commitment An increased commitment to a previous decision despite evidence that it might have been wrong.

intuitive decision making Making decisions on the basis of experience, feelings, and accumulated judgment.

"Trust your instincts" is one of the guiding principles for decision making advocated by Virgin Group founder Richard Branson. When Branson decided to enter the airline business, industry experts warned him that the competition was too fierce and the cost of entry was too high for him to succeed. Relying on his intuition, Branson decided to enter the market with the mission of running a profitable airline where people love to fly and where people love to work. He felt that by applying the right energy, focus, and flair his venture would succeed, and it did. Branson is shown here dressed up as a prize fighter determined to knock out his competitors while celebrating the launch of Virgin America's expanded service to Chicago with crew members.

ZUMA Press, Inc./Alamy

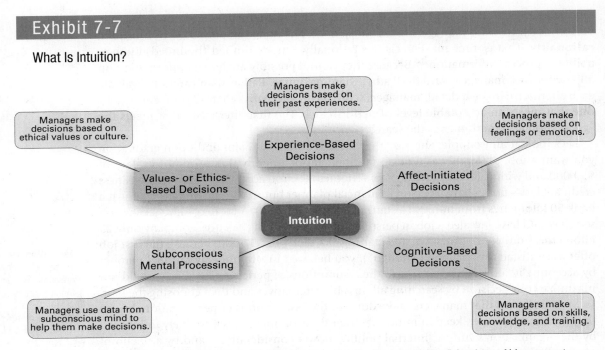

Exhibit 7-7

What Is Intuition?

Managers make decisions based on their past experiences.

Experience-Based Decisions

Managers make decisions based on ethical values or culture.

Values- or Ethics-Based Decisions

Managers make decisions based on feelings or emotions.

Affect-Initiated Decisions

Intuition

Subconscious Mental Processing

Cognitive-Based Decisions

Managers use data from subconscious mind to help them make decisions.

Managers make decisions based on skills, knowledge, and training.

Source: Based on L. A. Burke and M. K. Miller, "Taking the Mystery Out of Intuitive Decision Making," *Academy of Management Executive*, October 1999, pp. 91–99.

How common is intuitive decision making? One survey found that almost half of the executives surveyed "used intuition more often than formal analysis to run their companies."[19] Intuitive decision making can complement both rational and bounded rational decision making.[20] First of all, a manager who has had experience with a similar type of problem or situation often can act quickly with what appears to be limited information because of that past experience. In addition, a recent study found that individuals who experienced intense feelings and emotions when making decisions actually achieved higher decision-making performance, especially when they understood their feelings as they were making decisions. The old belief that managers should ignore emotions when making decisions may not be the best advice.[21]

Making Decisions:
The Role of Evidence-Based Management

Sales associates at the cosmetics counter at department store Bon-Ton Stores Inc. had the highest turnover of any store sales group. Using a data-driven decision approach, managers devised a more precise pre-employment assessment test. Now, not only do they have lower turnover, they actually have better hires.[22]

Suppose you were exhibiting some strange, puzzling physical symptoms. In order to make the best decisions about proper diagnosis and treatment, wouldn't you want your doctor to base her decisions on the best available evidence? Now suppose you're a manager faced with putting together an employee recognition program. Wouldn't you want those decisions also to be based on the best available evidence? "Any decision-making process is likely to be enhanced through the use of relevant and reliable evidence, whether it's buying someone a birthday present or wondering which new washing machine to buy."[23] That's the premise behind **evidence-based management (EBMgt)**, the "systematic use of the best available evidence to improve management practice."[24]

EBMgt is quite relevant to managerial decision making. The four essential elements of EBMgt are the decision maker's expertise and judgment; external evidence that's been evaluated by the decision maker; opinions, preferences, and values of those who have a

evidence-based management (EBMgt) The systematic use of the best available evidence to improve management practice.

stake in the decision; and relevant organizational (internal) factors such as context, circumstances, and organizational members. The strength or influence of each of these elements on a decision will vary with each decision. Sometimes, the decision maker's intuition (judgment) might be given greater emphasis in the decision; other times it might be the opinions of stakeholders; and at other times, it might be ethical considerations (organizational context). The key for managers is to recognize and understand the mindful, conscious choice as to which element(s) are most important and should be emphasized in making a decision.

Types of Decisions and Decision-Making Conditions

▶ ▶ ▶ Managers at the major airlines and airports make routine decisions about maintenance, baggage handling, purchasing supplies, and scheduling employee work shifts. It's something they have done numerous times. But the weather conditions they experienced in January 2014 were something they had not seen before.

3 Classify decisions and decision-making conditions.

> **Think About It**
>
> Managers at the major airlines and airport authorities will face different types of problems and decisions as they do their jobs. Some problems are structured and recurring, while others are unstructured and nonrecurring. Can you think of some examples?

Types of Decisions

Structured Problems and Programmed Decisions

Some problems are straightforward. The goal of the decision maker is clear, the problem is familiar, and information about the problem is easily defined and complete. Examples of these types of problems could include what to do when a customer returns a purchase to a store, a supplier delivers an important product late, a news team wants to respond to a fast-breaking event, or a student wants to drop a class. Such situations are called **structured problems** because they are straightforward, familiar, and easily defined. When situations are structured, there is probably some standardized routine for handling problems that may arise. For example, when a restaurant server spills a drink on a customer's coat, the manager offers to have the coat cleaned at the restaurant's expense. This is what we call a **programmed decision**, a repetitive decision that can be handled by a routine approach. Why? Because once the structured problem is defined, the solution is usually self-evident or at least reduced to a few alternatives that are familiar and have proved successful in the past. The spilled drink on the customer's coat doesn't require the restaurant manager to identify and weight decision criteria or to develop a long list of possible solutions. Instead, the manager relies on one of three types of programmed decisions: procedure, rule, or policy.

A **procedure** is a series of interrelated sequential steps that a decision maker can use to respond to a structured problem. The only difficulty is in identifying the problem. Once it's clear, so is the procedure. For instance, when bad weather grounds airplanes, airlines have procedures for helping customers who miss their flights. Customers may request being put up in hotels for the night. The customer service agent knows how to make this decision—follow the established airline procedure for dealing with customers when flights are grounded.

A **rule** is an explicit statement that tells a decision maker what he or she can or cannot do. Rules are frequently used because they are simple to follow and ensure consistency. For example, rules about lateness and absenteeism permit supervisors to make disciplinary decisions rapidly and fairly.

structured problems Problems that are straightforward, familiar, and easily defined.

programmed decisions Repetitive decisions that can be handled by a routine approach.

procedure A series of interrelated sequential steps that a decision maker can use to respond to a structured problem.

rule An explicit statement that tells a decision maker what he or she can or cannot do.

policy A guideline for making a decision.

A **policy** is a guideline for making a decision. In contrast to a rule, a policy establishes general parameters for the decision maker rather than specifically stating what should or should not be done. Policies typically contain an ambiguous term that leaves interpretation up to the decision maker. "The customer always comes first and should always be *satisfied*" is an example of a policy statement. While ambiguity of policies is often intended to allow more flexibility in action, not all employees and customers are comfortable with flexibly determined policies.

Here are some sample policy statements:

- The customer always comes first and should always be *satisfied*.

- We promote from within, *whenever possible*.

- Employee wages shall be *competitive* within community standards.

Unstructured Problems and Nonprogrammed Decisions

◄●─ Simulate on MyManagementLab

Firing an Employee

unstructured problems
Problems that are new or unusual and for which information is ambiguous or incomplete.

nonprogrammed decisions Decisions that are unique and nonrecurring and require custom-made solutions.

Many organizational situations involve **unstructured problems**, which are problems that are new or unusual and for which information is ambiguous or incomplete. The toughest of these unstructured problems were introduced in Chapter 6 as wicked problems, which are characterized by the fact that the problem and the solution are interrelated; key stakeholders have wildly different perspectives and frames of reference; the constraints related to the problem and the resources needed to resolve it change over time; and the problem is never definitively solved—it is a continuing work in progress.

Nonprogrammed decisions are unique and nonrecurring and require custom-made solutions. For instance, if an office building were to be flooded because sprinklers went off accidentally, CEOs with businesses in the building would have to decide when and how to start operating again and what to do for employees whose offices were completely ruined. When a manager confronts an unstructured problem, there is no cut-and-dried solution. It requires a custom-made response through nonprogrammed decision making.

Few managerial decisions in the real world are either fully programmed or nonprogrammed. These are extremes, and most decisions fall somewhere in between. Few programmed decisions are designed to eliminate individual judgment completely. At the other extreme, even a unique situation requiring a nonprogrammed decision can be helped by programmed routines. It's best to think of decisions as *mainly* programmed or *mainly* nonprogrammed, rather than as completely one or the other.

The problems confronting managers usually become more unstructured as they move up the organizational hierarchy. Why? Because lower-level managers handle the routine

Many people believe that China will become the next big market for powerful brand-name products, and Zong Qinghou, founder of China's Wahaha beverage group, plans to be ready. But brand names are a new concept in Chinese markets, and Zong prefers his own first-hand information to market research. He will face many nonprogrammed decisions as he tries to make his brand a success at home and eventually abroad.

Bloomberg/Contributor/Getty Images

decisions themselves and let upper-level managers deal with the decisions they find unusual or difficult. Similarly, higher-level managers delegate routine decisions to their subordinates so that they can deal with more difficult issues.[25]

One of the more challenging tasks facing managers as they make decisions is analyzing decision alternatives (step 5 in the decision-making process). In the next section, we look at analyzing alternatives under different conditions.

Decision-Making Conditions

When managers make decisions, they face three conditions: certainty, risk, and uncertainty. What are the characteristics of each?

Certainty

The ideal condition for making decisions is one of **certainty**, that is, a condition in which a decision maker can make accurate decisions because the outcome of every alternative is known. For example, when Saskatchewan's finance minister is deciding in which bank to deposit excess provincial funds, he knows the exact interest rate being offered by each bank and the amount that will be earned on the funds. He is certain about the outcomes of each alternative. As you might expect, most managerial decisions are not like this.

certainty A condition in which a decision maker can make accurate decisions because the outcome of every alternative is known.

Risk

A far more common condition is one of **risk**, a condition in which a decision maker is able to estimate the likelihood of certain outcomes. The ability to assign probabilities to outcomes may be the result of personal experiences or secondary information. With risk, managers have historical data that let them assign probabilities to different alternatives. Let's work through an example.

Suppose that you manage a ski resort in Whistler, BC. You are thinking about adding another lift to your current facility. Obviously, your decision will be influenced by the additional revenue that the new lift would generate, and additional revenue will depend on snowfall. The decision is made somewhat clearer because you have fairly reliable weather data from the past 10 years on snowfall levels in your area—three years of heavy snowfall, five years of normal snowfall, and two years of light snowfall. Can you use this information to help you make your decision about adding the new lift? If you have good information on the amount of revenues generated during each level of snow, the answer is yes.

You can calculate expected value—the expected return from each possible outcome—by multiplying expected revenues by snowfall probabilities. The result is the average revenue you can expect over time if the given probabilities hold. As Exhibit 7-8 shows, the expected revenue from adding a new ski lift is $687 500. Of course, whether that justifies a decision to build or not depends on the costs involved in generating that revenue. Making estimates of the probability of a set of outcomes is not a substitute for common sense. One of the contributing factors to the collapse of financial markets in the fall of 2008 was that "teams

risk A condition in which a decision maker is able to estimate the likelihood of certain outcomes.

Exhibit 7-8

Expected Value for Revenues from the Addition of One Ski Lift

Event	Expected Revenues	×	Probability	=	Expected Value of Each Alternative
Heavy snowfall	$850 000		0.3		$255 000
Normal snowfall	725 000		0.5		362 500
Light snowfall	350 000		0.2		70 000
					$687 500

of math geniuses had used sophisticated algorithms to forecast default rates on sub-prime mortgages." The problem was that they looked at historical data that ignored the high-risk nature of the underlying financial instrument, and although the models predicted default rates of 10 to 12 percent, actual default rates were as high as 60 percent.[26]

Uncertainty

What happens if you have a decision where you are not certain about the outcomes and cannot even make reasonable probability estimates? We call such a condition **uncertainty**. Managers do face decision-making situations of uncertainty. Under these conditions, the choice of alternative is influenced by the limited amount of information available to the decision maker and by the psychological orientation of the decision maker. The optimistic manager will follow a *maximax* choice (maximizing the maximum possible payoff) in order to get the largest possible gain. The pessimist will follow a *maximin* choice (maximizing the minimum possible payoff) to make the best of a situation should the worst possible outcome occur. The manager who desires to minimize his maximum "regret" will opt for a *minimax* choice, to avoid having big regrets after decisions play out. Let's look at these different choice approaches using an example.

A marketing manager at Visa has determined four possible strategies (S1, S2, S3, and S4) for promoting the Visa card throughout western Canada. The marketing manager also knows that major competitor MasterCard has three competitive actions (CA1, CA2, CA3) it's using to promote its card in the same region. For this example, we will assume that the Visa executive had no previous knowledge that would allow her to place probabilities on the success of any of the four strategies. She formulates the matrix shown in Exhibit 7-9 to show the various Visa strategies and the resulting profit to Visa depending on the competitive action used by MasterCard.

In this example, if our Visa manager is an optimist, she will choose S4 because that could produce the largest possible gain: $28 million. Note that this choice maximizes the maximum possible gain (the *maximax* choice).

If our manager is a pessimist, she will assume that only the worst can occur. The worst outcome for each strategy is as follows: S1 = $11 million; S2= $9 million; S3 = $15 million; S4 = $14 million. These are the most pessimistic outcomes from each strategy. Following the *maximin* choice, she would maximize the minimum payoff; in other words, she would select S3 ($15 million is the largest of the minimum payoffs).

In the third approach, managers recognize that once a decision is made, it will not necessarily result in the most profitable payoff. There may be a "regret" of profits given up—*regret* referring to the amount of money that could have been made had a different strategy been used. Managers calculate regret by subtracting all possible payoffs in each category from the maximum possible payoff for each given event, in this case for each competitive action. For our Visa manager, the highest payoff, given that MasterCard engages in CA_1, CA_2, or CA_3, is $24 million, $21 million, or $28 million, respectively (the highest number in each column). Subtracting the payoffs in Exhibit 7-9 from those figures produces the results shown in Exhibit 7-10.

Exhibit 7-9

Payoff Matrix

(in millions of dollars)

Visa Marketing Strategy	MasterCard's Response		
	CA_1	CA_2	CA_3
S_1	13	14	11
S_2	9	15	18
S_3	24	21	15
S_4	18	14	28

Exhibit 7-10

Regret Matrix

(in millions of dollars)

Visa Marketing Strategy	MasterCard's Response		
	CA_1	CA_2	CA_3
S_1	11	7	17
S_2	15	6	10
S_3	0	0	13
S_4	6	7	0

The maximum regrets are S1 = $17 million; S2 = $15 million; S3 = $13 million; and S4 = $7 million. The *minimax* choice minimizes the maximum regret, so our Visa manager would choose S4. By making this choice, she will never have a regret of giving up profits of more than $7 million. This result contrasts, for example, with a regret of $15 million had she chosen S2 and MasterCard had taken CA1.

Although managers will try to quantify a decision when possible by using payoff and regret matrices, uncertainty often forces them to rely more on intuition, creativity, hunches, and "gut feel."

Regardless of the decision that needs to be made and the conditions that affect it, each manager has his or her own style of making decisions.

MANAGEMENT REFLECTION

Technology Tools as Aids in Managerial Decision Making

Do you have an e-book reader? You'd be surprised at what digital-book publishers and retailers now know about you. The major players in e-book publishing—Amazon, Apple, and Google—can "easily track how far readers are getting in books, how long they spend reading them and which search terms they use to find books." For instance, this passage from *Catching Fire*, the second book of *The Hunger Games* series—"Because sometimes things happen to people and they're not equipped to deal with them"—was the most highlighted among Kindle readers. And according to Nook data, science-fiction, romance, and crime-fiction fans often read more books more quickly than readers of literary fiction.[27]

The possibilities of technology as a tool for managerial decision making are endless and fascinating! Artificial intelligence software will be available to approach problems the way the human brain does—by trying to recognize patterns that underlie a complex set of data. Like people, this software will "learn" to pick out subtle patterns. In so doing, it will be able to perform a number of decision-making tasks.

Just as today's computers allow you to access information quickly from sources such as spreadsheets or search engines, most of the routine decisions that employees now do on the job are likely to be delegated to a software program. For instance, much of the diagnostic work now done by doctors will be done by software. Patients will describe their symptoms to a computer in a medical kiosk, possibly at their neighbourhood drugstore; from answers the patient provides, the computer will render a decision. Similarly, many hiring decisions will be made by software programmed to simulate the successful decision processes used by recruiters and managers. Welcome to the future of decision making! ■

Decision-Making Styles

Describe different decision-making styles, and discuss how biases affect decision making.

▶ ▶ ▶ Howard Eng assumed the position of President and Chief Executive Officer of the Greater Toronto Airports Authority (GTAA) on March 29, 2012. The GTAA manages and operates Toronto Pearson International Airport. Mr. Eng was the Executive Director, Airport Operations of the Airport Authority Hong Kong up to March 2012. Mr. Eng was integral in moving Hong Kong onto the world stage as a global hub that enjoys consistently high ratings from guests, including a top rating from Skytrax.[28] The new strategic vision is that Toronto Pearson will become North America's premier entry point on the continent—"your global front door." The GTAA is focused on becoming more consumer-centric, recognizing the need to be competitive both operationally and from a customer service perspective. In Eng's words, "The job is to truly differentiate ourselves by delighting customers through excellence in service and product innovations."[29]

linear thinking style Decision style characterized by a person's preference for using external data and facts and processing this information through rational, logical thinking.

nonlinear thinking style Decision style characterized by a person's preference for internal sources of information and processing this information with internal insights, feelings, and hunches.

> ### Think About It
>
> **What biases might enter into the decision making of managers at Pearson International, and how might Eng overcome these? How can they improve their decision making, given that they are dealing with uncertainty and risk? How might escalation of commitment affect their decisions?**

Decision-making styles differ along two dimensions.[30] The first dimension is an individual's *way of thinking*. Some of us are more rational and logical in the way we process information. A rational type processes information in order and makes sure that it's logical and consistent before making a decision. Others tend to be creative and intuitive. An intuitive type does not have to process information in a certain order and is comfortable looking at it as a whole.

The other dimension is an individual's *tolerance for ambiguity*. Some of us have a low tolerance for ambiguity. These types need consistency and order in the way they structure information so that ambiguity is minimized. On the other hand, some of us can tolerate high levels of ambiguity and are able to process many thoughts at the same time.

William D. Perez's tenure as Nike's CEO lasted a short and turbulent 13 months. Analysts attributed his abrupt dismissal to a difference in decision-making approaches between him and Nike co-founder Phil Knight. Perez tended to rely more on data and facts when making decisions, whereas Knight highly valued, and had always used, his judgment and feelings to make decisions.[31] As this example clearly shows, managers have different styles when it comes to making decisions.

Nonlinear thinking characterizes the decision-making style of Hamdi Ulukaya, founder of the Chobani brand of yogurt. A native of Turkey, Hamdi says that people thought he was crazy when, after reading a for-sale ad for a small yogurt factory, he decided to buy it the next day based on a gut feeling that he could do something to introduce a quality, Greek-style yogurt in the United States without having any knowledge about how to do it. Hamdi also used nonlinear thinking in guiding his decisions involved in marketing and distributing Chobani. In this photo, Hamdi (centre) and employees display yogurt creations at Chobani SoHo, a first-of-its-kind Mediterranean yogurt bar, at its opening celebration in New York City.

Diane Bondareff/Invision for Chobani/AP Images

Linear–Nonlinear Thinking Style Profile

Suppose you're a new manager. How will you make decisions? Recent research done with four distinct groups of people says the way a person approaches decision making is likely affected by his or her thinking style.[32] Your thinking style reflects two things: (1) the source of information you tend to use (external data and facts OR internal sources such as feelings and intuition) and (2) whether you process that information in a linear way (rational, logical, analytical) OR a nonlinear way (intuitive, creative, insightful). These four dimensions are collapsed into two styles. The first, **linear thinking style**, is characterized by a person's preference for using external data and facts and processing this information through rational, logical thinking to guide decisions and actions. The second, **nonlinear thinking style**, is characterized by a preference for internal sources of information (feelings and intuition) and processing this information with internal insights, feelings, and hunches to guide decisions and actions. Look back at the earlier Nike example and you'll see both styles described.

Managers need to recognize that their employees may use different decision-making styles. Some employees may take their time weighing alternatives and rely on how they feel about it, while others rely on external data before logically making a decision. These differences don't make one person's approach better than the other. It just means their decision making styles are different.

Decision-Making Biases and Errors

When managers make decisions, not only do they use their own particular style, but many use "rules of thumb," or **heuristics**, to simplify their decision making. Rules of thumb can be useful to decision makers because they help make sense of complex, uncertain, and ambiguous information.[33] Even though managers may use rules of thumb, that does not mean those rules are reliable. Why? Because they may lead to errors and biases in processing and evaluating information. Exhibit 7-11 identifies twelve common decision-making biases and errors. Let's take a quick look at each.[34]

When decision makers tend to think they know more than they do or hold unrealistically positive views of themselves and their performance, they're exhibiting the *overconfidence bias*. The *immediate gratification bias* describes decision makers who tend to want immediate rewards and to avoid immediate costs. For these individuals, decision choices that provide quick payoffs are more appealing than those with payoffs in the future. The *anchoring effect* describes how decision makers fixate on initial information as a starting point and then, once set, fail to adequately adjust for subsequent information. First impressions, ideas, prices, and estimates carry unwarranted weight relative to information received later. When decision makers selectively organize and interpret events based on their biased perceptions, they're using the *selective perception bias*. This influences the information they pay attention to, the problems they identify, and the alternatives they develop. Decision makers who seek out information that reaffirms their past choices and

heuristics Rules of thumb that managers use to simplify decision making.

Exhibit 7-11

Common Decision-Making Biases and Errors

discount information that contradicts past judgments exhibit the *confirmation bias.* These people tend to accept at face value information that confirms their preconceived views, and are critical and skeptical of information that challenges these views. The *framing bias* occurs when decision makers select and highlight certain aspects of a situation while excluding others. By drawing attention to specific aspects of a situation and highlighting them, while at the same time downplaying or omitting other aspects, they distort what they see and create incorrect reference points. The *availability bias* happens when decision makers tend to remember events that are the most recent and vivid in their memory. The result? It distorts their ability to recall events in an objective manner and results in distorted judgments and probability estimates. When decision makers assess the likelihood of an event based on how closely it resembles other events or sets of events, that's the *representation bias.* Managers exhibiting this bias draw analogies and see identical situations where they don't exist. The *randomness bias* describes the actions of decision makers who try to create meaning out of random events. They do this because most decision makers have difficulty dealing with chance even though random events happen to everyone, and there's nothing that can be done to predict them. The *sunk costs error* occurs when decision makers forget that current choices can't correct the past. They incorrectly fixate on past expenditures of time, money, or effort in assessing choices rather than on future consequences. Instead of ignoring sunk costs, they can't forget them. Decision makers who are quick to take credit for their successes and to blame failure on outside factors are exhibiting the *self-serving bias.* Finally, the *hindsight bias* is the tendency for decision

Exhibit 7-12

Overview of Managerial Decision Making

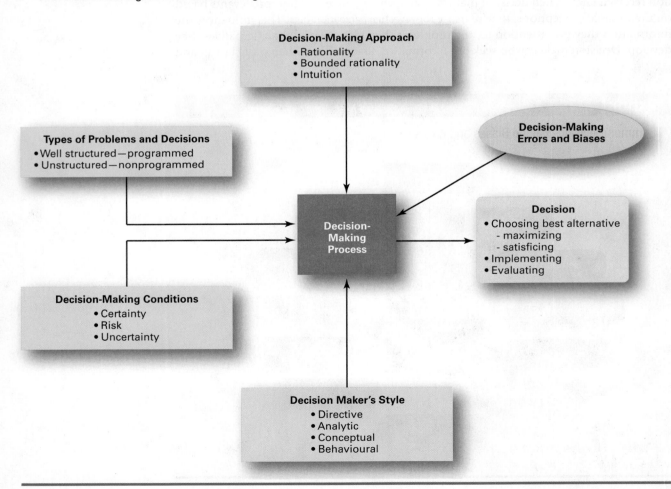

makers to falsely believe that they would have accurately predicted the outcome of an event once that outcome is actually known.

How can managers avoid the negative effects of these decision-making errors and biases? The main thing is being aware of them and then trying not to exhibit them. Beyond that, managers also should pay attention to "how" they make decisions and try to identify the heuristics they typically use and critically evaluate how appropriate those are. Finally, managers might want to ask those around them to help identify weaknesses in their decision-making style and try to improve on them.

Summing Up Managerial Decision Making

How can we best sum up managerial decision making? Exhibit 7-12 provides an overview. Because it's in their best interests, managers *want* to make good decisions—that is, choose the "best" alternative, implement it, and determine whether or not it takes care of the problem that created the reason a decision was needed in the first place. Their decision-making process is affected by four factors, including the decision-making approach being followed, the decision-making conditions, the type of problem being dealt with, and the decision maker's own style of decision making. In addition, certain decision-making errors and biases may impact the process. Each of these factors plays a role in determining how a manager makes a decision. So whether that decision involves addressing an employee's habitual tardiness, resolving a problem with product quality, or determining whether to enter a new market, remember that it has been shaped by a number of factors.

Effective Decision Making for Today's World

▶ ▶ ▶ The impact of the massive cancellations attributed to the polar vortex in late December 2013 changed the way managers at airports made decisions. At Pearson International airport an April 2014 report recommended changes in the way Pearson International airport deals with extreme weather in the future including doing a better job communicating with the public; having guidelines for responding to passengers during the weather crisis; boosting of the airport's Wi-Fi and cellphone service capacity; and taking warming stations to the tarmac to allow employees to increase the time spent outdoors.

> ### Think About It
> **Looking at the lessons learned at Pearson International Airport, can you think of others things can be done to proactively make better decisions during a crisis? How important is it to debrief with employees following an unplanned event like this? Why?**

Per Carlsson, a product development manager at IKEA, "spends his days creating Volvo-style kitchens at Yugo prices." His job is to take the "problems" identified by the company's product-strategy council (a group of globe-trotting senior managers that monitors consumer trends and establishes product priorities) and turn them into furniture that customers around the world want to buy. One "problem" identified by the council: The kitchen has replaced the living room as the social and entertaining centre in the home. Customers are looking for kitchens that convey comfort and cleanliness while still allowing them to pursue their gourmet aspirations. Carlsson must take this information and make things happen. There are a lot of decisions to make—programmed and nonprogrammed—and the fact that IKEA is a global company makes it even more challenging. Comfort in Asia means small, cozy appliances and spaces, while North American customers want oversized glassware and giant refrigerators. His ability to make good decisions quickly has significant implications for IKEA's success.[36]

Today's business world revolves around making decisions, often risky ones, usually with incomplete or inadequate information, and under intense time pressure. Making good business decisions in today's rapid-paced and messy world isn't easy. Things happen

datapoints[35]

7 percentage points higher returns is what organizations gained when they reduced the effect of bias in their decision-making processes.

90 percent of people believe they are just a little more competent, smarter, or kinder than average.

91 percent of companies use teams and groups to solve specific problems.

40 percent more ideas are generated with electronic brainstorming than with individuals brainstorming alone.

59 percent of employees said a key obstacle to their job is that more attention is paid to placing blame than to solving problems.

77 percent of managers said the number of decisions they made during a typical workday had increased.

54 percent of managers said the amount of time given to each decision had decreased.

In Asia, RPS (rock, paper, scissors) is more recognized as a decision tiebreaker than it is in the United States.

20 percent of adults said they think most creatively in their cars.

5 Identify effective decision-making techniques.

too fast. Customers come and go in the click of a mouse or the swipe of a screen. Market landscapes can shift dramatically overnight along several dimensions. Competitors can enter a market and exit it just as quickly as they entered. Thriving and prospering under such conditions means managerial decision making must adapt to these realities. Most managers make one decision after another; and as if that weren't challenging enough, more is at stake than ever before. Bad decisions can cost millions. What do managers need to do to make effective decisions in today's fast-moving world? First, let's look at some suggested guidelines. Then, we'll discuss an interesting new line of thinking that has implications for making effective decisions—especially for business types—called design thinking.

Guidelines for Effective Decision Making

Decision making is serious business. Your abilities and track record as an effective decision maker will determine how your organizational work performance is evaluated and whether you'll be promoted to higher and higher positions of responsibility. Here are some guidelines to help you be a better decision maker.

- **Understand cultural differences.** Managers everywhere want to make good decisions. However, is there only one "best" way worldwide to make decisions? Or does the "best way depend on the values, beliefs, attitudes, and behavioural patterns of the people involved?"[37]

- **Create standards for good decision making.** Good decisions are forward-looking, use available information, consider all available and viable options, and do not create conflicts of interest.[38]

- **Know when it's time to call it quits.** When it's evident that a decision isn't working, don't be afraid to pull the plug. For instance, the CEO of L. L. Bean pulled the plug on building a new customer call centre in Waterville, Maine—"literally stopping the bulldozers in their tracks"—after T-Mobile said it was building its own call centre right next door. He was afraid that the city would not have enough qualified workers for both companies and so decided to build 55 miles away in Bangor.[39] He knew when it was time to call it quits. However, as we said earlier, many decision makers block or distort negative information because they don't want to believe their decision was bad. They become so attached to a decision that they refuse to recognize when it's time to move on. In today's dynamic environment, this type of thinking simply won't work.

- **Use an effective decision-making process.** Experts say an effective decision-making process has these six characteristics: (1) it focuses on what's important; (2) it's logical and consistent; (3) it acknowledges both subjective and objective thinking and blends analytical with intuitive thinking; (4) it requires only as much information and analysis as is necessary to resolve a particular dilemma; (5) it encourages and guides the gathering of relevant information and informed opinion; and (6) it's straightforward, reliable, easy to use, and flexible."[40]

- **Build an organization that can spot the unexpected and quickly adapt to the changed environment.** This suggestion comes from Karl Weick, an organizational psychologist, who has made a career of studying organizations and how people work.[41] He calls such organizations *highly reliable organizations* (HROs) and says they share five habits. (1) They're *not tricked by their success.* HROs are preoccupied with their failures. They're alert to the smallest deviations and react quickly to anything that doesn't fit with their expectations. He talks about Navy aviators who describe "leemers—a gut feeling that something isn't right." Typically, these leemers turn out to be accurate. Something, in fact, is wrong. Organizations need to create climates where people feel safe trusting their leemers. (2) They *defer to the experts on the front line.* Frontline workers—those who interact day in and day out with customers, products, suppliers, and so forth—have first-hand knowledge of what can and cannot be done, what will and will not work. Get their input.

Let them make decisions. (3) They *let unexpected circumstances provide the solution.* One of Weick's better-known works is his study of the Mann Gulch fire in Montana that killed 13 smoke jumpers in 1949. The event was a massive, tragic organizational failure. However, the reaction of the foreman illustrates how effective decision makers respond to unexpected circumstances. When the fire was nearly on top of his men, he invented the escape fire—a small fire that consumed all the brush around the team, leaving an area where the larger fire couldn't burn. His action was contrary to everything firefighters are taught (that is, you don't start fires—you extinguish them), but at the time it was the best decision. (4) They *embrace complexity.* Because business is complex, these organizations recognize that it "takes complexity to sense complexity." Rather than simplifying data, which we instinctively try to do when faced with complexity, these organizations aim for deeper understanding of the situation. They ask "why" and keep asking why as they probe more deeply into the causes of the problem and possible solutions. (5) Finally, they *anticipate, but also recognize their limits.* These organizations do try to anticipate as much as possible, but they recognize that they can't anticipate everything. As Weick says, they don't "think, then act. They think by acting. By actually doing things, you'll find out what works and what doesn't."

Design Thinking and Decision Making

design thinking Approaching management problems as designers approach design problems.

The way managers approach decision making—using a rational and analytical mindset in identifying problems, coming up with alternatives, evaluating alternatives, and choosing one of those alternatives—may not be best and certainly not the only choice in today's environment. That's where design thinking comes in. **Design thinking** has been described as "approaching management problems as designers approach design problems."[42] More organizations are beginning to recognize how design thinking can benefit them.[43] For instance, Apple has long been celebrated for its design thinking. The company's lead designer, Jonathan "Jony" Ive (who was behind some of Apple's most successful products, including the iPod and iPhone and was just knighted in the United Kingdom for services to design and enterprise) had this to say about Apple's design approach: "We try to develop products that seem somehow inevitable—that leave you with the sense that that's the only possible solution that makes sense."[44]

While many managers don't deal specifically with product or process design decisions, they still make decisions about work issues that arise, and design thinking can help them be better decision makers. What can the design thinking approach teach managers about making better decisions? Well, it begins with the first step of identifying problems. Design thinking says that managers should look at problem identification collaboratively and integratively with the goal of gaining a deep understanding of the situation. They should look not only at the rational aspects, but also at the emotional elements. Then invariably, of course, design thinking would influence how managers identify and evaluate alternatives. "A traditional manager (educated in a business school, of course) would take the options that have been presented and analyze them based on deductive reasoning and then select the one with the highest net present value. However, using design thinking, a manager would say, "What is something completely new that would be lovely if it existed but doesn't now?"[45] Design thinking means opening up your perspective and gaining insights by using observation and inquiry skills and not relying simply on rational analysis. We're not saying that rational analysis isn't needed; we are saying that there's more needed in making effective decisions, especially in today's world. Just a heads up: Design thinking also has broad implications for managers in other areas, and we'll be looking in future chapters at its impact on innovation and strategies.

The design thinking approach to decision making is at the heart of Boeing's Concept Center, a developmental studio where engineers and designers create innovative concepts for airplane interiors through research, prototypes, mockups, and interactive workshops. The goal of the centre is to help Boeing's airline customers provide their passengers and crew members with innovative products and services that enhance the flying experience. In this photo, Alan Anderson, director of the centre, poses in a prototype of an inflatable crew rest module that features a sound system and adjustable recliner and that can be deflated to a fraction of its size for ease of installation and removal. Design thinking has helped underscore Boeing's reputation as a customer-focused and innovative company.

Dan Lamont/Alamy

SUMMARY AND IMPLICATIONS

1. Describe the eight steps in the decision-making process. A decision is a choice. The steps include identifying a problem and the decision criteria; allocating weights to those criteria; developing, analyzing, and selecting an alternative that can resolve the problem; implementing the alternative; and evaluating the decision's effectiveness.

> ▶ ▶ ▶ Imagine that you were Alexa Reedman planning to return to University in Halifax for the winter term. How might you have used the eight steps in the decision making process to resolve the challenge you faced.

2. Explain the four ways managers make decisions. The assumptions of rationality are as follows: The problem is clear and unambiguous; a single, well-defined goal is to be achieved; all alternatives and consequences are known; and the final choice will maximize the payoff. *Bounded rationality* says that managers make rational decisions but are bounded (limited) by their ability to process information. *Satisficing* happens when decision makers accept solutions that are good enough. *Intuitive decision making* means making decisions on the basis of experience, feelings, and accumulated judgment. Using *evidence-based management*, a manager makes decisions based on the best available evidence. With escalation of commitment, managers increase commitment to a decision even when they have evidence it may have been a wrong decision.

> ▶ ▶ ▶ Toronto's Pearson International Airport is Canada's busiest airport serving more than 36 million passengers[46] and 435 thousand aircraft movements.[47] Managers at Pearson make decisions in each of the four areas of management (planning, organizing, leading, and controlling), where they learn to employ the appropriate combination of decision-making perspectives—sometimes using intuition, sometimes rationality, and sometimes bounded rationality.

3. Classify decisions and decision-making conditions. Some problems are straightforward—these are known as structured problems. When situations are structured, there is often some standardized routine for handling problems that may arise, resulting in a programmed decision, a repetitive decision that can be handled by a routine approach. Many organizational situations involve unstructured problems, for which information is ambiguous or incomplete. The toughest of these unstructured problems are wicked problems, which are continuing works in progress. When decision makers face uncertainty, their psychological orientation will determine whether they follow a maximax choice (maximizing the maximum possible payoff); a maximin choice (maximizing the minimum possible payoff); or a minimax choice (minimizing the maximum regret—amount of money that could have been made if a different decision had been made).

> ▶ ▶ ▶ Managers at the major airlines and airports make routine decisions re maintenance, baggage handling, purchasing supplies and scheduling employee work shifts. It's something they have done numerous times. These managers will face different types of problems and decisions as they do their jobs. Some problems are structured and recurring, while others are unstructured and nonrecurring. Can you think of some examples?

4. Describe different decision-making styles, and discuss how affect decision making. A person's thinking style reflects two things: the source of information one tends to use (external or internal) and how one processes that information (linear or nonlinear). These four dimensions were collapsed into two styles. The linear thinking style is characterized by a person's preference for using external data and processing this information through rational, logical thinking. The nonlinear thinking style is characterized by a preference for internal sources of information and processing this information with internal insights, feelings, and hunches. The 12 common decision-making errors and biases include overconfidence, immediate gratification, anchoring, selective perception, confirmation, framing, availability, representation, randomness, sunk costs, self-serving bias, and hindsight. The managerial decision-making model helps explain how the decision-making process is used to choose the best alternative(s), either through maximizing or satisficing, and then implement and evaluate the alternative. It also helps explain what factors affect the decision-making process, including the decision-making approach (rationality, bounded rationality, intuition), the types of problems and decisions (well structured and programmed or unstructured and nonprogrammed), the decision-making conditions (certainty, risk, uncertainty), and the decision maker's style (linear or nonlinear).

▶ ▶ ▶ Howard Eng assumed the position of President and Chief Executive Officer of the Greater Toronto Airports Authority (GTAA) on March 29, 2012. The new strategic vision is that Toronto Pearson will become North America's premier entry point on the continent—"your global front door." GTAA is focused on becoming more consumer-centric, recognizing the need to be competitive both operationally and from a customer service perspective. In Eng's words, "The job is to truly differentiate ourselves by delighting customers through excellence in service and product innovations." What biases might enter into the decision making of managers at Pearson International, and how might Eng overcome these? How can they improve their decision making, given that they are dealing with uncertainty and risk? How might escalation of commitment affect their decisions?

5. Identify effective decision-making techniques. Managers can make effective decisions by understanding cultural differences in decision making, knowing when it's time to call it quits, using an effective decision-making process, and building an organization that can spot the unexpected and quickly adapt to the changed environment. An effective decision-making process (1) focuses on what's important, (2) is logical and consistent, (3) acknowledges both subjective and objective thinking and blends both analytical and intuitive approaches, (4) requires only "enough" information as is necessary to resolve a problem, (5) encourages and guides gathering relevant information and informed opinions, and (6) is straightforward, reliable, easy to use, and flexible. The five habits of highly reliable organizations are (1) not being tricked by their successes, (2) deferring to experts on the front line, (3) letting unexpected circumstances provide the solution, (4) embracing complexity, and (5) anticipating, but also recognizing, limits.

Design thinking is "approaching management problems as designers approach design problems." It can be useful when identifying problems and when identifying and evaluating alternatives.

▶ ▶ ▶ The polar vortex, which was at the heart of the cancellations and delays faced by Alexa Reedman as she attempted to return to Dalhousie University, ultimately resulted in the cancellation of 49 000 flights and delays in another 300 000 flights impacting 30 million passengers during the month of January 2014. A report published in April 2014 recommended changes in the way Pearson International airport will deal with extreme weather in the future. How important is it to debrief with employees following an unplanned event like this? Why?

MyManagementLab Study, practise, and explore real management situations with these helpful resources:
- **Interactive Lesson Presentations:** Work through interactive presentations and assessments to test your knowledge of management concepts.
- **PIA (Personal Inventory Assessments):** Enhance your ability to connect with key concepts through these engaging, self-reflection assessments.
- **Study Plan:** Check your understanding of chapter concepts with self-study quizzes.
- **Simulations:** Practise decision-making in simulated management environments.

P I A PERSONAL INVENTORY ASSESSMENT

REVIEW AND DISCUSSION QUESTIONS

1. Why is decision making often described as the essence of a manager's job?

2. Describe the eight steps in the decision making process.

3. Would you call yourself a linear or nonlinear thinker? What are the decision-making implications of these labels? What are the implications for choosing where you want to work?

4. Explain the two types of problems and decisions. Contrast the three decision-making conditions.

5. "As managers use computers and software tools more often, they'll be able to make more rational decisions." Do you agree or disagree with this statement? Why?

6. How can managers blend the guidelines for making effective decisions in today's world with the rationality and bounded rationality models of decision making, or can they? Explain.

7. Is there a difference between wrong decisions and bad decisions? Why do good managers sometimes make wrong decisions? Bad decisions? How can managers improve their decision-making skills?

8. All of us bring biases to the decisions we make. What would be the drawbacks of having biases? Could there be any advantages to having biases? Explain. What are the implications for decision making?

ETHICS DILEMMA

Competitive problems are rarely well structured, as the managers at Greenfield Brokerage know.[48] Over the years, the firm has successfully competed with well-established rivals by making nonprogrammed decisions.

Imagine you are an advertising manager at Greenfield. Your advertising agency has suggested a newspaper ad in which a fictitious competing broker is quoted as saying, "My investment advice is perfectly objective, even though I work on commission." A Greenfield broker is then quoted as saying, "I don't work on commission like other brokers do, so my investment advice is perfectly objective." How certain are you that your advice is perfectly objective when Greenfield benefits from every client it gets? (Review Exhibits 7-11 and 7-12 as you think about this dilemma.)

SKILLS EXERCISE

Developing Your Creativity Skill—About the Skill

Creativity is a frame of mind. You need to open your mind to new ideas. Every individual has the ability to be creative, but many people simply don't try to develop that ability. In current organizations, such people may have difficulty achieving success. Dynamic environments and managerial chaos require that managers look for new and innovative ways to attain their goals as well as those of the organization.[49]

Steps in Practising the Skill

1. *Think of yourself as creative.* Although it's a simple suggestion, research shows that if you think you can't be creative, you won't be. Believing in yourself is the first step in becoming more creative.

2. *Pay attention to your intuition.* Every individual's subconscious mind works well. Sometimes answers come to you when least expected. For example, when you are about to go to sleep, your relaxed mind sometimes whispers a solution to a problem you're facing. Listen to that voice. In fact, most creative people keep a notepad near their bed and write down those great ideas when they occur. That way, they don't forget them.

3. *Move away from your comfort zone.* Every individual has a comfort zone in which certainty exists. But creativity and the known often do not mix. To be creative, you need to move away from the status quo and focus your mind on something new.

4. *Engage in activities that put you outside your comfort zone.* You not only must think differently; you need to do things differently and thus challenge yourself. Learning to play a musical instrument or learning a foreign language, for example, opens your mind to a new challenge.

5. *Seek a change of scenery.* People are often creatures of habit. Creative people force themselves out of their

habits by changing their scenery, which may mean going into a quiet and serene area where you can be alone with your thoughts.

6. *Find several right answers.* In the discussion of bounded rationality, we said that people seek solutions that are good enough. Being creative means continuing to look for other solutions even when you think you have solved the problem. A better, more creative solution just might be found.

7. *Play your own devil's advocate.* Challenging yourself to defend your solutions helps you to develop confidence in your creative efforts. Second-guessing yourself may also help you find more creative solutions.

8. *Believe in finding a workable solution.* Like believing in yourself, you also need to believe in your ideas. If you

don't think you can find a solution, you probably won't.

9. *Brainstorm with others.* Being creative is not a solitary activity. Bouncing ideas off others creates a synergistic effect.

10. *Turn creative ideas into action.* Coming up with ideas is only half the process. Once the ideas are generated, they must be implemented. Keeping great ideas in your mind or on paper that no one will read does little to expand your creative abilities.

Practising the Skill

How many words can you make using the letters in the word brainstorm? There are at least 95.

WORKING TOGETHER: TEAM EXERCISE

Making Sense of Past Decision Making Experiences

Being effective in decision making is something that managers obviously want. What's involved with being a good decision maker? Form groups of three to four students. Discuss your experiences making decisions—for example, buying a car or some other purchase, choosing classes and professors, making summer or spring break plans, and so forth. Each of you should share times when you felt you made good decisions. Analyze what happened during

that decision-making process that contributed to it being a good decision. Then, consider some decisions that you felt were bad. What happened to make them bad? What common characteristics, if any, did you identify among the good decisions? The bad decisions? Come up with a bulleted list of practical suggestions for making good decisions. As a group, be prepared to share your list with the class.

LEARNING TO BE A MANAGER

- For one week, pay close attention to the decisions you make and how you make them. Write a description of five of those decisions using the steps in the decision-making process as your guide. Also, describe whether you relied on external or internal sources of information to help you make the decision and whether you think you were more linear or nonlinear in how you processed that information.

- When you feel you haven't made a good decision, assess how you could have made a better decision.

- Find two examples of a procedure, a rule, and a policy. Bring a description of these examples to class and be prepared to share them.

- Write a procedure, a rule, and a policy for your instructor to use in your class. Be sure that each one

is clear and understandable. And be sure to explain how it fits the characteristics of a procedure, a rule, or a policy.

- Find three examples of managerial decisions described in any of the popular business periodicals (*The Wall Street Journal, BusinessWeek, Fortune,* etc.). Write a paper describing each decision and any other information such as what led to the decision, what happened as a result of the decision, etc. What did you learn about decision making from these examples?

- Interview two managers and ask them for suggestions on what it takes to be a good decision maker. Write down their suggestions and be prepared to present them in class.

CASE APPLICATION 1

Underwater Chaos

It would be a claustrophobe's worst nightmare—trapped subsea in the 31-mile Eurotunnel beneath the English Channel on the Eurostar train that travels between Britain and the European mainland.[50] The first time it happened was after a series of breakdowns on five London-bound trains from Brussels on December 18, 2009, left more than 2000 passengers stranded for up to 16 hours. Many of those passengers, trapped in the dark and overheated tunnel, endured serious distress. The acutely uncomfortable temperatures led parents to remove their children's outer clothing. Other passengers felt ill, with some suffering "stress and panic attacks." Was this just an unfortunate incident for the unlucky passengers who happened to be on those trains, or did poor managerial decision making about the operation of both the train and the channel tunnel also play a role?

Poor decision making by managers of Eurostar and the operator of Eurotunnel created chaos for thousands of passengers who were trapped in the channel tunnel and for travellers at St. Pancras train station in London whose train service was suspended following the breakdown of the tunnel trains.

An independent review of the incident blamed Eurostar and the operator of the tunnel for being unprepared for severe winter weather. The report said that Eurostar had failed to adequately maintain and winterize its high-speed trains to protect sensitive components from malfunctioning due to excessive snow and moisture build-up. At the time of the Eurostar train breakdowns, severe winter weather had been wreaking havoc in Europe. Airlines, car and truck drivers, and rail operators across Europe were also suffering from a winter that was on course to be the coldest in more than 30 years. Freezing weather and snow had caused travel problems for days in Northern Europe. In addition, the report criticized Eurotunnel (the operator of the channel tunnel) for

having unsatisfactory communications systems in place inside the tunnel, which could have given its employees direct contact with train drivers and other Eurostar staff. "If a train breaks down and passengers have to be rescued and evacuated, this must be done with greater speed and consideration. In an emergency, passengers need to have prompt information and regular updates." Although the severe weather conditions undoubtedly played a role in this fiasco, there's no doubt that managers could have done a better job of making decisions in preparing for such scenarios.

The second disruption was in March 2012. Thousands of travellers, including Sir Paul McCartney and his family, were delayed by a faulty power cable. One passenger said, "There was absolute chaos at Gare du Nord and there was no information about possible delays. Eurostar staff were extremely unhelpful." However, another passenger said that despite the nine-hour wait with the train standing still and lack of information, the staff were helpful and supportive. As London prepared to host the 2012 Summer Olympics, car and coach traffic was expected to increase, lending even more urgency to prevent a repeat of the troubles.

DISCUSSION QUESTIONS?

1. What's your reaction to this story? What does it illustrate about decision making?
2. How could the decision-making process have helped in both the response to the crisis situations and in preventing them from happening?
3. Could procedures, policies, and rules play any role in future crisis situations like this one? If so, how? If not, why not?
4. What could other organizations learn from this incident?

CASE APPLICATION 2

The Business of Baseball

As the 2011 film *Moneyball* (based on an earlier book by the same name) emphasizes, statistics—the "right" statistics—are crucial aspects of effective decision making in the sport of baseball. The central premise of *Moneyball* was that the collected wisdom of baseball insiders (players, managers, coaches, scouts, and the front office) had pretty much been flawed almost from the onset of the game. Commonly used statistics—such as stolen bases, runs batted in, and

batting averages—that were typically used to evaluate players' abilities and performances were inadequate and poor gauges of potential. Rigorous statistical analysis showed that on-base percentages and slugging percentages were better indicators of a player's offensive potential. The goal of all this number crunching? To make better decisions. Team managers want to allocate their limited payroll in the best way possible to help the team be a winner.

The move to more systematic data usage can also be seen in college baseball. At this level, coaches have long used their faces (touching their ears, noses, and chins at a "dizzying speed") to communicate pitch selection to the catcher. Now, however, hundreds of college teams at all levels have abandoned these body signals and are using a system in which the coach yells out a series of numbers. "The catcher decodes the sequence by looking at a chart tucked into a wristband—the kind football quarterbacks have worn since 1965—and then relays the information to the pitcher the way he always has." Coaches say this approach is not only faster and more efficient, it's not decipherable by "dugout spies" wanting to steal the signs. Since the method allows for many combinations that can mean many different pitches, the same number sequence won't be used for the rest of the game—and maybe not even for the rest of the season.

DISCUSSION QUESTIONS?

1. In a general sense, what kinds of decisions are made in baseball? Would you characterize these decisions as structured or unstructured problems? Explain. What type(s) of decision-making condition would you consider this to be? Explain.

2. Is it appropriate for baseball managers to use only quantitative, objective criteria in evaluating their players? What do you think? Why?

3. Do some research on sabermetrics. What is it? What does it have to do with decision making?

4. Describe how baseball front-office executives and college coaches could use each of the following to make better decisions: (a) rationality, (b) bounded rationality, (c) intuition, and (d) evidence-based management.

5. Can there be too much information in managing the business of baseball? Discuss.

Foundations of Planning

Learning Outcomes

1 Define the nature and purpose of planning.

2 Classify the types of goals organizations might have and the plans they use.

3 Compare and contrast approaches to goal-setting and planning.

4 Discuss current issues in planning.

In this chapter, we begin our study of the first of the management functions: planning. Planning is important because it establishes what an organization is doing. We'll look at how managers set goals, as well as how they establish plans. After reading and studying this chapter, you will achieve the following learning outcomes.

▶ ▶ ▶ Blue Man Group is one of the hottest performance groups today.[1] Its theatrical productions have run in New York, Boston, Chicago, and Las Vegas for years. Currently, the group has shows in Berlin, Oberhausen, Amsterdam, New York, Boston, Chicago, Las Vegas, and Orlando. It also opened a show in Toronto in 2005, which ran until 2007. Blue Man performances are a mix of mime, percussion music, and splashing paint.

The group was founded in 1988 by three guys who decided it was time to stage a funeral for the 1980s. They put on bald wigs, painted themselves blue, and carried a coffin filled with items representing the worst of the decade (such as yuppies and Rambo) into New York City's Central Park. MTV recorded the ceremony.

Encouraged by their friends, the trio (Chris Wink, Matt Goldman, and Phil Stanton) started giving small performances around the city. None of the three had formal training in music or acting. They really had not planned to become performers. Three years later, they had performed on national TV, spitting paint on *The Tonight Show* and *Live with Regis and Kathie Lee*. They also had an off-Broadway show called *Tubes*.

Wink, Goldman, and Stanton were also starting to burn out. They were working six days a week, had gone three years without a break, and performed 1200 consecutive shows. Once success started, the three just kept going, not giving thought to how to manage the show or their time. They did not have time to create new material, so they were just performing the same show over and over. They had a small crew who had "never worked in theater and [did not] have a clue, just like us," says Wink. They spent 90 minutes each night making themselves up before a performance. Then they were part of the cleanup crew. They were so tired that they did not have time for a personal life. How did they get into this situation? "We've never planned ahead," explained Wink.

Adam Hunger/AP Photo

Managers everywhere need to plan. In this chapter, we present the basics of planning: what it is, why managers plan, and how they plan. Then we conclude by looking at some current issues in planning.

What Is Planning?

As we stated in Chapter 1, **planning** involves defining goals, establishing an overall strategy for achieving those goals, and developing a comprehensive set of plans to integrate and coordinate the work needed to achieve the goals. It's concerned both with ends (what's to be done) and means (how it's to be done).

Planning can be either formal or informal. In informal planning, nothing is written down, and there is little or no sharing of goals with others. Informal planning is general and lacks continuity. When we use the term *planning* in this book, we mean *formal* planning. In formal planning, specific goals covering a specific time period are defined. These goals are written and shared with organizational members to reduce ambiguity and create a common understanding about what needs to be done. Finally, specific plans exist for achieving these goals.

Ron Zambonini, former CEO of Ottawa-based Cognos (acquired by IBM in 2008), notes that planning went out of fashion during the dot-com years. He found that in both California and in Ottawa, entrepreneurs worked "90 hours a week, but the whole goal [was] not to build a business or a company. [All they really wanted was] someone to buy them out."[2] Unfortunately, many of those companies were not bought out, but folded. Planning might have helped them be more successful.

Planning and Performance

Planning seems to take a lot of effort. So why should managers plan? We can give you at least four reasons. First, planning *provides direction* to managers and nonmanagers alike. When employees know what their organization or work unit is trying to accomplish and what they must contribute to reach goals, they can coordinate their activities, cooperate with each other, and do what it takes to accomplish those goals. Without planning, departments and individuals might work at cross-purposes and prevent the organization from efficiently achieving its goals. Next, planning *reduces uncertainty* by forcing managers to look ahead, anticipate change, consider the impact of change, and develop appropriate responses. Although planning won't eliminate uncertainty, managers plan so they can respond effectively.

In addition, planning *minimizes waste and redundancy*. When work activities are coordinated around plans, inefficiencies become obvious and can be corrected or eliminated. Finally, planning *establishes the goals or standards used in controlling*. When managers plan, they develop goals and plans. When they control, they see whether the plans have been carried out and the goals met. Without planning, there would be no goals against which to measure work effort.

Numerous studies have looked at the relationship between planning and performance.[3] We can draw the following four conclusions from these studies. First, generally speaking, formal planning is associated with higher profits, higher return on assets, and other positive financial results. Second, the quality of the planning process and the appropriate implementation of the plans probably contribute more to high performance than does the extent of planning. Third, in those studies in which formal planning did not lead to higher performance, the external environment often was the culprit. Government

1 Define the nature and purpose of planning.

planning A management function that involves defining goals, establishing a strategy for achieving those goals, and developing plans to integrate and coordinate activities.

Victoria Hale founded the not-for-profit Institute for OneWorld Health with an informal plan. Inspired by a conversation with a cab driver about pharmaceutical science, Hale went back to an essay she had written years earlier about diseases that would benefit from drug development efforts. Using that as her preliminary business plan, she incorporated the institute the next day. The institute's goal is to persuade companies with important but not profitable drugs to donate those to the institute for tax and public relations benefits. The institute then uses grants and donations to distribute the drugs to needy patients around the world.

AP Photo/Jeff Chiu/The Canadian Press

regulations, powerful labour unions, and other critical environmental forces constrain managers' options and reduce the impact of planning on an organization's performance. Fourth, the planning/performance relationship is influenced by the planning time frame. Organizations need at least four years of systematic formal planning before performance is affected.

How Do Managers Plan?

◉ Watch on MyManagementLab

Planning (TWZ Role Play)

2 Classify the types of goals organizations might have and the plans they use.

▶ ▶ ▶ One evening, after three years of nonstop performing with Blue Man Group, Phil Stanton cut his hand with a router.[4] The group had never planned for what to do if one of them was injured. They had one understudy, one of the show's drummers, but only because their investors had insisted on it as a backup plan. While he had studied the show, he had never even rehearsed in it. When Stanton cut his hand, the drummer had to go onstage as a Blue Man. Because the group members wear bald wigs and paint themselves blue, no one in the audience knew that Stanton was missing. The show was a success even without him.

That success made the co-founders of Blue Man (Chris Wink, Matt Goldman, and Phil Stanton) realize that it would be quite easy to clone Blue Man, which would increase the number of shows they could do, and also give the co-founders time off. Finally, three years after they had started performing, they could think more about how to expand their show.

The group's next hurdle came when it opened a second venue, in Boston. The co-founders split their time between their New York venue and Boston, but it meant that they were less "hands on" at their shows. Quality started to slip. They finally realized they needed a specific plan to guide the 38 new performers they were bringing on board, so they locked themselves in an apartment and talked through their creative vision in great detail. The result? A 132-page operating manual that tells the story of the Blue Man show and allows the show to be reproduced by others. Ironically, by writing the plan, though it is a somewhat unorthodox one, the co-founders were able to express artistic ideals that had been understood among them but never stated before. Today, the former drummer who was their first understudy trains new Blue Man performers. Wink, Goldman, and Stanton make only occasional appearances on stage.

> **Think About It**
>
> **How did planning make Blue Man Group performers more successful in their one existing show? How did planning allow the concept to be successfully replicated in other venues?**

Goals and Plans

Planning is often called the primary management function because it establishes the basis for all the other things managers do as they organize, lead, and control. It involves two important aspects: goals and plans.

Goals (objectives) are desired outcomes or targets.[5] They guide management decisions and form the criterion against which work results are measured. That's why they're often described as the essential elements of planning. You have to know the desired target or outcome before you can establish plans for reaching it. **Plans** are documents that outline how goals are going to be met. They usually include resource allocations, schedules, and other necessary actions to accomplish the goals. As managers plan, they develop both goals and plans.

goals (objectives) Desired outcomes or targets.

plans Documents that outline how goals will to be met.

Types of Goals

It might seem that organizations have a single goal. Businesses want to make a profit and not-for-profit organizations want to meet the needs of some constituent group(s). However, a single goal can't adequately define an organization's success. And if managers emphasize only one goal, other goals essential for long-term success are ignored. Also, as we discussed in Chapter 5, using a single goal such as profit may result in unethical behaviours because managers and employees will ignore other aspects of their jobs in order to look good on that one measure.[6] In reality, all organizations have multiple goals. For instance, businesses may want to increase market share, keep employees enthused about working for the organization, and work toward more environmentally sustainable practices. And a place of worship provides a place for religious practices but also assists economically disadvantaged individuals in its community and acts as a social gathering place for its members.

We can classify most company's goals as either strategic or financial. Financial goals are related to the financial performance of the organization, while strategic goals are related to all other areas of an organization's performance. For instance, McDonald's states that its financial targets are 3 to 5 percent average annual sales and revenue growth, 6 to 7 percent average annual operating income growth, and returns on invested capital in the high teens.[7] Here's an example of a strategic goal from Royal Bank of Canada: "We want to be the undisputed leader in financial services."[8]

The goals just described are **stated goals**—official statements of what an organization says, and what it wants its stakeholders to believe, its goals are. However, stated goals—which can be found in an organization's charter, annual report, public relations announcements, or in public statements made by managers—often conflict with each other and are influenced by what various stakeholders think organizations should do. For instance, Nike's goal is "delivering inspiration and innovation to every athlete." Canadian company EnCana's vision is to "be the world's high performance benchmark independent oil and gas company." Deutsche Bank's goal is "to be the leading global provider of financial solutions, creating lasting value for our clients, our shareholders and people and the communities in which we operate."[9] Such statements are vague and probably better represent management's public relations skills than provide meaningful guides to what the organization is actually trying to accomplish. It shouldn't be surprising then to find that an organization's stated goals are often irrelevant to what actually goes on.[10]

stated goals Official statements of what an organization says, and what it wants its various stakeholders to believe its goals are.

If you want to know an organization's **real goals**—those goals an organization actually pursues—observe what organizational members are doing. Actions define priorities. For example, universities may say their goal is limiting class sizes, facilitating close student-faculty relations, and actively involving students in the learning process, but then they put students into 300+ student lecture classes! Knowing that real and stated goals may differ is important for recognizing what you might otherwise think are inconsistencies.

real goals Goals that an organization actually pursues, as defined by the actions of its members.

Types of Plans

The most popular ways to describe organizational plans are breadth (strategic versus operational), time frame (short term versus long term), specificity (directional versus specific), and

Exhibit 8-1

Types of Plans

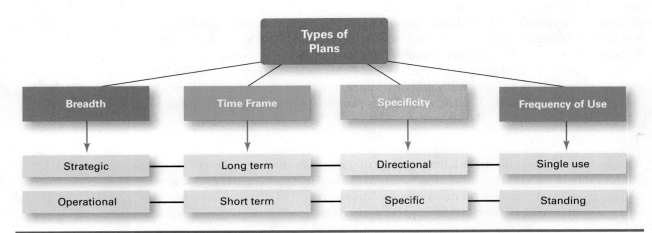

frequency of use (single use versus standing). As Exhibit 8-1 shows, these types of plans aren't independent. That is, strategic plans are usually long term, directional, and single use, whereas operational plans are usually short term, specific, and standing. What does each include?

Strategic plans are plans that apply to the entire organization and establish the organization's overall goals. Plans that encompass a particular operational area of the organization are called **operational plans.** These two types of plans differ because strategic plans are broad while operational plans are narrow.

The number of years used to define short-term and long-term plans has declined considerably because of environmental uncertainty. Long-term used to mean anything over seven years. Try to imagine what you're likely to be doing in seven years, and you can begin to appreciate how difficult it would be for managers to establish plans that far into the future. We define **long-term plans** as those with a time frame beyond three years.[11] **Short-term plans** cover one year or less. Any time period in between would be an intermediate plan. Although these time classifications are fairly common, an organization can use any planning time frame it wants.

Intuitively, it would seem that specific plans would be preferable to directional, or loosely guided, plans. **Specific plans** are clearly defined and leave no room for interpretation. A specific plan states its objectives in a way that eliminates ambiguity and problems with misunderstanding. For example, a manager who seeks to increase his or her unit's work output by 8 percent over a given 12-month period might establish specific procedures, budget allocations, and schedules of activities to reach that goal.

However, when uncertainty is high and managers must be flexible in order to respond to unexpected changes, directional plans are preferable. **Directional plans** are flexible plans that set out general guidelines. They provide focus but don't lock managers into specific goals or courses of action. For example, Sylvia Rhone, president of Motown Records, said she has a simple goal—to "sign great artists."[12] So instead of creating a specific plan to produce and market 10 albums from new artists this year, she might formulate a directional plan to use a network of people around the world to alert her to new and promising talent so she can increase the number of new artists she has under contract. Keep in mind, however, that the flexibility of directional plans must be weighed against the lack of clarity of specific plans.

Some plans that managers develop are ongoing while others are used only once. A **single-use plan** is a one-time plan specifically designed to meet the needs of a unique situation. For instance, when Walmart wanted to expand the number of its stores in China, top-level executives formulated a single-use plan as a guide. In contrast, **standing plans** are ongoing plans that provide guidance for activities performed repeatedly. Standing plans include policies, rules, and procedures, which we defined in Chapter 7. ·

strategic plans Plans that apply to the entire organization and establish the organization's overall goals.

operational plans Plans that encompass a particular operational area of the organization.

long-term plans Plans with a time frame beyond three years.

short-term plans Plans covering one year or less.

specific plans Plans that are clearly defined and leave no room for interpretation.

directional plans Plans that are flexible and set out general guidelines.

single-use plan A one-time plan specifically designed to meet the needs of a unique situation.

standing plans Ongoing plans that provide guidance for activities performed repeatedly.

An example of a standing plan is the Human Rights, Equity and Harassment Prevention equity policy developed by Dalhousie University to foster and support an inclusive working and learning environment where all members of the University community share the responsibility for establishing and maintaining a climate of respect. It provides guidance to university administrators, faculty, and staff as they make hiring plans and do their jobs.

Setting Goals and Developing Plans

▶ ▶ ▶ When Blue Man Group started out, it was just three guys having fun, mocking the 1980s, and then working their ideas through mime and percussion.[13] They did not feel they had time to plan. Many people feel the same way. Recall, though, that the three co-founders (Chris Wink, Matt Goldman, and Phil Stanton) were able to do only as many shows as they could physically attend when they started out. By figuring out a way to clone themselves, they could do many more shows and have the opportunity to tour Canada and the United States. Touring has meant even more planning. The move to planning has certainly made the group successful: Blue Man Group Productions has about 450 employees; their productions attract 1 million people a year; and they bring in millions of dollars in revenues annually. Their first CD, *Audio*, was nominated for a Grammy in 1999, and one of their songs made the soundtrack for *Terminator 3: Rise of the Machines*.

3 Compare and contrast approaches to goal-setting and planning.

Think About It

Blue Man Group clearly learned to develop plans in order to grow the company and create more opportunities. As founders moved forward from the creative-entrepreneurial roots, what resistance would they have to overcome? How important would it be for the founders to model the behaviours needed to model a planning culture? How difficult would be for the three of them to make the shift?

Taylor Haines has just been elected president of her business school's student society at Okanagan College in Kelowna. She wants the organization to be more actively involved in the business school than it has been. Francisco Garza graduated from Tecnologico de Monterrey with a degree in marketing and computers three years ago and went to work for a regional consulting services firm. He recently was promoted to manager of an eight-person e-business development team and hopes to strengthen the team's financial contributions to the firm. What should Taylor and Francisco do now? Their first step should be to set goals.

Approaches to Setting Goals

As we stated earlier, goals provide the direction for all management decisions and actions and form the criterion against which actual accomplishments are measured. Everything organizational members do should be oriented toward achieving goals. These goals can be set either through a traditional process or by using management by objectives. Jeff Bezos knows that having clear goals leads to success, as you will see in this *Management Reflection*.

MANAGEMENT REFLECTION

Planning at Amazon

How has planning made a difference at Amazon? Jeff Bezos, founder and CEO of Amazon.com, understands the importance of goals and plans. As a leader, he exudes energy, enthusiasm, and drive.[14] He's fun loving (his legendary laugh has been described as a flock of Canadian geese on nitrous oxide) but has pursued his vision for Amazon with serious intensity and has demonstrated an ability to inspire his employees through

Kim White/Reuters

the ups and downs of a rapidly growing company. When Bezos founded the company as an online bookstore, his goal was to be the leader in online retailing. Now fifteen years later, Amazon is quickly becoming the world's general store, selling not only books, CDs, and DVDs, but LEGO, power drills, and Jackalope Buck taxidermy mounts, to name a few of the thousands of products you can buy. What role might the setting of goals and plans have played in helping Bezos and Amazon successfully implement the original vision of being the leader in online retailing? ■

traditional goal-setting An approach to setting goals in which top managers set goals that then flow down through the organization and become subgoals for each organizational area.

In **traditional goal-setting**, goals set by top managers flow down through the organization and become subgoals for each organizational area. This traditional perspective assumes that top managers know what's best because they see the "big picture." And the goals passed down to each succeeding level guide individual employees as they work to achieve those assigned goals. If Taylor were to use this approach, she would see what goals the dean or director of the school of business had set and develop goals for her group that would contribute to achieving those goals. Or take a manufacturing business, for example. The president tells the vice president of production what he expects manufacturing costs to be for the coming year and tells the marketing vice president what level he expects sales to reach for the year. These goals are passed to the next organizational level and written to reflect the responsibilities of that level, passed to the next level, and so forth. Then, at some later time, performance is evaluated to determine whether the assigned goals have been achieved. Although the process is supposed to happen in this way, in reality it doesn't always do so. Turning broad strategic goals into departmental, team, and individual goals can be a difficult and frustrating process.

Another problem with traditional goal-setting is that when top managers define the organization's goals in broad terms—such as achieving "sufficient" profits or increasing "market leadership"—these ambiguous goals have to be made more specific as they flow down through the organization. Managers at each level define the goals and apply their own interpretations and biases as they make them more specific. However, what often happens is that clarity is lost as the goals make their way down from the top of the organization to lower levels. Exhibit 8-2 illustrates what can happen. But it doesn't have to be that way. For example, at the Carrier-Carlyle Compressor Facility in Stone Mountain, Georgia, employees and managers focus their work efforts around goals.

Exhibit 8-2

The Downside of Traditional Goal-Setting

"We need to improve the company's performance."

"I want to see a significant improvement in this division's profits."

Top Management's Objective

Division Manager's Objective

"Increase profits regardless of the means."

"Don't worry about quality; just work fast."

Department Manager's Objective

Individual Employee's Objective

Those goals encompass meeting and exceeding customer needs, concentrating on continuous improvement efforts, and engaging the workforce. To keep everyone focused on those goals, a "thermostat"—a 3-foot-by-4-foot metric indicator—found at the employee entrance communicates what factory performance is at any given time and where attention is needed. "The thermostat outlines plant goals across a range of metrics as well as monthly performance against those goals." Company executives state, "We have found that well-executed pre-planning drives improved results." Does their goal approach work? In the past three years, the facility has experienced a nearly 76 percent reduction in customer reject rates and a 54.5 percent reduction in OSHA-recordable injury and illness cases.[15]

When the hierarchy of organizational goals *is* clearly defined, as it is at Carrier-Carlyle Compressor, it forms an integrated network of goals, or a **means–ends chain.** Higher-level goals (or ends) are linked to lower-level goals, which serve as the means for their accomplishment. In other words, the goals achieved at lower levels become the means to reach the goals (ends) at the next level. And the accomplishment of goals at that level becomes the means to achieve the goals (ends) at the next level and on up through the different organizational levels. That's how traditional goal-setting is supposed to work.

Instead of using traditional goal-setting, many organizations use **management by objectives (MBO)**, a process of setting mutually agreed-upon goals and using those goals to evaluate employee performance. If Francisco were to use this approach, he would sit down with each member of his team and set goals and periodically review whether progress was being made toward achieving those goals. MBO programs have four elements: goal specificity, participative decision making, an explicit time period, and performance feedback.[16] Instead of using goals to make sure employees are doing what they're supposed to be doing, MBO uses goals to motivate them as well. The appeal is that it focuses on employees working to accomplish goals they've had a hand in setting. Exhibit 8-3 lists the steps in a typical MBO program.

Does MBO work? Studies have shown that it can increase employee performance and organizational productivity. For example, one review of MBO programs found productivity gains in almost all of them.[17] But is MBO relevant for today's organizations? If it's viewed as a way of setting goals, then yes, because research shows that goal-setting can be an effective approach to motivating employees.[18]

means–ends chain An integrated network of goals in which the accomplishment of goals at one level serves as the means for achieving the goals, or ends, at the next level.

management by objectives (MBO) A process of setting mutually agreed-upon goals and using those goals to evaluate employee performance.

Characteristics of Well-Written Goals

Goals aren't all written the same way. Some are better than others at making the desired outcomes clear. For instance, the CEO of Procter & Gamble said that he wants to see the

Exhibit 8-3

Steps in MBO

1. The organization's *overall objectives and strategies* are formulated.

2. Major objectives are allocated among *divisional and departmental units*.

3. Unit managers *collaboratively set specific objectives* for their units with their managers.

4. Specific objectives are collaboratively set with *all department members*.

5. *Action plans*, defining how objectives are to be achieved, are specified and agreed upon by managers and employees.

6. The action plans are *implemented*.

7. Progress toward objectives is *periodically reviewed*, and *feedback is provided*.

8. Successful achievement of objectives is reinforced by *performance-based rewards*.

Exhibit 8-4

Well-Written Goals

- Written in terms of outcomes rather than actions
- Measurable and quantifiable
- Clear as to a time frame
- Challenging yet attainable
- Written down
- Communicated to all necessary organizational members

company add close to 548 000 new customers a day, every day, for the next five years.[19] It's an ambitious but specific goal. Managers should be able to write well-written goals. What makes a "well-written" goal?[20] Exhibit 8-4 lists the characteristics.

Steps in Goal-Setting

Managers should follow five steps when setting goals.

mission The purpose of an organization.

1. *Review the organization's* **mission**, *or purpose*. A mission is a broad statement of an organization's purpose that provides an overall guide to what organizational members think is important. Managers should review the mission before writing goals because goals should reflect that mission.
2. *Evaluate available resources*. You don't want to set goals that are impossible to achieve given your available resources. Even though goals should be challenging, they should be realistic. After all, if the resources you have to work with won't allow you to achieve a goal no matter how hard you try or how much effort is exerted, you shouldn't set that goal. That would be like the person with a $50 000 annual income and no other financial resources setting a goal of building an investment portfolio worth $1 million in three years. No matter how hard he or she works at it, it's not going to happen.
3. *Determine the goals individually or with input from others*. The goals reflect desired outcomes and should be congruent with the organizational mission and goals in other organizational areas. These goals should be measurable, specific, and include a time frame for accomplishment.
4. *Write down the goals and communicate them to all who need to know*. Writing down and communicating goals forces people to think them through. The written goals also become visible evidence of the importance of working toward something.
5. *Review results and whether goals are being met*. If goals aren't being met, change them as needed.

Once the goals have been established, written down, and communicated, a manager is ready to develop plans for pursuing the goals.

datapoints[21]

51 percent of managers said they were approaching planning differently by using more business scenarios and data-driven approaches.

47 percent of managers said their organization's projects always or often meet their goals.

69 percent of managers said teams are not given enough resources to complete projects.

7 percent of information executives said they have no plan for disaster recovery.

75 percent of managers said their company's planning approach wasn't working.

19 percent of executives said that planning was an important skill.

Developing Plans

The process of developing plans is influenced by three contingency factors and by the planning approach followed.

Contingency Factors in Planning

Three contingency factors affect the choice of plans: organizational level, degree of environmental uncertainty, and length of future commitments.[22]

Exhibit 8-5

Planning and Organizational Level

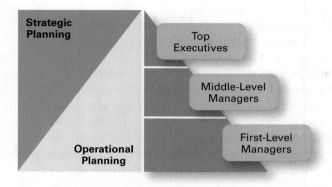

Exhibit 8-5 shows the relationship between a manager's level in the organization and the type of planning done. For the most part, lower-level managers do operational planning while upper-level managers do strategic planning.

The second contingency factor is environmental uncertainty. When uncertainty is high, plans should be specific, but flexible. Managers must be prepared to change or amend plans as they're implemented. At times, they may even have to abandon the plans.[23] For example, prior to Continental Airlines' merger with United Airlines, the former CEO and his management team established a specific goal of focusing on what customers wanted most—on-time flights—to help the company become more competitive in the highly uncertain airline industry. Because of the high level of uncertainty, the management team identified a "destination, but not a flight plan," and changed plans as necessary to achieve that goal of on-time service.

Michael Dell, founder and chief executive of Dell, Inc., uses an approach to the planning process that actively involves employees from different levels and functional areas throughout the company. Work teams, for example, develop their own daily schedules, track their progress, and develop alternate plans when they miss their daily goals. And each week, Dell's functional department leaders from production, supply management, and channel management meet to make plans based on product demand and supply. An advantage of this planning approach is that employees can actually see the plans that are used in directing and coordinating their work.

Grzegorz Michalowski/EPA/Newscom

commitment concept Plans should extend far enough to meet those commitments made when the plans were developed.

The last contingency factor also is related to the time frame of plans. The **commitment concept** says that plans should extend far enough to meet those commitments made when the plans were developed. Planning for too long or too short a time period is inefficient and ineffective. What happened at AT&T with the iPhone is a good example of why it's important to understand the commitment concept. When it secured exclusive rights to support the iPhone on its wireless network in June 2007, both Apple and AT&T vastly underestimated the phone's popularity—some 21.8 million alone were sold from 2011 through the first quarter of 2012.[24] And then there are all those apps—at least 500 000 different ones that have been downloaded over 15 billion times—many of which consume bandwidth. AT&T's network "simply can't handle the traffic." AT&T's chief strategy officer John Stankey said, "We missed on our usage estimates." As the company discovered, the bandwidth-hungry super-phone created serious challenges.[25] How does this illustrate the commitment concept? In becoming the primary provider of the iPhone, AT&T "committed" to whatever future expenses were generated by that planned decision. And they had to live with the decision and its consequences—good and bad.

Approaches to Planning

Federal, provincial, local government officials, and industry participants are working together on a plan to boost populations of wild salmon in British Columbia and on the Atlantic Coast. Managers in the Global Fleet Graphics division of the 3M Company are developing detailed plans to satisfy increasingly demanding customers and to battle more aggressive competitors. Emilio Azcárraga Jean, chairman, president, and CEO of Grupo Televisa, gets input from many different people before setting company goals and then turns over the planning for achieving the goals to various executives. In each of these situations, planning is done a little differently. *How* an organization plans can best be understood by looking at *who* does the planning.

formal planning department A group of planning specialists whose sole responsibility is helping to write organizational plans.

In the traditional approach, planning is done entirely by top-level managers who often are assisted by a **formal planning department,** a group of planning specialists whose sole responsibility is to help write the various organizational plans. Under this approach, plans developed by top-level managers flow down through other organizational levels, much like the traditional approach to goal-setting. As they flow down through the organization, the plans are tailored to the particular needs of each level. Although this approach makes managerial planning thorough, systematic, and coordinated, all too often the focus is on developing "the plan"—a thick binder (or binders) full of meaningless information that's stuck on a shelf and never used by anyone for guiding or coordinating work efforts. In fact, in a survey of managers about formal top-down organizational planning processes, more than 75 percent said their company's planning approach was unsatisfactory.[26] A common complaint was that, "plans are documents that you prepare for the corporate planning staff and later forget." Although this traditional top-down approach to planning is used by many organizations, it can be effective only if managers understand the importance of creating documents that organizational members actually use, not documents that look impressive but are ignored.

Another approach to planning is to involve more organizational members in the process. In this approach, plans are not handed down from one level to the next, but instead are developed by organizational members at the various levels and in the various work units to meet their specific needs. For instance, at Dell, employees from production, supply management, and channel management meet weekly to make plans based on current product demand and supply. In addition, work teams set their own daily schedules and track their progress against those schedules. If a team falls behind, team members develop "recovery" plans to try to get back on schedule.[27] When organizational members are more actively involved in planning, they see that the plans are more than just something written down on paper. They can actually see that the plans are used in directing and coordinating work.

Current Issues in Planning

▶ ▶ ▶ Despite their successes elsewhere and the time spent in making plans Blue Man's time in Toronto was short-lived. The production closed only 18 months after it opened, although the group had planned to be there forever. The group's debut at Toronto's Panasonic Theatre got off to a rocky start. Four unions called on the public to boycott the production after Blue Man refused to negotiate a collective agreement with any of them and decided to use non-union performers instead. "We maybe made assumptions that were naive or, I hope not, arrogant," said Wink during a visit to Toronto. "But we assumed that things would be more like they were in the States."

④ Discuss current issues in planning.

Think About It

What could the group have done to better plan for their Toronto production? How did context contribute to the group's short run in Toronto?

We conclude this chapter by addressing two current issues in planning. Specifically, we're going to look at planning effectively in dynamic environments and then at how managers can use environmental scanning, especially competitive intelligence.

◄-⊙-Simulate on MyManagementLab

Planning

How Can Managers Plan Effectively in Dynamic Environments?

As we saw in Chapter 2, the external environment is continually changing. For instance, cloud computing storage is revolutionizing all kinds of industries from financial services to health care to engineering.[28] Social networking sites are used by companies to connect with customers, employees, and potential employees. Amounts spent on eating out instead of cooking at home are predicted to decline. And experts believe that China and India are transforming the twenty-first-century global economy.

How can managers effectively plan when the external environment is continually changing? We already discussed uncertain environments as one of the contingency factors that affect the types of plans managers develop. Because dynamic environments are more the norm than the exception, let's look at how managers can effectively plan in such environments.

In an uncertain environment, managers should develop plans that are specific, but flexible. Although this may seem contradictory, it's not. To be useful, plans need some specificity, but the plans should not be set in stone. Managers need to recognize that planning is an ongoing process. The plans serve as a road map although the destination may change due to dynamic market conditions. They should be ready to change directions if environmental conditions warrant. This flexibility is particularly important as plans are implemented. Managers need to stay alert to environmental changes that may impact implementation and respond as needed. Keep in mind, also, that even when the environment is highly uncertain, it's important to continue formal planning in order to see any effect on organizational performance. It's the persistence in planning that contributes to significant performance improvement. Why? It seems that, as with most activities, managers "learn to plan" and the quality of their planning improves when they continue to do it.[23] Finally, make the organizational hierarchy flatter to effectively plan in dynamic environments. This means allowing lower organizational levels to set goals and develop plans because there's little time for goals and plans to flow down from the top. Managers should teach their employees how to set goals and to plan, and then trust them to do it. And you need look no

Knowledgeable and skilled employees play an important role in planning at Wipro, serving more than 800 clients, including governments, educational institutions, and businesses. Wipro has become successful while operating in a dynamic environment by teaching employees how to set goals and make plans and then trusting them to do it. Wipro gives employees responsibility to analyze customers' ever-changing business needs and then devise solutions that help them function faster and more efficiently. Shown here are Wipro software employees at company headquarters in Bangalore, India.

Jagadeesh NV/EPA/Newscom

further than Bangalore, India, to find a company that effectively understands this. Just a decade ago, Wipro Limited was "an anonymous conglomerate selling cooking oil and personal computers, mostly in India." Today, it's a $7.5 billion-a-year global company with much of its business coming from information-technology services.[29] Accenture, Hewlett-Packard, IBM, and the big Canadian accounting firms know all too well the competitive threat Wipro represents. Not only are Wipro's employees economical, they're knowledgeable and skilled. And they play an important role in the company's planning. Because the information services industry is continually changing, employees are taught to analyze situations and to define the scale and scope of a client's problems in order to offer the best solutions. These employees are on the front line with the clients, and it's their responsibility to establish what to do and how to do it. It's an approach that positions Wipro for success—no matter how the industry changes.

How Can Managers Use Environmental Scanning?

Crammed into a small Shanghai apartment that houses four generations of a Chinese family, Indra Nooyi, Chairman and CEO of PepsiCo Inc., asked the inhabitants several questions about "China's rapid development, their shopping habits, and how they feel about Western brands." This visit was part of an "immersion" tour of China for Ms. Nooyi, who hopes to strengthen PepsiCo's business in emerging markets. She said, "I wanted to look at how people live, how they eat, what the growth possibilities are."[30] The information gleaned from her research—a prime example of environmental scanning up close and personal—will help in establishing PepsiCo's future goals and plans.

A manager's analysis of the external environment may be improved by **environmental scanning**, which involves screening information to detect emerging trends. One of the fastest-growing forms of environmental scanning is **competitor intelligence**, gathering information about competitors that allows managers to anticipate competitors' actions rather than merely react to them.[31] It seeks basic information about competitors: Who are they? What are they doing? How will what they're doing affect us?

environmental scanning
Screening information to detect emerging trends.

competitor intelligence
Gathering information about competitors that allows managers to anticipate competitors' actions rather than merely react to them.

Many who study competitive intelligence suggest that much of the competitor-related information that managers need to make crucial strategic decisions is available and accessible to the public.[32] In other words, competitive intelligence isn't corporate espionage. Advertisements, promotional materials, press releases, reports filed with government agencies, annual reports, want ads, newspaper reports, information on the internet, and industry studies are readily accessible sources of information. Specific information about an industry and associated organizations is increasingly available through electronic databases. Managers can literally tap into this wealth of competitive information by purchasing access to databases. Attending trade shows and debriefing your own sales staff also can be good sources of information on competitors. In addition, many organizations even regularly buy competitors' products and ask their own employees to evaluate them to learn about new technical innovations.[33]

In a changing global business environment, environmental scanning and obtaining competitive intelligence can be quite complex, especially since information must be gathered from around the world. However, one thing managers could do is subscribe to news services that review newspapers and magazines from around the globe and provide summaries to client companies.

Managers do need to be careful about the way information, especially competitive intelligence, is gathered to prevent any concerns about whether it's legal or ethical.[34] For instance, Starwood Hotels sued Hilton Hotels, alleging that two former employees stole trade secrets and helped Hilton develop a new line of luxury, trendy hotels designed to appeal to a young demographic.[35] The court filing said, "This is the clearest imaginable case of corporate espionage, theft of trade secrets, unfair competition, and computer fraud." Competitive intelligence becomes illegal corporate spying when it involves the theft of proprietary materials or trade secrets by any means. The Economic Espionage Act makes it a crime in the United States to engage in economic espionage or to steal a trade secret. Difficult decisions about competitive intelligence arise because often there's a fine line between what's considered *legal and ethical* and what's considered *legal but unethical*. Although the top manager at one competitive intelligence firm contends that 99.9 percent of intelligence gathering is legal, there's no question that some people or companies will go to any lengths—some unethical—to get information about competitors.[36]

CHAPTER 8

SUMMARY AND IMPLICATIONS

1. Define the nature and purpose of planning. Planning involves defining the organization's goals, establishing an overall strategy for achieving those goals, and developing plans for organizational work activities. The four purposes of planning include providing direction, reducing uncertainty, minimizing waste and redundancy, and establishing the goals or standards used in controlling. Studies of the planning-performance relationship have concluded that formal planning is associated with positive financial performance, for the most part; it's more important to do a good job of planning and implementing the plans than doing more extensive planning; the external environment is usually the reason why companies that plan don't achieve high levels of performance; and the planning-performance relationship seems to be influenced by the planning time frame.

> ▶ ▶ ▶ In Blue Man Group's case, lack of planning in the early years led to exhaustion and near burnout of its co-founders. The co-founders claimed they did not have time to plan.

2. Classify the types of goals organizations might have and the plans they use. Goals are desired outcomes. Plans are documents that outline how goals are going to be met. Goals might be strategic or financial and they might be stated or real. Strategic plans apply to the entire organization while operational plans encompass a particular functional area. Long-term plans are those with a time frame beyond three years. Short-term plans cover one year or less. Specific plans are clearly defined and leave no room for interpretation. Directional plans are flexible and set out general guidelines. A single-use plan is a one-time plan designed to meet the needs of a unique situation. Standing plans are ongoing plans that provide guidance for activities performed repeatedly.

> ▶ ▶ ▶ Blue Man Group developed a very elaborate plan for their shows, enabling "clones" of the co-founders to deliver the same quality show wherever they performed.

3. Compare and contrast approaches to goal-setting and planning. In traditional goal-setting, goals are set at the top of the organization and then become subgoals for each organizational area. MBO (management by objectives) is a process of setting mutually agreed-upon goals and using those goals to evaluate employee performance. Well-written goals have six characteristics: (1) written in terms of outcomes, (2) measurable and quantifiable, (3) clear as to time frame, (4) challenging but attainable, (5) written down, and (6) communicated to all organizational members who need to know them. Goal-setting involves these steps: review the organization's mission; evaluate available resources; determine the goals individually or with input from others; write down the goals and communicate them to all who need to know them; and review results and change goals as needed. The contingency factors that affect planning include the manager's level in the organization, the degree of environmental uncertainty, and the length of future commitments. The two main approaches to planning include the traditional approach, which has plans developed by top managers that flow down through other organizational levels and which may use a formal planning department. The other approach is to involve more organizational members in the planning process.

> ▶ ▶ ▶ The Blue Man Group was able to adopt planning as part of the culture and it was planning that allowed them to scale from a single venue to multiple venues and deepen their product offerings. It is likely that this required a combination of the top down and bottom up approaches.

4. Discuss current issues in planning. Planning in dynamic environments usually means developing plans that are specific but flexible. Also, it's important to continue planning, especially when the environment is highly uncertain. Finally, because there's little time in a dynamic environment for goals and plans to flow down from the top, lower organizational levels should be allowed to set goals and develop plans. Another current planning issue involves using environmental scanning to help do a better analysis of the external environment. One form of environmental scanning, competitive intelligence, can be especially helpful in finding out what competitors are doing.

▶ ▶ ▶ Blue Man Group acted as if its environment was not particularly dynamic. They assumed that they could recreate the same experience for show goers with different performers, without thinking about the local environment. Thus, by writing clear plans for performers, they can produce a consistent show in any venue, but this may not be enough to guarantee that the show will go on.

MyManagementLab Study, practise, and explore real management situations with these helpful resources:
- **Interactive Lesson Presentations:** Work through interactive presentations and assessments to test your knowledge of management concepts.
- **PIA (Personal Inventory Assessments):** Enhance your ability to connect with key concepts through these engaging, self-reflection assessments.
- **Study Plan:** Check your understanding of chapter concepts with self-study quizzes.
- **Simulations:** Practise decision-making in simulated management environments.

P I A **PERSONAL INVENTORY ASSESSMENT**

REVIEW AND DISCUSSION QUESTIONS

1. Explain what studies have shown about the relationship between planning and performance.

2. Discuss the contingency factors that affect planning.

3. Will planning become more or less important to managers in the future? Why?

4. If planning is so crucial, why do some managers choose not to do it? What would you tell these managers?

5. Explain how planning involves making decisions today that will have an impact later.

6. How might planning in a not-for-profit organization such as the Canadian Cancer Society differ from planning in a for-profit organization such as Molson?

7. What types of planning do you do in your personal life? Describe these plans in terms of being (a) strategic or operational, (b) short term or long term, and (c) specific or directional.

8. Many companies have a goal of becoming more environmentally sustainable. One of the most important steps they can take is controlling paper waste. Choose a company—any type, any size. You've been put in charge of creating a program to do this for your company. Set goals and develop plans. Prepare a report for your boss (that is, your professor) outlining these goals and plans.

ETHICS DILEMMA

Rules are rules. Or are they? An incident at a Safeway store in Hawaii made international headlines after cops were called on a couple who failed to pay for two $2.50 sandwiches.[37] The couple had bought $50 worth of groceries and said they intended to pay for the sandwiches, which they'd eaten while shopping. The couple was with their two-year-old daughter and the mother was about eight months pregnant and said she had felt lightheaded before eating one of the sandwiches. Despite the couple's request to just let them pay for the sandwiches, the store manager, trying to follow company policy, called the police, leading to the arrest of both parents and their separation from their young daughter for more than 18 hours. Safeway did ultimately drop the shoplifting charges and apologized to the couple. But "by rigidly following a rule, the store may have turned a $5 theft into a much bigger dent in its reputation and bottom line." What do you think? Was this a good business decision for Safeway? What potential ethical issues do you see here? If you were the store manager, what would you have done in this situation?

Developing Your Goal Setting Skill—About the Skill

Employees should have a clear understanding of what they're attempting to accomplish. In addition, managers have the responsibility for seeing that this is done by helping employees set work goals. Setting goals is a skill every manager needs to develop.

Steps in Practising the Skill

You can be more effective at setting goals if you use the following eight suggestions.

1. *Identify an employee's key job tasks.* Goal-setting begins by defining what you want your employees to accomplish. The best source for this information is each employee's job description.

2. *Establish specific and challenging goals for each key task.* Identify the level of performance expected of each employee. Specify the target toward which the employee is working.

3. *Specify the deadlines for each goal.* Putting deadlines on each goal reduces ambiguity. Deadlines, however, should not be set arbitrarily. Rather, they need to be realistic given the tasks to be completed.

4. *Allow the employee to actively participate.* When employees participate in goal-setting, they're more likely to accept the goals. However, it must be sincere participation. That is, employees must perceive that you are truly seeking their input, not just going through the motions.

5. *Prioritize goals.* When you give someone more than one goal, it's important for you to rank the goals in order of importance. The purpose of prioritizing is to encourage the employee to take action and expend effort on each goal in proportion to its importance.

6. *Rate goals for difficulty and importance.* Goal-setting should not encourage people to choose easy goals. Instead, goals should be rated for their difficulty and importance. When goals are rated, individuals can be given credit for trying difficult goals, even if they don't fully achieve them.

7. *Build in feedback mechanisms to assess goal progress.* Feedback lets employees know whether their level of effort is sufficient to attain the goal. Feedback should be both self- and supervisor-generated. In either case, feedback should be frequent and recurring.

8. *Link rewards to goal attainment.* It's natural for employees to ask, "What's in it for me?" Linking rewards to the achievement of goals will help answer that question.

Practising the Skill

1. Where do you want to be in five years? Do you have specific five-year goals? Establish three goals you want to achieve in five years. Make sure these goals are specific, challenging, and measurable.

2. Set personal and academic goals you want to achieve by the end of this college term. Prioritize and rate them for difficulty.

Helping Design a Training Program

People Power, a training company that markets its human resource programs to corporations around the globe, has had several requests to design a training program to teach employees how to use the internet for researching information. This training program will then be marketed to potential corporate customers. Your team is spearheading this important project. There are three stages to the project: (1) researching corporate customer needs, (2) researching the internet for specific information sources and techniques that could be used in the training module, and (3) designing and writing a specific training module. The first thing your team has to do is identify at least three goals for each stage. As you proceed with this task, you don't need to come up with specifics about "how" to proceed with these activities; just think about "what" you want to accomplish in each stage.

Form groups of three or four individuals. Complete your assigned work as described above. Be sure that your goals are well designed. Be prepared to share your team's goals with the rest of the class.

LEARNING TO BE A MANAGER

- Think ahead to three years from now and consider what it is that you might like to be doing with your life. Develop your own vision and mission statements. Establish a set of goals that will help you achieve your vision and mission.

- Develop a three-year plan that maps out the steps you need to take in order to get to where you want to be with your life at that time.

- Practise setting goals by doing so for various aspects of your personal life, such as academic studies, career preparation, family, and so forth.

- Be prepared to change your goals as circumstances change.

- For goals that you have set, write out plans for achieving those goals.

- Write a personal mission statement.

- If you are employed, talk to your manager(s) about the types of planning they do. Ask them for suggestions on how to be a better planner.

CASE APPLICATION 1

Funny Name—Not-So-Funny Effect

This volcano has a funny name—Eyjafjallajokull—but its impact was not so funny to global businesses, both large and small.[38] When it erupted in April 2010, the plume of volcanic ash that spread across thousands of miles disrupted air travel and global commerce for a number of days.

The eruption of the Icelandic volcano Eyjafjallajokull, which produced a huge drifting ash cloud throughout Europe, resulted in flight cancellations that disrupted global commerce. The halting of air travel for several days impacted managers' plans for the production and distribution of goods and services and many other scheduled business operations.

As thousands of flights were cancelled across Europe, tens of thousands of air travellers couldn't get to their destinations. For example, Marthin De Beer, vice-president of emerging technologies at Cisco Systems, was headed to Oslo to discuss the final aspects of its acquisition of Tandberg, a Norwegian teleconferencing company. However, when his flight was cancelled, he and Tandberg's CEO, Fredrik Halvorsen, used their merged companies' equipment to hold a virtual press conference. Other businesses weren't as lucky, especially those with high-value, highly perishable products such as berries, fresh fish and flowers, and medicines and pharmaceuticals. African farmers, European fresh-produce

importers, and flower traders from Kenya to the Netherlands found their businesses threatened by the air traffic shutdown. Even manufacturers were affected. For instance, BMW had to scale back work hours and had even prepared for possibly shutting down production at its Spartanburg, South Carolina, plant because it depended on trans-Atlantic flights to bring transmissions and other components from German factories by air. A spokesperson at another automobile company, Mercedes-Benz, said, "There has been disruption in our parts supply. We expect that there may be shortages of some parts or delays in some instances."

DISCUSSION QUESTIONS

1. Could a company even plan for this type of situation? If yes, how? If not, why not?

2. Would goals be useful in this type of situation? What types of goals might a manufacturing company like BMW have in such a situation? How about a global airline? How about a small flower grower in Kenya?

3. What types of plans could companies use in this type of situation? Explain why you think these plans would be important.

4. What lessons about planning can managers learn from this crisis?

CASE APPLICATION 2

Shifting Direction

As the global leader in satellite navigation equipment, Garmin Ltd. recently hit a milestone number. It has sold more than 100 million of its products to customers—from motorists to runners to geocachers and more—who depend on the company's equipment to "help show them the way." Despite this milestone, the company's core business is in decline due to changing circumstances.[39] In response, managers at Garmin, the biggest maker of personal navigation devices, are shifting direction. Many of you probably have a dashboard-mounted navigation device in your car and chances are it might be a Garmin. However, a number of cars now have "dashboard command centers which combine smartphone docking stations with navigation systems." Sales of Garmin devices have declined as consumers increasingly use their smartphones for directions and maps. However, have you ever tried to use your smartphone navigation system while holding a phone to look at its display? It's dangerous to hold a phone and steer. Also, GPS apps can "crash" if multiple apps are running. That's why the Olathe, Kansas-based company is taking action to "aggressively partner" with automakers to embed its GPS systems in car dashboards. Right now, its biggest in-dash contract is with Chrysler and its Uconnect dashboard system found in several models of Jeep, Dodge, and Chrysler vehicles. Garmin also is working with Honda and Toyota for dashboard systems in the Asian market.

Despite these new market shifts, customers have gotten used to GPS devices that have become an essential part of their lives. That's why Garmin's executive team still believes there's a market for dedicated navigation systems. It's trying to breathe some life into the product with new features, better designs, and more value for the consumer's money. For instance, some of the new features include faster searching for addresses or points of interest, voice-activated navigation, and highlighting exit services such as gas stations and restaurants.

DISCUSSION QUESTIONS

1. What role do you think goals would play in planning the change in direction for the company? List some goals you think might be important. (Make sure these goals have the characteristics of well-written goals.)
2. What types of plans would be needed in an industry such as this one? (For instance, long term or short term, or both?) Explain why you think these plans would be important.
3. What contingency factors might affect the planning Garmin executives have to do? How might those contingency factors affect the planning?
4. What planning challenges do you think Garmin executives face with continuing to be the global market leader? How should they cope with those challenges?

Managing Strategically

In this chapter, we look at an important part of the planning that managers do: developing organizational strategies. Every organization has strategies for doing what it is in business to do, and managers must manage those strategies effectively. After reading and studying this chapter, you will achieve the following learning outcomes.

Learning Outcomes

1. Explain the role of strategic management and why it is important.

2. Explain the role of managers in each of the six strategic management steps.

3. Describe three types of organizational strategies.

4. Describe competitive advantage and the competitive strategies organizations use to get it.

5. Discuss current strategic management issues.

▶ ▶ ▶ Heather Reisman and husband Gerry Schwartz, owners of Toronto-based Indigo, opened their first store in Burlington, Ontario, in September 1997.[1] By 2000, there were 14 locations across Canada. Indigo was the first book retailer in Canada to sell music and gifts and to include licensed cafés in its stores. The company faced stiff competition from Chapters. In November 2000, Reisman and

Schwartz announced their bid to buy Chapters and, though a bitter battle ensued, the two companies merged in August 2001. Reisman took Canada's biggest book chain from a $48 million loss in 2002 to a $34.9 million profit in 2010, which represented an increase of 14 percent over 2009. Then things changed as the industry underwent dramatic change as sales of digital books increased with a corresponding decline in paper-based books.

As of March 2013 there were 97 superstores and 134 small-format stores. During 2013 the company did not open any new stores and closed 9 small format stores. From 2011 to 2013 sales declined from 956 million dollars to 892 million dollars, with profit of 58 cents a share in 2011, a loss of $1.10 a share in 2012, and profit of 17 cents a share in 2013.

In the words of Heather Reisman, "With our core book business under pressure, it will take us at least two more years to achieve the levels of growth necessary in our new business to make up and then surpass the decline in books. We are energized and firmly committed to taking our brand—so valued by Canadians—and reinventing it for the 21st century."[2]

Keith Beaty/ZUMA Press/Newscom

Think About It

How does a bookselling company choose a strategy that allows it to reinvent itself? Put yourself in Heather Reisman's shoes. What kinds of analyses can Reisman use to help her make good decisions that will lead to survival and growth?

The importance of having good strategies can be seen by the difficulties facing North American automotive manufacturers and traditional Canadian print media companies. By choosing effective strategies to attract customers, organizations can become prosperous and thrive. Improper strategies can lead to huge failures. An underlying theme in this chapter is that effective strategies can result in high organizational performance. This chapter examines various strategies that organizations can use to manage more effectively.

The Importance of Strategic Management

Watch on MyManagementLab
Joie de Vivre Hospitality: Strategic Management

① Explain the role of strategic management and why it is important.

Effective managers around the world recognize the role that strategic management plays in their organizations' performance. Swedish furniture giant IKEA Group says it's planning to set up 25 stores in India in coming years, a move made possible by a change in Indian government policy that says some retailers can now own 100 percent of their Indian units. In a fierce battle over tablet computers, Apple announced it's building a miniature iPad to rival Amazon's Kindle Fire, Google's Nexus 7, and Barnes & Noble's Nook Color. The race to build book-size tablets is driven by consumer desire for greater portability.[3] Strategic management is very much a part of what managers do. In this section, we want to look at what strategic management is and why it's important.

What Is Strategic Management?

To begin to understand the basics of strategy and strategic management, you need look no further than at what has happened in the discount retail industry. The industry's two largest competitors in Canada—Walmart and Zellers— battled for market dominance after Walmart arrived in 1992. The two chains have some striking similarities: store atmosphere, markets served, and organizational purpose. Yet Walmart's performance (financial and otherwise) took market share from Zellers every single year. Walmart is the world's largest and most successful retailer, and Zellers was the second-largest discount retailer in Canada. Why the difference in performance? Will Target be more successful a competitor now that they have a foothold in the Canadian market after acquiring many of the key Zellers locations? Organizations vary in how well they perform because of differences in their strategies and differences in competitive abilities.[4] Walmart excels at strategic management, as does Target, and it promises to be an interesting battle.

strategic management What managers do to develop the organization's strategies.

strategies Plans for how an organization will do what it's in business to do, how it will compete successfully, and how it will attract and satisfy its customers in order to achieve its goals.

Strategic management is what managers do to develop the organization's strategies. What are an organization's **strategies**? They are the decisions and actions that determine the long-run performance of an organization. Strategies differ from plans, which we discussed in Chapter 7, in that strategies are the "big picture" decisions. Through strategic management, managers establish the game plan or road map—that is, the strategies—for how the organization will do whatever it's in business to do, how it will compete successfully, and how it will attract and satisfy its customers in order to achieve its goals.[5] It's an important task of managers and ultimately entails all the basic management functions—planning, organizing, leading, and controlling.

business model A strategic design for how a company intends to profit from its strategies, work processes, and work activities.

One term that is often used in conjunction with strategic management and strategies is **business model**, which is a strategic design for how a company intends to profit from its strategies, work processes, and work activities. A company's business model focuses on two things: (1) whether customers will value what the company is providing and (2) whether the company can make any money doing that.[6] For instance, Jeff Bezos pioneered a new business model for selling books to consumers directly online instead of selling through bookstores. Did customers "value" that? Absolutely! Did Amazon make money doing it that way? Not at first, but now, absolutely! What began as the world's biggest bookstore is now the world's biggest everything store. As managers think about strategies, they need to think about the economic viability of their company's business model.

Why Is Strategic Management Important?

In the summer of 2002, *American Idol*, a spin-off from a British television show, became one of the biggest shows in American television history. Twelve seasons later, it's still one of the most-watched shows on television, although its audience has declined. However, the show's executive producer said, "If we're smart about it, there's no reason why 'Idol' wouldn't keep going. Just look at 'Price is Right.' It's been on for over 35 years."[7] The managers behind *Idol* seem to understand the importance of strategic management as they've developed and exploited every aspect of the *Idol* business—the television show, the music, the concerts, and all the other associated licensed products. Now, their challenge is to keep the franchise a strong presence in the market by making strategic changes.

Why is strategic management so important? One of the most significant reasons is that it can make a difference in how well an organization performs. The most fundamental questions about strategy address why firms succeed or fail, and why, when faced with the same environmental conditions, they have varying levels of performance. Studies of the factors that contribute to organizational performance have shown a positive relationship between strategic planning and performance.[8] In other words, it appears that organizations that use strategic management do have higher levels of performance. And that makes strategic management pretty important!

Another reason strategic management is important has to do with the fact that organizations of all types and sizes face continually changing situations. By following the steps in the strategic management process, managers examine relevant variables in deciding what to do and how to do it. When managers use the strategic management process, they can better cope with uncertain environments.

Finally, strategic management is important because it's involved in many of the decisions that managers make. Most of the significant current business events reported in the various business publications involve strategic management. For instance, Oakville, Ontario-based Tim Hortons introduced caramel-flavoured iced cappuccino, and Calgary-based WestJet Airlines hired bilingual flight attendants in anticipation of offering flights into Quebec City. Both of these events are examples of managers making strategic decisions.

How widespread is the use of strategic management? One survey of business owners found that 69 percent had strategic plans, and among those owners 89 percent responded that they found their plans effective.[9] They stated, for example, that strategic planning gave them specific goals and provided their staff with a unified vision. Although a few management writers claim that strategic planning is "dead," most continue to emphasize its importance.[10]

Today, strategic management has moved beyond for-profit business organizations to include government agencies, hospitals, and other not-for-profit organizations. For instance, when Canada Post found itself in intense competitive battles with overnight package-delivery companies, courier services, and email, its CEO used strategic management to help pinpoint important issues and design appropriate strategic responses. Although strategic management in not-for-profits has not been as well researched as that in for-profit organizations, it's important for these organizations as well.

The Strategic Management Process

▶ ▶ ▶ Heather Reisman describes the company as being in the early stages of a journey "which will take us from our position as Canada's leading bookseller to our vision of being the world's first CREATIVES department store—an omni-channel, multi-category retailer with books, writers, artists, and designers at the heart of our enterprise. Our new experience will include a series of shops where our customers will find, in addition to books, wonderfully affordable products for home, for his and her gifting, and for kids, much of which is being designed in our own studio and therefore unique to us."[11]

② Explain the role of managers in each of the six strategic management steps.

strategic management process A six-step process that encompasses strategic planning, implementation, and evaluation.

The **strategic management process**, as illustrated in Exhibit 9-1, is a six-step process that encompasses strategic planning, implementation, and evaluation. Although the first four steps describe the planning that must take place, implementation and evaluation are just as important! Even the best strategies can fail if management does not implement or evaluate them properly. Let's examine the six steps in detail.

Step 1: Identify the Organization's Current Mission, Goals, and Strategies

mission A statement of an organization's purpose

Every organization needs a **mission**—a statement of the purpose of an organization. An example is provided in Exhibit 9-2. The mission answers the question, What is our reason for being in business? Defining the organization's mission forces managers to carefully identify the scope of its products or services. For example, Indigo's mission statement used to be "to provide a service-driven, stress-free approach to satisfying the booklover."[12] The mission of WorkSafeBC (the Workers' Compensation Board of British Columbia) is to "promote workplace health and safety for the workers and employers of [the] province."[13] The mission of eBay is "to build an online marketplace that enables practically anyone to trade practically anything almost anywhere in the world."[14] These statements provide clues to what these organizations see as their reason for being in business.

It's also important for managers to identify goals and strategies consistent with the mission being pursued. As we explained in Chapter 7, goals are the foundation of planning. A company's goals provide the measurable performance targets that employees strive to reach. Knowing the company's current goals gives managers a basis for assessing whether those goals need to be changed. For the same reasons, it's important for managers to identify the organization's current strategies.

Step 2: Conduct an Internal Analysis

resources An organization's assets—financial, physical, human, intangible—that are used to develop, manufacture, and deliver products or services to customers.

The internal analysis provides important information about an organization's specific resources and capabilities. An organization's **resources** are its assets—financial, physical, human, intangible—that are used by the organization to develop, manufacture, and

Exhibit 9-1

The Strategic Management Process

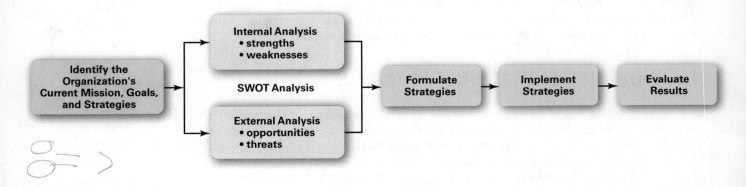

Exhibit 9-2

Components of a Mission Statement

Customers: Who are the firm's customers?

Markets: Where does the firm compete geographically?

Concern for survival, growth, and profitability: Is the firm committed to growth and financial stability?

Philosophy: What are the firm's basic beliefs, values, and ethical priorities?

Concern for public image: How responsive is the firm to societal and environmental concerns?

Products or services: What are the firm's major products or services?

Technology: Is the firm technologically current?

Self-concept: What are the firm's major competitive advantage and core competencies?

Concern for employees: Are employees a valuable asset of the firm?

Source: Based on *Strategic Management*, 13th edition, by F. David. Published by Pearson Education, Inc.

deliver products or services to its customers. Its **capabilities** are its skills and abilities in doing the work activities needed in its business. The major value-creating capabilities and skills of the organization are known as its **core competencies**.[15] Both resources and core competencies can determine the organization's competitive weapons. For instance, Fujio Cho, Toyota Motor Corporation's chair, called the company's Prius "a giant leap into the future," but the highly popular car is simply one more example of the company's resources and core competencies in product research and design, manufacturing, marketing, and managing its human resources. Experts who have studied the company point to its ability to nourish and preserve employee creativity and flexibility in a work environment that is fairly rigid and controlled.[16]

After doing the internal analysis, managers should be able to identify organizational strengths and weaknesses. Any activities the organization does well or any unique resources that it has are called **strengths**. **Weaknesses** are activities the organization does not do well or resources it needs but does not possess. This step forces managers to recognize that their organizations, no matter how large or successful, are constrained by the resources and capabilities they have.

Organizational culture, specifically, is one crucial part of the internal analysis that is often overlooked.[17] It's crucial because strong and weak cultures do have different effects on strategy, and the content of a culture has a major effect on strategies pursued. In a strong culture, almost all employees have a clear understanding of what the organization is about. This clarity makes it easy for managers to convey to new employees the organization's core competencies and strengths. The negative side of a strong culture, of course, is that it may be more difficult to change organizational strategies. Firms with "strategically appropriate cultures" outperformed corporations with less appropriate cultures.[18] What is a strategically appropriate culture? It's one that supports the firm's chosen strategy. For instance, Avis, the number two US car rental company, has for a number of years stood on top of its category in an annual survey of brand loyalty. By creating a culture where employees obsess over every step of the rental car experience, Avis has built an unmatched record for customer loyalty.[19]

Does the fact that Calgary-based WestJet Airlines made the list of Canada's 10 Most Admired Corporate Cultures for four separate years and was subsequently inducted into Waterstone's Corporate Culture Hall of Fame mean anything? Does the fact that Coca-Cola has the world's most powerful global brand give it any edge? Studies of reputation and corporate performance show that it can have a positive impact.[20] As one researcher said, "A strong, well-managed reputation can and should be an asset for any organization."[21]

capabilities An organization's skills and abilities that enable it to do the work activities needed in its business.

core competencies An organization's major value-creating skills, capabilities, and resources that determine its competitive advantage.

strengths Any activities the organization does well or any unique resources that it has.

weaknesses Activities the organization does not do well or resources it needs but does not possess.

◄●⊢Simulate on MyManagementLab

Conducting a SWOT Analysis

Exhibit 9-3

Identifying the Organization's Opportunities

Organization's Resources/Capabilities

Organization's Opportunities

Opportunities in the Environment

◄●⊢Simulate on MyManagementLab

Adapting to the Economic Environment

opportunities Positive trends in external environmental factors.

threats Negative trends in external environmental factors.

SWOT analysis An analysis of the organization's strengths, weaknesses, opportunities, and threats.

Step 3: Conduct an External Analysis

In Chapter 2, we described the external environment as informing a manager's actions. Analyzing that environment is a critical step in the strategy process. Managers need to know, for instance, what the competition is doing, what pending legislation might affect the organization, or what the labour supply is like in locations where it operates. In analyzing the external environment, managers should examine both the specific and general environments to see what trends and changes are occurring. At Indigo, managers noted that individuals were reading fewer books and using the internet more. This observation required Indigo to rethink how to encourage more people to rely on Indigo stores for gift items and connections with other book lovers.

After analyzing the environment, managers need to assess what they have learned in terms of opportunities that the organization can exploit, and threats that it must counteract. **Opportunities** are positive trends in external environmental factors; **threats** are negative trends.

The combined external and internal analyses are called the **SWOT analysis** because it's an analysis of the organization's *s*trengths, *w*eaknesses, *o*pportunities, and *t*hreats. Based on the SWOT analysis, managers can identify a strategic niche that the organization might exploit (Exhibit 9-3). For instance, owner Leonard Lee started Ottawa-based Lee Valley Tools in 1982 to help individual woodworkers, and later gardeners, find just the right tools for their tasks. This niche strategy enabled Lee Valley to grow into one of North America's leading garden and woodworking catalogue companies for over 25 years.

Step 4: Formulate Strategies

Once the SWOT analysis is complete, managers need to develop and evaluate strategic alternatives and then select strategies that capitalize on the organization's strengths and exploit environmental opportunities, or that correct the organization's weaknesses and buffer it against threats. Strategies need to be established for the organizational, business, and functional levels of the organization, which we will describe shortly. This step is complete when managers have developed a set of strategies that gives the organization a relative competitive advantage over its rivals.

Step 5: Implement Strategies

After strategies are formulated, they must be implemented. No matter how effectively an organization has planned its strategies, it cannot succeed if the strategies are not implemented properly.

Exhibit 9-4 indicates the different things organizations can do to implement a new strategy. The rest of the chapters in this book address a number of issues related to strategy implementation. For instance, in Chapter 10, we discuss the strategy–structure relationship.

Exhibit 9-4

Ways to Implement Strategy

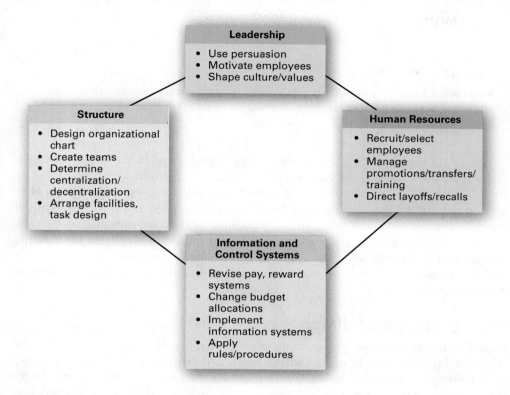

Leadership
- Use persuasion
- Motivate employees
- Shape culture/values

Structure
- Design organizational chart
- Create teams
- Determine centralization/ decentralization
- Arrange facilities, task design

Human Resources
- Recruit/select employees
- Manage promotions/transfers/ training
- Direct layoffs/recalls

Information and Control Systems
- Revise pay, reward systems
- Change budget allocations
- Implement information systems
- Apply rules/procedures

Source: Adapted from Jay R. Galbraith and Robert K. Kazanjian, *Strategy Implementation: Structure, Systems, and Process*, 2nd ed. (St. Paul, MN: West, 1986), p. 115.

In Chapter 12, we show that if new strategies are to succeed, they often require hiring new people with different skills, transferring some current employees to new positions, or laying off some employees. Also, since more organizations are using teams, the ability to build and manage effective teams is an important part of implementing strategy. (We cover teams in Chapter 15.) Finally, top management leadership is a necessary ingredient in a successful strategy. So, too, is a motivated group of middle- and lower-level managers to carry out the organization's specific strategies. Chapters 13 and 14 discuss ways to improve leadership effectiveness and offer suggestions on motivating people.

Step 6: Evaluate Results

The final step in the strategic management process is evaluating results. How effective have the strategies been? What adjustments, if any, are necessary? We discuss this step in our coverage of evidence-based decision making in Chapter 16.

Types of Organizational Strategies

▶ ▶ ▶ Indigo Books & Music first started to implement its expansion plans in 2001 by buying its major competitor, Chapters (and Chapters.ca).[22] This move gave Indigo a broader market base with a number of new stores, as well as the platform to launch a successful online business. But by 2013 the industry was undergoing dramatic change and Indigo described itself as being well underway to establishing itself as "the world's first CREATIVES department store, a digital and physical place

❸ Describe three types of organizational strategies.

inspired by and filled with books, ideas, beautifully designed products, and the creative people who make it all happen." The choice was made to continue to invest in "a brand and the customer experience which will position Indigo for sustained growth." The priorities remained focused on advancing the core retail business through adapting physical stores, improving productivity, driving employee engagement, and expanding the online and digital presence.[23]

> **Think About It**
> Indigo Books & Music has chosen a growth strategy. What other ways might the company grow? What other strategies might you recommend to Heather Reisman?

There are three types of organizational strategy: organization, business, and functional (Exhibit 9-5). Managers at the top level of the organization typically are responsible for corporate strategies; for example, Heather Reisman plans Indigo's growth strategy. Managers at the middle level typically are responsible for business strategies; for example, Indigo's executive vice-president, online, is responsible for the company's internet business. Departmental managers typically are responsible for functional strategies; for example, Indigo's senior vice-president, human resource/organization development, is responsible for human resource policies, employee training, and staffing. Let's look at each level of organizational strategy.

Organizational Strategy

Organization strategy is a strategy that evaluates what businesses an organization is in, should be in, or wants to be in, and what it wants to do with those businesses. It's based on the mission and goals of the organization and the roles that each business unit of the organization will play. Take PepsiCo, for instance. Its mission is to be a successful producer and marketer of beverage and packaged food products. At one time, PepsiCo had a restaurant division that included Taco Bell, Pizza Hut, and KFC; it made a strategic decision to spin off that division as a separate and independent business entity, now known as YUM! Brands. What types of corporate strategies do organizations such as PepsiCo use?

In choosing what businesses to be in, senior management can choose among three main types of organization strategies: growth, stability, and renewal. To illustrate, Walmart, Ganong Bros., and General Motors are companies that seem to be going in different directions. Walmart is rapidly expanding its operations and developing new business and retailing concepts. Managers at St. Stephen, New Brunswick-based Ganong Bros. ("Canada's Chocolate Family"), on the other hand, are content to maintain the status quo and focus on the candy

Organization strategy A strategy that evaluates what businesses a company is in, should be in, or wants to be in, and what it wants to do with those businesses.

Exhibit 9-5

Levels of Organizational Strategy

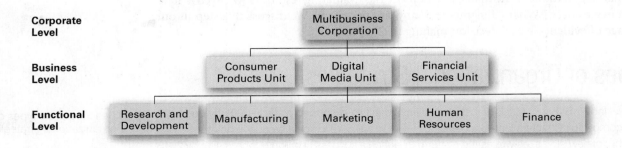

industry. Meanwhile, sluggish sales and an uncertain outlook in the automobile industry have prompted GM to take drastic measures in dealing with its problems. Each of these organizations is using a different type of corporate strategy. Let's look closer at each type.

Growth

Walmart, the world's largest retailer, continues to grow internationally and in Canada. With a **growth strategy**, an organization expands the number of markets served or products offered, either through its current business(es) or through new business(es). Because of its growth strategy, an organization may increase revenues, number of employees, or market share. Organizations grow by using concentration, vertical integration, horizontal integration, or diversification.

growth strategy A strategy that seeks to increase the organization's operations by expanding the number of products offered or markets served, either through its current business(es) or through new business(es).

Concentration   Growth through *concentration* is achieved when an organization concentrates on its primary line of business and increases the number of products offered or markets served in this primary business. No other firms are acquired or merged with; instead, the company chooses to grow by increasing its own business operations. For instance, Oakville, Ontario-based Tim Hortons opens hundreds of new stores every year, and is currently focusing most of its new openings in the United States and Middle East. In the United States, it grew from 288 stores in 2006 to 859 in 2014.[24]

Vertical Integration   A company also might choose to grow by using vertical integration, either backward, forward, or both. In backward vertical integration, an organization becomes its own supplier so it can control its inputs. For instance, eBay owns an online payment business that helps it provide more secure transactions and control one of its most critical processes. In forward vertical integration, an organization becomes its own distributor and is able to control its outputs. For example, Apple has more than 80 retail stores to distribute its product.

Horizontal Integration   In horizontal integration, a company grows by combining with other organizations in the same industry—that is, combining operations with competitors. For instance, French cosmetics giant L'Oréal acquired The Body Shop. Another example is Live Nation, the largest concert promoter in the United States, which combined operations with competitor HOB Entertainment, the operator of the House of Blues Clubs. Inbev of Belgium, which owns Labatt and Alexander Keith's, a Nova Scotia-based brewer, is the leading brewer in the world. Horizontal integration has been considered frequently in the Canadian banking industry in recent years as well.

Tim Hortons has signed a deal with Dubai-based Apparel Group to expand its Middle East development, and has developed from 5 stores in 2011 to 73 stores in 2014, with plans to open 220 new locations in the region. The move is part of a wider plan to develop an international growth strategy for Canadian and US Tim Hortons businesses.

All Tim Hortons trademarks referenced herein are owned by Tim Hortons. Used with permission.

Because combining with competitors might decrease the amount of competition in an industry, Competition Bureau Canada assesses the impact of proposed horizontal integration strategies and must approve such plans before they are allowed to go forward in this country. Other countries have similar bodies that protect fair competition. For instance, managers at Oracle Corporation had to get approval from the European Commission, the "watchdog" for the European Union, before it could acquire rival business-software maker PeopleSoft.

related diversification When a company grows by combining with firms in different, but related, industries.

unrelated diversification When a company grows by combining with firms in different and unrelated industries.

Diversification Finally, an organization can grow through *diversification*, either related or unrelated. In **related diversification** a company grows by merging with or acquiring firms in different, but related, industries. So, for instance, Toronto-based George Weston Foods is involved in the baking and dairy industries, while its ownership of Loblaw Companies provides for the distribution of Weston's food products. With **unrelated diversification**, a company combines with firms in different and unrelated industries. For instance, the Tata Group of India has businesses in chemicals, communications, IT (including the travel search engine Expedia), consumer products, energy, engineering, materials, and services. This is an odd mix, and in this case there's no strategic fit among the businesses.

Many companies use a combination of these approaches to grow. For instance, McDonald's has grown using the concentration strategy by opening more than 32 000 outlets in more than 100 countries, of which about 30 percent are company owned. In addition, it's used horizontal integration by purchasing Boston Market, Chipotle Mexican Grill (which it spun off as a separate entity in 2006), and Donato's Pizza chains (which it sold in late 2003). It also has a minority stake in the UK-based sandwich shops Pret A Manger. McDonald's newest twist on its growth strategy is a move into the premium coffee market with its McCafé coffee shops.

Stability

stability strategy A strategy characterized by an absence of significant change in what the organization is currently doing.

A **stability strategy** is characterized by an absence of significant change in what the organization is currently doing. Examples of this strategy include continuing to serve the same clients by offering the same product or service, maintaining market share, and sustaining the organization's business operations. The organization does not grow, but it does not fall behind, either.

Although it may seem strange that an organization might not want to grow, there are times when the industry is in a period of rapid upheaval with external forces drastically changing and making the future uncertain. At times like these, managers might decide that the prudent course of action is to sit tight and wait to see what happens. Owners and managers of small businesses, such as small neighbourhood grocers, often purposefully choose to follow a stability strategy. Why? They may feel that their business is successful enough just as it is, that it adequately meets their personal goals, and that they don't want the hassles of a growing business.

Renewal

The popular business periodicals frequently report stories of organizations that are not meeting their goals or whose performance is declining. When an organization is in trouble, something needs to be done. Managers need to develop strategies that address organizational weaknesses that are leading to performance declines. These strategies are called **renewal strategies**. There are two main types of renewal strategies, retrenchment and turnaround.

renewal strategy A strategy designed to address organizational weaknesses that are leading to performance declines.

retrenchment strategy A short-run renewal strategy.

A **retrenchment strategy** reduces the organization's activities or operations. Retrenchment strategies include cost reductions, layoffs, closing underperforming units, or closing entire product lines or services.[25] There is no shortage of companies that have pursued a retrenchment strategy. A partial list includes some big corporate names: Procter & Gamble, Sears Canada, Corel, and Nortel Networks. When an organization is facing minor performance setbacks, a retrenchment strategy helps it stabilize operations, revitalize organizational resources and capabilities, and prepare to compete once again.

What happens if an organization's problems are more serious? What if the organization's profits are not just declining, but instead there are no profits, just losses? Best Buy reported a net loss in 2012 of $1.2 billion.[26] Target had a $1 billion loss in 2013.[27] These types of situations call for a more drastic strategy. The **turnaround strategy** is a renewal strategy for times when the organization's performance problems are more critical.

For both renewal strategies, managers cut costs and restructure organizational operations. However, a turnaround strategy typically involves a more extensive use of these measures than does a retrenchment strategy.

turnaround strategy A renewal strategy for situations in which the organization's performance problems are more serious.

How Are Corporate Strategies Managed?

When an organization's corporate strategy involves a number of businesses, managers can manage this collection, or portfolio, of businesses using a corporate portfolio matrix.[28] The first portfolio matrix—the **BCG matrix**—developed by the Boston Consulting Group, introduced the idea that an organization's businesses could be evaluated and plotted using a 2 × 2 matrix (Exhibit 9-6) to identify which ones offered high potential and which were a drain on organizational resources.[29] The horizontal axis represents *market share*, which was evaluated as either low or high; and the vertical axis indicates anticipated *market growth*, which also was evaluated as either low or high. Based on its evaluation, businesses can be placed in one of four categories:

BCG matrix A strategy tool that guides resource allocation decisions on the basis of market share and growth rate of businesses.

- *Cash cows* (low growth, high market share). Businesses in this category generate large amounts of cash, but their prospects for future growth are limited.

- *Stars* (high growth, high market share). These businesses are in a fast-growing market and hold a dominant share of that market. Their contribution to cash flow depends on their need for resources.

- *Question marks* (high growth, low market share). These businesses are in an attractive market, but hold a small share of that market. Therefore, they have the promise of performance, but need to be developed more for that to happen.

- *Dogs* (low growth, low market share). Businesses in this category do not produce, or consume, much cash. However, they hold no promise for improved performance.

What are the strategic implications of the BCG matrix? Managers should "milk" cash cows for as much as they can, limit any new investment in them, and use the large amounts of cash generated to invest in stars and question marks with strong potential to improve

Exhibit 9-6

The BCG Matrix and Strategic Implications

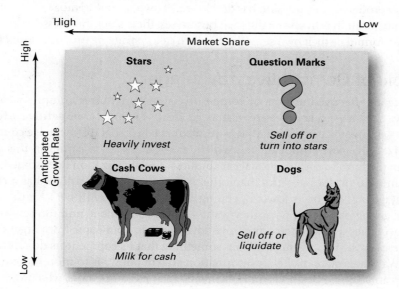

market share. Heavy investment in stars will help take advantage of the market's growth and help maintain high market share. The stars, of course, will eventually develop into cash cows as their markets mature and sales growth slows. The hardest decision for managers is related to the question marks. After careful analysis, some will be sold off and others turned into stars. The dogs should be sold off or liquidated as they have low market share in markets with low growth potential.

A corporate portfolio matrix, such as the BCG matrix, can be a useful strategic management tool. It provides a framework for understanding diverse businesses and helps managers establish priorities for making resource allocation decisions.

Creating Strategic Competitive Advantage

4 Describe competitive advantage and the competitive strategies organizations use to get it.

▶ ▶ ▶ As part of adapting the physical space in its stores, Indigo is providing more floor space in the growth categories of paper, toys, and gift products such as home and fashion accessories. The company continues to expand its assortment of toys and games; it has opened a new design office in New York in 2011; and a "full line of proprietary merchandise developed by this team began appearing on the shelves in 2012."[30]

Think About It

What choices do consumers have in acquiring the products and experiences that the company plans to provide? What steps will Chapters Indigo need to take to generate sustainable competitive advantage? Should Reisman consider alternative ways of growing her business? How would a SWOT analysis help her arrive at a conclusion?

competitive strategy An organizational strategy that focuses on how the organization will compete in each of its businesses.

A **competitive strategy** is a strategy focused on how an organization will compete in each of its businesses. For a small organization in only one line of business or for a large organization that has not diversified into different products or markets, the competitive strategy simply describes how the company will compete in its primary or main market. For organizations in multiple businesses, however, each division will have its own competitive strategy that defines its competitive advantage, the products or services it will offer, the customers it wants to reach, and the like. For example, the French company LVMH Moët Hennessy-Louis Vuitton SA has different business-level strategies for its divisions, such as Donna Karan fashions, Louis Vuitton leather goods, Guerlain perfume, TAG Heuer watches, Dom Pérignon champagne, and other luxury products. Each division has developed its own unique approach for competing. When an organization is in several different businesses, these single businesses that are independent and formulate their own strategies are often called **strategic business units (SBUs)**.

strategic business units (SBUs) Single businesses of an organization in several different businesses that are independent and formulate their own strategies.

competitive advantage What sets an organization apart: its distinct edge.

The Role of Competitive Advantage

Developing an effective business or competitive strategy requires an understanding of competitive advantage, a key concept in strategic management.[31] **Competitive advantage** is what sets an organization apart: that is, its distinct edge. That distinct edge comes from the organization's core competencies, which, as we know from earlier in this chapter, might be in the form of organizational capabilities—the organization does something that others cannot do or does it better than others can do it. WestJet Airlines has a competitive advantage because of its lower operating costs compared with rival Air Canada and its skills at giving passengers what they want—quick, convenient, and fun service. Those core competencies that lead to competitive advantage also can come from organizational assets or resources—the organization has something that its competitors do not have. For instance, Walmart's state-of-the-art information system allows it to monitor and control inventories and supplier relations more efficiently than its competitors, which Walmart has turned into a cost advantage. Harley-Davidson, Nike, and Coca-Cola all have well-known global trademarks that they use to get premium prices for their products.

Quality as a Competitive Advantage

If implemented properly, quality can be a way for an organization to create a sustainable competitive advantage.[32] That is why many organizations apply quality management concepts to their operations in an attempt to set themselves apart from competitors.

To the degree that an organization can satisfy a customer's need for quality better than a competitor, it can attract and retain a loyal customer base. Moreover, constant improvement in the quality and reliability of an organization's products or services may result in a competitive advantage that cannot be taken away.[33]

Design Thinking as a Competitive Advantage

In today's world, consumers can find just about anything they want online. And those consumers also expect a greater variety of choices and faster service when ordering online than ever before. One company that recognized the opportunities—and challenges—of this is Kiva Systems.[34] Kiva makes autonomous robots used in flexible automation systems that are critical to companies' strategic e-commerce efforts. Kiva's CEO says, "We transform inventory atoms into bits of information and run algorithms on that data and organize it in much the same way that Google sorts web pages." By doing this efficiently, the company's robots can gather goods within minutes of an order and deliver them to warehouse pickworkers who can then ship up to four times more packages in an hour. Kiva (which was recently acquired by Amazon) also has "taught" its robots to move cardboard boxes to the trash compactor and to assist in gift-wrapping.

Kiva is a company that understands the power of design thinking—defined in Chapter 7 (Decision Making) as approaching management problems the way designers approach design problems. Using design thinking means thinking in unusual ways about what the business is and how it's doing what it's in business to do—or as one person said, "solving wicked problems with creative resolutions by thinking outside existing alternatives and creating new alternatives."[35] After all, who would have thought to "teach" robots to help wrap gifts so that e-commerce warehouse fulfillment could be made even more efficient? However, as important as design thinking is to the design of amazing products, it also means recognizing that "design" isn't just for products or processes but for any organizational work problems that can arise. That's why a company's ability to use design thinking in the way its employees and managers strategically manage can be a powerful competitive tool.

Sustaining Competitive Advantage

Given the fact that every organization has resources and capabilities, what makes some organizations more successful than others? Why do some professional hockey teams consistently win championships or draw large crowds? Why do some organizations have consistent and continuous growth in revenues and profits? Why do some colleges, universities, or departments experience continually increasing enrolments? Why do some companies consistently appear at the top of lists ranking the "best," or the "most admired," or the "most profitable"? Although every organization has resources (assets) and capabilities (how work gets done) to do whatever it's in business to do, not every one is able to effectively exploit its resources and to develop the core competencies that can provide it with a competitive advantage. It's not enough for an organization simply to create a competitive advantage; it must be able to sustain it—that is, to keep its edge despite competitors' actions or evolutionary changes in the industry. But that is not easy to do. Market instabilities, new technology, and other types of significant but unpredictable changes can challenge managers' attempts at creating a long-term, sustainable competitive advantage. However, by using strategic management, managers can better position their organizations to get a sustainable competitive advantage.

Competitive Strategies

Many important ideas in strategic management have come from the work of Canadian Michael Porter.[36] Porter's major contribution has been to explain how managers can create and sustain a competitive advantage that will give a company above-average profitability. An important element in doing this is an industry analysis.

In trying to find a niche for his bread-making company, Dokse Perklin, founder of Mississauga, Ontario-based Le Bon Croissant, realized that he could do something that grocery stores and restaurants could not: ensure high-quality bakery products while controlling costs. "Hotels, grocery chains, restaurant chains [and] institutions just can't afford to bake on premises anymore," Perklin says. "They can't find the staff, they can't effectively control overheads, they can't ensure consistent quality." So Perklin filled that need and has created a bread-baking business that ships frozen unbaked and baked goods throughout Canada, the United States, the Caribbean, and Asia.

Colin O'Connor

In any industry, five competitive forces dictate the rules of competition. Together, these five forces determine industry attractiveness and profitability. Managers assess an industry's attractiveness using these forces:

- *Threat of new entrants.* Factors such as economies of scale, brand loyalty, and capital requirements determine how easy or hard it is for new competitors to enter an industry.

- *Threat of substitutes.* Factors such as switching costs and buyer loyalty determine the degree to which customers are likely to buy a substitute product.

- *Bargaining power of buyers.* Factors such as number of customers in the market, customer information, and the availability of substitutes determine the amount of influence that buyers have in an industry.

- *Bargaining power of suppliers.* Factors such as the degree of supplier concentration and availability of substitute inputs determine the amount of power that suppliers have over firms in the industry.

- *Current rivalry.* Factors such as industry growth rate, increasing or falling demand, and product differences determine how intense the competitive rivalry will be among firms currently in the industry.

Choosing a Competitive Strategy

Once managers have assessed the five forces and determined what threats and opportunities exist, they are ready to select an appropriate competitive strategy. According to Porter, no firm can be successful by trying to be all things to all people. He proposes that managers select a strategy that will give the organization a competitive advantage, which he says arises out of either having lower costs than all other industry competitors or by being significantly different from competitors. On that basis, managers can choose one of three strategies: cost leadership, differentiation, or focus. Which one managers select depends on the organization's strengths and core competencies and its competitors' weaknesses.

When an organization sets out to be the lowest-cost producer in its industry, it's following a **cost leadership strategy**. A low-cost leader aggressively searches out efficiencies in production, marketing, and other areas of operation. Overhead is kept to a minimum, and the firm does everything it can to cut costs. You will not find expensive art or interior décor at offices of low-cost leaders. For example, at Walmart's headquarters in Bentonville, Arkansas, office furnishings are sparse and drab but functional.

Although low-cost leaders don't place a lot of emphasis on "frills," the product or service being sold must be perceived as comparable in quality to that offered by rivals or at

cost leadership strategy A business strategy in which the organization sets out to be the lowest-cost producer in its industry.

least be acceptable to buyers. Examples of companies that have used the low-cost leader strategy include Walmart, Hyundai, and WestJet Airlines.

The company that seeks to offer unique products that are widely valued by customers is following a **differentiation strategy**. Sources of differentiation might be exceptionally high quality, extraordinary service, innovative design, technological capability, or an unusually positive brand image. The key to this competitive strategy is that whatever product or service attribute is chosen for differentiating must set the firm apart from its competitors and be significant enough to justify a price premium that exceeds the cost of differentiating. Vancouver-based Vancouver City Savings Credit Union differentiates itself from competitors through a focus on the community and the customer, as the following *Management Reflection* shows.

differentiation strategy A business strategy in which a company seeks to offer unique products that are widely valued by customers.

MANAGEMENT REFLECTION

Vancity Champions the Underdog

How does a small bank compete against the larger ones? Vancouver City Savings Credit Union (Vancity) does not hope to be like the country's Big Five banks.[33] It is much smaller, for one thing. Profit is not the bank's only goal, and only 20 percent of executive compensation is based on profit. Even so, the bank makes enough profit each year to return 30 percent of the profits to its members and the community. When Tamara Vrooman assumed the role of CEO in September 2007, she emphasized how Vancity is not simply about profit. "I am thrilled to be joining an organization that is well-known, successful, not afraid to take risks, and is thoughtful in terms of what it means to be a co-operative, a banker, an employer, and a member of the community."[34]

Vancity is sometimes mocked for its "left coast ways," but it is not afraid to be clear about its mission: The bank is committed to the community, social responsibility, and the environment. This is also what makes the bank unique. According to former CEO Dave Mowat: "Every day of our lives we're trading on our differentiation . . . We have to do it a little bit different, a little bit better to give value-added to draw people to our organization. There isn't an end point where we can win on scale." What the bank can win on is customer service, as Mowat explains, by providing "that extra bit of customization."

While Vancity has many wealthy clients, it likes to work with the less fortunate. It has set up a branch in Canada's poorest neighbourhood, East Vancouver, something other banks were reluctant to do. Mowat believes these clients can be just as trustworthy when you take the time to get to know them. Vancity is so dedicated to customer service that its customer satisfaction rating is at 85 percent, compared with 60 percent for the big banks. ∎

datapoints[37]

21 percent more profitable—this is what studies have shown about companies that are information-technology–savvy.

25 percent of allegedly high-performing companies are actually remarkable performers.

29 percent of respondents said losing their job was their biggest concern during a corporate merger or acquisition.

46 percent of executives at smaller companies are likely to take a collaborative approach to developing strategy.

29 percent of executives at larger companies are likely to take a collaborative approach to developing strategy.

60 percent of executives believe their employees are not prepared for future company growth.

The Ortiz brothers, Nicolas, George, and Oliver, have earned almost $400 million in revenues in a country of only 3.5 million people by creating IKI, now the second-largest supermarket chain in Lithuania. IKI's 67 stores and 15 convenience outlets cater to the once-Communist country's long-unmet niche market for luxury goods like French cheese, North American personal-care products, free-range chickens, and gourmet mushrooms. The brothers recently opened IKI stores in Latvia and are planning to expand to Estonia.

Piotr Malecki/Getty Images

focus strategy A business
strategy in which a company
pursues a cost or differentiation
advantage in a narrow industry
segment.

Although these two competitive strategies are aimed at the broad market, the final type of competitive strategy—the **focus strategy**—involves a cost advantage (cost focus) or a differentiation advantage (differentiation focus) in a narrow segment or niche. Segments can be based on product variety, customer type, distribution channel, or geographical location. For example, Denmark's Bang & Olufsen, whose revenues exceed $513 million, focuses on high-end audio equipment sales. Whether a focus strategy is feasible depends on the size of the segment and whether the organization can make money serving that segment.

stuck in the middle A situation in
which an organization is unable to
develop a competitive advantage
through cost or differentiation.

What happens if an organization can't develop a cost or a differentiation advantage? Porter called that being *stuck in the middle* and warned that's not a good place to be. An organization becomes **stuck in the middle** when its costs are too high to compete with the low-cost leader or when its products and services aren't differentiated enough to compete with the differentiator. Getting unstuck means choosing which competitive advantage to pursue and then doing so by aligning resources, capabilities, and core competencies.

Although Porter said you had to pursue either the low-cost or the differentiation advantage to prevent being stuck in the middle, more recent research has shown that organizations *can* successfully pursue both a low cost and a differentiation advantage and achieve high performance.[39] Needless to say, it's not easy to pull off! You have to keep costs low *and* be truly differentiated. But companies such as FedEx, Southwest Airlines, Google, and Coca-Cola have been able to do it.

functional strategy A strategy
used by a functional department
to support the business strategy of
the organization.

Before we leave this section, we want to point out the final type of organizational strategy, the **functional strategies**, which are the strategies used by an organization's various functional departments to support the competitive strategy. For example, when R. R. Donnelley & Sons Company, a Chicago-based printer, wanted to become more competitive and invested in high-tech digital printing methods, its marketing department had to develop new sales plans and promotional pieces, the production department had to incorporate the digital equipment in the printing plants, and the human resources department had to update its employee selection and training programs. We don't cover specific functional strategies in this book because you'll cover them in other business courses you take.

Current Strategic Management Issues

⑤ Discuss current strategic
management issues.

▶ ▶ ▶ Indigo, like many successful companies, finds itself at an inflection point where technology and changes in consumer buying habits are threatening their traditional business model. In its efforts to remain relevant to consumers and leverage its physical presence in regional markets, the company has taken strategic steps to return the company to growth. Harvard business professor Clayton Christianson describes a process he calls disruptive innovation through which successful companies like Blackberry and Indigo are displaced by new market entrants who force the existing companies to move upmarket where margins are higher.

Think About It

Should Heather Reisman continue with her current strategy of moving up market to higher-margin goods sold through her existing physical locations? Is there a better strategy that would allow Indigo to reinvent itself and deploy a new business model?

There's no better example of the strategic challenges faced by managers in today's environment than the recorded music industry. Overall, sales of CDs have plummeted in the past decade and are down about 50 percent from their peak. Not only has this trend impacted the music companies, but it's affected music retailers as well. "Retailers have been forced to adjust, often by devoting some shelf space to other products." For instance, Best Buy, the national electronics retailer, decided to experiment with selling musical instruments. Other major music retailers, such as Walmart, have shifted selling space used for CDs to other departments. "At music specialty stores, however, diversification has become a matter of survival." Managers are struggling to find strategies that will help their organizations succeed in such an environment. Many have had to shift into whole new areas of business.[40] But it isn't just the music industry that's dealing with strategic challenges. Managers everywhere face increasingly intense global competition and high performance expectations by investors and customers. How have they responded to these new realities? In this section, we look at three current strategic management issues, including the need for strategic leadership, the need for strategic flexibility, and how managers design strategies to emphasize e-business, customer service, and innovation.

The Need for Strategic Leadership

"Amazon is so serious about its next big thing that it hired three women to do nothing but try on size 8 shoes for its Web reviews. Full time." Hmmmm . . . now that sounds like a fun job! What exactly is Amazon's CEO Jeff Bezos thinking? Having conquered the book publishing, electronics, and toy industries (among others), his next target is high-end clothing. And he's doing it in its "typical way: go big and spare no expense."[41]

An organization's strategies are usually developed and overseen by its top managers. An organization's top manager is typically the CEO (chief executive officer). This individual usually works with a top management team that includes other executive or senior managers such as a COO (chief operating officer), CFO (chief financial officer), CIO (chief information officer), and other individuals who may have various titles. Traditional descriptions of the CEO's role in strategic management include being the "chief" strategist, structural architect, and developer of the organization's information/control systems.[42] Other descriptions of the strategic role of the "chief executive" include key decision maker, visionary leader, political actor, monitor and interpreter of environment changes, and strategy designer.[43]

No matter how top management's job is described, you can be certain that from their perspective at the organization's upper levels, it's like no other job in the organization. By definition, top managers are ultimately responsible for every decision and action of every organizational employee. One important role that top managers play is that of strategic leader. Organizational researchers study leadership in relation to strategic management because an organization's top managers must provide effective strategic leadership. What is **strategic leadership**? It's the ability to anticipate, envision, maintain flexibility, think strategically, and work with others in the organization to initiate changes that will create a viable and valuable future for the organization.[44] How can top managers provide effective strategic leadership? Eight key dimensions have been identified.[45] These dimensions include determining the organization's purpose or vision, exploiting and maintaining the organization's core competencies, developing the organization's human capital, creating and sustaining a strong organizational culture, creating and maintaining organizational relationships, reframing prevailing views by asking penetrating questions and questioning assumptions, emphasizing ethical organizational decisions and practices, and establishing appropriately balanced organizational controls. Each dimension encompasses an important part of the strategic management process.

strategic leadership The ability to anticipate, envision, maintain flexibility, think strategically, and work with others in the organization to initiate changes that will create a viable and valuable future for the organization.

The Need for Strategic Flexibility

Jürgen Schrempp, former CEO of DaimlerChrysler, stated, "My principle always was . . . move as fast as you can and [if] you indeed make mistakes, you have to correct them. It's much better to move fast, and make mistakes occasionally, than move too slowly."[46] You would not think that smart individuals who are paid lots of money to manage organizations would make mistakes when it comes to strategic decisions. But even when managers "manage strategically" by following the strategic management process, there is no guarantee that the chosen strategies will lead to positive outcomes. Reading any of the current business periodicals would certainly support this assertion. But the key for managers is responding quickly when it's obvious that the strategy is not working. In other words, they need **strategic flexibility**—the ability to recognize major external environmental changes, to quickly commit resources, and to recognize when a strategic decision is not working. Given the environment that managers face today—oftentimes, highly uncertain and changing—strategic flexibility seems absolutely necessary. What can managers do to enhance their ability to quickly shift strategies as needed?

strategic flexibility The ability to recognize major external environmental changes, to quickly commit resources, and to recognize when a strategic decision was a mistake.

New Directions in Organizational Strategies

What strategies are important for today's environment? We think there are three: e-business, customer service, and innovation.

E-Business Strategies

Use e-business strategies to develop a sustainable competitive advantage.[47] A cost leader can use e-business to lower costs in a variety of ways. For instance, it might use online bidding and order processing to eliminate the need for sales calls and to decrease sales force expenses; it could use web-based inventory control systems that reduce storage costs; or it might use online testing and evaluation of job applicants.

A differentiator needs to offer products or services that customers perceive and value as unique. For instance, a business might use internet-based knowledge systems to shorten customer response times, provide rapid online responses to service requests, or automate purchasing and payment systems so that customers have detailed status reports and purchasing histories.

Finally, because the focuser targets a narrow market segment with customized products, it might provide chat rooms or discussion boards for customers to interact with others who have common interests, design niche websites that target specific groups with specific interests, or use websites to perform standardized office functions such as payroll or budgeting.

At a press conference, Marc Benioff, CEO of Salesforce.com, announced the formation of a strategic alliance with Toyota Motors to build "Toyota Friend," a private social network for the automaker's customers. Offered first in Japan with Toyota's electric vehicles and plug-in hybrids, Toyota Friend is a customer communication system that is an important part of the automaker's customer service strategy. Accessible through smartphones, tablet PCs, and other mobile devices, the network gives Toyota customers the ability to connect with their cars, dealership, and Toyota. And it enables Toyota to communicate with customers by giving them product and service data and real-time information such as the battery level of their cars and locations of charging stations.

ZUMA Press, Inc./Alamy

Research also has shown that an important e-business strategy might be a clicks-and-bricks strategy. A clicks-and-bricks firm is one that uses both online (clicks) and traditional stand-alone locations (bricks).[48] For example, Walgreen's established an online site for ordering prescriptions, but some 90 percent of its customers who placed orders on the Web preferred to pick up their prescriptions at a nearby store rather than have them shipped to their home. So its "clicks-and-bricks" strategy has worked well! Other retailers, such as Best Buy, The Container Store, and Walmart, are transforming their stores into extensions of their online operations by adding web return centres, pickup locations, free shipping outlets, and payment booths.[49]

Customer Service Strategies

Companies that emphasize excellent customer service need strategies that cultivate that atmosphere from top to bottom. What kinds of strategies does that take? It takes giving customers what they want, communicating effectively with them, and providing employees with customer service training. Let's look first at the strategy of giving customers what they want.

New Balance Athletic Shoe was the first of the athletic shoe manufacturers to give customers a truly unique product: shoes in varying widths. Previously, no other athletic shoe manufacturer had shoes for narrow or wide feet in almost any size.[50] It should come as no surprise that an important customer service strategy is giving customers what they want, a major aspect of an organization's overall marketing strategy.

Having an effective customer communication system is an important customer service strategy. Managers should know what's going on with customers. They need to find out what customers liked and didn't like about their purchase encounter—from their interactions with employees to their experience with the actual product or service. It's also important to let customers know if something is going on with the company that might affect future purchase decisions. Finally, an organization's culture is important to providing excellent customer service. This typically requires that employees be trained to provide exceptional customer service. For example, Singapore Airlines is well-known for its customer treatment. "On everything facing the customer, they do not scrimp," says an analyst based in Singapore.[51] Employees are expected to "get service right," leaving employees with no doubt about the expectations as far as how to treat customers.

Innovation Strategies

When Procter & Gamble purchased the Iams pet food business, it did what it always does—it used its renowned research division to look for ways to transfer technology from its other divisions to make new products.[52] One of the outcomes of this cross-divisional combination was a new tartar-fighting ingredient from toothpaste that is included in all of its dry adult pet foods.

As this example shows, innovation strategies are not necessarily focused on just the radical, breakthrough products. They can include the application of existing technology to new uses. Organizations of all kinds and sizes have successfully used both approaches. What types of innovation strategies do organizations need in today's environment? Those strategies should reflect their philosophy about innovation, which is shaped by two strategic decisions: innovation emphasis and innovation timing.

As discussed in Chapter 6, managers must first decide where the emphasis of their innovation effort will be. Is the organization's focus going to be basic scientific research, product development, or process improvement? Basic scientific research requires the heaviest commitment in terms of resources because it involves the nuts-and-bolts activities and work of scientific research. In numerous industries (for instance, genetics engineering, information technology, or pharmaceuticals), an organization's expertise in basic research is the key to a sustainable competitive advantage. However, not every organization requires this extensive commitment to scientific research to achieve high performance levels. Instead, many depend on product development strategies. Although

Exhibit 9-7

First-Mover Advantages and Disadvantages

Advantages	Disadvantages
• Reputation for being innovative and industry leader	• Uncertainty over exact direction technology and market will go
• Cost and learning benefits	• Risk of competitors' imitating innovations
• Control over scarce resources and keeping competitors from having access to them	• Financial and strategic risks
• Opportunity to begin building customer relationships and customer loyalty	• High development costs

this strategy also requires a significant resource investment, it's not in the areas associated with scientific research. Instead, the organization takes existing technology and improves on it or applies it in new ways, just as Procter & Gamble did when it applied tartar-fighting knowledge to pet food products. Both of these first two strategic approaches to innovation (basic scientific research and product development) can help an organization achieve high levels of differentiation, which is a significant source of competitive advantage.

Finally, the last strategic approach to innovation emphasis is a focus on process development. Using this strategy, an organization looks for ways to improve and enhance its work processes. The organization introduces new and improved ways for employees to do their work in all organizational areas. This innovation strategy can lead to an organization's lowering costs, which, as we know, can be a significant source of competitive advantage.

Once managers have determined the focus of their innovation efforts, they must decide on their innovation timing strategy. Some organizations want to be the first with innovations, whereas others are content to follow or mimic the innovations. An organization that is first to bring a product innovation to the market or to use a new process innovation is called a **first mover**. Being a first mover has certain strategic advantages and disadvantages, as shown in Exhibit 9-7. Some organizations pursue this route, hoping to develop a sustainable competitive advantage. Others have successfully developed a sustainable competitive advantage by being the followers in the industry. They let the first movers pioneer the innovations and then mimic their products or processes. Which approach managers choose depends on their organizations' innovation philosophies and specific resources and capabilities.

first mover An organization that is first to bring a product innovation to the market or to use a new process innovation.

CHAPTER 9

SUMMARY AND IMPLICATIONS

1. Explain the role of strategic management and why it is important. Strategic management is what managers do to develop the organization's strategies. Strategies are the plans for how the organization will do whatever it's in business to do, how it will compete successfully, and how it will attract and satisfy its customers in order to achieve its goals. A business model is how a company is going to make money. Strategic management is important for three reasons. First, it makes a difference in how well organizations perform. Second, it's important for helping managers cope with continually changing situations. Finally, strategic management helps coordinate and focus employee efforts on what's important.

> ▶ ▶ ▶ Heather Reisman, CEO of Indigo stated that "with our core book business under pressure, it will take us at least two more years to achieve the levels of growth necessary in our new business to make up and then surpass the decline in books. We are energized and firmly committed to taking our brand—so valued by Canadians—and reinventing it for the 21st century."

2. Explain the role of managers in each of the six strategic management steps. The strategic management process is a six-step process that encompasses planning, implementation, and evaluation. The first four steps involve planning: identifying the organization's current mission, goals, and strategies; analyzing the internal environment; analyzing the external environment; and formulating strategies. The fifth step is implementing the strategy, and the sixth step is evaluating the results of the strategy. Even the best strategies can fail if management does not implement or evaluate them properly.

> ▶ ▶ ▶ Heather Reisman describes the company as being in the early stages of a journey "which will take us from our position as Canada's leading bookseller to our vision of being the world's first CREATIVES department store." This change in direction will require the support and engagement of Indigo's managers in the strategic process.

3. Describe three types of organizational strategies. There are three types of organizational strategy: corporate, business, and functional. They relate to the particular level of the organization that introduces the strategy. At the corporate level, organizations can engage in growth, stability, and renewal strategies. At the business level, strategies look at how an organization should compete in each of its businesses: through cost leadership, differentiation, or focus. At the functional level, strategies support the business strategy. The BCG matrix is a way to analyze a company's portfolio of businesses by looking at a business's market share and its industry's anticipated growth rate. The four categories of the BCG matrix are cash cows, stars, question marks, and dogs.

> ▶ ▶ ▶ In support of the intent to position Indigo as the world's first CREATIVES department store, the priorities remain focused on advancing the core retail business through adapting physical stores, improving productivity, driving employee engagement, and expanding the online and digital presence.

4. Describe competitive advantage and the competitive strategies organizations use to get it. An organization's competitive advantage is what sets it apart, its distinctive edge. A company's competitive advantage becomes the basis for choosing an appropriate competitive strategy. Porter's five forces model assesses the five competitive forces that dictate the rules of competition in an industry: threat of new entrants, threat of substitutes, bargaining power of buyers, bargaining power of suppliers, and current rivalry. Porter's three competitive strategies are cost leadership (competing on the basis of having the lowest costs in the industry), differentiation (competing on the basis of having unique products that are widely valued by customers), and focus (competing in a narrow segment with either a cost advantage or a differentiation advantage).

▶ ▶ ▶ As part of adapting the physical space in the stores, Indigo is providing more floor space in the growth categories of paper, toys, and gift products such as home and fashion accessories. The company continues to expand its assortment of toys and games; it has opened a new design office in New York in 2011; and a "full line of proprietary merchandise developed buy this team began appearing on the shelves in 2012."

5. Discuss current strategic management issues. Managers face three current strategic management issues: strategic leadership, strategic flexibility, and important types of strategies for today's environment. Strategic leadership is the ability to anticipate, envision, maintain flexibility, think strategically, and work with others in the organization to initiate changes that will create a viable and valuable future for the organization. Strategic flexibility Is important because managers often face highly uncertain environments. Managers can use e-business strategies to reduce costs, to differentiate their firm's products and services, to target (focus on) specific customer groups, or to lower costs. Another important e-business strategy is the clicks-and-bricks strategy, which combines online and traditional, stand-alone locations. Strategies managers can use to become more customer oriented include giving customers what they want, communicating effectively with them, and having a culture that emphasizes customer service. Strategies managers can use to become more innovative include deciding their organization's innovation emphasis (basic scientific research, product development, or process development) and its innovation timing (first mover or follower).

▶ ▶ ▶ Indigo, like many successful companies, finds itself at an inflection point where technology and changes in consumer buying habits are threatening its traditional business model.

MyManagementLab   Study, practise, and explore real management situations with these helpful resources:
- **Interactive Lesson Presentations:** Work through interactive presentations and assessments to test your knowledge of management concepts.
- **PIA (Personal Inventory Assessments):** Enhance your ability to connect with key concepts through these engaging, self-reflection assessments.
- **Study Plan:** Check your understanding of chapter concepts with self-study quizzes.
- **Simulations:** Practise decision-making in simulated management environments.

REVIEW AND DISCUSSION QUESTIONS

1. Describe the six-step strategic management process.

2. Should responsible management and ethical considerations be included in analyses of an organization's internal and external environments? Why or why not?

3. How could the internet be helpful to managers as they follow the steps in the strategic management process?

4. Describe the three major types of organizational strategies and how the BCG matrix is used to manage those corporate strategies.

5. Describe the role of competitive advantage and how Porter's competitive strategies help an organization develop competitive advantage.

6. "The concept of competitive advantage is as important for not-for-profit organizations as it is for for-profit organizations." Do you agree or disagree with this statement? Explain, using examples to make your case.

7. How could the internet be helpful to managers as they follow the steps in the strategic management process?

8. Describe e-business, customer service, and innovation strategies.

ETHICS DILEMMA

Many "social technology companies are presenting an anti-social attitude to callers."[53] If you try to call someone at or get a phone number for LinkedIn, Facebook, Twitter, or Quora (and probably others), well, you're out of luck! Google is one of a few companies that actually publishes phone numbers on its website. Yet, its phone system sends callers back to the web 11 times. At Facebook, a caller who goes through a long phone tree trying to reach a real person is told that "Facebook is, in fact, an internet-based company"

and suggests trying e-mail. Twitter's phone system hangs up after providing web or e-mail addresses three times.

Although voice calls aren't necessarily important to teenagers or twenty-somethings, has this strategy become a matter of policy for technology companies? Yes, phones cost money as do people to answer those phones. What do you think? What ethical dilemmas are involved with this strategic decision? What factors would influence the decision? (Think in terms of the various stakeholders who might be affected by this decision.)

SKILLS EXERCISE

Developing Your Business Planning Skill About the Skill

An important step in starting a business or in determining a new strategic direction is preparing a business plan.[54] Not only does the business plan aid in thinking about what to do and how to do it, but it can be a sound basis from which to obtain funding and resources.

Steps in Practising the Skill

1. *Describe your company's background and purpose.* Provide the history of the company. Briefly describe the company's history and what this company does that's unique. Describe what your product or service will be, how you intend to market it, and what you need to bring your product or service to the market.

2. *Identify your short- and long-term goals.* What is your intended goal for this organization? Clearly, for a new company three broad objectives are relevant: creation, survival, and profitability. Specific objectives can include such things as sales, market share, product quality, employee morale, and social responsibility. Identify how you plan to achieve each objective, how you intend to determine whether you met the objective, and when you intend the objective to be met (e.g., short or long term).

3. *Do a thorough market analysis.* You need to convince readers that you understand what you are doing, what your market is, and what competitive pressures you'll face. In this analysis, you'll need to describe the overall market trends, the specific market you intend to compete in, and who the competitors are. In essence, in this section you'll perform your SWOT analysis.

4. *Describe your development and production emphasis.* Explain how you're going to produce your product or service. Include time frames from start to finish. Describe the difficulties you may encounter in this stage as well as how much you believe activities in this stage will cost. Provide an explanation of what decisions (e.g., make or buy?) you will face and what you intend to do.

5. *Describe how you'll market your product or service.* What is your selling strategy? How do you intend to

reach your customers? In this section, describe your product or service in terms of your competitive advantage and demonstrate how you'll exploit your competitors' weaknesses. In addition to the market analysis, provide sales forecasts in terms of the size of the market, how much of the market you can realistically capture, and how you'll price your productor service.

6. *Put together your financial statements.* What's your bottom line? Investors want to know this information. In the financial section, provide projected profit-and-loss statements (income statements) for approximately three to five years, a cash flow analysis, and the company's projected balance sheets. In the financial section, give thought to how much start-up costs will be as well as develop a financial strategy—how you intend to use funds received from a financial institution and how you'll control and monitor the financial well-being of the company.

7. *Provide an overview of the organization and its management.* Identify the key executives, summarizing their education, experience, and any relevant qualifications. Identify their positions in the organization and their job roles. Explain how much salary they intend to earn initially. Identify others who may assist the organization's management (e.g., company lawyer, accountant, board of directors). This section should also include, if relevant, a subsection on how you intend to deal with employees. For example, how will employees be paid, what benefits will be offered, and how will employee performance be assessed?

8. *Describe the legal form of the business.* Identify the legal form of the business. For example, is it a sole proprietorship, a partnership, a corporation? Depending on the legal form, you may need to provide information regarding equity positions, shares of stock issued, and the like.

9. *Identify the critical risks and contingencies facing the organization.* In this section, identify what you'll do if problems arise. For instance, if you don't meet sales forecasts, what then? Similar responses to such

questions as problems with suppliers, inability to hire qualified employees, poor-quality products, and so on should be addressed. Readers want to see if you've anticipated potential problems and if you have contingency plans. This is the "what if" section.

10. *Put the business plan together.* Using the information you've gathered from the previous nine steps, it's now time to put the business plan together into a well-organized document. A business plan should contain a cover page that shows the company name, address, contact person, and numbers at which the individual can be reached. The cover page should also contain the date the business was established and, if one exists, the company logo. The next page of the business plan should be a table of contents. Here you'll want to list and identify the location of each major section and subsection in the business plan. Remember to use proper outlining techniques. Next comes the executive summary, the first section the readers will actually read. Thus, it's one of the more critical elements of the business plan, because if the executive summary is poorly done, readers may not read any further. In a two- to three-page summary, highlight information about the company, its management, its market and competition, the funds requested, how

the funds will be used, financial history (if available), financial projections, and when investors can expect to get their money back (called the exit). Next come the main sections of your business plan; that is, the material you've researched and written about in steps 1 through 9. Close out the business plan with a section that summarizes the highlights of what you've just presented. Finally, if you have charts, exhibits, photographs, tables, and the like, you might want to include an appendix in the back of the business plan. If you do, remember to cross-reference this material to the relevant section of the report.

Practising the Skill

You have a great idea for a business and need to create a business plan to present to a bank. Choose one of the following products or services and draft the part of your plan that describes how you will price and market it (step 5).

1. Haircuts at home (you make house calls)
2. Olympic snowboarding computer game
3. Online apartment rental listing
4. Voice-activated house alarm

Now choose a different product or service from the list and identify critical risks and contingencies (step 9).

WORKING TOGETHER: TEAM EXERCISE

Assessing the Organization's Environment

Organizational mission statements. Are they a promise, a commitment, or just a bunch of hot air? Form small groups of three to four individuals and find examples of three different organizational mission statements. Your first task is to evaluate the mission statements. How do they compare to the items listed in this chapter? Would you describe each as

an effective mission statement? Why or why not? How might you rewrite each mission statement to make it better? Your second task is to use the mission statements to describe the types of corporate and competitive strategies each organization might use to fulfill that mission statement. Explain your rationale for choosing each strategy.

LEARNING TO BE A MANAGER

- Do a personal SWOT analysis. Assess your personal strengths and weaknesses (skills, talents, abilities). What are you good at? What are you not so good at? What do you enjoy doing? What don't you enjoy doing? Then, identify career opportunities and threats by researching job prospects in the industry you're interested in. Look at trends and projections. You might want to check out the projections of labour demand and labour supply on the Human Resources and Skills Development Canada Job Bank. Once you have all this information, write a

  specific career action plan. Outline five-year career goals and what you need to do to achieve those goals.

- Using current business periodicals, find two examples of each of the corporate and competitive strategies. Write a description of what these businesses are doing and how it represents that particular strategy.

- Pick five companies from the latest version of *Fortune*'s "Most Admired Companies" list. Research these companies and identify their (a) mission statement, (b) strategic goals, and (c) strategies used.

CASE APPLICATION 1

Fast Fashion

When Amancio Ortega, a former Spanish bathrobe maker, opened his first Zara clothing store, his business model was simple: sell high-fashion look-alikes to price-conscious Europeans.[55] After succeeding in this, he decided to tackle the outdated clothing industry in which it took six months from a garment's design to consumers being able to purchase it in a store. What Ortega envisioned was "fast fashion"—getting designs to customers quickly. And that's exactly what Zara has done!

The company has been described as having more style than Gap, faster growth than Target, and logistical expertise rivaling Walmart. Zara, owned by the Spanish fashion retail group Inditex SA, recognizes that success in the fashion world is based on a simple rule—get products to market quickly. Accomplishing this, however, isn't so simple. It involves a clear and focused understanding of fashion, technology, and their market, *and* the ability to adapt quickly to trends.

Inditex, the world's largest fashion retailer by sales worldwide, has seven chains: Zara (including Zara Kids and Zara Home), Pull and Bear, Massimo Dutti, Stradivarius, Bershka, Oysho, and Uterqüe. The company has more than 5618 stores in 84 countries, although Zara pulls in more than 60 percent of the company's revenues. Despite its global presence, Zara is not yet a household name in the United States, with just over 50 stores open, including a flagship store in New York City.

What is Zara's secret to excelling at fast fashion? It takes approximately two weeks to get a new design from drawing board to store floor. And stores are stocked with new designs twice a week as clothes are shipped directly to the stores from the factory. Thus, each aspect of Zara's business contributes to the fast turnaround. Sales managers at "the Cube"—what employees call their futuristic-looking headquarters—sit at a long row of computers and scrutinize sales at every store. They see the hits and the misses almost instantaneously. They ask the in-house designers, who work in teams, sketching out new styles and deciding which fabrics will provide the best combination of style and price, for new designs. Once a design is drawn, it's sent electronically to Zara's factory across the street, where a clothing sample is made. To minimize waste, computer programs arrange and rearrange clothing patterns on the massive fabric rolls before a laser-guided machine does the cutting. Zara produces most of its designs close to home—in Morocco, Portugal, Spain, and Turkey. Finished garments are returned to the factory within a week. Finishing touches (buttons, trim, detailing, etc.) are added, and each garment goes through a quality check. Garments that don't pass are discarded while those that do pass are individually pressed. Then, garment labels (indicating to which country garments will be shipped) and security tags are added. The bundled garments proceed along a moving carousel of hanging rails via a maze of tunnels to the warehouse, a four-storey, 5-million-square-foot building (465 000 square metres, or about the size of 90 football fields). As the merchandise bundles move along the rails, electronic bar code tags are read by equipment that send them to the right "staging area," where specific merchandise is first sorted by country and then by individual store, ensuring that each store gets exactly the shipment it's supposed to. From there, merchandise for European stores is sent to a loading dock and packed on a truck with other shipments in order of delivery. Deliveries to other locations go by plane. Some 60 000 items each hour—more than 2.6 million items a week—move through this ultrasophisticated distribution center. And this takes place with only a handful of workers who monitor the entire process. The company's just-in-time production (an idea borrowed from the auto industry) gives it a competitive edge in terms of speed and flexibility.

Despite Zara's success at fast fashion, its competitors are working to be faster. But CEO Pablo Isla isn't standing still. To maintain Zara's leading advantage, he's introducing new methods that enable store managers to order and display merchandise faster and is adding new cargo routes for shipping goods. And the company has finally made the jump into online retailing. One analyst forecasts that the company could quadruple sales in the United States by 2014, with a majority of that coming from online sales.

DISCUSSION QUESTIONS

1. How is strategic management illustrated by this case story?
2. How might SWOT analysis be helpful to Inditex executives? To Zara store managers?
3. What competitive advantage do you think Zara is pursuing? How does it exploit that competitive advantage?
4. Do you think Zara's success is due to external or internal factors or both? Explain.
5. What strategic implications does Zara's move into online retailing have? (Hint: Think in terms of resources and capabilities.)

CASE APPLICATION 2

Rewind and Replay

There's no doubt that people like to watch movies, but *how* they watch those movies has changed.[56] Although many people still enjoy going to an actual movie theatre, more and more are settling back in their easy chairs in front of home entertainment systems, especially now that technology has improved to the point where those systems are affordable and offer many of the same features as those found in movie theaters. Along with the changes in *where* people watch movies, *how* people get those movies has changed. For many, the weekend used to start with a trip to the video rental store to search the racks for something good to watch, an approach Blockbuster built its business on. Today's consumers can choose a movie by going to their computer and visiting an online subscription and delivery site where the movies come to the customers—a model invented by Netflix.

Launched in 1999, Netflix's subscriber base grew rapidly. It now has more than 23.4 million subscribers and more than 100 000 movie titles from which to choose. "The company's appeal and success are built on providing the most expansive selection of DVDs, an easy way to choose movies, and fast, free delivery." A company milestone was reached in late February 2007, when Netflix delivered its one billionth DVD, a goal that took about seven-and-a-half years to accomplish–"about seven months less than it took McDonald's Corporation to sell one billion hamburgers after opening its first restaurant."

Netflix founder and CEO Reed Hastings believed in the approach he pioneered and set some ambitious goals for his company: build the world's best internet movie service and grow earnings per share (EPS) and subscribers every year. In 2011, though, Hastings made a decision that had customers complaining loudly. Netflix's troubles began when it announced it would charge separate prices for its DVDs-by-mail and streaming video plans. Then, it decided to rebrand its DVD service as Qwikster. Customers raged so much that Netflix reversed that decision and pulled the plug on the entire Qwikster plan. As Netflix regained its focus with customers, it was once again ready to refocus on its competitors.

Success ultimately attracts competition. Other businesses want a piece of the market. Trying to gain an edge in how customers get the movies they want, when and where they want them, has led to an all-out competitive war. Now, what Netflix did to Blockbuster, Blockbuster and other competitors are doing to Netflix. Hastings said he has learned never to underestimate the competition. He says, "We erroneously concluded that Blockbuster probably wasn't going to launch a competitive effort when they hadn't by 2003. Then, in 2004, they did. We thought . . . well they won't put much money behind it. Over the past four years, they've invested more than $500 million against us." Not wanting to suffer the same fate as Blockbuster (which filed for bankruptcy protection in 2010 and was sold to Satellite TV service provider DISH Network in 2011), Netflix is bracing for other onslaughts. In fact, CEO Hastings, defending his misguided decisions in 2011, said, "We did so many difficult things this year that we got overconfident. Our big obsession for the year was streaming, the idea that 'let's not die with DVDs.'"

The in-home filmed entertainment industry is intensely competitive and continually changing. Many customers have multiple providers (e.g., HBO, renting a DVD from Red Box, buying a DVD, streaming a movie from providers such as Hulu, Apple, and Amazon) and may use any or all of those services in the same month. Video-on-demand and streaming are becoming extremely competitive.

To counter such competitive challenges, Hastings is focusing the company's competitive strengths on a select number of initiatives. He says, "Streaming is the future; we're focused on it. DVD is going to do whatever it's going to do. We don't want to hurt it, but we're not putting much time or energy into it." Others include continually developing profitable partnerships with content providers, controlling the cost of streaming content, and even licensing original series. Its first original series was called *House of Cards* and stars Kevin Spacey. With other companies hoping to get established in the market, the competition is intense. Does Netflix have the script it needs to be a dominant player? CEO Hastings says, "If it's true that you should be judged by the quality of your competitors, we must be doing pretty well."

DISCUSSION QUESTIONS

1. Using Porter's framework, describe Netflix's competitive strategy. Explain your choice.
2. What competitive advantage(s) do you think Netflix has? Have its resources, capabilities, or core competencies contributed to its competitive advantage(s)? Explain.
3. How will Netflix's functional strategies have to support its competitive strategy? Explain.
4. What do you think Netflix is going to have to do to maintain its competitive position, especially as its industry changes?

Planning and Control Techniques

▶ ▶ ▶ Managers in hockey team front offices have discovered that certain factors dictate whether they can charge more for tickets—namely, the opposing team and the ongoing rivalry between them and the home team, star players, and day of the week.[1] The Ottawa Senators ride these shifts in demand by repricing tickets daily, a technique known as dynamic pricing. How well does it work? In the U.S., the San Francisco Giants were able to earn an extra $500 000 in revenue from dynamic pricing.

As this example shows, managers use planning tools and techniques to help their organizations be more efficient and effective. In this module, we discuss three categories of basic planning tools and techniques: techniques for assessing the environment, techniques for allocating resources, and contemporary planning techniques.

Techniques for Assessing the Environment

In our description of the strategic management process in Chapter 9, we discussed the importance of assessing the organization's environment. Three techniques help managers do that: environmental scanning, forecasting, and benchmarking.

Environmental Scanning

How important is environmental scanning? While looking around on competitor Google's company website, Bill Gates found a help-wanted page with descriptions of all the open jobs. What piqued his interest, however, was that many of these posted job qualifications were identical to Microsoft's job requirements. He began to wonder why Google—a web search company—would be posting job openings for software engineers with backgrounds that "had nothing to do with web searches and everything to do with Microsoft's core business of operating-system design, compiler optimization, and distributed-systems architecture." Gates e-mailed an urgent message to some of his top executives saying that Microsoft had better be on its toes because it sure looked like Google was preparing to move into being more of a software company.[2]

How can managers become aware of significant environmental changes such as a new law in Germany permitting shopping for "tourist items" on Sunday; the increased trend of counterfeit consumer products in South Africa; the precipitous decline in the working-age populations in Japan, Germany, Italy, and Russia; or the decrease in family size in Mexico? Managers in both small and large organizations use **environmental scanning**, the screening of large amounts of information to anticipate and interpret changes in the environment. Extensive environmental scanning is likely to reveal issues and concerns that could affect an organization's current or planned activities. Research has shown that companies that use environmental scanning have higher performance.[3] Organizations that don't keep on top of environmental changes are likely to experience the opposite!

environmental scanning The screening of large amounts of information to anticipate and interpret changes in the environment.

Competitor Intelligence

A fast-growing area of environmental scanning is **competitor intelligence**.[4] It's a process by which organizations gather information about their competitors and get answers to questions such as, Who are they? What are they doing? How will what they're doing affect us? Let's look at an example of how one organization used competitor intelligence in its planning. Dun & Bradstreet (D&B), a leading provider of business information, has an active business intelligence division. The division manager received a call from an assistant vice-president for sales in one of the company's geographic territories. This

competitor intelligence Environmental scanning activity by which organizations gather information about competitors.

person had been on a sales call with a major customer and the customer happened to mention in passing that another company had visited and made a major presentation about its services. It was interesting because, although D&B had plenty of competitors, this particular company wasn't one of them. The manager gathered together a team that sifted through dozens of sources (research services, internet, personal contacts, and other external sources) and quickly became convinced that there was something to this—that this company was "aiming its guns right at us." Managers at D&B jumped into action to develop plans to counteract this competitive attack.[5]

Competitor intelligence experts suggest that 80 percent of what managers need to know about competitors can be found out from their own employees, suppliers, and customers.[6] Competitor intelligence doesn't have to involve spying. Advertisements, promotional materials, press releases, reports filed with government agencies, annual reports, want ads, newspaper reports, and industry studies are examples of readily accessible sources of information. Attending trade shows and debriefing the company's salesforce can be other good sources of competitor information. Many firms regularly buy competitors' products and have their own engineers study them (through a process called *reverse engineering*) to learn about new technical innovations. In addition, the internet has opened up vast sources of competitor intelligence as many corporate webpages include new product information and other press releases.

Managers need to be careful about the way competitor information is gathered to prevent any concerns about whether it's legal or ethical. For instance, at Procter & Gamble, executives hired competitive intelligence firms to spy on its competitors in the hair-care business. At least one of these firms misrepresented itself to competitor Unilever's employees, trespassed at Unilever's hair-care headquarters in Chicago, and went through trash dumpsters to gain information. When P&G's CEO found out, he immediately fired the individuals responsible and apologized to Unilever.[7] Competitor intelligence becomes illegal corporate spying when it involves the theft of proprietary materials or trade secrets by any means. The Security of Information Act makes it a crime in Canada to engage in economic espionage or to steal a trade secret.[8] The difficult decisions about competitive intelligence arise because often there's a fine line between what's considered *legal and ethical* and what's considered *legal but unethical*. Although the top manager at one competitive intelligence firm contends that 99.9 percent of intelligence gathering is legal, there's no question that some people or companies will go to any lengths—some unethical—to get information about competitors.[9]

Global Scanning

One type of environmental scanning that's particularly important is global scanning. Because world markets are complex and dynamic, managers have expanded the scope of their scanning efforts to gain vital information on global forces that might affect their organizations.[10] The value of global scanning to managers, of course, largely depends on the extent of the organization's global activities. For a company with significant global interests, global scanning can be quite valuable. For instance, Sealed Air Corporation of Elmwood Park, New Jersey—you've probably seen and used its most popular product, Bubble Wrap—tracks global demographic changes. Company managers found that as countries move from agriculture-based societies to industrial ones, the population tends to eat out more and favour prepackaged foods, which translates to more sales of its food-packaging products.[11]

Because the sources that managers use for scanning the domestic environment are too limited for global scanning, managers must globalize their perspectives. For instance, they can subscribe to information-clipping services that review world newspapers and business periodicals and provide summaries of desired information. Also, numerous electronic services will provide topic searches and automatic updates in global areas of special interest to managers. Social media has always been about one-to-one interactions. Somewhere along the line, we lost touch with the true power of social media, and started to broadcast, instead of engage. LeadSift saves you time by scanning thousands of conversations, and looking for opportunities that are relevant to your business. LeadSift delivers leads through an easy-to-use platform where you can craft personalized responses and nurture your customer relationships.

Forecasting

The second technique managers can use to assess the environment is forecasting. Forecasting is an important part of planning, and managers need forecasts that will allow them to predict future events effectively and in a timely manner. Environmental scanning establishes the basis for **forecasts**, which are predictions of outcomes. Virtually any component in an organization's environment can be forecasted. Let's look at how managers forecast and the effectiveness of those forecasts.

forecasts Predictions of outcome.

Forecasting Techniques

Forecasting techniques fall into two categories: quantitative and qualitative. **Quantitative forecasting** applies a set of mathematical rules to a series of past data to predict outcomes. These techniques are preferred when managers have sufficient hard data that can be used. **Qualitative forecasting**, in contrast, uses the judgment and opinions of knowledgeable individuals to predict outcomes. Qualitative techniques typically are used when precise data are limited or hard to obtain. Exhibit PCT-1 describes some popular forecasting techniques.

quantitative forecasting
Forecasting that applies a set of mathematical rules to a series of past data to predict outcome.

qualitative forecasting
Forecasting that uses the judgment and opinions of knowledgeable individuals to predict outcomes.

Today, many organizations collaborate on forecasts using an approach known as CPFR, which stands for collaborative planning, forecasting, and replenishment.[12] CPFR provides a framework for the flow of information, goods, and services between retailers and manufacturers. Each organization relies on its own data to calculate a demand forecast for a particular product. If their respective forecasts differ by a certain amount (say 10 percent), the retailer and manufacturer exchange data and written comments until they arrive at a more accurate forecast. Such collaborative forecasting helps both organizations do a better job of planning.

Exhibit PCT-1

Forecasting Techniques

Technique	Description	Application
Quantitative		
Time series analysis	Fits a trend line to a mathematical equation and projects into the future by means of this equation	Predicting next quarter's sales on the basis of four years of previous sales data
Regression models	Predicts one variable on the basis of known or assumed other variables	Seeking factors that will predict a certain level of sales (e.g., price, advertising expenditures)
Econometric models	Uses a set of regression equations to simulate segments of the economy	Predicting change in car sales as a result of changes in tax laws
Economic indicators	Uses one or more economic indicators to predict a future state of the economy	Using change in GNP to predict discretionary income
Substitution effect	Uses a mathematical formula to predict how, when, and under what circumstances a new product or technology will replace an existing one	Predicting the effect of HDTVs on the sale of traditional-style tube TVs
Qualitative		
Jury of opinion	Combines and averages the opinions of experts	Polling the company's human resource managers to predict next year's college and university recruitment needs
Salesforce composition	Combines estimates from field sales personnel of customers' expected purchases	Predicting next year's sales of industrial lasers
Customer evaluation	Combines estimates from established customers' purchases	Surveying major car dealers by a car manufacturer to determine types and quantities of products desired

Forecasting Effectiveness

The goal of forecasting is to provide managers with information that will facilitate decision making. Despite its importance to planning, managers have had mixed success with it.[13] For instance, prior to a holiday weekend at the Procter & Gamble factory in Lima, Ohio, managers were preparing to shut down the facility early so as not to have to pay employees for just sitting around and to give them some extra time off. The move seemed to make sense since an analysis of purchase orders and historical sales trends indicated that the factory had already produced enough cases of Liquid Tide detergent to meet laundry demand over the holiday. However, managers got a real surprise. One of the company's largest retail customers placed a sizable—and unforeseen—order. They had to reopen the plant, pay the workers overtime, and schedule emergency shipments to meet the retailer's request.[14] As this example shows, managers' forecasts aren't always accurate. In a survey of financial managers in the United States, United Kingdom, France, and Germany, 84 percent of the respondents said their financial forecasts were inaccurate by 5 percent or more; 54 percent of the respondents reported inaccuracy of 10 percent or more.[15] Results of another survey showed that 39 percent of financial executives said they could reliably forecast revenues only one quarter out. Even more disturbing is that 16 percent of those executives said they were "in the dark" about revenue forecasts.[16] But it is important to try to make forecasting as effective as possible because research shows that a company's forecasting ability can be a distinctive competence.[17] Here are some suggestions for making forecasting more effective.[18]

First, it's important to understand that forecasting techniques are most accurate when the environment is not rapidly changing. The more dynamic the environment, the more likely managers are to forecast ineffectively. Also, forecasting is relatively ineffective in predicting nonseasonal events such as recessions, unusual occurrences, discontinued operations, and the actions or reactions of competitors. Next, use simple forecasting methods. They tend to do as well as, and often better than, complex methods that may mistakenly confuse random data for meaningful information. For instance, at St. Louis–based Emerson Electric, chairman emeritus Chuck Knight found that forecasts developed as part of the company's planning process indicated that the competition wasn't just domestic anymore, but global. He didn't use any complex mathematical techniques to come to this conclusion but instead relied on the information already collected as part of his company's planning process. Next, look at involving more people in the process. At *Fortune* 100 companies, it's not unusual to have 1000 to 5000 managers providing forecasting input. These businesses are finding that as more people are involved in the process, the more the reliability of the outcomes improves.[19] Next, compare every forecast with "no change." A no change forecast is accurate approximately half the time. Next, use *rolling* forecasts that look 12 to 18 months ahead, instead of using a single, static forecast. These types of forecasts can help managers spot trends better and help their organizations be more adaptive in changing environments.[20] It's also important to not rely on a single forecasting method. Make forecasts with several models and average them, especially when making longer-range forecasts. Next, don't assume you can accurately identify turning points in a trend. What is typically perceived as a significant turning point often turns out to be simply a random event. And, finally, remember that forecasting *is* a managerial skill and as such can be practised and improved. Forecasting software has made the task somewhat less mathematically challenging, although the "number crunching" is only a small part of the activity. Interpreting the forecast and incorporating that information into planning decisions is the challenge facing managers.

Benchmarking

Suppose you're a talented pianist or gymnast. To make yourself better, you want to learn from the best, so you watch outstanding musicians or athletes for motions and techniques they use as they perform. That same approach is involved in the final technique for assessing the environment we're going to discuss—**benchmarking**, the search for the best practices among competitors or noncompetitors that lead to their superior performance.[21]

benchmarking The search for the best practices among competitors or noncompetitors that lead to their superior performance

Exhibit PCT-2

Steps in Benchmarking

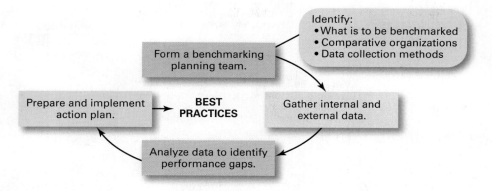

Source: Based on "Aiming High: Competitive Benchmarking for Superior Performance" by Y. K. Shetty, from *Long Range Planning*, February 1993 Volume 26(1).

Does benchmarking work? Studies show that users have achieved 69 percent faster growth and 45 percent greater productivity.[22]

The basic idea behind benchmarking is that managers can improve performance by analyzing and then copying the methods of the leaders in various fields. Organizations such as Nissan, Payless Shoe Source, General Mills, United Airlines, and Volvo Construction Equipment have used benchmarking as a tool in improving performance. In fact, some companies have chosen some pretty unusual benchmarking partners! IBM studied Las Vegas casinos for ways to discourage employee theft. Many hospitals have benchmarked their admissions processes against Marriott Hotels. And Giordano Holdings Ltd., a Hong Kong–based manufacturer and retailer of mass-market casual wear, borrowed its "good quality, good value" concept from Marks & Spencer, used Limited Brands to benchmark its point-of-sales computerized information system, and modelled its simplified product offerings on McDonald's menu.[23]

What does benchmarking involve? Exhibit PCT-2 illustrates the four steps typically used in benchmarking.

Techniques for Allocating Resources

Once an organization's goals have been established, it's important to determine how those goals are going to be accomplished. Before managers can organize and lead as goals are implemented, they must have **resources**, the assets of the organization (financial, physical, human, and intangible). How can managers allocate these resources effectively and efficiently so that organizational goals are met? Although managers can choose from a number of techniques for allocating resources (many of which are covered in courses on accounting, finance, and operations management), we'll discuss four techniques here: budgeting, scheduling, breakeven analysis, and linear programming.

> **resources** The assets of the organization, including financial, physical, human, intangible, and structural/cultural.

Budgeting

Most of us have had some experience, as limited as it might be, with budgets. We probably learned at an early age that unless we allocated our "revenues" carefully, our weekly allowance was spent on "expenses" before the week was half over.

A **budget** is a numerical plan for allocating resources to specific activities. Managers typically prepare budgets for revenues, expenses, and large capital expenditures such as equipment. It's not unusual, though, for budgets to be used for improving time, space, and

> **budget** A numerical plan for allocating resources to specific activities.

Exhibit PCT-3

Types of Budgets

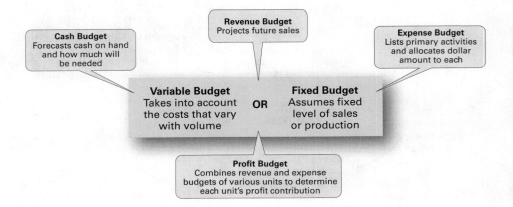

Cash Budget
Forecasts cash on hand and how much will be needed

Revenue Budget
Projects future sales

Expense Budget
Lists primary activities and allocates dollar amount to each

Variable Budget
Takes into account the costs that vary with volume

OR

Fixed Budget
Assumes fixed level of sales or production

Profit Budget
Combines revenue and expense budgets of various units to determine each unit's profit contribution

Source: Based on R. S. Russell and B. W. Taylor III, *Production and Operations Management* (Upper Saddle River, NJ: Prentice Hall, 1995) p. 287.

use of material resources. These types of budgets substitute nondollar numbers for dollar amounts. Such items as person-hours, capacity utilization, or units of production can be budgeted for daily, weekly, or monthly activities. Exhibit PCT-3 describes the different types of budgets that managers might use.

Why are budgets so popular? Probably because they're applicable to a wide variety of organizations and work activities within organizations. We live in a world in which almost everything is expressed in monetary units. Dollars, rupees, pesos, euros, yuan, yen, and the like are used as a common measuring unit within a country. That's why monetary budgets are a useful tool for allocating resources and guiding work in such diverse departments as manufacturing and information systems or at various levels in an organization. Budgets are one planning technique that most managers use—regardless of organizational level. It's an important managerial activity because it forces financial discipline and structure throughout the organization. However, many managers don't like preparing budgets because they feel the process is time consuming, inflexible, inefficient, and ineffective.[24] How can the budgeting process be improved? Exhibit PCT-4 provides some suggestions. Organizations such as Texas Instruments, IKEA, Volvo, and Svenska Handelsbanken have incorporated several of these suggestions as they revamped their budgeting processes.

Exhibit PCT-4

How to Improve Budgeting

- Collaborate and communicate.
- Be flexible.
- Goals should drive budgets—budgets should not determine goals.
- Coordinate budgeting throughout the organization.
- Use budgeting/planning software when appropriate.
- Remember that budgets are tools.
- Remember that profits result from smart management, not because you budgeted for them.

Scheduling

Ann is a manager at a Roots store in Vancouver. Every week, she determines employees' work hours and the store area where each employee will be working. If you observed any group of supervisors or department managers for a few days, you would see them doing much the same—allocating resources by detailing what activities have to be done, the order in which they are to be completed, who is to do each, and when they are to be completed. These managers are **scheduling**. In this section, we review some useful scheduling devices including Gantt charts, load charts, and PERT network analysis.

Gantt Charts

The **Gantt chart** was developed during the early 1900s by Henry Gantt, an associate of Frederick Taylor, the scientific management expert. The idea behind a Gantt chart is simple. It's essentially a bar graph with time on the horizontal axis and the activities to be scheduled on the vertical axis. The bars show output, both planned and actual, over a period of time. The Gantt chart visually shows when tasks are supposed to be done and compares those projections with the actual progress on each task. It's a simple but important device that lets managers detail easily what has yet to be done to complete a job or project and to assess whether an activity is ahead of, behind, or on schedule.

Exhibit PCT-5 depicts a simplified Gantt chart for book production developed by a manager in a publishing company. Time is expressed in months across the top of the chart. The major work activities are listed down the left side. Planning involves deciding what activities need to be done to get the book finished, the order in which those activities need to be completed, and the time that should be allocated to each activity. Where a box sits within a time frame reflects its planned sequence. The shading represents actual progress. The chart also serves as a control tool because the manager can see deviations from the plan. In this example, both the design of the cover and the review of first pages are running behind schedule. Cover design is about three weeks behind (note that there has been no actual progress—shown by blue colour line—as of the reporting date), and first pages review is about two weeks behind schedule (note that as of the report date, actual progress—shown by blue colour line—is about six weeks, out of a goal of completing in two months). Given this information, the manager might need to take some action to either make up for the two lost weeks or to ensure that no further delays will occur. At this point, the manager can expect that the book will be published at least two weeks later than planned if no action is taken.

scheduling Detailing what activities have to be done, the order in which they are to be completed, who is to do each, and when they are to be completed

Gantt chart A scheduling chart developed by Henry Gantt that shows actual and planned output over a period of time.

Exhibit PCT-5

A Gantt Chart

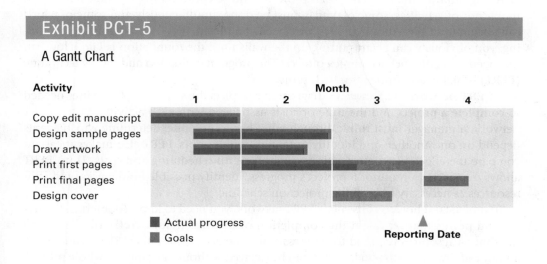

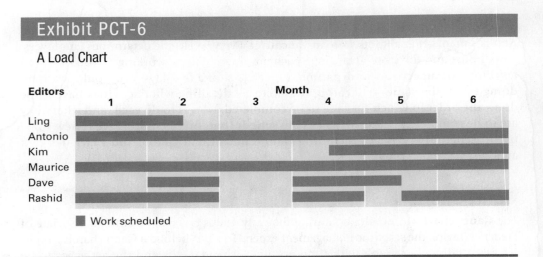

Exhibit PCT-6

A Load Chart

Work scheduled

load chart A modified Gantt chart that schedules capacity by entire departments or specific resources

Load Charts

A **load chart** is a modified Gantt chart. Instead of listing activities on the vertical axis, load charts list either entire departments or specific resources. This arrangement allows managers to plan and control capacity utilization. In other words, load charts schedule capacity by work areas.

For example, Exhibit PCT-6 shows a load chart for six production editors at the same publishing company. Each editor supervises the production and design of several books. By reviewing a load chart, the executive editor, who supervises the six production editors, can see who is free to take on a new book. If everyone is fully scheduled, the executive editor might decide not to accept any new projects, to accept new projects and delay others, to make the editors work overtime, or to employ more production editors. As this exhibit shows, only Antonio and Maurice are completely scheduled for the next six months. The other editors have some unassigned time and might be able to accept new projects or be available to help other editors who get behind.

PERT Network Analysis

Gantt and load charts are useful as long as the activities scheduled are few in number and independent of each other. But what if a manager had to plan a large project such as a departmental reorganization, the implementation of a cost-reduction program, or the development of a new product that required coordinating inputs from marketing, manufacturing, and product design? Such projects require coordinating hundreds and even thousands of activities, some of which must be done simultaneously and some of which can't begin until preceding activities have been completed. If you're constructing a building, you obviously can't start putting up the walls until the foundation is laid. How can managers schedule such a complex project? The program evaluation and review technique (PERT) is highly appropriate for such projects.

A **PERT network** is a flowchart diagram that depicts the sequence of activities needed to complete a project and the time or costs associated with each activity. With a PERT network, a manager must think through what has to be done, determine which events depend on one another, and identify potential trouble spots. PERT also makes it easy to compare the effects alternative actions might have on scheduling and costs. Thus, PERT allows managers to monitor a project's progress, identify possible bottlenecks, and shift resources as necessary to keep the project on schedule.

To understand how to construct a PERT network, you need to know four terms. **Events** are end points that represent the completion of major activities. **Activities** represent the time or resources required to progress from one event to another. **Slack time** is the amount of time an individual activity can be delayed without delaying the whole project. The **critical path** is the longest or most time-consuming sequence of events and activities

PERT network A flowchart diagram showing the sequence of activities needed to complete a project and the time or cost associated with each.

events End points that represent the completion of major activities in a PERT network.

activities The time or resources needed to progress from one event to another in a PERT network.

slack time The amount of time an individual activity can be delayed without delaying the whole project.

critical path The longest sequence of activities in a PERT network.

Exhibit PCT-7

Steps in Developing a PERT Network

1. *Identify every significant activity that must be achieved for a project to be completed.* The accomplishment of each activity results in a set of events or outcomes.

2. *Determine the order in which these events must be completed.*

3. *Diagram the flow of activities from start to finish, identifying each activity and its relationship to all other activities.* Use circles to indicate events and arrows to represent activities. This results in a flowchart diagram called a PERT network.

4. *Compute a time estimate for completing each activity.* This is done with a weighted average that uses an *optimistic* time estimate (t_0) of how long the activity would take under ideal conditions, a *most likely* estimate (t_m) of the time the activity normally should take, and a *pessimistic* estimate (t_p) that represents the time that an activity should take under the worst possible conditions. The formula for calculating the expected time (t_e) is then

$$t_e = \frac{t_0 + 4t_m + t_p}{6}$$

5. *Using the network diagram that contains time estimates for each activity, determine a schedule for the start and finish dates of each activity and for the entire project.* Any delays that occur along the critical path require the most attention because they can delay the whole project.

in a PERT network. Any delay in completing events on this path would delay completion of the entire project. In other words, activities on the critical path have zero slack time.

Developing a PERT network requires that a manager identify all key activities needed to complete a project, rank them in order of occurrence, and estimate each activity's completion time. Exhibit PCT-7 explains the steps in this process.

Most PERT projects are complicated and include numerous activities. Such complicated computations can be done with specialized PERT software. However, let's work through a simple example. Assume you're the superintendent at a construction company and have been assigned to oversee the construction of an office building. Because time really is money in your business, you must determine how long it will take to get the building completed. You've determined the specific activities and events. Exhibit PCT-8 outlines

Exhibit MPCT-8

Events and Activities in Constructing an Office Building

Event	Description	Expected Time (in weeks)	Preceding Event
A	Approve design and get permits	10	None
B	Dig subterranean garage	6	A
C	Erect frame and siding	14	B
D	Construct floor	6	C
E	Install windows	3	C
F	Put on roof	3	C
G	Install internal wiring	5	D, E, F
H	Install elevator	5	G
I	Put in floor covering and panelling	4	D
J	Put in doors and interior decorative trim	3	I, H
K	Turn over to building management group	1	J

Exhibit PCT-9

PERT Network for Constructing an Office Building

the major events in the construction project and your estimate of the expected time to complete each. Exhibit PCT-9 shows the actual PERT network based on the data in Exhibit PCT-8. You've also calculated the length of time that each path of activities will take:

A-B-C-D-I-J-K (44 weeks) → A-B-C-E-G-H-J-K (47 weeks)
A-B-C-D-G-H-J-K (50 weeks) → A-B-C-F-G-H-J-K (47 weeks)

Your PERT network shows that if everything goes as planned, the total project completion time will be 50 weeks. This is calculated by tracing the project's critical path (the longest sequence of activities): A-B-C-D-G-H-J-K and adding up the times. You know that any delay in completing the events on this path would delay the completion of the entire project. Taking six weeks instead of four to put in the floor covering and paneling (Event I) would have no effect on the final completion date. Why? Because that event isn't on the critical path. However, taking seven weeks instead of six to dig the subterranean garage (Event B) would likely delay the total project. A manager who needed to get back on schedule or to cut the 50-week completion time would want to concentrate on those activities along the critical path that could be completed faster. How might the manager do this? He or she could look to see if any of the other activities *not* on the critical path had slack time in which resources could be transferred to activities that *were* on the critical path.

Breakeven Analysis

breakeven analysis A technique for identifying the point at which total revenue is just sufficient to cover total costs.

Managers at McCain Foods want to know how many units of its new Solo Gourmet pizzas must be sold in order to break even—that is, the point at which total revenue is just sufficient to cover total costs. **Breakeven analysis** is a widely used resource allocation technique to help managers determine breakeven point.[25]

Breakeven analysis is a simple calculation, yet it's valuable to managers because it points out the relationship between revenues, costs, and profits. To compute breakeven point *(BE)*, a manager needs to know the unit price of the product being sold *(P)*, the variable cost per unit *(VC)*, and total fixed costs *(TFC)*. An organization breaks even when its total revenue is just enough to equal its total costs. But total cost has two parts: fixed and variable. *Fixed costs* are expenses that do not change regardless of volume. Examples include insurance premiums, rent, and property taxes. *Variable costs* change in proportion to output and include raw materials, labour costs, and energy costs.

Breakeven point can be computed graphically or by using the following formula:

$$BE = \frac{TFC}{P - VC}$$

This formula tells us that (1) total revenue will equal total cost when we sell enough units at a price that covers all variable unit costs, and (2) the difference between price and variable costs, when multiplied by the number of units sold, equals the fixed costs. Let's work through an example.

Exhibit PCT-10

Breakeven Analysis

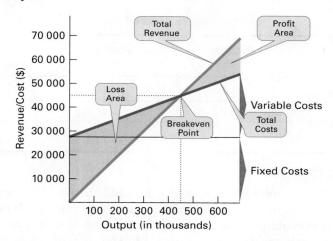

Assume that Randy's Photocopying Service charges $0.10 per photocopy. If fixed costs are $27 000 a year and variable costs are $0.04 per copy, Randy can compute his breakeven point as follows: $27 000 ÷ ($0.10 − $0.04) = 450 000 copies, or when annual revenues are $45 000 (450 000 copies × $0.10). This same relationship is shown graphically in Exhibit PCT-10.

As a planning tool, breakeven analysis could help Randy set his sales goal. For example, he could determine his profit goal and then calculate what sales level is needed to reach that goal. Breakeven analysis could also tell Randy how much volume has to increase to break even if he's currently operating at a loss or how much volume he can afford to lose and still break even.

Linear Programming

Jocelyn Dubois manages a manufacturing plant that produces two kinds of cinnamon-scented home fragrance products: wax candles and a woodchip potpourri sold in bags. Business is good, and she can sell all of the products she can produce. Her dilemma: Given that the bags of potpourri and the wax candles are manufactured in the same facility, how many of each product should she produce to maximize profits? Jocelyn can use **linear programming** to solve her resource allocation problem.

Although linear programming can be used here, it can't be applied to all resource allocation problems because it requires that resources be limited, that the goal be outcome optimization, that resources can be combined in alternative ways to produce a number of output mixes, and that a linear relationship exist between variables (a change in one variable must be accompanied by an exactly proportional change in the other).[26] For Jocelyn's business, that last condition would be met if it took exactly twice the amount of raw materials and hours of labour to produce two of a given home fragrance product as it took to produce one.

What kinds of problems can be solved with linear programming? Some applications include selecting transportation routes that minimize shipping costs, allocating a limited advertising budget among various product brands, making the optimal assignment of people among projects, and determining how much of each product to make with a limited number of resources. Let's return to Jocelyn's problem and see how linear programming could help her solve it. Fortunately, her problem is relatively simple, so we can solve

linear programming
A mathematical technique that solves resource allocation problems.

Exhibit PCT-11

Production Data for Cinnamon-Scented Products

Number of Hours Required (per unit)

Department	Potpourri Bags	Scented Candles	Monthly Production Capacity (in hours)
Manufacturing	2	4	1200
Assembly	2	2	900
Profit per unit	$10	$18	

it rather quickly. For complex linear programming problems, managers can use computer software programs designed specifically to help develop optimizing solutions.

First, we need to establish some facts about Jocelyn's business. She has computed the profit margins on her home fragrance products at $10 for a bag of potpourri and $18 for a scented candle. These numbers establish the basis for Jocelyn to be able to express her *objective function* as maximum profit $= 10P + \$18S$, where P is the number of bags of potpourri produced and S is the number of scented candles produced. The objective function is simply a mathematical equation that can predict the outcome of all proposed alternatives. In addition, Jocelyn knows how much time each fragrance product must spend in production and the monthly production capacity (1200 hours in manufacturing and 900 hours in assembly) for manufacturing and assembly. (See Exhibit PCT-11.) The production capacity numbers act as *constraints* on her overall capacity. Now Jocelyn can establish her constraint equations:

$$2P + 4S \leq 1,200$$
$$2P + 2S \leq 900$$

Of course, Jocelyn can also state that $P \geq 0$ and $S \geq 0$ because neither fragrance product can be produced in a volume less than zero.

Jocelyn has graphed her solution in Exhibit PCT-12. The shaded area represents the options that don't exceed the capacity of either department. What does this mean? Well,

Exhibit PCT-12

Graphical Solution to Linear Programming Problem

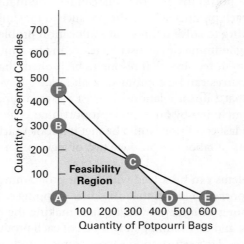

let's look first at the manufacturing constraint line BE. We know that total manufacturing capacity is 1200 hours, so if Jocelyn decides to produce all potpourri bags, the maximum she can produce is 600 (1200 hours ÷ 2 hours required to produce a bag of potpourri). If she decides to produce all scented candles, the maximum she can produce is 300 (1200 hours ÷ 4 hours required to produce a scented candle). The other constraint Jocelyn faces is that of assembly, shown by line DF. If Jocelyn decides to produce all potpourri bags, the maximum she can assemble is 450 (900 hours production capacity ÷ 2 hours required to assemble). Likewise, if Jocelyn decides to produce all scented candles, the maximum she can assemble is also 450 because the scented candles also take 2 hours to assemble. The constraints imposed by these capacity limits establish Jocelyn's *feasibility region*. Her optimal resource allocation will be defined at one of the corners within this feasibility region. Point C provides the maximum profits within the constraints stated. How do we know? At point A, profits would be 0 (no production of either potpourri bags or scented candles). At point B, profits would be $5400 (300 scented candles × $18 profit and 0 potpourri bags produced = $5400). At point D, profits would be $4500 (450 potpourri bags produced × $10 profit and 0 scented candles produced = $4500). At point C, however, profits would be $5700 (150 scented candles produced × $18 profit and 300 potpourri bags produced × $10 profit = $5700).

Contemporary Planning and Control Techniques

Lowest home mortgage rates since 1950s. H1N1 flu pandemic. Chemical/biological attacks. Recession/inflation worries. Category 4 or 5 hurricanes. Changing competition. Today's managers face the challenges of planning in an environment that's both dynamic and complex. Two planning techniques appropriate for this type of environment are project management and scenarios. Both techniques emphasize *flexibility*, something that's important to making planning more effective and efficient in this type of organizational environment.

Project Management

Different types of organizations, from manufacturers such as Coleman and Boeing to software design firms such as SAS and Microsoft, use projects. A **project** is a one-time-only set of activities that has a definite beginning and ending point in time.[27] Projects vary in size and scope—from Boston's "big dig" downtown traffic tunnel to a sorority's holiday formal. **Project management** is the task of getting a project's activities done on time, within budget, and according to specifications.[28]

More and more organizations are using project management because the approach fits well with the need for flexibility and rapid response to perceived market opportunities. When organizations undertake projects that are unique, have specific deadlines, contain complex interrelated tasks requiring specialized skills, and are temporary in nature, these projects often do not fit into the standardized planning procedures that guide an organization's other routine work activities. Instead, managers use project management techniques to effectively and efficiently accomplish the project's goals. What does the project management process involve?

Project Management Process

In the typical project, work is done by a project team whose members are assigned from their respective work areas to the project and who report to a project manager. The project manager coordinates the project's activities with other departments. When the project team accomplishes its goals, it disbands and members move on to other projects or back to their permanent work area.

The essential features of the project planning process are shown in Exhibit PCT-13. The process begins by clearly defining the project's goals. This step is necessary because the manager and the team members need to know what's expected. All activities in the project and the resources needed to do them must then be identified. What materials and labour are needed to complete the project? This step may be time-consuming and complex,

project A one-time-only set of activities that has a definite beginning and ending point in time.

project management The task of getting a project's activities done on time, within budget, and according to specifications.

Exhibit PCT-13

Project Planning Process

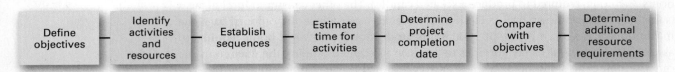

Source: Based on R. S. Russell and B. W. Taylor III, *Production and Operations Management* (Upper Saddle River, NJ: Prentice Hall, 1995), p. 287.

particularly if the project is unique and the managers have no history or experience with similar projects. Once the activities have been identified, the sequence of completion needs to be determined. What activities must be completed before others can begin? Which can be done simultaneously? This step often uses flowchart diagrams such as a Gantt chart, a load chart, or a PERT network. Next, the project activities need to be scheduled. Time estimates for each activity are done, and these estimates are used to develop an overall project schedule and completion date. Then the project schedule is compared to the goals, and any necessary adjustments are made. If the project completion time is too long, the manager might assign more resources to critical activities so they can be completed faster.

Today, the project management process can take place online as a number of web-based software packages are available. These packages cover aspects from project accounting and estimating to project scheduling and bug and defect tracking.[29]

The Role of the Project Manager

The temporary nature of projects makes managing them different from, say, overseeing a production line or preparing a weekly tally of costs on an ongoing basis. The one-shot nature of the work makes project managers the organizational equivalent of a hired gunman. There's a job to be done. It has to be defined—in detail. And the project manager is responsible for how it's done. At J.B. Hunt Transport Services, the head of project management trains project managers on both technical and interpersonal skills so that they know how to ". . . run a project effectively."[30]

Even with the availability of sophisticated computerized and online scheduling programs and other project management tools, the role of project manager remains difficult because he or she is managing people who typically are still assigned to their permanent work areas. The only real influence project managers have is through their communication skills and their power of persuasion. To make matters worse, team members seldom work on just one project. They're usually assigned to two or three at any given time. So project managers end up competing with each other to focus a worker's attention on his or her particular project.

Scenario Planning

During the 1990s, business was so good at Colgate-Palmolive that then-chair Reuben Mark worried about what "might go wrong." He installed an "early-warning system to flag problems before they blew up into company-wrecking crises." For instance, a red-flag report alerted Mark "that officials in Baddi, India, had questions about how a plant treated wastewater." Mark's response was to quickly assign an engineering team to check it out and prevent potential problems.[31]

We already know how important it is that today's managers do what Reuben Mark was doing—monitor and assess the external environment for trends and changes. As managers assess the environment, issues and concerns that could affect their organization's current or planned operations are likely to be revealed. All of these issues won't be equally important, so it's usually necessary to focus on a limited set that are most important and to develop scenarios based on each.

A **scenario** is a consistent view of what the future is likely to be. Developing scenarios also can be described as *contingency planning*; that is, if this event happens, then we need to take these actions. If, for instance, environmental scanning reveals increasing interest by the provinces for raising the provincial minimum wage, managers at Subway could create multiple scenarios to assess the possible consequences of such an action. What would be the implications for its labour costs if the minimum wage were raised to $12 an hour? How about $14 an hour? What effect would these changes have on the chain's bottom line? How might competitors respond? Different assumptions lead to different outcomes. The intent of scenario planning is not to try to predict the future but to reduce uncertainty by playing out potential situations under different specified conditions.[32] Subway could, for example, develop a set of scenarios ranging from optimistic to pessimistic in terms of the minimum-wage issue. It would then be prepared to implement new strategies to get and keep a competitive advantage. An expert in scenario planning said, "Just the process of doing scenarios causes executives to rethink and clarify the essence of the business environment in ways they almost certainly have never done before."[33]

Although scenario planning is useful in anticipating events that *can* be anticipated, it's difficult to forecast random events—the major surprises that cannot be foreseen. The planning challenge comes from the totally random and unexpected events. For instance, the 9/11 terrorist attacks in New York, Washington, and Pennsylvania were random, unexpected, and a total shock to numerous organizations throughout the world. Scenario planning was of little use because no one could have envisioned this scenario. Similarly, the sudden spread of the SARS virus in Toronto caught everyone by surprise, and many businesses in Ontario learned the hard way about the importance of having contingency plans in place.[34] Over 75 percent of companies said that they did not have a contingency plan in place for public health crises.[35]

As difficult as it may be for managers to anticipate and deal with these random events, they're not totally vulnerable to the consequences. One suggestion identified by risk experts as particularly important is to have an early warning system in place. (A similar idea is the tsunami warning systems in the Pacific and in Alaska, which alert officials to potentially dangerous tsunamis and give them time to take action.) Early warning indicators for organizations can give managers advance notice of potential problems and changes—as it did Reuben Mark at Colgate-Palmolive—so they, too, can take action. Then, managers need to have appropriate responses (plans) in place if these unexpected events occur.

Planning tools and techniques can help managers prepare confidently for the future. But they should remember that all the tools we've described in this module are just that—tools. They will never replace the manager's skills and capabilities in using the information gained to develop effective and efficient plans.

scenario A consistent view of what the future is likely to be.

REVIEW AND DISCUSSION QUESTIONS

1. Describe the different approaches to assessing the environment.

2. Describe the four techniques for allocating resources.

3. How does PERT network analysis work?

4. Why is flexibility so important to today's planning techniques?

5. What is project management, and what are the steps managers use in planning projects?

6. "It's a waste of time and other resources to develop a set of sophisticated scenarios for situations that may never occur." Do you agree or disagree? Support your position.

7. Do intuition and creativity have any relevance in quantitative planning tools and techniques? Explain.

8. *The Wall Street Journal* and other business periodicals often carry reports of companies that have not met their sales or profit forecasts. What are some reasons a company might not meet its forecast? What suggestions could you make for improving the effectiveness of forecasting?

9. In what ways is managing a project different from managing a department or other structured work area? In what ways are they the same?

10. What might be some early warning signs of (a) a new competitor coming into your market, (b) an employee work stoppage, or (c) a new technology that could change demand for your product?

PART TWO

Management Practice

A Manager's Dilemma

Habitat for Humanity is a nonprofit, ecumenical Christian housing ministry dedicated to building affordable housing for individuals dealing with poverty or homelessness. Habitat's approach is simple. Families in need of decent housing apply to a local Habitat affiliate. Homeowners are chosen based on their level of need, their willingness to become partners in the program, and their ability to repay the loan. And that's the unique thing about Habitat's approach. It's not a giveaway program. Families chosen to become homeowners have to make a down payment and monthly mortgage payments, and invest hundreds of hours of their own labour into building their Habitat home. And they have to commit to helping build other Habitat houses. Habitat volunteers (maybe you've been involved on a Habitat build) provide labour and donations of money and materials as well.

Social service organizations often struggle financially to provide services that are never enough to meet the overwhelming need. Habitat for Humanity, however, was given an enormous financial commitment—$100 million—from an individual who had worked with Habitat and seen the gift it offers to families in poverty. That amount of money means that Habitat can have a huge impact now and in the future. But the management team wants to use the gift wisely—a definite planning, strategy, and control challenge.

> Pretend you're part of that management team. Using what you've learned in the chapters on planning, strategic management, and managerial controls in Part 2, what five things would you suggest the team focus on? Think carefully about your suggestions to the team.

Global Sense

True or false: The workplace can be stressful. You probably said true, and it's especially true as the economic recession has gone on and on. During the recession, work teams have shrunk, and workloads and pressures have grown. Businesses have asked their employees to be more innovative and creative, but at the same time to be more efficient. It's a recipe for stress, for sure! One stress reliever is taking a break from work—a vacation. And most advanced countries have a national vacation policy requiring companies to give their workers paid time off. In Germany, for instance, workers are guaranteed a month of vacation. In the United Kingdom, they're guaranteed more than five weeks of paid vacation. In Switzerland, employees get at least 20 work days or four weeks. However, in the United States, there is no guarantee. The U.S. is practically the only developed country in the world that doesn't require companies to give their workers time off. Yet, although many companies in the U.S. *do* give their employees vacation days, employees aren't using them. A recent survey found that the average North American worker has accumulated more than a week's worth of unused vacation days. Why? The most-cited reasons employees give is lack of money and no time to plan a vacation. However, some management experts say the unwillingness to claim unused vacation time is more likely based on fears related to the economy.

Discuss the following questions in light of what you learned in Part 2:

- Why is a vacation from work a good remedy for stress?
- What's your opinion? Are North American workers not using up all their vacation time because of money or is it because of fear? Or maybe both? Discuss.
- As a manager, what could you do to "encourage" your employees to use their vacation time?
- Do some research. What other countries suffer from "vacation deprivation?"
- Why do you think European and other countries are more supportive of the concept of taking a vacation from work?
- Does Canada need a national vacation policy? Support your argument. Would this be good for businesses? Why or why not?

Sources: D. Thompson, "The Only Advanced Country Without a National Vacation Policy? It's the U.S.," www.theatlantic.com, July 2, 2012; P. Korkki, "Drive to Worry, and to Procrastinate," *New York Times Online*, February 25, 2012; "Expedia 2011 Vacation Deprivation Study Reveals Work-Life Disparity Across Five Continents," finance.yahoo.com/news/, November 30, 2011; "Overworked, Older Americans Not Using Up Allotted Vacation Days," www.huffingtonpost.com, November 26, 2011; and P. Korkki, "Working at Making the Most of Your Vacation," *New York Times Online*, August 13, 2011.

Organizational Design

Once managers are done planning, then what? This is when managers need to begin to "work the plan." And the first step in doing that involves designing an appropriate organizational structure. This chapter covers the decisions involved with designing that structure. After reading and studying this chapter, you will achieve the following learning outcomes.

Learning Outcomes

1. Describe the six key elements of organizational design.

2. Contrast mechanistic and organic structures.

3. Discuss the contingency factors that favour either the mechanistic model or the organic model of organizational design.

4. Describe traditional organizational designs.

5. Describe contemporary organizational designs.

▶ ▶ ▶ Tim Leiweke was the president and CEO of Maple Leaf Sports & Entertainment (MLSE), which owns the NHL's Toronto Maple Leafs, the NBA's Toronto Raptors, Major League Soccer's Toronto FC, the AHL's Toronto Marlies, Leafs TV, and Raptors NBA TV, from 2013–2015.[1] MLSE also owns the Air Canada Centre (where the Maple Leafs and Raptors play their home games). Lieweke's job was complex—it included responsibility for the business affairs of each team ("team operations,

sales, marketing, finance, administration, event operations, broadcast, communications, and community development"). Lieweke was also responsible for the operation of the Air Canada Centre, BMO Field, Ricoh Coliseum in Toronto, and General Motors Centre in Oshawa, Ontario.

Such a position demands the help of a variety of people and departments. One of Lieweke's jobs, then, was to create an organizational structure for MLSE that supports the operations of the sports teams and the sports facilities. The CEO has a great deal of flexibility in determining some parts of the structure, and less flexibility in determining others. For instance, the number of athletes that can fill positions on a hockey team is determined by the NHL. Through the draft and trades, however, MLSE and its managers have some ability to choose the particular players who fill these positions.

The CEO also oversees ticket sales for the four teams. In determining how to manage ticket sales, he can consider whether there should be separate ticket sales departments for each team, whether marketing should be included with or separate from ticket sales, and whether ticket salespeople should be subdivided into specialties: corporate sales, season tickets, playoff tickets, etc.

Tim Lieweke's desire to make Maple Leaf Sports & Entertainment successful illustrated how important it is for managers to design an organizational structure that helps accomplish organizational goals and objectives. In this chapter, we present information about designing appropriate organizational structures. We look at the various elements of organizational structure and the factors that influence their design. We also look at some traditional and contemporary organizational designs, as well as organizational design challenges that today's manager's face.

Designing Organizational Structure

Few topics in management have undergone as much change in the past few years as that of organizing and organizational structure. Managers are re-evaluating traditional approaches to find new structural designs that best support and facilitate employees' doing the organization's work—designs that can achieve efficiency but are also flexible.[2]

The basic concepts of organizational design formulated by early management writers, such as Henri Fayol and Max Weber, offered structural principles for managers to follow. Over 90 years have passed since many of those principles were originally proposed. Given that length of time and all the changes that have taken place, you'd think that those principles would be pretty worthless today. Surprisingly, they're not. For the most part, they still provide valuable insights into designing effective and efficient organizations. Of course, we've also gained a great deal of knowledge over the years as to their limitations.

In Chapter 1, we defined **organizing**. **Organizing** is arranging and structuring work to accomplish organizational goals. It's an important process during which managers design an organization's structure. **Organizational structure** is the formal arrangement of jobs within an organization. This structure, which can be shown visually in an **organizational chart**, also serves many purposes. (See Exhibit 10-1.) When managers create or change the structure, they're engaged in **organizational design**, a process that involves decisions about six key elements: work specialization, departmentalization, chain of command, span of control, centralization and decentralization, and formalization.[3]

Watch on MyManagementLab
Elm City Market: Organizational Structure

1 Describe the six key elements of organizational design.

organizing Arranging and structuring work to accomplish an organization's goals.

organizational structure How job tasks are formally divided, grouped, and coordinated within an organization.

organizational chart The visual representation of an organizations structure.

organizational design The process of developing or changing an organization's structure.

Exhibit 10-1

Purposes of Organizing

- Divides work to be done into specific jobs and departments.
- Assigns tasks and responsibilities associated with individual jobs.
- Coordinates diverse organizational tasks.
- Clusters jobs into units.
- Establishes relationships among individuals, groups, and departments.
- Establishes formal lines of authority.
- Allocates and deploys organizational resources.

Work Specialization

Today we use the term **work specialization** to describe the degree to which activities in an organization are subdivided into separate job tasks. The essence of work specialization is that an entire job is not done by one individual but instead is broken down into steps, and each step is completed by a different person. Individual employees specialize in doing part of an activity rather than the entire activity.

Work specialization makes efficient use of the diversity of skills that workers have. In most organizations, some tasks require highly developed skills; others can be performed by employees with lower skill levels. If all workers were engaged in all the steps of, say, a manufacturing process, all would need the skills necessary to perform both the most demanding and the least demanding jobs. Thus, except when performing the most highly skilled or highly sophisticated tasks, employees would be working below their skill levels. In addition, skilled workers are paid more than unskilled workers, and, because wages tend to reflect the highest level of skill, all workers would be paid at highly skilled rates to do easy tasks—an inefficient use of resources. This concept explains why you rarely find a cardiac surgeon closing up a patient after surgery. Instead, doctors doing their residencies in open-heart surgery and learning the skill usually stitch and staple the patient after the surgeon has finished the surgery.

Early proponents of work specialization believed it could lead to great increases in productivity. At the beginning of the twentieth century, that generalization was reasonable. Because specialization was not widely practised, its introduction almost always generated higher productivity. But, as Exhibit 10-2 illustrates, a good thing can be carried too far. At some point, the human diseconomies from division of labour—boredom, fatigue, stress, low productivity, poor quality, increased absenteeism, and high turnover—exceed the economic advantages.[4]

Today's View

Most managers today see work specialization as an important organizing mechanism but not as a source of ever-increasing productivity. They recognize the economies it

> **work specialization** The degree to which activities in an organization are subdivided into separate job tasks; also known as *division of labour.*

Exhibit 10-2

Economies and Diseconomies of Work Specialization

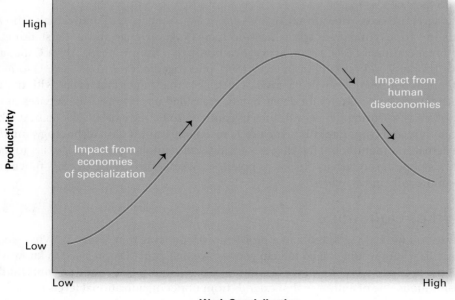

provides in certain types of jobs, but they also recognize the problems it creates—including job dissatisfaction, poor mental health, and a low sense of accomplishment—when it's carried to extremes.[5] McDonald's uses high work specialization to efficiently make and sell its products, and most employees in health care organizations are specialized. However, other organizations, such as Bolton, Ontario-based Husky Injection Molding Systems and Ford Australia, have successfully increased job breadth and reduced work specialization. Still, specialization has its place in some organizations. No hockey team has anyone play both goalie and centre positions. Rather, players specialize in their positions.

Departmentalization

Does your college or university have an office of student affairs? A financial aid or student housing department? Once job tasks have been divided up through work specialization, common job tasks have to be grouped back together so that they can be done in a coordinated way. The basis on which jobs are grouped together is called **departmentalization**. Every organization will have its own specific way of classifying and grouping work activities. Exhibit 10-3 shows the five common forms of departmentalization.

Large organizations often combine forms of departmentalization. For example, a major Japanese electronics firm organizes each of its divisions along functional lines; its manufacturing units around processes; its sales units around seven geographic regions; and sales regions into four customer groupings.

Today's View

Two popular trends in departmentalization are the increasing use of customer departmentalization and the use of cross-functional teams. Customer departmentalization is being used to monitor customers' needs and to respond to changes in those needs. For example, Toronto-based Dell Canada is organized around four customer-oriented business units: home and home office; small business; medium and large business; and government, education, and health care. Burnaby, BC-based TELUS is structured around four customer-oriented business units: consumer solutions (focused on services to homes and individuals); business solutions (focused on services to small and medium-sized businesses and entrepreneurs); TELUS Québec (a TELUS company focused on services for the Quebec marketplace); and partner solutions (focused on services to wholesale customers, such as telecommunications carriers and wireless communications companies). Customer-oriented structures allow companies to better understand their customers and to respond faster to their needs.

Managers use **cross-functional teams**—work teams made up of individuals who are experts in various functional specialties—to increase knowledge and understanding of some organizational tasks. For instance, Scarborough, Ontario-based Aviva Canada, a leading property and casualty insurance group, puts together catastrophe teams to more quickly help policyholders when a crisis occurs. The cross-functional teams, with trained representatives from all relevant departments, are called upon to provide services in the event of a crisis. During the BC wildfires of summer 2003, the catastrophe team worked on both local and corporate issues, including managing information technology, internal and external communication, tracking, resourcing, and vendors. This made it easier to meet the needs of policyholders as quickly as possible.[6] We discuss the use of cross-functional teams more fully in Chapter 15.

Chain of Command

Suppose you were at work and had a problem with an issue that came up. What would you do? To whom would you go to help you resolve that issue? People need to know who their boss is. That's what the chain of command is all about. The **chain of command** is the continuous line of authority that extends from upper organizational levels to the lowest levels and clarifies who reports to whom. It helps employees answer questions such as, "Who do I go to if I have a problem?" or "To whom am I responsible?"

Exhibit 10-3

The Five Common Forms of Departmentalization

Functional Departmentalization

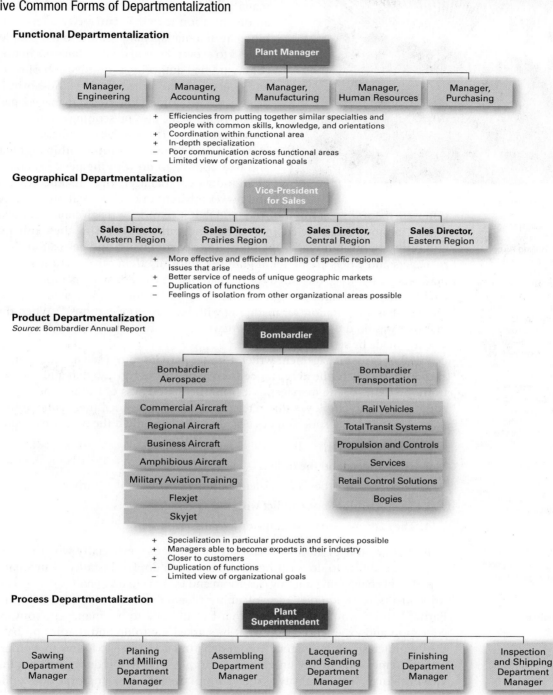

Plant Manager

Manager, Engineering | Manager, Accounting | Manager, Manufacturing | Manager, Human Resources | Manager, Purchasing

+ Efficiencies from putting together similar specialties and people with common skills, knowledge, and orientations
+ Coordination within functional area
+ In-depth specialization
– Poor communication across functional areas
– Limited view of organizational goals

Geographical Departmentalization

Vice-President for Sales

Sales Director, Western Region | Sales Director, Prairies Region | Sales Director, Central Region | Sales Director, Eastern Region

+ More effective and efficient handling of specific regional issues that arise
+ Better service of needs of unique geographic markets
– Duplication of functions
– Feelings of isolation from other organizational areas possible

Product Departmentalization

Source: Bombardier Annual Report

Bombardier

Bombardier Aerospace
- Commercial Aircraft
- Regional Aircraft
- Business Aircraft
- Amphibious Aircraft
- Military Aviation Training
- Flexjet
- Skyjet

Bombardier Transportation
- Rail Vehicles
- Total Transit Systems
- Propulsion and Controls
- Services
- Retail Control Solutions
- Bogies

+ Specialization in particular products and services possible
+ Managers able to become experts in their industry
+ Closer to customers
– Duplication of functions
– Limited view of organizational goals

Process Departmentalization

Plant Superintendent

Sawing Department Manager | Planing and Milling Department Manager | Assembling Department Manager | Lacquering and Sanding Department Manager | Finishing Department Manager | Inspection and Shipping Department Manager

+ More efficient flow of work activities
– Use possible only with certain types of products

Customer Departmentalization

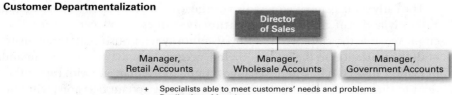

Director of Sales

Manager, Retail Accounts | Manager, Wholesale Accounts | Manager, Government Accounts

+ Specialists able to meet customers' needs and problems
– Duplication of functions
– Limited view of organizational goals

These waiters and waitresses stand in line while attending a meeting held by their managers before they start their work at a restaurant at the Beijing Airport. The managers have the authority to give employees instructions for their work day as it is an inherent right in their position as managers to tell people what to do and to expect them to do it. The concept of authority is part of the chain of command that extends from higher organizational levels to lower levels and clarifies who reports to whom. The concept of authority also includes the perspective that subordinates are willing to accept that authority when they understand what they are told to do and are able to perform the task.

Lou Linwei/Alamy

▶◉ Simulate on **MyManagementLab**

Responsibility, Authority, and Delegation

authority The rights inherent in a managerial position to tell people what to do and to expect them to do it.

acceptance theory of authority The view that authority comes from the willingness of subordinates to accept it.

line authority Authority that entitles a manager to direct the work of an employee.

Authority

Authority was a major concept discussed by the early management writers; they viewed it as the glue that held an organization together. **Authority** refers to the rights inherent in a managerial position to tell people what to do and to expect them to do it.[7] Managers in the chain of command had authority to do their job of coordinating and overseeing the work of others. Authority could be delegated downward to lower-level managers, giving them certain rights while also prescribing certain limits within which to operate. These writers emphasized that authority was related to one's position within an organization and had nothing to do with the personal characteristics of an individual manager. They assumed that the rights and power inherent in one's formal organizational position were the sole source of influence and that if an order were given, it would be obeyed.

You cannot discuss the chain of command without discussing these other concepts: authority, responsibility, accountability, unity of command, and delegation. Some senior managers and CEOs are better at granting authority than others. For instance, when a new general manager was hired for the Raptors, some sportswriters raised concerns over whether he would have enough autonomy to do his job. It was noted that the CEO of the day "has a reputation for meddling with basketball operations."[8] When the general manager was fired two years later, sportswriters observed that many of his decisions were actually made by senior management.[9]

Another early management writer, Chester Barnard, proposed another perspective on authority. This view, the **acceptance theory of authority**, says that authority comes not from the rights of the manager, but from the willingness of subordinates to accept the authority.[10] If an employee doesn't accept a manager's order, there is no authority. Barnard contended that subordinates *will* accept orders only if the following conditions are satisfied:

1. They understand the order.
2. They feel the order is consistent with the organization's purpose.
3. The order does not conflict with their personal beliefs.
4. They are able to perform the task as directed.

Barnard's view of authority seems to make sense, especially when it comes to an employee's ability to do what he or she is told to do. For instance, if my manager (my department chair) came into my classroom and told me to do open-heart surgery on one of my students, the traditional view of authority said that I would have to follow that order. Barnard's view would say, instead, that I would talk to my manager about my lack of education and experience to do what he's asked me to do and that it's probably not in the best interests of the student (or our department) for me to follow that order. Yes, this is an extreme—and highly unrealistic—example. However, it does point out that simply viewing a manager's authority as total control over what an employee does or doesn't do is unrealistic, except in certain circumstances such as in the military, where soldiers are expected to follow their commander's orders. However, understand that Barnard believed most employees would do what their managers asked them to do if they were able to do so.

The early management writers also distinguished between two forms of authority: line authority and staff authority. **Line authority** entitles a manager to direct the work of an employee. It is the employer–employee authority relationship that extends from the top of the organization to the lowest echelon, according to the chain of command, as shown in Exhibit 10-4. As a link in the chain of command, a manager with line authority has the right to direct the work of employees and to make certain decisions without consulting anyone. Of course, in the chain of command, every manager is also subject to the authority or direction of his or her superior.

Exhibit 10-4

Chain of Command and Line Authority

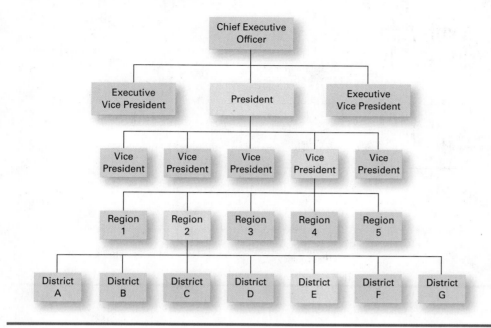

Keep in mind that sometimes the term *line* is used to differentiate line managers from staff managers. In this context, *line* refers to managers whose organizational function contributes directly to the achievement of organizational objectives. In a manufacturing firm, line managers are typically in the production and sales functions, whereas managers in human resources and payroll are considered staff managers with staff authority. Whether a manager's function is classified as line or staff depends on the organization's objectives. For example, at Staff Builders, a supplier of temporary employees, interviewers have a line function. Similarly, at the payroll firm of ADP, payroll is a line function.

As organizations get larger and more complex, line managers find that they do not have the time, expertise, or resources to get their jobs done effectively. In response, they create **staff authority** functions to support, assist, advise, and generally reduce some of their informational burdens. For instance, a hospital administrator who cannot effectively handle the purchasing of all the supplies the hospital needs creates a purchasing department, which is a staff function. Of course, the head of the purchasing department has line authority over the purchasing agents who work for him. The hospital administrator might also find that she is overburdened and needs an assistant, a position that would be classified as a staff position. Exhibit 10-5 illustrates line and staff authority.

staff authority Positions with some authority that have been created to support, assist, and advise those holding line authority.

Responsibility

When managers use their authority to assign work to employees, those employees take on an obligation to perform those assigned duties. This obligation or expectation to perform is known as **responsibility**. And employees should be held accountable for their performance! Assigning work authority without responsibility and accountability can create opportunities for abuse. Likewise, no one should be held responsible or accountable for work tasks that he or she has no authority to complete.

responsibility The obligation or expectation to perform any assigned duties.

Unity of Command

Finally, the **unity of command** principle (one of Fayol's 14 management principles) states that a person should report to only one manager. Without unity of command, conflicting demands from multiple bosses may create problems.

unity of command The management principle that each person should report to only one manager.

Exhibit 10-5

Line versus Staff Authority

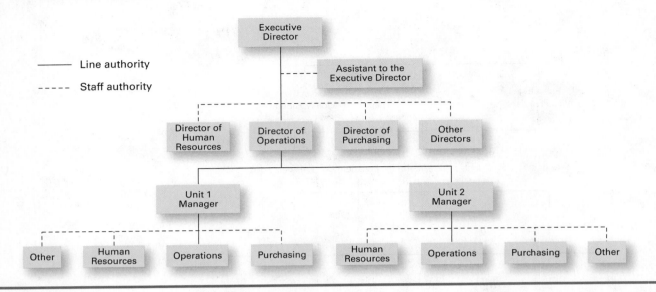

- ——— Line authority
- - - - - Staff authority

Today's View

Although early management theorists (Fayol, Weber, Taylor, Barnard, and others) believed that chain of command, authority (line and staff), responsibility, and unity of command were essential, times have changed.[11] Those elements are far less important today. For example, at the Michelin plant in Waterville, Nova Scotia, managers have replaced the top-down chain of command with "birdhouse" meetings, in which employees meet for five minutes at regular intervals throughout the day at a column on the shop floor and study simple tables and charts to identify production bottlenecks. Instead of being bosses, shop managers are enablers.[12] Information technology also has made such concepts less relevant today. Employees can access information that used to be available only to managers in a matter of a few seconds. It also means that employees can communicate with anyone else in the organization without going through the chain of command. Also, many employees, especially in organizations in which work revolves around projects, find themselves reporting to more than one boss, thus violating the unity of command principle. However, such arrangements can and do work if communication, conflict, and other issues are managed well by all involved parties.

Span of Control

How many employees can a manager efficiently and effectively manage? This question of **span of control** is important because, to a large degree, it determines the number of levels and managers an organization has. The traditional view was that managers could not—and should not—directly supervise more than five or six subordinates. All things being equal, the wider or larger the span, the more efficient the organization. An example can show why.

span of control The number of employees a manager can efficiently and effectively manage.

Assume that we have two organizations, both of which have almost 4100 employees. As Exhibit 10-6 shows, if one organization has a uniform span of four and the other a span of eight, the wider span will have two fewer levels and approximately 800 fewer managers. If the average manager made $50 000 a year, the organization with the wider span would save $40 million a year in management salaries alone! Obviously, wider spans are more efficient in terms of cost. However, at some point, wider spans reduce effectiveness. When the span becomes too large, employee performance can suffer because managers may no longer have the time to provide the necessary leadership and support.

Exhibit 10-6

Contrasting Spans of Control

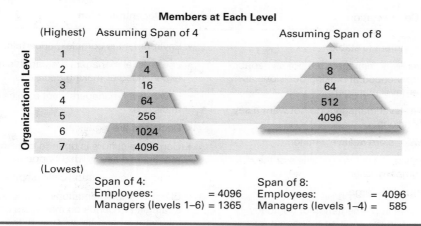

Members at Each Level

Organizational Level		Assuming Span of 4	Assuming Span of 8
(Highest)	1	1	1
	2	4	8
	3	16	64
	4	64	512
	5	256	4096
	6	1024	
	7	4096	
(Lowest)			

Span of 4:
Employees: = 4096
Managers (levels 1–6) = 1365

Span of 8:
Employees: = 4096
Managers (levels 1–4) =   585

Today's View

The contemporary view of span of control recognizes there is no magic number. Many factors influence the number of employees a manager can efficiently and effectively manage. These factors include the skills and abilities of the manager and the employees and the characteristics of the work being done. For instance, managers with well-trained and experienced employees can function well with a wider span. Other contingency variables that determine the appropriate span include similarity and complexity of employee tasks, the physical proximity of subordinates, the degree to which standardized procedures are in place, the sophistication of the organization's information system, the strength of the organization's culture, and the preferred style of the manager.[13]

The trend in recent years has been toward larger spans of control, which is consistent with managers' efforts to speed up decision making, increase flexibility, get closer to customers, empower employees, and reduce costs. Managers are beginning to recognize that they can handle a wider span when employees know their jobs well and when those employees understand organizational processes. For instance, at PepsiCo's Gamesa cookie plant in Mexico, 56 employees now report to each manager. However, to ensure that performance doesn't suffer because of these wider spans, employees are thoroughly briefed on company goals and processes. Also, new pay systems reward quality, service, productivity, and teamwork.[14]

Centralization and Decentralization

One of the questions that needs to be answered when organizing is At what organizational level are decisions made **Centralization** is the degree to which decision making takes place at upper levels of the organization. If top managers make key decisions with little input from below, then the organization is more centralized. On the other hand, the more that lower-level employees provide input or actually make decisions, the more **decentralization** there is. Keep in mind that centralization–decentralization is not an either–or concept. The decision is relative, not absolute—that is, an organization is never completely centralized or decentralized.

Early management writers proposed that the degree of centralization in an organization depended on the situation.[15] Their goal was the optimum and efficient use of employees. Traditional organizations were structured in a pyramid, with power and authority concentrated near the top of the organization. Given this structure, historically, centralized decisions were the most prominent, but organizations today have become more complex and responsive to dynamic changes in their environments. As such, many managers believe decisions need to be made by those individuals closest to the problems, regardless

centralization The degree to which decision making is concentrated at upper levels of the organization.

decentralization The degree to which lower-level employees provide input or actually make decisions.

Exhibit 10-7

Centralization or Decentralization

More Centralization	More Decentralization
• Environment is stable.	• Environment is complex, uncertain.
• Lower-level managers are not as capable or experienced at making decisions as upper-level managers.	• Lower-level managers are capable and experienced at making decisions.
• Lower-level managers do not want a say in decisions.	• Lower-level managers want a voice in decisions.
• Decisions are relatively minor.	• Decisions are significant.
• Organization is facing a crisis or the risk of company failure.	• Corporate culture is open to allowing managers a say in what happens.
• Company is large.	• Company is geographically dispersed.
• Effective implementation of company strategies depends on managers retaining say over what happens.	• Effective implementation of company strategies depends on managers having involvement and flexibility to make decisions.

of their organizational level. In fact, the trend over the past several decades—at least in U.S. and Canadian organizations—has been a movement toward more decentralization in organizations.[16] Exhibit 10-7 lists some of the factors that affect an organization's use of centralization or decentralization.[17]

Today's View

As organizations become more flexible and responsive, there is a distinct trend toward decentralizing decision making. This trend, also known as **employee empowerment**, gives employees more authority (power) to make decisions. (We'll address this concept more thoroughly in our discussion of leadership in Chapter 13.) In large companies especially, lower-level managers are "closer to the action" and typically have more detailed knowledge about problems and how best to solve them than do top managers. For instance, the Bank of Montreal's approximately 1000 branches are organized into "communities"—a group of branches within a limited geographical area. Each community is led by a community area manager, who typically works within a 20-minute drive of the area's other branches. This area manager can respond faster and more intelligently to problems in his or her community than could some senior executive at the company's head office. As the company continues its southward expansion into the United States, it continues to use decentralization to successfully manage its various businesses.[18]

Formalization

Formalization refers to how standardized an organization's jobs are and the extent to which employee behaviour is guided by rules and procedures. In highly formalized organizations, there are explicit job descriptions, numerous organizational rules, and clearly defined procedures covering work processes. Employees have little discretion over what's done, when it's done, and how it's done. However, where formalization is low, employees have more discretion in how they do their work.

Today's View

Although some formalization is important and necessary for consistency and control, many of today's organizations seem to be less reliant on strict rules and standardization to guide and regulate employee behaviour. For instance, consider the following situation:

It is 2:37 p.m., and a customer at a branch of a large national drugstore chain is trying to drop off a roll of film for same-day developing. Store policy states that film must be

employee empowerment
Giving employees more authority (power) to make decisions.

formalization The degree to which jobs within the organization are standardized and the extent to which employee behaviour is guided by rules and procedures.

dropped off by 2:00 p.m. for this service. The clerk knows that rules like this are supposed to be followed. At the same time, he wants to be accommodating to the customer, and he knows that the film could, in fact, be processed that day. He decides to accept the film and, in so doing, to violate the policy. He just hopes that his manager does not find out.[19]

Has this employee done something wrong? He did "break" the rule. But by breaking the rule, he actually brought in revenue and provided the customer good service: so good, in fact, that the customer may be satisfied enough to come back in the future.

Considering that there are numerous situations like these where rules may be too restrictive, many organizations have allowed employees some freedom to make those decisions that they feel are best under the circumstances. It does not mean that all organizational rules are thrown out the window, because there *will* be rules that are important for employees to follow—and these rules should be explained so employees understand why it's important to adhere to them. But for other rules, employees may be given some leeway in application.[20]

Mechanistic and Organic Strucutres

▶ ▶ ▶   The culture at Maple Leaf Sports and Entertainment reflects the culture of the patrons who frequent sporting events. "We play to win every day as passionate, dedicated leaders who work hard. We are all passionate about what we do. We have pride in our company, our brands and our people. We strive to achieve top performance, and we also like to have fun! Events like the MLSE Expo, Taste of the ACC, MLSE Dodgeball Classic, Holiday Hoopla, "Best Damn Cookie" Contest and Bake Sales in support of the MLSE Foundation, as well as community and volunteer opportunities for the MLSE Foundation, Golf Tournaments, and of course, working for and with great people every day make MLSE an incredible place to work. And let's face it, the sports and entertainment industry is pretty great!"[21]

Think About It

Maple Leaf Sports and Entertainment embraces a playful culture, yet things still need to get done. How could elements of a mechanistic structure bring order to the chaos of large sporting events? How might elements of an organic structure inform front line workers to make ad hoc decisions as the challenges at sporting events present themselves?

Organizations don't have the same structures. A company with 30 employees is not going to look like one with 30 000 employees. But even organizations of comparable size don't necessarily have similar structures. What works for one organization may not work for another. How do managers decide what organizational design to use? That decision depends upon certain contingency factors. In this section, we look at two generic models of organizational design and then at the contingency factors that favour each.

Exhibit 10-8 describes two organizational forms.[23] A **mechanistic organization** is a rigid and tightly controlled structure, much like McDonald's. It's characterized by high specialization, rigid departmentalization, a limited information network (mostly downward communication), narrow spans of control, little participation in decision making by lower-level employees, and high formalization.

Mechanistic organizational structures tend to be efficiency machines and rely heavily on rules, regulations, standardized tasks, and similar controls. This organizational design tries to minimize the impact of differing personalities, judgments, and ambiguity because these human traits are seen as inefficient and inconsistent. Although there is no totally mechanistic organization, almost all large corporations and government agencies have some of these mechanistic characteristics.

② Contrast mechanistic and organic structures.

mechanistic organization An organizational design that is rigid and tightly controlled.

datapoints[22]

24 percent of job seekers said they preferred to work at a company with more than 1000 employees; 27 percent they preferred a company with fewer than 200 employees.

80 percent of a company's total workforce is what typical frontline managers directly supervise.

34 percent of HR executives said they had retrained employees for new positions over the past six months.

68 percent of organizations said they've increased centralization in the past five years.

51 percent of white-collar workers say teleworking is a good idea.

42 percent of U.S. companies offer some form of telework arrangement.

55 percent of workers believe their work quality is perceived the same when working remotely as when working in the office.

Exhibit 10-8

Mechanistic vs. Organic Organization

Mechanistic

- High Specialization
- Rigid Departmentalization
- Clear Chain of Command
- Narrow Spans of Control
- Centralization
- High Formalization

Organic

- Cross-Functional Teams
- Cross-Hierarchical Teams
- Free Flow of Information
- Wide Spans of Control
- Decentralization
- Low Formalization

organic organization An organizational design that is highly adaptive and flexible.

In direct contrast to the mechanistic form of organization is the **organic organization**, which is as highly adaptive and flexible a structure as the mechanistic organization is rigid and stable. This structure characterizes the Blue Water Café, a well-known Vancouver seafood restaurant. Rather than having standardized jobs and regulations, the organic organization is flexible, which allows it to change rapidly as needs require. Organic organizations have a division of labour, but the jobs people do are not standardized. Employees are highly trained and empowered to handle diverse job activities and problems, and these organizations frequently use cross-functional and cross-hierarchical teams. Employees in organic-type organizations require minimal formal rules and little direct supervision, instead relying on a free flow of information and wide span of control. Their high levels of skills and training and the support provided by other team members make formalization and tight managerial controls unnecessary.

Organizations can display a mix of mechanistic and organic features. Wikipedia, the online encyclopedia, is known for its creation and editing of entries by anyone who has internet access. In this way, it displays a very organic structure. However, behind the scenes there is a more mechanistic structure, where individuals have some authority to monitor abuse and perform other functions to safeguard the credibility of entries and the website overall, as the following *Management Reflection* shows.

MANAGEMENT REFLECTION

Wikipedia's Structure Maintains Order in the Face of Anarchy

Why would a decentralized, free-wheeling website need an organizational structure? Even a seemingly democratic organization such as Wikipedia has an organizational structure.[24] The structure serves to help the online encyclopedia be as accurate as possible. At the bottom of that structure are the 4.6 million registered English-language users. These users are overseen by a group of about 1200 administrators, who have the power to "block other users from the site, either temporarily or permanently." One of their roles is to make sure that users are not vandalizing the site by adding incorrect information deliberately. To become an administrator, one must first be nominated, and then answer a series of five questions. Users then have seven days to register their approval or disapproval of the nominee. The administrators are overseen by a group called "bureaucrats." The bureaucrats can appoint administrators once they determine that users approve of a particular administrator nominee (this requires about a 70 percent approval rating by users). They can also change user names, and they make sure that both policies (policies regarding automated or semi-automated processes that edit webpages) are followed. Above the bureaucrats are about 30 stewards, who are elected to this position. The stewards can provide (and take away) special access status to Wikipedia. Above the stewards is the seven-person Wikimedia Foundation board of trustees, who are "the ultimate corporate authority." At the top of the Wikipedia organizational chart is the "de facto leader," Jimmy Wales, one of the co-founders of Wikipedia. When is a mechanistic structure preferable, and when is an organic one more appropriate? Let's look at the main contingency factors that influence the decision. ■

Contingency Factors Affecting Structural Choice

At Maple Leaf Sports and Entertainment there are three different sports (hockey, basketball, and soccer). Hockey and basketball are played in the fall and winter and baseball in the spring and summer. Each sport has its own fan base and expectations. Although there are generic principles that assist each of the four operating divisions, there are also needs peculiar to each sport/division.

Top managers of most organizations typically put a great deal of thought into designing an appropriate structure. What that appropriate structure is depends on four contingency variables: the organization's strategy, size, technology, and degree of environmental uncertainty. It is important to remember that because these variables can change over the life cycle of the organization, managers should consider from time to time whether the current organizational structure is best suited for what the organization is facing.

3 Discuss the contingency factors that favour either the mechanistic model or the organic model of organizational design.

Think About It

Given the reality of supporting three different sports played in three different seasons, each with a unique fan base, what criteria might Maple Leaf Sports and Entertainment use to decide which elements of each of the organic and mechanistic model best ensure that MLSE is able to meet its mission?

When Carol Bartz took over the CEO position at Yahoo! from cofounder Jerry Yang, she found a company "hobbled by slow decision making and ineffective execution on those decisions."[25] Bartz said, "There's plenty that has bogged this company down." For a company that was once the darling of web search, Yahoo! seemed to have lost its way, a serious misstep in an industry where change is continual and rapid. Bartz (who is no longer the CEO) implemented a new streamlined structure intended to "make the company a lot faster on its feet."

Simulate on MyManagementLab

Organizational Structure

Strategy and Structure

An organization's structure should facilitate goal achievement. Because goals are an important part of the organization's strategies, it's only logical that strategy and structure are closely linked. Alfred Chandler initially researched this relationship.[26] He studied several large US companies and concluded that changes in corporate strategy led to changes in an organization's structure that support the strategy.

Research has shown that certain structural designs work best with different organizational strategies.[27] For instance, the flexibility and free-flowing information of the organic structure works well when an organization is pursuing meaningful and unique innovations. The mechanistic organization, with its efficiency, stability, and tight controls, works best for companies that want to tightly control costs.

Size and Structure

There is considerable evidence that an organization's size significantly affects its structure.[28] For instance, large organizations—those with 2000 or more employees—tend to have more

Exhibit 10-9

Woodward's Findings on Technology, Structure, and Effectiveness

	Unit Production	Mass Production	Process Production
Structural Characteristics	• Low vertical differentiation	• Moderate vertical differentiation	• High vertical differentiation
	• Low horizontal differentiation	• High horizontal differentiation	• Low horizontal differentiation
	• Low formalization	• High formalization	• Low formalization
Most effective structure	• Organic	• Mechanistic	• Organic

Source: Based on J. Woodward, *Industrial Organization: Theory and Practice* (London: Oxford University Press, 1965).

unit production The production of items in units or small batches.

mass production The production of items in large batches.

process production The production of items in continuous processes.

Facing the dynamic environmental forces of global competition and accelerated product innovation by competitors, 3M Company has a flexible and decentralized organic structure that enables it to respond quickly to customer demands for high quality products and fast service. Describing itself as "a global innovation company that never stops inventing," 3M has 35 business units that operate as small companies to keep the company agile and entrepreneurial. The 10-finger multi-touch screen shown in this photo is an innovation of 3M's Touch System business unit designed for customers in the medical and engineering industries. With its organic structure, 3M is poised to adapt quickly to the fast-growing demand for touch-screen products.

Ethan Miller/Getty Images

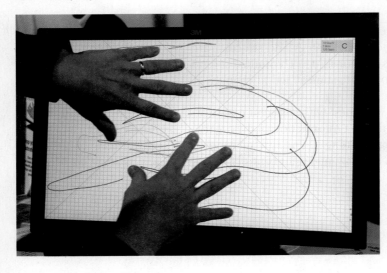

specialization, departmentalization, centralization, and rules and regulations than do small organizations. However, once an organization grows past a certain size, size has less influence on structure. Why? Essentially, once an organization has around 2000 employees, it's already fairly mechanistic. Adding 500 employees to an organization with 2000 employees will not have much of an impact. On the other hand, adding 500 employees to an organization that has only 300 members is likely to result in a shift toward a more mechanistic structure.

Technology and Structure

Every organization uses some form of technology to convert its inputs into outputs. For instance, workers at Whirlpool's Manaus, Brazil, facility build microwave ovens and air conditioners on a standardized assembly line. Employees at FedEx Kinko's Office and Print Services produce custom design and print jobs for individual customers. And employees at Bayer's facility in Karachi, Pakistan, are involved in producing pharmaceuticals on a continuous-flow production line.

The initial interest in technology as a determinant of structure can be traced to the work of British scholar Joan Woodward.[29] She studied several small manufacturing firms in southern England to determine the extent to which structural design elements were related to organizational success. Woodward was unable to find any consistent pattern until she segmented the firms into three categories based on the size of their production runs. The three categories, representing three distinct technologies, have increasing levels of complexity and sophistication. The first category, **unit production**, describes the production of items in units or small batches. The second category, **mass production**, describes large-batch manufacturing. Finally, the third and most technically complex group, **process production**, describes the production of items in continuous processes. A summary of her findings is shown in Exhibit 10-9.

Since Woodward's initial work, numerous studies have been done on the technology–structure relationship. These studies generally demonstrate that organizations adapt their structures to their technology.[30] The processes or methods that transform an organization's inputs into outputs differ by their degree of routineness or standardization. In general, the more routine the technology, the more mechanistic the structure can be. Organizations with more nonroutine technology, such as custom furniture building or online education, are more likely to have organic structures because the product delivery cannot be standardized.[31]

Other studies also have shown that organizations adapt their structures to their technology depending on how routine their technology is for transforming inputs into outputs.[32] In general, the more routine the technology, the more mechanistic the structure can be, and organizations with more nonroutine technology are more likely to have organic structures.[33]

Environmental Uncertainty and Structure

Some organizations face relatively stable and simple environments; others face dynamic and complex environments. Because uncertainty threatens an organization's effectiveness, managers will try to minimize it. One way to reduce environmental uncertainty is through adjustments in the organization's structure.[34] The greater the uncertainty, the more an organization needs the flexibility offered by an organic structure. On the other hand, in stable, simple environments, mechanistic structures tend to be most effective.

Today's View

The evidence on the environment–structure relationship helps explain why so many managers today are restructuring their organizations to be lean, fast, and flexible. Worldwide economic downturns, global competition, accelerated product innovation by competitors, and increased demands from customers for high quality and faster deliveries are examples of dynamic environmental forces. Mechanistic organizations are not equipped to respond to rapid environmental change and environmental uncertainty. As a result, we're seeing organizations become more organic.

Traditional Organizational Designs

▶ ▶ ▶ Maple Leaf Sports & Entertainment (MLSE) is divided into four operating units: MLSE, Toronto Raptors, Toronto Maple Leafs (Toronto Marlies is an affiliate), and Toronto FC. Tim Lieweke was the president and CEO of all four units.[35] The Raptors, the Maple Leafs, the Marlies, and Toronto FC each have their own general manager who manages the day-to-day operations of the team, develops recruiting plans, and oversees training. The general managers report to the CEO and have a number of managers who report to them. MLSE has a divisional structure, whereby its businesses operate separately, on a daily basis.

④ Describe traditional organizational designs.

> ### Think About It
>
> **Why do organizations vary in the types of structures they have? How do organizations choose their structures? Why does Maple Leaf Sports & Entertainment have the structure that it does?**

What organizational designs do Ford Canada, Corel, McCain Foods, Procter & Gamble, and eBay have? In making organizational design decisions, managers can choose from traditional organizational designs and contemporary organizational designs. These structures tend to be more mechanistic in nature. A summary of the strengths and weaknesses of each can be found in Exhibit 10-10.

Simple Structure

Most organizations start as entrepreneurial ventures with a simple structure consisting of owners and employees. A **simple structure** is an organizational structure with low departmentalization, wide spans of control, authority centralized in a single person, and little formalization.[36] This structure is most commonly used by small businesses in which the owner and manager are one and the same.

simple structure An organizational structure with low departmentalization, wide spans of control, authority centralized in a single person, and little formalization.

Exhibit 10-10

Traditional Organizational Designs

Structure	Strengths	Weaknesses
Simple Structure	Fast; flexible; inexpensive to maintain; clear accountability.	Not appropriate as organization grows; reliance on one person is risky.
Functional Structure	Cost-saving advantages from specialization (economies of scale, minimal duplication of people and equipment); employees are grouped with others who have similar tasks.	Pursuit of functional goals can cause managers to lose sight of what's best for overall organization; functional specialists become insulated and have little understanding of what other units are doing.
Divisional Structure	Focuses on results—division managers are responsible for what happens to their products and services.	Duplication of activities and resources increases costs and reduces efficiency.

As employees are added, however, most companies don't remain as simple structures. The structure tends to become more specialized and formalized. Rules and regulations are introduced, work becomes specialized, departments are created, levels of management are added, and the organization becomes increasingly bureaucratic. At this point, managers might choose a functional structure or a divisional structure.

Functional Structure

functional structure An organizational structure that groups similar or related occupational specialties together.

A **functional structure** is an organizational structure that groups similar or related occupational specialties together. It's the functional approach to departmentalization applied to the entire organization. For instance, Revlon is organized around the functions of operations, finance, human resources, and product research and development.

Divisional Structure

divisional structure An organizational structure that consists of separate business units or divisions.

The **divisional structure** is an organizational structure that consists of separate business units or divisions.[37] In this structure, each unit or division has relatively limited autonomy, with a division manager responsible for performance and with strategic and operational authority over his or her unit. In divisional structures, however, the parent corporation typically acts as an external overseer to coordinate and control the various divisions, and it often provides support services such as financial and legal. As we noted earlier, Maple Leaf Sports & Entertainment has four divisions, including Toronto's three major-league sports teams: the Raptors, the Maple Leafs, and Toronto FC.

Contemporary Organizational Designs

5 Describe contemporary organizational designs.

Microsoft's Windows 7 was the outcome of a three-year project marked by close collaboration among the thousands of people working on various aspects of the product.[38] This approach contrasted sharply with the development of Windows Vista, where the development team had evolved into "a rigid set of silos—each responsible for specific technical features—that didn't share their plans widely." With Vista, programming code created by each group might have worked fine on its own, but it caused technical problems when integrated with code created by other groups. Those design issues, as well as internal communications breakdowns, contributed to numerous product delays and defects. CEO Steve Ballmer was adamant about not repeating that mistake. Thus, to "rebuild Windows,

Microsoft razed walls"—that is, organizational structure walls that acted as barriers and impediments to efficient and effective work.

Like Steve Ballmer, many managers are finding that the traditional designs (discussed on pp. 263–264) often aren't appropriate for today's increasingly dynamic and complex environment. Instead, organizations need to be lean, flexible, and innovative; that is, they need to be more organic. So managers are finding creative ways to structure and organize work. These contemporary designs include team structures, matrix and project structures, boundaryless organizations, and learning organizations. (See Exhibit 10-11 for a summary of these designs.)

Team Structures

Larry Page and Sergey Brin, cofounders of Google, created a corporate structure that "tackles most big projects in small, tightly focused teams."[39] A **team structure** is one in which the entire organization is made up of work teams that do the organization's work.[40] In this structure, employee empowerment is crucial because no line of managerial authority flows from top to bottom. Rather, employee teams design and do work in the way they think is best, but the teams are also held responsible for all work performance results in their respective areas.

team structure An organizational structure in which the entire organization is made up of work teams.

Exhibit 10-11

Contemporary Organizational Designs

Team Structure

• What it is:	A structure in which the entire organization is made up of work groups or teams.
• Advantages:	Employees are more involved and empowered.
	Reduced barriers among functional areas.
• Disadvantages:	No clear chain of command.
	Pressure on teams to perform.

Matrix-Project Structure

• What it is:	In a matrix structure, specialists from different functional areas are assigned to work on projects and then return to their areas when the project is completed. In a project structure, employees continuously work on projects. As one project is completed, employees move on to the next project.
• Advantages:	Fluid and flexible design that can respond to environmental changes. Faster decision making.
• Disadvantages:	Complexity of assigning people to projects. Task and personality conflicts.

Boundaryless Structure

• What it is:	A structure not defined by or limited to artificial horizontal, vertical, or external boundaries; includes *virtual* and *network* types of organizations.
• Advantages:	Highly flexible and responsive.
	Utilizes talent wherever it's found.
• Disadvantages:	Lack of control.
	Communication difficulties.

Learning Structure

• What it is:	A structure in which employees continually acquire and share new knowledge and apply that knowledge.
• Advantages:	Sharing of knowledge throughout organization. Sustainable source of competitive advantage.
• Disadvantages:	Reluctance on part of employees to share knowledge for fear of losing their power.
	Large numbers of experienced employees on the verge of retiring.

Exhibit 10-12

Example of a Matrix Organization

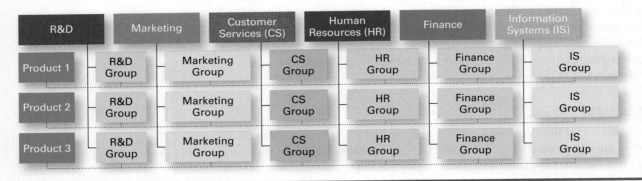

	R&D	Marketing	Customer Services (CS)	Human Resources (HR)	Finance	Information Systems (IS)
Product 1	R&D Group	Marketing Group	CS Group	HR Group	Finance Group	IS Group
Product 2	R&D Group	Marketing Group	CS Group	HR Group	Finance Group	IS Group
Product 3	R&D Group	Marketing Group	CS Group	HR Group	Finance Group	IS Group

In large organizations, the team structure complements what is typically a functional or divisional structure and allows the organization to have the efficiency of a bureaucracy *and* the flexibility that teams provide. Companies such as Amazon, Boeing, Hewlett-Packard, Louis Vuitton, Motorola, and Xerox, for instance, extensively use employee teams to improve productivity.

Matrix and Project Structures

matrix structure An organizational structure that assigns specialists from different functional departments to work on one or more projects.

Other popular contemporary designs are the matrix and project structures. The **matrix structure** assigns specialists from different functional departments to work on projects being led by a project manager. (See Exhibit 10-12.) One unique aspect of this design is that it creates a *dual chain of command* because employees in a matrix organization have two managers: their functional area manager and their product or project manager, who share authority. The project manager has authority over the functional members who are part of his or her project team in areas related to the project's goals. However, any decisions about promotions, salary recommendations, and annual reviews typically remain the functional manager's responsibility. The matrix design "violates" the unity of command principle, which says that each person should report to only one boss; however, it can—and does—work effectively if both managers communicate regularly, coordinate work demands on employees, and resolve conflicts together.[41]

project structure An organizational structure in which employees continuously work on projects.

Many organizations use a **project structure**, in which employees continuously work on projects. Unlike the matrix structure, a project structure has no formal departments to which employees return at the completion of a project. Instead, employees take their specific skills, abilities, and experiences to other projects. Also, all work in project structures is performed by teams of employees. For instance, at design firm IDEO, project teams form, disband, and form again as the work requires. Employees "join" project teams because they bring needed skills and abilities to that project. Once a project is completed, however, they move on to the next one.[42]

Project structures tend to be more flexible organizational designs, without the departmentalization or rigid organizational hierarchy that can slow down making decisions or taking action. In this structure, managers serve as facilitators, mentors, and coaches. They eliminate or minimize organizational obstacles and ensure that teams have the resources they need to effectively and efficiently complete their work.

The Boundaryless Organization

The Large Hadron Collider is a $6 billion particle accelerator lying in a tunnel that is 27 kilometres (17 miles) in circumference and 175 metres (574 feet) below ground near Geneva, Switzerland. "The atom smasher is so large that a brief status report lists 2900 authors, so complex that scientists in 34 countries have readied 100 000 computers to process its data, and so fragile that a bird dropping a bread crust can short-circuit its power supply."[43] But exploiting the collider's potential to expand the frontiers of knowledge has required that scientists around the world cut across "boundaries of place, organization, and technical specialty to conduct ever more ambitious experiments."

The structural arrangement for getting work done that has developed around the massive collider is an example of another contemporary organizational design called the **boundaryless organization**, an organization whose design is not defined by, or limited to, the horizontal, vertical, or external boundaries imposed by a predefined structure.[44] Former GE chair Jack Welch coined the term because he wanted to eliminate vertical and horizontal boundaries within GE and break down external barriers between the company and its customers and suppliers. Although the idea of eliminating boundaries may seem odd, many of today's most successful organizations find that they can operate most effectively by remaining flexible and *un*structured, that the ideal structure for them is *not* having a rigid, bounded, and predefined structure.[45]

What do we mean by *boundaries*? There are two types: (1) *internal*—the horizontal ones imposed by work specialization and departmentalization and the vertical ones that separate employees into organizational levels and hierarchies, and (2) *external*—the boundaries that separate the organization from its customers, suppliers, and other stakeholders. To minimize or eliminate these boundaries, managers might use virtual or network structural designs.

Virtual Organizations

Is an internship something you've ever thought about doing (or have done)? How about an internship that you could do not in a workplace cubicle, but from your couch using your computer?[46] Such virtual internships are becoming quite popular, especially with smaller and midsize companies and, of course, with online businesses. The type of work virtual interns do typically involves "researching, sales, marketing, and social media development"—tasks that can be done anywhere with a computer and online access. Some organizations are structured in a way that allows most employees to be virtual employees.

A **virtual organization** typically consists of a small core of full-time employees and outside specialists temporarily hired as needed to work on projects.[47] An example is when Second Life, a company creating a virtual world of colourful online avatars, was building its software. Founder Philip Rosedale hired programmers from around the world and divided up the work into about 1600 individual tasks, "from setting up databases to fixing bugs." The process worked so well, the company used it for all sorts of work.[48] Another example is Nashville-based Emma Inc., an e-mail marketing firm with 100 employees who work from home or offices in Austin, Denver, New York, and Portland.[49] The biggest challenge they've faced is creating a "virtual" culture, a task made more challenging by the fact that the organization is virtual.

Network Organizations

Food marketer Smart Balance Inc. helps people stay trim and lean with its heart-healthy products.[50] The company's organizational structure is also trim and lean. With only 67 employees, the company outsources almost every other organizational function, including manufacturing, product distribution, and sales. Smart Balance's structural approach is one that also eliminates organizational boundaries and can be described as a **network organization**, which uses its own employees to do some work activities and networks of outside suppliers to provide other needed product components or work processes.[51] This organizational form is sometimes called a *modular organization* by

Rekha Menon, executive vice-president of India geographic services and human capital and diversity at Accenture India, works from her home. Accenture, an international consulting, technology, and outsourcing firm, is a virtual organization that operates in 120 countries. Like Menon, most of Accenture's quarter of a million employees do not work in company offices but from home or at their clients' offices. Accenture achieves high productivity and collaboration by using an innovative videoconferencing system that connects with clients and enables employees of its worldwide virtual workplace to operate as a unified team.

The India Today Group/Getty Images

boundaryless organization An organization whose design is not defined by, or limited to, the horizontal, vertical, or external boundaries imposed by a predefined structure.

virtual organization An organization that consists of a small core of full-time employees and outside specialists temporarily hired as needed to work on projects.

network organization An organization that uses its own employees to do some work activities and networks of outside suppliers to provide other needed product components or work processes.

manufacturing firms.[52] Such an approach allows organizations to concentrate on what they do best by contracting out other activities to companies that do those activities best. For instance, the strategy of British company ARM, a microchip designer, is to find a lot of partners. It contracts with those partners for manufacturing and sales. ARM's chip designs serve as the brains of 98 percent of the world's cell phones. Because ARM doesn't manufacture, it can encourage its customers to request whatever they like. Such flexibility is particularly valuable in the cell phone market, where having custom chips and software can provide an edge.[53] At Boeing, the company's head of development for the 787 Dreamliner manages thousands of employees and some 100 suppliers at more than 100 sites in different countries.[54] Sweden's Ericsson contracts its manufacturing and even some of its research and development to more cost-effective contractors in New Delhi, Singapore, California, and other global locations.[55] And at Penske Truck Leasing, dozens of business processes, such as securing permits and titles, entering data from drivers' logs, and processing data for tax filings and accounting, have been outsourced to Mexico and India.[56]

Learning Organizations

learning organization An organization that has developed the capacity to continuously learn, adapt, and change.

Doing business in an intensely competitive global environment, British retailer Tesco realizes how important it is for its stores to run well behind the scenes.[57] And it does so using a proven "tool" called Tesco in a Box, a self-contained complete IT system and matching set of business processes that provides the model for all of Tesco's international business operations. This approach promotes consistency in operations and is a way to share innovations.[58] Tesco is an example of a **learning organization**, an organization that has developed the capacity to continuously learn, adapt, and change. "Today's managerial challenge is to inspire and enable knowledge workers to solve, day in and day out, problems that cannot be anticipated."[59] In a learning organization, employees continually acquire and share new knowledge and apply that knowledge in making decisions or doing their work. Some organizational theorists even go so far as to say that an organization's ability to do this—that is, to learn and to apply that learning—may be the only sustainable source of competitive advantage.[60] What structural characteristics does a learning organization need?

Employees throughout the entire organization—across different functional specialties and even at different organizational levels—must share information and collaborate on work activities. Such an environment requires minimal structural and physical barriers, which allows employees to work together in doing the organization's work the best way they can and, in the process, learn from each other. Finally, empowered work teams tend to be an important feature of a learning organization's structural design. These teams make decisions about doing whatever work needs to be done or resolving issues. With empowered employees and teams, there's little need for "bosses" to direct and control. Instead, managers serve as facilitators, supporters, and advocates.

Hopefully, you've seen in this chapter that organizational structure and design (or redesign) are important managerial tasks. Also, we hope that you recognize that organizing decisions aren't only important for upper-level managers. Managers at all levels may have to deal with work specialization or authority or span of control decisions. In the next chapter, we'll examine the factors that impact how managers communicate with their stakeholders.

CHAPTER 10

SUMMARY AND IMPLICATIONS

1. Describe the six key elements of organizational design. The key elements in organizational design are work specialization, departmentalization, chain of command, span of control, centralization–decentralization, and formalization. Traditionally, work specialization was viewed as a way to divide work activities into separate job tasks. Today's view is that it is an important organizing mechanism but it can lead to problems. The chain of command and its companion concepts—authority, responsibility, and unity of command—were viewed as important ways of maintaining control in organizations. The contemporary view is that they are less relevant in today's organizations. The traditional view of span of control was that managers should directly supervise no more than five to six individuals. The contemporary view is that the span of control depends on the skills and abilities of the manager and the employees and on the characteristics of the situation.

▶ ▶ ▶ The various forms of departmentalization are as follows: *Functional* groups jobs by functions performed; *product* groups jobs by product lines; *geographical* groups jobs by geographical region; *process* groups jobs on product or customer flow; and *customer* groups jobs on specific and unique customer groups. Authority refers to the rights inherent in a managerial position to tell people what to do and to expect them to do it. The acceptance view of authority says that authority comes from the willingness of subordinates to accept it. Line authority entitles a manager to direct the work of an employee. Staff authority refers to functions that support, assist, advise, and generally reduce some of managers' informational burdens. Responsibility is the obligation or expectation to perform assigned duties. Unity of command states that a person should report to only one manager. Centralization–decentralization is a structural decision about who makes decisions—upper-level managers or lower-level employees. Formalization concerns the organization's use of standardization and strict rules to provide consistency and control.

▶ ▶ ▶ For Maple Leafs Sports & Entertainment, it makes sense to separate the operation of the four sports teams because of the work specialization involved. For example, the general manager of the Raptors would not necessarily make good decisions about what Maple Leafs players should do to improve their game.

2. Contrast mechanistic and organic structures. A mechanistic organization is a rigid and tightly controlled structure. An organic organization is highly adaptive and flexible. There is no one best organizational structure. The appropriate structure depends upon the organization's strategy, its size, the technology it uses (unit production, mass production, or process production), and the degree of environmental uncertainty the organization faces.

▶ ▶ ▶ Maple Leaf Sports & Entertainment embraces a playful culture where having fun is embedded in the activities that employees engage in. Yet in spite of this organic and playful bent, elements of a mechanistic structure are needed to ensure that the fans at the many different sports event receive the experiences embedded in the brand promise of Maple Leaf Sports and Entertainment.

3. Discuss the contingency factors that favour either the mechanistic model or the organic model of organizational design. An organization's structure should support the strategy. If the strategy changes, the structure also should change. An organization's size can affect its structure up to a certain point. Once an organization reaches a certain size (usually around 2000 employees), it's fairly mechanistic. An organization's technology can affect its structure. An organic structure is most effective with unit production and process production technology. A mechanistic structure is most effective with mass production technology. The more uncertain an organization's environment, the more it needs the flexibility of an organic design.

▶ ▶ ▶ For Maple Leaf Sports & Entertainment, because hockey, basketball, and soccer are in different "industries" with different types of players, it makes sense to organize the teams by industry. Because sports teams are governed by formal rules, the teams have more of a mechanistic structure than an organic one. Each team has a similar organizational structure because size, technology, and environmental uncertainty would not differ in any meaningful way for the teams.

4. Describe traditional organizational designs. A simple structure is one with low departmentalization, wide spans of control, authority centralized in a single person, and little formalization. A functional structure groups similar or related occupational specialties together. A divisional structure is made up of separate business units or divisions.

▶ ▶ ▶ Maple Leaf Sports & Entertainment follows a traditional divisional structure for its sports teams. Other structures might be used to operate its sports facilities, such as a project structure or a boundaryless organization, because events and ticket sales can be managed in a variety of ways.

5. Describe contemporary organizational designs. In a team structure, the entire organization is made up of work teams. The matrix structure assigns specialists from different functional departments to work on one or more projects being led by project managers. A project structure is one in which employees continuously work on projects. A virtual organization consists of a small core of full-time employees and outside specialists temporarily hired as needed to work on projects. A network organization is an organization that uses its own employees to do some work activities and networks of outside suppliers to provide other needed product components or work processes. A learning organization is one that has developed the capacity to continuously learn, adapt, and change. It has certain structural characteristics including an emphasis on sharing information and collaborating on work activities, minimal structural and physical barriers, and empowered work teams.

MyManagementLab Study, practise, and explore real management situations with these helpful resources:

- **Interactive Lesson Presentations:** Work through interactive presentations and assessments to test your knowledge of management concepts.
- **PIA (Personal Inventory Assessments):** Enhance your ability to connect with key concepts through these engaging, self-reflection assessments.
- **Study Plan:** Check your understanding of chapter concepts with self-study quizzes.
- **Simulations:** Practise decision-making in simulated management environments.

P I A PERSONAL INVENTORY ASSESSMENT

REVIEW AND DISCUSSION QUESTIONS

1. Discuss the traditional and contemporary views of each of the six key elements of organizational design.

2. Contrast mechanistic and organic organizations.

3. Would you rather work in a mechanistic or an organic organization? Why?

4. Contrast the three traditional organizational designs.

5. With the availability of advanced information technology that allows an organization's work to be done anywhere at any time, is organizing still an important managerial function? Why or why not?

6. Researchers are now saying that efforts to simplify work tasks actually have negative results for both companies and their employees. Do you agree? Why or why not?

7. Describe the four contemporary organizational designs. How are they similar? Different?

8. Differentiate between matrix and project structures.

ETHICS DILEMMA

Thomas Lopez, a lifeguard in the Miami area, was fired for leaving his assigned area to save a drowning man.[61] His employer, Jeff Ellis and Associates, which has a contract with the Florida city of Hallandale, said Lopez "left his patrol area unmonitored and exposed the company to legal liability." Lopez said he had no choice but to do what he did. "I'm not going to put my job over helping someone. I'm going to do what I felt was right, and I did." After this story hit the media, the company offered Lopez his job back, but he declined.

What do you think? What ethical concerns do you see? What lessons can be applied to organizational design from this story?

SKILLS EXERCISE

Delegating—About the Skill

Managers get things done through other people. Because there are limits to any manager's time and knowledge, effective managers need to understand how to delegate. *Delegation* is the assignment of authority to another person to carry out specific duties. It allows an employee to make some of the decisions. Delegation should not be confused with participation. In participative decision making, there is a sharing of authority. In delegation, employees make decisions on their own.

Steps in Developing the Skill

A number of actions differentiate the effective delegator from the ineffective delegator. You can be more effective at delegating if you use the following five suggestions:[62]

1. **Clarify the assignment.** Determine what is to be delegated and to whom. You need to identify the person who is most capable of doing the task, and then determine whether or not he or she has the time and motivation to do the task. If you have a willing and able employee, it's your responsibility to provide clear information on what is being delegated, the results you expect, and any time or performance expectations you may have. Unless there is an overriding need to adhere to specific methods, you should delegate only the results expected. Get agreement on what is to be done and the results expected, but let the employee decide the best way to complete the task.

2. **Specify the employee's range of discretion.** Every situation of delegation comes with constraints. Although you are delegating to an employee the authority to perform some task or tasks, you are not delegating unlimited authority. You are delegating authority to act on certain issues within certain parameters. You need to specify what those parameters are so that employees know, without any doubt, the range of their discretion.

3. **Allow the employee to participate.** One of the best ways to decide how much authority will be necessary to accomplish a task is to allow the employee who will be held accountable for that task to participate in that decision. Be aware, however, that allowing employees to participate can present its own set of potential problems as a result of employees' self-interests and biases in evaluating their own abilities.

4. **Inform others that delegation has occurred.** Delegation should not take place behind the scenes. Not only do the manager and employee need to know specifically what has been delegated and how much authority has been given, but so does anyone else who is likely to be affected by the employee's decisions and actions. This includes people inside and outside the organization. Essentially, you need to communicate what has been delegated (the task and amount of authority) and to whom.

5. **Establish feedback channels.** To delegate without establishing feedback controls is to invite problems. The establishment of controls to monitor the employee's performance increases the likelihood that important problems will be identified and that the task will be completed on time and to the desired specifications. Ideally, these controls should be determined at the time of the initial assignment. Agree on a specific time for the completion of the task, and then set progress dates when the employee will report back on how well he or she is doing and any major problems that may have arisen. These controls can be supplemented with periodic checks to ensure that authority guidelines are not being abused, organizational policies are being followed, proper procedures are being met, and the like.

Practising the Skill

Read the following scenario. Write some notes about how you would handle the situation described. Be sure to refer to the five suggestions for delegating.

Scenario

Ricky Lee is the manager of the contracts group of a large regional office supply distributor. His manager, Anne Zumwalt, has asked him to prepare by the end of the month the department's new procedures manual, which will outline the steps followed in negotiating contracts with office products manufacturers who supply the organization's products. Because Ricky has another major project he is working on, he went to Anne and asked her if it would be possible to assign the rewriting of the procedures manual to Bill Harmon, one of his employees, who has worked in the contracts group for about three years. Anne said she had no problems with Ricky reassigning the project as long as Bill knew the parameters and the expectations for the completion of the project. Ricky is preparing for his meeting in the morning with Bill regarding this assignment. Prepare an outline of what Ricky should discuss with Bill to ensure the new procedures manual meets expectations.

Reinforcing the Skill

The following activities will help you practise and reinforce the skills associated with delegating:

1. Interview a manager regarding his or her delegation skills. What activities does he or she *not delegate?* Why?

2. Teach someone else how to delegate effectively. Be sure to identify to this person the behaviours needed to delegate effectively, and explain why these behaviours are important.

WORKING TOGETHER: TEAM EXERCISE

Charting an Organization's Structure.

An organizational chart can be a useful tool for understanding certain aspects of an organization's structure. Form small groups of three to four individuals. Among yourselves, choose an organization with which one of you is familiar (your place of work, a student organization to which you belong, your college or university, etc.). Draw an organizational chart of this organization. Be careful to show departments (or groups), and especially be careful to get the chain of command correct. Be prepared to share your chart with the class.

LEARNING TO BE A MANAGER

- Find three different examples of an organizational chart. (Company's annual reports are a good place to look.) In a report, describe each of these. Try to decipher the organization's use of organizational design elements, especially departmentalization, chain of command, centralization–decentralization, and formalization.

- Survey at least 10 different managers as to how many employees they supervise. Also ask them whether they feel they could supervise more employees or whether they feel the number they supervise is too many. Graph your survey results and write a report describing what you found. Draw some conclusions about span of control.

- Using the organizational chart you created in the team exercise, redesign the structure. What structural changes might make this organization more efficient and effective? Write a report describing what you would do and why. Be sure to include an example of the original organizational chart as well as a chart of your proposed revision of the organizational structure.

CASE APPLICATION 1

A New Kind of Structure

Admit it. Sometimes the projects you're working on (school, work, or both) can get pretty boring and monotonous. Wouldn't it be great to have a magic button you could push to get someone else to do that boring, time-consuming stuff? At Pfizer, that "magic button" is a reality for a large number of employees.[63]

As a global pharmaceutical company, Pfizer is continually looking for ways to help employees be more efficient and effective. The company's senior director of organizational effectiveness found that the "Harvard MBA staff we hired to develop strategies and innovate were instead Googling and making PowerPoints." Indeed, internal studies conducted to find out just how much time its valuable talent was spending on menial tasks was startling. The average Pfizer employee was spending 20 percent to 40 percent of his or her time on support work (creating documents, typing notes, doing research, manipulating data, scheduling meetings) and only 60 percent to 80 percent on knowledge work (strategy, innovation, networking, collaborating, critical thinking). And the problem wasn't just at lower levels. Even the highest-level employees were affected. Take, for instance, David Cain, an executive director for global engineering. He enjoys his job—assessing environmental real estate risks, managing facilities, and controlling a multimillion-dollar budget. But he didn't so much enjoy having to go through spreadsheets and put together PowerPoints. Now, however, with Pfizer's "magic button," those tasks are passed off to individuals outside the organization.

Just what is this "magic button?" Originally called the Office of the Future (OOF), the renamed PfizerWorks allows employees to shift tedious and time-consuming tasks with the click of a single button on their computer desktop. They describe what they need on an online form, which is then sent to one of two Indian service-outsourcing firms. When a request is received, a team member in India calls the Pfizer employee to clarify what's needed and by when. The team member then e-mails back a cost specification for the requested work. If the Pfizer employee decides to proceed, the costs involved are charged to the employee's department. About this unique arrangement, Cain said that he relishes working with what he prefers to call his "personal consulting organization."

The number 66 500 illustrates just how beneficial PfizerWorks has been for the company. That's the number of work hours estimated to have been saved by employees who've used PfizerWorks. What about Joe Cain's experiences? When he gave the Indian team a complex project researching strategic actions that worked when consolidating company facilities, the team put the report together in a month, something that would have taken him six months to do alone. He says, "Pfizer pays me not to work tactically, but to work strategically."

DISCUSSION QUESTIONS

1. Describe and evaluate what Pfizer is doing with its PfizerWorks.
2. What structural implications—good and bad—does this approach have? (Think in terms of the six organizational design elements.)
3. Do you think this arrangement would work for other types of organizations? Why or why not? What types of organizations might it also work for?
4. What role do you think organizational structure plays in an organization's efficiency and effectiveness? Explain.

CASE APPLICATION 2

Ask Chuck

The Charles Schwab Corporation (Charles Schwab) is a San Francisco-based financial services company.[64] Like many companies in that industry, Charles Schwab struggled during the economic recession.

Founded in 1971 by its namesake as a discount brokerage, the company has now "grown up" into a full-service traditional brokerage firm, with more than 300 offices in some 45 states and in London and Hong Kong. It still offers discount brokerage services, but also financial research, advice, and planning; retirement plans; investment management; and proprietary financial products including mutual funds, mortgages, CDs, and other banking products through its Charles Schwab Bank unit. However, its primary business is still making stock trades for investors who make their own financial decisions. The company has a reputation for being conservative, which helped it avoid the financial meltdown suffered by other investment firms. Founder Charles R. Schwab has a black bowling ball perched on his desk. "It's a memento of the long-forgotten bubble of 1961, when shares of bowling-pin companies, shoemakers, chalk manufacturers, and lane operators were thought to be can't-miss plays on the limitless potential of suburbia—and turned out to be duds." He keeps the ball as a reminder not to "buy into hype or take excessive risks."

Like many companies, Charles Schwab is fanatical about customer service. By empowering front-line employees to respond fast to customer issues and concerns, Cheryl Pasquale, a manager at one of Schwab's branches, is on the front line of Schwab's efforts to prosper in a "resource-challenged economy." Every workday morning, she pulls up a customer feedback report for her branch generated by a brief survey the investment firm e-mails out daily. The report allows her to review how well her six financial consultants handled the previous day's transactions. She's able to see comments of customers who gave both high and low marks and whether a particular transaction garnered praise or complaint. On one particular day, she notices that several customers commented on how difficult it was to use the branch's in-house information

kiosks. "She decides she'll ask her team for insights about this in their weekly meeting." One thing that she pays particular attention to is a "manager alert—a special notice triggered by a client who has given Schwab a poor rating for a delay in posting a transaction to his account." And she's not alone. Every day, Pasquale and the managers at all the company's branches receive this type of customer feedback. It's been particularly important to have this information in the challenging economic climate of the last few years.

DISCUSSION QUESTIONS

1. Describe and evaluate what Charles Schwab is doing.
2. How might the company's culture of not buying into hype and not taking excessive risks affect its organizational structural design?
3. What structural implications—good and bad—might Schwab's intense focus on customer feedback have?
4. Do you think this arrangement would work for other types of organizations? Why or why not?

Managers and Communication

Without communication, nothing would ever get done in organizations. Managers are concerned with two types of communication: interpersonal and organizational. We look at both in this chapter and the role they play in a manager's ability to be efficient and effective. After reading and studying this chapter, you will achieve the following learning outcomes.

▶ ▶ ▶ **Tweets. Twittering.** Prior to 2006, the only definition we would have known for these words would have involved birds and the sounds they make. Now, practically everyone knows that Twitter is also an online service—as of early 2012 with 500 million registered users, 340 million tweets daily, and 1.6 billion daily search queries—used to trade short messages of 140 characters or less via the Web, cell phones, and other devices.[1] According to its founders (Evan Williams, Biz Stone,

Kevin Mazur/Getty Images

and Jack Dorsey), Twitter is many things: a messaging service, a customer-service tool to reach customers, real-time search, and microblogging. And as the numbers show, it's become quite popular!

Twitter has caught on in the sports world. The power of instant communication is valuable when it comes to recruiting and keeping fans informed. But an unconsidered tweet can have big consequences. A tweet by a team member can not only affect the player but also affect the sports organization and the draw the ire of the public. We saw how tweeting backfired at the London Olympics. The "casualty"—a Greek triple jumper—was banned from the Games over some racially charged tweets. There seems to be good reason for the managers (i.e., coaches and administrators) to attempt to control the information flow. But those managers setting up rules and regulations need to understand what social media is all about and the value it provides as a marketing and recruiting tool. Is a team player tweeting as a private person or as a representative of a larger group, such as the team, the sports league, or other organization? Rather than banning the use of social media, some organizations hire companies to monitor athletes' posts. This, however, requires athletes to give access to their accounts, which some call an invasion of privacy.

Welcome to the new world of communication! In this "world," managers have to understand both the importance and the drawbacks of communication—all forms of communication. As such, there is no doubt that communication is fundamentally linked to managerial performance.[2] In this chapter, we present basic concepts in managerial communication. We describe the interpersonal communication process, channels for communicating, barriers to effective communication, and ways to overcome those barriers. We also look at organizational communication issues, including communication flow and communication networks. Finally, we discuss several contemporary communication issues facing managers.

Understanding Communication

◉ Watch on MyManagementLab
Communication (TWZ Role Play)

1 Define the nature and function of communication.

If you have not studied communication before, you might think that it's a pretty normal process and that almost anyone can communicate effectively without much thought. So many things can go wrong with communication, though, that it's clear not everyone thinks about how to communicate effectively.

Southwest Airlines suspended a pilot who accidentally broadcast a vulgar criticism that was picked up on an air traffic control frequency and heard by air traffic controllers and other pilots.[3] In the middle of the pilot's profanity-laced rant about the flight attendants on his plane, a Houston air-traffic controller interrupted and said, "Whoever's transmitting, better watch what you're saying." The Federal Aviation Administration sent the audio recording to Southwest, calling it "inappropriate." Southwest suspended the 12-year veteran pilot without pay for an undisclosed amount of time for making comments that were contrary to employee policy and sent him to sensitivity training. This example shows why it's important for managers to understand the impact of communication.

The ability to communicate effectively is a skill that must be mastered by any manager who wants to be effective. It is critical because everything a manager does involves communicating. Not *some* things, but everything! A manager can't make a decision without information. That information has to be communicated. Once a decision is made, communication must again take place. Otherwise, no one would know that a decision was made. The best idea, the most creative suggestion, the best plan, or the most effective job redesign can't take shape without communication.

What Is Communication?

communication The transfer and understanding of meaning.

Communication is the transfer and understanding of meaning. The first thing to note about this definition is the emphasis on the *transfer* of meaning. This means that if no information or ideas have been conveyed, communication has not taken place. The speaker who is not heard or the writer who is not read has not communicated.

More importantly, however, communication involves the *understanding* of meaning. For communication to be successful, the meaning must be conveyed and understood. A letter written in Portuguese addressed to a person who does not read Portuguese cannot be considered communication until it's translated into a language the person does read and understand. Perfect communication, if such a thing existed, would be the receiver's understanding of a transmitted thought or idea exactly as it was intended by the sender.

Another point to keep in mind is that *good* communication is often erroneously defined by the communicator as *agreement* with the message instead of clearly *understanding* the message.[4] If someone disagrees with us, many of us assume that the person just did not fully understand our position. In other words, many of us define good communication as having someone accept our views. But I can clearly understand what you mean and just *not agree* with what you say. In fact, many times, when a conflict has gone on for a long time, people will say it's because the parties are not communicating effectively. That assumption reflects the tendency to think that effective communication equals agreement.

The final point we want to make about communication is that it encompasses both **interpersonal communication**—communication between two or more people—and **organizational communication**—all the patterns, networks, and systems of communication within an organization. Both these types of communication are important to managers in organizations.

Functions of Communication

Irene Lewis, CEO of SAIT Polytechnic, a Calgary, Alberta-based technical institute, was awarded the 2012 Excellence in Communication Leadership (EXCEL) Award by the International Association of Business Communicators. This award recognizes leaders who foster excellence in communication and contribute to the development and support of organizational communication. The selection committee noted Lewis' leadership and commitment to communication and her impact on SAIT's reputation and growth. "She is involved in a wide variety of issues and uses communications wisely to engage relevant stakeholders."[5]

Throughout SAIT Polytechnic and many other organizations, communication serves four major functions: control, motivation, emotional expression, and information.[6] Each function is equally important.

Communication acts to *control* employee behaviour in several ways. As we know from Chapter 10, organizations have authority hierarchies and formal guidelines that employees are required to follow. For instance, when employees are required to communicate any job-related grievance first to their immediate manager, or to follow their job description, or to comply with company policies, communication is being used to control. But informal communication also controls behaviour. When work groups tease or harass a member who is working too hard or producing too much (making the rest of the group look bad), they are informally controlling the member's behaviour.

Communication encourages *motivation* by clarifying to employees what is to be done, how well they are doing, and what can be done to improve performance if it's not up to par. As employees set specific goals, work toward those goals, and receive feedback on their progress, communication is required. Managers motivate more effectively if they show support for the employee by communicating constructive feedback, rather than mere criticism.

For many employees, their work group is a primary source of social interaction. The communication that takes place within the group is a fundamental mechanism by which members share frustrations and feelings of satisfaction. Communication, therefore, provides a release for *emotional expression* of feelings and for fulfillment of social needs.

Finally, individuals and groups need *information* to get things done in organizations. Communication provides that information.

Methods of Interpersonal Communication

▶ ▶ ▶ The use of Twitter and other forms of social media can be a powerful positive communication tool to promote the goals of an organization. However, these forms of social communication can lead to detrimental outcomes for an organization, and many have implemented a code of conduct or other protocol around the use of social media. A recent (2013) study did a benchmark analysis of Fortune's most admired US companies and their use of social media (Facebook, Twitter, and YouTube) in their communications strategy. The study found that out of the 200 companies examined, 91 percent utilized at least one social media platform, with

interpersonal communication
Communication between two or more people.

organizational communication
All the patterns, networks, and systems of communication within an organization.

❷ Compare and contrast methods of interpersonal communication.

Exhibit 11-1

The Interpersonal Communication Process

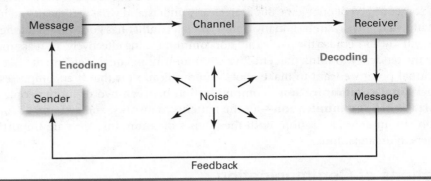

YouTube being the most commonly adopted social media, followed by Twitter, then Facebook. In addition, roughly 30 percent of companies in this study had developed a social media code of conduct in at least one platform.[7]

Think About It

What factors must be considered when determining the most appropriate method of interpersonal communication? Why might it be important to consider which form of interpersonal communication to use within an organization?

message A purpose to be conveyed.

encoding Converting a message into symbols.

channel The medium a message travels along.

decoding A receiver's translation of a sender's message.

interpersonal communication process The seven elements involved in transferring meaning from one person to another.

noise Disturbances that interfere with the transmission, receipt, or feedback of a message.

◄⊙▶ Simulate on MyManagementLab

Business Communications

Before communication can take place, a purpose, expressed as a **message** to be conveyed, must exist. It passes between a source (the sender) and a receiver. The message is converted to symbolic form (called **encoding**) and passed by way of some medium (**channel**) to the receiver, who retranslates the sender's message (called **decoding**). The result is the transfer of meaning from one person to another.[8]

Exhibit 11-1 illustrates the seven elements of the **interpersonal communication process**. In addition, the entire process is susceptible to **noise**—disturbances that interfere with the transmission, receipt, or feedback of a message. Typical examples of noise include illegible print, phone static, inattention by the receiver, and background sounds of machinery or co-workers. However, anything that interferes with understanding can be noise, and noise can create distortion at any point in the communication process.

Channels for Interpersonal Communication Techniques

Managers have a wide variety of communication channels from which to choose. These include face-to-face, telephone, group meetings, formal presentations, memos, postal (snail) mail, fax machines, employee publications, bulletin boards, social media, other company publications, audio files/DVD video, hotlines, email, computer conferences, voice mail, teleconferences, and videoconferences. It is interesting to note that small businesses/start-ups and not-for-profit organizations are using social media to reach a greater audience and to communicate with current and potential customers in ways that were not possible (affordable) previously. All of these communication channels include oral or written symbols, or both. How do you know which to use? Managers can use 12 questions to help them evaluate appropriate communication channels for different circumstances.[9]

1. *Feedback.* How quickly can the receiver respond to the message?

2. *Complexity capacity.* Can the method effectively process complex messages?

3. *Breadth potential.* How many different messages can be transmitted using this method?

4. *Confidentiality.* Can communicators be reasonably sure their messages are received only by those for whom they are intended?

5. *Encoding ease.* Can the sender easily and quickly use this channel?

6. *Decoding ease.* Can the receiver easily and quickly decode messages?

7. *Time–space constraint.* Do senders and receivers need to communicate at the same time and in the same space?

8. *Cost.* How much does it cost to use this method?

9. *Interpersonal warmth.* How well does this method convey interpersonal warmth?

10. *Formality.* Does this method have the appropriate amount of formality?

11. *Scanability.* Does this method allow the message to be easily browsed or scanned for relevant information?

12. *Time of consumption.* Does the sender or receiver exercise the most control over when the message is dealt with?

We cannot leave the topic of interpersonal communication without looking at the role of **nonverbal communication**—that is, communication transmitted without words. Some of the most meaningful communications are neither spoken nor written. A loud siren or a red light at an intersection tells you something without words. When an instructor is teaching a class, she does not need words to tell her that her students are bored when their eyes glaze over or they begin to read the school newspaper in the middle of class. Similarly, when students start putting their papers, notebooks, and books away, the message is clear: Class time is about over. The size of a person's office or the clothes he or she wears also convey messages to others. These are all forms of nonverbal communication. The best-known types of nonverbal communication are body language and verbal intonation.

Body language refers to gestures, facial expressions, and other body movements that convey meaning. A person frowning "says" something different from one who is smiling. Hand motions, facial expressions, and other gestures can communicate emotions or temperaments such as aggression, fear, shyness, arrogance, joy, and anger. Knowing the meaning behind someone's body movements and learning how to put forth your best body language can help you personally and professionally.[10] For instance, studies indicate that those who maintain eye contact while speaking are viewed with more credibility than those whose eye contact wanders. People who make eye contact are also deemed more competent than those who do not.

Be aware that what is communicated nonverbally may be quite different from what is communicated verbally. A manager may say it's a good time to discuss a raise, but then keep looking at the clock. This nonverbal signal may indicate that the manager has other things to do right now. Thus, actions can speak louder (and more accurately) than words.

A variety of popular books have been written to help one interpret body language. However, do use some care when interpreting their messages. For instance, while it is often thought that crossing one's arms in front of one's chest shows resistance to a message, it might also mean the person is feeling cold. Also remember that the meaning of body language can be different from one culture to another, as discussed in Chapter 3.

Verbal intonation (more appropriately called *paralinguistics*) refers to the emphasis someone gives to words or phrases that convey meaning. To illustrate how intonations can change the meaning of a message, consider the student who asks the instructor a question. The instructor replies, "What do you mean by that?" The student's reaction will vary, depending on the tone of the instructor's response. A soft, smooth vocal tone conveys interest and creates a different meaning from one that is abrasive and puts a strong emphasis on saying the last word. Most of us would view the first intonation as coming

nonverbal communication
Communication transmitted without words.

body language Gestures, facial expressions, and other body movements that convey meaning.

verbal intonation An emphasis given to words or phrases that conveys meaning.

Zappos, the quirky Las Vegas-based online shoe retailer (now a part of Amazon.com, which purchased the company for $1.2 billion), has a reputation for being a fun place to work.[11] Much of that is due to its CEO Tony Hsieh, who also understands the power of communication. And one thing that's communicated well and frequently is the company's values. He says that maintaining that corporate culture is "the number one priority." At the company's headquarters, employees use only one entrance and exit to encourage them to "literally run into" each other in the lobby. Hsieh believes that's a way to encourage opportune interactions to share ideas.

Danny Moloshok/Reuters

from someone sincerely interested in clarifying the student's concern, whereas the second suggests that the listener is defensive or aggressive.

Managers need to remember that as they communicate, the nonverbal component usually carries the greatest impact. "It's not *what* you say, but *how* you say it."

Effective Interpersonal Communication

Identify barriers to effective interpersonal communication and ways to overcome them.

▶ ▶ ▶ Written communication such as Twitter or email may not always be the optimal means of communication in cases where employees are separated over distance and are trying to detail ideas for new products, marketing campaigns, or other ideas involving visual cues. A better means of communication for employees communicating over distance may be to establish regular meetings via video conferencing or Skype to convey the true essence of a new product creation or marketing campaign. The ability for a company to recognize potential communication issues and identify appropriate communication solutions can drastically improve organizational culture and working conditions.

> **Think About It**
>
> **What types of barriers might lead to ineffective interpersonal communication? How can organizations or managers overcome these barriers?**

How Distortions Can Happen in Interpersonal Communication

Distortions can happen with the sender, the message, the channel, the choice of channel, the receiver, or the feedback loop. Let's look at each.

Sender

A *sender* initiates a message by *encoding* a thought. Four conditions influence the effectiveness of that encoded message: the skills, attitudes, and knowledge of the sender, and the social-cultural system. How? We will use ourselves, your textbook authors, as an example. If we don't have the required skills, our message won't reach you, the reader, in the form desired. Our success in communicating to you depends on our writing skills. In addition, any pre-existing ideas (attitudes) that we may have about numerous topics will affect how we communicate. For instance, our attitudes about managerial ethics or the importance of managers to organizations influence our writing. Next, the amount of knowledge we have about a subject affects the message(s) we are transferring. We cannot communicate what we don't know, and if our knowledge is too extensive, it's possible that our writing won't be understood by the readers. Finally, the socio-cultural system in which we live influences us as communication senders: Our beliefs and values (all part of culture) act to influence what and how we communicate.

Message

The *message* itself can distort the communication process, regardless of the kinds of supporting tools or technologies used to convey it. A message is the actual physical product encoded by the source. It can be a written document, a speech, or even the gestures and facial expressions we make. The message is affected by the symbols used to transfer meaning (words, pictures, numbers, etc.), the content of the message itself, and the decisions that the sender makes in selecting and arranging both the symbols and the content. Noise can distort the communication process in any of these areas.

Channel

The *channel* chosen to communicate the message also has the potential to be affected by noise. Whether it's a face-to-face conversation, an email message, or a company-wide

Communication channels have multiplied with the spread of new technologies such as Wi-Fi, which provides wireless high-speed internet access. Managers in some companies have saved time and money by switching to Wi-Fi for their internal communications. The devices mean that a manager can talk to customers, suppliers, or even his or her manager without having to hike across the aisles to the store's front-office telephone.

Ariel Skelley/Bland Images/Getty Images

memorandum, distortions can and do occur. Managers need to recognize that certain channels are more appropriate for certain messages. Obviously, if the office is on fire, a memo to convey the fact is inappropriate! And if something is important, such as an employee's performance appraisal, a manager might want to use multiple channels—perhaps an oral review followed by a written letter summarizing the points. This decreases the potential for distortion. In general, the type of channel chosen will affect the extent to which accurate emotional expression can be communicated. For instance, individuals often make stronger negative statements when using email than they would in holding a face-to-face conversation.[12] Additionally, individuals often give little thought to how their emails might be interpreted and assume that their intent will be readily apparent to the recipient, even though this is not always the case.[13]

Receiver

The *receiver* is the individual to whom the message is directed. Before the message can be received, however, the symbols in it must be translated into a form that the receiver can understand. This is the *decoding* of the message. Just as the sender was limited by his or her skills, attitudes, knowledge, and socio-cultural system, so is the receiver. And just as the sender must be skillful in writing or speaking, so the receiver must be skillful in reading or listening. A person's knowledge influences his or her ability to receive. Moreover, the receiver's attitudes and socio-cultural background can distort the message.

Feedback Loop

The final link in the communication process is a *feedback loop*. Feedback returns the message to the sender and provides a check on whether understanding has been achieved. Because feedback can be transmitted along the same types of channels as the original message, it faces the same potential for distortion. Many receivers forget that there is a responsibility involved in communication: to give feedback. For instance, if you sit in a boring lecture, but never discuss with the instructor ways that the delivery could be improved, you have not engaged in communication with your instructor.

When either the sender or the receiver fails to engage in the feedback process, the communication is effectively one-way communication. Two-way communication involves both talking and listening. Many managers communicate badly because they fail to use two-way communication.[14]

Barriers to Effective Interpersonal Communication

In addition to the general distortions identified in the communication process, managers face other barriers to effective communication.

Filtering

Filtering is the deliberate manipulation of information to make it appear more favourable to the receiver. For example, when a person tells his or her manager what the manager wants to hear, that individual is filtering information. Does this happen much in organizations? Yes, it does! As information is communicated up through organizational levels, it's condensed and synthesized by senders so those on top don't become overloaded with information. Those doing the condensing filter communications through their personal interests and their perceptions of what is important.

The extent of filtering tends to be a function of the number of vertical levels in the organization and the organizational culture. The more vertical levels there are in an organization, the more opportunities there are for filtering. As organizations become less dependent on strict hierarchical arrangements and instead use more collaborative, cooperative work arrangements, information filtering may become less of a problem. In addition, the ever-increasing use of email to communicate in organizations reduces filtering because communication is more direct as intermediaries are bypassed. Finally, the organizational culture encourages or discourages filtering by the type of behaviour it rewards. The more that organizational rewards emphasize style and appearance, the more managers will be motivated to filter communications in their favour.

Emotions

How a receiver feels when a message is received influences how he or she interprets it. You will often interpret the same message differently, depending on whether you are happy or upset. Extreme emotions are most likely to hinder effective communication. In such instances, we often disregard our rational and objective thinking processes and substitute emotional judgments. It's best to avoid reacting to a message when you are upset, because you are not likely to be thinking clearly.

Information Overload

A marketing manager goes on a week-long sales trip to Spain and does not have access to his email. On his return, he is faced with 1000 messages. It's not possible to fully read and respond to each and every one of those messages without facing **information overload**—when the information we have to work with exceeds our processing capacity. Today's typical employee frequently complains of information overload. Email has added considerably to the number of hours worked per week, according to a recent study by Christina Cavanagh, professor of management communications at the University of Western Ontario's Richard Ivey School of Business.[15] Researchers calculate that 294 billion email messages circulate the globe each day. In 2001, that number was 5.1 billion email messages.[16] One researcher suggests that knowledge workers devote about 28 percent of their days to email.[17] The demands of keeping up with email, phone calls, faxes, meetings, and professional reading create an onslaught of data that is nearly impossible to process and assimilate. What happens when individuals have more information than they can sort and use? They tend to select out, ignore, pass over, or forget information. Or they may put off further processing until the overload situation is over. Regardless, the result is lost information and less effective communication.

Selective Perception

Individuals don't see reality; rather, they interpret what they see and call it "reality." These interpretations are based on an individual's needs, motivations, experience, background, and other personal characteristics. Individuals also project their interests and expectations when they are listening to others. For example, the employment interviewer who believes that young people spend too much time on leisure and social activities will have a hard time believing that young job applicants will work long hours.

Filtering, or shaping information to make it look good to the receiver, might not always be intentional. For John Seral, vice-president and chief information officer of GE Aviation and GE Energy, the problem was that "when the CEO asked how the quarter was looking, he got a different answer depending on whom he asked." Seral solved the problem by building a continuously updated database of the company's most important financial information that gives not just the CEO but also 300 company managers instant access to sales and operating figures on their PCs and BlackBerrys. Instead of dozens of analysts compiling the information, the new system requires only six.

Ann States

Defensiveness

When people feel that they are being threatened, they tend to react in ways that reduce their ability to achieve mutual understanding. That is, they become defensive—engaging in behaviours such as verbally attacking others, making sarcastic remarks, being overly judgmental, and questioning others' motives.[18] When individuals interpret another's message as threatening, they often respond in ways that hinder effective communication.

Language

Words mean different things to different people. Age, education, and cultural background are three of the more obvious variables that influence the language a person uses and the definitions he or she gives to words. News anchor Peter Mansbridge and rap artist Nelly both speak English, but the language each uses is vastly different.

In an organization, employees typically come from diverse backgrounds and have different patterns of speech. Even employees who work for the same organization but in different departments often have different **jargon**—specialized terminology or technical language that members of a group use to communicate among themselves. Keep in mind that while we may speak the same language, our use of that language is far from uniform. Senders tend to assume that the words and phrases they use mean the same to the receiver as they do to them. This, of course, is incorrect and creates communication barriers. Knowing how each of us modifies the language would help minimize those barriers.

jargon Specialized terminology or technical language that members of a group use to communicate among themselves.

Overcoming Barriers to Communication

On average, an individual must hear new information seven times before he or she truly understands.[19] This might explain why reading your textbook just once may not be enough. In light of this fact and the barriers to communication, what can we do to overcome these barriers? The following suggestions should help make your interpersonal communication more effective.

Use Feedback

Many communication problems can be directly attributed to misunderstanding and inaccuracies. These problems are less likely to occur if individuals use the feedback loop in the communication process, either verbally or nonverbally.

If a speaker asks a receiver, "Did you understand what I said?" the response represents feedback. Good feedback should include more than yes-or-no answers. The speaker can ask a set of questions about a message to determine whether or not the message was received and understood as intended. Better yet, the speaker can ask the receiver to restate the message in his or her own words. If the speaker hears what was intended, understanding and accuracy should improve. Feedback includes subtler methods than directly asking questions or having the receiver summarize the message. General comments can give the speaker a sense of the receiver's reaction to a message. Of course, feedback does not have to be conveyed in words. Actions *can* speak louder than words. A sales manager sends an email to his or her staff describing a new monthly sales report that all sales representatives will need to complete. If some of them don't turn in the new report, the sales manager has received feedback. This feedback might suggest that that sales representatives don't like the new form or don't know how to complete the new form. However, it might also suggest that the sales manager needs to further clarify the initial communication. Similarly, when you are talking to people, you watch their eyes and look for other nonverbal clues to tell whether they are getting your message or not.

Simplify Language

Because language can be a barrier, managers should choose words and structure their messages in ways that will make those messages clear and understandable to the receiver. Remember, effective communication is achieved when a message is both received and *understood*. Understanding is improved by simplifying the language used in relation to the audience intended. This means, for example, that a hospital administrator should always try to communicate in clear, easily understood terms. The language used in messages to the emergency room staff should be purposefully different from that used with office employees. Jargon can facilitate understanding when it's used within a group of those who know what it means, but it can cause many problems when used outside that group.

Listen Actively

Do you know the difference between hearing and listening? When someone talks, we hear. But too often we don't listen. Listening is an active search for meaning, whereas hearing is passive. In listening, two people are engaged in thinking: the sender *and* the receiver.

active listening Listening for full meaning without making premature judgments or interpretations.

    Many of us are poor listeners. Why? Because it's difficult, and it's usually more satisfying to be on the offensive. Listening, in fact, is often more tiring than talking. It demands intellectual effort. Unlike hearing, **active listening**, which is listening for full meaning without making premature judgments or interpretations, demands total concentration. The average person normally speaks at a rate of about 125 to 200 words per minute. However, the average listener can comprehend up to 400 words per minute.[20] The difference obviously leaves lots of idle time for the brain and opportunities for the mind to wander.

    Active listening is enhanced by developing empathy with the sender—that is, by placing yourself in the sender's position. Because senders differ in attitudes, interests, needs, and expectations, empathy makes it easier to understand the actual content of a message. An empathetic listener reserves judgment about the message's content and carefully listens to what is being said. The goal is to improve your ability to receive the full meaning of a communication without having it distorted by premature judgments or interpretations. This involves accurately reflecting back what has been heard and asking "Do I have that right?" Once the answer is yes, the next question needs to be "Is there more?" This loop continues until the sender indicates that the message has been accurately received and that all relevant issues have been covered. Other specific behaviours that active listeners demonstrate are listed in Exhibit 11-2.

Constrain Emotions

It would be naive to assume that managers always communicate in a rational manner. We know that emotions can severely cloud and distort the transference of meaning. A manager who is emotionally upset over an issue is more likely to misconstrue incoming messages and fail to communicate clearly and accurately. What can the manager do? The simplest answer is to refrain from communicating until he or she has regained composure.

Exhibit 11-2

Active Listening Behaviours

Source: Based on J. V. Thill and C. L. Bovée, *Excellence in Business Communication*, 9th ed. (Upper Saddle River, NJ: Prentice Hall, 2011), pp. 48–49; and P. L. Hunsaker, *Training in Management Skills*, 5th ed. (Upper Saddle River, NJ: Prentice Hall, 2009), pp. 90–92.

Watch Nonverbal Cues

If actions speak louder than words, then it's important to watch your actions to make sure they align with and reinforce the words that go along with them. The effective communicator watches his or her nonverbal cues to ensure that they convey the desired message.

Organizational Communication

▶ ▶ ▶ One key feature of Twitter, Facebook, and other social media is the ability to mobilize people and facilitate group action. Nowhere was this more evident than in the use of social media as a means of rapidly communicating information to large groups resulting in the Arab Spring protests and uprisings of 2010. Social media played a large role in widespread messaging, rapidly disseminating news, swaying public opinion, and garnering international support throughout the Arab Spring revolutions. [21] Social media also played a very large role immediately following the Boston Marathon bombings (2013) in mobilizing information and resources to those in need. In this case, social media provided a medium through which the coordination of community support occurred in real time and was organized without the formal coordination by government or professional organization that would have been required otherwise.

These examples provide powerful illustrations of how social media were used to mobilize thousands of people at a moment's notice who were otherwise unknown to each other. These examples also raise question related to how the use of social media platforms might be used within an organization to mobilize and coordinate individuals, communicate a corporate message, facilitate collaboration, and call employees to action.

4 Explain how communication can flow most effectively in organizations.

Think About It

How can organizations utilize social media and other communication platforms to their advantage when trying to implement change, enter into new markets, or grow the size of their market share? What are the features of effective communication within an organization?

Maybe you've had the experience of sitting in an employee meeting with managers when they ask if anyone has any questions—only to be met with deafening silence. Communication can be an interesting thing, especially in organizations. As we've seen, managerial communication is important, but it is a two-way street. We can't understand managerial communication without looking at organizational communication. In this section, we look at several important aspects of organizational communication, including formal versus informal communication, the flow patterns of communication, formal and informal communication networks, and workplace design.

Formal vs. Informal Communication

Communication within an organization is often described as formal or informal.

formal communication
Communication that follows the official chain of command or is part of the communication required to do one's job.

Formal communication refers to communication that follows the official chain of command or is part of the communication required to do one's job. For example, when a manager asks an employee to complete a task, he or she is communicating formally. So is the employee who brings a problem to the attention of his or her manager. Any communication that takes place within prescribed organizational work arrangements would be classified as formal.

informal communication
Communication that is not defined by the organization's structural hierarchy.

Informal communication is communication that is not defined by the organization's structural hierarchy. When employees talk with each other in the lunch room, as they pass in hallways, or as they are working out at the company exercise facility, that is informal communication. Employees form friendships and communicate with each other. The informal communication system fulfills two purposes in organizations: (1) It permits employees to satisfy their need for social interaction, and (2) it can improve an organization's performance by creating alternative, and frequently faster and more efficient, channels of communication.

Direction of Communication Flow

Organizational communication can flow downward, upward, laterally, or diagonally. Let's look at each.

Downward Communication

Every morning, and often several times a day, managers at UPS package delivery facilities gather employees for mandatory meetings that last precisely three minutes. During those 180 seconds, managers relay company announcements and go over local information like traffic conditions or customer complaints. Then, each meeting ends with a safety tip. The three-minute meetings have proved so successful that many of the company's office employees are using the idea.[22]

town hall meeting Informal public meetings whereby information can be relayed, issues can be discussed, or employees can gather to celebrate accomplishments

downward communication
Communication that flows downward from managers to employees.

CEOs at companies such as Starbucks and Apple use **town hall meetings** to communicate with employees. These town hall meetings are informal public meetings where top executives relay information, discuss issues, or bring employees together to celebrate accomplishments. These are examples of **downward communication**, which is communication that flows from a manager to employees. Downward communication is used to inform, direct, coordinate, and evaluate employees. When managers assign goals to their employees, they are using downward communication. Managers are also using downward communication by providing employees with job descriptions, informing them of organizational policies and procedures, pointing out problems that need attention, or evaluating and giving feedback on their performance. Downward communication can take place through any of the communication methods we described earlier.

Upward Communication

upward communication
Communication that flows upward from employees to managers.

Any communication that flows upward from employees to managers is **upward communication**. Managers rely on their employees for information. Reports are given to managers to inform them of progress toward goals and any current problems. Upward communication keeps managers aware of how employees feel about their jobs, their co-workers, and the organization in general. Managers also rely on upward communication for ideas on how things can be improved. Some examples include performance reports prepared by employees, suggestion boxes, employee attitude surveys, grievance procedures, manager–employee discussions, and informal group sessions in which employees have the opportunity to identify and discuss problems with their manager or even representatives of top management.

The extent of upward communication depends on the organizational culture. If managers have created a climate of trust and respect and use participative decision making or empowerment, there will be considerable upward communication as employees provide input to decisions. For instance, Ernst & Young encourages employees to evaluate the principals, partners, and directors on how well they create a positive work climate. A partner in the Montreal office was surprised to learn that people in her office found her a poor role model, and she took care to explain her actions more as a result.[23] In a highly structured and authoritarian environment, upward communication still takes place, but is limited in both style and content.

Lateral Communication

Communication that takes place among employees on the same organizational level is called **lateral communication**. In today's often chaotic and rapidly changing environment, horizontal (lateral) communication is frequently needed to save time and facilitate coordination. Cross-functional teams, for instance, rely heavily on this form of communication. However, it can create conflicts if employees don't keep their managers informed about decisions they have made or actions they have taken.

lateral communication
Communication that takes place among employees on the same organizational level.

Diagonal Communication

Communication that cuts across both work areas *and* organizational levels is **diagonal communication**. When an analyst in the credit department communicates directly with a regional marketing manager—note the different department and different organizational level—about a customer problem, that is diagonal communication. In the interest of efficiency and speed, diagonal communication can be beneficial. Email facilitates diagonal communication. In many organizations, any employee can communicate by email with any other employee, regardless of organizational work area or level. However, just as with lateral communication, diagonal communication has the potential to create problems if employees don't keep their managers informed.

diagonal communication
Communication that cuts across both work areas and organizational levels.

Organizational Communication Networks

The vertical and horizontal flows of organizational communication can be combined into a variety of patterns called **communication networks**. Exhibit 11-3 illustrates three common communication networks.

communication networks The variety of patterns of vertical and horizontal flows of organizational communication.

Types of Communication Networks

In the *chain* network, communication flows according to the formal chain of command, both downward and upward. The *wheel* network represents communication flowing between a clearly identifiable and strong leader and others in a work group or team. The leader serves as the hub through whom all communication passes. Finally, in the *all-channel* network, communication flows freely among all members of a work team.

As a manager, which network should you use? The answer depends on your goal. Exhibit 11-3 also summarizes the effectiveness of the various networks according to four criteria: speed, accuracy, the probability that a leader will emerge, and the importance of member satisfaction. One observation is immediately apparent: No single network is best for all situations. If you are concerned with high member satisfaction, the all-channel network is best; if having a strong and identifiable leader is important, the wheel facilitates this; and if accuracy is most important, the chain and wheel networks work best.

◄●Simulate on **MyManagementLab**

Communication

Exhibit 11-3

Three Common Organizational Communication Networks and How They Rate on Effectiveness Criteria

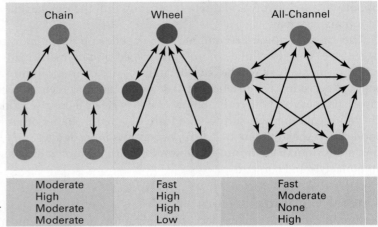

Criteria	Chain	Wheel	All-Channel
Speed	Moderate	Fast	Fast
Accuracy	High	High	Moderate
Emergence of leader	Moderate	High	None
Member satisfaction	Moderate	Low	High

The Grapevine We cannot leave our discussion of communication networks without discussing the **grapevine**—the informal organizational communication network. The grapevine is active in almost every organization. Is it an important source of information? You bet! One survey reported that 75 percent of employees hear about matters first through rumours on the grapevine.[24]

grapevine The informal organizational communication network.

What are the implications for managers? Certainly, the grapevine is an important part of any group or organization communication network and well worth understanding.[25] It identifies for managers those bewildering issues that employees consider important and anxiety producing. It acts as both a filter and a feedback mechanism, picking up on the issues employees consider relevant. More importantly, from a managerial point of view, it *is* possible to analyze what is happening on the grapevine—what information is being passed, how information seems to flow along the grapevine, and what individuals seem to be key conduits of information on the grapevine. By being aware of the grapevine's flow and patterns, managers can stay on top of issues that concern employees, and, in turn, can use the grapevine to disseminate important information. Since the grapevine cannot be eliminated, managers should "manage" it as an important information network.

It looks like graffiti, but it's really informal communication at work. Some companies use whiteboards in common areas to swap product ideas, share information, or simply facilitate social interactions.
© Blend Images/Alamy

Rumours that flow along the grapevine also can never be eliminated entirely. Managers can minimize the negative consequences of rumours by limiting their range and impact. How? By communicating openly, fully, and honestly with employees, particularly in situations where employees may not like proposed or actual managerial decisions or actions. Open and honest communication with employees can impact the organization in various ways.

Workplace Design and Communication

In addition to the direction of communication flow and organizational communication networks, another factor that influences organizational communication is workplace design. Despite all the information technology and associated employee mobility (which we'll discuss in the next section), much of an organization's communication still occurs in the workplace. In fact, some 74 percent of an employee's average workweek is spent in an office.[26] How that office workspace is designed and configured can affect the communication that occurs as well as influence an organization's overall performance. In fact, in a survey of American workers, 90 percent believed that better workplace design and layout result in better overall employee performance.[27]

Research shows that a workplace design should successfully support four types of employee work: focused work, collaboration, learning, and socialization.[28] Focused work happens when an employee needs to concentrate on completing a task. In collaboration, employees need to work together to complete a task. Learning takes place when employees are engaged in training or doing something new and could involve both focused work and collaboration. And socialization happens when employees informally gather to chat or to exchange ideas. A survey found that when workers had these types of "oases" or informal meeting places nearby, they had 102 percent more face-to-face communication than people who had only minimal access to such spots.[29] Because communication can and does take place in each of these settings, the workplace design needs to accommodate these organizational and interpersonal communications—all directions and all types—in order to be most effective.

As managers design the physical work environment, two common design elements have the greatest impact on communication.[30] First, consider the enclosures and barriers used in the workspace. Many organizational workplaces today—some 68 percent—are **open workplaces**; that is, they include few physical barriers and enclosures.[31] Research has shown both the merits and the drawbacks of an open workplace.[32] One of the things we know for sure about this type of arrangement and its effect on communication is *visibility*. People in open cubicles placed along main routes of circulation or adjacent to atria reported almost 60 percent more face-to-face communication with team members

open workplaces Workplaces with few physical barriers and enclosures

Skype's business goal is to break down the barriers to communication by developing technology that is inventive, dependable, easy to use, and affordable. In support of this goal, open workplace designs at Skype's offices throughout the world provide a comfortable and relaxed environment that encourages concentration, productivity, and creativity and in which employees can easily communicate and collaborate with each other. Skype's core development team of engineers and designers work from offices in Tallinn, Estonia, shown here, where informal spaces support focused work, collaboration, learning, and socialization.

AMRUTH/CARO FOTOS/SIPA/Newscom

than did those in lower-visibility locations. Another thing is *density*. More people populating an immediate work area meant that more face-to-face interactions took place. Workspaces with a high density yielded 84 percent more team-member communication than did workspace arrangements with a low density. If it's important that employees communicate and collaborate, managers need to consider visibility and density in workplace design. Another consideration in any open workplace is making sure to have some area where sensitive discussions can take place when needed. For instance, when private personnel matters need to be addressed, those shouldn't take place where interruptions or "eavesdropping" can occur.

As companies shrink workspaces to save money, managers need to ensure that the smaller and generally more open workspaces are useful and contribute to efficient and effective work.[33] By providing workspaces where employees can have some privacy and still have opportunities for collaborative efforts, both interpersonal and organizational communication can flourish and contribute to the organization's overall performance.

Information Technology and Communication

5 Describe how technology affects managerial communication.

▶ ▶ ▶ Technology has radically changed the way organizational members communicate. For example, it has significantly improved a manager's ability to monitor individual and team performance, has allowed employees to have more complete information to make faster and better decisions, and has provided employees more opportunities to collaborate and share information. In addition, technology has made it possible for people in organizations to be fully accessible, any time, regardless of where they are. Employees don't have to be at their desks with their computers running to communicate with others in the organization. Two technology developments that are most significant for managerial communication are networked systems and wireless capabilities.

More recently, Twitter, Facebook, YouTube, LinkedIn, blogs, and Wiki have all became popular tools for corporations to market products and services, and social media is seen as a powerful medium, largely due to the speed at which information travels in the social media arena. Crowd-sourced communities allow instant sharing of information among people with related interests. Customers, competitors, and employees can find, access, and share information at a rapid pace.

> ### Think About It
> **What are the benefits to employers of using technology to monitor employees? Should employers consider social media postings by their employees as just private musings and ignore them? Are there advantages to organizations in allowing employees to use social networking sites? If yes, do they outweigh the disadvantages?**

Technology is changing the way we live and work. Take the following four examples: Chefs are using digital approaches to solve a kitchen crisis—recipe clutter. Japanese employees, managers, housewives, and teens use wireless interactive webphones to send email, surf the web, swap photos, and play computer games. At DreamWorks Animation, a sophisticated videoconferencing system allows animators in three different locations to collaboratively edit films. Several thousand employees at Ford use cell phones exclusively at work. A recent survey of employees showed that 93 percent of those polled use the internet at work. Employees at Lockheed Martin Corporation can access an internal social media site called Unity, which includes tools such as blogs, wikis, file-sharing, discussion forums, and social bookmarking.[34]

The world of communication isn't what it used to be! Although changing technology has been a significant source of the environmental uncertainty facing organizations, these same technological changes have enabled managers to coordinate employees' work efforts in more efficient and effective ways. Information technology (IT) now touches every aspect of almost every company's business. The implications for the ways managers communicate are profound.

MANAGEMENT REFLECTION

Office of Tomorrow

How is communication likely to change in the office of tomorrow? The office of tomorrow is still likely to resemble the office of today. There probably won't be mail delivery by robots on hovercraft nor any teleportation devices. Most of the changes, however, will likely be in the way we communicate.[35] Employees will rely on multiple channels of communication with heavy reliance on social networks, text messaging, and instant messaging. Software will be able to track where employees are and blend that data with information about current projects and suggest potential collaborators. Email is likely to decline in popularity, largely because other channels are faster, more fluid, and more immediate.

Accurately forecasting tomorrow's technology is impossible. But several patterns seem to be evolving. For instance, combining functions in a single device is likely to result in employees having a single product that will combine phone, text messaging, internet access, video camera, teleconferencing, and language translator. It will allow people to read proposals, legal papers, news, or almost any document digitally. It won't need a keyboard and will operate via voice commands. It's also likely not to be hand-held but rather something akin to combining reading glasses and an earpiece. You'll read documents through the lenses of what look like normal reading glasses, and the earpiece/microphone will make it hands-free.

Another outcome made possible by technology will be a significant decrease in business travel. Improvements in computer-mediated groupware will allow individuals to conduct meetings in environments that closely simulate face-to-face interactions. In settings where employees use different languages, real-time translations will be transcribed and displayed on screen and teleconferencers will be able to hear and see the words. ■

Wireless Capabilities At Seattle-based Starbucks Corporation, district managers use mobile technology, giving them more time to spend in the company's stores. A company executive says, "These are the most important people in the company. Each has between 8 to 10 stores that he or she services. And while their primary job is outside of the office—and in those stores—they still need to be connected."[36] With more than 50 million "mobile" workers in the United States, smartphones, notebook computers, computing devices such as iPad, and other pocket communication devices have generated whole new ways for managers to "keep in touch." And the number of mobile communication users keeps increasing.[37] As wireless technology continues to improve, we'll see more organizational members using it as a way to collaborate and share information.

How Information Technology Affects Organizations

Employees—working in teams or as individuals—need information to make decisions and do their work. After describing the communications capabilities managers have at their disposal, it's clear that technology *can* significantly affect the way that organizational members communicate, share information, and do their work. The following *Management Reflection* explores how one company reduced cost and improved service for customers using Voice over Internet Protocol (VoIP) technology.

MANAGEMENT REFLECTION

The Power of Technology in Communication

How can technology be used to communicate a compelling message at work? Monsanto Company wanted to raise the visibility of some projects and to make a stronger argument for bioengineered crops. Using a YouTube approach, the company sent camera crews to the Philippines, Australia, and other countries to film testimonials from farmers using Monsanto products to grow these crops. The clips were posted on a company website, which now attracts more than 15 000 visitors a month. The PR manager in charge of the project said, "When the people involved relate how their life has changed and you actually see it, it's more compelling."[38] That's the power of IT at work. Employees—working in teams or as individuals—need information to make decisions and to do their work. It's clear that technology significantly affects the way that organizational members communicate, share information, and do their work. ■

Communication and the exchange of information among organizational members are not constrained by geography or time. Collaborative work efforts among widely dispersed individuals and teams, information sharing, and the integration of decisions and work throughout an entire organization have the potential to increase organizational efficiency and effectiveness. While the economic benefits of information technology are obvious, managers must not forget to address the psychological drawbacks.[39] For instance, what is the psychological cost of an employee always being accessible? Is there increased pressure for employees to "check in" even during their off hours? How important is it for employees to separate their work lives and their personal lives? While there are no easy answers to these questions, these are issues that managers have to face.

IT technology has affected the communication and exchange of information among doctors, medical staff, and patients by removing the constraints of geography and time. Shown here is Dr. Nir Cohen working on his Apple iPad before visiting a patient at the Mayanei Hayeshua Medical Center in Bnei Brak, Israel. Using iPads enables Dr. Cohen and his medical staff to check patients' records, test results, and other medical information; to study high-resolution X-rays and CT scans from both within and outside the hospital; and to diagnose and prescribe treatment immediately at any time.

Nir Elias/Reuters

Privacy Issues

The widespread use of voice mail and email at work has led to some ethical concerns as well. These forms of communication are not necessarily private, because employers have access to them. The federal Privacy Act (which protects the privacy of individuals and provides individuals with a right to access personal information about themselves) and the Access to Information Act (which allows individuals to access government information) apply to all federal government departments, most federal agencies, and some federal Crown corporations. However, many private sector employees are not covered by privacy legislation, as not all provinces have enacted legislation that protects private sector employees.[40] Managers need to clearly convey to employees the extent to which their communications will be monitored, and policies on such things as personal internet and email use.

Managers need to ensure that their organizations conform to the Personal Information Protection and Electronic Documents Act (PIPEDA), which balances an individual's right to privacy with the need of organizations to collect, use, or disclose personal information for legitimate business purposes. Unlike the Privacy Act, PIPEDA applies to the Canadian private sector. Part one of the act outlines the ground rules for managing personal information, while parts two through five concern the use of electronic documents and signatures as legal alternatives to original documents and signatures.[41] In addition to PIPEDA, the federal government passed a law governing the use of internet "spam," and requires customers to give consent before organizations can send solicitations to their electronic devices.[42]

Communication Issues in Today's Organizations

▶ ▶ ▶ Communications technologies are used for enterprise communications and management strategies and help companies and government agencies successfully implement major business changes or programs. EllisDon—a Canadian global construction services company founded in London, Ontario, by Don Smith and David Ellis in 1951—uses social media channels to build a strong sense of employee cohesiveness within the company. The company is 50 percent owned by its employees and has taken employee branding advocacy to the next level with the use of social media platforms.

⑤ Discuss contemporary issues in communication.

President and CEO Geoff Smith's blog boasts the largest Twitter following in the construction industry. He uses his blog to explain the deliberate decision-making that has created a thriving social media presence and create brand advocacy among EllisDon employees. Smith's objective is to educate employees to both understand the brand identity and embrace it, providing employees with a message they can stand behind. To achieve this, EllisDon has created forward-thinking projects like their Social Media Master class series and branding advocacy programs such as EllisDon University.

> ## Think About It
>
> **What are the main challenges of managing communication in an internet world? How can organizations manage knowledge? How can organizations make it easy for employees to communicate and share their knowledge? What are the benefits of enabling employees to share their knowledge with each other within an organization? Why is it important to get input from employees within an organization?**

Being an effective communicator in today's organizations means being connected—not only to employees and customers, but to any of the organization's stakeholders. In this section, we examine five communication issues of particular significance to today's managers: managing communication in an internet world, managing the organization's knowledge resources, communicating with customers, getting employee input, and communicating ethically.

Managing Communication in an Internet World

Lars Dalgaard, founder and chief executive of SuccessFactors, a human resource management software company, recently sent an email to his employees banning in-house email for a week. His goal? Getting employees to "authentically address issues amongst each other."[43] And he's not alone. Other companies have tried the same thing. (See Case Application 1 at the end of the chapter.) As we discussed earlier, email can consume employees, but it's not always easy for them to let go of it, even when they know it can be "intexticating." But email is only one communication challenge in this internet world. A recent survey found that 20 percent of employees at large companies say they contribute regularly to blogs, social networks, wikis, and other web services.[44]

Legal and Security Issues

Chevron paid $2.2 million to settle a sexual-harassment lawsuit stemming from inappropriate jokes being sent by employees over company email. U.K. firm Norwich Union had to pay £450 000 in an out-of-court settlement after an employee sent an email stating that their competitor, Western Provident Association, was experiencing financial difficulties. Whole Foods Market was investigated by federal regulators and its board after CEO John P. Mackey used a pseudonym to post comments on a blog attacking the company's rival, Wild Oats Markets.[45]

Although email, blogs, tweets, and other forms of online communication are quick and easy ways to communicate, managers need to be aware of potential legal problems from inappropriate usage. Electronic information is potentially admissible in court. For instance, during the Enron trial, prosecutors entered into evidence emails and other documents they say showed that the defendants defrauded investors. Says one expert, "Today, email and instant messaging are the electronic equivalent of DNA evidence."[46] But legal problems aren't the only issue—security concerns are as well.

A survey addressing outbound email and content security found that 26 percent of the companies surveyed saw their businesses affected by the exposure of sensitive or embarrassing information.[47] Managers need to ensure that confidential information is kept confidential. Employee emails and blogs should not communicate—inadvertently or purposely—proprietary information. Corporate computer and email systems should be protected against hackers (people who try to gain unauthorized access) and spam (electronic junk mail). These serious issues must be addressed if the benefits of communication technology are to be realized.

◉ Watch on **MyManagementLab**

MINI: Working in a Virtual World

Personal Interaction

It may be called social media, but another communication challenge posed by the internet age we live and work in is the lack of personal interaction.[48] Even when two people are communicating face to face, understanding is not always achieved. It can be especially challenging to achieve understanding and collaborate on getting work done when communication takes place in a virtual environment. In response, some companies have banned email on certain days, as we saw earlier. Others have simply encouraged employees to collaborate more in person. Yet, in some situations and at certain times, personal interaction isn't physically possible—your colleagues work across the continent or even across the globe. In those instances, real-time collaboration software (such as private workplace wikis, blogs, instant messengers, and other types of groupware) may be a better communication choice than sending an email and waiting for a response.[49] Instead of fighting it, other companies are encouraging employees to utilize the power of social networks to collaborate on work and to build strong connections. This form of interaction is especially appealing to younger workers, who are comfortable with this communication medium. Some companies created their own in-house social networks. For instance, employees at Starcom MediaVest Group tap into SMG Connected to find colleague profiles that outline their jobs, list the brands they admire, and describe their values. A company vice president says, "Giving our employees a way to connect over the internet around the world made sense because they were doing it anyway."[50]

Managing the Organization's Knowledge Resources

Kara Johnson is a materials expert at product design firm IDEO. To make finding the right materials easier, she built a master library of samples linked to a database that explains their properties and manufacturing processes.[51] What Johnson did was manage knowledge and make it easier for others at IDEO to "learn" and benefit from her knowledge. That is what today's managers need to do with the organization's knowledge resources—make it easy for employees to communicate and share their knowledge so they can learn from each other ways to do their jobs more effectively and efficiently. One way organizations can do this is to create online information databases that employees can access. This is one example of how managers can use communication tools to manage this valuable organizational resource called knowledge.

In addition to online information databases for sharing knowledge, some knowledge management experts suggest that organizations create **communities of practice**, which are "groups of people who share a concern, a set of problems, or a passion about a topic, and who deepen their knowledge and expertise in that area by interacting on an ongoing basis."[52] The keys to this concept are that the group must actually meet in some fashion on a regular basis and use its information exchanges to improve in some way. For example, repair technicians at Xerox tell "war stories" to communicate their experiences and to help others solve difficult problems with repairing machines.[53] This is not to say that communities of practice don't face challenges. They do. For instance, in large global organizations, keeping communities of practice going takes additional effort. To make these communities of practice

communities of practice Groups of people who share a concern, a set of problems, or a passion about a topic, and who deepen their knowledge and expertise in that area by interacting on an ongoing basis.

work, it's important to maintain strong human interactions through communication. Interactive websites, email, and videoconferencing are essential communication tools. In addition, these groups face the same communication problems that individuals face—filtering, emotions, defensiveness, information overload, and so forth. However, groups can resolve these issues by focusing on the same suggestions we discussed earlier: using feedback, simplifying language, listening actively, constraining emotions, and watching nonverbal cues.

The Role of Communication in Customer Service

You have been a customer many times; in fact, you probably find yourself in a customer service encounter several times a day. So what does this have to do with communication? As it turns out, a lot! *What* communication takes place and *how* it takes place can have a significant impact on a customer's satisfaction with the service and the likelihood of being a repeat customer. Managers in service organizations need to make sure that employees who interact with customers are communicating appropriately and effectively with those customers. How? By first recognizing the three components in any service delivery process: the customer, the service organization, and the individual service provider.[55] Each plays a role in whether or not communication is working. Obviously, managers don't have a lot of control over what or how the customer communicates, but they can influence the other two.

An organization with a strong service culture already values taking care of customers—finding out what their needs are, meeting those needs, and following up to make sure that their needs were met satisfactorily. Each of these activities involves communication, whether face to face, by phone, email, or through other channels. In addition, communication is part of the specific customer service strategies the organization pursues. One strategy that many service organizations use is personalization. For instance, at Ritz-Carlton Hotels, customers are provided with more than a clean bed and room. Customers who have stayed at a location previously and indicated that certain items are important to them—such as extra pillows, hot chocolate, or a certain brand of shampoo—will find those items waiting in their room at arrival. The hotel's database allows service to be personalized to customers' expectations. In addition, all employees are asked to communicate information related to service provision. For instance, if a room attendant overhears guests talking about celebrating an anniversary, he or she is supposed to relay the information so something special can be done.[56] Communication plays an important role in the hotel's customer personalization strategy.

Communication also is important to the individual service provider or contact employee. The quality of the interpersonal interaction between the customer and that contact employee does influence customer satisfaction.[57] That is especially true when the service encounter is not up to expectations. People on the front line involved with those "critical service encounters" are often the first to hear about or notice service failures or breakdowns. They must decide *how* and *what* to communicate during these instances. Their ability to listen actively and communicate appropriately with the customer goes a long way in whether or not the situation is resolved to the customer's satisfaction or spirals out of control. Another important communication concern for the individual service provider is making sure that he or she has the information needed to deal with customers efficiently and effectively. If the service provider does not personally have the information, there should be some way to get the information easily and promptly.[58]

Getting Employee Input

Nokia recently set up an intranet soapbox known as Blog-Hub, opening it up to employee bloggers around the world. There, employees have griped about their employer, but rather than shutting it down, Nokia managers want them to "fire away." They feel that Nokia's growth and success can be attributed to a "history of encouraging employees to say whatever's on their minds, with faith that smarter ideas will result."[59]

In today's challenging environment, companies need to get input from their employees. Have you ever worked somewhere that had an employee suggestion box? When an employee had an idea about a new way of doing something—such as reducing costs, improving delivery time, and so forth—it went into the suggestion box where it usually sat until someone

datapoints[54]

53 percent of companies have a policy for managing employees' use of social media.

176 square feet is now the average office space per worker. In 2010, it was 225 square feet; in 2017, it's forecasted to be 151 square feet.

70 percent of executives ranked in-person meetings as most valuable for an initial interaction with a new team member.

83 percent of employers use email to engage employees and foster productivity; 75 percent use their organization's intranet to do so.

45 percent of North American workers use their mobile devices during lunch; 44 percent use it before going to work.

38 percent of employees have a negative view of workers with a messy desk.

15 percent of employees say that if there were no consequences, they'd say to their boss that they need a chance to express their ideas.

28 percent of survey respondents said that phone calls were the most common workplace distraction; 23 percent cited emails.

1 of every 7 communications by managers is redundant with a previous communication using a different technology.

No. 1 form of evidence in any employment law dispute is . . . email.

44 percent of the time, emails are misinterpreted.

The opinions and ideas of employees are valued by sisters Jenny Briones (left) and Lisa De Bono (right), who, along with their mother, are owner-operators of nine McDonald's restaurants. Communication plays a big part in the growth and success of the family business. Jenny and Lisa engender trust and respect among their managers, employees, and customers by frequently visiting restaurants and encouraging everyone to voice their opinions and share information that will improve their business. In this photo, they seek out feedback from one of their managers about a new incentive plan for their restaurant crew members.

H. Lorren Au Jr./ZUMApress/Newscom

ethical communication
Communication that includes all relevant information, is true in every sense, and is not deceptive in any way

decided to empty the box. Businesspeople frequently joked about the suggestion box, and cartoonists lambasted the futility of putting ideas in the employee suggestion box. And unfortunately, this attitude about suggestion boxes still persists in many organizations, and it shouldn't. Managers do business in a world today where you can't afford to ignore such potentially valuable information. Exhibit 11-4 lists some suggestions for letting employees know that their opinions matter.

Communicating Ethically

It's particularly important today that a company's communication efforts be ethical. **Ethical communication** "includes all relevant information, is true in every sense, and is not deceptive in any way."[60] On the other hand, unethical communication often distorts the truth or manipulates audiences. What are some ways that companies communicate unethically? It could be by omitting essential information. For instance, not telling employees that an impending merger is going to mean some of them will lose their jobs is unethical. It's unethical to plagiarize, which is "presenting someone else's words or other creative product as your own."[61] It would also be unethical communication to selectively misquote, misrepresent numbers, distort visuals, and fail to respect privacy or information security needs. For instance, although British Petroleum attempted to communicate openly and truthfully about the Gulf Coast oil spill in the summer of 2010, the public still felt that much of the company's communication contained some unethical elements.

So how can managers encourage ethical communications? One thing is to "establish clear guidelines for ethical behavior, including ethical business communication."[62] In a global survey by the International Association of Business Communicators, 70 percent of communication professionals said their companies clearly define what is considered ethical and unethical behavior."[63] If no clear guidelines exist, it's important to answer the following questions:

- Has the situation been defined fairly and accurately?

- Why is the message being communicated?

- How will the people who may be affected by the message or who receive the message be impacted?

- Does the message help achieve the greatest possible good while minimizing possible harm?

- Will this decision that appears to be ethical now seem so in the future?

- How comfortable are you with your communication effort? What would a person you admire think of it?[64]

Remember that as a manager, you have a responsibility to think through your communication choices and the consequences of those choices. If you always operate with these two things in mind, you're likely to have ethical communication.

Exhibit 11-4

How to Let Employees Know Their Input Matters

- *Hold town-hall meetings* where information is shared and input solicited.

- *Provide information* about what's going on, good and bad.

- *Invest in training* so that employees see how they impact the customer experience.

- *Analyze problems together*—managers and employees.

- *Make it easy* for employees to give input by setting up different ways for them to do so (online, suggestion box, preprinted cards, and so forth).

CHAPTER 11

SUMMARY AND IMPLICATIONS

1. Define the nature and function of communication. Communication is the transfer and understanding of meaning. Interpersonal communication is communication between two or more people. Organizational communication includes all the patterns, networks, and systems of communication within an organization.

The functions of communication include controlling employee behaviour, motivating employees, providing a release for emotional expression of feelings, fulfillment of social needs, and providing information.

▶ ▶ ▶ Twitter and other forms of social media have changed the way we communicate. In the past, individuals and organizations had a set of contacts, all of whom we reached through telephone, mail, or e-mail. Today we have many sources of communication, each with a different purpose and set of norms and etiquette.

2. Compare and contrast methods of interpersonal communication. There are seven elements in the communication process. First there is a *sender*, who has a message for a *receiver*. A *message* is a purpose to be conveyed. *Encoding* is converting a message into symbols. A *channel* is the medium a message travels along. *Decoding* occurs when the receiver retranslates a sender's message. Finally, there should be *feedback*. Managers can evaluate the various communication methods according to their feedback, complexity capacity, breadth potential, confidentiality, encoding ease, decoding ease, time–space constraint, cost, interpersonal warmth, formality, scannability, and time of consumption. Communication methods include face-to-face communication, telephone communication, group meetings, formal presentations, memos, traditional mail, faxes, employee publications, bulletin boards, other company publications, audio- and videotapes, social media, hotlines, email, computer conference, voicemail, teleconferences, and videoconferences.

▶ ▶ ▶ When we understand the role of Twitter and other forms of social media and how these can be used as effective means of communication, they can help individuals and organizations more effectively engage with employees, consumers, colleagues, and the public.

3. Identify barriers to effective interpersonal communication and ways to overcome them. When a message passes between a sender and a receiver, it needs to be converted into symbols (called *encoding*) and passed to the receiver by some channel. The receiver translates (*decodes*) the sender's message. At any point in this process, communication can become distorted through noise. A variety of other factors also affect whether the message is interpreted correctly, including the degree of filtering, the sender's or receiver's emotional state, and whether too much information is being sent (information overload).

▶ ▶ ▶ Social media networks were originally created to help friends and family interact easily over distance, and they have become one of the most significant communication tools of the day. However, these networks are not appropriate for all types of communication and do not always replace face-to-face conversation.

4. Explain how communication can flow most effectively in organizations. Communication can be formal or informal. Formal communication follows the official chain of command or is part of the communication required to do one's job. Informal communication is not defined by the organization's structural hierarchy. Communication can flow downward, upward, laterally to those at the same organizational level, or diagonally, which means that the communication cuts across both work areas and organizational levels. Communication can also flow through networks and through the grapevine. The three types of communication networks are the chain, in which communication flows according to the formal chain of command; the wheel, in which communication flows between a clearly identifiable, strong leader and others in a work team; and the all-channel, in which communication flows freely among all members of a work team. Managers should manage the grapevine as an important information network. They can minimize the negative consequences of rumours by communicating with employees openly, fully, and honestly.

▶ ▶ ▶ Twitter and other forms of social media are used by EllisDon to build a strong sense of employee cohesiveness within the company.

5. Describe how technology affects managerial communication. Technology has radically changed the way organizational members communicate. It improves a manager's ability to monitor performance; it gives employees more complete information to make faster decisions; it has provided employees more opportunities to collaborate and share information; and it has made it possible for people to be fully accessible, anytime anywhere. IT affects organizations by influencing the way that organizational members communicate, share information, and do their work.

▶ ▶ ▶ Twitter and other forms of social media are used by companies such as EllisDon to educate employees to understand the company brand identity and provide employees with a message they can stand behind.

6. Discuss contemporary issues in communication. The two main challenges of managing communication in an internet world are the legal and security issues and the lack of personal interaction. Organizations can manage knowledge by making it easy for employees to communicate and share their knowledge, which can help them learn from each other ways to do their jobs more effectively and efficiently. One way is through online information databases, and another way is through creating communities of practice. Communicating with customers is an important managerial issue since *what* communication takes place and *how* it takes place can significantly affect a customer's satisfaction with the service and the likelihood of being a repeat customer. It's important for organizations to get input from their employees. Such potentially valuable information should not be ignored. Finally, a company's communication efforts need to be ethical. Ethical communication can be encouraged through clear guidelines and through answering questions that force a communicator to think through the communication choices made and the consequences of those choices.

▶ ▶ ▶ Rather than banning the use of social media, organizations can promote the use of social media by employees as a powerful marketing tool and to reinforce the organizational brand.

MyManagementLab Study, practise, and explore real management situations with these helpful resources:

- **Interactive Lesson Presentations:** Work through interactive presentations and assessments to test your knowledge of management concepts.
- **PIA (Personal Inventory Assessments):** Enhance your ability to connect with key concepts through these engaging, self-reflection assessments.
- **Study Plan:** Check your understanding of chapter concepts with self-study quizzes.
- **Simulations:** Practise decision-making in simulated management environments.

P I A PERSONAL INVENTORY ASSESSMENT

REVIEW AND DISCUSSION QUESTIONS

1. Define communication, interpersonal communication, and organizational communication. Why isn't effective communication synonymous with *agreement*?

2. What are the functions of communication?

3. Explain the components in the communication process.

4. What are the various communication methods managers can use? What criteria can managers use to evaluate those communication methods?

5. Contrast formal and informal communication.

6. Explain communication flow, the three common communication networks, and how managers should handle the grapevine.

7. Discuss the five contemporary communication issues facing managers.

8. Which do you think is more important for a manager: speaking accurately or listening actively? Why?

9. What can managers do to help them determine which communication channel to use in a given circumstance?

10. What are the two main challenges of communicating in the wired world?

11. Describe why effective communication is not synonymous with agreement between the communicating parties.

12. Which do you think is more important for a manager: speaking accurately or listening actively? Why?

13. "Ineffective communication is the fault of the sender." Do you agree or disagree with this statement? Explain your position.

14. How might a manager use the grapevine to his or her advantage? Support your response.

15. Is information technology helping managers to be more effective and efficient? Explain your position.

ETHICS DILEMMA

Social networking websites can be fun. Staying in touch with old friends or even family is one of the pleasures of joining. However, what happens when colleagues or even your boss want to "friend" you? Experts say that you should proceed with caution.[65]

What do you think? Is it okay to provide people you know in a professional sense a "window into your personal life?" What ethical issues might arise in such a situation? Have you had an instance where things did not go as you thought they would?

SKILLS EXERCISE

Developing Your Active Listening Skill—About the Skill

Active listening requires you to concentrate on what is being said. It's more than just hearing the words. It involves a concerted effort to understand and interpret the speaker's message.

Steps in Practising the Skill

1. *Make eye contact.* How do you feel when somebody doesn't look at you when you're speaking? If you're like most people, you're likely to interpret this behaviour as aloofness or disinterest. Making eye contact with the speaker focuses your attention, reduces the likelihood that you will become distracted, and encourages the speaker.

2. *Exhibit affirmative nods and appropriate facial expressions.* The effective listener shows interest in what is being said through nonverbal signals. Affirmative nods and appropriate facial expressions, when added to good eye contact, convey to the speaker that you're listening.

3. *Avoid distracting actions or gestures that suggest boredom.* In addition to showing interest, you must avoid actions that suggest that your mind is somewhere else. When listening, don't look at your watch, shuffle papers, play with your pencil, or engage in similar distractions. They make the speaker feel that you're bored or disinterested or indicate that you aren't fully attentive.

4. *Ask questions.* The critical listener analyzes what he or she hears and asks questions. This behaviour provides clarification, ensures understanding, and assures the speaker that you're listening.

5. *Paraphrase what's been said.* The effective listener uses phrases such as "What I hear you saying is . . ." or "Do you mean . . . ?" Paraphrasing is an excellent control device to check on whether you're listening carefully and to verify that what you heard is accurate.

6. *Avoid interrupting the speaker.* Let the speaker complete his or her thought before you try to respond. Don't try to

second-guess where the speaker's thoughts are going. When the speaker is finished, you'll know it.

7. *Stay motivated to listen.* Most of us would rather express our own ideas than listen to what someone else says. Talking might be more fun and silence might be uncomfortable, but you can't talk and listen at the same time. The good listener recognizes this fact and doesn't overtalk.

8. *Make smooth transitions between the roles of speaker and listener.* The effective listener makes transitions smoothly from speaker to listener and back to speaker. From a listening perspective, this means concentrating on what a speaker has to say and practising not thinking about what you're going to say as soon as you get your chance.

Practising the Skill

Ask a friend to tell you about his or her day, and listen without interrupting. When your friend has finished speaking, ask two or three questions if needed to obtain more clarity and detail. Listen carefully to the answers. Now summarize your friend's day in no more than five sentences.

How well did you do? Let your friend rate the accuracy of your paraphrase (and try not to interrupt).

WORKING TOGETHER: TEAM EXERCISE

YouTube: The New Frontier.

We've all watched and laughed at the oddball videos on YouTube and other online video sites. But what about using online video for work purposes?[66] What uses do you see for online video at work? What would be the advantages and drawbacks of using online video?

Form small groups of three to four individuals. Your team's task is to consider these issues. Be prepared to share your answers with the class.

LEARNING TO BE A MANAGER

- Research the characteristics of a good communicator. Keeping these characteristics in mind, practise being a good communicator—both as a sender and a listener.
- For one day, track nonverbal communication that you notice in others. What types did you observe? Was the nonverbal communication always consistent with the verbal communication taking place? Describe.
- Research new types of IT devices. Write a report describing these devices (at least three) and their applicability to employees and organizations. Be sure to look at both the positive and negative aspects.
- Survey five different managers for their advice on being a good communicator. Put this information in a bulleted list format and be prepared to present it in class.

- Survey 10 office workers. Ask them (1) the number of email messages they receive daily, on average, (2) how many times in one day they check their email, and (3) if they think a ban on email messages one day a week would be a good idea and why or why not. Compile this information into a report.
- Pick one of the five topics addressed in the section on Communication Issues in Today's Organizations and do some additional research. Put your findings in a bulleted list, and be prepared to discuss in class. Be sure to cite your sources!

CASE APPLICATION 1

Email Ban

Believing that most internal email messages are a waste of employees' time, and wanting to work with more current tools, Atos CEO Thierry Breton has banned internal emails and is replacing them with communication tools that include social networks like Facebook, instant messaging, and microblogging.

It's estimated that the average corporate user sends and receives some 112 emails daily.[67] That's about 14 emails per hour; even if half of those don't require a lot of time and concentration, that level of email volume can be stressful and lead to unproductive time. Once imagined to be a time-saver, has the inbox become a burden? Back in 2007, U.S. Cellular's executive vice president, Jay Ellison (who has since retired) implemented a ban on email every Friday. In his memo announcing the change to employees, he told them to get out and meet the people they work with rather than send an email. That directive went over with a thud. One employee confronted him saying that Ellison didn't understand how much work had to get done and how much easier it was when using email. Eventually, however, employees were won over. Forced to use the phone, one employee learned that a co-worker he thought was across the country was, instead, across the hall. Other executives are also discovering the benefits of banning email.

Jessica Rovello, co-founder and president of Arkadium, which develops games, has described email as "a form of business attention-deficit disorder." She found herself—and her employees—putting email in the inbox ahead of everything else being worked on. What she decided to do was check her email only four times a day and turn off her email notification. Another executive, Tim Fry of Weber Shandwick, a global public relations firm, spent a year preparing to "wean" his employees off their email system. His goal: dramatically reduce how much email employees send and receive. His approach started with the firm's interoffice communication system, which became an internal social network, with

elements of Facebook, work group collaboration software, and an employee bulletin board. And then there's Thierry Breton, head of Europe's largest IT firm, Atos. He announced a "zero email policy" to be replaced with a service more like Facebook and Twitter combined.

DISCUSSION QUESTIONS

1. What do you think of this? Do you agree that email can be unproductive in the workplace?
2. Were you surprised at the volume of email an average employee receives daily? What are the challenges of dealing with this volume of email? How much email would you say you receive daily? Has your volume of email increased? Have your had to change your email habits?
3. What do you think of the email "replacement" some businesses are using—social media tools? In what ways might they be better? Worse?
4. What implications can you see for managers and communication from this story?

CASE APPLICATION 2

Prank Goes Viral

When two Domino's Pizza employees filmed a gross prank in the kitchen of the restaurant in Conover, North Carolina, the company suddenly had a major public relations crisis on its hands.[68] The video ended up posted on YouTube and other sites and showed a Domino's employee performing unsanitary and vulgar actions while preparing food, with another employee providing narration. By the next day, over a million disgusted people had viewed the video and discussion about Domino's had spread throughout Twitter and Google.

As Domino's quickly realized, social media has the power to take tiny incidents and turn them into marketing crises. A company spokesperson said Domino's had no idea the video had been shot and posted online. When the company first learned about the video, executives decided not to respond aggressively, hoping the controversy would quiet down. What they missed, though, was how these videos can go viral so quickly. The chief marketing officer of a social media marketing firm said companies make a mistake when they assume a negative video will not spread because all too often it does—as Domino's discovered in this case. In just a matter of days, Domino's reputation was damaged. Customers' perception of its quality went from positive to negative. One brand expert said videos showing what this one did, even if the employees

never intended to sell the tainted food, can create a situation where customers will think twice about purchasing that product.

So what happened to the two employees? Although they told Domino's executives they never actually delivered the tainted food, they were fired and charged with a felony. And Domino's posted its own video featuring its top manager addressing the incident on YouTube not long after it occurred.

DISCUSSION QUESTIONS

1. Beyond its being vulgar and disgusting, what do you think of this situation from the perspective of managing communications?
2. Why do you think Domino's executives took a wait-and-see attitude? Why was this response a problem?
3. How could this type of communication problem be prevented at other Domino's Pizza restaurants?
4. Do incidents like this one and the possibility of them happening anywhere, anytime, mean that all forms of social media should be banned from workplaces? What are the implications for policies regarding communication technology? Discuss.

Managing Human Resources

Learning Outcomes

1. Explain the importance of the human resource management process and the external influences that might affect that process.

2. Discuss the tasks associated with identifying and selecting competent employees.

3. Explain the different types of orientation and training.

4. Describe strategies for retaining competent, high-performing employees.

5. Discuss contemporary issues in managing human resources.

Once an organization's structure is in place it's time to find the people to fill the jobs that have been created. That's where human resource management HRM comes in. It's an important task that involves getting the right number of people in the right place at the right time. After reading and studying this chapter, you will achieve the following learning outcomes.

▶ ▶ ▶ Toronto-based Bank of Nova Scotia (also called Scotiabank), Canada's third-largest bank, provides retail, corporate, and investment banking services worldwide.[1]

Scotiabank provides services in more than 55 countries, mainly in the Caribbean and Central and South America. The bank is Canada's most international bank, serving more than 21 million customers. In fiscal year 2013, the bank had total assets of over $743 billion, making it the number three bank by market capitalization. Scotiabank has close to 89 000 employees, but President and CEO Brian Porter worries that too many will be leaving within the next 5 to 10 years. He expects about half of the bank's senior management—vice-presidents and those at higher levels—will retire during that time.[2]

Managing human resources HR so that an organization has the right people in place at the right time is often thought of as a key role of HR managers. Porter thinks that is not enough, however. "Responsibility for leadership development must begin at the very top. HR can and does play an important role facilitating the process, but it must be owned and executed by current leaders," Porter told attendees at a recent Conference Board of Canada's National Leadership Summit.

Porter also wants to make sure that Scotiabank taps the full potential of its workforce. For instance, while women represent about 66 percent of Scotiabank's employees in Canada, they have much less representation at the executive level. Porter is working with senior managers to make sure that more qualified women get opportunities in senior management.

Think About It

How do companies manage their HR to achieve better performance? Put yourself in Brian Porter's shoes. What policies and practices can he adopt to ensure that the bank has a high-quality workforce? What might he do to make sure that Scotiabank will have enough people to fill important roles as baby boomers retire?

The challenge facing Brian Porter in making sure that Scotiabank recruits and retains high-quality employees reflects only a small aspect of the types of HR management challenges facing today's managers. If an organization does not take its HR management responsibilities seriously, work performance and goal accomplishment may suffer. The quality of an organization is, to a large degree, merely the sum of the quality of people it hires and keeps. Getting and keeping competent employees is critical to the success of every organization, whether the organization is just starting or has been in business for years. Therefore, part of every manager's job in the organizing function is HR management.

The Human Resource Management Process

"Our people are our most important asset." Many organizations use this phrase, or something close to it, to acknowledge the important role that employees play in organizational success. These organizations also recognize that *all* managers must engage in some HRM activities—even in large organizations that have a separate HRM department. These managers interview job candidates, orient new employees, and evaluate their employees' work performance.

Why Human Resource Management Is Important

HRM is important for three reasons. First, as various studies have concluded, it can be a significant source of competitive advantage.[3] And that's true for organizations around the world. The Human Capital Index, a comprehensive study of more than 2000 global firms, concluded that people-oriented HR gives an organization an edge by creating superior shareholder value.[4]

Second, HRM is an important part of organizational strategies. Achieving competitive success through people means managers must change how they think about their employees and how they view the work relationship. They must work with people and treat them as partners, not just as costs to be minimized or avoided. That's what people-oriented organizations such as Southwest Airlines and W. L. Gore do.

Finally, the way organizations treat their people has been found to significantly impact organizational performance.[5] For instance, one study reported that improving work practices could increase market value by as much as 30 percent.[6] Another study that tracked average annual shareholder returns of companies on *Fortune's* list of 100 Best Companies to Work For found that these companies significantly beat the S&P 500 over 10-year, 5-year, 3-year, and 1-year periods.[7] Work practices that lead to both high individual and high organizational performance are known as **high-performance work practices.** (See some examples in Exhibit 12-1.) The common thread among these practices seems to be a commitment to involving employees; improving the knowledge, skills, and abilities of an organization's employees; increasing their motivation; reducing loafing on the job; and enhancing the retention of quality employees while encouraging low performers to leave.

Human Resources for Non–Human Resource Managers

As a manager, it is important for you to be aware that federal and provincial legislation as well as company policies govern many aspects of the employment relationship. Because HR also involves appropriate ways for treating co-workers, even non-managers must be

▶ Watch on **MyManagementLab**

Root Capital: Human Resource Management and Operations

❶ Explain the importance of the human resource management process and the external influences that might affect that process.

high-performance work practices Work practices that lead to both high individual and high organizational performance.

Exhibit 12-1

High-Performance Work Practices

- Self-managed teams
- Decentralized decision making
- Training programs to develop knowledge, skills, and abilities
- Flexible job assignments
- Open communication
- Performance-based compensation
- Staffing based on person–job and person–organization fit
- Extensive employee involvement
- Giving employees more control over decision making
- Increasing employee access to information

Sources: C. H. Chuang and H. Liao, "Strategic Human Resource Management in Service Context: Taking Care of Business by Taking Care of Employees and Customers," *Personnel Psychology,* Spring 2010, pp. 153–196; M. Subramony, "A Meta-Analytic Investigation of the Relationship Between HRM Bundles and Firm Performance," *Human Resource Management,* September–October 2009, pp. 745–768; M. M. Butts et al., "Individual Reactions to High Involvement Work Practices: Investigating the Role of Empowerment and Perceived Organizational Support," *Journal of Occupational Health Psychology,* April 2009, pp. 122–136; and W. R. Evans and W. D. Davis, "High-Performance Work Systems and Organizational Performance: The Mediating Role of Internal Social Structure," *Journal of Management,* October 2005, p. 760.

aware of basic HR principles and practices. You may also be interested in HR issues as they help you understand and manage your own career.

Even if an organization doesn't use high-performance work practices, there are specific HRM activities that must be completed in order to ensure that the organization has qualified people to perform the work that needs to be done—activities that compose the **human resource management process**. Exhibit 12-2 shows the eight activities in

human resource management process Activities necessary for staffing the organization and sustaining high employee performance.

Exhibit 12-2

The Human Resource Management Process

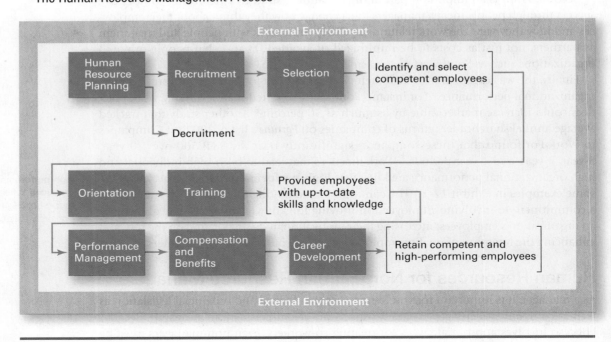

this process. The first three activities ensure that competent employees are identified and selected, the next two involve providing employees with up-to-date knowledge and skills, and the final three ensure that the organization retains competent and high-performing employees. Before we discuss those specific activities, we need to look at external factors that affect the HRM process.

External Factors That Affect the HRM Process

The entire HRM process is influenced by the external environment. Those factors most directly influencing it include the economy, employee labour unions, governmental laws and regulations, and demographic trends.

The Economy's Effect on HRM

The global economic downturn has left what many experts believe to be an enduring mark on HRM practices worldwide. For instance, in Japan, workers used to count on two things: a job for life and a decent pension. Now, lifetime employment is long gone and corporate pension plans are crumbling.[9] In the European Union, the 2011 jobless rate was 9.5 percent, with Spain being hit hardest with an unemployment rate of 21.7 percent.[10] And in Thailand, employees in the automotive industry dealt with reduced work hours, which affected their pay and their skill upgrades.[11] In the United States, labour economists say that although jobs may be coming back slowly, they aren't the same ones that employees were used to. Many of these jobs are temporary or contract positions, rather than full-time jobs with benefits. And many of the more than 8.4 million jobs lost during the recession aren't coming back at all, but may be replaced by other types of work in growing industries.[12] All of these changes have affected employers and workers. A Global Workforce Study survey by global professional services company Towers Watson confirmed that the recession has "fundamentally altered the way U.S. employees view their work and leaders. . . . U.S. workers have dramatically lowered their career and retirement expectations for the foreseeable future."[13] Such findings have profound implications for how an organization manages its human resources.

Labour Unions

The Canada Labour Code covers employment by the federal government and Crown corporations and establishes the right of employees to join labour unions if they desire. The provinces and territories have similar legislation to cover workplaces within their areas. This legislation provides a general framework for fair negotiations between management and labour unions and also provides guidelines to make sure that labour disputes do not unduly inconvenience the public. Part II of this legislation outlines the health and safety obligations of federal employers to prevent accidents and injury to their employees.

A **labour union** is an organization that represents employees and seeks to protect their interests through collective bargaining. Labour unions try to improve pay and benefits and working conditions for members. They also try to have greater control over the rules and procedures covering issues such as promotions, layoffs, transfers, and outsourcing.

In unionized organizations, many HRM decisions are regulated by the terms of collective agreements. These agreements usually define such things as recruitment sources; criteria for hiring, promotions, and layoffs; training eligibility; and disciplinary practices. About 31.5 percent of Canadian employees belong to labour unions, decreasing slightly from 33.7 percent in 1997. Slightly more women belong to unions. Older workers are also more likely to belong to unions: 38.1 percent of workers aged 55 to 64 are unionized compared to 16.0 percent of workers aged 15 to 24.[14] By comparison, only about 11.1 percent of the workforce in the United States is unionized, although that percentage is higher in other countries. For instance, in Japan and Sweden, respectively, 19 percent and 67.5 percent of the labour force belong to a union. In Mexico, 13 percent of employees belong to a union.[15] Individuals join a labour union

datapoints[8]

83 percent of companies cite a shortage of talent as their number one hiring challenge.

91 percent of recent university graduates say that if they started a job and didn't like it, they would stay in that job for up to a year.

52 percent of HR professionals say they don't use social networking sites to research job candidates.

85 percent of survey respondents said the top reason for why an employee should be terminated is sexually harassing a co-worker.

6.25 seconds is the time recruiters spend looking at a résumé before deciding whether the candidate is a good fit for a job.

61 percent of workers surveyed say they're never late for work.

15 percent of employers say they have fired a worker for calling in sick without a legitimate excuse.

36 percent of respondents say the top reason why someone hired would not work out in a position (other than poor performance) is a mismatched skill set.

39 percent of HR managers say that annual performance reviews are not an accurate appraisal of employees' work.

38 percent of senior managers say the most common mistake candidates make during job interviews is having little or no knowledge of the company.

82 percent of employees say they'd give up more than 5 percent of their salary to get a guaranteed retirement income.

labour union An organization that represents employees and seeks to protect their interests through collective bargaining.

for any number of reasons.[16] Wages, working conditions, lack of respect by managers, unfair working hours, job security, and the desire for safer workplaces all contribute to unionization. For example, coffee baristas at Halifax's Just Us! coffee were unhappy with their working conditions and voted to join the Service Employees International Union in December 2013.[17]

Government Legislation

The federal government has greatly expanded its influence over HRM by enacting a number of laws and regulations, including the Canada Labour Code, employment standards legislation, the Charter of Rights and Freedoms, and the Canadian Human Rights Act. The provincial and territorial governments also have their own labour legislation that governs the workplace.

Legislation Affecting Workplace Conditions   Each province and territory has health and safety regulations that cover most non-federal workplaces in its region. This legislation is typically called the Occupational Health and Safety Act or something similar. The act generally does not cover work done in private homes or work done in farming operations (unless separate regulations have been added). There is separate legislation covering workplace hazards: the Workplace Hazardous Materials Information System (WHMIS). This is a comprehensive plan for providing information on the safe use of potentially hazardous materials in the workplace.

Employment standards legislation sets minimum employment standards in the private sector in Canada. It covers such things as the minimum age of employees, hours of work and overtime pay, minimum wages, equal pay, general holidays and annual vacations with pay, parental leave, and termination of employment.

The intent of the Canada Labour Code, Occupational Health and Safety Act, and employment standards legislation is to ensure that all employees have a safe work environment, that they are not asked to work too many hours, and that pay for jobs is not discriminatory.

Anti-Discrimination Legislation   The Charter of Rights and Freedoms and the Canadian Human Rights Act require employers to ensure that equal employment opportunities exist for job applicants and current employees. (See Exhibit 12-3 for examples of prohibited grounds of discrimination in the provinces and territories.)

Trying to balance the "shoulds and should-nots" of these laws often falls within the realm of employment equity. The Employment Equity Act creates four "protected categories"—women, Aboriginal people, people with disabilities, and visible minorities. These groups must not be discriminated against by federally regulated employers and all employers who receive federal contracts worth more than $200 000.

Managers are not completely free to choose whom they hire, promote, or fire. Although these laws and regulations have significantly helped to reduce employment discrimination and unfair employment practices, they have, at the same time, reduced managers' discretion over HR decisions. Because an increasing number of workplace lawsuits are targeting supervisors, as well as their organizations, managers need to be aware of what they can and cannot do by law.[18]

The Canadian Human Rights Act also covers discrimination in pay, under its pay equity guidelines. The act specifies that "it is a discriminatory practice for an employer to establish or maintain differences in wages between male and female employees employed in the same establishment who are performing work of equal value."[19] While it is not always easy to determine what "work of equal value" means, the Equal Wages Guidelines, 1986, helps employers sort this out.[20]

Demographic Trends

In 1971, only 8 percent of the Canadian population was 65 or older. In 2011, this increased to 14.4 percent and by 2036 is expected to grow to 23.7 percent (almost a quarter of the total population).[21] Faced with shortages of skilled workers and with much of the current

Exhibit 12-3

Prohibited Grounds of Discrimination in Employment*

Prohibited Grounds	FED	BC	ALTA	SASK	MAN	ONT	QUE	NB	PEI	NS	NFLD	NWT	YT
Race or colour	•	•	•	•	•	•	•	•	•	•	•	•	•
Religion	•	•	•	•	•	•	•	•	•	•	•	•	•
Age	(19–65)	(19–65)	(18+)	(18–64)	•	(18–65)	•	•	•	•	(19–65)	•	•
Sex (includes pregnancy or childbirth)	•	•	•	•	•	•	•	•	•	•	•	•	•
Marital status	•	•	•	•	•	•	•3	•	•	•	•	•	•
Physical/Mental disability	•	•	•	•	•	•	•	•	•	•	•	•	•
Sexual orientation	•4	•	•	•5	•	•6	•	•	•	•	•	•	•
National or ethnic origin (includes linguistic background)	•			•5		•6					•	•5	
Family status	•	•	•	•	•	•	•3	•	•		•	•	•
Dependence on alcohol or drug	•1	•1	•1	•1	•1	•1	•	•1,7	•1	•7	•		
Ancestry or place of origin		•	•	•	•			•	•		•	•	
Political belief		•			•		•	•	•		•		
Based on association					•	•	•	•		•		•	•
Pardoned conviction	•	•					•						
Record of criminal conviction		•					•		•		•		•
Source of income			•	•8	•	•	•	•	•	•			
Place of residence												•	
Assignment, attachment, or seizure of pay											•		
Social condition/origin							•				•		
Language							•						•

*Any limitation, exclusion, denial, or preference may be permitted if a bona fide occupational requirement can be demonstrated. Harassment on any of the prohibited grounds is considered a form of discrimination.

1 Complaints accepted based on policy.
2 In Manitoba, includes gender-determined characteristics; in Ontario, includes transgendered persons.
3 Quebec uses the term "civil status."
4 Pursuant to a 1992 Ontario Court of Appeal decision, the Canadian Human Rights Commission now accepts complaints on the grounds of sexual orientation.
5 Defined as nationality.
6 Ontario's code includes both "ethnicity" and "citizenship."
7 Previous dependence only.
8 Defined as "receipt of public assistance."

Source: Compiled from "Prohibited Grounds of Discrimination in Canada," *Canadian Human Rights Commission*, September 2006, http://www.chrc-ccdp.ca/publications/prohibitedgrounds-en.asp.

knowledge base walking out the door, managers will need to find creative solutions to retain employees and ensure the transition of organizational knowledge to the next generation of employees. These and other demographic trends, such as a more educated workforce and more women working outside the home, are important because of the impact they're having on current and future HRM practices.

Identifying and Selecting Competent Employees

▶ ▶ ▶ As president and CEO of Scotiabank, Brian Porter recognizes that providing good service means having good employees.[22] Scotiabank needs to recruit more employees to replace those who will move into senior management positions in the next few years.

② Discuss the tasks associated with identifying and selecting competent employees.

Think About It

How will changes in the age of the population affect how organizations hire people? How can Scotiabank and other organizations respond successfully? Canada is expected to experience a shortage of 1 million skilled workers by 2020, according to the Conference Board of Canada. Aware of these predictions, managers at many companies are developing plans to ensure that they will have enough qualified people to fulfill their HR needs.

Every organization needs people to do whatever work is necessary for doing what the organization is in business to do. How do organizations get those people? And more importantly, what can they do to ensure that they get competent, talented people? This first phase of the HRM process involves three tasks: HR planning, recruitment and decruitment, and selection.

Human Resource Planning

human resource planning
Ensuring that the organization has the right number and kinds of capable people in the right places and at the right times

Human resource planning is the process by which managers ensure that they have the right number and kinds of people in the right places, and at the right times. Through planning, organizations can avoid sudden talent shortages and surpluses.[23] Human resource planning can be condensed into two steps: (1) assessing current human resources and (2) assessing future HR needs.

Human resource planning works together with general management planning to make sure that the goals of the organization can be met. If management is planning an expansion, for instance, HR needs to determine how to recruit more people. If management is planning downsizing, human resources determines how to lay off people in an efficient manner. If management is planning to introduce new technology, human resources should be examining the training needs required to make sure that the introduction of new technology will go smoothly. An HR manager who thinks strategically will be sure that the skills and training of employees is consistent with where the organization is planning to go in the future.

Assessing Current Human Resources

Managers begin HR planning by reviewing the organization's current HR status, usually through a *human resource inventory*. This information is taken from forms filled out by employees, and includes things such as name, education, training, prior employment, languages spoken, special capabilities, and specialized skills. Many firms have introduced HR management information systems (HRMIS) to track employee information for policy and strategic needs. For instance, these systems can be used for salary and benefits administration. They can also be used to track absenteeism, turnover, and health and safety data. More strategically, HRMIS can be used to keep track of employee skills and education and to match these to ongoing needs of the organization. The availability of sophisticated databases makes keeping and getting this information quite easy.

An important part of a current assessment is **job analysis**, an assessment that defines jobs and the behaviours necessary to perform them.

For instance, what are the duties of a level 3 accountant who works for General Motors? What minimal knowledge, skills, and abilities are necessary to adequately perform this job? How do these requirements compare with those for a level 2 accountant or for an accounting manager? Information for a job analysis is gathered by directly observing individuals on the job, interviewing employees individually or in a group, having employees complete a questionnaire or record daily activities in a diary, or having job "experts" (usually managers) identify a job's specific characteristics.

Using this information from the job analysis, managers develop or revise job descriptions and job specifications. A **job description** is a written statement of what a jobholder does, how it is done, and why it is done. It typically describes job content, environment, and conditions of employment. A **job specification** states the minimum qualifications that a person must possess to perform a given job successfully. It identifies the human traits, knowledge, skills, and attitudes needed to do the job effectively. The job description and the job specification are both important documents that aid managers in recruiting and selecting employees.

Meeting Future Human Resource Needs

Future HR needs are determined by the organization's mission, goals, and strategies. Demand for employees is a result of demand for the organization's products or services. On the basis of its estimate of total revenue, managers can attempt to establish the number and mix of employees needed to reach that revenue. In some cases, however, that situation may be reversed. When particular skills are necessary but in short supply, the availability of appropriate human resources determines revenues.

After assessing both current capabilities and future needs, managers can estimate areas in which the organization will be understaffed or overstaffed. Then they're ready to proceed to the next step in the HRM process.

Recruitment and Decruitment

Once managers know their current HR status and their future needs, they can begin to do something about any shortages or excesses. If one or more vacancies exist, they can use the information gathered through job analysis to guide them in **recruitment**—that is, the process of locating, identifying, and attracting capable applicants.[24] On the other hand, if HR planning shows a surplus of employees, management may want to reduce the organization's workforce through **decruitment**.[25]

Recruitment

Potential job candidates can be found through several sources, as Exhibit 12-4 shows.[26] Some organizations have interesting approaches to finding employees. For instance, on one day in April 2011, McDonald's, the world's largest hamburger chain, held its first National Hiring Day hoping to hire 50 000 people. The chain and its franchisees actually hired 62 000 workers.[27] Microsoft launched a new website that integrated 103 country sites into one career-related site. There, potential applicants find employee blogs on everything from interview tips to whether a failed start-up on a résumé hurts in applying for a job at the company.[28] Even Google, which receives 3000 applications a day and can afford to be picky about whom it hires, still needs qualified computer science and engineering candidates. One fun thing the company does is Google Games, a day devoted to student team competitions on the company's campus.[29] Accounting firm Deloitte & Touche created its Deloitte Film Festival to get employee team-produced films about "life" at Deloitte to use in college recruiting.[30]

job analysis An assessment that defines jobs and the behaviours necessary to perform them.

job description A written statement of what a jobholder does, how it is done, and why it is done.

job specification A statement of the minimum qualifications that a person must possess to perform a given job successfully.

recruitment The process of locating, identifying, and attracting capable applicants.

decruitment Techniques for reducing the organization's workforce.

Exhibit 12-4

Major Sources of Potential Job Candidates

Source	Advantages	Disadvantages
Internet	Reaches large numbers of people; can get immediate feedback	Generates many unqualified candidates
Employee Referrals	Knowledge about the organization provided by current employee; can generate strong candidates because a good referral reflects on the recommender	May not increase the diversity and mix of employees
Company Website	Wide distribution; can be targeted to specific groups	Generates many unqualified candidates
College/University Recruiting	Large centralized body of candidates	Limited to entry-level positions
Professional recruiting organizations	Good knowledge of industry challenges and requirements	Little commitment to specific requirements organization

selection process The process of screening job applicants to ensure that the most appropriate candidates are hired.

Although e-recruiting has been gaining in popularity (Scotiabank, for instance, allows applicants to fill out an information form online and upload their résumé with the form), employers use other recruitment sources as well. Burnaby, BC-based Electronic Arts Canada, following the lead of some other Canadian companies, decided to recruit at universities in recent years to win "the best and the brightest" from computer science programs.[31] Pat York, director of human resources, is pleased with the results, as the interviews have led to hires more than a third of the time.

What recruiting sources have been found to produce superior candidates? The majority of studies have found that employee referrals generally produce the best candidates.[32] The explanation is intuitively logical. First, applicants referred by current employees are prescreened by these employees. Because the recommenders know both the job and the person being recommended, they tend to refer applicants who are well qualified. Also, because current employees often feel that their reputation is at stake with a referral, they tend to refer others only when they are reasonably confident that the referral will not make them look bad.

Decruitment

The other approach to controlling labour supply is through decruitment. Managers gain respect from their employees when termination is handled with transparency, timeliness, fairness, and respect for the individual being terminated. The decruitment options are shown in Exhibit 12-5. Obviously, people can be fired, but other choices may be more beneficial to the organization. Keep in mind that, regardless of the method used to reduce the number of employees in the organization, there is no easy way to do it, even though it may be absolutely necessary.

Selection

Once the recruiting effort has developed a pool of candidates, the next step in the HRM process is to determine who is best qualified for the job. This step is called the **selection process**, the process of screening job applicants to ensure that the most

Vancouver Police Department

The Vancouver Police Department has started recruiting through an online presence on Second Life. They created special avatars (shown here) to interview prospective candidates.

Vancouver Police Department

Exhibit 12-5

Decruitment Options

Option	Description
Firing	Permanent involuntary termination
Layoffs	Temporary involuntary termination; may last only a few days or extend to years
Attrition	Not filling openings created by voluntary resignations or normal retirements
Transfers	Moving employees either laterally or downward; usually does not reduce costs but can reduce intraorganizational supply–demand imbalances
Reduced workweeks	Having employees work fewer hours per week, share jobs, or perform their jobs on a part-time basis
Early retirements	Providing incentives to older and more senior employees for retiring before their normal retirement dates
Job sharing	Having employees share one full-time position

appropriate candidates are hired. Errors in hiring can have far-reaching implications. However, hiring the right people pays off.

What Is Selection?

Selection is an exercise in prediction. It seeks to predict which applicants will be successful if hired. Successful in this case means performing well on the criteria the organization uses to evaluate employees. In filling a sales position, for example, the selection process should be able to predict which applicants will generate a high volume of sales; for a position as a network administrator, it should predict which applicants will be able to effectively oversee and manage the organization's computer network.

Consider, for a moment, that any selection decision can result in four possible outcomes. As shown in Exhibit 12-6, two of these outcomes would be correct, and two would indicate errors.

A decision is correct when the applicant was predicted to be successful and proved to be successful on the job, or when the applicant was predicted to be unsuccessful and would be so if hired. In the first case, we have successfully accepted; in the second case, we have successfully rejected.

Exhibit 12-6

Selection Decision Outcomes

		Selection Decision	
		Accept	**Reject**
Later Job Performance	**Successful**	Correct decision	Reject error
	Unsuccessful	Accept error	Correct decision

Karen Flavelle, president of Vancouver-based Purdy's Chocolates, agonizes over new hires because she really wants them to fit in with the company's culture. A search for a new personnel director took three years, until she could find someone who would support "the company's practice of rotating store clerks and plant workers into challenging projects to test their suitability for supervisory and management posts." Most managers at Purdy's are promoted from within.

Dick Loek/GetStock.com

Problems arise when errors are made in rejecting candidates who would have performed successfully on the job (reject errors) or accepting those who ultimately perform poorly (accept errors). These problems can be significant. Given today's HR laws and regulations, reject errors can cost more than the additional screening needed to find acceptable candidates. They can expose the organization to charges of discrimination, especially if applicants from protected groups are disproportionately rejected. The costs of accept errors include the cost of training the employee, the profits lost because of the employee's incompetence, the cost of severance, and the subsequent costs of further recruiting and screening. The major thrust of any selection activity should be to reduce the probability of making reject errors or accept errors while increasing the probability of making correct decisions. How do managers do this? By using selection procedures that are both valid and reliable.

Validity and Reliability

validity The proven relationship that exists between the selection device and some relevant job criterion.

Any selection device that a manager uses should demonstrate **validity**, a proven relationship between the selection device and some relevant job criterion. For example, the law prohibits managers from using a test score as a selection device unless there is clear evidence that, once on the job, individuals with high scores on this test outperform individuals with low test scores. The burden is on managers to show that any selection device they use to differentiate between applicants is related to job performance.

reliability The ability of a selection device to measure the same thing consistently.

A selection device must also demonstrate **reliability**, the device measures the same thing consistently. For example, if a test is reliable, any single individual's score should remain fairly consistent over time, assuming that the characteristics being measured are also stable. No selection device can be effective if it's low in reliability. Using such a device would be like weighing yourself every day on an erratic scale. If the scale is unreliable—randomly fluctuating, say four to seven kilos every time you step on it—the results will not mean much. To be effective predictors, selection devices must possess an acceptable level of consistency.

A growing number of companies are adopting a new measure of recruitment effectiveness called "quality of fill."[33] This measure looks at the contributions of good hires versus those of hires who have failed to live up to their potential. Five key factors are considered in defining this quality measure: employee retention, performance evaluations, number of first-year hires who make it into high-potential training programs, number of employees who are promoted, and what surveys of new hires indicate. Such measures help an organization assess whether its selection process is working well.

Exhibit 12-7

Selection Devices

Weaknesses	Weaknesses	Weaknesses
Application forms	Relevant biographical data and facts that can be verified have been shown to be valid performance measures for some jobs.	Usually only a couple of items on the form prove to be valid predictors of job performance, and then only for a specific job.
	When items on the form have been weighted to reflect job relatedness, this device has proved to be a valid predictor for diverse groups.	Weighted-item applications are difficult and expensive to create and maintain.
Written tests	Tests of intellectual ability, spatial and mechanical ability, perceptual accuracy, and motor ability are moderately valid predictors for many semi-skilled and unskilled lower-level jobs in manufacturing.	Intelligence and other tested characteristics can be somewhat removed from actual job performance, thus reducing their validity.
	Intelligence tests are reasonably good predictors for supervisory positions.	
Performance-simulation tests	Tests are based on job analysis data and easily meet the requirement of job relatedness.	They are expensive to create and administer.
	Tests have proven to be valid predictors of job performance.	
Interviews	Interviews must be structured and well organized to be effective predictors.	Interviewers must be aware of the legality of certain questions.
	Interviewers must use common questions to be effective predictors.	Interviews are subject to potential biases, especially if they are not well structured and standardized.
Background investigations	Verifications of background data are valuable sources of information.	Reference checks are essentially worthless as a selection tool.
Physical examinations	Physical exams have some validity for jobs with certain physical requirements.	Managers must be sure that physical requirements are job related and do not discriminate.

Types of Selection Devices

Managers can use a number of selection devices to reduce accept and reject errors. The best known include application forms, written tests, performance-simulation tests, interviews, background investigations, and, in some cases, physical examinations. Let's briefly review each of these devices. Exhibit 12-7 lists the strengths and weaknesses of each of these devices.[34]

What Works Best and When?

Many selection devices are of limited value to managers in making selection decisions. Exhibit 12-8 summarizes the validity of these devices for particular types of jobs. Managers should use those devices that effectively predict success for a given job.

One thing managers need to carefully watch is how they portray their organization and the work that an applicant will be doing. If they tell applicants only the good aspects, they're likely to have a workforce that's dissatisfied and prone to high turnover.[35] Negative things can happen when the information an applicant receives is excessively inflated. First, mismatched applicants probably won't withdraw from the selection process. Second, inflated information builds unrealistic expectations, so new employees may quickly become dissatisfied and leave the organization. Third, new hires become disillusioned and less committed to the organization when they face the unexpected harsh realities of the job. In addition, these individuals may feel that they were misled during the hiring process and then become problem employees.

Exhibit 12-8

Quality of Selection Devices as Predictors

Selection Device	Position			
	Senior Management	Middle and Lower Management	Complex Nonmanagerial	Routine Work
Application Forms	2	2	2	2
Written Tests	1	1	2	3
Work Sampling	—	—	4	4
Assessment Centres	5	5	—	—
Interviews	4	3	2	2
Verification of Application Data	3	3	3	3
Reference Checks	1	1	1	1
Physical Exams	1	1	1	2

Note: Validity is measured on a scale from 5 (highest) to 1 (lowest). A dash means "not applicable."

realistic job preview (RJP) A preview of a job that includes both positive and negative information about the job and the company.

To increase employee job satisfaction and reduce turnover, managers should consider a **realistic job preview (RJP)**, which includes both positive and negative information about the job and the company. For instance, in addition to the positive comments typically expressed during an interview, the job applicant might be told that there are limited opportunities to talk to co-workers during work hours, that promotional advancement is unlikely, or that work hours are erratic and employees may have to work weekends. Research indicates that applicants who receive an RJP have more realistic expectations about the jobs they'll be performing and are better able to cope with the frustrating elements than are applicants who receive only inflated information.

Providing Employees with Needed Skills and Knowledge

3 Explain the different types of orientation and training.

▶ ▶ ▶ Thirty-year-old Roxann Linton is enthusiastic about her career at Scotiabank.[36] "Working with an international and diverse organization like Scotiabank, there are so many opportunities," says Linton. The young woman was chosen for Leading Edge, Scotiabank's fast-track leadership program. In the application process, she had to prepare a challenging business case analysis, go through psychometric testing, and be interviewed twice by a total of eight executives. The Leading Edge program prepares employees for senior management positions by rotating them through a series of assignments.

Linton worked for the bank for about five years in the bank's internal audit department in Kingston, Jamaica. She then transferred to Halifax and worked in commercial banking. During the first 15 months of the Leading Edge program, Linton managed more than 100 people in the electronic banking contact centre. Her next assignment was as director of special projects at Scotia Cassels Investment Counsel, part of the bank's wealth management division. She launched a new corporate bond fund during her first three months on that assignment. She will have one more 12- to 18-month assignment in another part of the bank, and then she can start applying for vice-president positions.

Organizations have to introduce new members to the work they will do and the organization. They do this through their orientation programs. As time goes by, employees may need to increase their skills. This is handled through training. We review the strategies that organizations use for orientation and training below.

Employee Orientation

Did you participate in some type of organized "introduction to campus life" when you started school? If so, you may have been told about your school's rules and regulations, the procedures for activities such as applying for financial aid, cashing a cheque, or registering for classes, and you were probably introduced to some of the campus administrators. A person starting a new job needs the same type of introduction to his or her job and the organization. This introduction is called **orientation**.

There are two types of orientation. *Work unit orientation* familiarizes the employee with the goals of the work unit, clarifies how his or her job contributes to the unit's goals, and includes an introduction to his or her new co-workers. *Organization orientation* informs the new employee about the organization's objectives, history, philosophy, procedures, and rules. This should include relevant HR policies and benefits such as work hours, pay procedures, overtime requirements, and fringe benefits. In addition, a tour of the organization's work facilities is often part of the organization orientation.

Managers have an obligation to make the integration of the new employee into the organization as smooth and as free of anxiety as possible. They need to openly discuss employee beliefs regarding mutual obligations of the organization and the employee.[37] It's in the best interests of the organization and the new employee to get the person up and running in the job as soon as possible. Successful orientation, whether formal or informal, results in an outsider–insider transition that makes the new member feel comfortable and fairly well adjusted, lowers the likelihood of poor work performance, and reduces the probability of a surprise resignation by the new employee only a week or two into the job.

orientation Introduction of a new employee to his or her job and the organization.

Training

On the whole, planes don't cause airline accidents, people do. Most collisions, crashes, and other airline mishaps—nearly three-quarters of them— result from errors by the pilot or air traffic controller, or from inadequate maintenance. Weather and structural failures typically account for the remaining accidents.[38] We cite these statistics to illustrate the importance of training in the airline industry. Such maintenance and human errors could be prevented or significantly reduced by better employee training, as shown by the amazing "landing" of US Airways Flight 1549 in the Hudson River in January 2009 with no loss of life. Pilot Captain Chesley Sullenberger attributed the positive outcome to the extensive and intensive training that all pilots and flight crews undergo.[39]

Employee training is an important HRM activity. As job demands change, employee skills have to be altered and updated. In 2006, US business firms budgeted over $55 billion on workforce formal training.[40] Canadian companies spend far less than American firms on training and development, about $852 per employee compared with $1273 by the Americans in 2006.[41] Managers, of course, are responsible for deciding what type of training employees need, when they need it, and what form that training should take.

Toronto-based Labatt Breweries is putting its employees through beer school over the next few years. Beer "professors" at Labatt's beer school teach employees how to pour the perfect glass of beer and how to match food with certain beers.

Lucas Oleniuk/GetStock.com

Exhibit 12-9

Types of Training

Type	Includes
General	Communication skills, computer systems application and programming, customer service, executive development, management skills and development, personal growth, sales, supervisory skills, and technological skills and knowledge
Specific	Basic life/work skills, creativity, customer education, diversity/cultural awareness, remedial writing, managing change, leadership, product knowledge, public speaking/presentation skills, safety, ethics, sexual harassment, team building, wellness, and others

Source: Based on "2005 Industry Report—Types of Training," *Training*, December 2005, p. 22.

Types of Training

When organizations invest in employee training, what are they offering? Exhibit 12-9 describes the major types of training that organizations provide.[42] Some of the most popular types of training that organizations provide include sexual harassment, safety, management skills and development, and supervisory skills.[43] For many organizations, employee interpersonal skills training—communication, conflict resolution, team building, customer service, and so forth—is a high priority. For example, Shannon Washbrook, director of training and development for Vancouver-based Boston Pizza International, says, "Our people know the Boston Pizza concept; they have all the hard skills. It's the soft skills they lack." To address that, Washbrook launched Boston Pizza College, a training initiative that uses hands-on, scenario-based learning about many interpersonal skills topics.[44] SaskPower, like Scotiabank and Boston Pizza, uses training to develop leadership potential, as the following *Management Reflection* shows.

MANAGEMENT REFLECTION

SaskPower Sends Its Leaders to Leadership School

Are leaders made or born? Managers at Regina-based SaskPower believe that leaders are developed, not born.[45] The company has developed a leadership program that is similar to a mini-MBA. It introduces participants to leadership skills and other areas of business. The company selects employees for the program based on leadership potential. Individuals can nominate themselves for the leadership-training program by persuading management with examples of why they would make great managers.

The program works better than the way managers were chosen previously at Sask-Power. "It was unorganized, and the 'old boys' network' was still at work," said Bill Hyde, vice-president of human resources. The program also ensures that SaskPower continues to have a skilled workforce and trained managers for the future, when Baby Boomers start retiring in large numbers. ■

Training Methods

Although employee training can be done in traditional ways, many organizations are increasingly relying on technology-based training methods because of their accessibility, cost, and ability to deliver information. Web-based or online training had been predicted just a few years ago to become the most popular method of training, but as Julie Kaufman, an industry analyst with Toronto-based IDC Canada, recently told attendees at a training and development conference, it simply has not lived up to expectations.

Exhibit 12-10

Employee Training Methods

Traditional Training Methods

- *On the job*—Employees learn how to do tasks simply by performing them, usually after an initial introduction to the task.
- *Job rotation*—Employees work at different jobs in a particular area, getting exposure to a variety of tasks.
- *Mentoring and coaching*—Employees work with an experienced worker who provides information, support, and encouragement; also called apprenticing in certain industries.
- *Experiential exercises*—Employees participate in role playing, simulations, or other face-to-face types of training.
- *Workbooks/manuals*—Employees refer to training workbooks and manuals for information.
- *Classroom lectures*—Employees attend lectures designed to convey specific information.

Technology-Based Training Methods

- *CD-ROM/DVD/videotapes/audiotapes*—Employees listen to or watch selected media that convey information or demonstrate certain techniques.
- *Videoconferencing/teleconferencing/satellite TV*—Employees listen or participate as information is conveyed or techniques demonstrated.
- *E-learning*—Internet-based learning where employees participate in multimedia simulations or other interactive modules.

Most organizations have not yet figured out how to make use of this type of training.[46] Exhibit 12-10 provides descriptions of the various traditional and technology-based training methods that managers might use. Of all these training methods, experts believe that organizations will increasingly rely on e-learning applications to deliver important information and to develop employees' skills. It is predicted that Massive Open Online Courses will continue to increase enrollments and will be a globally disruptive force in education and training.[47]

Retaining Competent and High-Performance Employees

▶ ▶ ▶ Voluntary turnover rates (leaving due to resignation, voluntary settlement, retirement or contract expiration) in Canada averaged 10.2% in 2013. With the growing complexity of global banking, the large international base of employees, and the looming retirement of many senior employees, Scotiabank is investing in initiatives to both train and retain their most competent and high-performing employees. [48]

4 Describe strategies for retaining competent, high-performing employees.

Think About It

What kinds of strategies might Scotiabank employ to meet the training needs of their top employees? How might Scotiabank create a culture that fulfills the expectations of these employees? Would this vary dependent on the culture of the various countries served by the bank?

When an organization has invested significant money in recruiting, selecting, orienting, and training employees, it wants to keep those employees, especially the competent, high-performing ones! Two HRM activities that play a role in doing this are managing employee performance and developing an appropriate compensation and benefits program.

Employee Performance Management

A recent survey found that two-thirds of surveyed organizations have inefficient performance management processes in place.[49] That's scary because managers need to know whether their employees are performing their jobs efficiently and effectively. That's what a **performance management system** does—establishes performance standards used to evaluate employee performance. Performance appraisal is a critical part of a performance management system. Some companies invest far more effort in it than others. How do managers evaluate employees' performance? That's where the different performance appraisal methods come in.

performance management system A process of establishing performance standards and evaluating performance in order to arrive at objective HR decisions, as well as to provide documentation to support those decisions.

Performance Appraisal Methods

More than 70 percent of managers admit that they have trouble giving a critical performance review to an underachieving employee.[50] Appraising someone's performance is never easy, especially with employees who aren't doing their jobs well, but managers can be better at it by using any of the seven different performance appraisal methods. A description of each of these methods, including advantages and disadvantages, is shown in Exhibit 12-11.

What Happens When Performance Falls Short?

If, for some reason, an employee is not meeting his or her performance goals, a manager needs to find out why. If it is because the employee is mismatched for the job (a hiring error) or because he or she does not have adequate training, something relatively simple can be done: The manager can either reassign the individual to a job that better matches his or her skills or train the employee to do the job more effectively. If the problem is associated not with the employee's abilities but with his or her desire to do the job, it becomes a **discipline** problem. In that case, a manager can try **employee job counselling** and, if necessary, can take disciplinary action such as verbal and written warnings, suspensions, and even termination.

discipline Actions taken by a manager to enforce an organization's standards and regulations.

employee job counselling A process designed to help employees overcome performance-related problems.

Compensation and Benefits

Most of us expect to receive appropriate compensation from our employer. Developing an effective and appropriate compensation system is an important part of the HRM process.[51] Why? Because it helps attract and retain competent and talented individuals who help the

Exhibit 12-11

Advantages and Disadvantages of Performance Appraisal Methods

Method	Advantage	Disadvantage
Written essays	Simple to use	More a measure of evaluator's writing ability than of employee's actual performance
Critical incidents	Rich examples; behaviourally based	Time-consuming; lack quantification
Graphic rating scales	Provide quantitative data; less time-consuming than others	Do not provide depth of job behaviour assessed
BARS	Focus on specific and measurable behaviours	Time-consuming; difficult to develop job behaviours
Multiperson comparisons	Compare employees with one another	Unwieldy with large number of employees; legal concerns
MBO	Focuses on end goals; results oriented	Time-consuming
360-degree feedback	Thorough	Time-consuming

Exhibit 12-12

Factors That Influence Compensation and Benefits

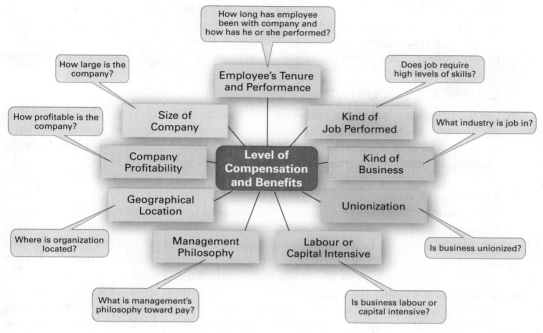

Sources: Based on R. I. Henderson, *Compensation Management*, 6th ed. (Upper Saddle River, NJ: Prentice Hall, 1994), pp. 3–24; and A. Murray, "Mom, Apple Pie, and Small Business," *Wall Street Journal*, August 15, 1994, p. A1.

organization accomplish its mission and goals. In addition, an organization's compensation system has been shown to have an impact on its strategic performance.[52]

Managers must develop a compensation system that reflects the changing nature of work and the workplace in order to keep people motivated. Organizational compensation can include many different types of rewards and benefits such as base wages and salaries, wage and salary add-ons, and incentive payments, as well as other benefits and services such as vacation time, extended health care, training allowances, and pensions. Benefits can often amount to one-third or more of an individual's base salary and should be viewed by the employee as part of the total compensation package.

How do managers determine who gets paid $9 an hour and who gets $350 000 a year? Several factors influence the differences in compensation and benefit packages for different employees. Exhibit 12-12 summarizes these factors, which are both job-based and business- or industry-based.

Many organizations use an alternative approach to determining compensation called **skill-based pay**. Under this type of pay system, an employee's job title does not define his or her pay category; skills do.[53] Research shows that this type of pay system seems to be more successful in manufacturing organizations than in service organizations and organizations pursuing technical innovations.[54] Skill-based pay systems seem to mesh nicely with the changing nature of jobs and today's work environment. As one expert noted, "Slowly, but surely, we're becoming a skill-based society where your market value is tied to what you can do and what your skill set is."[55] On the other hand, many organizations are using variable pay systems, in which an individual's compensation is contingent on performance—81 percent of Canadian and Taiwanese organizations use variable pay plans, and 78 percent of US organizations do.[56] In Chapter 14, we discuss how pay systems, such as pay-for-performance programs, can be used to motivate employees.

skill-based pay A pay system that rewards employees for the job skills and competencies they can demonstrate.

Although many factors influence the design of an organization's compensation system, flexibility is a key consideration. The traditional approach to paying people reflected a time of job stability when an employee's pay was largely determined by seniority and job level. Given the dynamic environments that many organizations face in which the skills that are absolutely critical to organizational success can change in a matter of months, the trend is to make pay systems more flexible and to reduce the number of pay levels. However, whatever approach managers take, they must establish a fair, equitable, and motivating compensation system that allows the organization to recruit and keep a productive workforce.

Career Development

career A sequence of positions held by a person during his or her lifetime.

For our purposes, we define a **career** as the sequence of positions held by a person during his or her lifetime.[57] Using this definition, it's apparent that we all have, or will have, a career. Moreover, the concept is as relevant to unskilled labourers as it is to software designers or physicians. But career development is not what it used to be![58]

The Way It Was

Career development programs were typically designed by organizations to help employees advance their work lives within a specific organization. The focus of such programs was to provide the information, assessment, and training needed to help employees realize their career goals. Career development was also a way for organizations to attract and retain highly talented people. Widespread organizational changes have led to uncertainty about the concept of a traditional organizational career. The individual—not the organization—is responsible for his or her own career! Both organizations and individuals are adjusting to the notion that organizational members have to look out for themselves and become more self-reliant.

You and Your Career Today

The idea of increased personal responsibility for one's career has been described as a *boundaryless career* in which individuals rather than organizations define career progression, organizational loyalty, important skills, and marketplace value.[59] The challenge for individuals is that there are no norms and few rules to guide them in these new circumstances. Instead, individuals assume primary responsibility for career planning, career goal setting, and education and training.[60]

One of the first career decisions you have to make is a career choice. The optimum career choice is one that offers the best match between what you want out of life and your interests, abilities, and market opportunities. A good career match, then, is one in which

Exhibit 12-13

What Do College and University Grads Want from Their Jobs?

Top Factors for Canadian Students	Top Factors for US Students	Top Factors for UK Students
• Opportunities for advancement in position • Good people to work with • Good people to report to • Work–life balance • Initial salary	• Work–life balance • Annual base salary • Job stability and security • Recognition for a job done well • Increasingly challenging tasks • Rotational programs	• International career opportunities • Flexible working hours • Variety of assignments • Paid overtime

Sources: Based on E. Pooley, "Hire Education: How to Recruit Top University Graduates," *Canadian Business*, September 11–24, 2006; S. Shellenbarger, "Avoiding the Next Enron: Today's Crop of Soon-to-Be Grads Seeks Job Security," *Wall Street Journal*, February 16, 2006; "MBAs Eye Financial Services and Management Consulting," *HRMarketer.com*, June 7, 2005; and J. Boone, "Students Set Tighter Terms for Work," *FinancialTimes.com*, May 21, 2005.

you are able to develop a positive self-concept, to do work that you think is important, and to lead the kind of life you desire.[61] Exhibit 12-13 describes the factors Canadian, US, and UK college and university students are looking for in their jobs. As you look at these results, think about what is important to you.

Once you have identified a career choice, it's time to go to work! How do you survive and excel in your career? By taking an active role in managing your career, your work life can be more exciting, enjoyable, and satisfying.

Contemporary Issues in Managing Human Resources

▶ ▶ ▶ Scotiabank prides itself on its work with the Aboriginal community.[62] The bank sponsors scholarships, events, and programs for community members, and also supports Aboriginal business initiatives.

The bank actively recruits from the Aboriginal community. Scotiabank's recruiting strategy is based "on the medicine wheel and the teachings of the medicine wheel, in terms of all the components [of the medicine wheel] need to exist in balance together," says Michele Baptiste, national manager of Aboriginal relations with Scotiabank. The bank has also approached the Aboriginal Human Resource Development Council of Canada to assist "in recruitment and retention of Aboriginal people across the country," according to Baptiste.

⑤ Discuss contemporary issues in managing human resources.

Think About It

How are companies managing diversity in their workplaces? To what extent are they addressing issues such as work–life balance? Should they be doing so?

👁 Watch on MyManagementLab
Diversity (TWZ Role Play)

We conclude this chapter by looking at some contemporary HR issues facing today's managers: managing workforce diversity, managing downsizing, dealing with sexual harassment, and helping employees manage work–life balance.

Workforce Diversity

We have discussed the changing makeup of the workforce in several places throughout this textbook . In this section, we consider how workforce diversity is directly affected by basic HRM activities, including recruitment, selection, and orientation and training.

Recruitment

To improve workforce diversity, managers need to widen their recruiting net. For example, the popular practice of relying on employee referrals as a source of job applicants tends to produce candidates who are similar to present employees. However, some organizations, such as Toronto-based Tele-Mobile (TELUS Mobility), have recruited and hired diverse individuals by relying on referrals from their current employees. But not every organization has the employee resources needed to achieve workforce diversity through employee referrals. Managers may have to look for job applicants in places where they might not have looked before. To increase diversity, managers from such companies as Calgary-based Suncor Energy, Saskatoon-based Cameco, and Toronto-based Scotiabank and TELUS Mobility are increasingly turning to

Michele Baptiste, national manager of Aboriginal relations with Scotiabank, created the bank's Aboriginal employment strategy. It is based on the teachings of the medicine wheel (an example of which is shown here). The idea behind the medicine wheel is that the four major components of an individual (mental, spiritual, emotional, physical) have to be in balance. Baptiste emphasizes that Scotiabank takes a holistic approach to Aboriginal relations, bringing together employment, business, and community involvement.

Dauphin Friendship Centre

nontraditional recruitment sources such as women's job networks, over-50 clubs, urban job banks, disabled people's training centres, ethnic newspapers, and gay rights organizations. This type of outreach should enable the organization to broaden its pool of diverse applicants. When IKEA went to Seville, Spain, it followed an alternative recruiting strategy, as the following *Management Reflection* shows.

←⊙ Simulate on MyManagementLab

Hiring A New Employee

MANAGEMENT REFLECTION

IKEA Taps into New Labour Force

Should you hire people with no previous experience? When Swedish-based IKEA opened up a store in Seville, its fifth location in Spain, the company decided to search for a different type of employee.[63] The company advertised for "single mothers, students, people with disabilities and long-term unemployed." They did not even require working experience. Andalusia, the region where the store was opening, had an 18.5 percent unemployment rate, and 30 000 applicants responded to IKEA's ads.

Employers in Spain had never recruited from these categories of workers before. IKEA's model for employment is unique: It targets people who really need jobs. The company provides training to its employees to help them overcome any initial hurdles from lack of experience. People with disabilities were hired for customer service, administration, and logistics. Juvencio Maeztu, the store manager, explained the store's hiring policy: "We were more interested in finding people with the right motivation than with the right college degrees."

IKEA's strategy of hiring the previously "unhirable" may well pay off in Spain. With the country's high unemployment rates and IKEA's plan to have 35 stores in Spain by 2015, those in Spain looking for jobs have renewed hope they will be able to find work. ∎

Managing Downsizing

"Before 1981, the word 'layoff' in the sense of permanent separation from a job with no prospects for recall, was so uncommon that the U.S. Bureau of Labor Statistics didn't even keep track of such cuts."[64] How things have changed!

downsizing The planned elimination of jobs in an organization

Downsizing (or layoffs) is the planned elimination of jobs in an organization. When an organization has too many employees—which can happen when it's faced with an economic recession, declining market share, too aggressive growth, or poorly managed operations—one option for improving profits is to eliminate some of those excess workers. During the most recent economic recession, many well-known companies downsized—including, among others, Boeing, Nokia, Procter & Gamble, Hewlett-Packard, Volkswagen, Dell, General Motors, Unisys, Siemens, Merck, Honeywell, and eBay. Now some HR experts are suggesting that a "cost" associated with mass layoffs is the damage they can cause to long-term growth prospects.[65]

How can managers best manage a downsized workplace? Disruptions in the workplace and in employees' personal lives should be expected. Stress, frustration, anxiety, and anger are typical reactions of both individuals being laid off and the job survivors. Exhibit 12-14 lists some ways that managers can lessen the trauma both for the employees being laid off and for the survivors.[66]

Managing Sexual Harassment

Sexual harassment is a serious issue in both public and private sector organizations. A 2001 survey by York University found that 48 percent of working women in Canada reported they had experienced some form of "gender harassment" in the year before they were surveyed.[67] A 1996 RCMP survey found that 6 out of every 10 female Mounties said they had experienced sexual harassment.[68] In 2006, Nancy Sulz, who worked as an RCMP officer

Exhibit 12-14

Tips for Managing Downsizing

- Treat everyone with respect.
- Communicate openly and honestly:
  - Inform those being let go as soon as possible.
  - Tell surviving employees the new goals and expectations.
  - Explain impact of layoffs.
- Follow any laws regulating severance pay or benefits.
- Provide support/counselling for surviving (remaining) employees.
- Reassign roles according to individuals' talents and backgrounds.
- Focus on boosting morale:
  - Offer individualized reassurance.
  - Continue to communicate, especially one-on-one.
  - Remain involved and available.
- Have a plan for the empty office spaces/cubicles so it isn't so depressing for surviving employees.

in British Columbia, was awarded $950 000 for her complaint against the detachment, which included claims of sexual harassment.[69] Barbara Orser, a research affiliate with the Conference Board of Canada, notes that "sexual harassment is more likely to occur in workplace environments that tolerate bullying, intimidation, yelling, innuendo and other forms of discourteous behaviour."[70] And sexual harassment is not a problem just in Canada. During 2005, more than 12 600 complaints were filed with the US Equal Employment Opportunity Commission (EEOC). Although most complaints are filed by women, the percentage of charges filed by males has risen every year but two since 1992.[71] Sexual harassment is a global issue: Charges have been filed against employers in such countries as Japan, Australia, the Netherlands, Belgium, New Zealand, Sweden, Ireland, and Mexico.[72]

Even though discussions of sexual harassment cases often focus on the large awards granted by a court, there are other concerns for employers. Sexual harassment creates an unpleasant work environment and undermines employees' ability to perform their jobs.

Sexual harassment is defined by the Supreme Court of Canada as unwelcome behaviour of a sexual nature in the workplace that negatively affects the work environment or leads to adverse job-related consequences for the employee.[73] Sexual harassment can occur between members of the opposite sex or of the same sex. Although such activity is generally covered under employment discrimination laws, in recent years this problem has gained more recognition. By most accounts, prior to the mid-1980s this problem was generally viewed as an isolated incident, with the individual at fault being considered solely responsible (if at all) for his or her actions.

Many problems associated with sexual harassment involve interpreting the Supreme Court's definition to determine exactly what constitutes illegal behaviour. For many organizations, conveying what an offensive or hostile environment looks like is not completely black and white. For instance, while it is relatively easy to focus on problems where an individual employee is harassed, this may not address more systemic problems in the workplace. Other employees can also be negatively affected when they witness offensive conduct.[74] Thus, managers at all levels need to be attuned to what makes fellow employees uncomfortable—and if they don't know, they should ask.[75]

What can an organization do to protect itself against sexual harassment claims?[76] The courts want to know two things: Did the organization know about, or should it have known about, the alleged behaviour? and What did management do to stop it? With the number and dollar amounts of the awards against organizations increasing, there is a greater need for management to educate all employees on sexual harassment matters and have mechanisms available to monitor employees. Managers at all levels have a duty to

sexual harassment Any unwelcome behaviour of a sexual nature in the workplace that negatively affects the work environment or leads to adverse job-related consequences for the employee.

create and maintain a harassment-free work environment. One final area of interest we want to discuss in terms of sexual harassment is workplace romances.

Workplace Romances

If you are employed, have you ever dated someone at work? If not, have you ever been attracted to someone in your workplace and thought about pursuing a relationship? Such situations are more common than you might think—40 percent of employees surveyed by the *Wall Street Journal* said that they have had an office romance. And another survey found that 54 percent of single men and 40 percent of single women said they would be open to dating a co-worker.[77] The environment in today's organizations with mixed-gender work teams and working long hours is undoubtedly contributing to this situation. "People realize they're going to be at work such long hours, it's almost inevitable that this takes place," said one survey director. But a workplace romance is something that can potentially become a really big problem for organizations.[78] In addition to the potential conflicts and retaliation between co-workers who decide to stop dating or to end a romantic relationship, the more serious problems stem from the potential for sexual harassment accusations, especially when it's between supervisor and subordinate. The standard used by judicial courts has been that workplace sexual conduct is prohibited sexual harassment *if* it is unwelcome. If it's welcome, it still may be inappropriate, but usually is not unlawful. However, a recent ruling by the California Supreme Court concerning specifically a supervisor–subordinate relationship that got out of hand is worth noting. That ruling said the "completely consensual workplace romances can create a hostile work environment for others in the workplace."[79]

What should managers do about workplace romances? Over the past decade, companies have become more flexible about workplace romances. People spend so much time at the office that coworker romances are almost inevitable.[80] However, it's important to educate employees about the potential for sexual harassment. And because the potential liability is more serious when it comes to supervisor–subordinate relationships, a more proactive approach is needed in terms of discouraging such relationships and perhaps even requiring supervisors to report any such relationships to the HR department. At some point, the organization may even want to consider banning such relationships, although an outright ban may be difficult to put into practice.

Managing Work–Life Balance

Professors Linda Duxbury of the Sprott School of Business at Carleton University and Chris Higgins of the University of Western Ontario are the leading Canadian researchers on the issue of work–life balance. Their research shows that employees are working long hours and are also increasingly being asked to work a number of unpaid hours a week.[81] This affects employees' abilities to manage their family lives.

What kinds of work–life balance issues can arise that might affect an employee's job performance? Here are some examples:

- Is it okay for someone to bring his baby to work because of an emergency crisis with normal child care arrangements?

- Is it okay to expect an employee to work 60 or more hours a week?

- Should an employee be given the day off to watch her child perform in a school event?

In the 1980s, organizations began to recognize that employees don't leave their families and personal lives behind when they walk into work. An organization hires a person who has a personal life outside the office, personal problems, and family commitments. Although managers cannot be sympathetic to every detail of an employee's family life, we *are* seeing organizations more attuned to the fact that employees have sick children, elderly parents who need special care, and other family issues that may require special arrangements. In response, most major organizations have taken actions to make their workplaces more family-friendly by offering **family-friendly benefits**, which include a wide range of work and family programs to help employees.[82] They have introduced programs such as on-site child care, summer day camps, flextime, job sharing, leaves for school functions, telecommuting, and part-time employment.

Work–life conflicts are as relevant to male employees with children and women without children as they are for female employees with children. Heavy workloads and increased travel demands, for instance, are making it increasingly hard for many employees, male and female, to meet both work and personal responsibilities. A *Fortune* survey found that 84 percent of male executives surveyed said that "they'd like job options that let them realize their professional aspirations while having more time for things outside work." Also, 87 percent of these executives believed that any company that restructured top-level management jobs in ways that would both increase productivity and make more time available for life outside the office would have a competitive advantage in attracting talented employees.[83] Younger employees, particularly, put a higher priority on family and a lower priority on jobs, and are looking for organizations that give them more work flexibility.[84]

Today's progressive workplace is becoming more accommodating to the varied needs of a diverse workforce. It provides a wide range of scheduling options and benefits that allow employees more flexibility at work and allow employees to better balance or integrate their work and personal lives. Despite these organizational efforts, work–life programs have room for improvement. Workplace surveys still show high levels of employee stress stemming from work–life conflicts. And large groups of women and minority employees remain unemployed or underemployed because of family responsibilities and bias in the workplace.[85] So what can managers do?

Research on work–family life balance has provided some new insights. For instance, we are beginning to see evidence that there are positive outcomes when individuals are able to combine work and family roles.[86] As a participant in a recent study noted, "I think being a mother and having patience and watching someone else grow has made me a better manager. I am better able to be patient with other people and let them grow and develop in a way that is good for them."[87] In addition, individuals who have family-friendly workplace support appear to be more satisfied on the job.[88] This finding seems to strengthen the notion that organizations benefit by creating a workplace in which employee work–family life balance is possible. And the benefits show up in financial results as well. Research has shown a significant, positive relationship between work–family initiatives and an organization's stock price.[89]

However, managers need to understand that people do differ in their preferences for work–family life scheduling options and benefits.[90] Some people prefer organizational initiatives that better *segment* work from their personal lives. Others prefer programs that facilitate *integration*. For instance, flextime schedules segment because they allow employees to schedule work hours that are less likely to conflict with personal responsibilities. On the other hand, on-site child care integrates by blurring the boundaries between work and family responsibilities. People who prefer segmentation are more likely to be satisfied and committed to their jobs when offered options such as flextime, job sharing, and part-time hours. People who prefer integration are more likely to respond positively to options such as on-site child care, gym facilities, and company-sponsored family picnics.

family-friendly benefits Benefits that accommodate employees' needs for work–life balance.

Discovery Communications provides flexible work arrangements, work-life initiatives, and wellness programs to accommodate employees' different lifestyles, life stages, and life events. To help employees balance work and personal responsibilities, the media company offers telework, compressed work weeks, job sharing, and a summer-hours program. Discovery's wellness initiatives include on-site wellness centres at several U.S. locations, physical fitness reimbursement, annual flu shots, wellness fairs, and wellness classes such as early morning yoga shown here.

Susan Heavey/Reuters

SUMMARY AND IMPLICATIONS

1. Explain the importance of the human resource management process and the external influences that might affect that process. Studies show that an organization's human resources can be a significant competitive advantage. Often, employees are thought of as costs to be minimized or avoided. However, when employees are considered partners, they are more likely to be motivated, leading to greater organizational performance. The external factors that most directly affect the HRM process are the economy, labour unions, legal environment, and demographic trends.

▶▶▶ Scotiabank is often rated as one of Canada's top employers and as a good place for women to work.

2. Discuss the tasks associated with identifying and selecting competent employees. A job analysis is an assessment that defines a job and the behaviours necessary to perform it. A job description is a written statement describing a job, and typically includes job content, environment, and conditions of employment. A job specification is a written statement that specifies the minimum qualifications a person must possess to successfully perform a given job. The major sources of potential job candidates include the Internet, employee referrals, company website, university and college recruiting, and professional recruiting organizations. The different selection devices include application forms (best used for gathering employee information), written tests (must be job-related), work sampling (appropriate for complex nonmanagerial and routine work), assessment centres (most appropriate for top-level managers), interviews (widely used, but most appropriate for managerial positions, especially top-level managers), background investigations (useful for verifying application data, but reference checks are essentially worthless), and physical exams (useful for work that involves certain physical requirements and for insurance purposes). A realistic job preview is important because it gives an applicant more realistic expectations about the job, which in turn should increase employee job satisfaction and reduce turnover.

▶▶▶ Because President and CEO Brian Porter would like to see more women in senior management positions, Scotiabank needs to assess which of its female employees have the skills and leadership qualities to move into senior management. One way that Scotiabank identifies potential employees is through applications from its Careers webpage, which targets young graduates and encourages them to think about working for the bank.

3. Explain the different types of orientation and training. Orientation is important because it results in an outsider–insider transition that makes the new employee feel comfortable and fairly well-adjusted, lowers the likelihood of poor work performance, and reduces the probability of an early surprise resignation. The two types of training are general (includes communication skills, computer skills, customer service, personal growth, etc.) and specific (includes basic life/work skills, customer education, diversity/cultural awareness, managing change, etc.). This training can be provided using traditional training methods (on-the-job, job rotation, mentoring and coaching, experiential exercises, workbooks/manuals, and classroom lectures) or by technology-based methods (CD/DVD/videotapes/audiotapes, videoconferencing or teleconferencing, or e-learning).

▶▶▶ Among other programs, Scotiabank has Leading Edge, the bank's fast-track leadership program.

4. Describe strategies for retaining competent, high-performing employees. Organizations develop compensation and benefit programs that will motivate employees to achieve high performance. Many organizations have implemented skill-based pay systems, which reward employees for the job skills and competencies they can demonstrate. A career is the sequence of positions held by a person during his or her lifetime. Career development programs used to be created by organizations to help employees advance within the organization. Today, employees are encouraged to create their own development programs, in addition to whatever their companies provide, because often employees work for multiple organizations during their careers. Thus, more responsibility rests on employees to manage their own careers.

▶ ▶ ▶ With the growing complexity of global banking, the large international base of employees and the looming retirement of many senior employees, Scotiabank is investing in initiatives to both train and retain their most competent and high-performing employees.

5. Discuss contemporary issues in managing human resources. The major current issues in HR management include managing workforce diversity, managing downsizing, dealing with sexual harassment and workplace romances, and helping employees manage work–life balance. To increase workforce diversity, managers are widening their recruitment net. Managers can manage downsizing by communicating openly and honestly, following appropriate laws regarding severance pay or benefits, providing support/counselling for surviving employees, reassigning roles according to individuals' talents and backgrounds, focusing on boosting morale, and having a plan for empty office spaces. Sexual harassment is any unwanted action or activity of a sexual nature that explicitly or implicitly affects an individual's employment, performance, or work environment. Managers need to be aware of what constitutes an offensive or hostile work environment, educate employees about sexual harassment, and ensure that no retaliatory actions are taken against any person who files harassment charges. Also, they may need to have a policy in place for workplace romances. Organizations are dealing with work–family life balance issues by offering family-friendly benefits such as on-site child care, flextime, telecommuting, and so on. Managers need to understand that people may prefer programs that segment work and personal lives, while others prefer programs that integrate their work and personal lives.

▶ ▶ ▶ Scotiabank prides itself on its work with the Aboriginal community, sponsoring scholarships, events, and programs for community members and also supporting Aboriginal business initiatives. The bank also permits flex hours, flex days, job sharing, and telecommuting so that employees can find the right "work life" to match their personal needs.

MyManagementLab   Study, practise, and explore real management situations with these helpful resources:
- **Interactive Lesson Presentations:** Work through interactive presentations and assessments to test your knowledge of management concepts.
- **PIA (Personal Inventory Assessments):** Enhance your ability to connect with key concepts through these engaging, self-reflection assessments.
- **Study Plan:** Check your understanding of chapter concepts with self-study quizzes.
- **Simulations:** Practise decision-making in simulated management environments.

P **I** **A** PERSONAL INVENTORY ASSESSMENT

REVIEW AND DISCUSSION QUESTIONS

1. Describe the external environmental factors that most directly influence the HRM process.

2. Some critics claim that corporate HR departments have outlived their usefulness and are there not to help employees, but to keep the organization from legal problems. What do you think? What benefits are there to having a formal HRM process? What drawbacks?

3. Describe the different selection devices and which work best for different jobs.

4. What are the benefits and drawbacks of realistic job previews? (Consider this question from the perspective of both the organization and the employee.)

5. Describe the different types of orientation and training and how each of the types of training might be provided.

6. List the factors that influence employee compensation and benefits.

7. Describe the different performance appraisal methods.

8. What, in your view, constitutes sexual harassment? Describe how companies can minimize sexual harassment in the workplace.

ETHICS DILEMMA

It's likely to be a challenging issue for HR managers.[91] "It" is the use of medical marijuana by employees. In Canada, medical marijuana is legal and has raised a number of controversies. Consider the case of Ronald Francis, a veteran RCMP officer who was stripped of his uniform for being photographed for consuming the legally acquired drug while in police uniform. In the United States, seventeen states and the District of Columbia have laws or constitutional amendments that allow patients with certain medical conditions such as cancer, glaucoma, or chronic pain to use marijuana without fear of being prosecuted. Federal prosecutors have been directed by the Obama administration not to bring criminal charges against marijuana users who follow their states' laws. However, that puts employers in a difficult position as they try to accommodate state laws on medical marijuana use while having to enforce federal rules or company drug-use policies based on federal law. In addition to the legal questions, employers are concerned about the challenge of maintaining a safe workplace.

What ethical issues do you see here? How might this issue affect HR processes such as recruitment, selection, performance management, compensation and benefits, and safety and health? What other stakeholders might be impacted by this? In what ways might they be impacted?

SKILLS EXERCISE

Developing Your Interviewing Skills—About the Skill

Every manager needs to develop his or her interviewing skills. The following discussion highlights the key behaviours associated with this skill.

Steps in Practising the Skill

1. *Review the job description and job specification.* Reviewing pertinent information about the job provides valuable information about how to assess the candidate. Furthermore, relevant job requirements help to eliminate interview bias.

2. *Prepare a structured set of questions to ask all applicants for the job.* By having a set of prepared questions, you ensure that the information you wish to elicit is attainable. Furthermore, if you ask all applicants similar questions, you're better able to compare their answers against a common base.

3. *Before meeting an applicant, review his or her application form and résumé.* Doing so helps you to create a complete picture of the applicant in terms of what is represented on the résumé or application and what the job requires. You will also begin to identify areas to explore in the interview. That is, areas not clearly defined on the résumé or application but essential for the job will become a focal point of your discussion with the applicant.

4. *Open the interview by putting the applicant at ease and by providing a brief preview of the topics to be discussed.* Interviews are stressful for job applicants. By opening with small talk (e.g., the weather), you give the person time to adjust to the interview setting. By providing a preview of topics to come, you're giving the applicant an agenda that helps the individual begin framing what he or she will say in response to your questions.

5. *Ask your questions and listen carefully to the applicant's answers.* Select follow-up questions that naturally flow from the answers given. Focus on the responses as they relate to information you need to ensure that the applicant meets your job requirements. Any uncertainty you may still have requires a follow-up question to probe further for the information.

6. *Close the interview by telling the applicant what's going to happen next.* Applicants are anxious about the status of your hiring decision. Be honest with the applicant regarding others who will be interviewed and the remaining steps in the hiring process. If you plan to make a decision in two weeks or so, let the individual know what you intend to do. In addition, tell the applicant how you will let him or her know about your decision.

7. *Write your evaluation of the applicant while the interview is still fresh in your mind.* Don't wait until the end of your day, after interviewing several applicants, to write your analysis of each one. Memory can fail you. The sooner you complete your write-up after an interview, the better chance you have of accurately recording what occurred in the interview.

Practising the Skill

Review and update your résumé. Then have several friends who are employed in management-level positions or in

management training programs critique it. Ask them to explain their comments and make any changes to your résumé they think will improve it.

Now inventory your interpersonal and technical skills and any practical experiences that do not show up in your résumé. Draft a set of leading questions you would like to be asked in an interview that would give you a chance to discuss the unique qualities and attributes you could bring to the job.

WORKING TOGETHER: TEAM EXERCISE

Body Art in the Workplace

The increasing popularity of body art is posing challenges for employers and HR departments in every profession and industry.[92] A Pew Research Center survey reported that 36 percent of 18- to 25-year-olds and 40 percent of 26- to 40-year-olds have at least one tattoo. In those same age groups, 30 percent and 22 percent, respectively, have a piercing somewhere other than their ears. The same survey

found that even in the 40- to 60-year-old age group, more than 10 percent had tattoos or piercings outside of their ears.

Form small groups of three to four individuals. Your team's task is to come up with a dress code and grooming policy that clearly spells out guidelines as far as body art and what is permitted. You can do this in the form of a bulleted list. Be prepared to share your proposed policy with the class.

LEARNING TO BE A MANAGER

- Using the internet, research different companies that interest you and check out what they say about careers or their people.
- If you are working, note what types of HRM activities your managers do. What do they do that seems to

be effective? Ineffective? What can you learn from this?

- Do career research in your chosen career by finding out what it's going to take to be successful in that career.

CASE APPLICATION 1

Thinking Outside the Box

It's the world's largest package delivery company with the instantly recognizable brown trucks.[93] Every day United Parcel Service (UPS) transports more than 15 million packages and documents throughout the United States and to more than 220 countries and territories. Delivering those packages efficiently is what it gets paid to do, and that massive effort wouldn't be possible without its 102 000-plus drivers. UPS recognizes that it has an HR challenge: hiring and training some 25 000 drivers over the next five years to replace retiring baby boomers. But the company has a plan in place that combines its tested business model of uniformity and efficiency (for instance, drivers are trained to hold their keys on a pinky finger so they don't waste time fumbling in their pockets for the keys) with a new approach to driver training.

UPS's traditional classroom driver training obviously wasn't working as some 30 percent of its driver candidates didn't make it. The company was convinced that the twenty-somethings—the bulk of its driver recruits—responded best to high-tech instruction instead of books and lectures. Now, trainees use videogames, a simulator to learn to avoid slips and falls on ice, and an obstacle course around a mock village.

At a UPS training centre outside of Washington, D.C., applicants for a driver's job, which pays an average of $74 000 annually, spend one week practising and training to be a driver. They move from one station to the next practising the company's "340 Methods," techniques developed by industrial engineers to save time and increase safety for all aspects of the job. Applicants play a videogame where they're in the driver's seat and must identify obstacles. From computer simulations, they move to "Clarksville," a mock village with miniature houses and faux businesses. There, they drive a real truck and practise making deliveries at the rate of about 1 every 4 minutes.

How are the new training methods working? So far, so good. Of the 1629 trainees who have completed it, 90 percent pass the six-week training program, which includes 30 days of real-world truck driving.

DISCUSSION QUESTIONS

1. What external factors were affecting UPS's HR practices? How did UPS respond to these trends?
2. Why is efficiency and safety so important to UPS? What role do the company's industrial engineers play in how employees do their work?
3. What changes did the company make to its driver training program? What do you think of these changes?
4. What advantages and drawbacks do you see to this training approach for (a) the trainee and (b) the company?

CASE APPLICATION 2

Spotting Talent

Attracting and selecting the right talent is critical to a company's success. For tech companies, the process is even more critical since it's the knowledge, skills, and abilities of their employees that determines these companies' efficiency, innovation, and ultimately, financial achievements.[94] So, how *do* companies like Google and Facebook and even IBM and Microsoft attract the talent they need? As you'll see, these companies use some unique approaches.

Modis, a global provider of IT staffing and recruiting, has an interesting philosophy about searching for talented tech types. As pressure has mounted on businesses to find qualified employees, the search for the "perfect" candidate has become increasingly competitive. This company calls this "search for perfection the quest for the 'purple squirrel.'" Sometimes you just have to realize that, like the purple squirrel, the "perfect" candidate isn't available or doesn't exist. But that doesn't mean you don't try to find the best available talent. How do some of the big tech names spot talent?

For "mature" tech companies like IBM, Microsoft, and Hewlett-Packard (H-P), the challenge can be especially difficult since they don't have the allure of start-ups or the younger, "sexier" tech companies. So these businesses have to "pour on the charm." Take IBM, for instance. After its Watson computer beat two former *Jeopardy* champions in a televised match, the company hauled the machine to Carnegie Mellon, a top school, where students got a chance to challenge the computer. IBM's goal: lure some of those students to consider a career at IBM. H-P is using the pizza party/tech talk approach at various schools trying to lure younger students before they get "snatched away by other tech companies and start-ups." Microsoft, which was once one of those start-ups, has sent alumni back to schools to promote why Microsoft is a great place to take their talents. And it also hosts game nights, final-exam study parties, and app-building sessions and other events to try to lure students.

For companies like Facebook and Google, the search for talent is still challenging because of the increasing demand for and limited supply of potential employees. So even these companies have to be creative in spotting talent. Google, for instance, found they had been looking at résumés too narrowly by focusing (as expected) on education, GPA, and even SAT scores trying to find those candidates with the highest IQs. But they found that some of those so-called geniuses weren't as effective on the job as expected. So, they began to "take a wider view." Rather than looking at résumés the "traditional way, from top to bottom," they began to look "upside down" at résumés, trying to find some "rare, special attribute that could point the way to greatness." Facebook found that old-fashioned hiring channels weren't getting the talent it needed fast enough. So it tried online puzzles and programming challenges to attract and spot talent. It was an easy, fast, and cheap approach to get submissions from potential candidates. Despite these unique approaches, it's also true that younger tech companies, like these and many others, have a built-in appeal for candidates primarily because they're what's "in" and what's "hot" right now. Also, in many of the younger tech companies, there's no entrenched bureaucracy or cultural restrictions. If employees want to come to work in cargo shorts, t-shirts, and flip-flops, they do. In fact, what attracts many talented employees to companies like these is the fact that they can set their own hours, bring their pets to work, have access to free food and drinks, and a variety of other perks.

DISCUSSION QUESTIONS

1. What does this case imply about the supply of and demand for employees and the implications for businesses?
2. What's the meaning behind the "search for the purple squirrel" in relation to spotting talent? Is this relevant to non-tech companies, as well? Discuss.
3. Do you think "mature" tech companies are always going to have a more difficult time attracting tech talent? Discuss.
4. What do you think of the approaches that Google and Facebook have tried? Explain.
5. Put on your "creative" hat. You're in charge of HR at a tech start-up. What suggestions can you come up with for "spotting talent?"

PART THREE

Management Practice

A Manager's Dilemma

Management theory suggests that, compared to an individual, a diverse group of people will be more creative because team members will bring a variety of ideas, perspectives, and approaches to the group. For an organization like Google, innovation is critical to its success, and teams are a way of life. If management theory about teams is on target, then Google's research and development centre in India should excel at innovation. Why? Because there you'll find broad diversity, even though all employees are from India. These Googlers include Indians, Sikhs, Hindus, Muslims, Buddhists, Christians, and Jains. And they speak English, Hindi, Tamil, Bengali, and more of India's 22 officially recognized languages. One skill Google looks for in potential hires is the ability to work as a team member. As Google continues to grow at a rapid pace, new Googlers are continually added to teams.

Suppose you're a manager at Google's Hyderabad facility. How would you gauge a potential hire's ability to work as a team member, and how would you maintain your team's innovation when new engineers and designers join the group?

Global Sense

Workforce productivity. It's a performance measure that's important to managers and policy makers around the globe. Governments want their labour forces to be productive. Managers want their employees to be productive. Being productive encompasses both efficiency and effectiveness. Think back to our discussion of efficiency and effectiveness in Chapter 1. Efficiency was getting the most output from the least amount of inputs or resources, or said another way, doing things the right way. Effectiveness was doing those work activities that would result in

achieving goals, or doing the right things that would lead to goal achievement. So how does workforce productivity stack up around the world? Here are some of the most recent data on productivity growth rates from the Organisation for Economic Cooperation and Development (OECD): Australia, 0.7 percent; Belgium, –1.2 percent; Canada, 0.7 percent; Estonia, –1.7 percent; Greece, –0.9 percent; Ireland, 2.4 percent; Korea, 1.8 percent; Poland, 3.4 percent; Turkey, 2.4 percent; United Kingdom, 1.9 percent; and United States, 0.2 percent. One factor that has had a significant effect on workforce productivity rates is the ongoing global economic recession. Productivity seems to have spiked through the early part of the downturn, but as the slowdown dragged on, productivity rates, for many countries, including the United States, fell. Labour economists suggest that perhaps companies are approaching the limits of how much they can squeeze from the workforce.

Discuss the following questions in light of what you learned in Part 3:

- *How might workforce productivity be affected by organizational design? Look at the six key elements of organizational design.*
- *How might an organization's human resource management approach affect worker productivity? How could managers use their HR processes to improve worker productivity?*
- *What's your reaction to the statement by experts that perhaps companies are approaching the limits of how much they can squeeze from the workforce? What are the implications for managers as they make organizing decisions?*

Sources: C. Dougherty, "Workforce Productivity Falls," *Wall Street Journal*, May 4, 2012, p. A5; "Labour Productivity Growth in the Total Economy," Organisation for Economic Cooperation and Development, http://stats.oecd.org/Index.aspx?DatasetCode=PDYGTH, February 2012; and "International Comparisons of Manufacturing Productivity and Unit Labor Cost Trends, 2010," Bureau of Labor Statistics, U.S. Department of Labor, [www.bls.gov], December 1, 2011.

Leadership

1. Define leader and leadership.
2. Compare and contrast early theories of leadership.
3. Describe the three major contingency theories of leadership.
4. Describe contemporary views of leadership.
5. Discuss contemporary issues affecting leadership.

Leaders in organizations make things happen. But what makes leaders different from nonleaders? What's the most appropriate style of leadership? What can you do to be seen as a leader? Those are just a few of the questions we'll try to answer in this chapter. After reading and studying this chapter, you will achieve the following learning outcomes.

▶ ▶ ▶ Leadership is a multifaceted topic. As a result, the vignettes in this chapter will highlight five Canadian leaders identified as "master leaders" by Dr. Brad McRae, director of the Atlantic Leadership Institute.[1]

Dr. David Johnston was appointed Canada's governor general in July 2010 but served as the president of the University of Waterloo from 1999 through 2010. At the university, he was a forceful advocate for higher education, research,

and innovation. He pointed out that three things distinguish the University of Waterloo from other universities: "We work very hard at innovation—we try constantly to reinvent ourselves. Secondly, we do a relatively small number of things exceedingly well—we have only six faculties, mathematics which is the largest in the world and engineering which is the largest in Canada. Thirdly, we believe deeply in the cooperative education model and employ it across our programs." A visionary at heart, Johnston has proposed the National Learning and Education Act as a national framework to ensure the well-being of the nation's talent. After all, he reasons, we have the Canada Health Act to protect and enhance the physical well-being of Canadians.

Universities are Canada's innovation engines. To reap the rewards of innovation, knowledge transfer, and the chance to shape and be shaped by the newest ideas in education, we must learn to build collaborative partnerships among the universities, the communities they serve, and local business partners. As Johnston puts it, "My definition of leadership is recognizing your total dependence on the people around you."[2]

D.Chan/EXImages/Alamy

Conservative MP Steven Fletcher is motivated to be a leader. A car accident left him quadriplegic when he was 23, and this inspired him to take charge of his life. He won his first political campaign, to be president of the University of Manitoba Students Union. He later became president of the Progressive Conservative Party of Manitoba. When he was elected MP in 2004, he defeated his riding's incumbent Liberal candidate, ultimately serving in cabinet. He says many of his constituents are not aware that he is quadriplegic until they meet him.

CHRIS WATTIE/Reuters /Landov

Think About It

What does it mean to be a leader for today's organizations? What kinds of challenges does someone like David Johnston face as a leader in the university environment, where change is often glacially slow? What can such a person do to encourage other universities to emulate the Waterloo model?

Who Are Leaders, and What Is Leadership?

Let's begin by clarifying who leaders are and what leadership is. Our definition of a **leader** is someone who can influence others and who has managerial authority. **Leadership** is the process of influencing individuals or groups toward the achievement of goals.

Are all managers leaders? Because leading is one of the four management functions, ideally, all managers *should* be leaders; thus, we're going to study leaders and leadership from a managerial perspective.[3] However, even though we're looking at these from a managerial perspective, we're aware that groups often have informal leaders who emerge. Although these informal leaders may be able to influence others, they have not been the focus of most leadership research and are not the types of leaders we're studying in this chapter.

Leaders and leadership, like motivation, are organizational behaviour topics that have been researched a lot. Most of that research has been aimed at answering the question "What is an effective leader?" We'll begin our study of leadership by looking at some early leadership theories that attempted to answer that question.

Early Leadership Theories

▶ ▶ ▶ Phil Fontaine is the former national chief of the Assembly of First Nations. The youngest son in an Ojibway family of 12 children, he served as chief of Sagkeeng First Nation at the tender age of 28 and set groundbreaking policies for his band. As national chief, Fontaine's crowning achievement was the negotiation of the $5.6 billion residential schools settlement, where he was known for opening lines of communication and building consensus to resolve complex and difficult issues. Since 2009 he has acted as a special advisor to the Royal Bank of Canada with a mandate to "provide advice and counsel to RBC's Canadian businesses to help deepen the company's

👁 Watch on **MyManagementLab**

Leadership (TWZ Role Play)

1 Define leader and leadership.

leader Someone who can influence others and who has managerial authority.

leadership The process of influencing individuals or groups toward the achievement of goals.

2 Compare and contrast early theories of leadership.

relationships with Aboriginal governments, communities and businesses."[4] His focus for the future is the elimination of poverty; improvements in education, health care, and housing; and strengthening of cultural identity for First Nations people, the fastest-growing demographic segment in Canada.[5]

Think About It

In working toward a settlement for the residential schools abuses, Phil Fontaine had to work with an extraordinarily diverse group of stakeholders with competing agendas in the Assembly of First Nations and in the federal government. What traits would serve him well in this situation? What behaviours would serve him well in the negotiations?

People have been interested in leadership since they started coming together in groups to accomplish goals. However, it wasn't until the early part of the twentieth century that researchers actually began to study leadership. These early leadership theories focused on the *leader* (trait theories) and how the *leader interacted* with his or her group members (behavioural theories).

Trait Theories

Even before the 2008 US presidential election, Barack Obama had captured the attention of political analysts and the public.[6] He had been compared to both Abraham Lincoln and Martin Luther King Jr. Many are saying that he has what it takes to be a leading political figure—characteristics such as self-awareness, clarity of speech, keen intellect, and an ability to relate to people. Is Obama a leader? The trait theories of leadership would answer this question by focusing on his traits.

Leadership research in the 1920s and 1930s focused on isolating leader traits—that is, characteristics—that would differentiate leaders from nonleaders. Some of the traits studied included physical stature, appearance, social class, emotional stability, fluency of speech, and sociability. Despite the best efforts of researchers, it proved impossible to identify a set of traits that would *always differentiate* a leader (the person) from a nonleader. Maybe it was a bit optimistic to think that there could be consistent and unique traits that would apply universally to all effective leaders, no matter whether they were in charge of Toyota Motor Corporation, the Moscow Ballet, the country of France, a local collegiate chapter of Alpha Chi Omega, Ted's Malibu Surf Shop, or the University of Waterloo.

Exhibit 13-1

Eight Traits Associated with Leadership

1. *Drive.* Leaders exhibit a high effort level. They have a relatively high desire for achievement, they are ambitious, they have a lot of energy, they are tirelessly persistent in their activities, and they show initiative.

2. *Desire to lead.* Leaders have a strong desire to influence and lead others. They demonstrate the willingness to take responsibility.

3. *Honesty and integrity.* Leaders build trusting relationships with followers by being truthful or nondeceitful and by showing high consistency between word and deed.

4. *Self-confidence.* Followers look to leaders for an absence of self-doubt. Leaders, therefore, need to show self-confidence in order to convince followers of the rightness of their goals and decisions.

5. *Intelligence.* Leaders need to be intelligent enough to gather, synthesize, and interpret large amounts of information, and they need to be able to create visions, solve problems, and make correct decisions.

6. *Job-relevant knowledge.* Effective leaders have a high degree of knowledge about the company, industry, and technical matters. In-depth knowledge allows leaders to make well-informed decisions and to understand the implications of those decisions.

7. *Extraversion.* Leaders are energetic, lively people. They are sociable, assertive, and rarely silent or withdrawn.

8. *Proneness to guilt.* Guilt proneness is positively related to leadership effectiveness because it produces a strong sense of responsibility for others.

Sources: Based on S. A. Kirkpatrick and E. A. Locke, "Leadership: Do Traits Really Matter?" *Academy of Management Executive,* May 1991, pp. 48–60; T. A. Judge, J. E. Bono, R. Ilies, and M. W. Gerhardt, "Personality and Leadership: A Qualitative and Quantitative Review," *Journal of Applied Psychology,* August 2002, pp. 765–780; and R. L. Schaumberg and F. J. Flynn, "Uneasy Lies the Head That Wears the Crown: The Link Between Guilt Proneness and Leadership," *Journal of Personality and Social Psychology,* August 2012, pp. 327–342.

However, later attempts to identify traits consistently associated with *leadership* (the process, not the person) were more successful. Eight traits associated with effective leadership include drive, the desire to lead, honesty and integrity, self-confidence, intelligence, job-relevant knowledge, and extroversion.[7] These traits are briefly described in Exhibit 13-1.

Researchers eventually recognized that traits alone were not sufficient for identifying effective leaders because explanations based solely on traits ignored the interactions of leaders and their group members as well as situational factors. Possessing the appropriate traits only made it more likely that an individual would be an effective leader. Therefore, leadership research from the late 1940s to the mid-1960s concentrated on the preferred behavioural styles that leaders demonstrated. Researchers wondered whether there was something unique in what effective leaders *did*—in other words, in their *behaviour.*

Behavioural Theories

Rick Waugh, president and CEO of Scotiabank, has very little in common with his predecessors who led the bank before him. Both Cedric Ritchie, CEO in the 1970s and 1980s, and Peter Godsoe, who succeeded Ritchie, are described as "autocratic, undemocratic and one-man army" when others reflect on their leadership styles.[8] Waugh, who was appointed president and CEO in 2003, is seen as kinder and gentler. "He is always open to discussion," says Laurent Lemaire, executive vice-chairman of pulp-and-paper manufacturer Cascades and a member of Scotiabank's executive and risk committee and human resources committee. "He will listen to you bring ideas."[9] Scotiabank has been quite successful under different leaders, and moved from the number five to the number two bank in Canada under Godsoe. But this example shows that leaders can behave in very different ways, even when working for the same organization. What do we know about leader behaviour, and how can it help us in our understanding of what an effective leader is?

Exhibit 13-2

Behavioural Theories of Leadership

	Behavioural Dimension	Conclusion
University of Iowa	*Democratic style:* involving subordinates, delegating authority, and encouraging participation *Autocratic style:* dictating work methods, centralizing decision making, and limiting participation *Laissez-faire style:* giving group freedom to make decisions and complete work	Democratic style of leadership was most effective, although later studies showed mixed results.
Ohio State	*Consideration:* being considerate of followers' ideas and feelings *Initiating structure:* structuring work and work relationships to meet job goals	High-high leader (high in consideration and high in initiating structure) achieved high subordinate performance and satisfaction, but not in all situations.
University of Michigan	*Employee oriented:* emphasizes interpersonal relationships and taking care of employees' needs *Production oriented:* emphasizes technical or task aspects of job	Employee-oriented leaders were associated with high group productivity and higher job satisfaction.
Managerial Grid	*Concern for people:* measures leader's concern for subordinates on a scale of 1 to 9 (low to high) *Concern for production:* measures leader's concern for getting job done on a scale of 1 to 9 (low to high)	Leaders performed best with a 9,9 style (high concern for production and high concern for people).

Researchers hoped that the **behavioural theories** approach would provide more definitive answers about the nature of leadership than did the trait theories. The four main leader behaviour studies are summarized in Exhibit 13-2.

University of Iowa Studies

The University of Iowa studies explored three leadership styles to find which was the most effective.[10] The **autocratic** style described a leader who dictated work methods, made unilateral decisions, and limited employee participation. The **democratic** style described a leader who involved employees in decision making, delegated authority, and used feedback as an opportunity for coaching employees. Finally, the **laissez-faire** style described a leader who let the group make decisions and complete the work in whatever way it saw fit. The researchers' results seemed to indicate that the democratic style contributed to both good quantity and quality of work. Had the answer to the question of the most effective leadership style been found? Unfortunately, it wasn't that simple. Later studies of the autocratic and democratic styles showed mixed results. For instance, the democratic style sometimes produced higher performance levels than the autocratic style, but at other times, it didn't. However, more consistent results were found when a measure of employee satisfaction was used. Group members were more satisfied under a democratic leader than under an autocratic one.[11]

Now leaders had a dilemma! Should they focus on achieving higher performance or on achieving higher member satisfaction? This recognition of the dual nature of a leader's behaviour—that is, focus on the task and focus on the people—was also a key characteristic of the other behavioural studies.

The Ohio State Studies

The Ohio State studies identified two important dimensions of leader behaviour.[12] Beginning with a list of more than 1000 behavioural dimensions, the researchers eventually narrowed it down to just two that accounted for most of the leadership behaviour described by group members. The first dimension, called **initiating structure**, referred to the extent to which a leader defined his or her role and the roles of group members in attaining goals.

autocratic style A leadership style whereby the leader tends to centralize authority, dictate work methods, make unilateral decisions, and limit employee participation.

democratic style A leadership style whereby the leader tends to involve employees in decision making, delegate authority, encourage participation in deciding work methods and goals, and use feedback as an opportunity for coaching employees.

laissez-faire style A leadership style whereby the leader tends to give the group complete freedom to make decisions and complete the work in whatever way it sees fit.

initiating structure The extent to which a leader defines his or her role and the roles of group members in attaining goals.

It included behaviours that involved attempts to organize work, work relationships, and goals. The second dimension, called **consideration**, was defined as the extent to which a leader had work relationships characterized by mutual trust and respect for group members' ideas and feelings. A leader who was high in consideration helped group members with personal problems, was friendly and approachable, and treated all group members as equals. He or she showed concern for (was considerate of) his or her followers' comfort, well-being, status, and satisfaction. Research found that a leader who was high in both initiating structure and consideration (a **high-high leader**) sometimes achieved high group task performance and high group member satisfaction, but not always.

consideration The extent to which a leader has work relationships characterized by mutual trust and respect for group members' ideas and feelings.

high-high leader A leader high in both initiating structure and consideration behaviours.

University of Michigan Studies

Leadership studies conducted at the University of Michigan at about the same time as those being done at Ohio State also hoped to identify behavioural characteristics of leaders that were related to performance effectiveness. The Michigan group also came up with two dimensions of leadership behaviour, which they labelled *employee oriented* and *production oriented*.[13] Leaders who were employee oriented were described as emphasizing interpersonal relationships. The production-oriented leaders, in contrast, tended to emphasize the task aspects of the job. Unlike the other studies, the Michigan studies concluded that leaders who were employee oriented were able to get high group productivity and high group member satisfaction.

The Managerial Grid

The behavioural dimensions from the early leadership studies provided the basis for the development of a two-dimensional grid for appraising leadership styles. This **managerial grid** used the behavioural dimensions "concern for people" and "concern for production" and evaluated a leader's use of these behaviours, ranking them on a scale from 1 (low) to 9 (high).[14] Although the grid had 81 potential categories into which a leader's behavioural style might fall, only five styles were named: impoverished management (1,1), task management (9,1), middle-of-the-road management (5,5), country club management (1,9), and team management (9,9). Of these five styles, the researchers concluded that managers performed best when using a 9,9 style. Unfortunately, the grid offered no explanations about what made a manager an effective leader; it only provided a framework for conceptualizing leadership style. In fact, there's little substantive evidence to support the conclusion that a 9,9 style is most effective in all situations.[15]

managerial grid A two-dimensional grid of leadership behaviours—concern for people and concern for production—that results in five different leadership styles.

Leadership researchers were discovering that predicting leadership success involved something more complex than isolating a few leader traits or preferable behaviours. They began looking at situational influences. Specifically, which leadership styles might be suitable in different situations, and what were these different situations?

Chanda Kochhar is the managing director and chief executive officer of ICICI Bank in India. She is an employee-oriented leader whose behaviour toward subordinates is compassionate, nurturing, and understanding. Kochhar sets high performance goals, encourages employees to work hard, motivates them to perform to the best of their abilities, and helps them realize their full potential. Her leadership behaviour of emphasizing interpersonal relationships and being sensitive to employees has resulted in high group member satisfaction and high group productivity. Under her leadership, ICICI Bank has grown to become the largest private retail bank in India.

Vivek Prakash/Reuters

Contingency Theories of Leadership

3 Describe the three major contingency theories of leadership.

Andrew Wallace/GetStock.com

fiedler contingency model A leadership theory that proposed that effective group performance depended on the proper match between a leader's style and the degree to which the situation allowed the leader to control and influence.

least-preferred co-worker (LPC) questionnaire A questionnaire that measured whether a leader was task or relationship oriented.

▶ ▶ ▶ Moya Greene was appointed president of Canada Post on May 12, 2005, following a portfolio of difficult assignments—she was responsible for the privatization of CN Rail, helped deregulate the airline industry, and took a lead role in the overhaul of the employment insurance system. Because Greene did not come from a logistics or postal background, she had to learn the culture at Canada Post first-hand. Starting from the ground up, she worked at a variety of key tasks and gained a sense of how complex and difficult it is to move 40 million pieces of mail a day to 14 million mailboxes, and was quoted as saying, "Each of our executives has to do a specific number of front line operations quarterly."[16] After departing from Canada Post, Greene became CEO of the Royal Mail in the summer of 2010, the first non-Briton and the first women to hold the post. Greene was named the Financial Times Person of the Year in 2014.[17]

Think About It

How did Moya Greene's commitment to gaining front-line experience help her understand the context for decision making at Canada Post? How do different situations and contexts influence her leadership style?

"The corporate world is filled with stories of leaders who failed to achieve greatness because they failed to understand the context they were working in."[18] In this section, we examine three contingency theories—Fiedler, Hersey-Blanchard, and path–goal. Each looks at defining leadership style and the situation, and attempts to answer the *if–then* contingencies (that is, *if* this is the context or situation, *then* this is the best leadership style to use).

The Fiedler Model

The first comprehensive contingency model for leadership was developed by Fred Fiedler.[19] The **Fiedler contingency model** proposed that effective group performance depended on properly matching the leader's style and the amount of control and influence in the situation. The model was based on the premise that a certain leadership style would be most effective in different types of situations. The keys were to (1) define those leadership styles and the different types of situations and then (2) identify the appropriate combinations of style and situation.

Fiedler proposed that a key factor in leadership success was an individual's basic leadership style, either task oriented or relationship oriented. To measure a leader's style, Fiedler developed the **least-preferred co-worker (LPC) questionnaire**. This questionnaire contained 18 pairs of contrasting adjectives—for example, pleasant–unpleasant, cold–warm, boring–interesting, and friendly–unfriendly. Respondents were asked to think of all the co-workers they had ever had and to describe that one person they *least enjoyed* working with by rating him or her on a scale of 1 to 8 for each of the 18 sets of adjectives. (The 8 always described the positive adjective out of the pair, and the 1 always described the negative adjective out of the pair.)

If the leader described the least-preferred co-worker in relatively positive terms (in other words, a "high" LPC score—a score of 64 or above), then the respondent was primarily interested in good personal relations with co-workers, and the style would be described as *relationship oriented.* In contrast, if the leader saw the least-preferred co-worker in relatively unfavourable terms (a low LPC score—a score of 57 or below), he or she was primarily interested in productivity and getting the job done; thus, the individual's style would be labelled *task oriented.* Fiedler acknowledged that a small number of people might fall in between these two extremes and not have a cut-and-dried leadership style. One other important point is that Fiedler assumed that a person's leadership style was fixed, regardless of the situation. In other words, if you were a relationship-oriented leader, you'd always be one, and if you were a task-oriented leader, you'd always be one.

After an individual's leadership style had been assessed through the LPC, it was time to evaluate the situation in order to be able to match the leader with the situation. Fiedler's research uncovered three contingency dimensions that defined the key situational factors in leader effectiveness:

- **Leader–member relations**—The degree of confidence, trust, and respect employees had for their leader; rated as either good or poor.

- **Task structure**—The degree to which job assignments were formalized and structured; rated as either high or low.

- **Position power**—The degree of influence a leader had over activities such as hiring, firing, discipline, promotions, and salary increases; rated as either strong or weak.

Each leadership situation was evaluated in terms of these three contingency variables, which when combined produced eight possible situations that were either favourable or unfavourable for the leader. (See the bottom of Exhibit 13-3.) Situations I, II, and III were classified as highly favourable for the leader. Situations IV, V, and VI were moderately favourable for the leader. And situations VII and VIII were described as highly unfavourable for the leader.

Once Fiedler had described the leader variables and the situational variables, he had everything he needed to define the specific contingencies for leadership effectiveness. To do so, he studied 1200 groups for which he compared relationship-oriented versus task-oriented leadership styles in each of the eight situational categories. He concluded that task-oriented leaders performed better in very favourable situations and in very unfavourable situations. (See the top of Exhibit 13-3, where performance is shown on the vertical axis and situation favourableness is shown on the horizontal axis.) On the other hand, relationship-oriented leaders performed better in moderately favourable situations.

Because Fiedler treated an individual's leadership style as fixed, there were only two ways to improve leader effectiveness. First, you could bring in a new leader whose style better fit the situation. For instance, if the group situation was highly unfavourable but

leader–member relations One of Fiedler's situational contingencies that described the degree of confidence, trust, and respect employees had for their leader.

task structure One of Fiedler's situational contingencies that described the degree to which job assignments were formalized and structured.

position power One of Fiedler's situational contingencies that described the degree of influence a leader had over activities such as hiring, firing, discipline, promotions, and salary increases.

Exhibit 13-3

The Fiedler Model

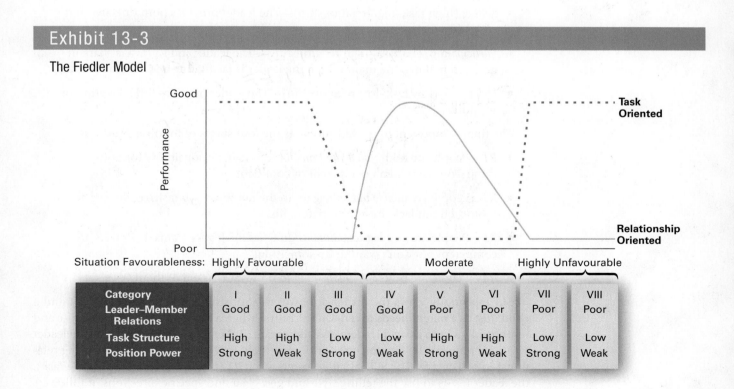

Category	I	II	III	IV	V	VI	VII	VIII
Leader–Member Relations	Good	Good	Good	Good	Poor	Poor	Poor	Poor
Task Structure	High	High	Low	Low	High	High	Low	Low
Position Power	Strong	Weak	Strong	Weak	Strong	Weak	Strong	Weak

Situation Favourableness: Highly Favourable | Moderate | Highly Unfavourable

was led by a relationship-oriented leader, the group's performance could be improved by replacing that person with a task-oriented leader. The second alternative was to change the situation to fit the leader. This could be done by restructuring tasks; by increasing or decreasing the power that the leader had over factors such as salary increases, promotions, and disciplinary actions; or by improving the leader–member relations.

Research testing the overall validity of Fiedler's model has shown considerable evidence in support of the model.[20] However, his theory wasn't without criticisms. The major criticism is that it's probably unrealistic to assume that a person can't change his or her leadership style to fit the situation. Effective leaders can and do change their styles. Another is that the LPC wasn't very practical. Finally, the situation variables were difficult to assess.[21] Despite its shortcomings, the Fiedler model showed that effective leadership style needed to reflect situational factors.

Hersey and Blanchard's Situational Leadership® Theory

situational leadership® theory (SLT) A leadership contingency theory that focuses on followers' readiness.

Paul Hersey and Ken Blanchard developed a leadership theory that has gained a strong following among management development specialists.[22] This model, called **Situational Leadership® theory (SLT)**, is a contingency theory that focuses on followers' readiness. Before we proceed, there are two points we need to clarify: why a leadership theory focuses on the followers and what is meant by the term *readiness*.

readiness The extent to which people have the ability and willingness to accomplish a specific task.

The emphasis on the followers in leadership effectiveness reflects the reality that it *is* the followers who accept or reject the leader. Regardless of what the leader does, the group's effectiveness depends on the actions of the followers. This is an important dimension that most leadership theories have overlooked or underemphasized. **Readiness**, as defined by Hersey and Blanchard, refers to the extent to which people have the ability and willingness to accomplish a specific task.

SLT uses the same two leadership dimensions that Fiedler identified: task and relationship behaviours. However, Hersey and Blanchard go a step further by considering each as either high or low and then combining them into four specific leadership styles:

- *Telling* (high task–low relationship)—The leader defines roles and tells people what, how, when, and where to do various tasks.

- *Selling* (high task–high relationship)—The leader provides both directive and supportive behaviour.

- *Participating* (low task–high relationship)—The leader and followers share in decision making; the main role of the leader is facilitating and communicating.

- *Delegating* (low task–low relationship)—The leader provides little direction or support.

The final component in the SLT model is the four stages of follower readiness:

- *R1*—People are both *unable and unwilling* to take responsibility for doing something. Followers aren't competent or confident.

- *R2*—People are *unable but willing* to do the necessary job tasks. Followers are motivated but lack the appropriate skills.

- *R3*—People are *able but unwilling* to do what the leader wants. Followers are competent but don't want to do something.

- *R4*—People are both *able and willing* to do what is asked of them.

SLT essentially views the leader–follower relationship as like that of a parent and a child. Just as a parent needs to relinquish control when a child becomes more mature and responsible, so too should leaders. As followers reach higher levels of readiness, the leader responds not only by decreasing control over their activities but also by decreasing relationship behaviours. The SLT says if followers are at R1 (*unable and unwilling* to do a task), the leader needs to use the telling style and give clear and specific directions; if followers

Exhibit 13-4

Hersey and Blanchard's Situational Leadership®

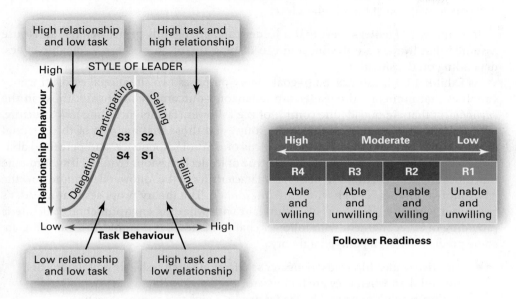

are at R2 (*unable and willing*), the leader needs to use the selling style and *display high task orientation to compensate for the followers' lack of ability and high relationship orientation to get followers to "buy into" the leader's desires; if followers are at R3 (*able and unwilling*), the leader needs to use the participating style to gain their support; and if employees are at R4 (both *able and willing*), the leader doesn't need to do much and should use the delegating style.

SLT has intuitive appeal. It acknowledges the importance of followers and builds on the logic that leaders can compensate for ability and motivational limitations in their followers. However, research efforts to test and support the theory have generally been disappointing.[23] Possible explanations include internal inconsistencies in the model as well as problems with research methodology. Despite its appeal and wide popularity, we have to be cautious about any enthusiastic endorsement of SLT.

Path–Goal Theory

Currently, one of the most respected approaches to understanding leadership is **path–goal theory**, which states that the leader's job is to assist followers in attaining their goals and to provide direction or support needed to ensure that their goals are compatible with those of the group or organization. Developed by Robert House, path–goal theory takes key elements from the expectancy theory of motivation.[24] The term *path–goal* is derived from the belief that effective leaders clarify the path to help their followers get from where they are to the achievement of their work goals and make the journey along the path easier by reducing roadblocks and pitfalls.

House identified four leadership behaviours:

- *Directive leader*—The leader lets subordinates know what's expected of them, schedules work to be done, and gives specific guidance on how to accomplish tasks.

- *Supportive leader*—The leader shows concern for the needs of followers and is friendly.

path–goal theory A leadership theory that says the leader's job is to assist followers in attaining their goals and to provide direction or support needed to ensure that their goals are compatible with those of the group or organization.

- *Participative leader*—The leader consults with group members and uses their suggestions before making a decision.

- *Achievement-oriented leader*—The leader sets challenging goals and expects followers to perform at their highest level.

In contrast to Fiedler's view that a leader can't change his or her behaviour, House assumed that leaders are flexible and can display any or all of these leadership styles, depending on the situation.

As Exhibit 13-5 illustrates, path–goal theory proposes two situational or contingency variables that moderate the leadership behaviour–outcome relationship: those in the *environment* that are outside the control of the follower (factors including task structure, formal authority system, and the work group) and those that are part of the personal characteristics of the *follower* (including locus of control, experience, and perceived ability). Environmental factors determine the type of leader behaviour required if subordinate outcomes are to be maximized; personal characteristics of the follower determine how the environment and leader behaviour are interpreted. The theory proposes that a leader's behaviour won't be effective if it's redundant with what the environmental structure is providing or is incongruent with follower characteristics. For example, the following are some predictions from path–goal theory:

- Directive leadership leads to greater satisfaction when tasks are ambiguous or stressful than when they are highly structured and well laid out. The followers aren't sure what to do, so the leader needs to give them some direction.

- Supportive leadership results in high employee performance and satisfaction when subordinates are performing structured tasks. In this situation, the leader only needs to support followers, not tell them what to do.

- Directive leadership is likely to be perceived as redundant among subordinates with high perceived ability or with considerable experience. These followers are quite capable, so they don't need a leader to tell them what to do.

- The clearer and more bureaucratic the formal authority relationships, the more leaders should exhibit supportive behaviour and de-emphasize directive behaviour. The organizational situation has provided the structure as far as what is expected of followers, so the leader's role is simply to support.

Exhibit 13-5

Path–Goal Model

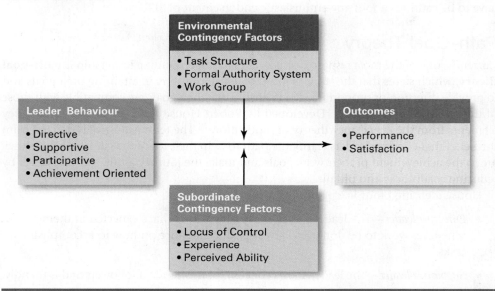

- Directive leadership will foster higher employee satisfaction when there is substantive conflict within a work group. In this situation, the followers need a leader who will take charge.

- Subordinates with an internal locus of control will be more satisfied with a participative style. Because these followers believe that they control what happens to them, they prefer to participate in decisions.

- Subordinates with an external locus of control will be more satisfied with a directive style. These followers believe that what happens to them is a result of the external environment, so they would prefer a leader who tells them what to do.

- Achievement-oriented leadership will increase subordinates' expectations that effort will lead to high performance when tasks are ambiguously structured. By setting challenging goals, followers know what the expectations are.

Testing path–goal theory has not been easy. A review of the research suggests mixed support. In summary, an employee's performance and satisfaction are likely to be positively influenced when a leader chooses a leadership style that compensates for shortcomings in either the employee or the work setting. However, if a leader spends time explaining tasks that are already clear or when an employee has the ability and experience to handle tasks without interference, the employee is likely to see such directive behaviour as redundant or even insulting.

Contemporary Views of Leadership

▶ ▶ ▶ When David Cheesewright became president of Walmart Canada, the organization was in the midst of implementing its sustainability strategy under the banner of "the greener good." Lee Scott, president of Walmart International, had set goals of zero waste to landfill (beginning with a 65 percent diversion rate by 2014) and a move to 100 percent renewable energy, with all Walmart suppliers to be held to compliance standards supporting these initiatives. It was the company's intent to price products in a way that would reflect their true costs—including the environmental ones.[26] Today, Walmart has exceeded its waste management benchmark and is on track to meet its commitments to sustainable energy. Currently Walmart diverts 88.1 percent of its waste and supplies its retail locations with 2.2 billion kilowatt hours of renewable energy annually.[27] David currently serves as president and chief executive officer of Walmart International, responsible for more than 6400 stores and 796 000 associates.[28]

4 Describe contemporary views of leadership.

J.P. Moczulski/Canadian Press Images

> ## Think About It
>
> **As president of Walmart Canada, David Cheesewright is tasked with implementing a fundamental change in strategic direction. What tools might he use? What style of leadership would best support this transformation of the organizational culture? What types of resistance should he expect?**

What are the latest views of leadership? There are three we want to look at: transformational vs. transactional leadership,[29] charismatic–visionary leadership, and team leadership.

Leader–Member Exchange (LMX) Theory

Have you ever been in a group in which the leader had "favourites" who made up his or her in-group? If so, that's the premise behind leader–member exchange (LMX) theory.[30] **Leader–member exchange theory (LMX)** says leaders create in-groups and out-groups and those in the in-group will have higher performance ratings, less turnover, and greater job satisfaction.

◀◉▶ Simulate on **MyManagementLab**

The Leadership Imperative

leader–member exchange theory (LMX) The leadership theory that says leaders create in-groups and out-groups and those in the in-group will have higher performance ratings, less turnover, and greater job satisfaction.

LMX theory suggests that early on in the relationship between a leader and a given follower, a leader will implicitly categorize a follower as an "in" or as an "out." That relationship tends to remain fairly stable over time. Leaders also encourage LMX by rewarding those employees with whom they want a closer linkage and punishing those with whom they do not.[31] For the LMX relationship to remain intact, however, both the leader and the follower must "invest" in the relationship.

It's not exactly clear how a leader chooses who falls into each category, but evidence shows that in-group members have demographic, attitude, personality, and even gender similarities with the leader or they have a higher level of competence than out-group members.[32] The leader does the choosing, but the follower's characteristics drive the decision.

Research on LMX has been generally supportive. It appears that leaders do differentiate among followers; that these disparities are not random; and followers with in-group status will have higher performance ratings, engage in more helping or "citizenship" behaviours at work, and report greater satisfaction with their boss.[33] This probably shouldn't be surprising since leaders invest their time and other resources in those whom they expect to perform best.

Transformational vs. Transactional Leadership

Many early leadership theories viewed leaders as **transactional leaders**—that is, leaders who lead primarily by using social exchanges (or transactions). Transactional leaders guide or motivate followers to work toward established goals by exchanging rewards for their productivity.[34] But there's another type of leader—a **transformational leader**—who stimulates and inspires (transforms) followers to achieve extraordinary outcomes. Examples include Jim Goodnight of SAS Institute and Andrea Jung of Avon. They pay attention to the concerns and developmental needs of individual followers; they change followers' awareness of issues by helping those followers look at old problems in new ways; and they are able to excite, arouse, and inspire followers to exert extra effort to achieve group goals.

Transactional and transformational leadership shouldn't be viewed as opposing approaches to getting things done.[35] Transformational leadership develops from transactional leadership. Transformational leadership produces levels of employee effort and performance that go beyond what would occur with a transactional approach alone. Moreover, transformational leadership is more than charisma because a transformational leader attempts to instill in followers the ability to question not only established views but views held by the leader.[36] The evidence supporting the superiority of transformational leadership over transactional leadership is overwhelmingly impressive. For instance, studies that looked at managers in different settings, including the military and business, found that transformational leaders were evaluated as more effective, higher performers, more promotable than their transactional counterparts, and more interpersonally sensitive.[37] In addition, evidence indicates that transformational leadership is strongly correlated with lower turnover rates and higher levels of productivity, employee satisfaction, creativity, goal attainment, and follower well-being.[38]

Charismatic–Visionary Leadership

Jeff Bezos, founder and CEO of Amazon.com,[39] has pursued his vision for Amazon with serious intensity and has demonstrated an ability to inspire his employees through the ups and downs of a rapidly growing company. Bezos is what we call a **charismatic leader**—that is, an enthusiastic, self-confident leader whose personality and actions influence people to behave in certain ways.

Characteristics of Charismatic Leaders

Several authors have attempted to identify personal characteristics of charismatic leaders.[40] The most comprehensive analysis identified five such characteristics: Charismatic leaders have a vision, ability to articulate that vision, willingness to take risks to achieve that vision, sensitivity to both environmental constraints and follower needs, and behaviours that are out of the ordinary.[41]

Effects of Charismatic Leadership

An increasing body of evidence shows impressive correlations between charismatic leadership and high performance and satisfaction among followers.[42] Although one study found that charismatic CEOs had no impact on subsequent organizational performance, charisma is still believed to be a desirable leadership quality.[43]

Becoming Charismatic

If charisma is desirable, can people learn to be charismatic leaders? Or are charismatic leaders born with their qualities? Although a small number of experts still think that charisma can't be learned, most believe that individuals can be trained to exhibit charismatic behaviours.[44] For example, researchers have succeeded in teaching undergraduate students to "be" charismatic. How? The students have been taught to articulate a far-reaching goal, communicate high performance expectations, exhibit confidence in the ability of subordinates to meet those expectations, and empathize with the needs of their subordinates; they have learned to project a powerful, confident, and dynamic presence; and they have practised using a captivating and engaging tone of voice. The researchers have also trained student leaders to use charismatic nonverbal behaviours, including leaning toward the follower when communicating, maintaining direct eye contact, and having a relaxed posture and animated facial expressions. In groups with these "trained" charismatic leaders, members had higher task performance, higher task adjustment, and better adjustment to the leader and to the group than did group members who worked in groups led by noncharismatic leaders.

One last thing we should say about charismatic leadership is that it may not always be necessary to achieve high levels of employee performance. Charismatic leadership may be most appropriate when the follower's task has an ideological purpose or when the environment involves a high degree of stress and uncertainty.[45] This may explain why, when charismatic leaders surface, they're likely to crop up in politics, religion, or wartime, or when a business firm is starting up or facing a survival crisis. For example, Martin Luther King Jr. used his charisma to bring about social equality through nonviolent means, and Steve Jobs achieved unwavering loyalty and commitment from Apple's technical staff in the early 1980s by articulating a vision of personal computers that would dramatically change the way people lived.

Visionary Leadership

Although the term *vision* is often linked with charismatic leadership, **visionary leadership** is different because it's the ability to create and articulate a realistic, credible, and attractive vision of the future that improves on the present situation.[46] This vision, if properly selected and implemented, is so energizing that it "in effect jump-starts the future by calling forth the skills, talents, and resources to make it happen."[47]

visionary leadership The ability to create and articulate a realistic, credible, and attractive vision of the future that improves on the present situation.

MANAGEMENT REFLECTION

An Apple a Day…

How was the late Steve Jobs able to accomplish what he did?[48] How was he able to take Apple from a niche business and turn it into the most valuable company in the world as measured by market capitalization. Jobs was extremely charismatic and extremely compelling in getting people to join with him and believe in his vision. But also he was despotic, tyrannical, abrasive, uncompromising, and a perfectionist. So what is his leadership legacy?

Everything Jobs did and how he did it was motivated by his desire to have Apple make innovative products—products that were "insanely great"—"insanely" being one of his favourite descriptors. That singular focus shaped his leadership style, which has been described as autocratic and yet persuasive. As one reporter said, Jobs "violated every rule of management. He was not a consensus builder but a dictator who listened mainly to his own intuition. He was a maniacal micromanager. . . He could be absolutely brutal in meetings." His verbal assaults on staff could be terrifying. When asked about his tendency to be rough on people, Jobs responded, "Look at the results. These are all smart people I work with, and any of them could get a top job at another place if they were truly feeling brutalized. But they don't." ■

An organization's vision should offer clear and compelling imagery that taps into people's emotions and inspires enthusiasm to pursue the organization's goals. It should be able to generate possibilities that are inspirational and unique and offer new ways of doing things that are clearly better for the organization and its members. Visions that are clearly articulated and have powerful imagery are easily grasped and accepted. For instance, Michael Dell of Dell Inc. created a vision of a business that sells and delivers customized PCs directly to customers in less than a week. The late Mary Kay Ash's vision of women as entrepreneurs selling products that improved their self-image gave impetus to her cosmetics company, Mary Kay Cosmetics.

Team Leadership

Because leadership is increasingly taking place within a team context and more organizations are using work teams, the role of the leader in guiding team members has become increasingly important. The role of a team leader *is* different from the traditional leadership role, as J. D. Bryant, a supervisor at the Texas Instruments Forest Lane plant in Dallas, discovered.[49] One day he was contentedly overseeing a staff of 15 circuit board assemblers. The next day he was told that the company was going to use employee teams, and he was to become a "facilitator." He said, "I'm supposed to teach the teams everything I know and then let them make their own decisions." Confused about his new role, he admitted, "There was no clear plan on what I was supposed to do." What *is* involved in being a team leader?

Many leaders are not equipped to handle the change to employee teams. As one consultant noted, "Even the most capable managers have trouble making the transition because all the command-and-control type things they were encouraged to do before are no longer appropriate. There's no reason to have any skill or sense of this."[50] This same consultant estimated that "probably 15 percent of managers are natural team leaders; another 15 percent could never lead a team because it runs counter to their personality—that is, they're unable

This young man is a team leader who manages the bakery department at a Whole Foods Market store. As leader of a 13-member team, he needs to possess good communication skills, work well with others, and convey enthusiasm. He serves as a coach in training and motivating team members to excellence in all aspects of the department, from maintaining good relationships with each other and with vendors to achieving team goals for sales, growth, and productivity. Whole Foods is completely organized around employee teams, with team leaders for each store department. Team leaders in each store also function as a team, store leaders in each region are a team, and regional presidents work as a team.

Daily Mail/Rex/Alamy

Exhibit 13-6

Team Leadership Roles

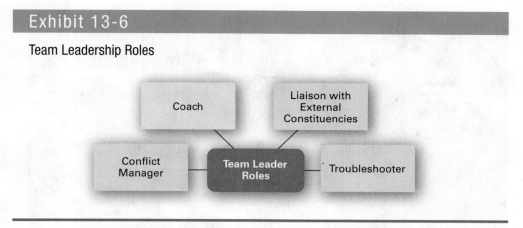

to sublimate their dominating style for the good of the team. Then there's that huge group in the middle: Team leadership doesn't come naturally to them, but they can learn it."[51]

The challenge for many managers is learning how to become an effective team leader. They have to learn skills such as patiently sharing information, being able to trust others and give up authority, and understanding when to intervene. And effective team leaders have mastered the difficult balancing act of knowing when to leave their teams alone and when to get involved. New team leaders may try to retain too much control at a time when team members need more autonomy, or they may abandon their teams at times when the teams need support and help.[53]

One study looking at organizations that had reorganized themselves around employee teams found certain common responsibilities of all leaders. These included coaching, facilitating, handling disciplinary problems, reviewing team and individual performance, training, and communication.[54] However, a more meaningful way to describe the team leader's job is to focus on two priorities: (1) managing the team's external boundary and (2) facilitating the team process.[55] These priorities entail four specific leadership roles, as shown in Exhibit 13-6.

Leadership Issues in the Twenty-First Century

▶ ▶ ▶ In 2010, Annette Verschuren was inducted into Canada's Marketing Hall of Legends and the Nova Scotia Business Hall of Fame. Verschuren clearly demonstrated her superior leadership skills in her role as president of The Home Depot Canada. When she took on the role in March 2006, there were just 19 Home Depot stores in Canada, but by the time she stepped down in January 2011, that number had grown to 179! Verschuren also led the expansion of the company into China, acquiring a chain of 12 stores in December 2006.

Before working for The Home Depot, Verschuren's impressive titles included president and co-owner of Michael's of Canada (arts and crafts stores) and vice-president of corporate development at Imasco Ltd. (a holding company for Shoppers Drug Mart, Canada Trust, and Imperial Tobacco). In addition to her work in the private sector, Verschuren served as executive vice-president of Canada Development Investment Corporation, privatizing various Crown corporations.[56] She currently serves as chancellor of Cape Breton University and serves as chair and CEO of NRStor, a company focusing on commercialization of energy storage technologies.[57]

5 Discuss contemporary issues affecting leadership.

> **Think About It**
> How did Verschuren's prior experience in the private and public sectors prepare her as a leader to deal with managing power, developing trust, empowering employees, and leading across cultures at The Home Depot? How did her varied experience help her to understand gender differences and continuously improve the leadership skills of her and her team?

Dick Loek/GetStock.com

It's not easy being a chief information officer (CIO) today. This person, who is responsible for managing a company's information technology activities, faces a lot of external and internal pressures. Technology continues to change rapidly—almost daily, it sometimes seems. Business costs continue to rise. Rob Carter, CIO of FedEx, is on the hot seat facing such challenges.[58] He's responsible for all the computer and communication systems that provide around-the-clock and around-the-globe support for FedEx's products and services. If anything goes wrong, you know who takes the heat. However, Carter has been an effective leader in this seemingly chaotic environment.

For most leaders, leading effectively in today's environment is unlikely to involve the challenging circumstances Carter faces. However, twenty-first-century leaders do deal with some important leadership issues. In this section, we look at these issues that include managing power, developing trust, empowering employees, leading across cultures, and becoming an effective leader.

Managing Power

Where do leaders get their power—that is, their capacity to influence work actions or decisions? Five sources of leader power have been identified: legitimate, coercive, reward, expert, and referent.[59]

Legitimate power and authority are the same. Legitimate power represents the power a leader has as a result of his or her position in the organization. Although people in positions of authority are also likely to have reward and coercive power, legitimate power is broader than the power to coerce and reward.

Coercive power is the power a leader has to punish or control. Followers react to this power out of fear of the negative results that might occur if they don't comply. Managers typically have some coercive power, such as being able to suspend or demote employees or to assign them work they find unpleasant or undesirable.

Reward power is the power to give positive rewards. These can be anything that a person values, such as money, favourable performance appraisals, promotions, interesting work assignments, friendly colleagues, and preferred work shifts or sales territories.

Expert power is power that's based on expertise, special skills, or knowledge. If an employee has skills, knowledge, or expertise that's critical to a work group, that person's expert power is enhanced.

legitimate power The power a leader has as a result of his or her position in an organization.

coercive power The power a leader has to punish or control.

reward power The power a leader has to give positive rewards.

expert power Power that's based on expertise, special skills, or knowledge. .

Finally, **referent power** is the power that arises because of a person's desirable resources or personal traits. If I admire you and want to be associated with you, you can exercise power over me because I want to please you. Referent power develops out of admiration of another and a desire to be like that person.

Most effective leaders rely on several different forms of power to affect the behaviour and performance of their followers. For example, the commanding officer of one of Australia's state-of-the-art submarines, the HMAS *Sheean*, employs different types of power in managing his crew and equipment. He gives orders to the crew (legitimate), praises them (reward), and disciplines those who commit infractions (coercive). As an effective leader, he also strives to have expert power (based on his expertise and knowledge) and referent power (based on his being admired) to influence his crew.[60]

Developing Trust

In today's uncertain environment, an important consideration for leaders is building trust and credibility—trust that can be extremely fragile. Before we can discuss ways leaders can build trust and credibility, we have to know what trust and credibility are and why they're so important.

The main component of credibility is honesty. Surveys show that honesty is consistently singled out as the number one characteristic of admired leaders. "Honesty is absolutely essential to leadership. If people are going to follow someone willingly, whether it be into battle or into the boardroom, they first want to assure themselves that the person is worthy of their trust."[61] In addition to being honest, credible leaders are competent and inspiring. They are personally able to effectively communicate their confidence and enthusiasm. Thus, followers judge a leader's **credibility** in terms of his or her honesty, competence, and ability to inspire.

Trust is closely entwined with the concept of credibility, and, in fact, the terms are often used interchangeably. **Trust** is defined as the belief in the integrity, character, and ability of a leader. Followers who trust a leader are willing to be vulnerable to the leader's actions because they are confident that their rights and interests will not be abused.[62] Research has identified five dimensions that make up the concept of trust:[63]

credibility The degree to which followers perceive someone as honest, competent, and able to inspire.

trust The belief in the integrity, character, and ability of a leader.

- *Integrity*—Honesty and truthfulness
- *Competence*—Technical and interpersonal knowledge and skills
- *Consistency*—Reliability, predictability, and good judgment in handling situations
- *Loyalty*—Willingness to protect a person, physically and emotionally
- *Openness*—Willingness to share ideas and information freely

Of these five dimensions, integrity seems to be the most critical when someone assesses another's trustworthiness.[64] Both integrity and competence came up in our earlier discussion of traits found to be consistently associated with leadership. Workplace changes have reinforced why such leadership qualities are important. For instance, the trend toward empowerment (which we'll discuss shortly) and self-managed work teams has reduced many of the traditional control mechanisms used to monitor employees. If a work team is free to schedule its own work, evaluate its own performance, and even make its own hiring decisions, trust becomes critical. Employees have to trust managers to treat them fairly, and managers have to trust employees to conscientiously fulfill their responsibilities.

Also, leaders have to increasingly lead others who may not be in their immediate work group or even may be physically separated—members of cross-functional or virtual teams, individuals who work for suppliers or customers, and perhaps even people who represent other organizations through strategic alliances. These situations don't allow leaders the luxury of falling back on their formal positions for influence. Many of these relationships, in fact, are fluid and temporary. So the ability to quickly develop trust and sustain that trust is crucial to the success of the relationship.

Exhibit 13-7

Building Trust

- Practise openness.
- Be fair.
- Speak your feelings.
- Tell the truth.
- Show consistency.
- Fulfill your promises.
- Maintain confidences.
- Demonstrate competence.

Why is it important that followers trust their leaders? Research has shown that trust in leadership is significantly related to positive job outcomes, including job performance, organizational citizenship behaviour, job satisfaction, and organizational commitment.[65] Given the importance of trust to effective leadership, how can leaders build trust? Exhibit 13-7 lists some suggestions.

Now, more than ever, managerial and leadership effectiveness depends on the ability to gain the trust of followers.[66] Downsizing, corporate financial misrepresentation, and the increased use of temporary employees have undermined employees' trust in their leaders and shaken the confidence of investors, suppliers, and customers. A survey found that only 39 percent of US employees and 51 percent of Canadian employees trusted their executive leaders.[67] Today's leaders are faced with the challenge of rebuilding and restoring trust with employees and with other important organizational stakeholders.

Providing Ethical Leadership

The topic of leadership and ethics has received surprisingly little attention. Only recently have ethics and leadership researchers begun to consider the ethical implications in leadership.[68] Why now? One reason is a growing general interest in ethics throughout the field of management. Another, without a doubt, is the recent corporate financial scandals that have increased the public's and politicians' concerns about ethical standards.

Ethics is part of leadership in a number of ways. For instance, transformational leaders have been described as fostering moral virtue when they try to change the attitudes and behaviours of followers.[69] We can also see an ethical component to charisma. Unethical leaders may use their charisma to enhance their power over followers and use that power for self-serving purposes. On the other hand, ethical leaders may use their charisma in more socially constructive ways to serve others.[70] We also see a lack of ethics when leaders abuse their power and give themselves large salaries and bonuses while, at the same time, they seek to cut costs by laying off employees. And, of course, trust, which is important to ethical behaviour, explicitly deals with the leadership traits of honesty and integrity.

As we have seen recently, leadership is not values-free. Providing moral leadership involves addressing the *means* that a leader uses in trying to achieve goals, as well as the content of those goals. As a recent study concluded, ethical leadership is more than being ethical; it's reinforcing ethics through organizational mechanisms such as communication and the reward system.[71] Thus, before we judge any leader to be effective, we should consider both the moral content of his or her goals *and* the means used to achieve those goals. In Chapter 5, we examined ethical leadership, responsible leadership, values-led leadership, and leading with integrity. In Module 3, we will discuss the ISO standards

Chapter 13 Leadership **351**

14001, which provide requirements for an environmental management system, and 26000, which provide guidance on social responsibility.

Empowering Employees

As we have described elsewhere in the text, managers are increasingly leading by empowering their employees. **Employee empowerment** involves giving more authority to employees to make decisions. Millions of individual employees and employee teams are making the key operating decisions that directly affect their work. They are developing budgets, scheduling workloads, controlling inventories, solving quality problems, and engaging in similar activities that until very recently were viewed exclusively as part of the manager's job.[72]

Why are more and more companies empowering employees? One reason is the need for quick decisions by those people who are most knowledgeable about the issues—often those at lower organizational levels. If organizations are to successfully compete in a dynamic global economy, they have to be able to make decisions and implement changes quickly. Another reason is the reality that organizational downsizing has left many managers with larger spans of control. In order to cope with the increased work demands, managers had to empower their people. Although empowerment is not appropriate for all circumstances, when employees have the knowledge, skills, and experience to do their jobs competently and when they seek autonomy and possess an internal locus of control, it can be beneficial. Empowerment should be used cautiously, however. Professor Jia Lin Xie of the University of Toronto's Rotman School of Management found that people who lack confidence can become ill from being put in charge of their own work. Xie and her colleagues found that "workers who had high levels of control at work, but lacked confidence in their abilities or blamed themselves for workplace problems, were more likely to have lower antibody levels and experienced more colds and flus."[73]

One of the difficulties with empowerment is that companies do not always introduce it properly. Professor Dan Ondrack of the University of Toronto's Rotman School of Management points out that for employees to be empowered, four conditions need to be met:[74]

- There must be a clear definition of the values and mission of the company.
- The company must help employees acquire the relevant skills.
- Employees need to be supported in their decision making and not criticized when they try to do something extraordinary.
- Employees need to be recognized for their efforts.

employee empowerment Giving more authority to employees to make decisions.

Paul Okalik (left) was the first sitting premier of Nunavut and was chosen to serve a second term. Okalik headed a nonpartisan government run by consensus, built from the principles of parliamentary democracy and Aboriginal values. Okalik's leadership skills include team building. He was the key negotiator in the settlement that led to the creation of Nunavut, and in his role as premier he balanced the needs of the Inuit and Qallunaaq (non-Inuit) residents in Nunavut.

Jonathan Hayward/Canadian Press Images

Leading across Cultures

"In North America, leaders are expected to look great, sound great, and be inspiring. In other countries—not so much."[75] In this global economy, how can managers account for cross-cultural differences as they lead?

One general conclusion that surfaces from leadership research is that effective leaders do not use a single style. They adjust their style to the situation. Although not mentioned explicitly, national culture is certainly an important situational variable in determining which leadership style will be most effective. What works in China isn't likely to be effective in France or Canada. For instance, one study of Asian leadership styles revealed that Asian managers preferred leaders who were competent decision makers, effective communicators, and supportive of employees.[76]

National culture affects leadership style because it influences how followers will respond. Leaders can't (and shouldn't) just choose their styles randomly. They're constrained by the cultural conditions their followers have come to expect. Exhibit 13-8 provides some findings from selected examples of cross-cultural leadership studies. Because most leadership theories were developed in the United States, they have an American bias. They emphasize follower responsibilities rather than rights; assume self-gratification rather than commitment to duty or altruistic motivation; assume centrality of work and democratic value orientation; and stress rationality rather than spirituality, religion, or superstition.[77] However, the GLOBE research program, first introduced in Chapter 3, is the most extensive and comprehensive cross-cultural study of leadership ever undertaken. The GLOBE study has found that there are some universal aspects to leadership. Specifically, a number of elements of transformational leadership appear to be associated with effective leadership, regardless of what country the leader is in.[78] These include vision, foresight, providing encouragement, trustworthiness, dynamism, positiveness, and proactiveness. The results led two members of the GLOBE team to conclude that "effective business leaders in any country are expected by their subordinates to provide a powerful and proactive vision to guide the company into the future, strong motivational skills to stimulate all employees to fulfill the vision, and excellent planning skills to assist in implementing the vision."[79] Some people suggest that the universal appeal of these transformational leader characteristics is due to the pressures toward common technologies and management practices, as a result of global competitiveness and multinational influences.

Exhibit 13-8

Selected Cross-Cultural Leadership Findings

- Korean leaders are expected to be paternalistic toward employees.

- Arab leaders who show kindness or generosity without being asked to do so are seen by other Arabs as weak.

- Japanese leaders are expected to be humble and speak frequently.

- Scandinavian and Dutch leaders who single out individuals with public praise are likely to embarrass, not energize, those individuals.

- Malaysian leaders are expected to show compassion while using more of an autocratic than a participative style.

- Effective German leaders are characterized by high performance orientation, low compassion, low self-protection, low team orientation, high autonomy, and high participation.

Sources: Based on J. C. Kennedy, "Leadership in Malaysia: Traditional Values, International Outlook," *Academy of Management Executive,* August 2002, pp. 15–17; F. C. Brodbeck, M. Frese, and M. Javidan, "Leadership Made in Germany: Low on Compassion, High on Performance," *Academy of Management Executive,* February 2002, pp. 16–29; M. F. Peterson and J. G. Hunt, "International Perspectives on International Leadership," *Leadership Quarterly,* Fall 1997, pp. 203–231; R. J. House and R. N. Aditya, "The Social Scientific Study of Leadership: Quo Vadis?" *Journal of Management* 23, no. 3 (1997), p. 463; and R. J. House, "Leadership in the Twenty-First Century," in *The Changing Nature of Work,* ed. A. Howard (San Francisco: Jossey-Bass, 1995), p. 442.

As part of their leadership training, some 300 executives of Samsung Heavy Industries Ship Construction attended a one-week military training camp at an airbase in South Korea. Developing effective leaders who will act as agents of change is a top priority for Samsung in executing its plan of reaching $400 billion in revenue and becoming one of the world's top five brands by 2020. Through military-style training, participants learn how to develop mentally, physically, and emotionally; how to become a source of influence to inspire others through vision, courage, and commitment; and how to motivate others to attain higher levels of performance.

Samsung Heavy Industries/Handout/Reuters

Becoming an Effective Leader

Organizations need effective leaders. Two issues pertinent to becoming an effective leader are leader training and recognizing that sometimes being an effective leader means *not* leading. Let's take a look at these issues.

Leader Training

Organizations around the globe spend billions of dollars, yen, and euros on leadership training and development.[80] These efforts take many forms—from $50 000 leadership programs offered by universities such as Harvard to sailing experiences at the Outward Bound School. Although much of the money spent on leader training may provide doubtful benefits, our review suggests that there are some things managers can do to get the maximum effect from such training.[81]

First, let's recognize the obvious: Some people don't have what it takes to be a leader. Period. For instance, evidence indicates that leadership training is more likely to be successful with individuals who are high self-monitors than with low self-monitors. Such individuals have the flexibility to change their behaviour as different situations require. In addition, organizations may find that individuals with higher levels of a trait called *motivation to lead* are more receptive to leadership development opportunities.[82]

What kinds of things can individuals learn that might be related to being a more effective leader? It may be a bit optimistic to think that "vision-creation" can be taught, but implementation skills can be taught. People can be trained to develop "an understanding about content themes critical to effective visions."[83] We can also teach skills such as trust-building and mentoring. And leaders can be taught situational analysis skills. They can learn how to evaluate situations, how to modify situations to make them fit better with their style, and how to assess which leader behaviours might be most effective in given situations.

Substitutes for Leadership

Despite the belief that some leadership style will always be effective, regardless of the situation, leadership may not always be important! Research indicates that, in some situations, any behaviours a leader exhibits are irrelevant. In other words, certain individual, job, and organizational variables can act as "substitutes for leadership," negating the influence of the leader.[84]

For instance, follower characteristics such as experience, training, professional orientation, and need for independence can neutralize the effect of leadership. These characteristics can replace the employee's need for a leader's support or ability to create structure and reduce task ambiguity. Similarly, jobs that are inherently unambiguous and routine or that are intrinsically satisfying may place fewer demands on the leadership variable. Finally, such organizational characteristics as explicit formalized goals, rigid rules and procedures, and cohesive work groups can substitute for formal leadership.

CHAPTER 13

SUMMARY AND IMPLICATIONS

1. Define leader and leadership. Leaders in organizations make things happen. But what makes leaders different from nonleaders? A leader is someone who can influence others and who has managerial authority. Leadership is a process of leading a group and influencing that group to achieve its goals. Managers should be leaders because leading is one of the four management functions.

> ▶ ▶ ▶ Universities are Canada's innovation engines. To reap the rewards of innovation, knowledge transfer, and the chance to shape and be shaped by the newest ideas in education, we must learn to build collaborative partnerships among the universities, the communities they serve, and local business partners. As Johnston puts it, "My definition of leadership is recognizing your total dependence on the people around you."

2. Compare and contrast early theories of leadership. Early attempts to define leadership traits were unsuccessful, although later attempts found seven traits associated with leadership. The University of Iowa studies explored three leadership styles. The only conclusion was that group members were more satisfied under a democratic leader than under an autocratic one. The Ohio State studies identified two dimensions of leader behaviour: initiating structure and consideration. A leader high in both those dimensions at times achieved high group task performance and high group member satisfaction, but not always. The University of Michigan studies looked at employee-oriented leaders and production-oriented leaders. They concluded that leaders who were employee oriented could get high group productivity and high group member satisfaction. The managerial grid looked at leaders' concern for production and concern for people and identified five leader styles. Although it suggested that a leader who was high in concern for production and high in concern for people was the best, there was no substantive evidence for that conclusion. The behavioural studies showed that a leader's behaviour has a dual nature: a focus on the task and a focus on the people.

> ▶ ▶ ▶ In reaching the residential schools settlement, Phil Fontaine needed to draw on the traits that first surfaced in his work as a band chief—his ability to open lines of communication and to build consensus.

3. Describe the three major contingency theories of leadership. Contingency theories acknowledge that different situations require different leadership styles. The theories suggest that leaders may need to adjust their style to the needs of different organizations and employees, and perhaps different countries.

Fiedler's model attempted to define the best style to use in particular situations. He measured leader style—relationship oriented or task oriented—using the least-preferred coworker questionnaire. Fiedler also assumed a leader's style was fixed. He measured three contingency dimensions: leader–member relations, task structure, and position power. The model suggests that task-oriented leaders performed best in very favourable and very unfavourable situations, and relationship-oriented leaders performed best in moderately favourable situations.

Hersey and Blanchard's situational leadership theory focused on followers' readiness. They identified four leadership styles: telling (high task–low relationship), selling (high task–high relationship), participating (low task–high relationship), and delegating (low task–low relationship). They also identified four stages of readiness: unable and unwilling (use telling style), unable but willing (use selling style), able but unwilling (use participative style), and able and willing (use delegating style).

The path–goal model developed by Robert House identified four leadership behaviours: directive, supportive, participative, and achievement-oriented. He assumed that a leader can and should be able to use any of these styles. The two situational contingency variables were found in the environment and in the follower. Essentially the path–goal model says that a leader should provide direction and support as needed; that is, structure the path so the followers can achieve goals.

▶▶▶ Because Moya Greene did not come from a logistics or postal background, she knew that she needed to learn Canada Post's culture first-hand. As her role at Canada Post evolved, she adjusted her style based on the context of the audience and the problem at hand.

4. Describe contemporary views of leadership. Leader–member exchange theory (LMX) says that leaders create in-groups and out-groups and those in the in-group will have higher performance ratings, less turnover, and greater job satisfaction. A transactional leader exchanges rewards for productivity, whereas a transformational leader stimulates and inspires followers to achieve goals. A charismatic leader is an enthusiastic and self-confident leader whose personality and actions influence people to behave in certain ways. People can learn to be charismatic. A visionary leader is able to create and articulate a realistic, credible, and attractive vision of the future. A team leader has two priorities: manage the team's external boundary and facilitate the team process. Four leader roles are involved: liaison with external constituencies, troubleshooter, conflict manager, and coach.

▶▶▶ David Cheesewright became president of Walmart Canada as the company was implementing "the greener good" sustainability strategy. His role was to assist in transforming the organization into a truly sustainable one. In order to do so he would have had to make conscious choices about which combination of contemporary leadership styles would best support the sustainability mandate for Walmart.

5. Discuss contemporary issues affecting leadership. The five sources of a leader's power are legitimate (authority or position), coercive (punish or control), reward (give positive rewards), expert (special expertise, skills, or knowledge), and referent (desirable resources or traits). Most effective leaders rely on several different sources of power—legitimate, coercive, reward, expert, and referent power—to affect the behaviour and performance of their followers. An important consideration for leaders today is building trust and credibility with employees. Trust in leadership has been found to have a significant effect on positive job outcomes, including job performance, organizational citizenship behaviour, job satisfaction, and organizational commitment.

▶▶▶ As Annette Verschuren performed her role in The Home Depot, she drew upon her prior experience to empower her performance and that of others in the organization. She was able to build trust with those she worked with and to adapt to the very different culture in the Asian operations.

MyManagementLab   Study, practise, and explore real management situations with these helpful resources:
- **Interactive Lesson Presentations:** Work through interactive presentations and assessments to test your knowledge of management concepts.
- **PIA (Personal Inventory Assessments):** Enhance your ability to connect with key concepts through these engaging, self-reflection assessments.
- **Study Plan:** Check your understanding of chapter concepts with self-study quizzes.
- **Simulations:** Practise decision-making in simulated management environments.

P I A PERSONAL INVENTORY ASSESSMENT

REVIEW AND DISCUSSION QUESTIONS

1. What does each of the four behavioural leadership theories say about leadership?

2. Explain Fiedler's contingency model of leadership.

3. How do situational leadership theory and path–goal theory each explain leadership?

4. What is leader–member exchange theory, and what does it say about leadership?

5. Differentiate between transactional and transformational leaders and between charismatic and visionary leaders.

6. What are the five sources of a leader's power?

7. Do you think most managers in real life use a contingency approach to increase their leadership effectiveness? Explain.

8. Do the followers make a difference in whether a leader is effective? Discuss.

ETHICS DILEMMA

Have you ever watched the show *Undercover Boss Canada*? It features a company's "boss" working undercover in his or her own company to find out how the organization really works. Typically, the executive works undercover for a week, and then the employees the leader has worked with are summoned to company headquarters and either rewarded or punished for their actions. Bosses from organizations ranging from 1-800-Got-Junk to YMCA Canada to Sodexo (one of the food contractions) have participated. What do you think? Is it ethical for a leader to go undercover in his or her organization? Why or why not? What ethical issues could arise?

SKILLS EXERCISE

Choosing an Effective Leadership Style—About the Skill

Effective leaders are skillful at helping the groups they lead be successful as the group goes through various stages of development. No leadership style is consistently effective. Situational factors, including follower characteristics, must be taken into consideration in the selection of an effective leadership style. The key situational factors that determine leadership effectiveness include stage of group development, task structure, position power, leader–member relations, the work group, employee characteristics, organizational culture, and national culture.

Steps in Practising the Skill

You can choose an effective leadership style if you use the following six suggestions.

1. *Determine the stage in which your group or team is operating: forming, storming, norming, or performing.* Because each team stage involves specific and different issues and behaviours, it's important to know in which stage your team is. *Forming* is the first stage of group development, during which people join a group and then help define the group's purpose, structure, and leadership. *Storming* is the second stage characterized by intragroup conflict. *Norming* is the third stage characterized by close relationships and cohesiveness. *Performing* is the fourth stage when the group is fully functional.

2. *If your team is in the forming stage, you want to exhibit certain leader behaviours.* These include making certain that all team members are introduced to one another, answering member questions, working to establish a foundation of trust and openness, modeling the behaviours you expect from the team members, and clarifying the team's goals, procedures, and expectations.

3. *If your team is in the storming stage, you want to exhibit certain leader behaviours.* These behaviours include identifying sources of conflict and adopting a mediator role, encouraging a win-win philosophy, restating the team's vision and its core values and goals, encouraging open discussion, encouraging an analysis of team processes in order to identify ways to improve, enhancing team cohesion and commitment, and providing recognition to individual team members as well as the team.

4. *If your team is in the norming stage, you want to exhibit certain leader behaviours.* These behaviours include clarifying the team's goals and expectations, providing performance feedback to individual team members and the team, encouraging the team to articulate a vision for the future, and finding ways to publicly and openly communicate the team's vision.

5. *If your team is in the performing stage, you want to exhibit certain leader behaviours.* These behaviours include providing regular and ongoing performance feedback, fostering innovation and innovative behaviour, encouraging the team to capitalize on its strengths, celebrating achievements (large and small), and providing the team whatever support it needs to continue doing its work.

6. *Monitor the group for changes in behaviour and adjust your leadership style accordingly.* Because a group is not a static entity, it will go through up periods and down periods. You should adjust your leadership style to the needs of the situation. If the group appears to need more direction from you, provide it. If it appears to be functioning at a high level on its own, provide whatever support is necessary to keep it functioning at that level.

Practising the Skill

The following suggestions are activities you can do to practise the behaviours in choosing an effective leadership style.

1. Think of a group or team to which you currently belong or of which you have been a part. What type of leadership style did the leader of this group appear to exhibit? Give some specific examples of the types of leadership behaviours he or she used. Evaluate the leadership style. Was it appropriate for the group? Why or why not? What would you have done differently? Why?

2. Observe a sports team (either a school team or professional) that you consider extremely successful and one that you would consider not successful. What leadership styles appear to be used in these team situations? Give some specific examples of the types of leadership behaviours you observe. How would you evaluate the leadership style? Was it appropriate for the team? Why or why not? To what degree do you think leadership style influenced the team's outcomes?

WORKING TOGETHER: TEAM EXERCISE

Horrible Bosses

Everybody's probably had at least one experience with a *bad boss.* But what *is* a bad boss? And more importantly, what can you do in such a situation?

Break into small groups of three to four other class members. Come up with a bulleted list of characteristics and behaviours you believe a bad boss would have or exhibit. Then, come up with another bulleted list of what you can do if you find yourself in a situation with a bad boss. Be realistic about your suggestions; that is, don't suggest tampering with the person's coffee or slashing the person's tires!

LEARNING TO BE A MANAGER

- Think of the different organizations to which you belong. Note the different styles of leadership used by the leaders in these organizations. Write a paper describing these individuals' styles of leading (no names, please) and evaluate the styles being used.

- Write down three people you consider effective leaders. Make a bulleted list of the characteristics these individuals exhibit that you think make them effective leaders.

- Think about the times you have had to lead. Describe your own personal leadership style. What could you do to improve your leadership style? Come up with an action plan of steps you can take. Put all this information into a brief paper.

- Managers say that increasingly they must use influence to get things done. Do some research on the art of persuasion. Make a bulleted list of suggestions you find on how to improve your skills at influencing others.

- Here's a list of leadership skills. Choose two and develop a training exercise that will help develop or improve those skills: building employee communities; building teams; coaching and motivating others; communicating with impact, confidence, and energy; leading by example; leading change; making decisions; providing direction and focus; and valuing diversity.

- Select one of the topics in the section on leadership issues in the twenty-first century. Do some additional research on the topic, and put your findings in a bulleted list that you are prepared to share in class. Be sure to cite your sources.

- Interview three managers about what they think it takes to be a good leader. Write up your findings in a report and be prepared to present it in class.

CASE APPLICATION 1

Growing Leaders

3M's new CEO Inge Thulin and former CEO George Buckley reinforce the company's pursuit of leadership excellence based on six leadership attributes: the ability to "chart the course; energize and inspire others; demonstrate ethics, integrity, and compliance; deliver results; raise the bar; and innovate resourcefully."

How important are excellent leaders to organizations? If you were to ask the recently retired 3M CEO George Buckley, he'd say extremely important.[86] But he'd also say that excellent leaders don't just pop up out of nowhere. A company has to cultivate leaders who have the skills and abilities to help it survive and thrive. And like a successful baseball team with strong performance statistics that has a player development plan in place, 3M has its own farm system. Except its farm system is designed to develop company leaders.

3M's leadership development program is so effective that it has been one of the "Top 20 Companies for Leadership" in three of the past four years and ranks as one of the top 25 companies for grooming leadership talent according to Hay Consulting Group and *Fortune* magazine. What is 3M's leadership program all about? About 10 years ago, the company's former CEO (Jim McNerney, who went on to become Boeing's CEO) and his top team spent 18 months developing a new leadership model for the company. After numerous brainstorming sessions and much heated debate, the group finally agreed on six "leadership attributes" they believed were essential for the company to become skilled at executing strategy and being accountable. Those six attributes included the ability to "chart the course; energize and inspire others; demonstrate ethics, integrity, and compliance; deliver results; raise the bar; and innovate resourcefully." And under Buckley's guidance, and continuing under the leadership of newly appointed CEO Inge Thulin, the company is continuing and reinforcing its pursuit of leadership excellence with these six attributes.

When asked about his views on leadership, Buckley said he believes leaders differ from managers. "A leader is as much about inspiration as anything else. A manager is more about process." He believes the key to developing leaders is to focus on those things that can be developed—like strategic thinking. Buckley also believes leaders should not be promoted up and through the organization too quickly. They need time to experience failures and what it takes to rebuild.

Finally, when asked about his own leadership style. Buckley responded, "The absolutely best way for me to be successful is to have people working for me who are better. Having that kind of emotional self-confidence is vital to leaders. You build respect in those people because you admire what they do. Having built respect, you build trust. However hokey it sounds, it works." And it must be working as the company was ranked number 18 on *Fortune's* most admired global companies list for 2012.

DISCUSSION QUESTIONS

1. What do you think about Buckley's statement that leaders and managers differ? Do you agree? Why or why not?
2. What leadership models/theories/issues do you see in this case? List and describe.
3. Take each of the six leadership attributes that the company feels is important. Explain what you think each one involves. Then discuss how those attributes might be developed and measured.
4. What did this case teach you about leadership?

CASE APPLICATION 2

Radical Leadership

The radical leadership of Ricardo Semler that entrusts employees to make important decisions about their work hours, pay levels, supervisors, corporate leadership, and strategic initiatives is based on his belief that self-governance is necessary to create a flexible organization that will survive and thrive in a chaotic political and economic environment.

Ricardo Semler, CEO of Semco Group of São Paulo, Brazil, is considered by many to be a radical.[87] He's never been the type of leader that most people might expect to be in charge of a multimillion-dollar business. Why? Semler breaks all the traditional "rules" of leading. He's the ultimate hands-off leader who doesn't even have an office at the company's headquarters. As the "leading proponent and most tireless evangelist" of participative management, Semler says his philosophy is simple: Treat people like adults and they'll respond like adults.

Underlying his participative management approach is the belief that "organizations thrive best by entrusting employees to apply their creativity and ingenuity in service of the whole enterprise, and to make important decisions close to the flow of work, conceivably including the selection and election of their bosses." And according to Semler, his approach works . . . and works well. But how does it work in reality?

At Semler, you won't find most of the trappings of organizations and management. There are no organizational charts, no long-term plans, no corporate values statements, no dress codes, and no written rules or policy manuals. The company's employees decide their work hours and their pay levels. Subordinates decide who their bosses will be and they also review their boss's performance. The employees also elect the corporate leadership and decide most of the company's new strategic initiatives. Each person has one vote—including Ricardo Semler.

Why did Semler decide that his form of radical leadership was necessary, and does it work? Semler didn't pursue such radical self-governance out of some altruistic ulterior motive. Instead, he felt it was the only way to build an organization that was flexible and resilient enough to flourish in chaotic and turbulent times. He maintains that this approach has enabled Semco to survive the roller-coaster nature of Brazilian politics and economy. Although the country's political leadership and economy have gone from one extreme to another and countless Brazilian banks and companies have failed, Semco has survived. And not just survived—prospered. And Semler attributes that fact to flexibility—of his company and most importantly, of his employees.

DISCUSSION QUESTIONS

1. Describe Ricardo Semler's leadership style. What do you think the advantages and drawbacks of his style might be?
2. What challenges might a radically "hands-off" leader face? How could those challenges be addressed?
3. How could future leaders be identified in this organization? Would leadership training be important to this organization? Discuss.
4. What could other businesses learn from Ricardo Semler's approach to leadership?

Motivating Employees

Motivating and rewarding employees is one of the most important and challenging activities that managers do. To get employees to put forth maximum work effort, managers need to know how and why they're motivated. After reading and studying this chapter, you will achieve the following learning outcomes.

Learning Outcomes

1. Define motivation.

2. Compare and contrast early theories of motivation.

3. Compare and contrast contemporary theories of motivation.

4. Discuss current issues in motivation.

▶ ▶ ▶ How do you motivate employees in an industry where absenteeism rates average 5 percent of all working hours, but can be as high as 10 percent in urban areas?[1] What do you do when the turnover rate of managers averages 20 percent, and the turnover rate of nonmanagerial employees averages 30 percent?

Sir Terry Leahy, CEO of UK-based Tesco until 2011, faced these problems daily. The company has over 4800 supermarkets, hypermarkets, and convenience stores in the United Kingdom, Ireland, Central Europe, and Asia. Once a discount supermarket, Tesco has built itself as a dressier, mid-market retailer while becoming the number one food retailer in the United Kingdom.

The company tries to keep its Generation Y employees (Generation Y includes those born between 1979 and 1994) motivated, while also trying to accommodate the needs of other groups of employees, including ethnic minorities and mothers returning to the workplace. Not all of the jobs are interesting, and many can be quite repetitive.

Leahy believed in starting with the basics in dealing with employees. "We built Tesco around sound values and principles," he said. Therefore, he made sure that employees were treated with respect. But he was also concerned about performance: "If that's bad and there's no good reason, I get cross."

BRIAN HARRIS/Alamy

> **Think About It**
>
> What are the different motivation tools that managers use? Imagine you are the CEO of Tesco. How should you motivate your managers so that you will have less turnover? What can you do to keep your shelf-stockers and cashiers motivated?

Motivating and rewarding employees is one of the most important and one of the most challenging activities that managers perform. Successful managers, like Sir Terry Leahy, understand that what motivates them personally may have little or no effect on others. Just because *you* are motivated by being part of a cohesive work team, don't assume everyone is. Or the fact that you are motivated by challenging work does not mean everyone is. Effective managers who want their employees to put forth maximum effort recognize that they need to know how and why employees are motivated and to tailor their motivational practices to satisfy the needs and wants of those employees.

In this chapter, we take a look at what motivation is, early motivation theories, and contemporary theories. Then we discuss some current motivation issues and provide practical suggestions managers can use to motivate employees.

What Is Motivation?

⊙ Watch on **MyManagementLab**

Motivation (TWZ Role Play)

❶ Define motivation.

According to LinkedIn Corporation, a website that provides networking for more than 175 million professionals, "ninja" has far outpaced the growth of other trendy job titles.[2] Although most individuals using that title are computer programmers—who attack writing code like a ninja, with tonnes of tools available to do battle—the term also has been used to describe expertise in everything from customer service to furniture movers. For instance, in Salt Lake City, one business owner sells the services of "ninja workers" who will do everything from hauling junk to personal security to house-sitting. And at Bonobos, Inc., a New York City start-up that makes and sells men's apparel online, customer-service employees are also called ninjas. Why would a job title matter to employees? Many people, especially the young and young-at-heart, like vivid and unusual titles that celebrate their hard work. And ninja, like other popular job titles before it (guru, evangelist, barista, or even sandwich artist) shows employees that their efforts aren't plain and ordinary, but appreciated.

Would you ever have thought that a job title might be motivating? Have you ever thought about how to motivate someone? It's an important topic in management, and researchers have long been interested in it.[3] All managers need to be able to motivate their employees, which first requires understanding what motivation is. Let's begin by pointing out what motivation is not. Why? Because many people incorrectly view motivation as a personal trait; that is, they think some people are motivated and others aren't. Our knowledge of motivation tells us that we can't label people that way because individuals differ in motivational drive and their overall motivation varies from situation to situation. For instance, you're probably more motivated in some classes than in others.

motivation The process by which a person's efforts are energized, directed, and sustained toward attaining a goal.

Motivation refers to the process by which a person's efforts are energized, directed, and sustained toward attaining a goal.[4] This definition has three key elements: energy, direction, and persistence.[5] The *energy* element is a measure of intensity or drive. A motivated person puts forth effort and works hard. However, the quality of the effort must also be considered. High levels of effort don't necessarily lead to favourable job performance unless the effort is channelled in a *direction* that benefits the organization. Effort that's directed toward and consistent with organizational goals is the kind of effort we want from employees. Motivation also includes a *persistence* dimension. We want employees to persist in putting forth effort to achieve those goals. Finally, we will treat motivation as a *need-satisfying* process, as shown in Exhibit 14-1.

Exhibit 14-1

The Motivation Process

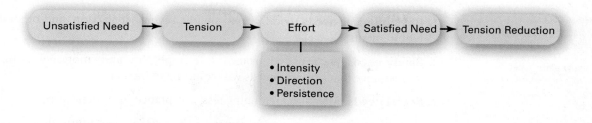

A **need** is an internal state that makes certain outcomes appear attractive. An unsatisfied need creates tension, which an individual reduces by exerting effort. Because we are interested in work behaviour, this tension-reduction effort must be directed toward organizational goals. Therefore, inherent in our definition of motivation is the requirement that the individual's needs be compatible with the organization's goals. When the two don't match, individuals may exert high levels of effort that run counter to the interests of the organization. Incidentally, this is not all that unusual. Some employees regularly spend a lot of time talking with friends at work to satisfy their social need. There is a high level of effort, but little, if any, is being directed toward work.

Finding ways to motivate employees to achieve high levels of performance is an important organizational problem, and managers keep looking for a solution. A survey by market research firm GfK found that 64 percent of Canadians either like or love what they do for a living. By comparison, 53 percent of American workers are happy with their work, and 57 percent of workers in the Netherlands report high satisfaction.[6] In light of these results, it's no wonder that both academic researchers and practising managers want to understand and explain employee motivation.

need An internal state that makes certain outcomes appear attractive.

Early Theories of Motivation

▶ ▶ ▶ Management at Tesco was interested in discovering what concerns their employees had and how these might be addressed.[7] They conducted research on their employees and found that many of their staff were single and worked mainly to have the money to travel overseas and participate in leisure activities. Their research also found that these employees "were unlikely to take much pride in their work, would lack commitment and would have little hesitation about going to work elsewhere if the pay were better."

② Compare and contrast early theories of motivation.

Think About It

What kinds of needs do employees have? How can they be addressed?

We begin by looking at four early motivation theories: *Maslow's hierarchy of needs theory, McGregor's Theory X and Theory Y, Herzberg's motivation-hygiene theory,* and *McClelland's three-needs theory.* Although more valid explanations of motivation have been developed, these early theories are important because they represent the foundation from which contemporary motivation theories were developed and because many managers still use them.

◀▶ Simulate on MyManagementLab

Motivation

Maslow's Hierarchy of Needs Theory

The best-known theory of motivation is probably Abraham Maslow's **hierarchy of needs theory**.[8] Maslow was a psychologist who proposed that within every person is a hierarchy of five needs:

1. **Physiological needs.** Food, drink, shelter, sexual satisfaction, and other physical requirements.

2. **Safety needs.** Security and protection from physical and emotional harm, as well as assurance that physical needs will continue to be met.

3. **Social needs.** Affection, belongingness, acceptance, and friendship.

4. **Esteem needs.** Internal esteem factors such as self-respect, autonomy, and achievement, and external esteem factors such as status, recognition, and attention.

5. **Self-actualization needs.** Growth, achieving one's potential, and self-fulfillment; the drive to become what one is capable of becoming.

Maslow argued that each level in the needs hierarchy must be substantially satisfied before the next is activated and that once a need is substantially satisfied, it no longer motivates behaviour. In other words, as each need is substantially satisfied, the next need becomes dominant. In terms of Exhibit 14-2, an individual moves up the needs hierarchy. From the standpoint of motivation, Maslow's theory proposed that, although no need is ever fully satisfied, a substantially satisfied need will no longer motivate an individual. Therefore, according to Maslow, if you want to motivate someone, you need to understand at what level that person is on in the hierarchy and focus on satisfying needs at or above that level. Managers who accepted Maslow's hierarchy attempted to change their organizations and management practices so that employees' needs could be satisfied.

Maslow's needs theory received wide recognition during the 1960s and 1970s, especially among practising managers, probably because of its intuitive logic and ease of understanding. However, Maslow provided no empirical support for his theory, and several studies sought to validate it could not.[9]

hierarchy of needs theory Maslow's theory that there is a hierarchy of five human needs: physiological, safety, social, esteem, and self-actualization; as each need becomes satisfied, the next need becomes dominant.

physiological needs A person's need for food, drink, shelter, sexual satisfaction, and other physical requirements.

safety needs A person's need for security and protection from physical and emotional harm, as well as assurance that physical needs will continue to be met.

social needs A person's need for affection, belongingness, acceptance, and friendship.

esteem needs A person's need for internal esteem factors such as self-respect, autonomy, and achievement, and external esteem factors such as status, recognition, and attention.

self-actualization needs A person's need to grow and become what he or she is capable of becoming.

Exhibit 14-2

Maslow's Hierarchy of Needs

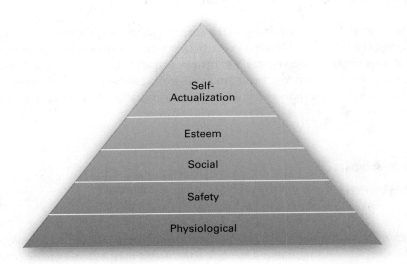

Source: Abraham H. Maslow, Robert D. Frager, and James Fadiman, *Motivation and Personality*, 3rd Edition, © 1987. Adapted by permission of Pearson Education, Inc., Upper Saddle River, NJ.

McGregor's Theory X and Theory Y

Andy Grove, cofounder of Intel Corporation and now a senior advisor to the company, was known for being open with his employees. However, he was also known for his tendency to yell. Intel's current CEO, Paul Otellini said, "When Andy was yelling at you, it wasn't because he didn't care about you. He was yelling at you because he wanted you to do better."[10] Although managers like Andy Grove want their employees to do better, that approach might not have been the best way to motivate employees, as McGregor's Theory X and Theory Y suggest.

Douglas McGregor is best known for proposing two assumptions about human nature: Theory X and Theory Y.[11] Very simply, **Theory X** is a negative view of people that assumes workers have little ambition, dislike work, want to avoid responsibility, and need to be closely controlled to work effectively. **Theory Y** is a positive view that assumes employees enjoy work, seek out and accept responsibility, and exercise self-direction. McGregor believed that Theory Y assumptions should guide management practice and proposed that participation in decision making, responsible and challenging jobs, and good group relations would maximize employee motivation.

Unfortunately, no evidence confirms that either set of assumptions is valid or that being a Theory Y manager is the only way to motivate employees. For instance, Jen-Hsun Huang, founder of Nvidia Corporation, an innovative and successful microchip manufacturer, has been known to use both reassuring hugs and tough love in motivating employees. He also has little tolerance for screw-ups. In one meeting, he supposedly screamed at a project team for its tendency to repeat mistakes. "Do you suck?" he asked the stunned employees. "Because if you suck, just get up and say you suck."[12] His message, delivered in classic Theory X style, was that if you need help, ask for it. It's a harsh approach, but in this case, it worked.

Herzberg's Two-Factor Theory

Frederick Herzberg's **two-factor theory** (also called **motivation-hygiene theory**) proposes that intrinsic factors are related to job satisfaction, while extrinsic factors are associated with job dissatisfaction.[13] Herzberg wanted to know when people felt exceptionally good (satisfied) or bad (dissatisfied) about their jobs. He concluded that the replies people gave when they felt good about their jobs were significantly different from the replies they gave when they felt badly. Certain characteristics were consistently related to job satisfaction (factors on the left side of the exhibit 14-3), and others to job dissatisfaction (factors on the right side). When people felt good about their work, they tended to cite intrinsic factors arising from the job itself such as achievement, recognition, and responsibility. On the other hand, when they were dissatisfied, they tended to cite extrinsic factors arising from the job context such as company policy and administration, supervision, interpersonal relationships, and working conditions. Findings from the survey work conducted by Herzberg are shown in Exhibit 14-3.

In addition, Herzberg believed that the data suggested that the opposite of satisfaction was not dissatisfaction, as traditionally had been believed. Removing dissatisfying characteristics from a job would not necessarily make that job more satisfying (or motivating). As shown in Exhibit 14-4, Herzberg proposed that his findings indicated the existence of a dual continuum: The opposite of "satisfaction" is "no satisfaction," and the opposite of "dissatisfaction" is "no dissatisfaction."

Again, Herzberg believed the factors that led to job satisfaction were separate and distinct from those that led to job dissatisfaction. Therefore, managers who sought to eliminate factors that created job dissatisfaction could bring about workplace harmony but not necessarily motivation. The extrinsic factors that create job dissatisfaction were

Satisfying physiological, safety, and social needs may be the most important motivators for these men and women hired to work at a new Procter & Gamble factory in Urlati, Romania. According to Maslow's hierarchy of needs theory, after these employees are assured that their lower-order needs of a salary, a safe job, benefits, and job security are satisfied, they will move up to the next level of social needs. Managers can motivate employees to satisfy their needs for belongingness, acceptance, and friendship by creating an environment that fosters good relationships with co-workers and supervisors, by forming work groups or teams, and by providing leisure and recreational activities that give employees opportunities to socialize.

Bloomberg/Getty Images

Theory X The assumption that employees dislike work, are lazy, avoid responsibility, and must be coerced to perform.

Theory Y The assumption that employees are creative, enjoy work, seek responsibility, and can exercise self-direction.

two-factor theory (motivation-hygiene theory) Herzberg's theory that intrinsic factors are related to job satisfaction and motivation, whereas extrinsic factors are related to job dissatisfaction.

Exhibit 14-3

Herzberg's Two-Factor Theory

Motivators	Hygiene Factors
• Achievement • Recognition • Work Itself • Responsibility • Advancement • Growth	• Supervision • Company Policy • Relationship with Supervisor • Working Conditions • Salary • Relationship with Peers • Personal Life • Relationship with Subordinates • Status • Security
Extremely Satisfied	Neutral Extremely Dissatisfied

Source: Based on F. Herzberg, B. Mausner, and B. B. Snyderman, *The Motivation to Work* (New York: John Wiley, 1959).

---

hygiene factors Factors that eliminate job dissatisfaction, but don't motivate.

motivators Factors that increase job satisfaction and motivation.

three-needs theory McClelland's motivation theory, which says that three acquired (not innate) needs—achievement, power, and affiliation—are major motives in work.

need for achievement (nAch) The drive to succeed and excel in relation to a set of standards.

need for power (nPow) The need to make others behave in a way that they would not have behaved otherwise.

need for affiliation (nAff) The desire for friendly and close interpersonal relationships.

called **hygiene factors**. When these factors are adequate, people won't be dissatisfied, but they won't be satisfied (or motivated) either. To motivate people in their jobs, Herzberg suggested emphasizing **motivators**, the intrinsic factors such as achievement, recognition, and challenge that increase job satisfaction.

Herzberg's theory enjoyed wide popularity from the mid-1960s to the early 1980s, but criticisms arose concerning his procedures and methodology. Although some critics said his theory was too simplistic, it has influenced how we currently design jobs, especially when it comes to job enrichment, which we'll discuss at a later point in this chapter.

McClelland's Three-Needs Theory

David McClelland and his associates proposed the **three-needs theory**, which says that three acquired (not innate) needs are major motivators in work.[14] These three needs are the **need for achievement (nAch)**, which is the drive to succeed and excel in relation to a set of standards; the **need for power (nPow)**, which is the need to make others behave in a way that they would not have behaved otherwise; and the **need for affiliation (nAff)**, which is the desire for friendly and close interpersonal relationships. Of these three needs, the need for achievement has been researched the most.

Exhibit 14-4

Contrasting Views of Satisfaction–Dissatisfaction

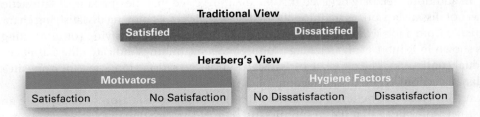

People with a high need for achievement strive for personal achievement rather than for the trappings and rewards of success. They have a desire to do something better or more efficiently than it's been done before.[15] They prefer jobs that offer personal responsibility for finding solutions to problems, in which they can receive rapid and unambiguous feedback on their performance in order to tell whether they're improving, and in which they can set moderately challenging goals. High achievers avoid what they perceive to be very easy or very difficult tasks. Also, a high need to achieve doesn't necessarily lead to being a good manager, especially in large organizations. That's because high achievers focus on their *own* accomplishments, while good managers emphasize helping *others* accomplish their goals.[16] McClelland showed that employees can be trained to stimulate their achievement need by being in situations where they have personal responsibility, feedback, and moderate risks.[17]

The other two needs in this theory haven't been researched as extensively as the need for achievement. However, we do know that the best managers tend to be high in the need for power and low in the need for affiliation.[18]

While needs theories give us some insights into motivating employees by stressing the importance of addressing individuals' needs, they don't provide a complete picture of motivation. For that we turn to some contemporary theories of motivation that explain the processes managers can use to motivate employees.

Contemporary Theories of Motivation

▶ ▶ ▶ One of the challenges of motivating employees is linking productivity to rewards. Compounding this challenge for Tesco is that some jobs are very boring.[19] Tesco's director of human resources, said "We're trying to take the routine out of the workplace, and build in more interest." The company eliminated the boring task of unloading soft drinks by ordering merchandising units that come fully stocked, ready to be wheeled into the store.

Tesco also encourages employees to buy shares of the company, so that staff can "share in the success they helped to create." To help employees understand the potential benefits of shares, the annual benefit report includes share price graphs and a reward statement for staff. The benefit report helps employees see how the share price performs over the longer term and in comparison with the shares of other companies.

Sir Terry Leahy said he wanted his employees to take four things from the job: "They find it interesting, they're treated with respect, they have the chance to get on, and they find their boss is helpful and not their biggest problem." All of these rewards make it easier for employees to perform well.

❸ Compare and contrast contemporary theories of motivation.

> **Think About It**
>
> **How can you link productivity to rewards so that employees feel motivated? What other things can be done at Tesco to ensure that employees feel motivated?**

The theories we look at in this section represent current explanations of employee motivation. Although these theories may not be as well known as those we just discussed, they are supported by research.[20] These contemporary motivation approaches are goal-setting theory, reinforcement theory, job design theory, equity theory, and expectancy theory.

Goal-Setting Theory

Before a big assignment or major class project presentation, has a teacher ever encouraged you to "just do your best"? What does that vague statement "do your best" mean? Would your performance on a class project have been higher had that teacher said you needed to score 93 percent to keep your A in the class? Research on goal-setting theory addresses these issues; the findings, as you'll see, are impressive in terms of the effect that goal specificity, challenge, and feedback have on performance.[21]

goal-setting theory The proposition that specific goals increase performance and that difficult goals, when accepted, result in higher performance than do easy goals.

There is substantial research support for **goal-setting theory**, which says that specific goals increase performance and that difficult goals, when accepted, result in higher performance than do easy goals. What does goal-setting theory tell us?

First, working toward a goal is a major source of job motivation. Studies on goal setting have demonstrated that specific and challenging goals are superior motivating forces.[22] Such goals produce a higher output than does the generalized goal "do your best." The specificity of the goal itself acts as an internal stimulus. For instance, when a sales rep commits to making eight sales calls daily, this intention gives him a specific goal to try to attain.

It's not a contradiction that goal-setting theory says that motivation is maximized by *difficult* goals, whereas achievement motivation (from three-needs theory) is stimulated by *moderately challenging goals*.[23] First, goal-setting theory deals with people in general, while the conclusions on achievement motivation are based on people who have a high nAch. Given that no more than 10 to 20 percent of North Americans are high achievers, difficult goals are still recommended for the majority of employees. Second, the conclusions of goal-setting theory apply to those who accept and are committed to the goals. Difficult goals will lead to higher performance *only* if they are accepted.

Next, will employees try harder if they have the opportunity to participate in the setting of goals? Not always. In some cases, participatively set goals elicit superior performance; in other cases, individuals perform best when their managers assign goals. However, participation is probably preferable to assigning goals when employees might resist accepting difficult challenges.[24]

Finally, we know that people will do better if they get feedback on how well they're progressing toward their goals because feedback helps identify discrepancies between what they have done and what they want to do. But all feedback isn't equally effective. Self-generated feedback—where an employee monitors his or her own progress—has been shown to be a more powerful motivator than feedback coming from someone else.[25] An example of this would be when an employee identifies the metrics to be measured and designs a customized report.

Three other contingencies besides feedback influence the goal–performance relationship: goal commitment, adequate self-efficacy, and national culture.

First, goal-setting theory assumes that an individual is committed to a goal. Commitment is most likely when goals are made public, when an individual has an internal locus of control, and when the goals are self-set rather than assigned.[26]

self-efficacy An individual's belief that he or she is capable of performing a task.

Next, **self-efficacy** refers to an individual's belief that he or she is capable of performing a task.[27] The higher your self-efficacy, the more confidence you have in your ability to succeed in a task. So, in difficult situations, we find that people with low self-efficacy are likely to reduce their effort or give up altogether, whereas those with high self-efficacy will try harder to master the challenge.[28] In addition, individuals with high self-efficacy seem to respond to negative feedback with increased effort and motivation, whereas those with low self-efficacy are likely to reduce their effort when given negative feedback.[29]

Finally, the value of goal-setting theory depends on the national culture. It's well adapted to North American countries because its main ideas align reasonably well with those cultures. It assumes that subordinates will be reasonably independent (not a high score on power distance), that people will seek challenging goals (low in uncertainty avoidance), and that performance is considered important by both managers and subordinates (high in assertiveness). Don't expect goal setting to lead to higher employee performance in countries where the cultural characteristics aren't like this.

Exhibit 14-5 summarizes the relationships among goals, motivation, and performance. Our overall conclusion is that the intention to work toward hard and specific goals is a powerful motivating force. Under the proper conditions, it can lead to higher performance. However, there is no evidence that such goals are associated with increased job satisfaction.[30]

Reinforcement Theory

reinforcement theory The theory that behaviour is a function of its consequences.

reinforcers Consequences immediately following a behaviour that increase the probability that the behaviour will be repeated.

Reinforcement theory says that behaviour is a function of its consequences. Consequences that immediately follow a behaviour and increase the probability that the behaviour will be repeated are called **reinforcers**.

Exhibit 14-5

Goal-Setting Theory

Reinforcement theory ignores factors such as goals, expectations, and needs. Instead, it focuses solely on what happens to a person when he or she does something. For instance, Walmart improved its bonus program for hourly employees. Employees who provide outstanding customer service get a cash bonus. And all Walmart hourly full- and part-time store employees are eligible for annual "My$hare" bonuses, which are allocated on store performance and distributed quarterly so that workers are rewarded more frequently.[31] The company's intent: Keep the workforce motivated.

According to B. F. Skinner, people will most likely engage in desired behaviours if they are rewarded for doing so. These rewards are most effective if they immediately follow a desired behaviour, and behaviour that isn't rewarded or that is punished is less likely to be repeated.[32]

Using reinforcement theory, managers can influence employees' behaviour by using positive reinforcers for actions that help the organization achieve its goals. Managers should ignore, not punish, undesirable behaviour. Although punishment eliminates undesired behaviour faster than nonreinforcement does, its effect is often temporary, and it may have unpleasant side effects, including dysfunctional behaviour such as workplace conflicts, absenteeism, and turnover. Although reinforcement is an important influence on work behaviour, it isn't the only explanation for differences in employee motivation.[33]

Designing Motivating Jobs

It's not unusual to find shop-floor workers at Cordis LLC's San German, Puerto Rico, facility interacting directly with customers, especially if that employee has special skills or knowledge that could help come up with a solution to a customer's problem.[34] One company executive said, "Our sales guys often encourage this in specific situations because they don't always have all the answers. If, by doing this, we can better serve the customers, then we do it." As this example shows, the tasks an employee performs in his or her job are often determined by different factors, such as providing customers what they need—when they need it.

Because managers are primarily interested in how to motivate individuals on the job, we need to look at ways to design motivating jobs. If you look closely at what an organization is and how it works, you will find that it's composed of thousands of tasks. These

job design The way tasks are combined to form complete jobs.

job scope The number of different tasks required in a job and the frequency with which these tasks are repeated.

job enlargement The horizontal expansion of a job through increasing job scope.

job enrichment The vertical expansion of a job by adding planning and evaluating responsibilities.

job depth The degree of control employees have over their work.

job characteristics model (JCM) A framework for analyzing jobs and designing motivating jobs that identifies five core job dimensions, their interrelationships, and their impact on employees.

Dr. Sigrid Heuer, a senior scientist at the International Rice Research Institute, is the leader of an international multidisciplinary team of research scientists whose work scores high on the core dimensions of skill variety, task identity, and task significance. Heuer and her team discovered a gene that increases grain production substantially by enabling rice plants to grow stronger root systems that take in more phosphorus, an important plant nutrient. Their discovery will help poor rice farmers grow more rice for sale to poor countries. Believing their work is meaningful because it has a significant impact on the lives of others gives the scientists great motivation and job satisfaction.

Cheryl Ravelo/Reuters

tasks, in turn, are combined into jobs. We use the term **job design** to refer to the way tasks are combined to form complete jobs. The jobs that people perform in an organization should not evolve by chance. Managers should design jobs deliberately and thoughtfully to reflect the demands of the changing environment, the organization's technology, and its employees' skills, abilities, and preferences.[35] When jobs are designed with those things in mind, employees are motivated to work hard. What are some ways that managers can design motivating jobs?[36]

Job Enlargement

As we saw earlier, in Chapter 10, job design historically has concentrated on making jobs smaller and more specialized. Yet when jobs are narrow in focus and highly specialized, motivating employees is a real challenge. One of the earliest efforts at overcoming the drawbacks of job specialization involved the horizontal expansion of a job through increasing **job scope**—the number of different tasks required in a job and the frequency with which these tasks are repeated. For instance, a dental hygienist's job could be enlarged so that in addition to dental cleaning, he or she is pulling patients' files, re-filing them when finished, and cleaning and storing instruments. This type of job design option is called **job enlargement**.

Most job enlargement efforts that focused solely on increasing the number of tasks don't seem to work. As one employee who experienced such a job redesign said, "Before, I had one lousy job. Now, thanks to job enlargement, I have three lousy jobs!" However, one study that looked at how *knowledge* enlargement activities (expanding the scope of knowledge used in a job) affected employees found benefits such as more satisfaction, enhanced customer service, and fewer errors.[37]

Job Enrichment

Another approach to designing motivating jobs is the vertical expansion of a job by adding planning and evaluating responsibilities—**job enrichment**. Job enrichment increases **job depth**, which is the degree of control employees have over their work. In other words, employees are empowered to assume some of the tasks typically done by their managers. Thus, the tasks in an enriched job should allow employees to do a complete activity with increased freedom, independence, and responsibility. These tasks should also provide feedback so that individuals can assess and correct their own performance. For instance, in an enriched job, our dental hygienist, in addition to dental cleaning, could schedule appointments (planning) and follow up with clients (evaluating). Although job enrichment can improve the quality of work, employee motivation, and satisfaction, the research evidence on the use of job enrichment programs has been inconclusive as to its usefulness.[38]

Job Characteristics Model

Even though many organizations have implemented job enlargement and job enrichment programs and experienced mixed results, neither of these job design approaches provided a conceptual framework for analyzing jobs or for guiding managers in designing motivating jobs. The **job characteristics model (JCM)** offers such a framework.[39] It identifies five core job dimensions, their interrelationships, and their impact on employee productivity, motivation, and satisfaction.

According to the JCM, any job can be described in terms of five core dimensions, defined as follows:

1. **Skill variety.** The degree to which a job requires a variety of activities so that an employee can use a number of different skills and talents.

2. **Task identity.** The degree to which a job requires completion of a whole and identifiable piece of work.

3. **Task significance.** The degree to which a job affects the lives or work of other people.

4. **Autonomy.** The degree to which a job provides substantial freedom, independence, and discretion to the individual in scheduling the work and determining the procedures to be used in carrying it out.

5. **Feedback.** The degree to which carrying out work activities required by a job results in the individual's obtaining direct and clear information about the effectiveness of his or her performance.

Exhibit 14-6 presents the JCM. Notice how the first three dimensions—skill variety, task identity, and task significance—combine to create meaningful work. What we mean is that if these three characteristics exist in a job, we can predict that the person will view his or her job as important, valuable, and worthwhile. Notice, too, that jobs that possess autonomy give the job incumbent a feeling of personal responsibility for the results, and that if a job provides feedback, the employee will know how effectively he or she is performing.

From a motivational standpoint, the JCM suggests that internal rewards are obtained when an employee *learns* (knowledge of results through feedback) that he or she *personally* (experienced responsibility through autonomy of work) has performed well on a task that he or she *cares* about (experienced meaningfulness through skill variety, task identity, and/or task significance).[40] The more these three conditions characterize a job, the greater the employee's motivation, performance, and satisfaction and the lower his or her absenteeism and likelihood of resigning. As the model shows, the links between the job dimensions and the outcomes are moderated by the strength of the individual's growth need (the person's desire for self-esteem and self-actualization). This means that individuals with a high growth need are more likely to experience the critical psychological states and respond positively when their jobs include the core dimensions than are individuals with a low growth need. This may explain the mixed results with job enrichment: Individuals with low growth needs don't tend to achieve high performance or satisfaction by having their jobs enriched.

The JCM provides specific guidance to managers for job design. These suggestions specify the types of changes most likely to lead to improvement in the five core job dimensions. You'll notice that two suggestions incorporate job enlargement and job

skill variety The degree to which a job requires a variety of activities so that an employee can use a number of different skills and talents.

task identity The degree to which a job requires completion of a whole and identifiable piece of work.

task significance The degree to which a job affects the lives or work of other people.

autonomy The degree to which a job provides substantial freedom, independence, and discretion to the individual in scheduling work and determining the procedures to be used in carrying it out.

feedback The degree to which carrying out work activities required by a job results in the individual's obtaining direct and clear information about the effectiveness of his or her performance.

Exhibit 14-6

Job Characteristics Model

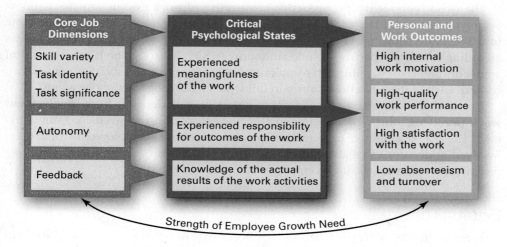

Source: "Job Characteristics Model" from *Work Redesign*, by J. R. Hackman & G. R. Oldham. Copyright © 1980 by Addison-Wesley (a division of Pearson). Reprinted with permission.

enrichment, although the other suggestions involve more than vertical and horizontal expansion of jobs.

1. *Combine tasks.* Put fragmented tasks back together to form a new, larger work module (job enlargement) to increase skill variety and task identity.

2. *Create natural work units.* Design tasks that form an identifiable and meaningful whole to increase employee "ownership" of the work. Encourage employees to view their work as meaningful and important rather than as irrelevant and boring.

3. *Establish client (external or internal) relationships.* Whenever possible, establish direct relationships between workers and their clients to increase skill variety, autonomy, and feedback.

4. *Expand jobs vertically.* Vertical expansion gives employees responsibilities and controls that were formerly reserved for managers, which can increase employee autonomy.

5. *Open feedback channels.* Direct feedback lets employees know how well they're performing their jobs and whether their performance is improving or not.

Research into the JCM continues. For instance, one recent study looked at using job redesign efforts to change job characteristics and improve employee well-being.[41] Another study examined psychological ownership—that is, a personal feeling of "mine-ness" or "our-ness"—and its role in the JCM.[42]

Redesigning Job Design Approaches[43]

Although the JCM has proven to be useful, it may not be totally appropriate for today's jobs that are more service- and knowledge-oriented. The nature of today's jobs has also changed the tasks that employees do in traditional jobs. Two emerging viewpoints on job design are causing a rethink of the JCM and other standard approaches. Let's take a look at each perspective.

The first perspective, the **relational perspective of work design**, focuses on how people's tasks and jobs are increasingly based on social relationships. In jobs today, employees have more interactions and interdependence with coworkers and others both inside and outside the organization. In doing their jobs, employees rely more and more on those around them for information, advice, and assistance. So what does this mean for designing motivating jobs? It means that managers need to look at important components of those employee relationships such as access to and level of social support in an organization, types of interactions outside an organization, amount of task interdependence, and interpersonal feedback.

The second perspective, the **proactive perspective of work design**, says that employees are taking the initiative to change how their work is performed. They're much more involved in decisions and actions that affect their work. Important job design factors according to this perspective include autonomy (which *is* part of the JCM), amount of ambiguity and accountability, job complexity, level of stressors, and social or relationship context. Each of these has been shown to influence employee proactive behaviour.

One stream of research that's relevant to proactive work design is **high-involvement work practices**, which are designed to elicit greater input or involvement from workers.[44] The level of employee proactivity is believed to increase as employees become more involved in decisions that affect their work. Another term for this approach, which we discussed in an earlier chapter, is employee empowerment.

Equity Theory

After graduating from the University of New Brunswick, Mike Wilson worked in Northern Alberta as a civil engineer. He liked his job, but he became frustrated with his employer. "If you did a great job, you were treated just the same as if you did a poor job," he says.[45] Wilson decided to return home to work in the business his father had started in 1965—Dorchester, New Brunswick-based Atlantic Industries, which designs, fabricates, and

relational perspective of work design An approach to job design that focuses on how people's tasks and jobs are increasingly based on social relationships.

proactive perspective of work design An approach to job design in which employees take the initiative to change how their work is performed.

high-involvement work practices Work practices designed to elicit greater input or involvement from workers.

Exhibit 14-7

Equity Theory

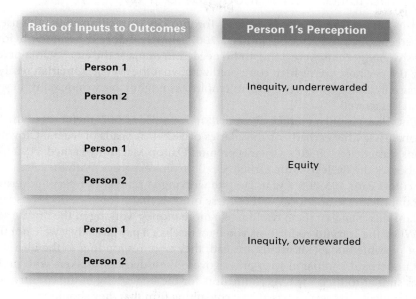

Ratio of Inputs to Outcomes	Person 1's Perception
Person 1 / Person 2	Inequity, underrewarded
Person 1 / Person 2	Equity
Person 1 / Person 2	Inequity, overrewarded

builds corrugated steel structures. Wilson's hard work at Atlantic Industries has paid off: He received the Ernst & Young Entrepreneur of the Year Award for the Atlantic Region.

Wilson's decision to leave his job in Northern Alberta can be explained by equity theory. The term *equity* is related to the concept of fairness and equal treatment compared with others who behave in similar ways. There is considerable evidence that employees compare their job inputs and outcomes relative to others' and that inequities influence the degree of effort that employees exert.[46]

Equity theory, developed by J. Stacey Adams, proposes that employees perceive what they get from a job situation (outcomes) in relation to what they put into it (inputs) and then compare their inputs–outcomes ratio with the inputs–outcomes ratio of relevant others (see Exhibit 14-7). If an employee perceives her ratio to be equal to those of relevant others, a state of equity exists. In other words, she perceives that her situation is fair— that justice prevails. However, if the ratio is perceived as unequal, inequity exists and she views herself as under-rewarded or over-rewarded. Not all inequity (or equity) is real. It is important to underscore that it is the individual's *perception* that determines the equity of the situation. When inequities occur, employees attempt to do something about it.[47] The result might be lower or higher productivity, improved or reduced quality of output, increased absenteeism, or voluntary resignation.

When Toronto city councillors faced inequity in their pay, they responded by voting themselves a raise, as the *Management Reflection* on the next page shows.

The **referent**—the other persons, systems, or selves individuals compare themselves against in order to assess equity—is an important variable in equity theory.[48] Each of the three referent categories is important. The "persons" category includes other individuals with similar jobs in the same organization but also includes friends, neighbours, or professional associates. Based on what they hear at work or read about in newspapers or trade journals, employees compare their pay with that of others. The "system" category includes organizational pay policies, procedures, and allocation. The "self" category refers to inputs–outcomes ratios that are unique to the individual. It reflects past personal experiences and contacts and is influenced by criteria such as past jobs or family commitments.

equity theory The theory that an employee compares his or her job's inputs–outcomes ratio with that of relevant others and then responds to correct any inequity.

referents Those things individuals compare themselves against in order to assess equity.

MANAGEMENT REFLECTION

City Councillors End "Inequitable" Pay

What is fair pay for city councillors? Toronto city councillors voted themselves an 8.9 percent pay raise effective January 2007, shortly before it became obvious that extensive budget cuts were going to be needed to manage the city.[49] On a percentage basis, the pay raise seems high compared with what the average Ontarian received as a pay raise in 2006. Other government employees might have wondered if they should have raises as well.

But what should a municipal councillor be paid? In 2007, members of the Quebec National Assembly earned annual salaries of $82 073, heads of federal Crown corporations started at $109 000, Ontario premier Dalton McGuinty earned $198 620, and members of the BC legislature earned $98 000, plus expenses. With the raise, Toronto's councillors earn $95 000 a year. Despite working at different levels of government—federal, provincial, and local—all of these officials make complex decisions and need similar skills. Many of them could make more money working in the private sector.

When the Toronto councillors voted themselves a pay raise, they were not thinking about possible budget shortfalls. Instead, they were responding to the idea that they were underpaid compared with other government decision makers who performed duties similar to their own. As councillors for the largest city in the country, with the largest budget, they were advised by a consulting firm that they should rank in the "top 25 percent of salaries of councillors across the country." Their salary before the raise was one of the lowest in the country. ■

distributive justice Perceived fairness of the amount and allocation of rewards among individuals.

procedural justice Perceived fairness of the process used to determine the distribution of rewards.

Historically, equity theory focused on **distributive justice**, which is the perceived fairness of the amount and allocation of rewards among individuals. Recent equity research has focused on looking at issues of **procedural justice**, which is the perceived fairness of the process used to determine the distribution of rewards. This research shows that distributive justice has a greater influence on employee satisfaction than procedural justice, while procedural justice tends to affect an employee's organizational commitment, trust in his or her manager, and intention to quit.[50] What are the implications of these findings for managers? They should consider openly sharing information on how allocation decisions are made, follow consistent and unbiased procedures, and engage in similar practices to increase the perception of procedural justice. When managers increase the perception of procedural justice, employees are likely to view their managers and the organization as positive even if they are dissatisfied with pay, promotions, and other personal outcomes.

In conclusion, equity theory shows that, for most employees, motivation is influenced significantly by relative rewards, as well as by absolute rewards, but some key issues are still unclear.[51] For instance, how do employees define inputs and outcomes? How do they combine and weigh their inputs and outcomes to arrive at totals? When and how do the factors change over time? And how do people choose referents? Despite these problems, equity theory does have an impressive amount of research support and offers us some important insights into employee motivation. Managers need to pay attention to equity issues when making plans to motivate their employees.

Expectancy Theory

expectancy theory The theory that an individual tends to act in a certain way based on the expectation that the act will be followed by a given outcome and on the attractiveness of that outcome to the individual.

The most comprehensive and widely accepted explanation of employee motivation to date is Victor Vroom's **expectancy theory**.[52] Although the theory has its critics,[53] most research evidence supports it.[54]

Exhibit 14-8

Simplified Expectancy Model

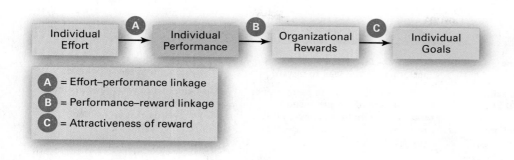

Expectancy theory states that an individual tends to act in a certain way based on the expectation that the act will be followed by a given outcome and on the attractiveness of that outcome to the individual. It includes three variables or relationships (see Exhibit 14-8):

- *Expectancy, or effort–performance linkage.* The probability perceived by the individual that exerting a given amount of effort will lead to a certain level of performance.

- *Instrumentality, or performance–reward linkage.* The degree to which the individual believes that performing at a particular level is instrumental in attaining the desired outcome.

- *Valence, or attractiveness of reward.* The importance that the individual places on the potential outcome or reward that can be achieved on the job. Valence considers both the goals and needs of the individual. (See also *Self-Assessment—What Rewards Do I Value Most?* on pages xx–xx.)

Just Born candy company—makers of Peeps, Mike and Ike's, Hot Tamales, and Teenie Beanie brands—uses expectancy theory in motivating employees to achieve annual corporate sales goals. Members of Just Born's sales team shown here expected that their efforts to reach their goal of increasing sales by 4 percent over the previous year would earn them an all-expense paid trip to Hawaii if they met their target. The 24-employee sales team had a good year of boosting sales by 2 percent but, in failing to meet their goal, they were given fleece jackets and bomber hats and a trip to Fargo, North Dakota.

Ann Arbor Miller/AP Photos

This explanation of motivation might sound complex, but it really is not. It can be summed up in these questions: How hard do I have to work to achieve a certain level of performance, and can I actually achieve that level? What reward will I get for working at that level of performance? How attractive is the reward to me, and does it help me achieve my goals? Whether you are motivated to put forth effort (that is, to work) at any given time depends on your particular goals and your perception of whether a certain level of performance is necessary to attain those goals.

The key to expectancy theory is understanding an individual's goal and the link between effort and performance, between performance and rewards, and, finally, between rewards and individual goal satisfaction. Expectancy theory recognizes that there is no universal principle for explaining what motivates individuals and thus stresses that managers need to understand why employees view certain outcomes as attractive or unattractive. After all, we want to reward individuals with those things they value as positive. Also, expectancy theory emphasizes expected behaviours. Do employees know what is expected of them and how they will be evaluated? Finally, the theory is concerned with perceptions. Reality is irrelevant. An individual's own perceptions of performance, reward, and goal outcomes, not the outcomes themselves, will determine his or her motivation (level of effort). Exhibit 14-9 suggests how managers might increase employee motivation, using expectancy theory.

Exhibit 14-9

Steps to Increasing Motivation, Using Expectancy Theory

Improving Expectancy	Improving Instrumentality	Improving Valence
Improve the ability of the individual to perform.	**Increase the individual's belief that performance will lead to reward.**	**Make sure that the reward is meaningful to the individual.**
• Make sure employees have skills for the task. • Provide training. • Assign reasonable tasks and goals.	• Observe and recognize performance. • Deliver rewards as promised. • Indicate to employees how previous good performance led to greater rewards.	• Ask employees what rewards they value. • Give rewards that are valued.

Integrating Contemporary Theories of Motivation

Many of the ideas underlying the theories are complementary, and you will better understand how to motivate people if you see how the theories fit together.[55] Exhibit 14-10 presents a model that integrates much of what we know about motivation. Its basic foundation is the expectancy model. Let's work through the model, starting on the left.

The individual effort box has an arrow leading into it. This arrow flows from the individual's goals. Consistent with goal-setting theory, this goals–effort link is meant to illustrate that goals direct behaviour. Expectancy theory predicts that an employee will exert a high level of effort if he or she perceives that there is a strong relationship between effort and performance, performance and rewards, and rewards and satisfaction of personal goals. Each of these relationships is, in turn, influenced by certain factors. You can see from the model that the level of individual performance is determined not only by the level of individual effort but also by the individual's ability to perform and by whether the organization has a fair and objective performance evaluation system. The performance–reward relationship will be strong if the individual perceives that it is performance (rather than seniority, personal favourites, or some other criterion) that is rewarded. The final link in expectancy theory is the rewards–goals relationship. The traditional need theories come into play at this point. Motivation would be high to the degree that the rewards an individual received for his or her high performance satisfied the dominant needs consistent with his or her individual goals.

A closer look at the model also shows that it considers the achievement-need, reinforcement, equity, and JCM theories. The high achiever isn't motivated by the organization's assessment of his or her performance or organizational rewards; hence the jump from effort to individual goals for those with a high nAch. Remember that high achievers are internally driven as long as the jobs they're doing provide them with personal responsibility, feedback, and moderate risks. They're not concerned with the effort–performance, performance–reward, or rewards–goals linkages.

Reinforcement theory is seen in the model by recognizing that the organization's rewards reinforce the individual's performance. If managers have designed a reward system that is seen by employees as "paying off" for good performance, the rewards will reinforce and encourage continued good performance. Rewards also play a key part in equity theory. Individuals will compare the rewards (outcomes) they have received from the inputs or efforts they made with the inputs–outcomes ratio of relevant others. If inequities exist, the effort expended may be influenced.

Finally, the JCM is seen in this integrative model. Task characteristics (job design) influence job motivation at two places. First, jobs that are designed around the five job

Exhibit 14-10

Integrating Contemporary Theories of Motivation

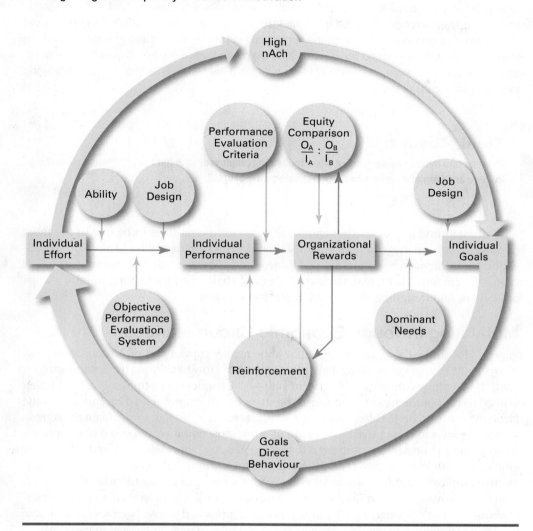

dimensions are likely to lead to higher actual job performance because the individual's motivation will be stimulated by the job itself—that is, these jobs will increase the linkage between effort and performance. Second, jobs that are designed around the five job dimensions increase an employee's control over key elements in his or her work. Therefore, jobs that offer autonomy, feedback, and similar task characteristics help to satisfy the individual goals of employees who desire greater control over their work.

Current Issues in Motivation

▶ ▶ ▶ One of the challenges managers at Tesco faced was how to motivate its many different employee groups: students, new graduates, mothers returning to the workplace, and ethnic minorities.[56] In a survey of its employees, the company found that older female employees wanted flexible hours and stimulating work, but they were not looking to be promoted. Young college graduates working in head office wanted a challenging, well-paid career and time to pursue personal interests and family life. Many employees noted they wanted managers who helped them.

4 Discuss current issues in motivation.

Tesco has come up with a variety of practices to meet employee needs, including career breaks of up to eight months, discounts on family holidays, driving lessons, and magazine subscriptions. Tesco has a website that offers career and financial advice and discounts on meals, cinema tickets, and travel for its 16- to 24-year-old employees who are in school or have recently left school. The company created the "A-Level Options" program to give young people who did not want a post-secondary education the opportunity to be fast-tracked into management. Clare Chapman, Tesco's human resource director, says the company has not limited specific rewards for specific groups. "It's more a question of being mindful of the needs of all staff instead of catering for one or two types of attitude."

Think About It

What factors need to be considered when motivating employees who have very different needs? Is there anything else Tesco can do to motivate young people?

Understanding and predicting employee motivation continues to be one of the most popular areas in management research. However, even current studies of employee motivation are influenced by several significant workplace issues, such as motivating in tough economic circumstances, managing cross-cultural challenges, motivating unique groups of workers, and designing appropriate rewards programs.

Motivating in Tough Economic Circumstances

Zappos, the quirky Las Vegas–based online shoe retailer (now a part of Amazon.com), has always had a reputation for being a fun place to work.[57] However, during the economic recession, it, like many companies, had to cut staff—124 employees in total. CEO Tony Hsieh wanted to get out the news fast to lessen the stress for his employees. So he announced the layoff in an e-mail, on his blog, and on his Twitter account. Although some might think these are terrible ways to communicate that kind of news, most employees thanked him for being so open and so honest. The company also took good care of those who were laid off. Laid-off employees with less than two years of service were paid through the end of the year. Longer-tenured employees got four weeks for every year of service. All got six months of continued paid health coverage and, at the request of the employees, got to keep their 40 percent merchandise discount through the Christmas season. Zappos had always been a model of how to nurture employees in good times; now it showed how to treat employees in bad times.

The economic recession of the past few years was difficult for many organizations, especially when it came to their employees. Layoffs, tight budgets, minimal or no pay raises, benefit cuts, no bonuses, long hours doing the work of those who had been laid off—this was the reality that many employees faced. As conditions deteriorated, employee confidence, optimism, and job engagement plummeted as well. As you can imagine, it wasn't an easy thing for managers to keep employees motivated under such challenging circumstances.

Managers came to realize that in an uncertain economy, they had to be creative in keeping their employees' efforts energized, directed, and sustained toward achieving goals. They were forced to look at ways to motivate employees that didn't involve money or that were relatively inexpensive.[58] So they relied on actions such as holding meetings with employees to keep the lines of communication open and to get their input on issues; establishing a common goal, such as maintaining excellent customer service, to keep everyone focused; creating a community feel so employees could see that managers cared about them and their work; and giving employees opportunities to continue to learn and grow. And, of course, an encouraging word always went a long way.

Managing Cross-Cultural Motivational Challenges

Scores of employees at Denmark's largest brewer, Carlsberg A/S, walked off their jobs in protest after the company tightened rules on workplace drinking and removed beer coolers from work sites.[59] Now that's a motivational challenge you don't often see in North American workplaces!

In today's global business environment, managers can't automatically assume motivational programs that work in one geographic location are going to work in others. Most current motivation theories were developed in the United States by Americans and about Americans.[60] Maybe the most blatant pro-American characteristic in these theories is the strong emphasis on individualism and achievement. For instance, both goal-setting and expectancy theories emphasize goal accomplishment as well as rational and individual thought. Let's look at the motivation theories to see their level of cross-cultural transferability.

Maslow's need hierarchy argues that people start at the physiological level and then move progressively up the hierarchy in order. This hierarchy, if it has any application at all, aligns with American culture. In countries like Japan, Greece, and Mexico, where uncertainty avoidance characteristics are strong, security needs would be the foundational layer of the need hierarchy. Countries that score high on nurturing characteristics—Denmark, Sweden, Norway, the Netherlands, and Finland—would have social needs as their foundational level.[62] We would predict, for instance, that group work will be more motivating when the country's culture scores high on the nurturing criterion.

Another motivation concept that clearly has an American bias is the achievement need. The view that a high achievement need acts as an internal motivator presupposes two cultural characteristics—a willingness to accept a moderate degree of risk (which excludes countries with strong uncertainty avoidance characteristics) and a concern with performance (which applies almost singularly to countries with strong achievement characteristics). This combination is found in Anglo-American countries such as the United States, Canada, and Great Britain.[63] On the other hand, these characteristics are relatively absent in countries such as Chile and Portugal.

Equity theory has a relatively strong following in the United States, which is not surprising given that U.S.-style reward systems are based on the assumption that workers are highly sensitive to equity in reward allocations. In the United States, equity is meant to closely link pay to performance. However, recent evidence suggests that in collectivist cultures, especially in the former socialist countries of Central and Eastern Europe, employees expect rewards to reflect their individual needs as well as their performance.[64] Moreover, consistent with a legacy of communism and centrally planned economies, employees exhibited a greater "entitlement" attitude—that is, they expected outcomes to be greater than their inputs.[65] These findings suggest that U.S.-style pay practices may need to be modified in some countries in order to be perceived as fair by employees.

Another research study of more than 50 000 employees around the world examined two cultural characteristics from the GLOBE framework—individualism and masculinity—(see Chapter 3 for a discussion of these characteristics) in relation to motivation.[66] The researchers found that in individualistic cultures such as the United States and Canada, individual initiative, individual freedom, and individual achievement are highly valued. In more collective cultures such as Iran, Peru, and China, however, employees may be less interested in receiving individual praise but place a greater emphasis on harmony, belonging, and consensus. They also found that in masculine (achievement/assertive) cultures such as Japan and Slovakia, the focus is on material success. Those work environments are designed to push employees hard and then reward top performers with high earnings. However, in more feminine (nurturing) cultures such as Sweden and the Netherlands, smaller wage gaps among employees are common, and employees are likely to have extensive quality-of-life benefits.

Despite these cross-cultural differences in motivation, some cross-cultural consistencies are evident. In a recent study of employees in 13 countries, the top motivators included (ranked from number one on down): being treated with respect, work-life balance, the type of work done, the quality of people worked with and the quality of the organization's leadership (tied), base pay, working in an environment where good service can be provided to others, long-term career potential, flexible working arrangements, learning and development opportunities and benefits (tied), promotion opportunities,

datapoints[61]

92 percent of executives have the perception that favouritism occurs in large organizations.

29 percent of HR professionals and employees were satisfied with their organization's recognition efforts.

50 percent of HR professionals said they believe managers and supervisors acknowledge and appreciate employees effectively.

100 percent of senior executives indicated that satisfied and engaged employees positively affect an organization's bottom line.

65 percent of American adults polled said rewards in the workplace are distributed less fairly today than five years ago.

92 percent of employers have variable pay plans or performance-based award programs.

12 percent of employees believe their company listens to and cares about them.

56 percent of HR professionals believe rewards are based on job performance.

67 percent of employees said their manager acknowledges and appreciates them at work.

21 percent of adults surveyed said job security was the most important thing to them about their job.

and incentive pay or bonus.[67] And other studies have shown that the desire for interesting work seems important to almost all workers, regardless of their national culture. For instance, employees in Belgium, Britain, Israel, and the United States ranked "interesting work" number one among 11 work goals. It was ranked either second or third in Japan, the Netherlands, and Germany.[68] Similarly, in a study comparing job-preference outcomes among graduate students in the United States, Canada, Australia, and Singapore, growth, achievement, and responsibility were rated the top three and had identical rankings.[69] Both studies suggest some universality to the importance of intrinsic factors identified by Herzberg in his two-factor theory. Another recent study examining workplace motivation trends in Japan also seems to indicate that Herzberg's model is applicable to Japanese employees.[70]

Motivating Unique Groups of Workers

At Deloitte, employees are allowed to "dial up" or "dial down" their job responsibilities to fit their personal and professional goals.[71] The company's program, called Mass Career Customization, has been a huge hit with its employees! In the first 12 months after it was rolled out, employee satisfaction with "overall career/life fit" rose by 25 percent. Also, the number of high-performing employees staying with Deloitte increased.

Motivating employees has never been easy! Employees come into organizations with different needs, personalities, skills, abilities, interests, and aptitudes. They have different expectations of their employers and different views of what they think their employer has a right to expect of them. And they vary widely in what they want from their jobs. For instance, some employees get more satisfaction out of their personal interests and pursuits and only want a weekly paycheque—nothing more. They're not interested in making their work more challenging or interesting or in "winning" performance contests. Others derive a great deal of satisfaction in their jobs and are motivated to exert high levels of effort. Given these differences, how can managers do an effective job of motivating the unique groups of employees found in today's workforce? One thing is to understand the motivational requirements of these groups including diverse employees, professionals, contingent workers, and low-skilled minimum-wage employees.

Motivating a Diverse Workforce

To maximize motivation among today's workforce, managers need to think in terms of *flexibility*. For instance, studies tell us that men place more importance on having autonomy in their jobs than do women. In contrast, the opportunity to learn, convenient and flexible work hours, and good interpersonal relations are more important to women.[72] Baby Boomers may need more flextime as they manage the needs of their children and their aging parents. Gen-Xers want employers to add to their experience so they develop portable skills. Meanwhile, Gen-Yers want more opportunities and the ability to work in teams.[73] Managers need to recognize that what motivates a single mother with two dependent children who is working full time to support her family may be very different from the needs of a single part-time employee or an older employee who is working to supplement his or her retirement income. A diverse array of rewards is needed to motivate employees with such diverse needs. Many of the work–life balance programs that organizations have implemented are a response to the varied needs of a diverse workforce. In addition, many organizations have developed flexible work arrangements such as compressed workweeks, flextime, and job sharing that recognize different needs.

Motivating Professionals

In contrast to a generation ago, the typical employee today is more likely to be a professional with a university degree than a blue-collar factory worker. What special concerns should managers be aware of when trying to motivate a team of engineers at Intel's India Development Center, software designers at SAS Institute in North Carolina, or a group of consultants at Accenture in Singapore?

Chrislyn Hamilton, a crew member at a McDonald's restaurant in Brisbane, Australia, won first place in the Voice of McDonald's, a global singing competition to discover, recognize, and reward the most talented singers among the company's 1.8 million restaurant employees throughout the world. As top winner in the contest, Hamilton received $25 000, will lend her voice to a DreamWorks Animation movie, and will appear in a McDonald's TV commercial in her market. In addition to this recognition program, McDonald's motivates its crew members by providing them with a relaxed work environment, a low-stress job, social interaction with co-workers, a flexible work schedule, and opportunity to advance to a higher position.

Reinhold Matay/MacDonald's/AP Photos

Professionals are different from nonprofessionals.[74] They have a strong and long-term commitment to their field of expertise. To keep current in their field, they need to regularly update their knowledge, and because of their commitment to their profession, they rarely define their workweek as 8 a.m. to 5 p.m. five days a week.

What motivates professionals? Money and promotions typically are low on their priority list. Why? They tend to be well paid and enjoy what they do. In contrast, job challenge tends to be ranked high. They like to tackle problems and find solutions. Their chief reward in their job is the work itself. Professionals also value support. They want others to think that what they are working on is important.[75] That may be true for all employees, but professionals tend to be focused on their work as their central life interest, whereas nonprofessionals typically have other interests outside work that can compensate for needs not met on the job.

Motivating Contingent Workers

As full-time jobs have been eliminated through downsizing and other organizational restructurings, the number of openings for part-time, contract, and other forms of temporary work have increased. Contingent workers don't have the security or stability that permanent employees have, and they don't identify with the organization or display the commitment that other employees do. Temporary employees also typically get little or no benefits such as health care or pensions.[76]

There is no simple solution for motivating contingent employees. For that small set of individuals who prefer the freedom of their temporary status—for instance, some students, working mothers, retirees—the lack of stability may not be an issue. In addition, temporariness might be preferred by highly compensated physicians, engineers, accountants, or financial planners who don't want the demands of a full-time job. But these are the exceptions. For the most part, temporary employees are not temporary by choice.

What will motivate involuntarily temporary employees? An obvious answer is the opportunity to become a permanent employee. In cases in which permanent employees are selected from a pool of temps, the temps will often work hard in hopes of becoming permanent. A less obvious answer is the opportunity for training. The ability of a temporary employee to find a new job is largely dependent on his or her skills. If the employee sees that the job he or she is doing can help develop marketable skills, then motivation is increased. From an equity standpoint, you should also consider the repercussions of mixing permanent and temporary workers when pay differentials are significant. When temps work alongside permanent employees who earn more and also get benefits for doing the same job, the performance of temps is likely to suffer. Separating such employees or perhaps minimizing interdependence between them might help managers decrease potential problems.[77]

Motivating Minimum-Wage Employees

Suppose that in your first managerial position after graduating, you are responsible for managing a work group composed of minimum-wage employees. Offering more pay to these employees for high levels of performance is out of the question: Your company just cannot afford it.[78] In addition, these employees have limited education and skills. What are your motivational options at this point? One of the toughest motivational challenges facing many managers today is how to achieve high performance levels from minimum-wage employees.

One trap we often fall into is thinking that people are motivated only by money. Although money is important as a motivator, it's not the only reward that people seek and that managers can use. In motivating minimum-wage employees, managers might look at employee recognition programs. Many managers also recognize the power of praise, although these "pats on the back" must be sincere and given for the right reasons.

Designing Effective Rewards Programs

Employee rewards programs play a powerful role in motivating for appropriate employee behaviour. In this section, we look at how managers can design effective rewards programs by using employee recognition programs and pay-for-performance programs. First, though, we should examine the issue of the extent to which money motivates.

Open-Book Management

Within 24 hours after managers of the Heavy Duty Division of Springfield Remanufacturing Company (SRC) gather to discuss a multi-page financial document, every plant employee will have seen the same information. If the employees can meet shipment goals, they'll all share in a large year-end bonus.[79] Many organizations of various sizes involve their employees in workplace decisions by opening up the financial statements (the "books"). They share that information so employees will be motivated to make better decisions about their work and better able to understand the implications of what they do, how they do it, and the ultimate impact on the bottom line. This approach is called **open-book management** and many organizations are using it.[80] For instance, at Parrish Medical Center in Titusville, Florida, CEO George Mikitarian was struggling with the prospect of massive layoffs, facilities closing, and profits declining. So he turned to "town hall meetings" in which employees received updates on the financial condition of the hospital. He also told his employees it would require their commitment to help find ways to reduce expenses and cut costs.[81] At giant insurance broker Marsh, its 25 000 employees are being taught the ABCs of finance and accounting.[82]

The goal of open-book management is to get employees to think like owners by seeing the impact their decisions have on financial results. Since many employees don't have the knowledge or background to understand the financials, they have to be taught how to read and understand the organization's financial statements. Once employees have this knowledge, however, managers need to regularly share the numbers with them. By sharing this information, employees begin to see the link between their efforts, level of performance, and operational results.

Employee Recognition Programs

Employee recognition programs provide managers with opportunities to give employees personal attention and express interest, approval, and appreciation for a job well done.[83] These programs can take many forms. For instance, you can personally congratulate an employee in private for a good job. You can send a handwritten note or an email message acknowledging something positive that the employee has done. For employees with a strong need for social acceptance, you can publicly recognize accomplishments. To enhance group cohesiveness and motivation, you can celebrate team successes. For instance, you can throw a pizza party to celebrate a team's accomplishments.

A recent survey of organizations found that 84 percent had some type of program to recognize worker achievements.[84] And do employees think these programs are important? You bet! In a survey conducted a few years ago, a wide range of employees was asked what they considered the most powerful workplace motivator. Their response? Recognition, recognition, and more recognition![85]

Consistent with reinforcement theory, rewarding a behaviour with recognition that immediately follows the behaviour is likely to encourage its repetition. During the economic recession, managers got quite creative in how they showed employees they were appreciated.[86] For instance, employees at one company got to take home fresh vegetables from the company vegetable garden. In others, managers treated employees who really put forth efforts on a project to a special meal or movie tickets. Also, managers can show employees that no matter his or her role, their contributions matter. Some of these things may seem simple, but they can go a long way in showing employees they're valued.

Pay-for-Performance Programs

Here's a survey statistic that may surprise you: 40 percent of employees see no clear link between performance and pay.[87] So what are the companies where these employees work paying for? They're obviously not clearly communicating performance expectations.[88] **Pay-for-performance programs** are variable compensation plans that pay employees on the basis of some performance measure.[89] Piece-rate pay plans, wage incentive plans, profit-sharing, and lump-sum bonuses are examples. What differentiates these forms of pay from more traditional compensation plans is that instead of paying a person for time on the job, pay is adjusted to reflect some performance measure. These performance measures might include such things as individual productivity, team or work group productivity, departmental productivity, or the overall organization's profit performance.

Pay-for-performance is probably most compatible with expectancy theory. Individuals should perceive a strong relationship between their performance and the rewards they receive for motivation to be maximized. If rewards are allocated only on nonperformance factors—such as seniority, job title, or across-the-board pay raises—then employees are likely to reduce their efforts. From a motivation perspective, making some or all of an employee's pay conditional on some performance measure focuses his or her attention and effort toward that measure, then reinforces the continuation of the effort with a reward. If the employee's team's or organization's performance declines, so does the reward. Thus, there's an incentive to keep efforts and motivation strong.

pay-for-performance programs Variable compensation plans that pay employees on the basis of some performance measure.

SUMMARY AND IMPLICATIONS

1. Define motivation. Motivation refers to the process by which a person's efforts are energized, directed, and sustained toward attaining a goal, conditioned by the effort's ability to satisfy some individual need. The *energy* element is a measure of intensity, drive, or vigour. The high level of effort needs to be *directed* in ways that help the organization achieve its goals. Employees must *persist* in putting forth effort to achieve those goals.

▶▶▶ At Tesco, one challenge was to motivate employees so that there would be less turnover.

2. Compare and contrast early theories of motivation. Four early motivation theories—Maslow's hierarchy of needs theory, McGregor's Theory X and Theory Y, Herzberg's two-factor theory, and McClelland's three-needs theory—were discussed. Although more valid explanations of motivation have been developed, these early theories are important because they represent the foundation from which contemporary motivation theories were developed and because many practising managers still use them.

▶▶▶ Managers at Tesco discovered that different employee groups, such as students and mothers returning to the workplace, had different needs, and tried to address these needs to keep employees motivated.

3. Compare and contrast contemporary theories of motivation. It is possible to make jobs more motivating by designing them better. The job characteristics model proposes that employees will be more motivated if they have greater autonomy and feedback and the work is meaningful. Equity theory proposes that employees compare their rewards and their productivity with others, and then determine whether they have been treated fairly. Individuals who perceive that they are under rewarded will try to adjust their behaviour to correct this imbalance. Expectancy theory explores the link between people's belief in whether they can do the work assigned, their belief in whether they will get the rewards promised, and the extent to which the reward is something they value. Most research evidence supports expectancy theory. Goal-setting theory says that specific goals increase performance and that difficult goals, when accepted, result in higher performance than do easy goals. Reinforcement theory ignores factors such as goals, expectations, and needs. Instead, it focuses solely on what happens to a person when he or she does something.

▶▶▶ Tesco encourages employees to buy shares of the company, so that they can "share in the success they helped to create" and see the link between performance and reward.

4. Discuss current issues in motivation. Managers must cope with four current motivation issues: motivating in tough economic circumstances, managing cross-cultural challenges, motivating unique groups of workers, and designing appropriate rewards programs. During tough economic conditions, managers must look for creative ways to keep employees' efforts energized, directed, and sustained toward achieving goals. Most motivational theories were developed in the United States and have a North American bias. Some theories (Maslow's need hierarchy, achievement need, and equity theory) don't work well for other cultures. However, the desire for interesting work seems important to all workers and Herzberg's motivator (intrinsic) factors may be universal. Managers face challenges in motivating unique groups of workers. A diverse workforce is looking for flexibility. Professionals want job challenge and support and are motivated by the work itself. Contingent workers want the opportunity to become permanent or to receive skills training. Recognition programs and sincere appreciation for work done can be used to motivate low-skilled, minimum-wage workers. Open-book management shares the financial statements (the books) with employees who have been taught what they mean. Employee recognition programs consist of personal attention, approval, and appreciation for a job well done. Pay-for-performance programs are variable compensation plans that pay employees on the basis of some performance measure.

▶ ▶ ▶ One of Tesco's challenges was motivating employees who had somewhat repetitive jobs.

MyManagementLab Study, practise, and explore real management situations with these helpful resources:
- **Interactive Lesson Presentations:** Work through interactive presentations and assessments to test your knowledge of management concepts.
- **PIA (Personal Inventory Assessments):** Enhance your ability to connect with key concepts through these engaging, self-reflection assessments.
- **Study Plan:** Check your understanding of chapter concepts with self-study quizzes.
- **Simulations:** Practise decision-making in simulated management environments.

P I A PERSONAL INVENTORY ASSESSMENT

REVIEW AND DISCUSSION QUESTIONS

1. What is motivation? Explain the three key elements of motivation.

2. Describe each of the four early theories of motivation.

3. How do goal-setting, reinforcement, and equity theories explain employee motivation?

4. What are the different job design approaches to motivation?

5. Explain the three key linkages in expectancy theory and their role in motivation.

6. What challenges do managers face in motivating today's workforce?

7. Describe open-book management, employee recognition, and pay-for-performance programs.

8. Can an individual be too motivated? Discuss.

ETHICS DILEMMA

Kodak, once the premier maker of photographic film, has struggled to make it in a world of digital photography and camera phones.[90] It filed for bankruptcy in early 2012. In July 2012, the company's CEO went back to bankruptcy court asking permission to pay 15 top executives and managers (including himself) up to $8.82 million in cash and deferred stock if they successfully restructured the company and brought it back out of bankruptcy.

Although incentive plans in bankruptcy have been controversial, Kodak said a committee of the company's unsecured creditors supported the pay plan. What do you think? What potential ethical issues do you see here? What stakeholders might be impacted and how?

SKILLS EXERCISE

Developing Your Motivating Employees Skill—About the Skill

Because a simple, all-encompassing set of motivational guidelines is not available, the following suggestions draw on the essence of what we know about motivating employees.

Steps in Practising the Skill

1. *Recognize individual differences.* Almost every contemporary motivation theory recognizes that employees are not homogeneous. They have different needs. They also differ in terms of attitudes, personality, and other important individual variables.

2. *Match people to jobs.* A great deal of evidence shows the motivational benefits of carefully matching people to jobs. People who lack the necessary skills to perform successfully will be at a disadvantage.

3. *Use goals.* You should ensure that employees have hard, specific goals and feedback on how well they're doing in pursuit of those goals. In many cases, these goals should be participatively set.

4. *Ensure goals are perceived as attainable.* Regardless of whether goals are actually attainable, employees

who see goals as unattainable will reduce their effort. Be sure, therefore, that employees feel confident that increased efforts can lead to achieving performance goals.

5. *Individualize rewards.* Because employees have different needs, what acts as a reinforcer for one may not do so for another. Use your knowledge of employee differences to individualize the rewards over which you have control. Some of the more obvious rewards that you can allocate include pay, promotions, autonomy, and the opportunity to participate in goal setting and decision making.

6. *Link rewards to performance.* You need to make rewards contingent on performance. Rewarding factors other than performance will only reinforce the importance of those other factors. Key rewards such as pay increases and promotions should be given for the attainment of employees' specific goals.

7. *Check the system for equity.* Employees should perceive that rewards or outcomes are equal to the inputs given. On a simplistic level, experience, ability, effort, and other obvious inputs should explain differences in pay, responsibility, and other obvious outcomes.

8. *Don't ignore money.* It's easy to get so caught up in setting goals, creating interesting jobs, and providing opportunities for participation that you forget that money is a major reason why most people work. Thus, the allocation of performance-based wage increases, piece-work bonuses, employee stock ownership plans, and other pay incentives are important in determining employee motivation.

WORKING TOGETHER: TEAM EXERCISE

What Matters to "Me"

List five criteria (for example, pay, recognition, challenging work, friendships, status, the opportunity to do new things, the opportunity to travel, and so forth) that would be most important to you in a job. Rank them by order of importance.

Break into small groups of three or four and compare your responses. What patterns, if any, did you find?

LEARNING TO BE A MANAGER

- A good habit to get into if you don't already do it is goal-setting. Set goals for yourself using the suggestions from goal-setting theory. Write these down and keep them in a notebook. Track your progress toward achieving these goals.

- Describe a task you've done recently for which you exerted a high level of effort. Explain your behaviour, using any three of the motivation approaches described in this chapter.

- Pay attention to times when you're highly motivated and times when you're not as motivated. Write down a description of these. What accounts for the difference in your level of motivation?

- Interview three managers about how they motivate their employees. What have they found that works the best? Write up your findings in a report and be prepared to present it in class.

- Using the job characteristics model, redesign the following jobs to be more motivating: retail store sales associate, utility company meter reader, and checkout cashier at a discount store. In a written report, describe for each job at least two specific actions you would take for each of the five core job dimensions.

- Do some serious thinking about what you want from your job after graduation. Make a list of what's important to you. Are you looking for a pleasant work environment, challenging work, flexible work hours, fun coworkers, or what? Discuss how you will discover whether a particular job will help you get those things.

- Find five different examples of employee recognition programs from organizations with which you're familiar or from articles that you find. Write a report describing your examples and evaluating what you think about the various approaches.

- Find the website of Great Place to Work Institute [www.greatplacetowork.com]. What does the Institute say about what makes an organization a great place to work? Next, locate the lists of the Best Companies to Work For. Choose one company from each of the international lists. Now research that company and describe what it does that makes it a great place to work.

CASE APPLICATION 1

Passion for the Outdoors and for People

At its headquarters in Ventura, California, Patagonia's office space feels more like a national park lodge than the main office of a $400 million retailer.[91] It has a Douglas fir staircase and a portrait of Yosemite's El Capitan. The company's café serves organic food and drinks. There's an infant and toddler child-care room for employees' children. It's an easy one-block walk from the Pacific Ocean, and employees' surfboards are lined up by the cafeteria, ready at a moment's notice to catch some waves. (Current wave reports are noted on a whiteboard in the lobby.) After surfing or jogging or biking, employees can freshen up in the showers in the restrooms. And no one has a private office. If an employee doesn't want to be disturbed, he or she wears headphones. Visitors are evident by the business attire they wear. The company encourages celebrations to boost employee morale. For instance, at the Reno store, the "Fun Patrol" organizes parties throughout the year.

Attracting people who share its strong passion for the outdoors and the environment, Patagonia motivates its loyal employees by giving them responsibility for the outcomes of their work and a high level of task significance that their work is meaningful because it contributes to the purpose of protecting and preserving the environment.

Patagonia has long been recognized as a great workplace for mothers. And it's also earned a reputation for loyal employees, something that many retailers struggle with. Its combined voluntary and involuntary turnover in its retail stores was around 25 percent, while it was only 7 percent at headquarters. (The industry average for retail is around 44 percent.) Patagonia's CEO Casey Sheahan says the company's culture, camaraderie, and way of doing business

is very meaningful to employees and they know that "what they do each day is contributing toward a higher purpose— protecting and preserving the areas that most of them love spending time in." Managers are coached to define expectations, communicate deadlines, and then let employees figure out the best way to meet those.

Founded by Canadian-born Yvon Chouinard, Patagonia's first and strongest passion is for the outdoors and the environment. And that attracts employees who are also passionate about those things. But Patagonia's executives do realize that they are first and foremost a business and, even though they're committed to doing the right thing, the company needs to remain profitable to be able to continue to do the things it's passionate about. But that hasn't seemed to be an issue since the recession in the early 1990s when the company had to make its only large-scale layoffs in its history.

DISCUSSION QUESTIONS

1. What would it be like to work at Patagonia? (Hint: Go to Patagonia's website and find the section on jobs.) What's your assessment of the company's work environment?
2. Using what you've learned from studying the various motivation theories, what does Patagonia's situation tell you about employee motivation?
3. What do you think might be Patagonia's biggest challenge in keeping employees motivated?
4. If you were managing a team of Patagonia employees in the retail stores, how would you keep them motivated?

CASE APPLICATION 2

Best Practices at Best Buy

Best Buy's Results-Only Work Environment program, which changed the company's culture of evaluating and rewarding employees on the results of their work rather than on the number of hours they work, increased worker productivity and job satisfaction and decreased voluntary turnover.

Do traditional workplaces reward long hours instead of efficient hours? Wouldn't it make more sense to have a workplace in which "people can do whatever they want, whenever they want, as long as the work gets done?" Well, that's the approach Best Buy is taking.[92] And this radical workplace experiment, which obviously has many implications for

employee motivation, has been an interesting and enlightening journey for the company.

In 2002, then-CEO Brad Anderson introduced a carefully crafted program called ROWE—Results-Only Work Environment. ROWE was the inspiration of two HRM managers at Best Buy, Cali Ressler and Jody Thompson, who had been given the task of taking a flexible work program in effect at corporate headquarters in Minnesota and developing it for everyone in the company. Ressler and Thompson said, "We realized that the flexible work program was successful as employee engagement was up, productivity was higher, but the problem was the participants were being viewed as 'not working.'" And that was a common reaction from managers who didn't really view flexible work employees as "really working because they aren't in the office working traditional hours." The two women set about to change that by creating a program in which "everyone would be evaluated solely on their results, not on how long they worked."

The first thing to understand about ROWE is that it's not about schedules. Instead, it's about changing the work culture of an organization, which is infinitely more difficult than changing schedules. With Anderson's blessing and support, they embarked on this journey to overhaul the company's corporate workplace.

The first step in implementing ROWE was a culture audit at company headquarters, which helped them establish a baseline for how employees perceived their work environment. After four months, the audit was repeated. During this time, Best Buy executives were being educated about ROWE and what it was all about. Obviously, it was important to have their commitment to the program. The second phase involved explaining the ROWE philosophy to all the corporate employees and training managers on how to maintain control in a ROWE workplace. In the third phase, work unit teams were free to figure out how to implement the changes. Each team found a different way to keep the flexibility from spiralling into chaos. For instance, the public relations team got pagers to make sure someone was always available in an emergency. Some employees in the finance department used software that turns voice mail into e-mail files accessible from anywhere, making it easier for them to work at home.

Four months after ROWE was implemented, Ressler and Thompson followed up with another culture check to see how everyone was doing.

So what's the bottom line for Best Buy? Productivity jumped 41 percent, and voluntary turnover fell to 8 percent from 12 percent. They also discovered that when employees' engagement with their jobs increased, average annual sales increased 2 percent. And employees said the freedom changed their lives. "They don't know if they work fewer hours—they've stopped counting—but they are more productive." ROWE reduced work-family conflict and increased employees' control over their schedules. As Ressler and Thompson stated, "Work isn't a place you go—it's something you do."

DISCUSSION QUESTIONS

1. Describe the elements of ROWE. What do you think might be the advantages and drawbacks of this program?
2. Using one or more motivation theories from the chapter, explain why you think ROWE works.
3. What might be the challenges for managers in motivating employees in a program like this?
4. Does this sound like something you would be comfortable with? Why or why not?
5. What's your interpretation of the statement that "Work isn't a place you go—it's something you do"? Do you agree? Why or why not?

Managing Groups and Teams

Few trends have influenced how work gets done in organizations as much as the use of work teams. Organizations are increasingly structuring work around teams rather than individuals. Managers need to understand what influences team performance and satisfaction. After reading and studying this chapter, you will achieve the following learning outcomes.

▶ ▶ ▶ Following the Canadian men's hockey team's disappointing result in Turin (their worst result in the Olympics since 1980), one reporter wrote, "How could an elite group of players who will be paid nearly $100 million in salaries, and that has scored 334 goals in NHL games already this season, look as dysfunctional as a bantam league team on its first road trip to Medicine Hat?"[1]

Sidney Crosby's golden goal in overtime in the final game of the 2010 Olympics against the United States was hailed as the biggest in a generation.[2] In Canada hockey is more of an obsession than a sport. Expectations were high for the 2014 team, and on the day the 2014 team was announced prime minister

Stephen Harper tweeted "looking forward to @HockeyCanada's announcement at 11AM ET. With so much to choose from, I'm sure they'll make us proud in #Sochi2014."[3]

The Olympics pose challenges not present in NHL hockey—a short tournament, on the bigger international ice surface—which required the coaching and management team to "get the right person for the job, not necessarily the most talented.[4] As Steve Yzerman prepared for the 2014 Sochi Winter Olympics, he found himself having to make one of the toughest decisions of his career when he did not name Martin St. Louis, from the Tampa Bay Lightning, where Yzerman serves as the team manager, to the final squad of 25.[5]

imago sportfotodienst/imago/Sven Simon/Newscom

You've probably had a lot of experience working in groups—on class project teams, maybe an athletic team, a fundraising committee, or even a sales team at work. Work teams are one of the realities—and challenges—of managing in today's dynamic global environment. Many organizations have made the move to restructure work around teams rather than individuals. Why? What do these teams look like? And, as with the challenge Steve Yzerman faced in preparing for the Sochi 2014 Olympics, how can managers build effective teams? These are some of the questions we'll be answering in this chapter. Before we can understand teams, however, we first need to understand some basics about groups and group behaviour.

Groups and Group Development

❶ Define *group* and describe the stages of group development.

Because most organizational work is done by individuals who are part of a work group, it's important for managers to understand group behaviour. Why? Because individuals act differently in groups than they do when they are alone. Therefore, if we want to understand organizational behaviour more fully, we need to study groups.

What Is a Group?

group Two or more interacting and interdependent individuals who come together to achieve particular goals.

A **group** is defined as two or more interacting and interdependent individuals who come together to achieve specific goals. *Formal groups* are work groups defined by the organization's structure that have designated work assignments and specific tasks. In formal groups, appropriate behaviours are established by and directed toward organizational goals. Exhibit 15-1 provides some examples of different types of formal groups in today's organizations.

Informal groups are social groups. These groups occur naturally in the workplace in response to the need for social contact. For example, three employees from different departments who regularly eat lunch together are an informal group. Informal groups tend to form around friendships and common interests.

Stages of Group Development

Research has shown that groups develop through five stages.[6] As shown in Exhibit 15-2, these five stages are *forming, storming, norming, performing,* and *adjourning.* Understanding

---

Exhibit 15-1

Examples of Formal Groups

Command Groups: Groups that are determined by the organizational chart and composed of individuals who report directly to a given manager.

Task Groups: Groups composed of individuals brought together to complete a specific job task; their existence is often temporary because once the task is completed, the group disbands.

Cross-Functional Teams: Groups that bring together the knowledge and skills of individuals from various work areas, or groups whose members have been trained to do one another's jobs.

Self-Managed Teams: Groups that are essentially independent and, in addition to their own tasks, take on traditional managerial responsibilities such as hiring, planning and scheduling, and performance evaluations.

Exhibit 15-2

Stages of Group Development

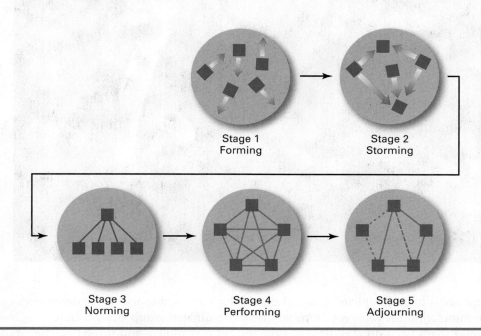

Stage 1
Forming

Stage 2
Storming

Stage 3
Norming

Stage 4
Performing

Stage 5
Adjourning

the progression of a group is useful for managers on many levels, one of them being the need to diagnose what actions must be taken in order to propel a group forward (e.g., if it is stuck in the forming phase, what needs to be done to take it into storming, etc.).

The **forming stage** has two phases. The first occurs as people join the group. In a formal group, people join because of some work assignment. After they've joined, the second phase begins: defining the group's purpose, structure, and leadership. This phase involves a great deal of uncertainty as members "test the waters" to determine what types of behaviour are acceptable. This stage is complete when members begin to think of themselves as part of a group.

The **storming stage** is named because of the intragroup conflict that occurs over who will control the group and what the group needs to be doing. When this stage is complete, there is a relatively clear hierarchy of leadership and agreement on the group's direction.

The **norming stage** is one in which close relationships develop and the group becomes cohesive. There's now a strong sense of group identity and camaraderie. This stage is complete when the group structure solidifies and the group has assimilated a common set of expectations (or norms) regarding member behaviour.

The fourth stage of group development is **performing**. The group structure is in place and accepted by group members. Their energies have moved from getting to know and understand each other to working on the group's task. This is the last stage of development for permanent work groups. However, for temporary groups—project teams, task forces, or similar groups that have a limited task to do—the final stage is **adjourning**. In this stage, the group prepares to disband. Attention is focused on wrapping up activities instead of task performance. Group members react in different ways. Some are upbeat, thrilled about the group's accomplishments. Others may be sad over the loss of camaraderie and friendships.

Many of you have probably experienced these stages as you've worked on a group project for a class. Group members are selected or assigned and then meet for the first time. There's a "feeling out" period to assess what the group is going to do and how it's going to be done. This is usually followed by a battle for control: Who's going to be in charge? When this issue is resolved and a "hierarchy" is agreed on, the group identifies specific work that needs to be done, who's going to do each part, and dates by which the assigned

forming stage The first stage of group development, in which people join the group and then define the group's purpose, structure, and leadership.

storming stage The second stage of group development, which is characterized by intragroup conflict.

norming stage The third stage of group development, which is characterized by close relationships and cohesiveness.

performing stage The fourth stage of group development, when the group is fully functional and works on the group task.

adjourning stage The final stage of group development for temporary groups, during which group members are concerned with wrapping up activities rather than task performance.

Senior vice-president Dadi Perl-mutter leads a chip design group in Haifa, Israel, for the foremost semiconductor maker in the world, Intel. Perlmutter's group thrives on the kind of debate and confrontation typical of the storm-ing stage of group development, but it achieves the kind of real-world results that usually char-acterize the performing stage. Recently, for instance, the group came up with a winning design for a processor chip for wireless computers that consumes half the power of other chips without sacrificing processing speed.

Ryan Anson/Bloomberg/Getty Images

work needs to be completed. General expectations are established. These decisions form the foundation for what you hope will be a coordinated group effort culminating in a project that's been done well. When the project is complete and turned in, the group breaks up. Of course, some groups don't get much beyond the forming or storming stages. These groups may have serious interpersonal conflicts, turn in disappointing work, and get low grades.

Does a group become more effective as it progresses through the first four stages? Some researchers say yes, but it's not that simple.[7] That assumption may be generally true, but what makes a group effective is a complex issue. Under some conditions, high levels of conflict are conducive to high levels of group performance. There might be situations in which groups in the storming stage outperform those in the norming or performing stages. Also, groups don't always proceed sequentially from one stage to the next. Sometimes, groups are storming and performing at the same time. Groups even occasionally regress to previous stages. Therefore, it's not safe to assume that all groups precisely follow this process or that performing is always the most preferable stage. It's better to think of this model as a general framework that underscores the fact that groups are dynamic entities and managers need to know the stage a group is in so they can understand the problems and issues that are most likely to surface.

Work Group Performance and Satisfaction

2 Describe the major components that influence group performance and satisfaction.

▶ ▶ ▶ Playing six games in eight days does not leave a lot of time to practise and build a sense of team.[8] Mike Babcock, the coach for Team Canada 2014, needed players he could actually use, and hence the selection committee provided a number of game scenarios (power plays, if we're down by a goal with a minute left, who's going on the ice? etc.) to assist coach Babcock in identifying players he would find useful. The 2014 team had 11 returning players from the 2010 team.[9]

Think About It

How would group dynamics have changed as new groups of players from various NHL teams arrived for camp? What techniques could the coaching staff use to build the cohesiveness that Chris Pronger spoke of? How might the 11 returning players help with this?

Exhibit 15-3

Group Performance Satisfaction Model

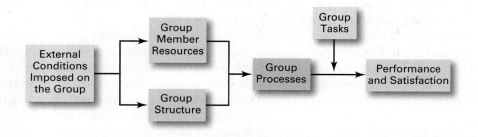

Many people consider them the most successful "group" of our times. Who? The Beatles. "The Beatles were great artists and entertainers, but in many respects they were four ordinary guys who, as a group, found a way to achieve extraordinary artistic and financial success and have a great time together while doing it. Every business team can learn from their story."[10]

Why *are* some groups more successful than others? Why do some groups achieve high levels of performance and high levels of member satisfaction and others do not? The answers are complex but include variables such as the abilities of the group's members, the size of the group, the level of conflict, and the internal pressures on members to conform to the group's norms. Exhibit 15-3 presents the major factors that determine group performance and satisfaction.[11] Let's look at each of them.

External Conditions Imposed on the Group

A work group is affected by the external conditions imposed on it. These include the organization's strategy, authority relationships, formal rules and regulations, the availability of resources, employee selection criteria, the performance management system and culture, and the general physical layout of the group's work space. For instance, some groups have modern, high-quality tools and equipment to do their jobs, while other groups don't. Or the organization might be pursuing a strategy of lowering costs or improving quality, which will affect what a group does and how it does it.

Group Member Resources

A group's performance potential depends to a large extent on the resources each individual brings to the group. These resources include knowledge, skills, abilities, and personality traits, and they determine what members can do and how effectively they will perform in a group. Interpersonal skills—especially conflict management and resolution, collaborative problem solving, and communication—consistently emerge as important for work groups to perform well.[12]

Personality traits also affect group performance because they strongly influence how an individual will interact with other group members. Research has shown that traits that are viewed as positive in our culture (such as sociability, self-reliance, and independence) tend to be positively related to group productivity and morale. In contrast, negative personality characteristics (such as authoritarianism, dominance, and unconventionality) tend to be negatively related to group productivity and morale.[13]

Group Structure

Work groups aren't unorganized crowds. They have an internal structure that shapes members' behaviour and influences group performance. The structure defines roles, norms, conformity, status systems, group size, group cohesiveness, and leadership. Let's look at the first six of these. Leadership was discussed in Chapter 13.

role Behavioural patterns
expected of someone occupying a
given position in a social unit.

norms Standards or expectations
that are accepted and shared by a
group's members.

Roles

We introduced the concept of roles in Chapter 1 when we discussed what managers do. (Remember Mintzberg's managerial roles.) Of course, managers aren't the only individuals in an organization who play various roles. The concept of roles applies to all employees and to their life outside an organization as well. (Think of the various roles you play: student, sibling, employee, spouse or significant other, etc.)

A **role** refers to behavioural patterns expected of someone occupying a given position in a social unit. In a group, individuals are expected to do certain things because of their position (role) in the group. These roles are generally oriented toward either getting work done or keeping group members happy.[14] Think about groups that you've been in and the roles that you played. Were you continually trying to keep the group focused on getting its work done? If so, you were in a task-accomplishment role. Or were you more concerned that group members had the opportunity to offer ideas and that they were satisfied with the experience? If so, you were performing a group member satisfaction role. Both roles are important to the group's ability to function effectively and efficiently.

A problem that arises is that individuals play multiple roles and adjust their roles to the group to which they belong at the time. Because of the different expectations of these roles, employees face *role conflicts*.

Norms

All groups have **norms**—standards or expectations that are accepted and shared by a group's members. Norms dictate things such as work output levels, absenteeism, prompt-ness, and the amount of socializing on the job.

For example, norms dictate the "arrival ritual" among office assistants at Coleman Trust Inc., where the workday begins at 8 a.m. Most employees typically arrive a few minutes before and hang up their coats and put their purses and other personal items on their desks so everyone knows they're "at work." They then go to the break room to get coffee and chat. Anyone who violates this norm by starting work at 8 a.m. is pressured to behave in a way that conforms to the group's standard.

Although a group has its own unique set of norms, common organizational norms focus on effort and performance, dress, and loyalty. The most widespread norms are those related to work effort and performance. Work groups typically provide their members with explicit cues on how hard to work, level of output, when to look busy, when it's acceptable to goof off, and the like. These norms are very powerful influences on an individual employee's performance. They're so powerful that you can't predict someone's performance based solely on his or her ability and personal motivation. Dress norms frequently dictate what's acceptable to wear to work. If the norm is more formal dress, anyone who dresses casually may face subtle pressure to conform. Finally, loyalty norms will influence whether individuals work late, work on weekends, or move to locations they might not prefer to live.

One negative thing about group norms is that being part of a group can increase an individual's antisocial actions. If the norms of the group include tolerating deviant behav-iour, someone who normally wouldn't engage in such behaviour might be more likely to do so. For instance, one study found that those working in a group were more likely to lie, cheat, and steal than were individuals working alone.[16] Why? Because groups provide anonymity, thus giving individuals—who might otherwise be afraid of getting caught—a false sense of security.

Conformity

Because individuals want to be accepted by groups to which they belong, they're suscep-tible to pressures to conform. Early experiments done by Solomon Asch demonstrated the impact that conformity has on an individual's judgment and attitudes.[17] In these experi-ments, groups of seven or eight people were asked to compare two cards held up by the experimenter. One card had three lines of different lengths, and the other had one line that was equal in length to one of the three lines on the other card (see Exhibit 15-4). Each group member was to announce aloud which of the three lines matched the single line.

Exhibit 15-4

Examples of Asch's Cards

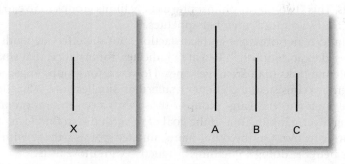

Asch wanted to see what would happen if members began to give incorrect answers. Would pressures to conform cause individuals to give wrong answers just to be consistent with the others? The experiment was "fixed" so that all but one of the members (the unsuspecting subject) was told ahead of time to start giving obviously incorrect answers after one or two rounds. Over many experiments and trials, the unsuspecting subject conformed over one-third of the time.

Are these conclusions still valid? Research suggests that conformity levels have declined since Asch's studies. However, managers can't ignore conformity because it can still be a powerful force in groups.[18] Group members often want to be seen as one of the group and avoid being visibly different. People tend to find it more pleasant to agree than to be disruptive, even if being disruptive may improve the group's effectiveness. So we conform. But conformity can go too far, especially when an individual's opinion differs significantly from that of others in the group. When this happens, the group often exerts intense pressure on the individual to align his or her opinion to conform to others' opinions, a phenomenon known as **groupthink**. Groupthink seems to occur when there is a clear group identity, members hold a positive group image that they want to protect, and the group perceives a collective threat to this positive image.[19]

groupthink A phenomenon in which a group exerts extensive pressure on an individual to align his or her opinion with others' opinions.

Status Systems

Status systems are an important factor in understanding groups. **Status** is a prestige grading, position, or rank within a group. As far back as researchers have been able to trace groups, they have found status hierarchies. Status can be a significant motivator with behavioural consequences, especially when individuals see a disparity between what they perceive their status to be and what others perceive it to be.

status A prestige grading, position, or rank within a group.

Status may be informally conferred by characteristics such as education, age, skill, or experience. Anything can have status value if others in the group evaluate it that way. Of course, just because status is informal doesn't mean that it's unimportant or that it's hard to determine who has it or who does not. Group members have no problem placing people into status categories and usually agree about who has high or low status.

Status is also formally conferred, and it's important for employees to believe that the organization's formal status system is congruent—that is, that there's consistency between the perceived ranking of an individual and the status symbols he or she receives from the organization. For instance, status incongruence would occur when a supervisor earns less than his or her subordinates, a desirable office is occupied by a person in a low-ranking position, or paid country club memberships are provided to division managers but not to vice-presidents. Employees expect the "things" an individual receives to be congruent with his or her status. When they're not, employees may question the authority of their managers and may not be motivated by job promotion opportunities.

Group Size

What's an appropriate size for a group? At Amazon.com, work teams have considerable autonomy to innovate and to investigate their ideas. And Jeff Bezos, founder and CEO, uses a "two-pizza" philosophy; that is, a team should be small enough that it can be fed with two pizzas. This "two-pizza" philosophy usually limits groups to five to seven people, depending, of course, on team member appetites.[20]

Group size affects performance and satisfaction, but the effect depends on what the group is supposed to accomplish.[21] Research indicates, for instance, that small groups are faster at completing tasks than are larger ones. However, for groups engaged in problem solving, large groups consistently get better results than smaller ones. What does this mean in terms of specific numbers? Large groups—those with a dozen or more members—are good for getting diverse input. Thus, if the goal of the group is to find facts, a larger group should be more effective. On the other hand, smaller groups—those with five to seven members—are better at doing something productive with those facts.

One important research finding related to group size concerns **social loafing**, which is the tendency for an individual to expend less effort when working collectively than when working individually.[22] Social loafing may occur because people believe that others in the group aren't doing their fair share. Thus, they reduce their work efforts in an attempt to make the workload fairer. Also, the relationship between an individual's input and the group's output is often unclear. Thus, individuals may become "free riders" and coast on the group's efforts because individuals believe that their contribution can't be measured.

The implications of social loafing are significant. When managers use groups, they must find a way to identify individual efforts. If they do not, group productivity and individual satisfaction may decline.[23]

social loafing The tendency for individuals to expend less effort when working collectively than when working individually.

Group Cohesiveness

Cohesiveness is important because it has been found to be related to a group's productivity. Groups in which there's a lot of internal disagreement and lack of cooperation are less effective in completing their tasks than are groups in which members generally agree, cooperate, and like each other. Research in this area has focused on **group cohesiveness**, or the degree to which members are attracted to a group and share the group's goals.[24]

Research has generally shown that highly cohesive groups are more effective than less cohesive ones.[25] However, the relationship between cohesiveness and effectiveness is complex. A key moderating variable is the degree to which the group's attitude aligns with its goals or with the goals of the organization[26] (Exhibit 15-5). The more cohesive the group,

group cohesiveness The degree to which group members are attracted to one another and share the group's goals.

Exhibit 15-5

Group Cohesiveness and Productivity

		Cohesiveness	
		High	**Low**
Alignment of Group and Organizational Goals	**High**	Strong Increase in Productivity	Moderate Increase in Productivity
	Low	Decrease in Productivity	No Significant Effect on Productivity

the more its members will follow its goals. If the goals are desirable (for instance, high output, quality work, cooperation with individuals outside the group), a cohesive group is more productive than a less cohesive group. But if cohesiveness is high and attitudes are unfavourable, productivity decreases. If cohesiveness is low but goals are supported, productivity increases, but not as much as when both cohesiveness and support are high. When cohesiveness is low and goals are not supported, there's no significant effect on productivity. It is interesting to note that in a study of 196 MBA students at McMaster University, in Hamilton, Ontario, nonhomogeneous groups came up with more creative solutions than did homogeneous groups. The nonhomogeneous groups also experienced higher levels of conflict.[27]

Group Processes

In addition to group member resources and structure, another factor that determines group performance and satisfaction concerns the processes that go on within a work group, such as communication, decision making, and conflict management. These processes are important to understanding work groups because they influence group performance and satisfaction positively or negatively. An example of a positive process factor is the synergy of four people on a marketing research team who are able to generate far more ideas as a group than the members could produce individually. However, the group may also have negative process factors, such as social loafing, high levels of conflict, or poor communication, that may hinder group effectiveness. We'll look at two important group processes: group decision making and conflict management.

Group Decision Making

It's a rare organization that doesn't use committees, task forces, review panels, study teams, or other similar groups to make decisions. Studies show that managers may spend up to 30 hours per week in group meetings.[28] Undoubtedly, a large portion of that time is spent formulating problems, developing solutions, and determining how to implement the solutions. It's possible, in fact, for groups to be assigned any of the eight steps in the decision-making process. (Refer to Chapter 7 to review these steps.)

What advantages do group decisions have over individual decisions? One is that groups generate more complete information and knowledge. They bring a diversity of experience and perspectives to the decision process that an individual cannot. In addition, groups generate more diverse alternatives because they have a greater amount and diversity of information. Next, groups increase acceptance of a solution. Group members are reluctant to fight or undermine a decision that they helped develop. Finally, groups increase legitimacy. Decisions made by groups may be perceived as more legitimate than decisions made by one person.

Group decisions also have disadvantages. One is that groups almost always take more time to reach a solution than would an individual. Another is that a dominant and vocal minority can heavily influence a group's final decision. In addition, groupthink can undermine critical thinking in a group and harm the quality of the final decision.[29] Finally, in a group, members share responsibility, but the responsibility of any single member is ambiguous.

Determining whether groups are effective at making decisions depends on the criteria used to assess effectiveness.[30] If accuracy, creativity, and degree of acceptance are important, then a group decision may work best. However, if speed and efficiency are important, then an individual decision may be the best. In addition, decision effectiveness is influenced by group size. Although a larger group provides more diverse representation, it also requires more coordination and time for members to contribute their ideas. Evidence indicates that groups of five, and to a lesser extent seven, are the most effective for making decisions.[31] Having an odd number in the group helps avoid decision deadlocks. Also, these groups are large enough for members to shift roles and withdraw from unfavourable positions but still small enough for quieter members to participate actively in discussions.

What techniques can managers use to help groups make more creative decisions? Exhibit 15-6 describes three possibilities.

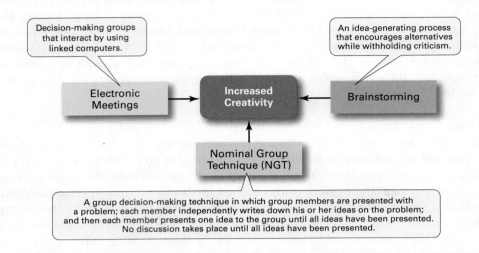

Exhibit 15-6

Creative Group Decision Making

> Decision-making groups that interact by using linked computers.

> An idea-generating process that encourages alternatives while withholding criticism.

Electronic Meetings → **Increased Creativity** ← Brainstorming

Nominal Group Technique (NGT)

> A group decision-making technique in which group members are presented with a problem; each member independently writes down his or her ideas on the problem; and then each member presents one idea to the group until all ideas have been presented. No discussion takes place until all ideas have been presented.

Conflict Management

In addition to decision making, another important group process is how a group manages conflict. As a group performs its assigned tasks, disagreements inevitably arise. **Conflict** is *perceived* incompatible differences resulting in some form of interference or opposition. Whether the differences are real is irrelevant. If people in a group perceive that differences exist, then there is conflict.

Three different views have evolved regarding conflict.[32] The **traditional view of conflict** argues that conflict must be avoided—that it indicates a problem within the group. Another view, the **human relations view of conflict**, argues that conflict is a natural and inevitable outcome in any group and need not be negative, but has potential to be a positive force in contributing to a group's performance. The third and most recent view, the **interactionist view of conflict**, proposes that not only can conflict be a positive force in a group, but some conflict is *absolutely necessary* for a group to perform effectively.

The interactionist view doesn't suggest that all conflicts are good. Some conflicts—**functional conflicts**—are constructive and support the goals of the work group and improve its performance. Other conflicts—**dysfunctional conflicts**—are destructive and prevent a group from achieving its goals. Exhibit 15-7 illustrates the conflict challenges managers face.

When is conflict functional and when is it dysfunctional? Research indicates that it depends on the *type* of conflict.[33] **Task conflict** relates to the content and goals of the work. **Relationship conflict** focuses on interpersonal relationships. **Process conflict** refers to how the work gets done. Research has shown that *relationship* conflicts are almost always dysfunctional because the interpersonal hostilities increase personality clashes and decrease mutual understanding, and the tasks don't get done. On the other hand, low levels of process conflict and low to moderate levels of task conflict are functional. For *process* conflict to be productive, it must be minimal. Otherwise, intense arguments over who should do what may become dysfunctional because they can lead to uncertainty about task assignments, increase the time to complete tasks, and lead to members working at cross-purposes. However, a low to moderate level of *task* conflict consistently has a positive effect on group performance because it stimulates discussion of ideas that help groups be more innovative.[34] Because we don't yet have a sophisticated measuring instrument for assessing whether conflict levels are optimal, too high, or too low, a manager must try to judge that intelligently.

When group conflict levels are too high, managers can select from five conflict management options: avoiding, accommodating, forcing, compromising, and collaborating.[35]

conflict Perceived incompatible differences that result in interference or opposition.

traditional view of conflict The view that all conflict is bad and must be avoided.

human relations view of conflict The view that conflict is a natural and inevitable outcome in any group.

interactionist view of conflict The view that some conflict is necessary for a group to perform effectively.

functional conflicts Conflicts that support a group's goals and improve its performance.

dysfunctional conflicts Conflicts that prevent a group from achieving its goals.

task conflict Conflicts over content and goals of work.

relationship conflict Conflict based on interpersonal relationships.

process conflict Conflict over how work gets done.

Exhibit 15-7

Conflict and Group Performance

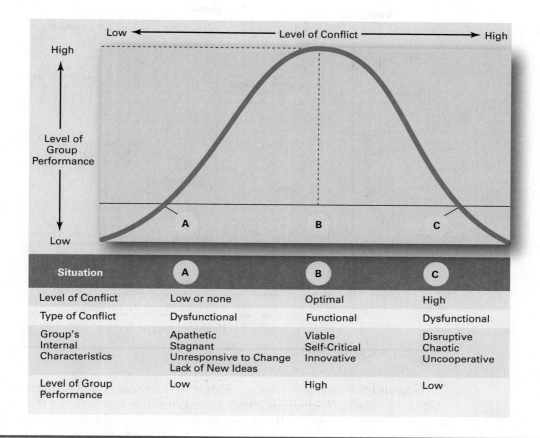

Situation	A	B	C
Level of Conflict	Low or none	Optimal	High
Type of Conflict	Dysfunctional	Functional	Dysfunctional
Group's Internal Characteristics	Apathetic Stagnant Unresponsive to Change Lack of New Ideas	Viable Self-Critical Innovative	Disruptive Chaotic Uncooperative
Level of Group Performance	Low	High	Low

(See Exhibit 15-8 for descriptions of these techniques.) Keep in mind that no one option is ideal for every situation. Which approach to use depends on the circumstances.

Have you ever been part of a class group in which all teammates received the same grade, even though some team members didn't fulfill their responsibilities? How did that make you feel? Did it create conflict within the group, and did you feel that the process and outcome were unfair? Recent research also has shown that organizational justice or fairness is an important aspect of managing group conflict.[36] How group members feel about how they're being treated, both by each other within the group and by outsiders, can affect their work attitudes and behaviours. To promote the sense of fairness, it's important that group leaders build a strong sense of community based on fair and just treatment.

Group Tasks

At the QEII Health Sciences Centre in Halifax, Nova Scotia, daily reviews of each patient in each nursing unit are conducted in multidisciplinary rounds by teams of nurses, case managers, social workers, and an in-hospital doctor. These teams perform tasks such as prescribing drugs and recommending that patients be discharged. Employee teams at Lockheed Martin's Halifax facility custom build complex products such as ground-based radar systems using continuous quality improvement techniques. The three people in the Blue Man Group (see Chapter 8) perform their unique brand of performance art in multiple venues. Each of these groups has a different type of task to accomplish.

As the group performance satisfaction model (see Exhibit 15-3 on page 391) shows, the impact that group processes have on group performance and member satisfaction is modified by the task the group is doing. More specifically, the *complexity* and *interdependence* of tasks influence a group's effectiveness.[37]

Exhibit 15-8

Conflict-Management Techniques

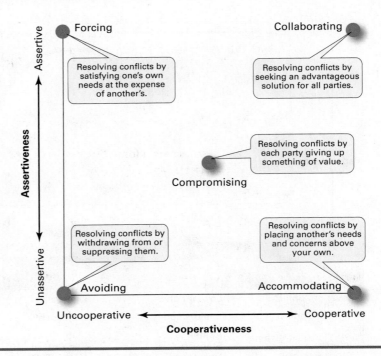

Tasks are either simple or complex. Simple tasks are routine and standardized. Complex tasks tend to be novel or nonroutine. It appears that the more complex the task, the more a group benefits from group discussion about alternative work methods. Group members don't need to discuss such alternatives for a simple task but can rely on standard operating procedures. Similarly, if there's a high degree of interdependence among the tasks that group members must perform, they'll need to interact more. Thus, effective communication and controlled conflict are most relevant to group performance when tasks are complex and interdependent.

Turning Groups into Effective Teams

3 Define *team* and describe best practices for team performance.

▶ ▶ ▶ A best practice for team performance is embedded in the criteria used to select the team. In the case of the 2014 hockey team, management did not necessarily look for the "best players" but the "right players." Scoring prowess alone did not earn a place on the team; Joe Thorton, who was tied for fourth in scoring, was not asked to join the team. A second "rightness" factor had to do with the strategy of head coach Mike Babcock, who believed that playing a go-go-up-tempo style would be essential to win Olympic gold. The third "rightness" factor had to do with the shortness of the tournament. Familiarity was core in the selection process. "You have to hit the ground running."[38]

Think About It

How might Yzerman and his managerial team create a winning team with clear goals, relevant skills, and a level of mutual trust?

When companies such as W. L. Gore, Volvo, and Kraft Foods introduced teams into their production processes, they made news because no one else was doing it. Today, it's just the opposite—an organization that *doesn't* use teams would be newsworthy. It's estimated that some 80 percent of *Fortune* 500 companies have at least half of their employees on teams.[39] Teams are likely to continue to be popular. Why? Research suggests that teams typically outperform individuals when the tasks being done require multiple skills, judgment, and experience.[40] Organizations are using team-based structures because they've found that teams are more flexible and responsive to changing events than are traditional departments or other permanent work groups. Teams have the ability to quickly assemble, deploy, refocus, and disband. In this section, we'll discuss what a work team is, the different types of teams that organizations might use, and how to develop and manage work teams.

What Is a Work Team?

Most of you are probably familiar with teams, especially if you've watched or participated in organized sports. Work *teams* differ from work *groups* and have their own unique traits (Exhibit 15-9). Work groups interact primarily to share information and to make decisions to help each member do his or her job more efficiently and effectively. There's no need or opportunity for work groups to engage in collective work that requires joint effort. On the other hand, **work teams** are groups whose members work intensely on a specific, common goal, using their positive synergy, individual and mutual accountability, and complementary skills.

work teams Groups whose members work intensely on a specific, common goal, using their positive synergy, individual and mutual accountability, and complementary skills.

Types of Work Teams

Teams can do a variety of things. They can design products, provide services, negotiate deals, coordinate projects, offer advice, and make decisions.[41] For instance, at Blackberry Ltd., teams are used in new product development. At Ocean Nutrition (the world's leading producer of omega-3 fish oil) in Halifax, Nova Scotia, teams work on process optimization projects. And every summer weekend at any NASCAR race, you can see work teams in action during drivers' pit stops.[42] The four most common types of work teams are problem-solving teams, self-managed work teams, cross-functional teams, and virtual teams.

Problem-Solving Teams

When work teams first became popular, most were **problem-solving teams**, which are teams from the same department or functional area involved in efforts to improve work activities or to solve specific problems. Members share ideas or offer suggestions on how work processes and methods can be improved. However, these teams are rarely given the authority to implement any of their suggested actions.

problem-solving team A team from the same department or functional area that's involved in efforts to improve work activities or to solve specific problems.

Exhibit 15-9

Groups versus Teams

Work Teams	Work Groups
• Leadership role is shared	• One leader clearly in charge
• Accountable to self and team	• Accountable only to self
• Team creates specific purpose	• Purpose is same as broader organizational purpose
• Work is done collectively	• Work is done individually
• Meetings characterized by open-ended discussion and collaborative problem-solving	• Meetings characterized by efficiency; no collaboration or open-ended discussion
• Performance is measured directly by evaluating collective work output	• Performance is measured indirectly according to its influence on others
• Work is decided upon and done together	• Work is decided upon by group leader and delegated to individual group members
• Can be quickly assembled, deployed, refocused, and disbanded	

Sources: J. R. Katzenbach and D. K. Smith, "The Wisdom of Teams," *Harvard Business Review*, July–August 2005, p. 161; A. J. Fazzari and J. B. Mosca, "Partners in Perfection: Human Resources Facilitating Creation and Ongoing Implementation of Self-Managed Manufacturing Teams in a Small Medium Enterprise," *Human Resource Development Quarterly*, Fall 2009, pp. 353–376.

Self-Managed Work Teams

Although problem-solving teams were helpful, they didn't go far enough in getting employees involved in work-related decisions and processes. This led to another type of team, the **self-managed work team**, which is a formal group of employees who operate without a manager and are responsible for a complete work process or segment. A self-managed team is responsible for getting the work done *and* for managing itself. This usually includes planning and scheduling work, assigning tasks to members, collectively controlling the pace of work, making operating decisions, and taking action on problems. For instance, teams at Corning have no shift supervisors and work closely with other manufacturing divisions to solve production-line problems and coordinate deadlines and deliveries. The teams have the authority to make and implement decisions, finish projects, and address problems.[43] Other organizations, such as Xerox, Boeing, PepsiCo, and Hewlett-Packard, also use self-managed teams. It's estimated that about 30 percent of US employers now use this form of team; among large firms, the number is probably closer to 50 percent.[44] Most organizations that use self-managed teams find them to be effective.[45]

Cross-Functional Teams

The third type of team is the **cross-functional team**, which we introduced in Chapter 10 and defined as a work team composed of individuals from various specialties. Many organizations use cross-functional teams. For example, ArcelorMittal, the world's biggest steel company, uses cross-functional teams of scientists, plant managers, and salespeople to review and monitor product innovations.[46] The concept of cross-functional teams is even being applied in health care. For instance, at Suburban Hospital in Bethesda, Maryland, intensive care unit (ICU) teams composed of a doctor trained in intensive care medicine, a pharmacist, a social worker, a nutritionist, the chief ICU nurse, a respiratory therapist, and a chaplain meet daily at every patient's bedside nurse to discuss and debate the best course of treatment. The hospital credits this team care approach with reducing errors, shortening the amount of time patients spent in the ICU, and improving communication between families and the medical staff.[47]

Virtual Teams

The final type of team is the **virtual team**, which is a team that uses technology to link physically dispersed members in order to achieve a common goal. For instance, a virtual team at Boeing-Rocketdyne played a pivotal role in developing a radically new product.[48] Another company, Decision Lens, uses a virtual team environment to generate and evaluate creative ideas.[49] In a virtual team, members collaborate online with tools such as wide-area networks, videoconferencing, fax, email, or websites where the team can hold online conferences.[50] Virtual teams can do all the things that other teams can do, including share information, make decisions, and complete tasks; however, they lack the normal give-and-take of face-to-face discussions. That's why virtual teams tend to be more task oriented, especially if the team members have never met in person.

Creating Effective Work Teams

Teams are not always effective. They don't always achieve high levels of performance. However, research on teams provides insights into the characteristics typically associated with effective teams.[51] These characteristics are listed in Exhibit 15-10. One element you might notice is missing but think is important to being an effective team is that a team be harmonious and friendly.[52] In fact, friendliness is not a necessary ingredient. Even a grumpy team can be effective if these other team characteristics are present. When a team is productive, has done something good together, and is recognized for its efforts, team members can feel good about their effectiveness.

Clear Goals

A high-performance team has a clear understanding of the goal to be achieved. Members are committed to the team's goals, know what they're expected to accomplish, and understand how they will work together to achieve these goals.

Exhibit 15-10

Characteristics of Effective Teams

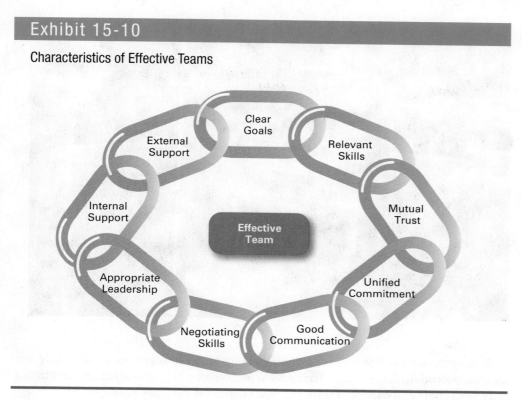

Relevant Skills

Effective teams are composed of competent individuals who have the necessary technical and interpersonal skills to achieve the desired goals while working well together. This last point is important because not everyone who is technically competent has the interpersonal skills to work well as a team member.

Mutual Trust

Effective teams are characterized by high mutual trust among members. That is, members believe in each other's ability, character, and integrity. But as you probably know from personal relationships, trust is fragile. Maintaining trust requires careful attention by managers.

Unified Commitment

Unified commitment is characterized by dedication to a team's goals and a willingness to expend extraordinary amounts of energy to achieve them. Members of an effective team exhibit intense loyalty and dedication to the team and are willing to do whatever it takes to help their team succeed.

Good Communication

Not surprisingly, effective teams are characterized by good communication. Members convey messages, verbally and nonverbally, between each other in ways that are readily and clearly understood. Also, feedback helps guide team members and correct misunderstandings. Like a couple who has been together for many years, members of high-performing teams are able to quickly and efficiently share ideas and feelings.

Negotiating Skills

Effective teams are continually making adjustments to who does what. This flexibility requires team members to possess negotiating skills. Because problems and relationships are regularly changing in teams, members need to be able to confront and reconcile differences.

Appropriate Leadership

Effective leaders can motivate a team to follow them through the most difficult situations. How? By clarifying goals, demonstrating that change is possible by overcoming inertia,

All the work that employees do at Whole Foods Market is based around teamwork. Characteristics of effective teams, like job skills, commitment, trust, communication, and effective training and support, are important for making this kind of structure successful and contributing to the rapid growth of the organic-food retailer.

Jim West/Alamy

increasing the self-confidence of team members, and helping members to more fully realize their potential. Increasingly, effective team leaders are acting as coaches and facilitators. They help guide and support a team but don't control it.

Internal and External Support

The final condition necessary for an effective team is a supportive climate. Internally, the team should have a sound infrastructure, which means proper training, a clear and reasonable measurement system that team members can use to evaluate their overall performance, an incentive program that recognizes and rewards team activities, and a supportive human resource system. The right infrastructure should support members and reinforce behaviours that lead to high levels of performance. Externally, managers should provide the team with the resources needed to get the job done.

Current Challenges in Managing Teams

4 Discuss contemporary issues in managing teams.

▶ ▶ ▶ Public pressure to select the "right" team to win gold could not be ignored in preparing for the Sochi Olympics. For example, when the team was named, the immediate discussion focused on who was not selected. As the Olymics opened, criticism centred on the lack of scoring. The 2014 team was the polar opposite to the 2010 team. In 2014 the team scored only 17 goals compared to the 36 goals scored in 2010, yet the 2014 team allowed an Olympic record low of only three goals.[53]

> **Think About It**
>
> **As Hockey Canada prepared for the 2014 games, what impact might increasing numbers of international players have on the team dynamic? How will the team manager's role need to change? What role could social networks and social media play in building team success?**

Few trends have influenced how work gets done in organizations as much as the use of work teams. The shift from working alone to working on teams requires employees to cooperate with others, share information, confront differences, and put aside personal interests for the greater good of the team. Managers can build effective teams by understanding what influences performance and satisfaction. However, managers also face some

Exhibit 15-11

Drawbacks and Benefits of Global Teams

Drawbacks	Benefits
• Dislike team members	• Greater diversity of ideas
• Mistrust team members	• Limited groupthink
• Stereotyping	• Increased attention on understanding others' ideas, perspectives, etc.
• Communication problems	
• Stress and tension	

Source: Based on N. Adler, *International Dimensions in Organizational Behaviour*, 4th ed. (Cincinnati, OH: South-Western Publishing, 2002), pp. 141–147.

current challenges in managing teams, primarily those associated with managing global teams and with understanding organizational social networks.

Managing Global Teams

Two characteristics of today's organizations are obvious: They're global, and work is increasingly done by teams. This means that any manager is likely to have to manage a global team. What do we know about managing global teams? We know there are both drawbacks and benefits in using global teams (Exhibit 15-11). Using our group model as a framework, we can see some of the issues associated with managing global teams.

Group Member Resources in Global Teams

In global organizations, understanding the relationship between group performance and group member resources is especially challenging because of the unique cultural characteristics represented by members of a global team. In addition to recognizing team members' knowledge, skills, abilities, and personality, managers need to be familiar with and clearly understand the cultural characteristics of the groups and the group members they manage.[54] For instance, is the global team from a culture in which uncertainty avoidance is high? If so, members will not be comfortable dealing with unpredictable and ambiguous tasks. Also, as managers work with global teams, they need to be aware of the potential for stereotyping, which can lead to problems.

Group Structure

Some of the structural areas where we see differences in managing global teams include conformity, status, social loafing, and cohesiveness.

Conformity   Are conformity findings generalizable across cultures? Research suggests that Asch's findings are culture bound.[55] For instance, as might be expected, conformity to social norms tends to be higher in collectivistic cultures than in individualistic cultures. Despite this, however, groupthink tends to be less of a problem in global teams because members are less likely to feel pressured to conform to the ideas, conclusions, and decisions of the group.[56]

Status   The importance of status also varies between cultures. The French, for example, are extremely status conscious. Furthermore, countries differ on the criteria that confer status. For instance, in Latin America and Asia, status tends to come from family position and formal roles held in organizations. In contrast, while status is important in countries such as the United States and Australia, it tends to be less "in your face." And it tends to be given based on accomplishments rather than on titles and family history. Managers must understand who and what holds status when interacting with people from a culture different from their own. A US manager who doesn't understand that office size isn't a measure of a Japanese executive's position or who fails to grasp the importance the British place on family genealogy and social class is likely to unintentionally offend others and reduce his or her interpersonal effectiveness.

Social Loafing   Social loafing has a Western bias. It's consistent with individualistic cultures, such as the United States and Canada, which are dominated by self-interest. It's not consistent with collectivistic societies, in which individuals are motivated by group goals. For instance, in studies comparing employees from the United States with employees from the People's Republic of China and Israel (both collectivistic societies), the Chinese and Israelis showed no propensity to engage in social loafing. In fact, they actually performed better in a group than when working alone.[57]

Cohesiveness   Cohesiveness is another group structural element with which managers may face special challenges. In a cohesive group, members are unified and "act as one." There's a great deal of camaraderie, and group identity is high. In global teams, however, cohesiveness is often more difficult to achieve because of higher levels of "mistrust, miscommunication, and stress."[58]

Group Processes

The processes that global teams use to do their work can be particularly challenging for managers. For one thing, communication issues often arise because not all team members may be fluent in the team's working language. This can lead to inaccuracies, misunderstandings, and inefficiencies.[59] However, research has also shown that a multicultural global team is better able to capitalize on the diversity of ideas represented if a wide range of information is used.[60]

Managing conflict in global teams isn't easy, especially when those teams are virtual teams. Conflict can interfere with how a team uses information. However, research has shown that in collectivistic cultures, a collaborative conflict management style can be most effective.[61]

The Manager's Role

Despite the challenges associated with managing global teams, there are things managers can do to provide a group with an environment in which efficiency and effectiveness are enhanced.[62] First, because communication skills are vital, managers should focus on developing those skills. Also, as mentioned earlier, managers must consider cultural differences when deciding what type of global team to use. For instance, evidence suggests that self-managed teams have not fared well in Mexico largely due to that culture's low tolerance of ambiguity and uncertainty, and employees' strong respect for hierarchical authority.[63] Finally, it's vital that managers be sensitive to the unique differences of each member of a global team. But it's also important that team members be sensitive to each other.

Building Team Skills

Have you ever participated in a team-building exercise? Such exercises are commonly used to illustrate and develop specific aspects or skills of being on a team. For instance, maybe you've completed *Lost on the Moon* or *Stranded at Sea* or some other written exercise in which you rank-order what items are most important to your survival. Then, you do the same thing with a group—rank-order the most important items. The rank-ordered items are compared against some expert ranking to see how many you got "right." The intent of the exercise is to illustrate how much more effective decisions can be when made as a team. Or maybe you've been part of a trust-building exercise in which you fall back and team members catch you or an exercise in which your team had to figure out how to get all members across an imaginary river or up a rock wall. Such exercises help teams bond or connect and learn to rely on one another. One of the important tasks managers have is building effective teams.[64] These types of team-building exercises can be an important part of that process. And team-building efforts can work. For example,

Because a team-focused mind-set is so critical to the success of US Navy SEAL operations, candidates train together so they can work together and accomplish their goals together. The extremely rigorous team-building training for the SEALs includes physical-endurance exercises with a 600-pound log that helps trainees bond, support, cooperate with, and rely on each other. Team-building training for the SEALs emphasizes that each person is a valuable asset to the team and then prepares individuals to be ready and willing to implement a unified approach of working together to achieve the team's mission.

U.S. Navy/AFLO/Newscom

a research project that looked at star performers with poor team skills who went through two cycles of team-building exercises found that those individuals learned how to collaborate better.[65]

Understanding Social Networks

We can't leave this chapter on managing teams without looking at the patterns of informal connections among individuals within groups—that is, at the **social network structure**.[66] What actually happens *within* groups? How *do* group members relate to each other, and how does work get done?

social network structure The patterns of informal connections among individuals within a group.

Managers need to understand the social networks and social relationships of work groups. Why? Because a group's informal social relationships can help or hinder its effectiveness. For instance, research on social networks has shown that when people need help getting a job done, they'll choose a friendly colleague over someone who may be more capable.[67] Another recent review of team studies showed that teams with high levels of interpersonal interconnectedness actually attained their goals better and were more committed to staying together.[68] Organizations are recognizing the practical benefits of knowing the social networks within teams. For instance, when Ken Loughridge, an IT manager with MWH Global, was transferred from Cheshire, England, to New Zealand, he had a "map" of the informal relationships and connections among company IT employees. This map had been created a few months earlier, using the results of a survey that asked employees who they "consulted most frequently, who they turned to for expertise, and who either boosted or drained their energy levels." Not only did this map help him identify well-connected technical experts, it helped him minimize potential problems when a key manager in the Asia region left the company, because Loughridge knew who this person's closest contacts were and the map helped identify potential candidates to replace the key manager. Loughridge said, "It's as if you took the top off an ant hill and could see where there's a hive of activity. It really helped me understand who the players were."[69]

CHAPTER 15

SUMMARY AND IMPLICATIONS

1. Define *group* and describe the stages of group development. A group is two or more interacting and interdependent individuals who come together to achieve specific goals. Formal groups are work groups that are defined by an organization's structure and have designated work assignments and specific tasks directed at accomplishing organizational goals. Informal groups are social groups.

The forming stage of group development consists of two phases: joining the group and defining the group's purpose, structure, and leadership. The storming stage involves intragroup conflict over who will control the group and what the group will be doing. In the norming stage, close relationships and cohesiveness develop as norms are determined. During the performing stage, group members begin to work on the group's task. At the adjourning stage, the group prepares to disband.

► ► ► When the Canadian men's hockey team started practising for the 2014 Winter Olympics, individual hockey players knew how to play the game and were used to playing for their own coaches and with their own teammates. The challenge for Team Canada was to meld these independent and autonomous groups into a team as quickly as possible.

2. Describe the major components that influence group performance and satisfaction. The major components that determine group performance and satisfaction are external conditions, group member resources, group structure, group processes, and group tasks. External conditions such as availability of resources and organizational goals affect work groups. Group member resources (knowledge, skills, abilities, and personality traits) can influence what members can do and how effectively they will perform in a group. Group roles generally involve getting group work done or keeping group members happy. Group norms are powerful influences on a person's performance and dictate factors such as work output levels, absenteeism, and promptness. Pressures to conform can heavily influence a person's judgment and attitudes. If carried to extremes, groupthink can be a problem. Status systems can be a significant motivator with individual behavioural consequences, especially if there's incongruence in status. What size group is most effective and efficient depends on the task the group is supposed to accomplish. Cohesiveness can affect a group's productivity positively or negatively. Group decision making and conflict management are important group processes that play a role in performance and satisfaction. If accuracy, creativity, and degree of acceptance are important, a group decision may work best. Relationship conflicts are almost always dysfunctional. Low levels of process conflict and low to moderate levels of task conflict are functional. Effective communication and controlled conflict are most relevant to group performance when tasks are complex and interdependent.

► ► ► Mike Babcock, the coach for Team Canada 2014, needed players he could actually use, and hence the selection committee provided a number of game scenarios (power plays, if we're down by a goal with a minute left, who's going on the ice? etc.) to assist coach Babcock in identifying players he would find useful. The 2014 team had 11 returning players from the 2010 team who had the potential to help or hinder the level of group satisfaction.

3. Define *team* and describe best practices for team performance. Work groups have the following characteristics: a strong, clearly focused leader; individual accountability; a purpose that's the same as the broader organizational mission; an individual work product; efficient meetings; effectiveness measured by influence on others; and the ability to discuss, decide, and delegate together. Teams have the following characteristics: shared leadership roles; individual and mutual accountability; specific team purpose; collective work products; meetings with open-ended discussion and active problem solving; performance measured directly on collective work products; and the ability to discuss, decide, and do real work. A problem-solving team is a team that's focused on improving work activities or solving specific problems. A self-managed work team is responsible for a complete work process or segment and manages itself. A cross-functional team is composed of individuals from various specialties. A virtual team uses technology to link physically dispersed members in order to achieve a common goal. The characteristics of an effective team include clear goals, relevant skills, mutual trust, unified commitment, good communication, negotiating skills, appropriate leadership, and internal and external support.

▶▶▶ Many individuals resist being team players. To improve the odds that a team would function well, managers (like Steve Yzerman and coach Mike Babcock) focused on picking the "right" players rather than the highest-scoring players and looked for players who were familiar with each other.

4. Discuss contemporary issues in managing teams. The challenges of managing global teams can be seen in the group member resources, especially the diverse cultural characteristics; group structure, especially conformity, status, social loafing, and cohesiveness; group processes, especially with communication and managing conflict; and the manager's role in making it all work. With the emphasis on teams in today's organizations, managers need to recognize that people don't automatically know how to be part of a team or to be an effective team member. Like any behaviour, team members have to learn about the skill and then keep practising and reinforcing it. In building team skills, managers must view their role as more of being a coach and developing others to create more committed, collaborative, and inclusive teams. Managers need to understand the patterns of informal connections among individuals within groups because those informal social relationships can help or hinder the group's effectiveness.

▶▶▶ Public pressure influenced how Steve Yzerman and Mike Babcock explained the choices they made in selecting the team and the very different strategy they used in the 2014 games—low scoring and great defence.

MyManagementLab Study, practise, and explore real management situations with these helpful resources:
- **Interactive Lesson Presentations:** Work through interactive presentations and assessments to test your knowledge of management concepts.
- **PIA (Personal Inventory Assessments):** Enhance your ability to connect with key concepts through these engaging, self-reflection assessments.
- **Study Plan:** Check your understanding of chapter concepts with self-study quizzes.
- **Simulations:** Practise decision-making in simulated management environments.

REVIEW AND DISCUSSION QUESTIONS

1. Describe the different types of groups and the five stages of group development.
2. Explain how external conditions and group member resources affect group performance and satisfaction.
3. Discuss how group structure, group processes, and group tasks influence group performance and satisfaction.
4. Compare groups and teams.
5. Describe the four most common types of teams.
6. List the characteristics of effective teams.
7. Explain the role of informal (social) networks in managing teams.

ETHICS DILEMMA

When coworkers work closely on a team project, is there such a thing as TMI (too much information)?[70] At one company, a team that had just finished a major project went out to lunch to celebrate. During lunch, one colleague mentioned that he was training for a 20-mile bike race. In addition to a discussion of his new helmet and Lycra shorts, the person also described shaving his whole body to reduce aerodynamic drag. Later, another team member said, "Why, why, why do we need to go there? This is information about a coworker, not someone I really consider a friend, and now it's forever burned in my brain."

What do you think? Why are work colleagues sharing increasingly personal information? How have social media and technology contributed to this type of information disclosure? What are the ethical implications of sharing such personal information in the workplace?

SKILLS EXERCISE

Developing Your Coaching Skills—About the Skill

Effective managers are increasingly being described as coaches rather than bosses. Just like coaches, they're expected to provide instruction, guidance, advice, and encouragement to help team members improve their job performance.

Steps in Practising the Skill

1. *Analyze ways to improve the team's performance and capabilities.* A coach looks for opportunities for team members to expand their capabilities and improve performance. How? You can use the following behaviours. Observe your team members' behaviours on a day-to-day basis. Ask questions of them: Why do you do a task this way? Can it be improved? What other approaches might be used? Show genuine interest in team members as individuals, not merely as employees. Respect them individually. Listen to each employee.

2. *Create a supportive climate.* It's the coach's responsibility to reduce barriers to development and to facilitate a climate that encourages personal performance improvement. How? You can use the following behaviours. Create a climate that contributes to a free and open exchange of ideas. Offer help and assistance. Give guidance and advice when asked. Encourage your team. Be positive and upbeat. Don't use threats. Ask, "What did we learn from this that can help us in the future?" Reduce obstacles. Assure team members that you value their contribution to the team's goals. Take personal responsibility for the outcome, but don't rob team members of their full responsibility. Validate team members' efforts when they succeed. Point to what was missing when they fail. Never blame team members for poor results.

3. *Influence team members to change their behaviour.* The ultimate test of coaching effectiveness is whether an employee's performance improves. You must encourage ongoing growth and development. How can you do this? Try the following behaviours. Recognize and reward small improvements and treat coaching as a way of helping employees to continually work toward improvement. Use a collaborative style by allowing team members to participate in identifying and choosing among improvement ideas. Break difficult tasks down into simpler ones. Model the qualities you expect from your team. If you want openness, dedication, commitment, and responsibility from your team members, demonstrate these qualities yourself.

Practising the Skill

Collaborative efforts are more successful when every member of the group or team contributes a specific role or task toward the completion of the goal. To improve your skill at nurturing team effort, choose two of the following activities and break each one into at least six to eight separate tasks or steps. Be sure to indicate which steps are sequential, and which can be done simultaneously with others. What do you think is the ideal team size for each activity you choose?

a. Making an omelette

b. Washing the car

c. Creating a computerized mailing list

d. Designing an advertising poster

e. Planning a ski trip

f. Restocking a supermarket's produce department

WORKING TOGETHER: TEAM EXERCISE

Are Healthier Chips in Our Future?

Derek Yach, senior vice-president for global health policy at PepsiCo, is assembling a team of "idealistic scientists to find alternatives to Doritos."[71] These physicians and researchers with doctoral degrees, many of whom have built their reputations at places like the Mayo Clinic, the World Health Organization, and like-minded organizations, are tasked with creating healthier options by "making the bad stuff less bad." Suppose you were put in charge of this elite team. How would you lead it?

Form small groups of three or four individuals. Your team's task is to come up with some suggestions for leading this team. (Hint: Look at Exhibit 15-10.) Come up with a bulleted list of your ideas. Be prepared to share your ideas with the class.

LEARNING TO BE A MANAGER

- Think of a group to which you belong (or have belonged). Trace its development through the stages of group development as shown in Exhibit 15-2. How closely did its development parallel the group development model? How might the group development model be used to improve this group's effectiveness?

- Using this same group, write a report describing the following things about this group: types of roles played by whom, group norms, group conformity issues, status system, size of group and how effective/efficient it is, and group cohesiveness.

- Using the same group, describe how decisions are made. Is the process effective? Efficient? Describe what types of conflicts seem to arise most often (relationship, process, or task) and how those conflicts are handled. Add this information to your report on the group's development and structure.

- What traits do you think good team players have? Do some research to answer this question and write up a report detailing your findings using a bulleted list format.

- Select two of the characteristics of effective teams listed in Exhibit 15-10 and develop a team-building exercise for each characteristic that will help a group improve that characteristic. Be creative. Write a report describing your exercises, and be sure to explain how your exercise will help a group improve or develop that characteristic.

- When working in a group (any group to which you're assigned or to which you belong), pay careful attention to what happens in the group as tasks are completed. How does the group's structure or its processes affect how successful the group is at completing its task?

- Research brainstorming and write a report to your professor explaining what it is and listing suggestions for making it an effective group decision-making tool.

CASE APPLICATION 1

Far and Wide

A lot of people around the world love to travel. How about you? Have you visited other countries, or do you hope to visit other countries some day? For those who do travel outside their home country, travel advice guides can be quite valuable. Lonely Planet, an Australian company, has set the benchmark for providing accurate, up-to-date travel guides that have accompanied millions of travelers on their journeys worldwide.[72]

Lonely Planet was started by husband-and-wife team Tony and Maureen Wheeler who in 1971, after Tony finished graduate school in London, decided to embark on an adventurous trip before settling into "real" jobs. They drove through Europe armed with a few maps and sold their car in Afghanistan. From there, they continued their journey using local buses, trains, and boats or by hitchhiking whenever they needed to keep within their daily budget of $6 AUD. Their nine-month journey took them through Pakistan, Kashmir, India, Nepal, Thailand, Malaysia, and Indonesia on their way to their ultimate destination, Australia. The story is they arrived in Sydney on Boxing Day 1971 and had 27 cents left between them. Their plan was to find jobs in Sydney until they had earned enough for plane tickets back to London. However, they found that a lot of people were interested in hearing about their travel experiences. Urged on by friends, they started working on a travel guide title *Across Asia on the Cheap*. Within a week of the 96-page book's completion and placement in a Sydney bookstore, they had sold 1500 copies, and the publishing company Lonely Planet was born. They financed their second trip through Asia with profits from the first book and published their second guidebook, *South-East Asia on a Shoestring*. A succession of basic travel guides written by Tony and Maureen produced enough income to cover their own travelling and publishing expenses, but just enough to break even. Their decision to produce a 700-page guidebook to India almost overwhelmed them, but that guidebook was an immediate success, giving Lonely Planet financial stability for the future. Finally, they could afford to hire editors, cartographers, and writers, all of whom worked on a contract basis on individual team projects.

By developing an effective team of professional writers, cartographers, designers, image researchers, and other independent contractors, Tony and Maureen Wheeler, founders of Lonely Planet Publications, grew their company from a simple, self-published guidebook to the world's largest publisher of travel guidebooks.

So, how does Lonely Planet produce a product like a guidebook? It's all about teamwork. Commissioning editors (CEs) have a specific geographic area for which they're responsible for commissioning authors of regional content for Lonely Planet's digital and print travel products. CEs research a destination thoroughly to see what travellers are looking for—what's hot and what's not. CEs also get input from specialists and regional experts. Based on this information, the CEs write an author brief. Then, they commission freelance authors who do a lot of pre-trip research before packing their bags. Armed with author briefs, an empty notebook, and a laptop, an author goes on the road doing all the diligent groundwork on location. After concluding their research, the writing of the manuscript begins, which must be completed by a deadline. Once a manuscript is done, it's worked on by CEs and editors at Lonely Planet headquarters to ensure it meets the company's standards of style and quality. Cartographers create new maps from the author's material. The layout designers work with the editors to bring the text, maps, and images together. The design team and image researchers create the cover and photo sections. A proofreader makes

sure there are no typographical or layout errors. The book is then sent to a printer, where it's printed, bound, and shipped to bookstores for sale.

From its first simple self-published guidebook, Lonely Planet Publications has grown to become the world's largest independent guidebook publisher. Tony and Maureen realized the business needed a partner that had the necessary resources for future growth, especially in the digital side of the business. BBC Worldwide acquired a 75 percent share in October 2007. In 2011, BBC acquired the remaining 25 percent share of Lonely Planet Publishing.

DISCUSSION QUESTIONS

1. What challenges would there be to creating an effective team in an organization staffed by independent contractors? How could managers deal with these challenges?
2. Why do you think teamwork is crucial to Lonely Planet's business model?
3. Using Exhibit 15-10, what characteristics of effective teams would be most important to Lonely Planet's guidebook teams? Explain your choices.

CASE APPLICATION 2

737 Teaming Up for Take Off

The Boeing 737, a short- to medium-range twin-engine, narrow-body jet, first rolled off the assembly line in 1967.[73] Now, almost half a century later, it's the best-selling jet airliner in the history of aviation. The 737 is Boeing's only narrow-body airliner in production, with the -600, -700, -800, and -900ER series currently being built. The re-engined and redesigned 737MAX is set for debut in 2017. As airlines replace their aging jet fleets, the burden is on Boeing to ramp up production to meet demand and to do so efficiently. As Boeing managers state, "How do you produce more aircraft without expanding the building?" Managing production of the multi-million dollar product—a 737-800 is sold for $84.4 million—means "walking an increasingly fine line between generating cash and stoking an airplane glut." And Boeing is relying on its employee innovation teams to meet the challenge.

Management team members of Boeing's 737 jet airplanes applauded the company's employee innovation teams during a celebration honouring them for devising ways to improve their work processes. These improvements resulted in increased production to meet customers' demands for new planes needed to replace their aging jet fleets.

Boeing has been using employee-generated ideas since the 1990s when its manufacturing facility in Renton, Washington, began adopting "lean" manufacturing techniques. Today, employee teams are leaving "few stones unturned." For instance, a member of one team thought of a solution to a problem of stray metal fasteners sometimes puncturing the tires as the airplane advanced down the assembly line.

The solution? A canvas wheel cover that hugs the four main landing-gear tires. Another team figured out how to rearrange its work space to make four engines at a time instead of three. Another team of workers in the paint process revamped their work routines and cut 10 minutes to 15 minutes per worker off each job. It took five years for another employee team to perfect a process for installing the plane's landing gear hydraulic tubes, but it eventually paid off.

These employee teams are made up of seven to ten workers with "varying backgrounds"—from mechanics to assembly workers to engineers—and tend to focus on a specific part of a jet, such as the landing gear or the passenger seats or the galleys. These teams may meet as often as once a week. What's the track record of these teams? Today, it takes about 11 days for the final assembly of a 737 jet. That's down from 22 days about a decade ago. The near-term goal is to "whittle that number down to nine days."

DISCUSSION QUESTIONS

1. What type of team(s) do these employee teams appear to be? Explain.
2. As this story illustrated, sometimes it may take a long time for a team to reach its goal. As a manager, how would you motivate a team to keep on trying?
3. What role do you think a team leader needs to play in this type of setting? Explain.
4. Using Exhibit 15-10, what characteristics of effective teams would these teams need? Explain.

PART FOUR

Management Practice

A Manager's Dilemma

How would you feel as a new employee if your boss asked you to do something and you had to admit that you didn't know how to do it? Most of us would probably feel pretty inadequate and incompetent. Now imagine how strange and uncomfortable it would be if, after experiencing such an incident, you went home with the boss because you were roommates and have been friends since fourth grade. That's the situation faced by John, Glen, and Kurt. John and Kurt are employees at a software company that their friend Glen and four others started. The business now has 39 employees, and the "friends" are finding out that mixing work and friendships can be tricky! At home, they're equals. They share a three-bedroom condo and divide up housework and other chores. However, at work, equality is out the door. Glen is John's boss and Kurt's boss is another company manager. Recently, the company moved into a new work space. As part of the four-person management team, Glen has a corner office with windows. However, John was assigned a cubicle and is annoyed at Glen for not standing up for him when offices were assigned. But John didn't complain because he didn't want to get an office only because of his friendship with Glen. Another problem brewing is that the roommates compete to outlast one another working late. Kurt's boss is afraid that he's going to burn out. Other awkward moments arise whenever the company's performance is discussed. When Glen wants to get something off his chest about work matters, he has to stop himself. And then there's the "elephant in the room." If the software company is ever bought out by a larger company, Glen (and his three partners) stand to profit dramatically, thereby creating some interesting emotional issues for the roommates. Although it might seem easy to say the solution is to move, real estate is too expensive and besides that, these guys are good friends.

> Put yourself in Glen's shoes. Using what you've learned in Part 4 about leadership, behaviour, communication, employee motivation, and managing groups and teams, how would you handle this situation?

Global Sense

As you discovered in this part of the text, employee engagement is an important focus for managers. Managers want their employees to be connected to, satisfied with, and enthusiastic about their jobs; that is, to be engaged. Why is employee engagement so important? The level of employee engagement serves as an indicator of organizational health and ultimately business results—success or failure. The latest available data (2011) on global employee engagement levels showed a slight increase, up to 58 percent from 56 percent in 2010. That is, 58 percent of employees worldwide say they're engaged—passionate about and deeply connected to their work. The largest upward movement was seen in the Asia Pacific region; a slight increase was seen in Europe; a small downward movement was noted in Latin America; and in North America, the level of employee engagement stayed the same. Think about the other side of this, though. With 58 percent of employees saying they're engaged with their jobs and organizations, that means four employees out of ten worldwide are somewhat or completely disengaged.

So what can managers do to keep employees engaged? Some important efforts include providing opportunities for career advancement, offering recognition, and having a good organization reputation.

Discuss the following questions in light of what you learned in Part 4.

- What role do you think external factors such as the global economic downturn or a country's culture play in levels of employee engagement? Discuss.
- What role does an organization's motivational program play in whether an employee is engaged or not? Discuss.
- How might a manager's leadership style affect an employee's level of engagement? Discuss.
- You're a manager of a workplace that has different "generations." How will you approach engaging your employees? Do you think Gen Y employees are going to be more difficult to "engage"? Discuss.

Sources: M. Wilson, "Study: Employee Engagement Ticking Up, But It's Not All Good News," [www.hrcommunication.com], June 18, 2012; "2012 Trends in Global Employee Engagement," www.aon.com, June 17, 2012; K. Gurchiek, "Engagement Erosion Plagues Employers Worldwide," *HR Magazine*, June 2012, p. 17; and T. Maylett and J. Nielsen, "There Is No Cookie-Cutter Approach to Engagement," *T&D*, April 2012, pp. 54–59.

Managerial Controls:
Evidence-Based Decision Making

Managers need to monitor the activities of the organization and determine whether they are accomplishing their planned goals. In evaluating outcomes, they are able to spot opportunities that sometimes require a change in direction. After reading and studying this chapter, you will achieve the following learning outcomes.

Learning Outcomes

1. Explain the nature and importance of control.
2. Describe the three steps in the control process.
3. Explain how organizational and employee performance are measured.
4. Describe tools used to measure organizational performance.
5. Discuss contemporary issues in control.

▶ ▶ ▶ When Li Ka-shing first invested in Calgary-based Husky Oil (now Husky Energy) in 1986, buying 52 percent of its shares, the company had just posted its first year-end loss in the company's history.[1] The company had no cash on hand, shares had dropped to half of their 1981 value, and the company's debt was growing. Bob Blair, then the CEO at Husky, turned to Li. "We required a lot of capital, more than Husky could generate from its own cash flow," says Blair, in explaining why he approached his friend Li, a wealthy Hong Kong businessman,

to invest in the company. In 1991, Li and his holding company bought 43 percent more of the company.

After the 1991 investment, Li immediately sent John Chin-Sung Lau (pictured) to Calgary to turn the company around. Li wanted to halt the company's large losses and "wild expansions" of Husky's previous management. Appointed vice-president at the time, Lau had difficulty working with Husky president Art Price and found the culture at Husky to be a free-spending one.

Lau had a difficult task in front of him to make Husky profitable.

CP PHOTO/Adrian Wyld

In today's competitive global marketplace, managers want their organizations to achieve high levels of performance, and one way they can do that is by searching out the best practices successful organizations are using. By comparing themselves against the best, managers look for specific performance gaps and areas for improvement.

As we will see in this chapter, John Lau understands the importance of management strategy in making the right strategic choices. Lau also understands the role of management controls in supporting the choices made by Husky. No matter how thorough the planning, a decision still may be poorly implemented without a satisfactory control system in place. This chapter describes controls for monitoring and measuring performance. It also looks at how to create a well-designed organizational control system.

What Is Controlling, and Why Is It Important?

Imagine that a press operator at the Royal Canadian Mint in Ottawa notices a flaw—a missing antler—on the new quarters being pressed at one of his five press machines. He stops the machine and leaves for a meal break. When he returns, he sees the machine running and assumes that someone has changed the die in the machine. However, after a routine inspection, the machine operator realizes that the die has not been changed. The faulty press has likely been running for over an hour, and thousands of the flawed coins are now co-mingled with unblemished quarters. As many as 50 000 of the faulty coins enter circulation, setting off a coin collector buying frenzy.[2] Can you see why ensuring that the process is under control (controlling) is such an important managerial function?

Control is one of the four pillars of management (planning, leading, and organizing are the other three) and is a strategic activity that is infused across all activities within an organization. What is **controlling**? It's the process of monitoring activities to ensure that they are being accomplished as planned, correcting any significant deviations and, where necessary, modifying the plan (a pivot as described in Chapter 4). All managers should be involved in the control function even if their units are performing as planned. Managers cannot really know whether their units are performing properly until they have evaluated what activities have been done and have compared the actual performance with the desired standard.[3] An effective control system ensures that activities are completed in ways that lead to the attainment of the organization's goals. The criterion that determines the effectiveness of a control system is how well it facilitates goal achievement. The more it helps managers achieve their organization's goals, the better the control system.[4]

Why Is Control Important?

Planning can be done, an organizational structure can be created to efficiently facilitate the achievement of goals, and employees can be motivated through effective leadership. Still, there is no assurance that activities are going as planned and that the goals managers are seeking are, in fact, being attained. Control is important, therefore, because it's the final link in the four management functions. It is the only way managers know whether organizational goals are being met and, if not, the reasons why. The value of the control function lies in its relation to planning, empowering employees, and protecting the organization and workplace.

In Chapter 8, we described goals as the foundation of planning. Goals give specific direction to managers. However, just stating goals or having employees accept your goals

👁 Watch on **MyManagementLab**

Zane's Cycles: Foundations of Control

❶ Explain the nature and importance of control.

controlling The process of monitoring activities to ensure that they are being accomplished as planned, correcting any significant deviations and, where necessary, modifying the plan (a pivot as described in Chapter 4).

Exhibit 16-1

The Planning–Controlling Link

Planning
Goals
Objectives
Strategies
Plans

Organizing
Structure
Human Resource
    Management

Leading
Motivation
Leadership
Communication
Individual and
    Group Behaviour

Controlling
Standards
Measurements
Comparison
Actions

is no guarantee that the necessary actions to accomplish those goals have been taken. As the old saying goes, "The best-laid plans often go awry." The effective manager needs to follow up to ensure that what others are supposed to do is, in fact, being done and that their goals are in fact being achieved. In reality, managing is an ongoing process, and controlling activities provide the critical link back to planning (see Exhibit 16-1). If managers did not control, they would have no way of knowing whether their goals and plans were on target and what future actions to take.

Another reason control is important is employee empowerment. While some managers are reluctant to empower their employees because they fear employees will do something wrong for which the manager will be held responsible, others understand that properly designed decision support systems enhance the ability of the employees to make better decisions. A **decision support system (DSS),** a subset of the management information system, is a computer-based information system that provides decision makers with information relevant to the decisions they are making.

An effective control system provides information and feedback on employee performance to both managers and employees.

The final reason that managers control is to protect the organization and the physical workplace.[5] Today's environment brings heightened threats from natural disasters, financial scandals, workplace violence, global supply chain disruptions, security breaches, and even possible terrorist attacks. Managers must protect organizational assets in the event that any of these things should happen. Comprehensive controls and back-up plans will help assure minimal work disruptions.

decision support system (DSS)
A computer-based information system that provides decision makers with information relevant to the decisions they are making.

The Control Process

2 Describe the three steps in the control process.

control process A three-step process that includes measuring actual performance, comparing actual performance against a standard, and taking managerial action to correct deviations or inadequate standards.

The **control process** is a three-step process: measuring actual performance, comparing actual performance against a standard, and taking managerial action to correct deviations or inadequate standards (Exhibit 16-2). The control process assumes that performance standards already exist, and they do. They're the specific goals created during the planning process. The control process for managers is similar to what you might do as a student at the beginning of the term: set goals for yourself for studying and marks, and then evaluate your performance after midterms, determining whether you have studied enough or need to study more in order to meet whatever goals you set for your marks.

Exhibit 16-2

The Control Process

Step 1: Measuring Performance

◀●▶ Simulate on MyManagementLab

Controlling

If you can't measure it, you can't manage it! To determine what actual performance is, a manager must acquire information about it. The first step in control, then, is measuring. Let's consider how we measure and what we measure.

How We Measure

Four sources of information frequently used by managers to measure actual performance are personal observations, statistical reports, oral reports, and written reports. Exhibit 16-3 summarizes the advantages and drawbacks of each approach. Most managers use a combination of these approaches.

What We Measure

What we measure is probably more critical to the control process than *how* we measure. Why? The selection of the wrong criteria can result in serious dysfunctional consequences.

Exhibit 16-3

Common Sources of Information for Measuring Performance

	Advantages	Drawbacks
Personal Observations (Management by Walking Around)	• Get first-hand knowledge • Information isn't filtered • Intensive coverage of work activities	• Subject to personal biases • Time-consuming • Can distract employees
Statistical Reports	• Easy to visualize • Effective for showing relationships	• Provide limited information • Ignore subjective factors
Oral Reports	• Fast way to get information • Allow for verbal and nonverbal feedback	• Information is filtered • Information cannot be documented
Written Reports	• Comprehensive • Formal • Easy to file and retrieve	• Take more time to prepare

Exhibit 16-4

Defining the Acceptable Range of Variation

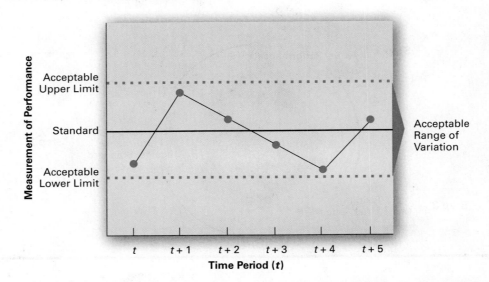

Besides, what we measure determines, to a great extent, what people in the organization will attempt to excel at.[6] For instance, if employees are evaluated by the number of big-ticket items they sell, they may not help customers who are looking for less expensive items.

Some control criteria can be used for any management situation. For instance, all managers deal with people, so criteria such as employee satisfaction or turnover and absenteeism rates can be measured. Keeping costs within budget is also a fairly common control measure. Other control criteria should recognize the different activities that managers supervise. For instance, a manager at a pizza delivery location might use measures such as number of pizzas delivered per day, average delivery time, or number of coupons redeemed. A manager in a governmental agency might use applications typed per day, client requests completed per hour, or average time to process paperwork.

Most work activities can be expressed in quantifiable terms, but when they can't, managers should use subjective measures. Although such measures may have limitations, having them is better than having no standards at all and doing no controlling.

Step 2: Comparing Performance against Standard

The comparing step determines the degree of variation between actual performance and the standard. Although some variation in performance can be expected in all activities, it's critical to determine the acceptable **range of variation** (Exhibit 16-4). Deviations that exceed this range become significant and need the manager's attention. In the comparison stage, managers are particularly concerned with the size and direction of the variation. An example can help make this concept clearer.

Chris Tanner is sales manager for Beer Unlimited, a distributor of specialty beers in the Prairies. Chris prepares a report during the first week of each month that describes sales for the previous month, classified by brand name. Exhibit 16-5 displays both the sales goal (standard) and the actual sales figures for the month of July.

Should Chris be concerned about July's sales performance? Sales were a bit higher than originally targeted, but does that mean there were no significant deviations? Even though overall performance was generally quite favourable, several brands might need to be examined more closely by Chris. However, the number of brands that deserve attention

range of variation The acceptable degree of variation between actual performance and the standard.

Exhibit 16-5

Sales Performance Figures for July, Beer Unlimited

Brand	Standard	(number of cases) Actual	Over (Under)
Premium Lager (Okanagan Spring, Vernon, BC)	1075	913	(162)
India Pale Ale (Alexander Keith's, Halifax)	800	912	112
Maple Brown Ale (Upper Canada Brewery, Guelph, ON)	620	622	2
Blanche de Chambly (Brasseries Unibroue, Quebec)	160	110	(50)
Full Moon (Alley Kat, Edmonton)	225	220	(5)
Black Cat Lager (Paddock Wood Brewing, Saskatoon, Saskatchewan)	80	65	(15)
Bison Blonde Lager (Agassiz, Winnipeg)	170	286	116
Total cases	3130	3128	(2)

depends on what Chris believes to be *significant*. How much variation should Chris allow before corrective action is taken?

The deviation on three brands (Maple Brown Ale, Full Moon, Black Cat Lager) is very small and does not need special attention. On the other hand, are the lower sales for Premium Lager and Blanche de Chambly brands significant? That is a judgment Chris must make. Premium Lager sales were 15 percent below Chris' goal. This deviation is significant and needs attention. Chris should look for a cause. In this instance, Chris attributes the decrease to aggressive advertising and promotion programs by the big domestic producers, Anheuser-Busch and Miller. Because Premium Lager is his company's number-one–selling microbeer, it's most vulnerable to the promotion clout of the big domestic producers. If the decline in sales of Premium Lager is more than a temporary slump (that is, if it happens again next month), then Chris will need to consider actions, including cutting back on inventory in the short term and in the long term formulating strategies to combat his competitor's tactics.

Higher sales than anticipated can also be a problem. For instance, is the surprising popularity of Bison Blonde Lager (up 68 percent) a one-month anomaly, or is this brand becoming more popular with customers? If the brand is increasing in popularity, Chris will want to order more product to meet customer demand, so as not to run short and risk losing customers. Again, Chris will have to interpret the information and make a decision.

Step 3: Taking Managerial Action

Managers can choose among three possible courses of action: they can do nothing; they can correct the actual performance; or they can revise the standard. Because "doing nothing" is fairly self-explanatory, let's look more closely at the other two options.

Correct Actual Performance

If the source of the performance variation is unsatisfactory work, the manager will want to take corrective action. Examples of such corrective action might include changing strategy, structure, compensation practices, or training programs; redesigning jobs; or firing employees.

Industry and company rankings determined by specific performance measures are one way managers can assess their company's performance. With sales topping $11 billion, eBay is the world's largest marketplace that connects buyers and sellers. The company appears on the Forbes Global 2000, a list of the world's largest companies based on a composite ranking of sales, profits, assets, and market value. eBay is also included on the Forbes Global High Performers list, an industry-specific ranking of fast-growing and well-managed global companies in 26 industries based on measures such as growth in sales, income, and earnings per share. eBay is ranked as one of the five best companies in the retailing industry.

DDAA/ZOB WENN Photos/Newscom

immediate corrective action Corrective action that corrects problems at once to get performance back on track.

basic corrective action Corrective action that looks at how and why performance deviated and then proceeds to correct the source of deviation.

A manager who decides to correct actual performance has to make another decision: Should immediate or basic corrective action be taken? **Immediate corrective action** corrects problems at once to get performance back on track. **Basic corrective action** looks at how and why performance has deviated and then proceeds to correct the source of deviation. It's not unusual for managers to rationalize that they don't have the time to take basic corrective action and therefore must be content to perpetually "put out fires" with immediate corrective action. Effective managers, however, analyze deviations and, when the benefits justify it, take the time to pinpoint and correct the causes of variance.

Revise the Standard

In some cases, variance may be a result of an unrealistic standard—a goal that's too low or too high. In this case, the standard—not the performance—needs corrective action. If performance consistently exceeds the goal, then a manager should look at whether the goal is too easy and needs to be raised. On the other hand, managers must be cautious about revising a standard downward. It's natural to blame the goal when an employee or a team falls short. For instance, students who get a low score on a test often attack the grade cut-off standards as being too high; rather than accept the fact that their performance was inadequate, they will argue that the standards are unreasonable. Likewise, salespeople who don't meet their monthly quota often want to blame what they think is an unrealistic quota. The point is that when performance isn't up to par, you shouldn't immediately blame the goal or standard. If you believe the standard is realistic, fair, and achievable, tell employees that you expect future work to improve and then take the necessary corrective action to help make that happen.

Summary of Managerial Decisions

Exhibit 16-6 summarizes the manager's decisions in the control process. Standards evolve out of goals that are developed during the planning process. These goals then provide the basis for the control process, which is essentially a continuous flow between measuring, comparing, and taking managerial action. Depending on the results of comparing, a manager's decision about what course of action to take might be to do nothing, revise the standard, or correct the performance.

Corrective action can take many forms. On the selling floor of Home Depot stores, where one contractor spent 20 minutes waiting for a Home Depot forklift operator to arrive so he could load some purchased drywall, the need to improve customer service led to changes in the composition of the workforce. Senior management realized that stores had hired too many part-time employees, whose commitment to the job and knowledge about the do-it-yourself business sometimes lagged behind those of full-timers. Home Depot scaled back from a 50-50 mix to a new balance of 40 percent part-time and 60 percent full-time employees, and customer service has since improved.

Win McNamee/Reuters/Landov

Exhibit 16-6

Managerial Decisions in the Control Process

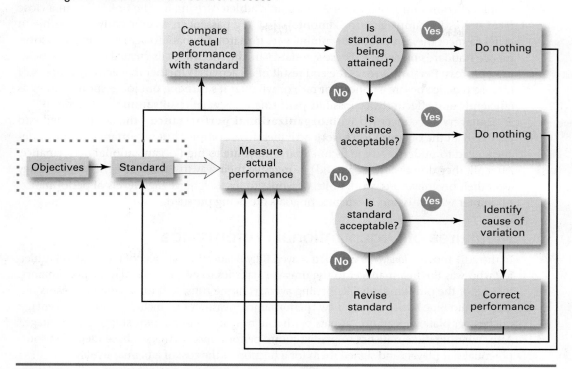

Controlling for Organizational and Employee Performance

▶ ▶ ▶ For Husky Energy president and CEO John Lau, the bottom line is the measure of organizational performance.[7] When he started at Husky in 1991, it was not doing well financially. By 1993, it had a loss of $250 million on the books. In 2006, the company had $2.7 billion in net earnings, clearly an outstanding turnaround. Judith Romanchuk, an investment banker, notes that Lau took the company from "minor league player with a 'crumbling foundation' to a major producer" with holdings in both Canada and China.

Lau also measures performance by the number of barrels of oil equivalent (BOE) produced daily. When he started, Husky was producing 28 000 barrels daily. In 2006, the company produced 359 700 BOE daily. Lau has grown volume by 10 percent a year since 2004 and expected to reach 500 000 BOE daily by 2008. By 2020, he expects the company will extract half a million BOEs daily from the Alberta oil sands alone.

❸ Explain how organizational and employee performance are measured.

Think About It

How can managers use financial and information controls to make sure that their organizations are performing well?

Performance Standards

Cost efficiency. The length of time customers are kept on hold. Customer satisfaction with service provided. These are just a few of the important performance indicators that executives in the intensely competitive call-centre service industry measure. To make good decisions, managers in this industry want and need this type of information so they can manage organizational and employee performance. Managers in all types of businesses are responsible for managing organizational and employee performance.

When you hear the word *performance,* what do you think of? A summer evening concert by a local community orchestra? An Olympic athlete striving for the finish line in a close race? A WestJet ramp agent in Edmonton, loading passengers as efficiently as possible in order to meet the company's 20-minute gate turnaround goal? To achieve control, performance standards must exist. These standards are the specific goals created during the planning process. **Performance** is the end result of an activity. Whether that activity is hours of intense practice before a concert or race or whether it's carrying out job responsibilities as efficiently and effectively as possible, performance is what results from that activity.

Managers are concerned with **organizational performance**—the accumulated end results of all the organization's work activities. It's a complex but important concept. Managers need to understand the factors that contribute to high organizational performance. After all, they don't want (or intend) to manage their way to mediocre performance. They *want* their organizations, work units, or work groups to achieve high levels of performance, no matter what mission, strategies, or goals are being pursued.

Measures of Organizational Performance

In the 2011 movie *Moneyball,* Brad Pitt played Billy Beane, the manager of the Oakland Athletics, who was the first manager to use unusual statistics to evaluate his players' performance. Instead of the old standards like batting average, home runs, and runs batted in, teams like the Toronto Blue Jays use these "new" performance measures that include on-base percentage, pitches per plate appearance, at-bats per home run, and on-base plus slugging percentage.[8] Also, by using these statistics to predict future performance, managers have identified some potential star players and signed them for a fraction of the cost of a big-name player.

All managers must know what organizational performance measures will give them the information they need. The most frequently used organizational performance measures include organizational productivity, organizational effectiveness, and industry and company rankings.

Organizational Productivity

Productivity is the amount of goods or services produced divided by the inputs needed to generate that output. Organizations and individual work units want to be productive. They want to produce the most goods and services using the least amount of inputs. Output is measured by the sales revenue an organization receives when those goods and services are sold (selling price × number sold). Input is measured by the costs of acquiring and transforming the organizational resources into the outputs.

Organizational Effectiveness

In Chapter 1, we defined managerial effectiveness as goal attainment. The same interpretation can apply to organizational effectiveness. **Organizational effectiveness** is a measure of how appropriate organizational goals are and how well those goals are being met. That's the bottom line for managers, and it's what guides managerial decisions in designing strategies and work activities and in coordinating the work of employees.

Rankings are a popular way for managers to measure their organization's performance. There is no shortage of different types of industry and company rankings. The rankings for each list are determined by specific performance measures. For instance, the companies listed in *Report on Business Magazine's* Top 1000: Canada's Power Book are measured by assets. They are ranked according to after-tax profits in the most recent fiscal year, excluding extraordinary gains or losses.[9] The companies listed in the 50 Best Employers in Canada are ranked based on answers given by managers to a leadership team survey, an employee opinion survey, and a human resource survey designed by Hewitt Associates, a compensation and benefits consultant.[10] The companies listed in the *PROFIT* 100: Canada's Fastest Growing Companies are ranked based on their percentage sales growth over the past five years. Private and publicly

---

performance The end result of an activity.

organizational performance The accumulated results of all the organization's work activities.

productivity The amount of goods or services produced divided by the inputs needed to generate that output.

organizational effectiveness A measure of how appropriate organizational goals are and how well those goals are being met.

Exhibit 16-7

Types of Discipline Problems and Examples of Each

Attendance	Absenteeism, tardiness, abuse of sick leave
On-the-Job Behaviours	Insubordination, failure to use safety devices, alcohol or drug abuse
Dishonesty	Theft, lying to supervisors, falsifying information on employment application or on other organizational forms
Outside Activities	Criminal activities, unauthorized strike activities, working for a competing organization (if no-compete clause is part of employment)

traded companies that are over 50 percent Canadian-owned and are headquartered in Canada nominate themselves, and then *PROFIT* editors collect further information about eligible companies.[11]

Controlling for Employee Performance

Since managers manage employees, they also have to be concerned about controlling for employee performance; that is, making sure employees' work efforts are of the quantity and quality needed to accomplish organizational goals. How do managers do that? By following the control process: measure actual performance; compare that performance to standard (or expectations); and take action, if needed. It's particularly important for managers to deliver effective performance feedback and to be prepared, if needed, to use **disciplinary actions**—actions taken by a manager to enforce the organization's work standards and regulations.[12] Let's look first at effective performance feedback.

disciplinary actions Actions taken by a manager to enforce the organization's work standards and regulations

Delivering Effective Performance Feedback Throughout the semester, do you keep track of all your scores on homework, exams, and papers? If you do, why do you like to know that information? For most of us, it's because we like to know where we stand in terms of where we'd like to be and what we'd like to accomplish in our work. We like to know how we're doing. Managers need to provide their employees with feedback so that the employees know where they stand in terms of their work. When giving performance feedback, both parties need to feel heard, understood, and respected. And if done that way, positive outcomes can result. "In a productive performance discussion, organizations have the opportunity to reinforce company values, strengthen workplace culture, and achieve strategic goals."[13] Sometimes, however, performance feedback doesn't work. An employee's performance may continue to be an issue. Under those circumstances, disciplinary actions may be necessary to address the problems.

Using Disciplinary Actions Fortunately, most employees do their jobs well and never need formal correction. Yet, sometimes it is needed. Exhibit 16-7 lists some common types of work discipline problems and examples of each. In those circumstances, it's important for a manager to know what the organization's policies are on discipline. Is there a process for dealing with unsatisfactory job performance? Do warnings need to be given when performance is inadequate? What happens if, after the warnings, performance or the troublesome behaviour doesn't improve? Disciplinary actions are never easy or pleasant; however, discipline can be used to both control and correct employee performance, and managers must know how to discipline.

Tools for Measuring Organizational Performance

▶ ▶ ▶ Everyone seems to agree that John Lau, president and CEO of Husky Energy, is a difficult and demanding boss.[14] He represents the Li family's interests in the company, and the Li family "favours a top down, autocratic environment, crammed with checks and balances." As one former executive of the company noted, "if you want to learn manufacturing cost control,

4 Describe tools used to measure organizational performance.

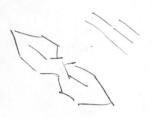

unit cost measurement, they are great at it." Lau, trained as an accountant, brought to Husky the financial models that Li uses with his own companies to control costs and improve performance. Husky gets top shareholder returns as a result, but the company is viewed as tough on its employees.

> ### Think About It
> **What methods of control are available to managers? How do managers introduce controls? What impact might controls have on employees?**

All managers need appropriate tools for monitoring and measuring organizational performance. Before describing some specific types of control tools, let's look at the concept of feed-forward, concurrent, and feedback control. Managers can implement controls *before* an activity begins, *during* the time the activity is going on, and *after* the activity has been completed. The first type is called *feed-forward control*, the second is *concurrent control*, and the last is *feedback control* (Exhibit 16-8).

Feed-Forward Control

feed-forward control A type of control that focuses on preventing anticipated problems, since it takes place before the actual activity.

The most desirable type of control—**feed-forward control**—prevents anticipated problems since it takes place before the actual activity.[15] Let's look at some examples of feed-forward control.

When McDonald's Canada opened its first restaurant in Moscow, it sent company quality control experts to help Russian farmers learn techniques for growing high-quality potatoes and bakers to learn processes for baking high-quality breads. Why? Because McDonald's strongly emphasizes product quality no matter what the geographical location. It wants a cheeseburger in Moscow to taste like one in Winnipeg. Still another example of feed-forward control is the scheduled preventive maintenance programs on aircraft done by airlines. These are designed to detect and, it is hoped, to prevent structural damage that might lead to an accident.

The key to feed-forward controls is taking managerial action *before* a problem occurs. That way, problems can be prevented rather than corrected after the damage (such as poor-quality products, lost customers, lost revenue, and so forth) has already been done. However, these controls require timely and accurate information that often is difficult to get. As a result, managers frequently end up using the other two types of control.

Concurrent Control

concurrent control A type of control that takes place while an activity is in progress.

Concurrent control, as its name implies, takes place while an activity is in progress. When control is enacted while the work is being performed, management can correct problems

Exhibit 16-8

Types of Control

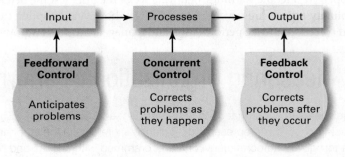

Yun Jong-Yong, corporate advisor and former CEO of Samsung Electronics, describes how he practised an effective kind of concurrent control. "I [spent] much of my time visiting our domestic and overseas work sites to examine operations from the ground, receiving face-to-face reports and indicating areas for improvement. This [gave] me the opportunity to freely discuss matters with the person directly involved, from the top management to the junior staff of that work site . . . I still believe that no [technological] innovation can replace the valuable information that is gathered through direct discussions."

Ki Ho Park/Kistone

before they become too costly. Nicholas Fox is director of business product management at Google. He and his team keep a watchful eye on one of Google's most profitable businesses—online ads. They watch "the number of searches and clicks, the rate at which users click on ads, the revenue this generates—everything is tracked hour by hour, compared with the data from a week earlier and charted."[16] If they see something that's not working particularly well, they fine-tune it.

The best-known form of concurrent control is direct supervision. When managers use **management by walking around**, which is a term used to describe a manager being out in the work area, interacting directly with employees, they are using concurrent control. When a manager directly oversees the actions of employees, he or she can monitor their actions and correct problems as they occur. Problems usually can be addressed before much resource waste or damage has been done.

Also, technical equipment (computers, computerized machine controls, and so forth) can be programmed for concurrent controls. For instance, you may have experienced concurrent control when using a computer program such as word-processing software that alerts you to misspelled words or incorrect grammatical usage. In addition, many organizational quality programs rely on concurrent controls to inform employees if their work output is of sufficient quality to meet standards.

management by walking around A term used to describe a manager being out in the work area, interacting directly with employees.

Feedback Control

The most popular type of control relies on feedback. In **feedback control**, the control takes place *after* the activity is done. For instance, when McDonald's executives learned that a suspected criminal ring had allegedly stolen millions of dollars in top prizes in their customer games, it was discovered through feedback control and the perpetrators were arrested.[17] Even though the company took corrective action once it was discovered, the damage had already occurred.

As the McDonald's example shows, the major drawback of this type of control is that by the time the manager has the information, the problems have already occurred—leading to waste or damage. But for many activities, feedback is the only viable type of control available. For instance, financial statements are an example of feedback controls. If, for example, the income statement shows that sales revenues are declining, the decline has already occurred. So at this point, the manager's only option is to try to determine why sales have decreased and to correct the situation.

Feedback controls do have two advantages.[18] First, feedback provides managers with meaningful information on how effective their planning efforts were. Feedback that indicates little variance between standard and actual performance is evidence that the planning was generally on target. If the deviation is significant, a manager can use that information when formulating new plans to make them more effective. Second, feedback control can enhance employee motivation. People want information on how well they

feedback control Control that takes place after a work activity is done.

have performed, and feedback control provides that information. However, managers should be aware that recent research suggests that, while individuals raise their goals when they receive positive feedback, they lower their goals when they receive negative feedback.[19]

Financial Controls

Every business wants to earn a profit. To achieve this goal, managers need financial controls. For instance, they might analyze quarterly income statements for excessive expenses. They might also calculate financial ratios to ensure that sufficient cash is available to pay ongoing expenses, that debt levels haven't become too high, or that assets are used productively.

Managers might use traditional financial measures such as ratio analysis and budget analysis. Some of the most popular financial ratios include liquidity ratios that measure an organization's ability to meet its current debt obligations. Leverage ratios examine the organization's use of debt to finance its assets and whether it's able to meet the interest payments on the debt. Activity ratios assess how efficiently a company uses its assets. Finally, profitability ratios measure how efficiently and effectively the company uses its assets to generate profits. These ratios are calculated using selected information from the organization's two primary financial statements (the balance sheet and the income statement), which are then expressed as a percentage or ratio. Because you've probably studied these ratios in other accounting or finance courses, or will in the near future, we aren't going to elaborate on how they're calculated. We mention them here to remind you that managers use such ratios as internal control tools.

Budgets are planning and control tools. (See Module 2, Planning and Control Techniques, for more information on budgeting.) When a budget is formulated, it's a planning tool because it indicates which work activities are important and what and how much resources should be allocated to those activities. But budgets are also used for controlling because they provide managers with quantitative standards against which to measure and compare resource consumption. If deviations are significant enough to require action, the manager examines what has happened and tries to uncover why. With this information, necessary action can be taken. For example, if you use a personal budget for monitoring and controlling your monthly expenses, you might find that one month your miscellaneous expenses were higher than you had budgeted for. At that point, you might cut back spending in another area or work extra hours to get more income.

Information Controls

Cyber-attackers from China targeted Google and 34 other companies in an attempt to steal information. The largest ever stealing of credit card data—account information belonging to millions of people—happened to Heartland Payment Systems, a payments processor. An ex-worker at Goldman Sachs stole "black box" computer programs that Goldman uses to make lucrative, rapid-fire trades in the financial markets. Even the U.S. government is getting serious about controlling information. Financial-market sensitive data (Consumer Price Index, housing starts, inflation numbers, gas prices, corn yields, etc.) will be guarded as a precaution against anyone who might want to take advantage of an accidental or covert leak to get an insider's edge in the financial markets.[20] Talk about the need for information controls! Managers deal with information controls in two ways: (1) as a tool to help them control other organizational activities and (2) as an organizational asset they need to protect.

How Is Information Used in Controlling?

Managers need the right information at the right time and in the right amount to monitor and measure organizational activities and performance.

In measuring actual performance, managers need information about what is happening within their area of responsibility and about the standards in order to be able to compare actual performance with the standard. They also rely on information to help them determine if deviations are acceptable. Finally, they rely on information to help them develop appropriate courses of action. Information *is* important! Most of the information tools managers use come from the organization's management information system.

A **management information system (MIS)** is a system used to provide managers with needed information on a regular basis. In theory, this system can be manual or computer-based, although most organizations have moved to computer-supported applications. The term *system* in MIS implies order, arrangement, and purpose. Further, an MIS focuses specifically on providing managers with *information* (processed and analyzed data), not merely **data** (raw, unanalyzed facts). A library provides a good analogy. Although it can contain millions of volumes, a library doesn't do you any good if you can't find what you want quickly. That's why librarians spend a great deal of time cataloguing a library's collections and ensuring that materials are returned to their proper locations. Organizations today are like well-stocked libraries. The issue is not a lack of data; instead, the issue is whether an organization has the ability to process that data so that the right information is available to the right person when he or she needs it. An MIS collects data and turns them into relevant information for managers to use.

An emerging trend in MIS systems is the use of a **dashboard** that presents managers and other decision makers with an easy-to-read, real-time user interface, often employing a graphical presentation of the data, to enable decision makers to make informed decisions quickly. The dashboard presents metrics (information) to decision makers that are relevant to the decisions they are making. Later in this chapter we will provide examples of how metrics are used to support the quality of customer interactions at Enterprise.

Controlling Information

It seems that every week, there's another news story about information security breaches. A survey shows that 85 percent of privacy and security professionals acknowledge that a reportable data breach occurred within their organizations within the past year alone.[21] Because information is critically important to everything an organization does, managers must have comprehensive and secure controls in place to protect that information. Such controls can range from data encryption to system firewalls to data back-ups, and other techniques as well.[22] Problems can lurk in places that an organization might not even have considered, like blogs, search engines, and Twitter accounts. Sensitive, defamatory, confidential, or embarrassing organizational information has found its way into search engine results. For instance, detailed monthly expenses and employee salaries on the National Speleological Society's Web site turned up in a Google search.[23] Equipment such as tablet and laptop computers, smart phones, and even RFID (radio-frequency identification) tags are vulnerable to viruses and hacking. Needless to say, information controls should be monitored regularly to ensure that all possible precautions are in place to protect important information.

Balanced Scorecard

The **balanced scorecard** approach is a way to evaluate organizational performance from more than just the financial perspective.[24] A balanced scorecard typically looks at four areas that contribute to a company's performance: financial, customer, internal processes, and people/innovation/growth assets. According to this approach, managers should develop goals in each of the four areas and then measure whether the goals are being met.

Although a balanced scorecard makes sense, managers will tend to focus on areas that drive their organization's success and use scorecards that reflect those strategies.[25] For example, if strategies are customer-centred, then the customer area is likely to get more attention than the other three areas. Yet, you can't focus on measuring only one performance area, because others are affected as well. For instance, at IBM Global Services in Houston, managers developed a scorecard around an overriding strategy of customer satisfaction. However, the other areas (financial, internal processes, and people/innovation/

management information system (MIS) A system used to provide management with needed information on a regular basis

data Raw, unanalyzed facts.

dashboard An interface that presents managers and other decision makers with an easy-to-read, real-time user interface, often employing a graphical presentation of the data to enable decision makers to make informed decisions quickly.

balanced scorecard A performance measurement tool that looks at more than just the financial perspective

growth) support that central strategy. The division manager described it as follows, "The internal processes part of our business is directly related to responding to our customers in a timely manner, and the learning and innovation aspect is critical for us since what we're selling our customers above all is our expertise. Of course, how successful we are with those things will affect our financial component."[26]

Benchmarking of Best Practices

The Cleveland Clinic is world renowned for delivering high-quality health care, with a top-ranked heart program that attracts patients from around the world. But what you may not realize is that it's also a model of cost-effective health care.[27] It could serve as a model for other health care organizations looking to be more effective and efficient.

Managers in such diverse industries as health care, education, and financial services are discovering what manufacturers have long recognized—the benefits of **benchmarking**, which is the search for the best practices among competitors or non-competitors that lead to their superior performance. Benchmarking should identify various **benchmarks**, the standards of excellence against which to measure and compare. For instance, the American Medical Association developed more than 100 standard measures of performance to improve medical care. Carlos Ghosn, CEO of Nissan, benchmarked Walmart operations in purchasing, transportation, and logistics.[28] At its most basic, benchmarking means learning from others. As a tool for monitoring and measuring organizational performance, benchmarking can be used to identify specific performance gaps and potential areas of improvement. But best practices aren't just found externally.

Sometimes those best practices can be found inside the organization and just need to be shared. One fertile area for finding good performance improvement ideas is an employee suggestion box. Research shows that best practices frequently already exist within an organization but usually go unidentified and unnoticed.[29] In today's environment, organizations seeking high performance levels can't afford to ignore such potentially valuable information. For example, Ameren Corporation's power plant managers used internal benchmarking to help identify performance gaps and opportunities.[30] Exhibit 16-9 provides some suggestions for internal benchmarking.

WestJet has empowered its employees to look for internal ways to save costs employing the tools listed above and examples can be found in the following *Management Reflection*.

benchmarking The search for the best practices among competitors or noncompetitors that lead to their superior performance.

benchmark The standard of excellence against which to measure and compare.

Exhibit 16-9

Suggestions for Internal Benchmarking

1. *Connect best practices to strategies and goals.* The organization's strategies and goals should dictate what types of best practices might be most valuable to others in the organization.

2. *Identify best practices throughout the organization.* Organizations must have a way to find out what practices have been successful in different work areas and units.

3. *Develop best-practices reward and recognition systems.* Individuals must be given an incentive to share their knowledge. The reward system should be built into the organization's culture.

4. *Communicate best practices throughout the organization.* Once best practices have been identified, that information needs to be shared with others in the organization.

5. *Create a best-practices knowledge-sharing system.* There needs to be a formal mechanism for organizational members to continue sharing their ideas and best practices.

6. *Nurture best practices on an ongoing basis.* Create an organizational culture that reinforces a "we can learn from everyone" attitude and emphasizes sharing information.

Source: Based on "Extracting Diamonds in the Rough" by Tad Leahy, from *Business Finance*, August 2000.

WestJet Airline's Employees Control Costs

Can employees be encouraged to think just like owners? WestJet airline's founder and former CEO, Clive Beddoe, encouraged his employees to keep costs low.[31] The airline has a much better profit margin than Air Canada and its other rivals. Beddoe introduced a generous profit-sharing plan to ensure that employees felt personally responsible for the profitability of the airline. The company's accountants insist that profit-sharing turns employees into "cost cops" looking for waste and savings. "We are one of the few companies that have to justify [to employees] its Christmas party every year," Derek Payne, vice-president of finance, boasts ruefully.

WestJet encourages teamwork and gives employees a lot of freedom to determine and carry out their day-to-day duties. There are no rigid job descriptions for positions, and employees are required to help with all tasks. Sometimes pilots are recruited to load baggage. When a plane reaches its destination, all employees on board, even those not working the flight, are expected to prepare the plane for its next takeoff. The company saves $2.5 million annually in cleaning costs by having everyone work together. Planes get turned around much more quickly as well, usually within about a half-hour. When necessary, though, the employees have been able to do it in as little as six minutes. WestJet's profit-sharing program encourages employees to do their best because they see a clear link between their performance, the profits of the company, and their rewards. Not all companies that have profit-sharing programs provide employees with such clear links between behaviour and performance. ■

Contemporary Issues in Control

▶ ▶ ▶ Husky Energy, like all public organizations, has a board of directors that looks after the interests of shareholders.[32] In recent years, corporate governance has come under scrutiny because of corporate scandals. Many boards were not overseeing management as well as they might have.

Husky has strengthened its board policies in recent years. The primary duty of Husky's board is to "approve, monitor and provide guidance on the strategic planning process." While the president and CEO and senior management team create the strategic plan, the board has to review and approve it. The board's role also includes identifying the principal risks of Husky's business and managing and monitoring these risks, as well as approving Husky's strategic plans, annual budget, and financial plans.

5 Discuss contemporary issues in control.

Think About It

Why has corporate governance become so important in recent years? What are the advantages of having a strong corporate board? Would there be any disadvantages?

The employees of Tempe, Arizona-based Integrated Information Systems thought there was nothing wrong with exchanging copyrighted digital music over a dedicated office server they had set up. Like office betting on college basketball games, it was technically illegal but harmless, or so they thought. But after the company had to pay a $1.3 million (US) settlement to the Recording Industry Association of America, managers wished they had controlled the situation better.[33]

Control is an important managerial function. What types of control issues do today's managers face? We look at five: balanced scorecard, corporate governance, cross-cultural differences, workplace concerns, and customer interactions.

Shown here at the Canadian International Auto Show is the new Jaguar C-X16. From its beginning as a manufacturer of motorcycle sidecars in 1922, Jaguar has grown to become one of the world's premier manufacturers of luxury sedans and sports cars. The company's strategy of producing beautiful fast cars that are desired throughout the world includes controlling customer interactions that create and build long-term relationships among the company, employees, and customers. The high quality of Jaguar's customer service staff and service policies results in customer satisfaction and loyalty that improves the company's growth and profitability.

Nathan Denette/AP Photos

service profit chain The service sequence from employees to customers to profit

Controlling Customer Interactions

Every month, every local branch of Enterprise Rent-a-Car conducts telephone surveys with customers.[34] Each branch earns a ranking based on the percentage of its customers who say they were "completely satisfied" with their last Enterprise experience—a level of satisfaction referred to as "top box." Top-box performance is important to Enterprise because completely satisfied customers are far more likely to be repeat customers. By using this service-quality index measure, employees' careers and financial aspirations are linked with the organizational goal of providing consistently superior service to each and every customer. Managers at Enterprise Rent-a-Car understand the connection between employees and customers and the importance of controlling these customer interactions.

There's probably no better area to see the link between planning and controlling than in customer service. If a company proclaims customer service as one of its goals, it quickly and clearly becomes apparent whether that goal is being achieved by seeing how satisfied customers are with their service! How can managers control the interactions between the goal and the outcome when it comes to customers? The concept of a service profit chain can help.[35]

A **service profit chain** is the service sequence from employees to customers to profit. According to this concept, the company's strategy and service delivery system influence how employees deal with customers—that is, how productive they are in providing service and the quality of that service. The level of employee service productivity and service quality influences customer perceptions of service value. When service value is high, it has a positive impact on customer satisfaction, which leads to customer loyalty. And customer loyalty improves organizational revenue growth and profitability.

What does this concept mean for managers? Managers who want to control customer interactions should work to create long-term and mutually beneficial relationships among the company, employees, and customers. How? By creating a work environment that enables employees to deliver high levels of quality service and that makes them feel they're capable of delivering top-quality service. In such a service climate, employees are motivated to deliver superior service. Employee efforts to satisfy customers, coupled with the service value provided by the organization, improve customer satisfaction. And when customers receive high service value, they're loyal and return, which ultimately improves the company's growth and profitability.

There's no better example of this concept in action than WestJet, which is the most consistently profitable Canadian airline. Its customers are fiercely loyal because the company's operating strategy (hiring, training, rewards and recognition, teamwork, and so forth) is built around customer service. Employees consistently deliver outstanding service value to customers. And WestJet's customers reward the company by coming back. It's through efficiently and effectively controlling these customer interactions that companies like WestJet and Enterprise have succeeded.

Organizational Governance

Andrew Fastow, Enron's former chief financial officer, had an engaging and persuasive personality, but that does not explain why Enron's board of directors failed to raise even minimal concerns about management's questionable accounting practices. The board even allowed Fastow to set up off-balance-sheet partnerships for his own profit at the expense of Enron's shareholders.

Organizational governance, the system used to govern an organization so that the interests of stakeholders are protected, failed abysmally at Enron, as it did at many of the other companies caught in recent financial scandals. In the aftermath of these scandals,

organizational governance The system used to govern an organization so that the interests of stakeholders are protected.

there have been increased calls for better organizational governance. Two areas in which organizational governance is being reformed are the role of boards of directors and financial reporting. The concern over corporate governance exists in Canada and globally.[36] For example, 75 percent of senior executives at US and Western European corporations expect their boards of directors to take a more active role in improving corporate governance.[37]

The Role of Boards of Directors

The original purpose of a board of directors was to have a group, independent from management, looking out for the interests of shareholders who, because of the corporate structure, were not involved in the day-to-day management of the organization. However, it has not always worked that way in practice. Board members often enjoy a cozy relationship with managers in which board members "take care" of the CEO and the CEO "takes care" of the board members.

This quid pro quo arrangement is changing. In the United States, since the passage of the Sarbanes-Oxley Act in 2002, demands on board members of publicly traded companies have increased considerably.[38] The Canadian Securities Administrators rules, which came into effect in March 2004, strive to tighten board responsibility somewhat, though these rules are not as stringent as those developed in the United States. To help boards do their job better, researchers at the Corporate Governance Center at Kennesaw State University developed 10 governance principles for American public companies that have been endorsed by the Institute of Internal Auditors in the United States. These principles are equally relevant for Canadian public companies. (See Exhibit 16-10 for a list of these principles.)

Financial Reporting

In addition to expanding the role of boards of directors, the Canadian Securities Administrators rules require more financial disclosure by organizations but, unlike the Sarbanes-Oxley Act of the United States, do not require senior managers to provide a qualitative

Exhibit 16-10 Twenty-First-Century Governance Principles for Public Companies

1. *Interaction:* Sound governance requires effective interaction among the board, management, the external auditor, and the internal auditor.

2. *Board purpose:* The board of directors should understand that its purpose is to protect the interests of the corporation's stockholders, while considering the interests of other stakeholders (for example, creditors and employees).

3. *Board responsibilities:* The board's major areas of responsibility should be monitoring the CEO, overseeing the corporation's strategy, and monitoring risks and the corporation's control system. Directors should employ healthy skepticism in meeting these responsibilities.

4. *Independence:* The major stock exchanges should define an "independent" director as one who has no professional or personal ties (either current or former) to the corporation or its management other than service as a director. The vast majority of the directors should be independent in both fact and appearance so as to promote arm's-length oversight.

5. *Expertise:* The directors should possess relevant industry, company, functional area, and governance expertise. The directors should reflect a mix of backgrounds and perspectives. All directors should receive detailed orientation and continuing education to assure they achieve and maintain the necessary level of expertise.

6. *Meetings and information:* The board should meet frequently for extended periods of time and should have access to the information and personnel it needs to perform its duties.

7. *Leadership:* The roles of board chair and CEO should be separate.

8. *Disclosure:* Proxy statements and other board communications should reflect board activities and transactions (e.g., insider trades) in a transparent and timely manner.

9. *Committees:* The nominating, compensation, and audit committees of the board should be composed only of independent directors.

10. *Internal audit:* All public companies should maintain an effective, full-time internal audit function that reports directly to the audit committee.

Source: P. D. Lapides, D. R. Hermanson, M. S. Beasley, J. V. Carcello, F. T. DeZoort, and T. L. Neal. Corporate Governance Center, Kennesaw State University, March 26, 2002.

assessment of a company's internal compliance control. Still, these types of changes should lead to somewhat better information—that is, information that more accurately reflects the firm's financial condition.

Adjusting Controls for Cross-Cultural Differences and Global Turmoil

The concepts of control that we have discussed so far are appropriate for an organization whose units are not geographically separated or culturally distinct. But what about global organizations? Will control systems be different, and what should managers know about adjusting controls for cross-cultural differences?

Methods of controlling people and work can be quite different in different countries. The differences we see in organizational control systems of global organizations are primarily in the measurement and corrective action steps of the control process. In a global corporation, managers of foreign operations tend to be less directly controlled by the home office, if for no other reason than that distance keeps managers from being able to observe work directly. Because distance creates a tendency to formalize controls, the home office of a global company often relies on extensive formal reports for control.

Technology's impact on control is also seen when comparing technologically advanced nations with less technologically advanced countries. Managers in countries where technology is more advanced often use indirect control devices such as computer-generated reports and analyses in addition to standardized rules and direct supervision to ensure that work activities are going as planned. In less technologically advanced countries, however, managers tend to use more direct supervision and highly centralized decision making for control.

Also, constraints on what corrective actions managers can take may affect managers in foreign countries because laws in some countries do not allow managers the option of closing facilities, laying off employees, taking money out of the country, or bringing in a new management team from outside the country.

Another challenge for global managers in collecting data for measurement and comparison is comparability. For instance, a company that manufactures apparel in Cambodia might produce the same products at a facility in Scotland. However, the Cambodian facility might be more labour intensive than its Scottish counterpart to take advantage of lower labour costs in Cambodia. This difference makes it hard to compare, for instance, labour costs per unit.

Finally, global organizations need to have controls in place for protecting their workers and other assets during times of global turmoil and disasters. For instance, when the earthquake/tsunami hit Japan in March 2011, companies scrambled to activate their disaster management plans. In the volatile Middle East, many companies have had to evacuate workers during times of crisis. The best time to be prepared is before an emergency occurs, and many organizations are doing just that so that if a crisis occurs, employees and other organizational assets are protected as best as possible.

Emerging Workplace Concerns

Today's workplace presents considerable control challenges for managers. From monitoring employees' computer use at work to protecting the workplace from disgruntled employees, managers must control the workplace to ensure that the organization's work can be carried out efficiently and effectively as planned. In this section, we look at two major workplace concerns: workplace privacy and employee theft.

Workplace Privacy

If you work, do you think you have a right to privacy at your workplace? What can your employer find out about you and your work? You might be surprised by the answers!

Employers can (and do), among other things, read your email (even those marked "personal" or "confidential"), tap your telephone, monitor your work by computer, store

Exhibit 16-11

Types of Workplace Monitoring by Employers

Internet use	54.7%
Telephone use	44.0%
Email messages	38.1%
Computer files	30.8%
Job performance using video cameras	14.6%
Phone conversations	11.5%
Voice mail messages	6.8%

Source: Based on S. McElvoy, "E-Mail and Internet Monitoring and the Workplace: Do Employees Have a Right to Privacy?" *Communications and the Law,* June 2002, p. 69.

and review computer files, and monitor you in an employee washroom or dressing room. And these actions are not all that uncommon. Nearly 57 percent of Canadian companies have internet-use policies restricting employees' personal use of the internet.[39] A big reason is that employees are hired to work, not to surf the web checking stock prices, watching online videos, playing fantasy baseball, or shopping for presents for family or friends. Recreational on-the-job web surfing is thought to cost billions of dollars in lost work productivity annually. In fact, a survey of U.S. employers said that 87 percent of employees look at non-work-related websites while at work and more than half engage in personal website surfing every day.[40] Watching online video has become an increasingly serious problem not only because of the time being wasted by employees but because it clogs already-strained corporate computer networks.[41] All this non-work adds up to significant costs to businesses.

Employees of the City of Vancouver are warned that their computer use is monitored, and a desktop agent icon of a spinning head reminds them that they are being watched. Exhibit 16-11 summarizes the percentage of employers engaging in different forms of workplace monitoring.

Another reason that managers monitor employee email and computer use is that they don't want to risk being sued for creating a hostile workplace environment because of offensive messages or an inappropriate image displayed on a co-worker's computer screen. Concern about racial or sexual harassment is one of the reasons companies might want to monitor or keep backup copies of all email. This electronic record can help establish what actually happened and can help managers react quickly.[42]

Finally, managers want to ensure that company secrets are not being leaked.[43] Although protecting intellectual property is important for all businesses, it's especially important in high-tech industries. Managers need to be certain that employees are not, even inadvertently, passing information on to others who could use that information to harm the company.

Even with the workplace monitoring that managers can do, Canadian employees do have some protection through the Criminal Code, which prohibits unauthorized interception of electronic communication. The Personal Information Protection and Electronic Documents Act, which went into effect in early 2004, gives employees some privacy protection, but it does not make workplace electronic monitoring illegal. Under existing laws, if an individual is aware of a corporate policy of surveillance and does not formally object, or remains at the job, the monitoring is acceptable.[44] Unionized employees may have a bit more privacy with respect to their computers. The Canada Labour Code requires employers operating under a collective agreement to disclose information about plans for technological change. This might provide unions with an opportunity to bargain over electronic surveillance.

Because of the potentially serious costs, and given the fact that many jobs now entail computers, many companies have workplace monitoring policies. Such policies should control employee behaviour in a non-demeaning way and employees should be informed about those policies.[45]

Employee Theft

Would you be surprised to find out that in 2011, 26 percent of small and medium-sized Canadian companies reported experiencing employee theft at some point in the previous year?[46] It's a costly problem—Air Canada, which has run a campaign against employee theft, noted that the airline "is right in line with industry standards for employee theft, and that means as much as 9 per cent of stock such as office supplies and on-board products is taken each year."[47] Employee theft cost Canadian retail businesses more than $3 billion in 2008.[48]

employee theft Any unauthorized taking of company property by employees for their personal use.

Employee theft is defined as any unauthorized taking of company property by employees for their personal use.[49] It can range from embezzlement to fraudulent filing of expense reports to removing equipment, parts, software, and office supplies from company premises. While retail businesses have long faced serious potential losses from employee theft, loose financial controls at start-ups and small companies and the ready availability of information technology have made employee stealing an escalating problem in all kinds and sizes of organizations. It's a control issue that managers need to educate themselves about and that they must be prepared to deal with.[50]

Why do employees steal? The answer depends on whom you ask.[51] Experts in various fields—industrial security, criminology, clinical psychology—all have different perspectives. Industrial security people propose that people steal because the opportunity presents itself through lax controls and favourable circumstances. Criminologists say that it's because people have financial pressures (such as personal financial problems) or vice-based pressures (such as gambling debts). Clinical psychologists suggest that people steal because they can rationalize whatever they are doing as correct and appropriate behaviour ("everyone does it," "they had it coming," "this company makes enough money and they will never miss anything this small," "I deserve this for all that I put up with," and so forth).[52] Although each of these approaches provides compelling insights into employee theft and has been instrumental in program designs to deter it, unfortunately employees continue to steal.

What can managers do to deter or reduce employee theft or fraud? We can use the concepts of feed-forward, concurrent, and feedback controls to identify actions managers can take.[53] Exhibit 16-12 summarizes several possible control measures.

Customer Experience

Ottawa-based John Weigelt, national technology officer for Microsoft Canada, is a frequent traveller for business and wanted to surprise his wife Laurel with a weekend in Toronto just before Christmas. Because he was a gold member of the Westin loyalty program he had high expectations for the level of service he would receive. Upon arrival at their hotel John was informed that they did not have the room he requested and that it would be another four hours before he could check in. Unable to resolve the issue at the desk, John sat down beside Laurel, took out his Microsoft windows phone and tweeted: #Fail Westin Toronto—describing his problem and including his cell phone number. Within ten minutes his phone rang and he was asked to come to the front desk, where the hotel manager was waving at him. Problem resolved in less than 15 minutes![54]

There is probably no better area to see the link between planning and controlling than in customer service. If a company proclaims customer service as one of its goals, it quickly and clearly becomes apparent whether or not that goal is being achieved by seeing how satisfied customers are with their service. How can managers control the interactions

Exhibit 16-12

Control Measures for Deterring or Reducing Employee Theft or Fraud

Feed-forward	Concurrent	Feedback
Use careful pre-hiring screening.	Treat employees with respect and dignity.	Make sure employees know when theft or fraud has occurred—not naming names but letting people know this is not acceptable.
Establish specific policies defining theft and fraud and discipline procedures.	Openly communicate the costs of stealing.	
Involve employees in writing policies.	Let employees know on a regular basis about their successes in preventing theft and fraud.	Use the services of professional investigators.
Educate and train employees about the policies.	Use video surveillance equipment if conditions warrant.	Redesign control measures.
Have professionals review your internal security controls.	Install "lock-out" options on computers, telephones, and email.	Evaluate your organization's culture and the relationships of managers and employees.
	Use corporate hotlines for reporting incidents.	
	Set a good example.	

Sources: Based on A. H. Bell and D. M. Smith, "Protecting the Company Against Theft and Fraud," *Workforce Online,* December 3, 2000, www.workforce.com; J. D. Hansen, "To Catch a Thief," *Journal of Accountancy,* March 2000, pp. 43–46; and J. Greenberg, "The Cognitive Geometry of Employee Theft," in *Dysfunctional Behavior in Organizations: Nonviolent and Deviant Behavior,* eds. S. B. Bacharach, A. O'Leary-Kelly, J. M. Collins, and R. W. Griffin, pp. 147–193 (Stamford, CT: JAI Press, 1998).

between the goal and the outcome when it comes to customers? The concept of a service profit chain can help.

The **service profit chain** is the service sequence from employees to customers to profit.[55] According to this concept, the company's strategy and service delivery system influences how employees serve customers—their attitudes, behaviours, and service capability. Service capability, in turn, enhances how productive employees are in providing service and the quality of that service. The level of employee service productivity and service quality influences customer perceptions of service value. When service value is high, it has a positive impact on customer satisfaction, which leads to customer loyalty. And customer loyalty improves organizational revenue growth and profitability.

So what does the concept of a service profit chain mean for managers? Managers who want to control customer interactions should work to create long-term and mutually beneficial relationships among the company, employees, and customers. How? By creating a work environment that not only enables employees to deliver high levels of quality service, but makes them feel they are capable of delivering top-quality service. In such a service climate, employees are motivated to deliver superior service.

service profit chain The service sequence from employees to customers to profit.

CHAPTER 16

SUMMARY AND IMPLICATIONS

1. Explain the nature and importance of control. Control is the process of monitoring activities to ensure that they are being accomplished as planned, correcting any significant deviations and where necessary modifying the plan (a pivot as described in Chapter 4). Control systems also protect the organization's assets and the physical and virtual workplace. The more a control system helps managers achieve their organization's goals, the better the control system.

▶ ▶ ▶ When Li Ka-shing first bought Husky Energy, he immediately introduced financial controls to improve the company's bottom line. He also hired John Lau to stop the losses and halt the expansions that previous managers had introduced. These measures were put in place to make the company profitable.

2. Describe the three steps in the control process. The control process is a three-step process: measuring actual performance, comparing actual performance against a standard, and taking managerial action to correct deviations or inadequate standards. Standards are based on the specific goals created during the planning process. Common sources of information for measuring performance include personal observation, statistical reports, oral reports and written reports. What is measured (metrics) needs to reflect the strategic choices made by the organization.

3. Explain how organizational and employee performance are measured. Performance is the end result of an activity, and mangers *want* their organizations, work units, or work groups to achieve high levels of performance, no matter what mission, strategies, or goals are being pursued. Rankings are a popular way for managers to measure their organization's performance. Managers also want to ensure that employees' work efforts are of the quantity and quality needed to accomplish organizational goals. It's particularly important for managers to deliver effective performance feedback and to be prepared, if needed, to use disciplinary actions.

▶ ▶ ▶ One of the key metrics measured by Lau are the number of barrels of oil equivalent (BOE) produced daily. Lau grew volume by 10 percent a year since 2004. By 2020, he expects the company will extract half a million BOEs daily from the Alberta oil sands alone.

4. Describe tools used to measure organizational performance. Managers can implement controls before an activity begins (feed-forward control), during the time the activity is going on (concurrent control), and after the activity has been completed (feedback control).The tools available to measure organizational performance include financial controls (ratios and budgets), information controls (provision of appropriate information as well as protection of the information assets), the balanced scorecard (looking at financial, customer, internal business process, and learning and growth assets), and benchmarking of best practices (both among internal units and appropriate external exemplars).

▶ ▶ ▶ Li Ka-shing has employed an autocratic "top down" approach in implementing a strong financial control system and this has resulted in to notch shareholder returns. But … this has resulted in a reputation that Husky is "tough" on its employees.

5. Discuss contemporary issues in control. Some important current issues in control include controlling customer interactions, organizational governance, adjusting controls for cross-cultural differences and global turmoil, and emerging workplace concerns.

▶ ▶ ▶ Husky Energy has a board of directors that looks after the interests of shareholders. The primary duty of Husky's board is to "approve, monitor and provide guidance on the strategic planning process." The board also approves Husky's strategic plans, annual budget, and financial plans.

MyManagementLab Study, practise, and explore real management situations with these helpful resources:
- **Interactive Lesson Presentations:** Work through interactive presentations and assessments to test your knowledge of management concepts.
- **PIA (Personal Inventory Assessments):** Enhance your ability to connect with key concepts through these engaging, self-reflection assessments.
- **Study Plan:** Check your understanding of chapter concepts with self-study quizzes.
- **Simulations:** Practise decision-making in simulated management environments.

PIA PERSONAL INVENTORY ASSESSMENT

REVIEW AND DISCUSSION QUESTIONS

1. What are the three steps in the control process? Describe in detail.

2. What is organizational performance? Name four sources managers can use to acquire information about actual organizational performance.

3. Compare and contrast feed-forward, concurrent, and feedback controls.

4. Discuss the five tools managers can use to measure organizational performance.

5. Describe the financial control measures managers can use.

6. Why is control important in managing customer interactions?

7. In Chapter 6 we discussed the white-water rapids view of change, which refers to situations in which unpredictable change is normal and expected, and managing it is a continual process. Do you think it's possible to establish and maintain effective standards and controls in this type of environment? Discuss.

8. "Every individual employee in the organization plays a role in controlling work activities." Do you agree, or do you think control is something that only managers are responsible for? Explain.

ETHICS DILEMMA

Pornography and offensive email are two major reasons why many companies establish strict policies and monitor their employees' use of the internet.[56] Citing legal and ethical concerns, managers are determined to keep inappropriate images and messages out of the workplace. "Having a clear policy and a monitoring system are only first steps. Management must be sure that employees are aware of the rules—and understand that the company is serious about cleaning up any ethics violations."

Imagine that you are the administrative assistant for a high-ranking executive. One afternoon you receive an urgent phone call for your manager. You knock on that office door but get no answer, so you open the door, thinking you will leave a note on the desk. Then you notice that your manager is absorbed in watching a very graphic adult website on his personal laptop. As you quietly back out of the office, you wonder how to handle this situation.

What would/should you do? Should you raise the issue with your boss? Do you have a duty to report the incident? Do you ignore it? Why?

SKILLS EXERCISE

About the Skill

One of the more critical feedback sessions will occur when you, as a manager, are using feedback control to address performance issues.

Steps in Practising the Skill

1. **Schedule the feedback session in advance and be prepared.** One of the biggest mistakes you can make is to treat feedback control lightly. Simply calling in an employee and giving feedback that's not well organized serves little purpose for you and your employee. For feedback to be effective, you must plan ahead. Identify the issues you wish to address and cite specific examples to reinforce what you are saying. Furthermore, set aside the time for the meeting with the employee. Make sure what you do is done in private and can be completed without interruptions. That may mean closing your office door (if you have one), not taking phone calls, and the like.

2. **Put the employee at ease.** Regardless of how you feel about the feedback, you must create a supportive climate for the employee. Recognize that giving and getting this feedback can be an emotional event even when the feedback is positive. By putting your employee at ease, you begin to establish a supportive environment in which understanding can take place.

3. **Make sure the employee knows the purpose of this feedback session.** What is the purpose of the meeting? That's something any employee will be wondering. Clarifying what you are going to do sets the appropriate stage for what is to come.

4. **Focus on specific rather than general work behaviours.** Feedback should be specific rather than general. General statements are vague and provide little useful information—especially if you are attempting to correct a problem.

5. **Keep comments impersonal and job-related.** Feedback should be descriptive rather than judgmental or evaluative, especially when you are giving negative feedback. No matter how upset you are, keep the feedback job-related and never criticize someone personally because of an inappropriate action. You're correcting job-related behaviour, not the person.

6. **Support feedback with hard data.** Tell your employee how you came to your conclusion on his or her performance. Hard data help your employees to identify with specific behaviours. Identify the "things" that were done correctly and provide a detailed critique. And if you need to criticize, state the basis of your conclusion that a good job was not completed.

7. **Direct the negative feedback toward work-related behaviour that the employee controls.** Negative feedback should be directed toward work-related behaviour that the employee can do something about. Indicate what he or she can do to improve the situation. This practice helps take the sting out of the criticism and offers guidance to an individual who understands the problem but doesn't know how to resolve it.

8. **Let the employee speak.** Get the employee's perceptions of what you are saying, especially if you are addressing a problem. Of course, you're not looking for excuses, but you need to be empathetic to the employee. Get his or her side. Maybe something has contributed to the issue. Letting the employee speak involves your employee and just might provide information you were unaware of.

9. **Ensure that the employee has a clear and full understanding of the feedback.** Feedback must be concise and complete enough so that your employee clearly and fully understands what you have said. Consistent with active listening techniques, have your employee rephrase the content of your feedback to check whether it fully captures your meaning.

10. **Detail a future plan of action.** Performing doesn't stop simply because feedback occurred. Good performance must be reinforced and new performance goals set. However, when performance deficiencies are the issue, time must be devoted to helping your employee develop a detailed, step-by-step plan to correct the situation. This plan includes what has to be done and when and how you will monitor the activities. Offer whatever assistance you can to help the employee, but make it clear that it is the employee, not you, who has to make the corrections.

PRACTISING THE SKILL

Think of a skill you would like to acquire or improve, or a habit you would like to break. Perhaps you would like to learn a foreign language, start exercising, quit smoking, ski better, or spend less. For the purpose of this exercise, assume you have three months to make a start on your project and all the necessary funds. Draft a plan of action that outlines what you need to do, when you need to do it, and how you will know that you have successfully completed each step of your plan. Be realistic, but don't set your sights too low either.

Review your plan. What outside help or resources will you require? How will you get them? Add these to your plan. Could someone else follow the steps you've outlined to achieve the goal you set? What modifications would you have to make, if any?

WORKING TOGETHER: TEAM EXERCISE

Controlling Cheating

You are a professor in the School of Business at a local university. Several of your colleagues have expressed an interest in developing some specific controls to minimize opportunities for students to cheat on homework assignments and exams. You and some other faculty members have volunteered to write a report outlining some suggestions that might be used.

Form teams of three or four and discuss this topic. Write a bulleted list of your suggestions from the perspective of controlling possible cheating (1) before it happens, (2) while in-class exams or assignments are being completed, and (3)

after it has happened. Please keep the report brief (no more than two pages). Be prepared to present your suggestions before the rest of the class.

LEARNING TO BE A MANAGER

- You have a major class project due in a month. Identify some performance measures you could use to help determine whether the project is going as planned and will be completed efficiently (on time) and effectively (high quality).

- How could you use the concept of control in your personal life? Be specific. (Think in terms of feed-forward, concurrent, and feedback controls as well as specific controls for the different aspects of your life—school, work, family relationships, friends, hobbies, etc.)

- Survey 30 people as to whether they have experienced office rage. Ask them specifically whether they have experienced any of the following: yelling or other verbal abuse, yelled at coworkers themselves, cried over work-related issues, saw someone purposely damage machines or furniture, saw physical violence in the

workplace, or struck a coworker. Compile your findings in a table. Are you surprised at the results? Be prepared to present these in class.

- Pretend you're the manager of a customer call centre for timeshare vacations. What types of control measures would you use to see how efficient and effective an employee is? How about measures for evaluating the entire call centre?

- Disciplining employees is one of the least favourite tasks of managers, but is something that all managers have to do. Survey three managers about their experiences with employee discipline. What types of employee actions have caused the need for disciplinary action? What disciplinary actions have they used? What do they think is the most difficult thing to do when disciplining employees? What suggestions do they have for disciplining employees?

CASE APPLICATION 1

Baggage Blunders and Wonders

Terminal 5 (T5), built by British Airways for $8.6 billion, is London Heathrow Airport's newest state-of-the-art facility.[57] Made of glass, concrete, and steel, it's the largest free-standing building in the United Kingdom and has more than 10 miles of belts for moving luggage. At the terminal's unveiling in March 2008, Queen Elizabeth II called it a "twenty-first-century gateway to Britain." Alas, the accolades didn't last long! After two decades in planning and 100 million hours in manpower, opening day didn't work out as planned. Endless lines and major baggage handling delays led to numerous flight cancellations, stranding many irate passengers. Airport operators said the problems were triggered by glitches in the terminal's high-tech baggage-handling system.

With its massive automation features, T5 was planned to ease congestion at Heathrow and improve the flying experience for the 30 million passengers expected to pass through it annually. With 96 self-service check-in kiosks, more than 90 fast check-in bag drops, 54 standard check-in desks, and miles of suitcase-moving belts estimated to be able to process 12 000 bags per hour, the facility's design seemed to support those goals.

However, within the first few hours of the terminal's operation, problems developed. Presumably understaffed, baggage workers were unable to clear incoming luggage fast enough. Arriving passengers waited more than an hour for their bags. Departing passengers tried in vain to check in for flights. Flights left with empty cargo holds. Sometime on day one, the airline checked in only those passengers with no luggage. And it didn't help that the moving belt system jammed at one point. Lesser problems also became apparent: a few broken escalators, some hand dryers that didn't work, a gate that wouldn't function at the new underground station, and inexperienced ticket sellers who didn't know the fares between Heathrow and various stations on the Piccadilly line. By the end of the first full day of operation, Britain's Department of Transportation released a statement calling for British Airways and the airport operator BAA to "work hard to resolve these issues and limit disruptions to passengers."

You might be tempted to think that all of this could have been prevented if British Airways had only tested the system. But thorough runs of all systems "from toilets to check in and seating" took place six months before opening, including four full-scale test runs using 16 000 volunteers.

Although T5's debut was far from perfect, things have certainly changed. A recent customer satisfaction survey showed that 80 percent of passengers waited less than five minutes to check in. And those passengers are extremely satisfied with the terminal's lounges, catering, facilities, and ambience.

With the Summer Olympics in London, London's Heathrow (and T5) grappled with a record passenger surge as competitors, spectators, and media arrived. To cope with the deluge, some 1000 volunteers greeted arrivals, and special teams were assigned to deal with athletes' oversize items like javelins, bikes, and other sports equipment. Despite the chaotic "birth" of T5, it's become a valued component of Heathrow and British Airways.

DISCUSSION QUESTIONS

1. What type of control—feed-forward, concurrent, or feedback—do you think would be most important in this situation? Explain your choice.
2. How might immediate corrective action have been used in this situation? How about basic corrective action?
3. Could British Airways' controls have been more effective? How?
4. What role would information controls play in this situation? Customer interaction controls? Benchmarking?
5. What could companies learn from the smooth handling of the throngs of arrivals and departures for the Summer 2012 Olympics?

CASE APPLICATION 2

Deepwater in Deep Trouble

When all is said and done, which may not be for many years, it's likely to be one of the worst environmental disasters, if not the worst, in U.S. history.[58] When British Petroleum's (BP) Deepwater Horizon off-shore rig in the Gulf of Mexico exploded in a ball of flames on April 20, 2010, killing 11 employees, it set in motion frantic efforts to stop the flow of oil and to initiate the long and arduous clean-up process. Although the impacts of the explosion and oil spill were felt most intensely by businesses and residents along the coast and by coastal wildlife, those of us inland who watched the disaster unfold were also stunned and dismayed by what we saw happening. What led to this disaster, and what can BP do to ensure that the likelihood of it ever happening again is minimized?

Strong warning signs indicated serious problems with well equipment and other safety aspects of the Deepwater Horizon oil rig, but a lack of effective controls needed to protect the rig as the employees' workplace resulted in a tragic explosion and oil spill.

One thing that came to light in the disaster investigation is that it's no surprise that something like this happened. After Hurricane Dennis blew through in July 2005, a passing ship was shocked to see BP's new massive $1 billion Thunder Horse oil platform listing to one side and close to collapse. Thunder Horse was intended to be a showpiece for deepwater drilling in the gulf. But the problems with this rig soon became evident. A valve installed backwards caused it to flood during the hurricane even before any oil had been pumped. Other problems included a welding job so shoddy that it left underwater pipelines brittle and full of cracks. After the disaster occurred these shortfalls were deemed to be harbingers of the destruction that was to follow.

Then came the tragic explosion on the Deepwater Horizon. Before the rig exploded, strong warning signs indicated that something was terribly wrong with the oil well. Among the red flags were several equipment readings suggesting that gas was bubbling into the well, a potential sign of an impending blowout. Those red flags were ignored. Other decisions made in the 24 hours before the explosion included a critical decision to replace heavy mud in the pipe rising from the seabed with seawater, again possibly increasing the risk of an explosion. Internal BP documents also show serious problems and safety concerns with Deepwater. Those problems involved the well casing and blowout preventer. One BP senior drilling engineer warned, "This would certainly be a worst-case scenario."

The federal panel charged with investigating the spill examined 20 problems with the well and how the crew dealt with them. The panel investigated in particular why the crew missed the signs that an uncontrollable blowout was imminent. The U.S. Coast Guard's report found that inadequate maintenance, training, and a poor culture of safety were the major contributing factors to the explosion and susbsequent sinking of the rig. And finally, the U.S. Justice Department was getting closer to civil and criminal settlements with BP and with Transocean over the Deepwater Horizon disaster—deals that would likely include billions of dollars in fines and penalties.

DISCUSSION QUESTIONS

1. What type(s) of control—feed-forward, concurrent, or feedback—do you think would have been most useful in this situation? Explain your choice(s).
2. Using Exhibit 16-2, explain what BP could have done better.
3. Why do you think company employees ignored the red flags? How could such behaviour be changed in the future?
4. What could other organizations learn from BP's mistakes?

MODULE ③

Managing Operations

▶ ▶ ▶ Every organization "produces" something, whether it's a good or a service. Organizations need to have well-thought-out and well-designed operating systems, organizational control systems, and quality programs to survive in today's increasingly competitive global environment. And it's the manager's job to manage those systems and programs.

David Ritacco is CEO of Truro, Nova Scotia–based Eldis Group, which serves the do-it-yourself (DIY) market for home appliance repair.[1] The company operates a family of DIY websites, including PartSelect. According to the company website, "We provide consumers with the parts and know-how to fix their major home appliances themselves, offering the internet's largest collection of step-by-step installation instructions and videos."

Customers in Canada and the United States browse the websites to determine what part they need and place their order online. The customer pays with a credit card, and a shipping ticket is printed automatically in one of the partner fulfillment centres, where the product is picked and shipped with an Eldis company logo and documentation. Eldis Group holds no inventory and relies on automation within its websites, allowing the company to maintain a small staff. PartSelect, Eldis' flagship site, has more unique visitors monthly than Amazon.ca.[2] A commitment to the principles of operations management has made Eldis a major player in its industry.

The Role of Operations Management

Inside Intel's factory in New Mexico, employee Trish Roughgarden is known as a "seed"—an unofficial title for technicians who transfer manufacturing know-how from one Intel facility to another.[3] Her job is to make sure that this factory works just like an identical one that opened earlier in Oregon. When another plant opened in Ireland, several hundred other seeds copied the same techniques. The company's facility in Arizona also benefited from "seeding." What the seeds do is part of a strategy known as "Copy Exactly," which Intel implemented after frustrating variations between factories hurt productivity and product quality. In the intensely competitive chip-making industry, Intel knows that how it manages operations will determine whether it succeeds.

What is **operations management**? The term refers to the design, operation, and control of the transformation process that converts resources into finished goods and services. Exhibit MO-1 portrays this process in a very simplified fashion. The system takes

operations management The design, operation, and control of the transformation process that converts resources into goods and services.

Exhibit MO-1

The Operations System

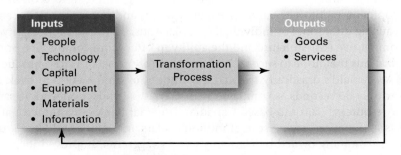

in inputs—people, technology, capital, equipment, materials, and information—and transforms them through various processes, procedures, work activities, and so forth into finished goods and services. Because every unit in an organization produces something, managers need to be familiar with operations management concepts in order to achieve goals efficiently and effectively.

Operations management is important to organizations and managers for three reasons: It encompasses both services and manufacturing, it's important in effectively and efficiently managing productivity, and it plays a strategic role in an organization's competitive success. Let's look at each.

Services and Manufacturing

With a menu that offers over 200 items, The Cheesecake Factory restaurants rely on a finely tuned production system. One food-service consultant says, "They've evolved with this highly complex menu combined with a highly efficient kitchen."[4]

manufacturing organizations
Organizations that produce physical goods.

service organizations
Organizations that produce nonphysical outputs in the form of services.

Every organization produces something. Unfortunately, this fact is often overlooked except in obvious cases, such as in the manufacturing of cars, cellphones, or lawnmowers. After all, **manufacturing organizations** produce physical goods. It's easy to see the operations management (transformation) process at work in these types of organizations because raw materials are turned into recognizable physical products. But that transformation process isn't as readily evident in **service organizations** because they produce nonphysical outputs in the form of services. For instance, hospitals provide medical and health care services that help people manage their personal health; airlines provide transportation services that move people from one location to another; cruise lines provide vacation and entertainment services; military forces provide defence capabilities; and the list goes on and on. Service organizations also transform inputs into outputs, although the transformation process isn't as easily recognizable as it is in manufacturing organizations. Take a university, for example. University administrators bring together inputs—professors, books, academic journals, technology materials, computers, classrooms, and similar resources—to transform "unenlightened" students into educated and skilled individuals who are capable of making contributions to society.

The reason we're making this point is that most of the world's developed countries are predominantly service economies. In Canada over 69 percent of all economic activity is in the services sector; in the United States, it's 78 percent.[5]

Managing Productivity

One jetliner has some 4 million parts. Efficiently assembling such a finely engineered product requires intense focus. Boeing and Airbus, the two major global manufacturers, have copied techniques from Toyota. However, not every technique can be copied because airlines demand more customization than do car buyers, and there are significantly more rigid safety regulations for jetliners than for cars.[6]

productivity The overall output of goods or services produced divided by the inputs needed to generate that output.

Although most organizations don't make products that have 4 million parts, improving productivity has become a major goal in virtually every organization. By **productivity**, we mean the overall output of goods or services produced divided by the inputs needed to generate that output. For countries, high productivity can lead to economic growth and development. Employees can receive higher wages, and company profits can increase without causing inflation. For individual organizations, increased productivity provides a more competitive cost structure and the ability to offer more competitive prices.

Organizations that hope to succeed globally look for ways to improve productivity. For example, McDonald's drastically reduced the amount of time it takes to cook its french fries—now only 65 seconds as compared with the 210 seconds it once took, saving time and other resources.[7] Toronto-based Canadian Imperial Bank of Commerce automated its purchasing function, saving several million dollars annually.[8] And Škoda, the Czech Republic car company owned by Germany's Volkswagen AG, improved its productivity through an intensive restructuring of its manufacturing process.[9]

Productivity is a composite of people and operations variables. To improve productivity, managers must focus on both. The late W. Edwards Deming, a renowned quality expert, believed that managers, not workers, were the primary source of increased productivity. Some of his suggestions for managers included planning for the long-term future, never being complacent about product quality, understanding whether problems were confined to particular parts of the production process or stemmed from the overall process itself, training workers for the job they're being asked to perform, raising the quality of line supervisors, requiring workers to do quality work, and so forth.[10] As you can see, Deming understood the interplay between people and operations. High productivity can't come solely from good "people management." The truly effective organization will maximize productivity by successfully integrating people into the overall operations system. For instance, at Simplex Nails Manufacturing in Americus, Georgia, employees were an integral part of the company's much-needed turnaround effort.[11] Some production workers were redeployed on a plant-wide cleanup and organization effort, which freed up floor space. The company's sales force was retrained and refocused to sell what customers wanted rather than what was in inventory. The results were dramatic. Inventory was reduced by more than 50 percent, the plant had 20 percent more floor space, orders were more consistent, and employee morale improved. Here's a company that recognized the important interplay between people and the operations system.

Strategic Role of Operations Management

The era of modern manufacturing originated over 100 years ago in North America, primarily in Detroit's automobile factories. The success that North American manufacturers experienced during World War II led manufacturing executives to believe that troublesome production problems had been conquered. These executives focused, instead, on improving other functional areas such as finance and marketing, and gave manufacturing little attention.

However, as Canadian and US executives neglected production, managers in Japan, Germany, and other countries took the opportunity to develop modern, computer-based, and technologically advanced facilities that fully integrated manufacturing operations into strategic planning decisions. The competition's success realigned world manufacturing leadership. North American manufacturers soon discovered that foreign goods were being made not only less expensively but also with better quality. Finally, by the late 1970s, Canadian and American executives recognized that they were facing a true crisis, and they responded. They invested heavily in improving manufacturing technology, increased the corporate authority and visibility of manufacturing executives, and began incorporating existing and future production requirements into the organization's overall strategic plan. Today, successful organizations recognize the crucial role that operations management plays as part of the overall organizational strategy to establish and maintain global leadership.[12]

The strategic role that operations management plays in successful organizational performance can be seen clearly as more organizations move toward managing their operations from a value chain perspective, which we discuss next.

What Is Value Chain Management, and Why Is It Important?

It's 11 p.m., and you're reading a text message from your parents, saying they want to buy you a laptop for your birthday and that you should order it. You log on to Dell's website and configure your dream machine. You hit the order button, and within three or four days, your dream computer is delivered to your front door, built to your exact specifications, ready to set up and use immediately to write the management assignment that's due tomorrow. Or consider that Siemens AG's computed tomography manufacturing plant in Forcheim, Germany, has established partnerships with about 30 suppliers. These suppliers are partners in the truest sense as they share responsibility with the plant for overall process performance. This arrangement has allowed Siemens to eliminate all inventory warehousing and has reduced the number of times paper changes hands when parts are ordered from 18 to 1. At the Timken plant in Canton, Ohio, electronic purchase orders are sent across the street to an adjacent "Supplier City," where many of its key suppliers have set up shop. The process takes milliseconds and costs less than 50 cents per purchase order. And when Black & Decker extended its line of handheld tools to include a glue gun, it outsourced the entire design and production to the leading glue gun manufacturer. Why? Because the company understood that glue guns don't require motors, which was what Black & Decker did best.[13]

As these examples show, closely integrated work activities among many different players are possible. How? The answer lies in value chain management. The concepts of value chain management have transformed operations management strategies and turned organizations around the world into finely tuned models of efficiency and effectiveness, strategically positioned to exploit competitive opportunities.

What Is Value Chain Management?

Every organization needs customers if it's going to survive and prosper. Even a not-for-profit organization must have "customers" who use its services or purchase its products. Customers want some type of value from the goods and services they purchase or use, and these customers decide what has value. Organizations must provide that value to attract and keep customers. **Value** is defined as the performance characteristics, features and attributes, and any other aspects of goods and services for which customers are willing to give up resources (usually money). For example, when you purchase Rihanna's new CD at Best Buy, a new pair of Australian sheepskin Ugg boots online at the company's website, a Wendy's bacon cheeseburger at the drive-through location near campus, or a haircut from your local hair salon, you're exchanging (giving up) money in return for the value you need or desire from these products—providing music during your evening study time, keeping your feet warm and fashionable during winter's cold weather, alleviating the lunchtime hunger pangs quickly since your next class starts in 15 minutes, or looking professionally groomed for the job interview you're going to next week.

How *is* value provided to customers? Through transforming raw materials and other resources into some product or service that end users need or desire when, where, and how they want it. However, that seemingly simple act of turning varied resources into something that customers value and are willing to pay for involves a vast array of interrelated work activities performed by different participants (suppliers, manufacturers, and even customers)—that is, it involves the value chain. The **value chain** is the entire series of organizational work activities that add value at each step, from raw materials to finished product. In its entirety, the value chain can encompass the supplier's suppliers to the customer's customers.[14]

Value chain management is the process of managing the sequence of activities and information along the entire value chain. In contrast to supply chain management, which is *internally* oriented and focuses on efficient flow of incoming materials (resources) to the organization, value chain management is *externally* oriented and focuses on both incoming materials and outgoing products and services. Whereas supply chain management is efficiency oriented (its goal is to reduce costs and make the organization more productive), value chain management is effectiveness oriented and aims to create the highest value for customers.[15]

Goal of Value Chain Management

Who has the power in the value chain? Is it the suppliers providing needed resources and materials? After all, they have the ability to dictate prices and quality. Is it the manufacturer who assembles those resources into a valuable product or service? Their contributions in creating a product or service are quite obvious. Is it the distributor that makes sure the product or service is available where and when the customer needs it? Actually, it's none of these! In value chain management, ultimately customers are the ones with power.[16]

value The performance characteristics, features, and attributes, as well as any other aspects of goods and services for which customers are willing to give up resources.

value chain The entire series of organizational work activities that add value at each step from raw materials to finished product.

value chain management The process of managing the sequence of activities and information along the entire value chain.

They're the ones who define what value is and how it's created and provided. Using value chain management, managers hope to find that unique combination whereby customers are offered solutions that truly meet their needs incredibly fast and at a price that competitors can't match.

The goal of value chain management is therefore to create a value chain strategy that meets and exceeds customers' needs and desires and allows for full and seamless integration among all members of the chain. A good value chain is one in which a sequence of participants work together as a team, each adding some component of value—such as faster assembly, more accurate information, better customer response and service, and so forth—to the overall process.[17] The better the collaboration among the various chain participants, the better the customer solutions. When value is created for customers and their needs and desires are satisfied, everyone along the chain benefits. For example, at Johnson Controls Inc., managing the value chain started first with improved relationships with internal suppliers and then expanded to external suppliers and customers. As the company's experience with value chain management improved, so did its connection with its customers, and this will ultimately pay off for all its value chain partners.[18]

Benefits of Value Chain Management

Collaborating with external and internal partners in creating and managing a successful value chain strategy requires significant investments in time, energy, and other resources, as well as a serious commitment by all chain partners. So why would managers ever choose to implement value chain management? A survey of manufacturers noted four primary benefits of value chain management: improved procurement, improved logistics, improved product development, and enhanced customer order management.[19]

Managing Operations by Using Value Chain Management

Even though it's the world's largest retailer, Walmart still looks for ways to more effectively and efficiently manage its value chain. Its current efforts involve taking over U.S. transportation services from suppliers in an effort to reduce the cost of transporting goods. The goal: "to handle suppliers' deliveries in instances where Walmart can do the same job for less, then use those savings to reduce prices in stores." Walmart believes it has the size and scale to allow it to ship most products more efficiently than the companies that produce the goods.[20]

Even if you're Walmart, managing an organization from a value chain perspective isn't easy. Approaches to giving customers what they want that may have worked in the past are likely no longer efficient or effective. Today's dynamic competitive environment demands new solutions from global organizations. Understanding how and why value is determined by the marketplace has led some organizations to experiment with a new business model, a concept we introduced in Chapter 4. For example, IKEA transformed itself from a small Swedish mail-order furniture operation into one of the world's largest furniture retailers by reinventing the value chain in that industry. The company offers customers well-designed products at substantially lower-than-typical prices in return for their willingness to take on certain key tasks traditionally done by manufacturers and retailers, such as getting furniture home and assembling it.[21] The company's creation of a new business model and its willingness to abandon old methods and processes has worked well.

Requirements of Value Chain Management

Exhibit MO-2 shows the six main requirements of a successful value chain strategy: coordination and collaboration, technology investment, organizational processes, leadership, employees, and organizational culture and attitudes.

Exhibit MO-2

Value Chain Strategy Requirements

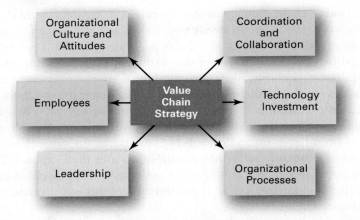

Coordination and Collaboration

For the value chain to achieve its goal of meeting and exceeding customers' needs and desires, collaborative relationships must exist among all chain participants.[22] Each partner must identify things that they may not value but that customers do. And sharing information and being flexible in terms of who in the value chain does what are important steps in building coordination and collaboration. This sharing of information and analysis requires open communication among the various value chain partners. For example, Kraft Foods believes that better communication with customers and with suppliers has facilitated timely delivery of goods and services.[23]

Technology Investment

Successful value chain management isn't possible without a significant investment in information technology. The payoff from this investment, however, is that information technology can be used to restructure the value chain to better serve end users. For example, each year the Houston-based food distributor Sysco ships 21.5 million tonnes of produce, meats, prepared meals, and other food-related products to restaurants, cafeterias, and sports stadiums. To get all that food safely to the right place at the right time, Sysco relies on a complex web of software, databases, scanning systems, and robotics.[24]

Organizational Processes

organizational processes The ways that organizational work is done.

Value chain management radically changes **organizational processes**—that is, the ways that organizational work is done. When managers decide to manage operations using value chain management, old processes are no longer appropriate. All organizational processes must be critically evaluated, from beginning to end, to see where value is being added. Non-value-adding activities should be eliminated. Questions such as Where can internal knowledge be leveraged to improve the flow of material and information? How can we better configure our product to satisfy both customers and suppliers? How can the flow of material and information be improved? and How can we improve customer service?" should be answered for each and every process. For example, when managers at Deere and Company implemented value chain management, a thorough process evaluation revealed that work activities needed to be better synchronized and interrelationships between multiple links in the value chain needed to be better managed. They changed numerous work processes division-wide in order to do this.[25] Three important conclusions can be made about organizational processes. First, better demand forecasting is necessary *and* possible because of closer ties with customers and suppliers. For example, in an effort to make sure that Listerine was on the store shelves when customers wanted it (known in the retail industry as *product replenishment rates*), Walmart and Pfizer's Consumer Healthcare Group collaborated on improving product demand forecast information. Through their mutual efforts, the partners boosted Walmart's sales of Listerine, an excellent outcome for both supplier and retailer. Customers also benefited because they were able to purchase the product when and where they wanted it.

Second, selected functions may need to be done collaboratively with other partners in the value chain. This collaboration may even extend to sharing employees. For instance, Saint-Gobain Performance Plastics places its own employees in customer sites and brings in employees of suppliers and customers to work on its premises.[26]

Finally, new measures are needed for evaluating performance of various activities along the value chain. Because the goal in value chain management is meeting and exceeding customers' needs and desires, managers need a better picture of how well this value is being created and delivered to customers. For example, when Nestlé USA implemented value chain management, it redesigned its metrics system to focus on one consistent set of measurements—including, for instance, accuracy of demand forecasts and production plans, on-time delivery, and customer service levels—that allowed the company to identify problem areas more quickly and take actions to resolve them.[27]

Leadership

Successful value chain management isn't possible without strong and committed leadership. From top organizational levels to lower levels, managers must support, facilitate, and promote the implementation and ongoing practice of value chain management. Managers must seriously commit to identifying what value is, how that value can best be provided, and how successful those efforts have been. A culture in which all efforts are focused on delivering superb customer value isn't possible without serious commitment on the part of the organization's leaders.

Also, it's important that managers outline expectations for what's involved in the organization's pursuit of value chain management. Ideally, this starts with a vision or mission statement that expresses the organization's commitment to identifying, capturing, and providing the highest possible value to customers. For instance, when American Standard began using value chain management, the CEO held dozens of meetings across the United States to explain the new competitive environment and why the company needed to create better working relationships with its value chain partners in order to better serve the needs of its customers.[28]

Then, managers should clarify expectations regarding each employee's role in the value chain. But clear expectations aren't important only for internal partners. Being clear about expectations also extends to external partners. For example, managers at American Standard identified clear requirements for suppliers and were prepared to drop any suppliers that couldn't meet the requirements, and they did so. The upside was that the suppliers that met the expectations benefited from more business, and American Standard had partners willing to work with them in delivering better value to customers.

Employees/Human Resources

We know from our discussions of management theories throughout this text book that employees are the organization's most important resource. Without employees, there would be no products produced or services delivered—in fact, there would be no organized efforts in the pursuit of common goals. Not surprisingly, employees play an important role in value chain management. The three main human resource requirements for value chain management are flexible approaches to job design, effective hiring process, and ongoing training.

Flexibility is the key to job design in value chain management. Traditional functional job roles—such as marketing, sales, accounts payable, customer service, and so forth—don't work with value chain management. Instead, jobs must be designed around work processes that create and provide value to customers. It takes flexible jobs and flexible employees.

In a value chain organization, employees may be assigned to work teams that tackle particular processes and may be asked to do different things on different days, depending on need. In such an environment—where customer value is best delivered through collaborative relationships that may change as customer needs change and where there are no standardized processes or job descriptions—an employee's ability to be flexible is critical. Therefore, the organization's hiring process must be designed to identify employees who have the ability to learn and adapt.

Finally, the need for flexibility also requires that there be a significant investment in continual and ongoing employee training. Whether that training involves learning how to use information technology software, how to improve the flow of materials throughout the chain, how to identify activities that add value, how to make better decisions faster, or how to improve any number of other potential work activities, managers must see to it that employees have the knowledge and tools they need to do their jobs efficiently and effectively.

Organizational Culture and Attitudes

The last requirement for value chain management is having a supportive organizational culture and attitudes. From our extensive description of value chain management, you could probably guess the type of organizational culture that's going to support its successful implementation! Those cultural attitudes include sharing, collaboration, openness, flexibility, mutual respect, and trust. And these attitudes encompass not only the internal partners in the value chain but external partners as well.

Obstacles to Value Chain Management

As desirable as the benefits of value chain management may be, managers must tackle several obstacles in managing the value chain, including organizational barriers, cultural attitudes, required capabilities, and people (Exhibit MO-3).

Organizational Barriers

At General Cable's manufacturing facility in Manchester, New Hampshire, one of the most interesting challenges faced by managers and employees in maintaining its world-class competitiveness is the 23 different nationalities that speak 12 languages besides English. Multiple languages make getting new messages out about anything that comes up especially tricky. But they've made it work using visual cues throughout the plant.[29]

Organizational barriers are among the most difficult obstacles to handle. These barriers include refusal or reluctance to share information, reluctance to shake up the status quo, and security issues. Without shared information, close coordination and collaboration is impossible. And the reluctance or refusal of employees to shake up the status quo can impede efforts toward value chain management and prevent its successful implementation. Finally, because value chain management relies heavily on a substantial information technology infrastructure, system security and internet security breaches are issues that need to be addressed.

Exhibit MO-3

Obstacles to Value Chain Management

Cultural Attitudes

Unsupportive cultural attitudes—especially trust and control—can be obstacles to value chain management. The trust issue—both lack of trust and too much trust—is a critical one. To be effective, partners in a value chain must trust each other. There must be a mutual respect for, and honesty about, each partner's activities all along the chain. When that trust doesn't exist, the partners will be reluctant to share information, capabilities, and processes. But too much trust can also be a problem. Just about any organization is vulnerable to theft of **intellectual property**—that is, proprietary information that's critical to an organization's efficient and effective functioning and competitiveness. You need to be able to trust your value chain partners so your organization's valuable assets aren't compromised.[30] Another cultural attitude that can be an obstacle is the belief that when an organization collaborates with external and internal partners, it no longer controls its own destiny. However, this just isn't the case. Even with the intense collaboration that's important to value chain management, organizations still control critical decisions such as what customers value, how much value they desire, and what distribution channels are important.[31]

> **intellectual property** Proprietary information that's critical to an organization's efficient and effective functioning and competitiveness.

Required Capabilities

We know from our earlier discussion of requirements for the successful implementation of value chain management that value chain partners need numerous capabilities. Several of these—coordination and collaboration, the ability to configure products to satisfy customers and suppliers, and the ability to educate internal and external partners—aren't easy. But they're essential to capturing and exploiting the value chain. Many of the companies we've described throughout this section endured critical, and oftentimes difficult, self-evaluations of their capabilities and processes in order to become more effective and efficient at managing their value chains.

People

The final obstacles to successful value chain management can be an organization's people. Without their unwavering commitment to do whatever it takes, value chain management won't be successful. If employees refuse to be flexible in their work—how and with whom they work—collaboration and cooperation throughout the value chain will be difficult to achieve.

In addition, value chain management takes an incredible amount of time and energy on the part of an organization's employees. Managers must motivate those high levels of effort from employees, which is not an easy thing to do.

Finally, a major human resource problem is a lack of experienced managers who can lead value chain management initiatives. Value chain management isn't very widespread, so there aren't a lot of managers who've done it successfully. However, this hasn't prevented progressive organizations from pursuing the benefits to be gained from value chain management.

Current Issues in Managing Operations

David Ritacco and Ben Graham of PartsSelect in Truro Nova Scotia use analytics to manage the day-to-day operations of their business and to manage the conversion rate of their customers (the percentage of visitors who proceed through the process to place an order). To do so, they use the visualization tool in Google Analytics. In addition to analytics, Ritacco and Graham use "A and B" testing to tweak performance of their site. For example, the company put an avatar on its website to speak with visitors (an actor from the United States who has played a minor role on the TV drama *Prison Break*). During the A and B test period, half the traffic to the website was directed to the conventional site, and half was driven to the site with the new avatar. Although Ritacco wasn't convinced that the avatar would work, Graham was in favour of it. At the end of the test period, they found a significant increase in conversion rate and order size on the website with the avatar. Based on these data, the avatar was incorporated into the customer experience.

Technology's Role in Operations Management

Global positioning systems (GPS) are changing a number of enterprises from shipping to shopping, from health care to law enforcement, and even farming.[32] Like many other technologies, GPS was invented for military use to track weapons and personnel as they moved. Now GPS is being used to track shipping fleets, revitalize consumer products such as watches or photos, and monitor parolees or sex offenders.

As we know from our previous discussion of value chain management, today's competitive marketplace has put tremendous pressure on organizations to deliver, in a timely manner, products and services that customers value. Smart companies are looking at ways to harness technology to improve operations management. Many fast-food companies are competing to see who can provide faster and better service to drive-through customers. With drive-through now representing a huge portion of sales, faster and better delivery can be a significant competitive edge. For instance, Wendy's has added awnings to some of its menu boards and replaced some of the text with pictures. Others use confirmation screens, a technology that helped McDonald's boost accuracy by more than 11 percent. And technology used by two national chains tells managers how much food they need to prepare by counting vehicles in the drive-through line and factoring in demand for current promotional and popular staple items.[33]

Although an organization's production activities are driven by the recognition that the customer is king, managers still need to be more responsive. For instance, operations managers need systems that can reveal available capacity, status of orders, and product quality while products are in the process of being manufactured, not just after the fact. To connect more closely with customers, production must be synchronized across the enterprise. To avoid bottlenecks and slowdowns, the production function must be a full partner in the entire business system.

Technology is making such extensive collaboration possible. Technology is also allowing organizations to control costs, particularly in the areas of predictive maintenance, remote diagnostics, and utility cost savings. For instance, new internet-compatible equipment contains embedded web servers that can communicate proactively—for example, if a piece of equipment breaks or reaches certain preset parameters indicating that it's about to break, it asks for help. Technology can do more than sound an alarm or light up an indicator button. For instance, some devices have the ability to initiate email or signal a pager of a supplier, the maintenance department, or a contractor, describing the specific problem and requesting parts and service. How much is such e-enabled maintenance control worth? It can be worth quite a lot if it prevents equipment breakdowns and subsequent production downtime.

Managers who understand the power of technology to contribute to more effective and efficient performance know that managing operations is more than the traditional view of simply producing the product. Instead, the emphasis is on working together with all the organization's business functions to find solutions to customers' business problems. Even service providers understand the power of technology for these tasks. For example, Southwest Airlines upgraded its cockpit software, enabling its pilots (who have been extensively trained) to fly precise satellite-based navigation approaches to airports, thus saving fuel, reducing delays, and cutting noise.[34]

Quality Initiatives

Quality problems are expensive. For example, even though Apple has had phenomenal success with its iPod, the batteries in the first three versions died after 4 hours instead of lasting up to 12 hours, as buyers expected. Apple's settlement with consumers cost close to $100 million (US). At Schering-Plough, problems with inhalers and other pharmaceuticals were traced to chronic quality control shortcomings, for which the company eventually paid a $500 million (US) fine. And in one recent year, the auto industry paid $14.5 billion (US) to cover the cost of warranty and repair work.[35]

Many experts believe that organizations unable to produce high-quality products won't be able to compete successfully in the global marketplace. What is quality? When you consider a product or service to have quality, what does that mean? Does it mean that the product doesn't break or quit working—that is, that it's reliable? Does it mean that the service is delivered in a way that you intended? Does it mean that the product does what it's supposed to do? Or does quality mean something else? In this case, we define **quality** as the ability of a product or service to reliably do what it's supposed to do and to satisfy customer expectations.

How is quality achieved? That's an issue managers must address. A good way to look at quality initiatives is with the management functions—planning, organizing and leading, and controlling—that need to take place.

quality The ability of a product or service to reliably do what it's supposed to do and to satisfy customer expectations.

Planning for Quality

Managers must have quality improvement goals and strategies and plans to achieve those goals. Goals can help focus everyone's attention on some objective quality standard. For instance, Caterpillar has a goal of applying quality improvement techniques to help cut costs.[36] Although this goal is specific and challenging, managers and employees are partnering together to pursue well-designed strategies to achieve the goals, and they are confident they can do so.

Organizing and Leading for Quality

Because quality improvement initiatives are carried out by organizational employees, it's important for managers to look at how they can best organize and lead them. For instance, at the Moose Jaw, Saskatchewan, plant of General Cable Corporation, every employee participates in continual quality assurance training. In addition, the plant manager believes wholeheartedly in giving employees the information they need to do their jobs better. He says, "Giving people who are running the machines the information is just paramount. You can set up your cellular structure, you can cross-train your people, you can use lean tools, but if you don't give people information to drive improvement, there's no enthusiasm." As you might expect, this company shares production data and financial performance measures with all employees.[37]

Organizations with extensive and successful quality improvement programs tend to rely on two important people approaches: cross-functional work teams and self-directed, or empowered, work teams. Because all employees, from upper to lower levels, must participate in achieving product quality, it's not surprising that quality-driven organizations rely on well-trained, flexible, and empowered employees.

Controlling for Quality

Quality improvement initiatives aren't possible without a means of monitoring and evaluating their progress. Whether it involves standards for inventory control, defect rate, raw materials procurement, or other operations management areas, controlling for quality is important. For instance, at the Northrup Grumman Corporation plant in Rolling Meadows, Illinois, several quality controls have been implemented, such as automated testing and IT that integrates product design and manufacturing and tracks process quality improvements. Also, employees are empowered to make accept/reject decisions about products throughout the manufacturing process. The plant manager explains, "This approach helps build quality into the product rather than trying to inspect quality into the product." But one of the most important things the company does is "go to war" with its customers— soldiers preparing for war or in live-combat situations. Again, the plant manager says, "What discriminates us is that we believe if we can understand our customers' mission as well as they do, we can help them be more effective. We don't wait for our customer to ask us to do something. We find out what our customer is trying to do and then we develop solutions."[38]

These types of quality improvement success stories aren't limited to US operations. For example, at a Delphi assembly plant in Matamoros, Mexico, employees worked hard to improve quality and made significant strides. The customer reject rate on shipped products is now 10 ppm (parts per million), down from 3000 ppm—an improvement of almost 300 percent.[39] Quality initiatives at several Australian companies, including Alcoa of Australia, Wormald Security, and Carlton and United Breweries, have led to significant quality improvements.[40] And at Valeo Klimasystemme GmbH of Bad Rodach, Germany, assembly teams build different climate-control systems for high-end German cars, including Mercedes and BMW. Quality initiatives by Valeo's employee teams have led to significant improvements in various quality standards.[41]

Quality Goals

To publicly demonstrate their quality commitment, many organizations worldwide have pursued challenging quality goals, the two best known of which are ISO 9000 and Six Sigma. It is interesting to note that the ISO standards have been extended to include the issues discussed in Chapter 5—environmental performance and social responsibility.

ISO 9000

ISO 9000, 14000, and 26000 A series of international quality management standards that set uniform guidelines for processes to ensure that products conform to customer requirements.

ISO 9000 is a series of international quality management standards established by the International Organization for Standardization (**www.iso.org**), which sets uniform guidelines for processes to ensure that products conform to customer requirements. These standards cover everything from contract review to product design to product delivery. The ISO 9000 standards have become the internationally recognized standard for evaluating and comparing companies in the global marketplace. In fact, this type of certification can be a prerequisite for doing business globally. Achieving ISO 9000 certification provides proof that a quality operations system is in place.

A recent survey of ISO 9000 certificates—awarded in 170 countries—showed that the number of registered sites worldwide was almost 900 000, an increase of 16 percent over the previous year.[42]

ISO 14000

ISO 14000 is a family of standards that address different aspects of environmental management, including environmental management systems (EMS) and encompassing both the requirements (ISO 14001:2004) and the guidelines (ISO 14004:2004). To be ISO 14001:2004 certified, an organization must commit to complying with applicable environmental legislation and regulations, as well as to continual improvement—for which the environmental management system provides the framework. The intent of ISO 14001:2004 "is to provide a framework for a holistic, strategic approach." The other standards in ISO 14000 address specific environmental aspects, including labelling, performance evaluation, life-cycle analysis communications, and auditing.[43]

ISO 26000

ISO 26000 provides guidance on best practice in social responsibility (SR) worldwide for private and public sector organizations. ISO 26000 provides a guide to what SR means and what organizations can do to operate in a socially responsible way. It also refines best practices that already exist and makes the information available for the good of the international community.[44]

Six Sigma

Six Sigma A quality standard that establishes a goal of no more than 3.4 defects per million units or procedures.

Motorola popularized the use of stringent quality standards more than 30 years ago, through a trademarked quality improvement program called Six Sigma.[45] Very simply, **Six Sigma** is a quality standard that establishes a goal of no more than 3.4 defects per million units or procedures. What does the name mean? *Sigma* is the Greek letter that statisticians use to define a standard deviation from a bell curve. The higher the sigma, the fewer the deviations from the norm—that is, the fewer the defects. At One Sigma, two-thirds of whatever is being measured falls within the curve. Two Sigma covers about 95 percent. At Six Sigma, you're about as close to defect free as you can get.[46] It's an ambitious quality goal! Although Six Sigma is an extremely high standard to achieve, many quality-driven businesses are using it and benefiting from it. For instance, General Electric company executives estimate that the company has saved billions in costs since 1995.[47] Other well-known companies pursuing Six Sigma include ITT Industries, Dow Chemical,

3M Company, American Express, Sony Corporation, Nokia Corporation, and Johnson & Johnson. Although manufacturers seem to make up the bulk of Six Sigma users, service companies such as financial institutions, retailers, and health care organizations are beginning to apply it as well. What impact can Six Sigma have? Let's look at an example.

It used to take Wellmark Blue Cross & Blue Shield, a managed-care health care company, 65 days or more to add a new doctor to its medical plans. Thanks to Six Sigma, the company discovered that half the processes they were using were redundant. With those unnecessary steps gone, the job now gets done in 30 days or less, and with reduced staff. The company has also been able to reduce its administrative expenses by $3 million per year, an amount passed on to consumers through lower health insurance premiums.[48]

Quality Goals Summary

Although it's important for managers to recognize that many positive benefits come from obtaining ISO 9000, 14000, and 26000 certification or Six Sigma, the key benefit comes from the quality improvement journey itself. In other words, the goal of quality certification should be having work processes and an operations system in place that enable organizations to meet customers' needs and employees to perform their jobs in a consistently high-quality way.

Mass Customization and Lean Organization

The term *mass customization* seems like an oxymoron. However, the design-to-order concept is becoming an important operations management issue for today's managers. **Mass customization** provides consumers with a product when, where, and how they want it.[49] Companies as diverse as BMW, Ford, Levi Strauss, Wells Fargo, Mattel, and Dell Computer are adopting mass customization to maintain or attain a competitive advantage. Mass customization requires flexible manufacturing techniques and continual customer dialogue.[50] Technology plays an important role in both.

mass customization Providing customers with a product when, where, and how they want it.

With flexible manufacturing, companies have the ability to quickly readjust assembly lines to make products to order. Using technology such as computer-controlled factory equipment, intranets, industrial robots, bar-code scanners, digital printers, and logistics software, companies can manufacture, assemble, and ship customized products with customized packaging to customers in incredibly short time frames. Dell is a good example of a company that uses flexible manufacturing techniques and technology to custom-build computers to customers' specifications.

Technology is also important in the continual dialogue with customers. Using extensive databases, companies can keep track of customers' likes and dislikes. And the internet has made it possible for companies to have ongoing dialogues with customers to learn about and respond to their exact preferences. For instance, on Amazon's website, customers are greeted by name and can get personalized recommendations of books and other products. The ability to customize products to a customer's desires and specifications starts an important relationship between the organization and the customer. If the customer likes the product and believes the customization provides value, he or she is more likely to be a repeat customer.

An intense focus on customers is also important to be a **lean organization**, which is an organization that understands what customers want, identifies customer value by analyzing all activities required to produce products, and then optimizes the entire process from the customer's perspective.[51] Lean organizations drive out all activities that do not add value in customers' eyes. For instance, companies like United Parcel Service, LVMH Moet Hennessy Louis Vuitton, and Harley-Davidson have pursued lean operations. "Lean operations adopt a philosophy of minimizing waste by striving for perfection through continuous learning, creativity, and teamwork."[52] As more manufacturers and service organizations adopt lean principles, they must realize that it's a never-ending journey toward being efficient and effective.

lean organization An organization that understands what customers want, identifies customer value by analyzing all activities required to produce products, and then optimizes the entire process from the customer's perspective

REVIEW AND DISCUSSION QUESTIONS

1. What is operations management?

2. Do you think that manufacturing or service organizations have the greater need for operations management? Explain.

3. What is a value chain and what is value chain management? What is the goal of value chain management? What are the benefits of value chain management?

4. What is required for successful value chain management? What obstacles exist to successful value chain management?

5. How could you use value chain management in your everyday life?

6. How does technology play a role in manufacturing?

7. What are ISO 9000 and Six Sigma?

8. Describe lean management and explain why it's important.

9. How might operations management apply to other managerial functions besides control?

10. Which is more critical to success in organizations: continuous improvement or quality control? Support your position.

PART FIVE   CONTROLLING

Management Practice

A Manager's Dilemma

"Prisons are easier to enter than Visa's top-secret Operations Center East (OCE), its biggest, newest and most advanced U.S. data center." And Rick Knight, Visa's head of global operations and engineering, is responsible for its security and functioning. Why all the precautions? Because Visa acknowledges that (1) hackers are increasingly savvy, (2) data is an increasingly desirable black-market commodity, and (3) the best way to keep itself safe is with an information network in a fortress that instantly responds to threats.

Every day, Visa processes some 150 million retail electronic payments from around the globe. (Its current record for processing transactions? 300.7 million on December 23, 2011.) And every day, Visa's system connects up to 2 billion debit and credit cards, millions of acceptance locations, 1.9 million ATMs, and 15 000 financial institutions. So what seems to us a simple swipe of a card or keying in our card numbers on an online transaction actually triggers a robust set of activities, including the basic sales transaction processing, risk management, and information-based services. That's why OCE's 130 workers have two jobs: "Keep hackers out and keep the network up, no matter what." And that's why Visa doesn't reveal the location of OCE—on the eastern seaboard is as specific as the description gets.

With a wall of screens in front of them, each employee sits at a desk with four monitors. In a room behind the main centre, three security experts keep an eye on things. "Knight says about 60 incidents a day warrant attention." Although hackers are a primary concern, Knight also worries about network capacity. Right now, maximum capacity is currently at 24 000 transactions per second. At some point, over that 24 000-message limit, "the network doesn't stop processing one message. It stops processing all of them."

Put yourself in Rick's shoes. Using what you've learned in Part 5 about controlling and managing operations, do you feel this is an appropriate level of control? Is this an environment that you would feel comfortable working im? What other managerial controls might be useful to Rick Knight?

Global Sense

Manufacturers have spent years building low-cost global supply chains. However, when those businesses are dependent on a global supply chain, any unplanned disruptions (political, economic, weather, natural disaster,

etc.) can wreak havoc on plans, schedules, and budgets. The Icelandic Eyjafjallajökull volcano in 2010 and the Japanese earthquake/tsunami and Thailand flooding in 2011 are still fresh in the minds of logistics, transportation, and operations managers around the globe. Although unexpected problems in the supply chain have always existed, now the far-reaching impact of something happening not in your own facility but thousands of miles away has created additional volatility and risk for managers and organizations. For instance, when the Icelandic volcano erupted, large portions of European airspace were shut down for more than a week, which affected air traffic worldwide. At BMW's plant in Spartanburg, South Carolina, air shipments of car components were delayed, workers' hours had to be scaled back, and plans were made for a possible shutdown of the entire facility. During the Thailand floods in late 2011, industrial parks that manufactured semiconductors for companies like Apple and Samsung were under water and crawling with crocodiles. After the Japanese earthquake and tsunami in early 2011 shut down dozens of contractors and subcontractors that supply many parts to the auto and technology industries, companies like Toyota, Honda, and Hewlett-Packard had to adjust to critical parts shortages.

Discuss the following questions in light of what you have learned:

- What types of plans would be best in these unplanned events?
- As Chapter 8 asks, how can managers plan effectively in dynamic environments?
- Could SWOT analysis be useful in these instances? Explain.
- How might managers use scenario planning in preparing for such disasters? (Scenario planning is discussed in Module 2, Planning and Control Techniques.)
- What types of managerial controls might be useful to managers during these events?
- How is the operations system, especially of manufacturing companies, affected by such global disruptions? What can managers do to minimize the impact of those disruptions?

Sources: R. Teijken, "Local Issues in Global Supply Chains," *Logistics & Transport Focus*, April 2012, pp. 41–43; J. Beer, "Sighted: The Ends of the Earth," *Canadian Business*, Winter 2011/2012, pp. 19–22; B. Powell, "When Supply Chains Break," *Fortune*, December 26, 2011, pp. 29–32; A. H. Merrill, R. E. Scale, and M. D. Sullivan, "Post-Natural Disaster Appraisal and Valuation: Lessons from the Japan Experience," *The Secured Lender*, November/December 2011, pp. 30–33; J. Rice, "Alternate Supply," *Industrial Engineer*, May 2011, p. 10; and "Risk Management: An Increasingly Small World," *Reactions*, April 2011, p. 252.

Chapter 1

1. Based on "How Cirque du Soleil's Hippy Circus Took Over the World," *Guardian Unlimited*, September 4, 2009, www.guardian.co.uk/stage/2009/sep/04/cirque-du-soleil-circus; Cirque du Soleil home page, www.cirquedusoleil.com/CirqueDuSoleil/en/Pressroom/cirq-uedusoleil/biographies/Laliberté_guy.htm (accessed July 9, 2010); K. Moore, "Creativity No Laughing Matter at Cirque du Soleil," *Globe and Mail*, March 2, 2010, www.theglobeandmail.com; K. Moore, "Daniel Lamarre: A CEO's High-Wire Act," *Globe and Mail*, December 29, 2009; information from the Cirque du Soleil website http://www.cirq-uedusoleil.com (accessed April 17, 2014).

2. J. Welch and S. Welch, "An Employee Bill of Rights," *Bloomberg BusinessWeek,* March 16, 2009, p. 72.

3. E. Frauenheim, "Managers Don't Matter," *Workforce Management Online,* April 2010; and K. A. Tucker and V. Allman, "Don't Be a Cat-and-Mouse Manager," The Gallup Organization, www.brain.gallup.com, September 9, 2004.

4. A. Taylor III, "Survival on Dealers' Row," *CNNMoney.com,* March 26, 2008.

5. "Work USA 2008/2009 Report: Driving Business Results through Continuous Engagement," Watson Wyatt Worldwide, Washington, DC.

6. D. J. Campbell, "The Proactive Employee: Managing Workplace Initiative," *Academy of Management Executive*, August 2000, pp. 52–66.

7. J. S. McClenahen, "Prairie Home Champion," *Industry Week*, October 2005, pp. 45–47.

8. "Interaction: First, Let's Fire All the Managers," *Harvard Business Review,* March 2012, pp. 20–21; and G. Hamel, "First, Let's Fire All the Managers," *Harvard Business Review,* December 2011, pp. 48–60.

9. data points box based on J. Yang and V. Bravo, "Would You Like to Have Your Manager's Job?" *USA Today Snapshots,* November 15, 2011, p. 1B; J. Yang and S. Ward, "Do You Think You Could Do a Better Job Than Your Boss?" *USA Today Snapshots,* November 7, 2011, p. 1B; J. Yang and S. Ward, "Is Working Part Time in a Management Position Possible?" *USA Today Snapshots,* October 11, 2011, p. 1B; R. J. Alsop, "The Last Word: Misery in Your Company," *Workforce Management Online,* August 9, 2011; J. Yang and K. Geiles, "The 'Horrible Boss' I Had Was …" *USA Today Snapshots,* August 4, 2011, p. 1B; and R. R. Hastings, "Study: Employees' Trust in Leaders Has Declined," *HR Magazine,* September 2011, p. 15.

10. K. Moore, "Daniel Lamarre: A CEO's High-Wire Act," *Globe and Mail*, December 29, 2009.

11. P. Drucker, *Management: Tasks, Responsibilities, Practices* (New York: Harper & Row, 1974).

12. H. Fayol, *Industrial and General Administration* (Paris: Dunod, 1916).

13. For a comprehensive review of this question, see C. P. Hales, "What Do Managers Do? A Critical Review of the Evidence," *Journal of Management*, January 1986, pp. 88–115.

14. H. Mintzberg, *The Nature of Managerial Work* (New York: Harper & Row, 1973); and J. T. Straub, "Put on Your Manager's Hat," *USA Today*, October 29, 2002, www.usatoday.com.

15. See, for example, L. D. Alexander, "The Effect Level in the Hierarchy and Functional Area Have on the Extent Mintzberg's Roles Are Required by Managerial Jobs," *Academy of Management Proceedings* (San Francisco, 1979), pp. 186–189; A. W. Lau and C. M. Pavett, "The Nature of Managerial Work: A Comparison of Public and Private Sector Managers," *Group and Organization Studies*, December 1980, pp. 453–466; M. W. McCall Jr. and C. A. Segrist, "In Pursuit of the Manager's Job: Building on Mintzberg," Technical Report No. 14 (Greensboro, NC: Center for Creative Leadership, 1980); C. M. Pavett and A. W. Lau, "Managerial Work: The Influence of Hierarchical Level and Functional Specialty," *Academy of Management Journal*, March 1983, pp. 170–177; C. P. Hales, "What Do Managers Do? A Critical Review of the Evidence," *Journal of Management*, January 1986, pp. 88–115; A. I. Kraut, P. R. Pedigo, D. D. McKenna, and M. D. Dunnette, "The Role of the Manager: What's Really Important in Different Management Jobs," *Academy of Management Executive*, November 1989, pp. 286–293; M. J. Martinko and W. L. Gardner, "Structured Observation of Managerial Work: A Replication and Synthesis," *Journal of Management Studies*, May 1990, pp. 330–357.

16. C. M. Pavett and A. W. Lau, "Managerial Work: The Influence of Hierarchical Level and Functional Specialty," *Academy of Management Journal*, March 1983, pp. 170–177.

17. S. J. Carroll and D. A. Gillen, "Are the Classical Management Functions Useful in Describing Managerial Work?" *Academy of Management Review*, January 1987, p. 48.

18. H. Koontz, "Commentary on the Management Theory Jungle—Nearly Two Decades Later," in *Management: A Book of Readings*, 6th ed., ed. H. Koontz, C. O'Donnell, and H. Weihrich (New York: McGraw-Hill, 1984); S. J. Carroll and D. A. Gillen, "Are the Classical Management Functions Useful in Describing Managerial Work?" *Academy of Management Review*, January 1987, p. 48; and P. Allan, "Managers at Work: A Large-Scale Study of the Managerial Job in New York City Government," *Academy of Management Journal*, September 1981, pp. 613–619.

19. E. White, "Firms Step Up Training for Front-Line Managers," *Wall Street Journal*, August 27, 2007, p. B3; Information from Dell website, www.dell.com (accessed April 18, 2014).

20. R. L. Katz, "Skills of an Effective Administrator," *Harvard Business Review*, September–October 1974, pp. 90–102.

21. D. Nebenzahl, "People Skills Matter Most," *Gazette* (Montreal), September 20, 2004, p. B1.

22. H. G. Barkema, J. A. C. Baum, and E. A. Mannix, "Management Challenges in a New Time," *Academy of Management Journal*, October 2002, pp. 916–930; M. A. Hitt, "Transformation of Management for the New Millennium," *Organizational Dynamics*, Winter 2000, pp. 7–17; T. Aeppel, "Power Generation," *Wall Street Journal*, April 7, 2000, p. A11; "Rethinking Work," *Fast Company*, April 2000, p. 253; "Workplace Trends Shifting Over Time," *Springfield News Leader*, January 2, 2000, p. 7B1; "Expectations: The State of the New Economy," *Fast Company*, September 1999, pp. 251–264; T. J. Tetenbaum, "Shifting Paradigms: From Newton to Chaos," *Organizational Dynamics*, Spring 1998, pp. 21–33; T. A. Stewart, "Brain Power: Who Owns It … How They Profit from It," *Fortune*, March 17, 1997, pp. 105–110; G. P. Zachary, "The Right Mix," *Wall Street Journal*, March 13, 1997, p. A11; W. H. Miller, "Leadership at a Crossroads," *IndustryWeek*, August 19, 1996, pp. 42–56; M. Scott, "Interview with Dee Hock," *Business Ethics*, May–June 1996, pp. 37–41; and J. O. C. Hamilton, S. Baker, and B. Vlasic, "The New Workplace," *BusinessWeek*, April 29, 1996, pp. 106–117.

23. Industry Canada, "What Is the Contribution of Small Businesses to Canada's Gross Domestic Product?" *SME Research and Statistics*,

August 2013, http://www.ic.gc.ca/eic/site/061.nsf/eng/02812.html (accessed April 17, 2014).

24. Statistics Canada, "Latest Release from the Labour Force Survey," *The Daily*, March, 2014, http://www.statcan.gc.ca/daily-quotidien/140404/dq140404a-eng.htm (accessed April 17, 2014).

25. Statistics Canada, "Latest Release from the Labour Force Survey," *The Daily*, March, 2014, http://www.statcan.gc.ca/daily-quotidien/140404/dq140404a-eng.htm (accessed April 17, 2014).

26. See "2012 Annual Report," *Canada Post*, http://www.canadapost.ca/cpo/mc/assets/pdf/aboutus/annualreport/2012_AR_Overview_en.pdf (accessed April 17, 2014); and "Twentieth Annual Report to the Prime Minister on the Public Service of Canada," *Clerk of the Privy Council*, http://www.clerk.gc.ca/local_grfx/docs/rpt/rpt2013-eng.pdf (accessed April 18, 2014).

27. Karl Moore, "Daniel Lamarre: A CEO's High-Wire Act," *Globe and Mail*, December 29, 2009.

28. J. B. Sorensen, "The Strength of Corporate Culture and the Reliability of Firm Performance," *Administrative Science Quarterly*, 2002, vol. 47, no. 1, pp. 70–91; and L. B. Rosenfeld, J. M. Richman, and S. K. May, "Information Adequacy, Job Satisfaction, and Organizational Culture in a Dispersed-Network Organization," *Journal of Applied Communication Research*, vol. 32, 2004, pp. 28–54.

29. Cited in E. Naumann and D. W. Jackson, Jr., "One More Time: How Do You Satisfy Customers?" *Business Horizons*, May/June 1999, p. 73.

30. Data from *The World Factbook 2012*, https://www.cia.gov/library/publications/the-world-factbook/, (accessed April 7, 2012).

31. C. B. Blocker, D. J. Flint, M. B. Myers, and S. F. Slater, "Proactive Customer Orientation and Its Role for Creating Customer Value in Global Markets," *Journal of the Academy of Marketing Science*, April 2011, pp. 216–233; D. Dougherty and A. Murthy, "What Service Customers Really Want," *Harvard Business Review*, September 2009, p. 22; and K. A. Eddleston, D. L. Kidder, and B. E. Litzky, "Who's the Boss? Contending With Competing Expectations From Customers and Management," *Academy of Management Executive*, November 2002, pp. 85–95.

32. See, for instance, D. Meinert, "Aim to Serve," *HR Magazine*, December 2011, p. 18; D. M. Mayer, M. G. Ehrhart, and B. Schneider, "Service Attribute Boundary Conditions of the Service Climate-Customer Satisfaction Link," *Academy of Management Journal*, October 2009, pp. 1034–1050; M. Groth, T. Hennig-Thurau, and G. Walsh, "Customer Reactions to Emotional Labor: The Roles of Employee Acting Strategies and Customer Detection Accuracy," *Academy of Management Journal*, October 2009, pp. 958–974; J. W. Grizzle, A. R. Zablah, T. J. Brown, J. C. Mowen, and J. M. Lee, "Employee Customer Orientation in Context: How the Environment Moderates the Influence of Customer Orientation on Performance Outcomes," *Journal of Applied Psychology*, September 2009, pp. 1227–1242; B. A. Gutek, M. Groth, and B. Cherry, "Achieving Service Success Through Relationships and Enhanced Encounters," *Academy of Management Executive*, November 2002, pp. 132–144; Eddleston, Kidder, and Litzky, "Who's the Boss? Contending With Competing Expectations From Customers and Management"; S. D. Pugh, J. Dietz, J. W. Wiley, and S. M. Brooks, "Driving Service Effectiveness Through Employee-Customer Linkages," *Academy of Management Executive*, November 2002, pp. 73–84; S. D. Pugh, "Service With a Smile: Emotional Contagion in the Service Encounter," *Academy of Management Journal*, October 2001, pp. 1018–1027; W. C. Tsai, "Determinants and Consequences of Employee Displayed Positive Emotions," *Journal of Management*, 27, no. 4, 2001, pp. 497–512; Naumann and Jackson, Jr., "One More Time: How Do You Satisfy Customers?"; and M. D. Hartline and O. C. Ferrell, "The Management of Customer-Contact Service Employees: An Empirical Investigation," *Journal of Marketing*, October 1996, pp. 52–70.

33. J. Swartz, "Twitter Helps Customer Service," *USA Today*, November 18, 2009, p. 3B; and J. Swartz, "Businesses Get Cheap Help from a Little Birdie," *USA Today*, June 26, 2009, p. 1B.

34. M. J. Piskorski, "Social Strategies That Work," *Harvard Business Review*, November 2011, pp. 116–122.

35. D. Ferris, "Social Studies: How to Use Social Media to Build a Better Organization," *Workforce Online*, February 12, 2012.

36. R. A. Hattori and J. Wycoff, "Innovation DNA," *Training and Development*, January 2002, p. 24.

37. R. Wagner, "One Store, One Team at Best Buy," *Gallup Brain*, August 12, 2004 http://brain.gallup.com/content/, (accessed November 28, 2005).

38. M. Kripalani, "Tata Taps A Vast R&D Shop—Its Own," *Bloomberg BusinessWeek Magazine*, April 8, 2009, p. 50.

39. P. E. Mott, *The Characteristics of Effective Organizations* (New York: HarperCollins, 1972).

40. M. Basadur, J. Conklin, and G. K. VanPatter, "Rethinking Wicked Problems Part 2: Unpacking Paradigms, Bridging Universes," *NextDJournal* 10, Conversation 10.3.

41. S. Rosenbloom, "Wal-Mart Unveils Plan to Make Supply Chain Greener," *New York Times Online*, February 25, 2010; "Environmental Responsibility", 2013 Global Responsibility Report, http://cdn.corporate.walmart.com/39/97/81c4b26546b3913979b260ea0a74/updated-2013-global-responsibility-report_130113953638624649.pdf (accessed April 18, 2014).

42. S. Clifford, "Unexpected Ally Helps Wal-Mart Cut Waste," *New York Times Online*, April 13, 2012.

43. KPMG Global Sustainability Services, *Sustainability Insights*, October 2007.

44. *Symposium on Sustainability—Profiles in Leadership*, New York, October 2001.

45. M. S. Plakhotnik and T. S. Rocco, "A Succession Plan for First-Time Managers," *T&D*, December 2011, pp. 42–45; P. Brotherton, "New Managers Feeling Lost at Sea," *T&D*, June 2011, p. 25; and "How Do We Help a New Manager Manage?" *Workforce Management Online*, June 16, 2011.

46. Based on H. Rothman, "The Boss as Mentor," *Nation's Business*, April 1993, pp. 66–67; J. B. Cunningham and T. Eberle, "Characteristics of the Mentoring Experience: A Qualitative Study," *Personnel Review*, June 1993, pp. 54–66; S. Crandell, "The Joys of Mentoring," *Executive Female*, March–April 1994, pp. 38–42; and W. Heery, "Corporate Mentoring Can Break the Glass Ceiling," *HRfocus*, May 1994, pp. 17–18.

47. R. D'Aprix, "A Simple Effective Formula for Leadership," *Strategic Communication Management*, May 2011, p. 14; R. Jaish, "Pieces of Eight," *e-learning age*, May 2011, p. 6; M. L. Stallard, "Google's Project Oxygen: A Case-Study in Connection Culture," www.human-resourcesiq.com, March 25, 2011; J. Aquino, "8 Traits of Stellar Managers, Defined by Googlers," *Business Insider*, March 15, 2011. Copyright © 2011 by Business Insider, Inc. Reprinted with permission; and A. Bryant, "Google's Quest to Build a Better Boss," *New York Times Online*, March 12, 2011.

Module 1

1. C. S. George, Jr., *The History of Management Thought*, 2nd ed. (Upper Saddle River, NJ: Prentice Hall, 1972), p. 4.

2. C. S. George, Jr., *The History of Management Thought*, 2nd ed. (Upper Saddle River, NJ: Prentice Hall, 1972), pp. 35–41.

3. F. W. Taylor, *Principles of Scientific Management* (New York: Harper, 1911), p. 44. For other information on Taylor, see S. Wagner-Tsukamoto, "An Institutional Economic Reconstruction of Scientific Management: On the Lost Theoretical Logic of Taylorism," *Academy of Management Review*, January 2007, pp. 105–117; R. Kanigel, *The One Best Way: Frederick Winslow Taylor and the Enigma of Efficiency* (New York: Viking, 1997); and M. Banta, *Taylored Lives: Narrative Productions in the Age of Taylor, Veblen, and Ford* (Chicago: University of Chicago Press, 1993).

4. See for example, F. B. Gilbreth, *Motion Study* (New York: Van Nostrand, 1911); and F. B. Gilbreth and L. M. Gilbreth, *Fatigue Study* (New York: Sturgis and Walton, 1916).

5. H. Fayol, *Industrial and General Administration* (Paris: Dunod, 1916).

6. M. Weber, *The Theory of Social and Economic Organizations*, ed. T. Parsons, trans. A. M. Henderson and T. Parsons (New York: Free Press, 1947); and M. Lounsbury and E. J. Carberry, "From King to Court Jester? Weber's Fall from Grace in Organizational Theory," *Organization Studies*, vol. 26, no. 4, 2005, pp. 501–525.

7. E. Mayo, *The Human Problems of an Industrial Civilization* (New York: Macmillan, 1933); and F. J. Roethlisberger and W. J. Dickson, *Management and the Worker* (Cambridge, MA: Harvard University Press, 1939).

8. See, for example, G. W. Yunker, "An Explanation of Positive and Negative Hawthorne Effects: Evidence from the Relay Assembly Test Room and Bank Wiring Observation Room Studies," paper presented, Academy of Management Annual Meeting, August 1993, Atlanta, Georgia; S. R. Jones, "Was There a Hawthorne Effect?" *American Sociological Review*, November 1992, pp. 451–468; and S. R. G. Jones, "Worker Interdependence and Output: The Hawthorne Studies Reevaluated," *American Sociological Review*, April 1990, pp. 176–190; J. A. Sonnenfeld, "Shedding Light on the Hawthorne Studies," *Journal of Occupational Behavior*, April 1985, pp. 111–130; B. Rice, "The Hawthorne Defect: Persistence of a Flawed Theory," *Psychology Today*, February 1982, pp. 70–74; R. H. Franke and J. Kaul, "The Hawthorne Experiments: First Statistical Interpretations," *American Sociological Review*, October 1978, pp. 623–643; and A. Carey, "The Hawthorne Studies: A Radical Criticism," *American Sociological Review*, June 1967, pp. 403–416.

9. N. Zamiska, "Plane Geometry: Scientists Help Speed Boarding of Aircraft," *Wall Street Journal*, November 2, 2005, p. A1+.

10. See, for example, J. Jusko, "Tried and True," *IW*, December 6, 1999, pp. 78–84; T. A. Stewart, "A Conversation with Joseph Juran," *Fortune*, January 11, 1999, pp. 168–170; J. R. Hackman and R. Wageman, "Total Quality Management: Empirical, Conceptual, and Practical Issues," *Administrative Science Quarterly*, June 1995, pp. 309–42; T. C. Powell, "Total Quality Management as Competitive Advantage: A Review and Empirical Study," *Strategic Management Journal*, January 1995, pp. 15–37; R. K. Reger, L. T. Gustafson, S. M. Demarie, and J. V. Mullane, "Reframing the Organization: Why Implementing Total Quality Is Easier Said Than Done," *Academy of Management Review*, July 1994, pp. 565–584; C. A. Reeves and D. A. Bednar, "Defining Quality: Alternatives and Implications," *Academy of Management Review*, July 1994, pp. 419–445; J. W. Dean Jr. and D. E. Bowen, "Management Theory and Total Quality: Improving Research and Practice through Theory Development," *Academy of Management Review*, July 1994, pp. 392–418; B. Krone, "Total Quality Management: An American Odyssey," *The Bureaucrat*, Fall 1990, pp. 35–38; and A. Gabor, *The Man Who Discovered Quality* (New York: Random House, 1990).

11. M. Barbaro, "A Long Line for a Shorter Wait at the Supermarket," *New York Times Online*, June 23, 2007.

12. S. Haines, "Become a Strategic Thinker," *Training*, October/November 2009, p. 64; and K. B. DeGreene, *Sociotechnical Systems: Factors in Analysis, Design, and Management* (Upper Saddle River, NJ: Prentice Hall, 1973), p. 13.

Chapter 2

1. Based on R. Chang, "At 3M Staff Get Time Off for Eureka Moments," *Straits Times, Singapore*, February 26, 2010; A. Nanavati, "Find a Middle Path," *Outlook Business India*, May 29, 2010; B. NNeji, "Improve Processes, Improve Innovation; Equally Critical: Process Improvement and Quality Must Work Together," *Advertising Age*, June 25, 2007.

2. "BP Braced for Shakeup at Top," *Dow Jones International News*, July 3, 2010; Krauss, Clifford, "Judge Accepts BP's $ Billion Criminal Settlement Over Gulf Oil Spill," *New York Times*, January 29, 2013.

3. B. Cooper, "Blue Mantle Will Close on April 30: Other Closures Hurt Business," *Leader Post*, March 20, 2004, p. B2.

4. For insights into the symbolic view, see J. Pfeffer, "Management as Symbolic Action: The Creation and Maintenance of Organizational Paradigms," in *Research in Organizational Behavior*, vol. 3, ed. L. L. Cummings and B. M. Staw, pp. 1–52 (Greenwich, CT: JAI Press, 1981); D. C. Hambrick and S. Finkelstein, "Managerial Discretion: A Bridge between Polar Views of Organizational Outcomes," in *Research in Organizational Behavior*, vol. 9, ed. L. L. Cummings and B. M. Staw, pp. 369–406 (Greenwich, CT: JAI Press, 1987); J. A. Byrne, "The Limits of Power," *BusinessWeek*, October 23, 1987, pp. 33–35; J. R. Meindl and S. B. Ehrlich, "The Romance of Leadership and the Evaluation of Organizational Performance," *Academy of Management Journal*, March 1987, pp. 91–109; C. R. Schwenk, "Illusions of Management Control? Effects of Self-serving Attributions on Resource Commitments and Confidence in Management," *Human Relations*, April 1990, pp. 333–347; S. M. Puffer and J. B. Weintrop, "Corporate Performance and CEO Turnover: The Role of Performance Expectations," *Administrative Science Quarterly*, March 1991, pp. 1–19; and "Why CEO Churn Is Healthy," *BusinessWeek*, November 13, 2000, p. 230.

5. T. M. Hout, "Are Managers Obsolete?" *Harvard Business Review*, March–April 1999, pp. 161–168; and J. Pfeffer, "Management as Symbolic Action: The Creation and Maintenance of Organizational Paradigms," in *Research in Organizational Behavior*, vol. 3, ed. L. L. Cummings and B. M. Staw, pp. 1–52 (Greenwich, CT: JAI Press, 1981).

6. Based on R. Chang, "At 3M Staff Get Time Off for Eureka Moments," *Straits Times* (Singapore) February 26, 2010; A. Nanavati, "Find a Middle Path," *Outlook Business India*, May 29, 2010; B. NNeji, "Improve Processes, Improve Innovation; Equally Critical: Process Improvement and Quality Must Work Together," *Advertising Age*, June 25, 2007.

7. Example based on "HBC Announces Future President of Saks Fifth Avenue," *Business Wire*, September 16, 2013.

8. L. Smircich, "Concepts of Culture and Organizational Analysis," *Administrative Science Quarterly*, September 1983, p. 339; D. R. Denison, "What Is the Difference between Organizational Culture and Organizational Climate? A Native's Point of View on a Decade of Paradigm Wars" (paper presented at Academy of Management Annual Meeting, Atlanta, Georgia, 1993); and M. J. Hatch, "The Dynamics of Organizational Culture," *Academy of Management Review*, October 1993, pp. 657–693.

9. K. Shadur and M. A. Kienzle, "The Relationship between Organizational Climate and Employee Perceptions of Involvement," *Group & Organization Management*, December 1999, pp. 479–503; and A. M. Sapienza, "Believing Is Seeing: How Culture Influences the Decisions Top Managers Make," in *Gaining Control of the Corporate Culture*, ed. R. H. Kilmann, M. J. Saxton, and R. Serpa (San Francisco: Jossey-Bass, 1985), p. 68.

10. C. A. O'Reilly III, J. Chatman, and D. F. Caldwell, "People and Organizational Culture: A Profile Comparison Approach to Assessing Person-Organization Fit," *Academy of Management Journal*,

September 1991, pp. 487–516; and J. A. Chatman and K. A. Jehn, "Assessing the Relationship between Industry Characteristics and Organizational Culture: How Different Can You Be?" *Academy of Management Journal*, June 1994, pp. 522–553.

11. Y. Berson, S. Oreg, and T. Dvir, "CEO Values, Organizational Culture, and Firm Outcomes," *Journal of Organizational Behavior,* July 2008, pp. 615–633; and E. H. Schien, *Organizational Culture and Leadership* (San Francisco: Jossey-Bass, 1985), pp. 314–315.

12. A. E. M. Va Vianen, "Person-Organization Fit: The Match Between Newcomers' and Recruiters' Preferences for Organizational Cultures," *Personnel Psychology*, Spring 2000, pp. 113–149; K. Shadur and M. A. Kienzle, *Group & Organization Management*; P. Lok and J. Crawford, "The Relationship between Commitment and Organizational Culture, Subculture, and Leadership Style," *Leadership & Organization Development Journal*, vol. 20, no. 6/7, 1999, pp. 365–374; C. Vandenberghe, "Organizational Culture, Person-Culture Fit, and Turnover: A Replication in the Health Care Industry," *Journal of Organizational Behavior,* March 1999, pp. 175–184; and C. Orphen, "The Effect of Organizational Cultural Norms on the Relationships between Personnel Practices and Employee Commitment," *Journal of Psychology*, September 1993, pp. 577–579.

13. See, for example, J. B. Sorensen, "The Strength of Corporate Culture and the Reliability of Firm Performance," *Administrative Science Quarterly*, 2002, vol. 47, no. 1, pp. 70–91; R. Goffee and G. Jones, "What Holds the Modern Company Together?" *Harvard Business Review*, November–December 1996, pp. 133–148; Collins and Porras, "Building Your Company's Vision," *Harvard Business Review*, September–October 1996, pp. 65–77; J. C. Collins and J. I. Porras, *Built to Last* (New York: HarperBusiness, 1994); G. G. Gordon and N. DiTomaso, "Predicting Corporate Performance from Organizational Culture," *Journal of Management Studies*, November 1992, pp. 793–798; J. P. Kotter and J. L. Heskett, *Corporate Culture and Performance* (New York: Free Press, 1992), pp. 15–27.

14. Sorensen, "The Strength of Corporate Culture and the Reliability of Firm Performance," pp. 70–91; and L. B. Rosenfeld, J. M. Richman, and S. K. May, "Information Adequacy, Job Satisfaction, and Organizational Culture in a Dispersed-Network Organization," *Journal of Applied Communication Research*, vol. 32, 2004, pp. 28–54.

15. See J. M. Jermier, J. Slocum, L. Fry, and J. Gaines, "Organizational Subcultures in a Soft Bureaucracy: Resistance Behind the Myth and Facade of an Official Culture," *Organization Science*, May 1991, pp. 170–194; S. A. Sackmann, "Culture and Subcultures: An Analysis of Organizational Knowledge," *Administrative Science Quarterly*, March 1992, pp. 140–161; R. F. Zammuto, "Mapping Organizational Cultures and Subcultures: Looking Inside and Across Hospitals" (paper presented at the 1995 National Academy of Management Conference, Vancouver, BC, August 1995); and G. Hofstede, "Identifying Organizational Subcultures: An Empirical Approach," *Journal of Management Studies*, January 1998, pp. 1–12.

16. T. A. Timmerman, "Do Organizations Have Personalities?" (paper presented at the 1996 National Academy of Management Conference, Cincinnati, OH, August 1996).

17. See http://thecanadianencyclopedia.com/index.cfm?PgNm=TC E&Params=M1ARTM0011001; www.magna.com/magna/en/about/ (accessed September 11, 2007); and B. Simon, "Work Ethic and the Magna Carta," *Financial Post Daily*, March 20, 1997, p. 14.

18. C. Edwards, "Why Tech Bows to Best Buy," *BusinessWeek Online*, December 10, 2009.

19. S. E. Ante, "The New Blue," *BusinessWeek*, March 17, 2003, p. 82.

20. C. C. Miller, "Now at Starbucks: A Rebound," *New York Times Online*, January 21, 2010; J. Jargon, "Latest Starbucks Buzzword: 'Lean' Japanese Techniques," *Wall Street Journal,* August 4, 2009, pp. A1+; P. Kafka, "Bean Counter," *Forbes*, February 28, 2005, pp. 78–80; A. Overholt, "Listening to Starbucks," *Fast Company*, July

2004, pp. 50–56; and B. Filipczak, "Trained by Starbucks," *Training*, June 1995, pp. 73–79.

21. P. Guber, "The Four Truths of the Storyteller," *Harvard Business Review,* December 2007, pp. 53–59; S. Denning, "Telling Tales," *Harvard Business Review*, May 2004, pp. 122–129; T. Terez, "The Business of Storytelling," *Workforce*, May 2002, pp. 22–24; J. Forman, "When Stories Create an Organization's Future," *Strategy & Business*, Second Quarter 1999, pp. 6–9; C. H. Deutsch, "The Parables of Corporate Culture," *New York Times*, October 13, 1991, p. F25; and D. M. Boje, "The Storytelling Organization: A Study of Story Performance in an Office-Supply Firm," *Administrative Science Quarterly*, March 1991, pp. 106–126.

22. G. Colvin, "Value Driven," *Fortune,* November 23, 2009, p. 24.

23. J. Useem, "Jim McNerney Thinks He Can Turn 3M From a Good Company into a Great One—With a Little Help from His Former Employer, General Electric," *Fortune*, August 12, 2002, pp. 127–132.

24. Denning, 2004; and A. M. Pettigrew, "On Studying Organizational Cultures," *Administrative Science Quarterly*, December 1979, p. 576.

25. J. E. Vascellaro, "Facebook CEO in No Rush to 'Friend' Wall Street," *Wall Street Journal,* March 4, 2010, p. A1+.

26. E. H. Schein, "Organizational Culture," *American Psychologist,* February 1990, pp. 109–119.

27. M. Zagorski, "Here's the Drill," *Fast Company*, February 2001, p. 58.

28. "Slogans That Work," Forbes.com Special, January 7, 2008, p. 99.

29. P. Keegan, "Best Companies to Work For: Maxine Clark and Kip Tindell Exchange Jobs," *Fortune,* February 8, 2010, pp. 68–72.

30. data points box based on R. J. Alsop, "The Last Word: Tapping Social Workers," *Workforce Management,* May 2011, p. 50; R. E. Silverman, "Latest Game Theory Mixes Work and Play," *Wall Street Journal,* October 10, 2011, p. B11; K. E. Ayers, "A Culture of Proactive Employees Will Let the Boss Know if His Fly Is Unzipped," *Workforce Management Online,* August 23, 2011; R. Wartzman, "Executives Are Wrong to Devalue Values," *Bloomberg BusinessWeek Online,* October 30, 2009; J. MacIntyre, "Hurdles to Re-Entry," *Springfield, Missouri Business Journal,* August 16–22, 2010, p. 16; G. Kranz, "Fit to be Tied? Recession May Inspire More Formal Work Attire," *Workforce Management Online,* October 18, 2008; and *Global Firms in 2020* (Economist Intelligence Unit, 2010), www.shrm.org, July 2, 2011.

31. See B. Victor and J. B. Cullen, "The Organizational Bases of Ethical Work Climates," *Administrative Science Quarterly*, March 1988, pp. 101–125; L. K. Trevino, "A Cultural Perspective on Changing and Developing Organizational Ethics," in *Research in Organizational Change and Development*, vol. 4, ed. W. A. Pasmore and R. W. Woodman (Greenwich, CT: JAI Press, 1990); and M. W. Dickson, D. B. Smith, M. W. Grojean, and M. Ehrhart, "An Organizational Climate Regarding Ethics: The Outcome of Leader Values and the Practices That Reflect Them," *Leadership Quarterly*, Summer 2001, pp. 197–217.

32. Seth Stevenson, "Patagonia's Founder is America's Most Unlikely Business Guru," *Wall Street Journal Magazine*, April 26, 2012, http://online.wsj.com/news/articles/SB10001424052702303513404577352 221465986612 (accessed November 2, 2013).

33. "The World's 50 Most Innovative Companies," *Fast Company*, March 2008, p. 93; T. Kelley and J. Littman, *The Ten Faces of Innovation: IDEO's Strategies for Defeating the Devil's Advocate and Driving Creativity Throughout Your Organization* (New York: Currency, 2005); C. Fredman, "The IDEO Difference," *Hemispheres*, August 2002, pp. 52–57; and T. Kelley and J. Littman, *The Art of Innovation* (New York: Currency, 2001).

34. B. Nussbaum, " IDEO Makes the Top 25 Global Innovators— Here's Why," *Businessweek*, April 17, 2006.

35. J. F. Suri, *Thoughtless Acts? Observations on Intuitive Design* (San Francisco: Chronicle Books, 2005)

36. "Cirque du Soleil: Creating a Culture of Extraordinary Creativity," InnovationNetwork, http://innovationnetwork.biz/inmembership/emergent-practices/cirque.html (accessed March 14, 2011).

37. J. Yang and R. W. Ahrens, "Culture Spurs Innovation," *USA Today*, February 25, 2008, p. 1B.

38. J. Cable, "Building an Innovative Culture," *Industry Week*, March 2010, pp. 32–27; M. Hawkins, "Create a Climate of Creativity," *Training*, January 2010, p. 12; and L. Simpson, "Fostering Creativity," *Training*, December 2001, p. 56.

39. K. Aaserud, C. Cornell, J. McElgunn, K. Shiffman, and R. Wright, "The Golden Rules of Growth: Isadore Sharp," *PROFIT*, May 2007, www.canadianbusiness.com/entrepreneur/managing/article.jsp?content=20070419_095326_4460.

40. L. Gary, "Simplify and Execute: Words to Live By in Times of Turbulence," *Harvard Management Update*, January 2003, p. 12.

41. Based on M. J. Bitner, B. H. Booms, and L. A. Mohr, "Critical Service Encounters: The Employee's Viewpoint," *Journal of Marketing*, October 1994, pp. 95–106; M. D. Hartline and O. C. Ferrell, "The Management of Customer-Contact Service Employees: An Empirical Investigation," *Journal of Marketing*, October 1996, pp. 52–70; M. L. Lengnick-Hall and C. A. Lengnick-Hall, "Expanding Customer Orientation in the HR Function," *Human Resource Management*, Fall 1999, pp. 201–214; B. Schneider, D. E. Bowen, M. G. Ehrhart, and K. M. Holcombe, "The Climate for Service: Evolution of a Construct," in *Handbook of Organizational Culture and Climate*, ed. N. M. Ashkanasy, C. P. M. Wilderom, and M. F. Peterson, pp. 21–36 (Thousand Oaks, CA: Sage, 2000); M. D. Hartline, J. G. Maxham III, and D. O. McKee, "Corridors of Influence in the Dissemination of Customer-Oriented Strategy to Customer Contact Service Employees," *Journal of Marketing*, April 2000, pp. 35–50; L. A. Bettencourt, K. P. Gwinner, and M. L. Mueter, "A Comparison of Attitude, Personality, and Knowledge Predictors of Service-Oriented Organizational Citizenship Behaviors," *Journal of Applied Psychology*, February 2001, pp. 29–41; R. C. Ford and C. P. Heaton, "Lessons from Hospitality That Can Serve Anyone," *Organizational Dynamics*, Summer 2001, pp. 30–47; S. D. Pugh, J. Dietz, J. W. Wiley, and S. M. Brooks, "Driving Service Effectiveness through Employee-Customer Linkages," *Academy of Management Executive*, November 2002, pp. 73–84; K. A. Eddleston, D. L. Kidder, and B. E. Litzky, "Who's the Boss? Contending with Competing Expectations from Customers and Management," *Academy of Management Executive*, November 2002, pp. 85–95; and B. A. Gutek, M. Groth, and B. Cherry, "Achieving Service Success through Relationships and Enhanced Encounters," *Academy of Management Executive*, November 2002, pp. 132–144.

42. Thanks to a reviewer, Dr. Michelle Inness, University of Alberta, for providing this insight.

43. This box is based on Y. Cole, "Holding Managers Accountable for Diversity Success," *DiversityInc*. Special Issue 2006, pp. 14–19; "Diversity Is Important to the Bottom Line," *HR Powerhouse*, www.hrpowerhouse.com, January 21, 2006; P. Rosinski, *Coaching Across Cultures: New Tools for Leveraging National, Corporate, and Professional Differences* (London: Nicholas Brealey, 2003); "Diversity at the Forefront," *BusinessWeek*, November 4, 2002, pp. 27–38; "Talking to Diversity Experts: Where Do We Go from Here?" *Fortune*, September 30, 2002, pp. 157–172; "Keeping Your Edge: Managing a Diverse Corporate Culture," *Fortune*, June 11, 2001, pp. S1–S18; "Diversity Today," *Fortune*, June 12, 2000, pp. S1–S24; O. C. Richard, "Racial Diversity, Business Strategy, and Firm Performance: A Resource-Based View," *Academy of Management Journal*, April 2000, pp. 164–177; A. Markels, "How One Hotel Manages Staff's Diversity," *Wall Street Journal*, November 20, 1996, pp. B1+; C. A. Deutsch, "Corporate Diversity in Practice," *New York Times*, November 20, 1996, pp. C1+; and D. A. Thomas and R. J. Ely, "Making Differences Matter: A New Paradigm for Managing Diversity," *Harvard Business Review*, September–October 1996, pp. 79–90.

44. D. Kawamoto, "Dow Jones Decline Mimics Great Depression," *cnet News*, Business Tech, http://news.cnet.com/8301-1001_3-10185559-92.html (accessed July 3, 2010).

45. Information taken from the 2008 10-K annual report filed by 3M. *Bloomberg BusinessWeek* (accessed July 3, 2010).

46. J. Greenfield, "Kindle Most Popular Device For Ebooks, Beating Out iPad; Tablets On the Rise," *Forbes*, October 30, 2013; J. Greengield, "Taking Another Look At Ebook Upstart Kobo," *Forbes*, August 28, 2013; P. Svensson, "Microsoft Backs B&N in Battle of the e-Books," The Associated Press, *USA Today*, May 1, 2012, p. 3B; J. A. Trachtenberg and M. Peers, "Barnes & Noble Seeks Next Chapter," *Wall Street Journal*, January 6, 2012, pp. A1+; J. Bosman and M. J. De La Merced, "Barnes & Noble Considers Spinning Off Its Nook Unit," IPO Offerings .com, January 5, 2012; M. Maxwell, "Barnes & Noble's Digital Strategy Gaining Traction," *Wall Street Journal*, August 31, 2011, p. B3; J. A. Trachtenberg, S. Schechner, and G. Chon, "B&N Vulnerable to Rivals: Amazon, Apple Loom as Bookseller's Takeover Offer Dies," *Wall Street Journal Online*, August 20, 2011; A. Flood, "Hardback Sales Plummeting in Age of the ebook," *The Guardian*, www.guardian.co.uk, August 12, 2011; and J. Bosman, "Publishing Gives Hints of Revival, Data Show," *New York Times Online*, August 9, 2011.

47. C. MacLeod, "Chinese Divided Over Google Move," *Garnett News Service*, March 25, 2010.

48. A. Campbell, "Richmond Walmart gets green light after 10 years of rejection," *The Vancouver Sun* November 19, 2013, http://www.vancouversun.com/news/Richmond+Walmart+gets+green+light+after+years+rejection/9185437/story.html; J. Greenwood, "Home Depot Runs into Vancouver Red Tape," *Financial Post (National Post)*, May 10, 2004, pp. FP1, FP11.

49. D. Calleja, "Equity or Else," *Canadian Business*, March 19, 2001, p. 31.

50. T. S. Mescon and G. S. Vozikis, "Federal Regulation—What Are the Costs?" *Business*, January–March 1982, pp. 33–39.

51. J. Thorpe, "Inter-Provincial Trade Barriers Still a Concern for Executives 'Handicapping Country Economically,'" *Financial Post (National Post)*, September 13, 2004, p. FP2.

52. C. Sands, "Canada's Problem: Domestic Trade Barriers," *American*, May 22, 2007, www.american.com/archive/2007/may-0507/canada2019s-problem-domestic-trade-barriers.

53. C. Hausman, "Americans See Inequality as a Major Problem," Ethics Newsline, www.globalethics.org/newsline, April 9, 2012.

54. E. Porter, "Inequality Undermines Democracy," *New York Times Online*, March 20, 2012.

55. J. Cox, "Occupy Wall Street: They're Back, But Does Anyone Care?" CNBC.com, April 30, 2012; L. Visconti, "Ask the White Guy: Why Are Disparities in Income Distribution Increasing?" DiversityInc .com, April 10, 2012; P. Meyer, "Income Inequality *Does* Matter," *USA Today*, March 28, 2012, p. 9A; E. Porter, "Inequality Undermines Democracy," *New York Times Online*, March 20, 2012; T. Cowen, "Whatever Happened to Discipline and Hard Work?" *New York Times Online*, November 12, 2011; and A. Davidson, "It's Not Just About the Millionaires," *New York Times Online*, November 9, 2011.

56. A. Zolli, "Demographics: The Population Hourglass," *Fast Company*, March 2006, pp. 56–63.

57. S. Jayson, "iGeneration Has No Off Switch," *USA Today*, February 10, 2010, pp. 1D+; and L. Rosen, *Rewired: Understanding the iGeneration and the Way They Learn* (Palgrave-McMillan), 2010.

58. B. Horovitz, "Generation Whatchamacallit," *USA Today*, May 4, 2012, p. 1B+.

59. Statistics Canada, "Census Snapshot of Canada: Population (Age and Sex)," *Canadian Social Trends*, Cat. no. 11-008, www.statcan.gc.ca/pub/11-008-x/2007006/article/10379-eng.pdf (accessed July 5, 2010).

60. Human Resources and Skills Development Canada, "Canadians in Context—Aging Population," *Indicators of Well-Being in Canada*, www4.hrsdc.gc.ca/.3ndic.1t.4r@-eng.jsp?iid=33 (accessed July 5, 2010).

61. Center for Strategic and International Studies, *Global Aging Initiative*, http://csis.org/program/global-aging-initiative (accessed July 5, 2010).

62. R. W. Davis, "It's Time to Bet on Genomics," *Forbes*, June 1, 2012, http://www.forbes.com/sites/forbesleadershipforum/2012/06/01/its-time-to-bet-on-genomics/; D. Drell and A. Adamson, "Fast Forward to 2020: What to Expect in Molecular Medicine," Human Genome Project, 2003, www.ornl.gov/sci/techresources/Human_Genome/medicine/tnty (accessed March 19, 2011).

63. "Application and Products: Putting Technology to Use," National Nanotechnology Initiative, www.nano.gov/html/facts/nanoapplication-sandproducts.html (accessed March 19, 2011).

64. T. Donaldson and L. E. Preston, "The Stakeholder Theory of the Corporation: Concepts, Evidence, and Implications," *Academy of Management Review*, January 1995, pp. 65–91.

65. J. S. Harrison and C. H. St. John, "Managing and Partnering with External Stakeholders," *Academy of Management Executive*, May 1996, pp. 46–60.

66. A. J. Hillman and G. D. Keim, "Shareholder Value, Stakeholder Management, and Social Issues: What's the Bottom Line?" *Strategic Management Journal*, March 2001, pp. 125–139; and J. Kotter and J. Heskett, *Corporate Culture and Performance* (New York: Free Press, 1992).

67. M. V. Copeland, "Can the Ski Suit Make the Man (and Woman)?" *Fortune Online*, February 16, 2010; C. Hausman, "New and Old Technologies Keep Officials, Ethicists, Debating Questions of Fairness," *Global Ethics Newsline Online*, February 8, 2010; and S. Sataline, "Some Aging Competitors Call High-Tech Swimsuits Dirty Pool," *Wall Street Journal*, November 3, 2009, pp. A1.

68. Situation adapted from information in "Two Admit to Securities Fraud," *Los Angeles Times*, April 25, 2006, p. C3; and "Software Chief Admits to Guilt in Fraud Case," *New York Times*, April 25, 2006, pp. A1+.

69. *The Ritz-Carlton*, March 10, 2008, http://corporate.ritzcarlton .com; R. Reppa and E. Hirsh, "The Luxury Touch," *Strategy+Business*, Spring 2007, pp. 32–37; and J. Gordon, "Redefining Elegance," *Training*, March 2007, pp. 14–20.

70. Based on www.southernco.com/mspower; Edison Electric Institute, "EEI Honors Mississippi Power with 'Emergency Response Award' for Hurricane Recovery Efforts," *PR Newswire*, January 11, 2006, www.prnewswire.com; S. Lewis, "Contractors to the Rescue," *Transmission & Distribution World*, December 1, 2005, http://tdworld .com/mag/power_contractors_rescue/index.html; D. Cauchon, "The Little Company That Could," *USA Today*, October 10, 2005, pp. 1B+; and S. Covey, *The 7 Habits of Highly Effective People* (New York: Free Press, 1989).

Chapter 3

1. S. Terlep and M. Ramsey, "Ford Bets $5 Billion on Made in China," *Wall Street Journal*, April 20, 2012, pp. B1+; K. Bradsher, "Ford to Build New Plant in China to Bolster Global Sales," *New York Times Online*, April 19, 2012; Ford Motor Company, www.ford.com, March 5, 2012; A. Censky, "Our Love-Hate Relationship with China," CNN .com, February 13, 2012; M. Ramsey, "Ford SUV Marks New World

Car Strategy," *Wall Street Journal*, November 16, 2011, pp. B1+; A. Mulally, address at annual shareholders meeting; and "Charlie Rose Talks to Alan Mulally," *Bloomberg BusinessWeek*, August 1–August 7, 2011, p. 27.

2. M. Kato, "Elementary School English: Ready or Not—Teachers Fret Their Inadequate Skills, Others Dislike the Language," *Japan Times*, March 5, 2009, http://search.japantimes.co.jp/cgi-bin/nn20090305f1 .html (accessed February 3, 2011).

3. Reuters Limited, *USA Today Online*, www.usatoday.com, February 21, 2006; D. Graddol, "Indian English Challenge Hurts Bahrain," *The Telegraph* (Calcutta, India), February 22, 2006; and "Learning the Lingo," *USA Today*, January 26, 2006, p. 1A.

4. N. Adler, *International Dimensions of Organizational Behavior*, 3rd ed. (Cincinnati, OH: South-Western, 1996).

5. M. R. F. Kets De Vries and E. Florent-Treacy, "Global Leadership from A to Z: Creating High Commitment Organizations," *Organizational Dynamics*, Spring 2002, pp. 295–309; P. R. Harris and R. T. Moran, *Managing Cultural Differences*, 4th ed. (Houston, TX: Gulf Publishing, 1996); R. T. Moran, P. R. Harris, and W. G. Stripp, *Developing the Global Organization: Strategies for Human Resource Professionals* (Houston, TX: Gulf Publishing, 1993); Y. Wind, S. P. Douglas, and H. V. Perlmutter, "Guidelines for Developing International Marketing Strategies," *Journal of Marketing*, April 1973, pp. 14–23; and H. V. Perlmutter, "The Tortuous Evolution of the Multinational Corporation," *Columbia Journal of World Business*, January–February 1969, pp. 9–18.

6. M. Mendenhall, B. Punnett, and D. Ricks, *Global Management* (Cambridge, MA: Blackwell, 1995), p. 74.

7. T. K. Grose, "When in Rome, Do as Roman CEOs Do," *U.S. News & World Report*, November 2009, pp. 38–41.

8. World Trade Organization, *WTO Policy Issues for Parliamentarians*, *2001*, www.wto.org/english/res_e/booksp_e/parliamentarians_e.pdf (accessed September 3, 2004), p. 1.

9. "Panorama of the European Union," http://www.ec.europa. eu/publications/booklets/eu_glance/79/en.pdf, May 30, 2012; and "EU Enlargement: The Next Eight," *BBC News Europe*, www.bbc.co.uk, December 9, 2011.

10. Europa, www.europa.eu/index_en.htm, May 30, 2012.

11. Europa, www.europa.eu/index_en.htm, May 30, 2012.

12. Europa, www.europa.eu/index_en.htm, May 30, 2012.

13. S. Erlanger and S. Castle, "Growing Economic Crisis Threatens the Idea of One Europe," *New York Times Online*, March 2, 2009.

14. M. Walker and A. Galloni, "Europe's Choice: Growth or Safety Net," *Wall Street Journal*, March 25, 2010, p. A1.

15. J. Kanter and P. Geitner, "E.U. Cautions France and Warns of Challenges in Spain," *New York Times Online*, May 30, 2012.

16. F. Norris, "In Economic Deluge, a World That Can't Bail Together," *New York Times Online*, June 2, 2012; S. Castle, "Future in Mind, E.U. Plans for Less Unanimity," *New York Times Online*, January 1, 2012; M. Walker, C. Forelle, and S. Meichtry, "Deepening Crisis Over Euro Pits Leader Against Leader," *Wall Street Journal*, December 30, 2011, pp. A1+; J. Bhatti and N. Apostolou, "In Europe, Economic Meltdown Tears at Unity," *USA Today*, October 12, 2011, pp. 1A+; D. Melvin, "Will the European Union Survive?" *Springfield News-Leader* (Missouri), September 29, 2011, p. 4B; D. Macshane, "Europe Agrees to Disagree on Foreign Policy," *Newsweek*, April 12, 2010, p. 6; and C. Forelle and M. Walker, "Europeans Agree on Bailout for Greece," *Wall Street Journal*, March 26, 2010, p. A1.

17. N. Popper, "Europe's Fade Becomes Drag on Sales for U.S. Companies," *New York Times Online*, June 4, 2012; V. Fuhrmans and D. Cimiluca, "Business Braces for Europe's Worst," *Wall Street*

Journal, June 1, 2012, pp. B1+; and J. Revill, "Food Makers Rethink Europe," *Wall Street Journal,* May 29, 2012, p. B8.

18. *CIA World Factbook,* www.cia.gov/library/publications/the-world-factbook/, 2012.

19. "North American Free Trade Agreement (NAFTA)," Foreign Affairs, Trade and Development Canada, http://www.international.gc.ca/trade-agreements-accords-commerciaux/agr-acc/nafta-alena/info.aspx?lang=eng (accessed 28 April, 2014); "Results: North Americans Are Better Off After 15 Years of NAFTA," www.naftanow.org/results/default_en.asp, April 3, 2012.

20. "Goods Going South? Think Mexico," *Export Development Canada,* www.edc.ca/english/publications_9432.htm (accessed July 8, 2007).

21. J. Lyons, "Costa Rica CAFTA Vote Bolsters U.S. Policy," *Wall Street Journal,* October 9, 2007, p. A2.

22. J. Forero, "U.S. and Colombia Reach Trade Deal After 2 Years of Talks," *New York Times Online,* www.nytimes.com, February 28, 2006.

23. "Free Trade Area of the Americas," www.en.wikipedia.org, April 6, 2010; "Ministerial Declaration," website of the Free Trade Area of the Americas, www.ftaa-alca.org, January 23, 2006; and M. Moffett and J. D. McKinnon, "Failed Summit Casts Shadow on Global Trade Talks," *Wall Street Journal,* November 7, 2005, pp. A1+.

24. "EU and Canada strike free trade deal," *Europa,* http://trade.ec.europa.eu/doclib/press/index.cfm?id=973 (accessed April 25, 2014); Public Works and Government Services Canada, *Opening New Markets in Europe,* October, 2013.

25. Foreign Affairs, Trade and Development Canada, "Trans-Pacific Partnership (TPP) Free Trade Negotiations," http://www.international.gc.ca/trade-agreements-accords-commerciaux/agr-acc/tpp-ptp/index.aspx?lang=eng (accessed September 25, 2014).

26. "Selected Basic ASEAN Indicators," ASEAN website, www.asean-sec.org/stat/Table1.pdf (accessed February 3, 2011).

27. J. Hookway, "Asian Nations Push Ideas for Trade," *Wall Street Journal,* October 26, 2009, p. A12; and Bloomberg News, "Southeast Asian Nations Talk of Economic Union," *New York Times Online,* March 2, 2009.

28. "Asia's Never-Closer Union," *Economist,* February 6, 2010, p. 48; "East Asia Summit: Regional Unity Decades Away," *Business Monitor International,* www.asia-monitor.com, 2009/2010; and "Southeast Asian Nations Talk of Economic Union."

29. "China-ASEAN FTA: Winners and Losers," *China & North East Asia,* February 2010, p. 2.

30. "2009–2012 Strategic Plan," *Commission of the African Union,* www.africa-union.org; and D. Kraft, "Leaders Question, Praise African Union," *Springfield News-Leader,* July 10, 2002, p. 8A.

31. J. Guo, "Africa Is Booming Like Never Before," *Newsweek,* March 1, 2010, p. 6.

32. "It Really May Happen," *Economist,* January 2, 2010, p. 36; and "Five Into One?" *Business Africa,* December 1, 2009, p. 1.

33. SAARC official website, www.saarc-sec.org; and N. George, "South Asia Trade Zone in Works," *Springfield News-Leader,* January 4, 2004, p. 1E+.

34. data points box based on J. F. Lepage and J. P. Corbeil, "The Evolution of English-French Bilingualism in Canada from 1961 to 2011," *Insights on Canadian Society,* May 2013; M. J. Slaughter and L. D. Tyson, "A Warning Sign from Global Companies," *Harvard Business Review,* March 2012, p. 74; J. Schramm, "Think Globally," *HRMagazine,* June 2011, p. 156; A. R. Carey and V. Salazar,

"Speaking a Foreign Language," *USA Today,* October 4, 2010, p. 1A; J. Jargon and J. S. Lublin, "Uprooted Again?" *Wall Street Journal,* September 2, 2011, p. B1; P. Brotherton, "Top Global Leadership Programs Tied to Business Results," *T&D,* August 2011, p. 20; A. R. Carey and S. Ward, "What Are the Most Common Foreign Languages Taught in U.S. Schools?" *USA Today,* February 16, 2010, p. 1A; J. Yang and V. Salazar, "Foreign Relations," *USA Today,* December 5, 2007, p. 1B; D. Stuckey and S. Parker, "Young Americans Staying Home," *USA Today,* August 4, 2006, p. 1A; and J. Yang and K. Simmons, "Global Travel and Career," *USA Today,* November 26, 2008, p. 1B.

35. This section is based on material from the World Trade Organization website, www.wto.org (accessed February 3, 2011).

36. 2010 Press Release, "Trade to Expand by 9.5 Percent in 2010 After a Dismal 2009, WTO Reports," www.wto.org, March 26, 2010.

37. International Monetary Fund website, www.imf.org, March 15, 2010.

38. S. Johnson, "Can the I.M.F. Save the World?" *New York Times Online,* September 22, 2011; and Associated Press, "IMF Warns Global Instability Demands Strong Policies," *USA Today,* September 21, 2011, p. 3B.

39. World Bank Group website, www.worldbank.org, March 15, 2010.

40. News Release, "World Bank Group: Record US $100 Billion Response Lays Foundation for Recovery from Global Economic Crisis," www.worldbank.org, April 7, 2010.

41. Organisation for Economic Co-operation and Development website, www.oecd.org, March 15, 2010.

42. D. Searcey, "Small-Scale Bribes Targeted by OECD," *Wall Street Journal,* December 10, 2009, p. A4.

43. B. Schmitt, "Hyundai 4th Largest Automaker, Overtakes Ford," *TTAC,* January 28, 2011, http://www.thetruthaboutcars.com/2011/01/hyundai-4th-largest-automaker-overtakes-ford/ (accessed April 15 2014).

44. Ford Motor Company 2011 Annual Report, http://corporate.ford.com/doc/2011_annual_report.pdf (accessed April 27, 2014).

45. C. A. Barlett and S. Ghoshal, *Managing Across Borders: The Transnational Solution,* 2nd ed. (Boston: Harvard Business School Press, 2002); and N. J. Adler, *International Dimensions of Organizational Behavior,* 4th ed. (Cincinnati, OH: South-Western, 2002), pp. 9–11.

46. P. F. Drucker, "The Global Economy and the Nation-State," *Foreign Affairs,* September–October, 1997, pp. 159–171.

47. D. A. Aaker, *Developing Business Strategies,* 5th ed. (New York: John Wiley & Sons, 1998); and J. A. Byrne et al., "Borderless Management," *BusinessWeek,* May 23, 1994, pp. 24–26.

48. G. A. Knight and S. T. Cavusgil, "A Taxonomy of Born-Global Firms," *Management International Review* 45, no. 3 (2005), pp. 15–35; S. A. Zahra, "A Theory of International New Ventures: A Decade of Research," *Journal of International Business Studies,* January 2005, pp. 20–28; and B. M. Oviatt and P. P. McDougall, "Toward a Theory of International New Ventures," *Journal of International Business Studies,* January 2005, pp. 29–41.

49. See "Bell Canada Outsources Job to Sitel," *The Hindu Business Line,* October 16, 2006, www.blonnet.com/2006/10/17/stories/2006101701390400.htm

50. Mega Brands, *Third Quarter Report,* 2010, www.megabrands.com/media/pdf/corpo/en/reports/2010_q3_en.pdf (accessed February 3, 2011).

51. B. Brown, "UAW Deal Hurts Canada's Auto Towns," *Washington Times,* October 2, 2007.

52. F. Mutsaka and P. Wonacott, "Mugabe Presses Law Requiring Foreign Entities to Cede Control," *Wall Street Journal,* February 19, 2010, p. A9.

53. D. Roberts, "Closing for Business," *Bloomberg BusinessWeek,* April 5, 2010, pp. 32–37; and A. Browne and J. Dean, "Business Sours on China," *Wall Street Journal,* March 17, 2010, pp. A1+.

54. J. Bush, "Ikea in Russia: Enough Is Enough," *Bloomberg BusinessWeek,* July 13, 2009, p. 33.

55. W. Mauldin, "Russians Search BP Office Second Day," *Wall Street Journal*, September 2, 2011, p. B6; and A. E. Kramer, "Memo to Exxon: Business with Russia Might Involve Guns and Balaclavas," *New York Times Online,* August 31, 2011.

56. Aon Political 2012 Political Risk Map," www.aon.com, June 12, 2012.

57. Roberts, "Closing for Business"; and Browne and Dean, "Business Sours on China."

58. "Leading Indicator," *Newsweek,* September 14, 2009, p. 14.

59. M. Landler, "Germany's Export-Led Economy Finds Global Niche," *New York Times Online,* April 13, 2007.

60. "Country Comparison: Inflation Rate," *CIA World Factbook,* www.cia.gov/library/publications/the-world-factbook/rankorder/2092rank, 2012.

61. D. M. Airoldi, "Starwood Studies Abroad," *CFO,* September 2011, pp. 29–30; A. Sheivachman, "Starwood Puts Priority on Chinese Development," *Hotel Management,* August 1, 2011, p. 15; and A. Berzon, "Frits Van Paasschen: Starwood CEO Moves to China to Grow Brand," *Wall Street Journal,* June 6, 2011, p. B6.

62. J. McGregor and S. Hamm, "Managing the Global Workforce," *Bloomberg BusinessWeek,* January 28, 2008, pp. 34–51.

63. Leader Who Made a Difference box based on B. Kowitt and R. Arora, "50 Most Powerful Women," *Fortune,* October 17, 2011, pp. 125–130; P. Sellers, "The Queen of Pop," *Fortune,* September 28, 2009, p. 108; M. Egan and others, "The Top 100," *Forbes,* September 7, 2009, pp. 72–76; I. K. Nooyi, "Leading to the Future," *Vital Speeches of the Day,* September 2009, pp. 404–410; B. Einhorn, "Pepsi Chief on Trip to China," *BusinessWeek Online,* July 3, 2009; G. Fairclough and V. Bauerlein, "Pepsi CEO Tours China to Get a Feel for Market," *Wall Street Journal,* July 1, 2009, p. B5; H. Jackson, "America's Best CEOs," *Institutional Investor,* April 2009, pp. 66–70; "Women to Watch: The 50 Women to Watch," *Wall Street Journal,* November 10, 2008, p. R3; B. McKay, "Boss Talk: PepsiCo CEO Adapts to Tough Climate," *Wall Street Journal,* September 11, 2008, p. B1; and H.Schultz, "Indra Nooyi," *Time,* May 12, 2008, pp. 116–117.

64. Based on information from M. Javidan, P. W. Dorfman, M. S. deLuque, and R. J. House, "In the Eye of the Beholder: Cross-Cultural Lessons in Leadership from Project GLOBE," *Academy of Management Perspective*, February 2006, pp. 67–90; and M. Javidan, G. K. Stahl, F. Brodbeck, and C. P. M. Wilderon, "Cross-Border Transfer of Knowledge: Cultural Lessons from Project GLOBE," *Academy of Management Executive*, May 2005, pp. 59–76.

65. See G. Hofstede, *Culture's Consequences: International Differences in Work-Related Values*, 2nd ed. (Thousand Oaks, CA: Sage, 2001), pp. 9–15.

66. G. Hofstede, *Culture's Consequences: International Differences in Work-Related Values*, 2nd ed. (Thousand Oaks, CA: Sage, 2001), pp. 9–15; and G. Hofstede, "The Cultural Relativity of Organizational Practices and Theories," *Journal of International Business Studies*, Fall 1983, pp. 75–89.

67. Hofstede called this dimension *masculinity versus femininity*, but we have changed his terms because of their strong sexist connotation.

68. G. Hofstede, *Culture's Consequences: International Differences in Work-Related Values*, 2nd ed. (Thousand Oaks, CA: Sage, 2001), pp. 355–358.

69. R. R. McCrae, A. Terracciano, A. Realo, and J. Allik, "Interpreting GLOBE Societal Practices Scale," *Journal of Cross-Cultural Psychology,* November 2008, pp. 805–810; J. S. Chhokar, F. C. Brodbeck, and R. J. House, *Culture and Leadership Across the World: The GLOBE Book of In-Depth Studies of 25 Societies,* (Philadelphia: Lawrence Erlbaum Associates, 2007); and R. J. House, P. J. Hanges, M. Javidan, P. W. Dorfman, and V. Gupta, *Culture, Leadership, and Organizations: The GLOBE Study of 62 Societies* (Thousand Oaks, CA: Sage Publications, 2004).

70. For instance, see D. A. Waldman, M. S. de Luque, and D. Wang, "What Can We Really Learn About Management Practices Across Firms and Countries?" *Academy of Management Perspectives,* February 2012, pp. 34–40; A. E. Munley, "Culture Differences in Leadership," *IUP Journal of Soft Skills,* March 2011, pp. 16–30; and R. J. House, N. R. Quigley, and M. S. deLuque, "Insights from Project GLOBE: Extending Advertising Research Through a Contemporary Framework," *International Journal of Advertising,* 29, no. 1 (2010), pp. 111–139.

71. H. Seligson, "For American Workers in China, a Culture Clash," *New York Times Online,* December 23, 2009.

72. G. N. Powell, A. M. Francesco, and Y. Ling, "Toward Culture-Sensitive Theories of the Work-Family Interface," *Journal of Organizational Behavior,* July 2009, pp. 597–616.

73. J. S. Lublin, "Cultural Flexibility in Demand," *Wall Street Journal,* April 11, 2011, pp. B1+; S. Russwurm, L. Hernández, S. Chambers, and K. Chung, "Developing Your Global Know-How," *Harvard Business Review,* March 2011, pp. 70–75; "Are You Cued in to Cultural Intelligence?" *Industry Week,* November 2009, p. 24; M. Blasco, "Cultural Pragmatists? Student Perspectives on Learning Culture at a Business School," *Academy of Management Learning & Education,* June 2009, pp. 174–187; and D. C. Thomas and K. Inkson, "Cultural Intelligence: People Skills for a Global Workplace," *Consulting to Management,* vol. 16, no. 1, pp. 5–9.

74. M. Javidan, M. Teagarden, and D. Bowen, "Making It Overseas," *Harvard Business Review,* April 2010, pp. 109–113.

75. M. Maynard, "Ford's Unhappy $2 Billion European Surprise," *Forbes,* 29 January 2013, http://www.forbes.com/sites/micheline-maynard/2013/01/29/fords-unhappy-2-billion-european-surprise/ (accessed April 7, 2014).

76. S. Deffree, "Foxconn Explosion Ignites Conversation on Corporate Responsibility," *EDN,* June 23, 2011, p. 8; J. Bussey, "Measuring the Human Cost of an iPad Made in China," *Wall Street Journal*, June 3, 2011, pp. B1+; A. Satariano, "Apple Risks iPad Production Loss of 500,000 After Blast," *Bloomberg BusinessWeek*, May 26, 2011; and E. Savitz, "Apple: Analysts See Limited Risks From Hon Hai Plant Explosion," Forbes.com, May 23, 2011, p. 4.

77. Information from company website, www.inditex.com (accessed July 5, 2007); and M. Helft, "Fashion Fast-Forward," *Business 2.0,* May 2002, pp. 60–66.

78. See "Canadians in the NBA," NBA.com, June 30, 2004, www.nba.com/canada/Canadians_in_the_NBA-Canada_Generic_Article-18022.html (accessed September 15, 2007); D. Eisenberg, "The NBA's Global Game Plan," *Time,* March 17, 2003, pp. 59–63; J. Tyrangiel, "The Center of Attention," *Time,* February 10, 2003, pp. 56–60; "Spin Master Stern," *Latin Trade,* July 2000, p. 32; Information from NBA website, www.nba.com (accessed July 1, 2004); J. Tagliabue, "Hoop Dreams, Fiscal Realities," *New York Times,* March 4, 2000, p. B11; D. Roth, "The NBA's Next Shot," *Fortune,* February 21, 2000, pp. 207–216; A. Bianco, "Now It's NBA All-the-Time TV," *BusinessWeek,* November 15, 1999, pp. 241–242; and D. McGraw and M. Tharp, "Going Out on Top," *U.S. News & World Report*, January 25, 1999, p. 55.

Chapter 4

1. Canadian Youth Business Foundation, "Home," http://www.cybf.ca/ (accessed October 25, 2013).

2. Canadian Youth Business Foundation, *2012/2013 Annual Review*, http://www.cybf.ca/annual-reports/ (accessed October 25, 2013).

3. P. E. Mott, *The Characteristics of Effective Organizations* (New York: HarperCollins, 1972).

4. Steve Blank, Address to the National Governors Association Conference, Arlington Virginia July 18, 2012, http://www.c-spanvideo.org/clip/3344757 (accessed November 2, 2013).

5. J. A. Schumpeter, *The Theory of Economic Development*, 2nd ed. (Cambridge, MA: Harvard University Press, 1936).

6. I. M. Kirzner, *Competition and Entrepreneurship* (Chicago: University of Chicago Press, 1973).

7. J. O. Fiet, *The Systematic Search for Entrepreneurial Discoveries* (Westport, CT: Quorum Books, 2002); J. O. Fiet, V. G. H. Clouse, and W. I. Norton, "Systematic Search by Repeat Entrepreneurs," in *Opportunity Identification and Entrepreneurial Behavior*, ed. E. B. John (Greenwich, CT: Information Age Publishing, 2004).

8. Y. Sarason, T. Dean, and J. F. Dillard, "Entrepreneurship as the Nexus of Individual and Opportunity: A Structuration View," *Journal of Business Venturing* 21, no. 3 (2006), pp. 286–305; S. D. Sarasvathy, "Causation and Effectuation: Toward a Theoretical Shift from Economic Inevitability to Entrepreneurial Contingency," *Academy of Management Review* 26, no. 2 (2001), pp. 243–263; S. D. Sarasvathy, N. Dew, R. Velamuri, and S. Venkataraman, "Three Views of Entrepreneurial Opportunity," *Handbook of Entrepreneurship Research* 156 (2003), pp. 1–25.

9. J. W. Carland, F. Hoy, W. R. Boulton, and J. C. Carland, "Differentiating Entrepreneurs from Small Business Owners: A Conceptualization," *Academy of Management Review* 9, no. 2 (1984), pp. 354–359.

10. Organisation for Economic Co-operation and Development, "The Importance of Entrepreneurship," in *Measuring Entrepreneurship: A Digest of Indicators*, 2008, www.oecd.org/dataoecd/53/24/41664503.pdf (accessed November 18, 2010).

11. P. Almeida and B. Kogut, "The Exploration of Technological Diversity and Geographic Localization in Innovation: Start-up Firms in the Semiconductor Industry," *Small Business Economics*, 9, no. 1 (1997), pp. 21–31.

12. R. J. Arend, "Emergence of Entrepreneurs Following Exogenous Technological Change," *Strategic Management Journal* 20, no. 1 (1999), pp. 31–47.

13. U.S. Small Business Administration, Office of Advocacy, "Frequently Asked Questions," www.sba.gov, April 16, 2007.

14. Startup Canada, "Statistics on Small Business in Canada," http://www.startupcan.ca/wp-content/uploads/2012/01/Statistics-on-Small-Business-in-Canada_StartupCanada.pdf (accessed October 31, 2013).

15. Industry Canada, "Key Small Business Statistics—August 2013," http://www.ic.gc.ca/eic/site/061.nsf/eng/02803.html (accessed May 15, 2014).

16. J. Amorós and N. Bosma, *Global Entrepreneurship Monitor 2013 Global Report*, www.gemconsortium.org.

17. P. F. Drucker, *Innovation and Entrepreneurship: Practice and Principles* (New York: Harper & Row, 1985).

18. International Organization for Standardization, "*ISO 14000 Essentials*," www.iso.org/iso/iso_catalogue/management_and_leadership_standards/environmental_management/iso_14000_essentials .htm (accessed October 7, 2010); International Organization for Standardization, "*ISO 26000: Social Responsibility*," www.iso.org/iso/iso_catalogue/management_and_leadership_standards/social_responsibility.htm (accessed October 7, 2010); and International Organization for Standardization, "ISO's Social Responsibility Standard Approved for Publication," Ref: 1351, September 14, 2010, www.iso.org/iso/pressrelease.htm?refid=Ref1351 (accessed November 11, 2010).

19. Skoll Foundation, "About Us," www.skollfoundation.org/about/Ref1351 (accessed November 18, 2010).

20. Corporate Knights, "The 2010 Cleantech 10TM," http://corporateknights.ca/report/cleantech-index-2010/2010-cleantech-10%E2%84%A2 (accessed November 18, 2010).

21. Ned Smith, "Why Americans Still Love Small Business," *CNBC Small Business*, August 20, 2012, http://www.cnbc.com/id/48705659 (accessed May 13, 2014).

22. S. Blank, *The Startup Owners Manual*, http://www.stevenblank.com/startup_index_qty.html (accessed May 13, 2014).

23. S. Shane, "How Do Entrepreneurs Come Up With New Business Ideas?" *Small Business Trends* May 5, 2008, http://smallbiztrends.com/2008/05/how-do-entrepreneurs-come-up-with-new-business-ideas.html (accessed May 14, 2014).

24. C. Barnes, H. Blake, and D. Pinder, *Creating and Delivering Your Value Proposition: Managing Customer Experience for Profit* (London: Kogan Page, 2009).

25. A. Barrett, B. Turek, and C. Faivre d'Arcier, "Bottoms Up—and Profits, Too," *BusinessWeek*, September 12, 2005, pp. 80–82; and C. Hajim, "Growth in Surprising Places," *Fortune*, September 5, 2005, bonus section.

26. R. L. Heneman, J. W. Tansky, and S. M. Camp, "Human Resource Management Practices in Small and Medium-Sized Enterprises: Unanswered Questions and Future Research Perspectives," *Entrepreneurship Theory and Practice*, Fall 2000, pp. 11–26.

27. R. L. Heneman, J. W. Tansky, and S. M. Camp, "Human Resource Management Practices in Small and Medium-Sized Enterprises: Unanswered Questions and Future Research Perspectives," *Entrepreneurship Theory and Practice*, Fall 2000, pp. 11–26.

28. Based on G. Fuchsberg, "Small Firms Struggle With Latest Management Trends," *Wall Street Journal*, August 26, 1993, p. B2; M. Barrier, "Re-engineering Your Company," *Nation's Business*, February 1994, pp. 16–22; J. Weiss, "Re-engineering the Small Business," *Small Business Reports*, May 1994, pp. 37–43; and K. D. Godsey, "Back on Track," *Success*, May 1997, pp. 52–54.

29. Based on Basadur Applied Creativity website, www.basadur.com/company/index.htm (accessed June 10, 2010).

30. "History," Perimeter Institute for Theoretical Physics, www.perimeterinstitute.ca/About/History/History/ (accessed June 3, 2010).

31. Definition from *Investopedia*, www.investopedia.com/terms/r/randd.asp (accessed June 10, 2010).

32. B. Jaruzelski and K. Dehoff, "The Global Innovation 1000: How the Top Innovators Keep Winning," *strategy+business* 61 (November 3, 2010), www.strategy-business.com/article/10408?pg=0.

33. Booz & Company, The Global Innovation 1000 Study 2013: Navigating the Digital Future, *Strategy and Business*, Issue 73, winter 2013.

34. AACSB International, *Business Schools on an Innovation Mission: Report of the AACSB International Task Force on Business Schools and Innovation* (Tampa, FL: AACSB International, 2010).

35. M. DePree, *Leadership Jazz* (New York: Currency Doubleday, 1992), pp. 8–9.

36. J. C. Collins and J. I. Porras, *Built to Last: Successful Habits of Visionary Companies* (New York: Harper Business, 1994).

37. G. R. Merz, P. B. Weber, and V. B. Laetz, "Linking Small Business Management with Entrepreneurial Growth," *Journal of Small Business Management*, October 1994, pp. 48–60.

38. J. Bailey, "Growth Needs a Plan or Only Losses May Build," *Wall Street Journal*, October 29, 2002, p. B9; and L. Beresford, "Growing Up," *Entrepreneur*, July 1995, pp. 124–28.

39. T. Pender, "Desire2Learn's rapid growth has come with challenges," *Guelph Mercury*, December 20, 2013, http://www.guelphmercury.com/news-story/4283503-desire2learn-s-rapid-growth-has-come-with-challenges/ (accessed May 15, 2014).

40. C. Farrell, "How to Survive a Downturn," *BusinessWeek*, April 28, 1997, pp. ENT4-ENT6.

41. J. Bailey, "Selling the Firm and Letting Go of the Dream," *Wall Street Journal*, December 10, 2002, p. B6; P. Hernan, "Finding the Exit," *IndustryWeek*, July 17, 2000, pp. 55–61; D. Rodkin, "For Sale by Owner," *Entrepreneur*, January 1998, pp. 148–153; A. Livingston, "Avoiding Pitfalls When Selling a Business," *Nation's Business*, July 1998, pp. 25–26; and G. Gibbs Marullo, "Selling Your Business: A Preview of the Process," *Nation's Business*, August 1998, pp. 25–26.

42. B. Jaruzelski and K. Dehoff, "The Global Innovation 1000: How the Top Innovators Keep Winning," *Strategy+Business* 61, Winter 2010, www.strategy-business.com/article/10408?pg=0 (accessed April 5, 2011).

43. S. Thomke and B. Feinberg, "Design Thinking and Innovation at Apple," *Harvard Business Review*, January 9, 2009, http://hbr.org/product/design-thinking-and-innovation-at-apple/an/609066-PDF-ENG (accessed April 5, 2011).

44. "Apple/Newton Cancellation—2: No Layoffs Expected," Dow Jones Newswires, February 27, 1998.

45. C. Bayers, "Steve Jobs Comes Home to Apple," *Wired*, December 20, 1996, www.wired.com/techbiz/media/news/1996/12/1137 (accessed April 5, 2011).

46. Booz & Company, The Global Innovation 1000 Study 2013: Navigating the Digital Future, *Strategy and Business*, Issue 73, winter 2013.

47. Based on personal conversations and interviews with Kathy Murphy, CEO of CEED, and Ed Matwawana, director of the Second Chance Program; and Second Chance website, www.ceed.ca/default.asp?mn=1.247.241 (accessed November 19, 2010).

Chapter 5

1. Based on R. C. Anderson with R. White, *Confessions of a Radical Industrialist: Profits, People, Purpose—Doing Business by Respecting the Earth* (New York: St. Martin's Press, 2009); Interface sustainability page on the Interface website, www.interfaceglobal.com/Sustainability.aspx (accessed May 25, 2014); Interface 2013 Annual Report, file, ///C:/Users/Colin/Downloads/TILE_2013AnnualReport.pdf (accessed May 25, 2014); interview by George Stroumboulopoulos, *The Hour, CBC television*, January 25, 2007; R. C. Anderson, presentation at the Power of Green Conference, Halifax, Nova Scotia, November 8, 2009.

2. M. L. Barnett, "Stakeholder Influence Capacity and the Variability of Financial Returns to Corporate Social Responsibility," *Academy of Management Review*, July 2007, pp. 794–816; A. Mackey, T. B. Mackey, and J. B. Barney, "Corporate Social Responsibility and Firm Performance: Investor Preferences and Corporate Strategies," *Academy of Management Review*, July 2007, pp. 817–835; and A. B. Carroll, "A Three-Dimensional Conceptual Model of Corporate Performance," *Academy of Management Review*, October 1979, p. 499.

3. See K. Basu and G. Palazzo, "Corporate Social Performance: A Process Model of Sensemaking," *Academy of Management Review*, January 2008, pp. 122–136; and S. P. Sethi, "A Conceptual Framework for Environmental Analysis of Social Issues and Evaluation of Business Response Patterns," *Academy of Management Review*, January 1979, pp. 68–74.

4. M. Friedman, *Capitalism and Freedom* (Chicago: University of Chicago Press, 1962); and M. Friedman, "The Social Responsibility of Business Is to Increase Profits," *New York Times Magazine*, September 13, 1970, p. 33.

5. J. Bakan, *The Corporation* (Toronto: Big Picture Media Corporation, 2003).

6. "The McKinsey Global Survey of Business Executives: Business and Society," *McKinsey Quarterly*, January 2006, www.mckinseyquarterly.com.

7. See, for example, D. J. Wood, "Corporate Social Performance Revisited," *Academy of Management Review*, October 1991, pp. 703–708; and S. L. Wartick and P. L. Cochran, "The Evolution of the Corporate Social Performance Model, *Academy of Management Review*, October 1985, p. 763.

8. N. Bunkley, "Ford Backs Ban on Text Messaging by Drivers," *New York Times Online*, September 11, 2009.

9. See, for example, R. A. Buccholz, *Essentials of Public Policy for Management*, 2nd ed. (Upper Saddle River, NJ: Prentice Hall, 1990).

10. RBC Blue Water Project website, http://bluewater.rbc.com/ (accessed November 13, 2010).

11. See www.mec.ca; and H. Hoag, "Blocks of Buildings of the Future," *Gazette* (Montreal), October 24, 2006, p. B3.

12. M. Straus, "Why Loblaws Takes Top Honours for Corporate Social Responsibility," *Globe and Mail*, June 20, 2010, www.theglobeandmail.com/report-on-business/managing/report-on-corporate-responsibil/why-loblaw-takes-top-honours-for-corporate-social-responsibility/article1605337/ (accessed November 13, 2010).

13. "Sustainable Pay: How TSX 60 Companies Compensate Executives for Sustainability Performance," Strandberg Consulting, http://corostrandberg.com/publications/sustainable-pay-tsx60-executive-compensation (accessed May 22, 2014).

14. "BMO Invests in Clear Blue Skies," *CNW*, November 23, 2009, www.newswire.ca/en/releases/archive/November2009/23/c3931.html (accessed November 13, 2010).

15. Based on D. Dias, "Giant Steps," *Financial Post Business*, July 7, 2008, www.financialpost.com/magazine/story.html?id=610758 (accessed November 13, 2010).

16. See, for example, A. B. Carroll, "The Pyramid of Corporate Social Responsibility: Toward the Moral Management of Organizational Stakeholders," *Business Horizons*, July–August 1991, pp. 39–48.

17. This section has been influenced by K. B. Boal and N. Peery, "The Cognitive Structure of Social Responsibility," *Journal of Management*, Fall–Winter 1985, pp. 71–82.

18. R. C. Anderson with R. White, *Confessions of a Radical Industrialist: Profits, People, Purpose—Doing Business by Respecting the Earth* (New York: St. Martin's Press, 2009), p. 76.

19. See, for instance, D. O. Neubaum and S. A. Zahra, "Institutional Ownership and Corporate Social Performance: The Moderating Effects of Investment Horizon, Activism, and Coordination," *Journal of Management*, February 2006, pp. 108–131; P. C. Godfrey, "The Relationship between Corporate Philanthropy and Shareholder Wealth: A Risk Management Perspective," *Academy of Management Review*, October 2005, pp. 777–798; D. K. Peterson, "The Relationship between Perceptions of Corporate Citizenship and Organizational Commitment," *Business & Society*, September 2004, pp. 296–319; B. Seifert, S. A. Morris, and B. R. Bartkus, "Having,

Giving, and Getting: Slack Resources, Corporate Philanthropy, and Firm Financial Performance," *Business* & Society, June 2004, pp. 135–161; S. L. Berman, A. Wicks, S. Kotha, and T. Jones, "Does Stakeholder Orientation Matter? The Relationship between Stakeholder Management Models and Firm Financial Performance," *Academy of Management Journal*, October 1999, pp. 488–506; S. A. Waddock and S. B. Graves, "The Corporate Social Performance–Financial Performance Link," *Strategic Management Journal*, April 1997, pp. 303–319; D. B. Turban and D. W. Greening, "Corporate Social Performance and Organizational Attractiveness to Prospective Employees," *Academy of Management Journal*, June 1996, pp. 658–672; J. B. McGuire, A. Sundgren, and T. Schneeweis, "Corporate Social Responsibility and Firm Financial Performance," *Academy of Management Journal*, December 1988, pp. 854–872; K. Aupperle, A. B. Carroll, and J. D. Hatfield, "An Empirical Examination of the Relationship between Corporate Social Responsibility and Profitability," *Academy of Management Journal*, June 1985, pp. 446–463; and P. Cochran and R. A. Wood, "Corporate Social Responsibility and Financial Performance," *Academy of Management Journal*, March 1984, pp. 42–56.

20. See J. Surroca and J. A. Tribo, "The Corporate Social and Financial Performance Relationship: What's the Ultimate Determinant?" *Academy of Management Proceedings Best Conference Paper*, 2005; D. J. Wood and R. E. Jones, "Stakeholder Mismatching: A Theoretical Problem in Empirical Research on Corporate Social Performance," *International Journal of Organizational Analysis*, July 1995, pp. 229–267; R. Wolfe and K. Aupperle, "Introduction to Corporate Social Performance: Methods for Evaluating an Elusive Construct," in J. E. Post (ed.), *Research in Corporate Social Performance and Policy* 12 (1991), pp. 265–268; and A. A. Ullmann, "Data in Search of a Theory: A Critical Examination of the Relationships among Social Performance, Social Disclosure, and Economic Performance of U.S. Firms," *Academy of Management Review*, July 1985, pp. 540–557.

21. B. Seifert, S. A. Morris, and B. R. Bartkus, "Having, Giving, and Getting: Slack Resources, Corporate Philanthropy, and Firm Financial Performance," *Business* & Society, June 2004, pp. 135–161; and J. B. McGuire, A. Sundgren, and T. Schneeweis, "Corporate Social Responsibility and Firm Financial Performance," *Academy of Management Journal*, December 1988, pp. 854–872.

22. G. Michelon, K. Kumar, and G. Boesso, "Examining the Link between Strategic Corporate Social Responsbility and Company Performance: An Analysis of the Best Corporate Citizens,"*Corporate Social Responsbility*, 20 (2) 2013, pp. 81–94; and K. L. Becker-Olsen, B. A. Cudmore and R. P. Hill, "The Impact of Perceived Corporate Social Responsibility on Consumer Behavior," *Journal of Business Research*, 59 (1) 2006, pp. 46–53.

23. A. Lioui and Z. Sharma, "Environmental Corporate Social Responsibility and Financial Performance: Disentangling Direct and Indirect Effects," *Ecological Economics,* 78 (2012), pp. 100–111.

24. E. Briggs, F. Jaramillo, and W. A. Weeks, "The Influences of Ethical Climate and Organization Identity Comparisons on Salespeople and the Job Performance," *Journal of Personal Selling and Sales Management* 32, 4 (Fall 2012), pp. 421–436; and M. Orlitzky, F. L. Schmidt, and S. L. Rynes, "Corporate Social and Financial Performance," *Organization Studies* 24, no. 3 (2003), pp. 403–441.

25. "Socially Responsible Investing—Better Companies, Better Communities," *Green Money Journal*, Fall 2010, www.greenmoneyjournal.com/article.mpl?newsletterid=45&articleid=622 (accessed November 13, 2010).

26. Responsible Investment Organization, *Canadian Socially Responsible Investment Review* 2012 (2013), http://riacanada.ca/wp-content/uploads/CSRIR-2012-English.pdf (accessed May 22, 2014).

27. MaRS Centre for Impact Investing, "Certified B Corporation (B Corp) Hub", http://impactinvesting.marsdd.com/strategic-initiatives/benefit-corporation-b-corp-hub/ (accessed May 22, 2014); and

Certified B Corporation, "The Non-Profit Behind B Corps," https://www.bcorporation.net/what-are-b-corps/the-non-profit-behind-b-corps (accessed May 21, 2014).

28. J. Jedras, "Social Workers," *Silicon Valley North*, July 30, 2001, p. 1.

29. Based on R. C. Anderson with R. White, *Confessions of a Radical Industrialist: Profits, People, Purpose—Doing Business by Respecting the Earth* (New York: St. Martin's Press, 2009); and the Interface sustainability page on the Interface website, www.interfaceglobal.com/Sustainability.aspx (accessed May 15, 2014).

30. This section is based on K. Buysse and A. Verbeke, "Proactive Environmental Strategies: A Stakeholder Management Perspective," *Strategic Management Journal*, May 2003, pp. 453–470; D. A. Rondinelli and T. London, "How Corporations and Environmental Groups Cooperate: Assessing Cross-Sector Alliances and Collaborations," *Academy of Management Executive*, February 2003, pp. 61–76; J. Alberto Aragon-Correa and S. Sharma, "A Contingent Resource-Based View of Proactive Corporate Environmental Strategy," *Academy of Management Review*, January 2003, pp. 71–88; P. Christmann and G. Taylor, "Globalization and the Environment: Strategies for International Voluntary Environmental Initiatives," *Academy of Management Executive*, August 2002, pp. 121–135; P. Bansal, "The Corporate Challenges of Sustainable Development," *Academy of Management Executive*, May 2002, pp. 122–131; M. Stark and A. A. Marcus, "Introduction to the Special Research Forum on the Management of Organizations in the Natural Environment: A Field Emerging from Multiple Paths, with Many Challenges Ahead," *Academy of Management Journal*, August 2000, pp. 539–546; P. Bansal and K. Roth, "Why Companies Go Green: A Model of Ecological Responsiveness," *Academy of Management Journal*, August 2000, pp. 717–736; S. L. Hart, "Beyond Greening: Strategies for a Sustainable World," *Harvard Business Review*, January–February 1997, pp. 66–76; S. L. Hart, "A Natural-Resource-Based View of the Firm," *Academy of Management Review*, December 1995, pp. 986–1014; and P. Shrivastava, "Environmental Technologies and Competitive Advantage," *Strategic Management Journal*, Summer 1995, pp. 183–200.

31. J. L. Seglin, "It's Not That Easy Going Green," *Inc.*, May 1999, pp. 28–32; W. H. Miller, "What's Ahead in Environmental Policy?" *IW*, April 19, 1999, pp. 19–24; and P. Shrivastava, "Environmental Technologies and Competitive Advantage," *Strategic Management Journal*, Summer 1995, p. 183.

32. PBL Netherlands Environmental Assessment Agency, *Trends in Global CO_2 Emissions: 2013 Report,* The Hague, 2013, http://edgar.jrc.ec.europa.eu/news_docs/pbl-2013-trends-in-global-co2-emissions-2013-report-1148.pdf (accessed 25 May, 2014); and S. L. Hart, "Beyond Greening: Strategies for a Sustainable World," *Harvard Business Review*, January–February 1997, p. 68.

33. Worldwatch Institute, *State of the World 2006: China and India Hold World in Balance*, www.worldwatch.org/node/3894 (accessed July 12, 2007); "Is There a Green Movement in the Air?" *Fortune*, December 12, 2005, pp. 69–78; A. Aston and B. Helm, "The Race Against Climate Change," *BusinessWeek*, December 12, 2005, pp. 58–66; J. Kluger and A. Dorfman, "The Challenges We Face," *Time*, August 26, 2002, pp. A6–A12; Worldwatch Institute, "Earth Day 2000: What Humanity Can Do Now to Turn the Tide," www.worldwatch.org/node/483 (accessed July 12, 2007); and L. Brown and Staff of Worldwatch Institute, *State of the World* (New York: Norton, 1987–1996).

34. M. Conlin, "Sorry, I Composted Your Memorandum," *BusinessWeek*, February 18, 2008, p. 60; "Whole Foods Switching to Wind Power," *CBS News Online*, January 12, 2006, www.cbsnews.com; A. Aston and B. Helm, "Green Culture, Clean Strategies," *BusinessWeek*, December 12, 2005, p. 64; and J. Esty, "Never Say Never," *Fast Company*, July 2004, p. 34.

35. The concept of shades of green can be found in R. E. Freeman, J. Pierce, and R. Dodd, *Shades of Green: Business Ethics and the Environment* (New York: Oxford University Press, 1995).

36. Responsible Care Progress Report, 2014, Chemistry Association of Canada, 2014.

37. Responsible Care, Progress Report, 2014, Canadian Industry Association of Canada (CIAC), p. 12, 2014.

38. International Organization for Standardization, "ISO's Social Responsibility Standard Approved for Publication," ISO News and Media, September 14, 2010, www.iso.org/iso/pressrelease .htm?refid=Ref1351 (accessed November 11, 2010).

39. The 2014 Best 50 Corporate Citizens in Canada, Issue #49, Corporate Knights, June 2014.

40. Based on R. C. Anderson with R. White, *Confessions of a Radical Industrialist: Profits, People, Purpose—Doing Business by Respecting the Earth* (New York: St. Martin's Press, 2009); and the Interface sustainability page on the Interface website, www.interfaceglobal.com/ Sustainability.aspx (accessed November 13, 2010).

41. W. G. Bliss, "Why Is Corporate Culture Important?" *Workforce*, February 1999, pp. W8–W9; E. J. Giblin and L. E. Amuso, "Putting Meaning into Corporate Values," *Business Forum*, Winter 1997, pp. 14–18; R. Barrett, "Liberating the Corporate Soul," *HRfocus*, April 1997, pp. 15–16; K. Blanchard and M. O'Connor, *Managing by Values* (San Francisco: Berrett-Koehler, 1997); and G. P. Alexander, "Establishing Shared Values Through Management Training Programs," *Training & Development*, February 1987, pp. 45–47.

42. Based on Mary Lamey, "A Monument to the Environment: Focus on Recycling: Mountain Equipment Is Building First 'Green' Retail Outlet in Quebec," *Gazette* (Montreal), November 22, 2002, www .Canada.com/montreal.

43. W. G. Bliss, "Why Is Corporate Culture Important?" *Workforce*, February 1999, pp. W8–W9; E. J. Giblin and L. E. Amuso, "Putting Meaning into Corporate Values," *Business Forum*, Winter 1997, pp. 14–18; R. Barrett, "Liberating the Corporate Soul," *HRfocus*, April 1997, pp. 15–16; K. Blanchard and M. O'Connor, *Managing by Values* (San Francisco: Berrett-Koehler, 1997); G. P. Alexander, "Establishing Shared Values through Management Training Programs," *Training & Development*, February 1987, pp. 45–47; J. L. Badaracco Jr. and R. R. Ellsworth, *Leadership and the Quest for Integrity* (Boston: Harvard Business School Press, 1989); and T. Chappell, *Managing Upside Down: The Seven Intentions of Values-Centered Leadership* (New York: William Morrow, 1999).

44. Information from Tom's of Maine website, www.tomsofmaine.com/ about/statement.asp (accessed July 11, 2007).

45. R. Kamen, "Values: For Show or for Real?" *Working Woman*, August 1993, p. 10.

46. Management Reflection box based on One Percent for the Planet, http://www.onepercentfortheplanet.org/en/, June 12, 2012; S. Stevenson, "Patagonia's Founder Is America's Most Unlikely Business Guru," *Wall Street Journal Magazine,* May 2012; "Responsible Company," *Wall Street Journal Online,* April 25, 2012; T. Henneman, "Patagonia Fills Payroll With People Who Are Passionate," *Workforce Management Online,* November 4, 2011; M. J. Ybarra, "Book Review: The Fun Hog Expedition Revisited," *Wall Street Journal,* February 19, 2010, p. W8; K. Garber, "Not in the Business of Hurting the Planet," *US News & World Report,* November 2009, p. 63; and T. Foster, "No Such Thing As Sustainability," *Fast Company,* July/August 2009, pp. 46–48.

47. F. O. Walumba and J. Schaubroeck, "Leader Personality Traits and Employee Voice Behavior: Mediating Roles of Ethical Leadership and Work Group Psychological Safety," *Journal of Applied Psychology,* September 2009, pp. 1275–1286; G. Weaver, "Ethics and Employees: Making the Connection," May 2004; G. Weaver, L. K. Treviño,

and P. L. Cochran, "Integrated and Decoupled Corporate Social Performance: Management Commitments, External Pressures, and Corporate Ethics Practices," *Academy of Management Journal*, October 1999, pp. 539–552; G. R. Weaver, L. K. Treviño, and P. L. Cochran, "Corporate Ethics Programs as Control Systems: Influences of Executive Commitment and Environmental Factors," *Academy of Management Journal*, February 1999, pp. 41–57; R. B. Morgan, "Self- and Co-Worker Perceptions of Ethics and Their Relationships to Leadership and Salary," *Academy of Management Journal*, February 1993, pp. 200–214; and B. Z. Posner and W. H. Schmidt, "Values and the American Manager: An Update," *California Management Review*, Spring 1984, pp. 202–216.

48. "Interface Code of Business Conduct and Ethics," Interface website, www.interfaceglobal.com/Investor-Relations/ Corporate-Governance.aspx (accessed July 15, 2010).

49. K. Davis and W. C. Frederick, *Business and Society: Management, Public Policy, Ethics*, 5th ed. (New York: McGraw-Hill, 1984), pp. 28–41, 76.

50. F. D. Sturdivant, *Business and Society: A Managerial Approach*, 3rd ed. (Homewood, IL: Richard D. Irwin, 1985), p. 128.

51. L. Kohlberg, *Essays in Moral Development: The Philosophy of Moral Development*, vol. 1 (New York: Harper & Row, 1981); L. Kohlberg, *Essays in Moral Development: The Psychology of Moral Development*, vol. 2 (New York: Harper & Row, 1984); J. W. Graham, "Leadership, Moral Development, and Citizenship Behavior," *Business Ethics* Quarterly, January 1995, pp. 43–54; and T. Kelley, "To Do Right or Just to Be Legal," *New York Times*, February 8, 1998, p. BU12.

52. See, for example, J. Weber, "Managers' Moral Reasoning: Assessing Their Responses to Three Moral Dilemmas," *Human Relations*, July 1990, pp. 687–702.

53. J. H. Barnett and M. J. Karson, "Personal Values and Business Decisions: An Exploratory Investigation," *Journal of Business Ethics*, July 1987, pp. 371–382; and W. C. Frederick and J. Weber, "The Value of Corporate Managers and Their Critics: An Empirical Description and Normative Implications," in *Business Ethics*: Research Issues and Empirical Studies, ed. W. C. Frederick and L. E. Preston, pp. 123–144 (Greenwich, CT: JAI Press, 1990).

54. L. K. Trevino and S. A. Youngblood, "Bad Apples in Bad Barrels: A Causal Analysis of Ethical Decision-Making Behavior," *Journal of Applied Psychology*, August 1990, pp. 378–385; and M. E. Baehr, J. W. Jones, and A. J. Nerad, "Psychological Correlates of Business Ethics Orientation in Executives," *Journal of Business and Psychology*, Spring 1993, pp. 291–308.

55. R. L. Cardy and T. T. Selvarajan, "Assessing Ethical Behavior Revisited: The Impact of Outcomes on Judgment Bias" (paper presented at the Annual Meeting of the Academy of Management, Toronto, Ontario, 2000).

56. B. Victor and J. B. Cullen, "The Organizational Bases of Ethical Work Climates," *Administrative Science Quarterly*, March 1988, pp. 101–125; J. B. Cullen, B. Victor, and C. Stephens, "An Ethical Weather Report: Assessing the Organization's Ethical Climate," *Organizational Dynamics*, Autumn 1989, pp. 50–62; B. Victor and J. B. Cullen, "A Theory and Measure of Ethical Climate in Organizations," in *BusinessEthics*, ed. W. Frederick and L. Preston, pp. 77–97 (Greenwich, CT: JAI Press, 1990); R. R. Sims, "The Challenge of Ethical Behavior in Organizations," *Journal of Business Ethics*, July 1992, pp. 505–513; and V. Arnold and J. C. Lampe, "Understanding the Factors Underlying Ethical Organizations: Enabling Continuous Ethical Improvement," *Journal of Applied Business Research*, Summer 1999, pp. 1–19.

57. T. M. Jones, "Ethical Decision Making by Individuals in Organizations: An Issue-Contingent Model," *Academy of Management Review*, April 1991, pp. 366–395; and T. Barnett, "Dimensions of

Moral Intensity and Ethical Decision Making: An Empirical Study," *Journal of Applied Social Psychology*, May 2001, pp. 1038–1057.

58. T. M. Jones, "Ethical Decision Making by Individuals in Organizations," pp. 374–378.

59. data points box based on J. Yang and A. Gonzalez, "Do You Feel Guilty Calling In Sick When You Aren't?" *USA Today*, June 14, 2012, p. 1B; M. Heller, "Ethics Group Warns of 'Steep Declines' in Workforce Trust," *Workforce Management Online*, March 20, 2012; S. Bates, "Surge Predicted in Workplace Ethical Lapses," *HR Magazine*, March 2012, p. 11; J. Yang and P. Trap, "If Granted Access to Confidential Document Accidently, I'd…" *USA Today*, September 13, 2010, p. 1B; and R. R. Hastings, "Study: Employees' Trust in Leaders Has Declined," *HR Magazine*, September 2011, p. 15.

60. M. McClearn, "African Adventure," *Canadian Business*, September 1, 2003.

61. "Corruption Still Tainting Asian Financial Picture, Study Says," *Vancouver Sun*, March 20, 2001, p. D18.

62. United Nations Global Compact, www.unglobalcompact.org/AboutTheGC/index.html, June 10, 2012.

63. Organisation for Economic Cooperation and Development, "About Bribery in International Business," www.oecd.org, April 30, 2010.

64. C. J. Robertson and W. F. Crittenden, "Mapping Moral Philosophies: Strategic Implications for Multinational Firms," *Strategic Management Journal*, April 2003, pp. 385–392.

65. L. K. Trevino and S. A. Youngblood, "Bad Apples in Bad Barrels: A Causal Analysis of Ethical Decision-Making Behavior," *Journal of Applied Psychology*, August 1990, p. 384.

66. L. Bogomolny, "Good Housekeeping," *Canadian Business*, March 1, 2004, pp. 87–88.

67. See www.csa-acvm.ca/home.html.

68. W. Dabrowski, "Tighter Guidelines Issued on Disclosure: Canada's 'Sarbanes,'" *Financial Post (National Post)*, March 30, 2004, p. FP1.

69. King, Bart, "U.S. Corporations Lead on Business Ethics, Lag on Environmental Transparency," Sustainable Brands, July 31, 2012, http://www.sustainablebrands.com/news_and_views/articles/us-corporations-lead-business-ethics-lag-environmental-transparency.

70. P. Richter, "Big Business Puts Ethics in Spotlight," *Los Angeles Times*, June 19, 1986, p. 29.

71. J. B. Singh, "Determinants of the Effectiveness of Corporate Codes of Ethics: An Empirical Study," *Journal of Business Ethics* 101, no. 3 (2011), pp. 385–395.

72. ERC Ethics Resource Center, *2013 National Ethics Survey*, (Arlington, VA: Ethics Resource Center, 2014), http://www.ethics.org/nbes/.

73. UN Global Compact, *Reporting Guidance on the 10th Principle Against Corruption* (New York: UN Global Compact Office, December 2009), www.unglobalcompact.org/Issues/transparency_anticorruption/Anti-Corruption_Guidance_Material.html.

74. J. B. Singh, "Determinants of the Effectiveness of Corporate Codes of Ethics: An Empirical Study," *Journal of Business Ethics*, July 2011, pp. 385–395; P. M. Erwin, "Corporate Codes of Conduct: The Effects of Code Content and Quality on Ethical Performance," *Journal of Business Ethics*, April 2011, pp. 535–548; "Codes of Conduct," Center for Ethical Business Cultures, www.cebcglobal.org, February 15, 2006; L. Paine, R. Deshpande, J. D. Margolis, and K. E. Bettcher, "Up to Code: Does Your Company's Conduct Meet World-Class Standards"; and A. K. Reichert and M. S. Webb, "Corporate Support for Ethical and Environmental Policies: A Financial Management Perspective," *Journal of Business Ethics*, May 2000.

75. J. B. Singh, "Changes and Trends in Canadian Coirporate Ethics Programs," *Business and Society Review* 116, no. 2 (2011).

76. V. Wessler, "Integrity and Clogged Plumbing," *Straight to the Point*, newsletter of VisionPoint Corporation, Fall 2002, pp. 1–2.

77. J. B. Singh, "Ethics Programs in Canada's Largest Corporations," *Business and Society Review* 111, no. 2 (2006), pp. 119–136; and K. Doucet, "Canadian Organizations Not Meeting Ethics Expectations," *CMA Management* 74, no. 5 (2000), p. 10.

78. T. A. Gavin, "Ethics Education," *Internal Auditor*, April 1989, pp. 54–57.

79. L. Myyry and K. Helkama, "The Role of Value Priorities and Professional Ethics Training in Moral Sensitivity," *Journal of Moral Education* 31, no. 1 (2002), pp. 35–50; and W. Penn and B. D. Collier, "Current Research in Moral Development as a Decision Support System," *Journal of Business Ethics*, January 1985, pp. 131–136.

80. J. A. Byrne, "After Enron: The Ideal Corporation," *BusinessWeek*, August 19, 2002, pp. 68–71; D. Rice and C. Dreilinger, "Rights and Wrongs of Ethics Training," *Training & Development*, May 1990, pp. 103–109; and J. Weber, "Measuring the Impact of Teaching Ethics to Future Managers: A Review, Assessment, and Recommendations," *Journal of Business Ethics*, April 1990, pp. 182–190.

81. See, for instance, A. Wheat, "Keeping an Eye on Corporate America," *Fortune*, November 25, 2002, pp. 44–46; R. B. Schmitt, "Companies Add Ethics Training: Will It Work?" *Wall Street Journal*, November 4, 2002, p. B11; and P. F. Miller and W. T. Coady, "Teaching Work Ethics," *Education Digest*, February 1990, pp. 54–55.

82. G. Farrell and J. O'Donnell, "Ethics Training As Taught by Ex-Cons: Crime Doesn't Pay," *USA Today*, November 16, 2005, p. 1B+.

83. R. C. Anderson with R. White, *Confessions of a Radical Industrialist: Profits, People, Purpose—Doing Business by Respecting the Earth* (New York: St. Martin's Press, 2009), p. 5.

84. "Our Progress," Interface website, www.interfaceglobal.com/Sustainability/Progress-to-Zero.aspx (accessed July 15, 2010).

85. "Interface Support of Communities on the Shared Journey" Interface website, www.interfaceglobal.com/Sustainability/Social-Responsibility.aspx (accessed July 15, 2010).

86. S. Deffree, "Foxconn Explosion Ignites Conversation on Corporate Responsibility," *EDN*, June 23, 2011, p. 8; J. Bussey, "Measuring the Human Cost of an iPad Made in China," *Wall Street Journal*, June 3, 2011, pp. B1+; A. Satariano, "Apple Risks iPad Production Loss of 500,000 After Blast," *Bloomberg BusinessWeek*, May 26, 2011; and E. Savitz, "Apple: Analysts See Limited Risks from Hon Hai Plant Explosion," *Forbes.com*, May 23, 2011, p. 4.

87. Skills Exercise based on F. Bartolome, "Nobody Trusts the Boss Completely—Now What?" *Harvard Business Review*, March–April 1989, pp. 135–142; and J. K. Butler Jr., "Toward Understanding and Measuring Conditions of Trust: Evolution of a Condition of Trust Inventory," *Journal of Management*, September 1991, pp. 643–663.

87. Based on "Corporate Responsibility Isn't Only About How a Company Spends Its Money: It's About How a Company Makes Its Money," RBC Corporate Responsibility webpage, www.rbc.com/responsibility/index.html (accessed November 13, 2010).

89. "20 Odd Questions: Sole Man Blake Mycoskie," *Wall Street Journal*, January 2012, p. D8; "Your Childhood Saw It Coming," *Fast Company*, December 2011/January 2012, p. 25; C. Garton, "Consumers Are Drawn to Products with a Charitable Connection," *USA Today Online*, July 18, 2011; "Ten Companies with Social Responsibility at the Core," *Advertising Age*, April 19, 2010, p. 88; C. Binkley, "Charity Gives Shoe Brand Extra Shine," *Wall Street Journal*, April 1, 2010, p. D7; J. Shambora, "How I Got Started: Blake Mycoskie, Founder of TOMS Shoes," *Fortune*, March 22, 2010, p. 72;

and "Making A Do-Gooder's Business Model Work," *BusinessWeek Online,* January 26, 2009.

Chapter 6

1. "Innovation knows no boundaries": http://www.infoworld.com/d/adventures-in-it/exploring-cloud-computing-say-good-bye-version-control-618.

2. Based on W. Connors and C. Cummins, "Rim CEOs Give up Top Posts in Shuffle," *Wall Street Journal,* January 23, 2013, http://online.wsj.com/article/SB10001424052970204624204577177184275959856.html (accessed November 12, 2012).

3. J. Zettel, "BlackBerry Inks US$4.7-billion deal with Toronto-based Fairfax," *CTV News* Online, http://www.ctvnews.ca/business/blackberry-inks-us-4-7-billion-deal-with-toronto-based-fairfax-1.1466420 (accessed September 23, 2013).

4. W. H. Gates, written testimony before US House of Representatives Committee on Science and Technology, March 2008.

5. D. Kirkpatrick, "The Second Coming of Apple," *Fortune,* November 9, 1998.

6. AACSB International, *Business Schools on an Innovation Mission: Report of the AACSB International Task Force on Business Schools and Innovation* (Tampa, FL: AACSB International, 2010).

7. R. A. Hattori and J. Wycoff, "Innovation DNA," *Training & Development,* January 2002, p. 24.

8. C. West Churchman introduced the concept of wicked problems in a guest editorial of *Management Science* 14, no. 4 (December 1967).

9. J. C. Camillus, "Strategy as a Wicked Problem," *Harvard Business Review* 86 (2008), pp. 98–101.

10. C. Welch, "Netflix's momentum continues with 2.33 million new US customers in Q4," *The Verge,* January 22, 2014, http://www.theverge.com/2014/1/22/5334934/netflix-q4-2013-earnings (accessed May 25, 2014).

11. Delloite, *Technology, Media & Telecommunications Predictions 2014,* http://www2.deloitte.com/content/dam/Deloitte/global/Documents/Technology-Media-Telecommunications/dttl_TMT_Predictions-2014-lc2.pdf (accessed May 29, 2014).

12. The idea for these metaphors came from J. E. Dutton, S. Ashford, K. O'Neill, and K. Lawrence, "Moves That Matter: Issue Selling and Organizational Change," *Academy of Management Journal,* August 2001, pp. 716–736; B. H. Kemelgor, S. D. Johnson, and S. Srinivasan, "Forces Driving Organizational Change: A Business School Perspective," *Journal of Education for Business,* January–February 2000, pp. 133–137; G. Colvin, "When It Comes to Turbulence, CEOs Could Learn a Lot from Sailors," *Fortune,* March 29, 1999, pp. 194–196; and P. B. Vaill, *Managing as a Performing Art: New Ideas for a World of Chaotic Change* (San Francisco: Jossey-Bass, 1989).

13. K. Lewin, *Field Theory in Social Science* (New York: Harper & Row, 1951).

14. For contrasting views on episodic and continuous change, see K. E. Weick and R. E. Quinn, "Organizational Change and Development," in *Annual Review of Psychology,* vol. 50, ed. J. T. Spence, J. M. Darley, and D. J. Foss, pp. 361–386 (Palo Alto, CA: Annual Reviews, 1999).

15. G. Hamel, "Take It Higher," *Fortune,* February 5, 2001, pp. 169–170.

16. S. Crock and J. Carey, "Storming the Streets of Baghdad," *BusinessWeek,* October 21, 2002, pp. 46–47.

17. J. Jesitus, "Change Management: Energy to the People," *IndustryWeek,* September 1, 1997, pp. 37, 40.

18. D. Lavin, "European Business Rushes to Automate," *Wall Street Journal,* July 23, 1997, p. A14.

19. See, for example, T. C. Head and P. F. Sorensen, "Cultural Values and Organizational Development: A Seven-Country Study," *Leadership & Organization Development Journal,* March 1993, pp. 3–7; A. H. Church, W. W. Burke, and D. F. Van Eynde, "Values, Motives, and Interventions of Organization Development Practitioners," *Group & Organization Management,* March 1994, pp. 5–50; W. L. French and C. H. Bell Jr., *Organization Development: Behavioral Science Interventions for Organization Improvement,* 6th ed. (Upper Saddle River, NJ: Prentice Hall, 1998); N. A. Worren, K. Ruddle, and K. Moore, "From Organizational Development to Change Management," *Journal of Applied Behavioral Science,* September 1999, pp. 273–286; G. Farias, "Organizational Development and Change Management," *Journal of Applied Behavioral Science,* September 2000, pp. 376–379; W. Nicolay, "Response to Farias and Johnson's Commentary," *Journal of Applied Behavioral Science,* September 2000, pp. 380–381; and S. Hicks, "What Is Organization Development?" *Training & Development,* August 2000, p. 65.

20. T. White, "Supporting Change: How Communicators at Scotiabank Turned Ideas into Action," *Communication World,* April 2002, pp. 22–24.

21. M. Javidan, P. W. Dorfman, M. S. deLuque, and R. J. House, "In the Eye of the Beholder: Cross-Cultural Lessons in Leadership from Project GLOBE," *Academy of Management Perspective,* February 2006, pp. 67–90; and E. Fagenson-Eland, E. A. Ensher, and W. W. Burke, "Organization Development and Change Interventions: A Seven-Nation Comparison," *Journal of Applied Behavioral Science,* December 2004, pp. 432–464.

22. E. Fagenson-Eland, E. A. Ensher, and W. W. Burke, "Organization Development and Change Interventions" p. 461.

23. See, for example, A. Deutschman, "Making Change: Why Is It So Hard to Change Our Ways?" *Fast Company,* May 2005, pp. 52–62; S. B. Silverman, C. E. Pogson, and A. B. Cober, "When Employees at Work Don't Get It: A Model for Enhancing Individual Employee Change in Response to Performance Feedback," *Academy of Management Executive,* May 2005, pp. 135–147; C. E. Cunningham, C. A. Woodward, H. S. Shannon, J. MacIntosh, B. Lendrum, D. Rosenbloom, and J. Brown, "Readiness for Organizational Change: A Longitudinal Study of Workplace, Psychological and Behavioral Correlates," *Journal of Occupational and Organizational Psychology,* December 2002, pp. 377–392; M. A. Korsgaard, H. J. Sapienza, and D. M. Schweiger, "Beaten Before Begun: The Role of Procedural Justice in Planning Change," *Journal of Management,* 28, no. 4 (2002), pp. 497–516; R. Kegan and L. L. Lahey, "The Real Reason People Won't Change," *Harvard Business Review,* November 2001, pp. 85–92; S. K. Piderit, "Rethinking Resistance and Recognizing Ambivalence: A Multidimensional View of Attitudes toward an Organizational Change," *Academy of Management Review,* October 2000, pp. 783–794; C. R. Wanberg and J. T. Banas, "Predictors and Outcomes of Openness to Changes in a Reorganizing Workplace," *Journal of Applied Psychology,* February 2000, pp. 132–142; A. A. Armenakis and A. G. Bedeian, "Organizational Change: A Review of Theory and Research in the 1990s," *Journal of Management,* 25, no. 3 (1999), pp. 293–315; and B. M. Staw, "Counterforces to Change," in *Change in Organizations,* ed. P. S. Goodman and Associates, pp. 87–121 (San Francisco: Jossey-Bass, 1982).

24. J. P. Kotter and L. A. Schlesinger, "Choosing Strategies for Change," *Harvard Business Review,* March–April 1979, pp. 107–109; P. Strebel, "Why Do Employees Resist Change?" *Harvard Business Review,* May–June 1996, pp. 86–92; J. Mariotti, "Troubled by Resistance to Change," *IndustryWeek,* October 7, 1996, p. 30; and A. Reichers, J. P. Wanous, and J. T. Austin, "Understanding and Managing Cynicism about Organizational Change," *Academy of Management Executive,* February 1997, pp. 48–57.

25. J. P. Kotter and L. A. Schlesinger, "Choosing Strategies for Change," *Harvard Business Review*, March–April 1979, pp. 106–111; K. Matejka and R. Julian, "Resistance to Change Is Natural," *Supervisory Management*, October 1993, p. 10; C. O'Connor, "Resistance: The Repercussions of Change," *Leadership & Organization Development Journal*, October 1993, pp. 30–36; J. Landau, "Organizational Change and Barriers to Innovation: A Case Study in the Italian Public Sector," *Human Relations*, December 1993, pp. 1411–1429; A. Sagie and M. Koslowsky, "Organizational Attitudes and Behaviors as a Function of Participation in Strategic and Tactical Change Decisions: An Application of Path-Goal Theory," *Journal of Organizational Behavior*, January 1994, pp. 37–47; V. D. Miller, J. R. Johnson, and J. Grau, "Antecedents to Willingness to Participate in a Planned Organizational Change," *Journal of Applied Communication Research*, February 1994, pp. 59–80; P. Pritchett and R. Pound, *The Employee Handbook for Organizational Change* (Dallas, TX: Pritchett, 1994); R. Maurer, *Beyond the Wall of Resistance: Unconventional Strategies That Build Support for Change* (Austin, TX: Bard Books, 1996); D. Harrison, "Assess and Remove Barriers to Change," *HRfocus*, July 1999, pp. 9–10; L. K. Lewis, "Disseminating Information and Soliciting Input during Planned Organizational Change," *Management Communication Quarterly*, August 1999, pp. 43–75; J. P. Wanous, A. E. Reichers, and J. T. Austin, "Cynicism about Organizational Change," *Group & Organization Management*, June 2000, pp. 132–153; K. W. Mossholder, R. P. Settoon, A. A. Armenakis, and S. G. Harris, "Emotion during Organizational Transformations," *Group & Organization Management*, September 2000, pp. 220–243; and S. K. Piderit, "Rethinking Resistance and Recognizing Ambivalence: A Multidimensional View of Attitudes toward an Organizational Change," *Academy of Management Review*, October 2000, pp. 783–794.

26. R. M. Kanter, "From Spare Change to Real Change: The Social Sector as Beta Site for Business Innovation," *Harvard Business Review*, May–June 1999, pp. 122–132.

27. J. E. Perry-Smith and C. E. Shalley, "The Social Side of Creativity: A Static and Dynamic Social Network Perspective," *Academy of Management Review*, January 2003, pp. 89–106; and P. K. Jagersma, "Innovate or Die: It's Not Easy, but It Is Possible to Enhance Your Organization's Ability to Innovate," *Journal of Business Strategy*, January–February 2003, pp. 25–28.

28. Statistics Canada, "Corporate Failures, 1996," *The Daily*, August 8, 2003.

29. These definitions are based on T. M. Amabile, *Creativity in Context* (Boulder, CO: Westview Press, 1996).

30. M. Basadur, J. Conklin, and G. K. VanPatter, "Rethinking Wicked Problems Part (2): Unpacking Paradigms, Bridging Universes," *NextD Journal* 10 (2007), Conversation 10.3.

31. Management Reflection Box based on N. Karmali, "Bill Gates, Azim Premji, Ratan Tata to Host Bangalore Philanthropy Meet," *Forbes.com,* May 12, 2012; A. Chaze, "Mistry To Take Helm At Tata Sons," *Global Finance,* January 2012, p. 6; C. Chynoweth, "Dare to Try, the Indian Way," *The Sunday Times Online,* April 17, 2011; C. K. Prahalad, "Best Practices Get You Only So Far," *Harvard Business Review,* April 2010, p. 32; A. Graham, "Too Good to Fail," *Strategy+Business Online,* www.strategy-business.com, February 23, 2010; J. Scanlon, "How to Build a Culture of Innovation," *BusinessWeek Online,* www.businessweek.com, August 19, 2009; and J. Scanlon, "Tata Group's Innovation Competition," *BusinessWeek Online,* www.businessweek.com, June 17, 2009.

32. R. W. Woodman, J. E. Sawyer, and R. W. Griffin, "Toward a Theory of Organizational Creativity," *Academy of Management Review*, April 1993, pp. 293–321.

33. T. M. Egan, "Factors Influencing Individual Creativity in the Workplace: An Examination of Quantitative Empirical Research," *Advances in Developing Human Resources*, May 2005,

pp. 160–181; F. Damanpour, "Organizational Innovation: A Meta-Analysis of Effects of Determinants and Moderators," *Academy of Management Journal*, September 1991, pp. 555–590; S. D. Saleh and C. K. Wang, "The Management of Innovation: Strategy, Structure, and Organizational Climate," *IEEE Transactions on Engineering Management*, February 1993, pp. 14–22; G. R. Oldham and A. Cummings, "Employee Creativity: Personal and Contextual Factors at Work," *Academy of Management Journal*, June 1996, pp. 607–634; J. B. Sorensen and T. E. Stuart, "Aging, Obsolescence, and Organizational Innovation," *Administrative Science Quarterly*, March 2000, pp. 81–112; T. M. Amabile, C. N. Hadley, and S. J. Kramer, "Creativity Under the Gun," *Harvard Business Review*, August 2002, pp. 52–61; and N. Madjar, G. R. Oldham, and M. G. Pratt, "There's No Place Like Home? The Contributions of Work and Nonwork Creativity Support to Employees' Creative Performance," *Academy of Management Journal*, August 2002, pp. 757–767.

34. P. R. Monge, M. D. Cozzens, and N. S. Contractor, "Communication and Motivational Predictors of the Dynamics of Organizational Innovations," *Organization Science*, May 1992, pp. 250–274.

35. T. M. Amabile, C. N. Hadley, and S. J. Kramer, "Creativity Under the Gun," *Harvard Business Review*, August 2002, pp. 52–61.

36. N. Madjar, G. R. Oldham, and M. G. Pratt, "There's No Place Like Home? The Contributions of Work and Nonwork Creativity Support to Employees' Creative Performance," *Academy of Management Journal*, August 2002, pp. 757–767.

37. V. Galt, "Training on Tap," *Globe and Mail*, November 20, 2002, pp. C1, C8.

38. C. Salter, "Mattel Learns to 'Throw the Bunny,'" *Fast Company*, November 2002, p. 22.

39. See, for instance, J. E. Perry-Smith, "Social Yet Creative: The Role of Social Relationships in Facilitating Individual Creativity," *Academy of Management Journal*, February 2006, pp. 85–101; C. E. Shalley, J. Zhou, and G. R. Oldham, "The Effects of Personal and Contextual Characteristics on Creativity: Where Should We Go from Here?" *Journal of Management* 30, no. 6 (2004), pp. 933–958; M. Amabile, *Creativity in Context* (Boulder, CO: Westview Press, 1996); M. Tushman and D. Nadler, "Organizing for Innovation," *California Management Review*, Spring 1986, pp. 74–92; R. Moss Kanter, "When a Thousand Flowers Bloom: Structural, Collective, and Social Conditions for Innovation in Organization," in *Research in Organizational Behavior*, vol. 10, ed. B. M. Staw and L. L. Cummings, pp. 169–211 (Greenwich, CT: JAI Press, 1988); G. Morgan, "Endangered Species: New Ideas," *Business Month*, April 1989, pp. 75–77; S. G. Scott and R. A. Bruce, "Determinants of Innovative People: A Path Model of Individual Innovation in the Workplace," *Academy of Management Journal*, June 1994, pp. 580–607; T. M. Amabile, R. Conti, H. Coon, J. Lazenby, and M. Herron, "Assessing the Work Environment for Creativity," *Academy of Management Journal*, October 1996, pp. 1154–1184; A. deGues, "The Living Company," *Harvard Business Review*, March–April 1997, pp. 51–59; J. Zhou, "Feedback Valence, Feedback Style, Task Autonomy, and Achievement Orientation: Interactive Effects on Creative Behavior," *Journal of Applied Psychology* 83, no. 2 (1998), pp. 261–276; G. Hamel, "Reinvent Your Company," *Fortune*, June 12, 2000, pp. 98–118; J. M. George and J. Zhou, "When Openness to Experience and Conscientiousness Are Related to Creative Behavior: An Interactional Approach," *Journal of Applied Psychology*, June 2001, pp. 513–524; and Perry-Smith and C. E. Shalley, "The Social Side of Creativity: A Static and Dynamic Social Network Perspective," *Academy of Management Review*, January 2003, pp. 89–106.

40. J. M. Howell and C. A. Higgins, "Champions of Change," *Business Quarterly*, Spring 1990, pp. 31–32; P. A. Carrow-Moffett,

"Change Agent Skills: Creating Leadership for School Renewal," *NASSP Bulletin*, April 1993, pp. 57–62; T. Stjernberg and A. Philips, "Organizational Innovations in a Long-Term Perspective: Legitimacy and Souls-of-Fire as Critical Factors of Change and Viability," *Human Relations*, October 1993, pp. 1193–2023; and J. Ramos, "Producing Change That Lasts," *Across the Board*, March 1994, pp. 29–33.

41. Associated Press, "Mars Rover Is Launched on Voyage to Look for Water," *USA Today*, June 11, 2003, www.usatoday.com; NASA's website, www.nasa.gov (accessed June 11, 2003); and W. J. Broad, "A Tiny Rover, Built on the Cheap, Is Ready to Explore Distant Mars," *New York Times*, July 5, 1997, p. 9.

42. P. Sonne, "Tesco's CEO-to-Be Unfolds Map for Global Expansion," *Wall Street Journal,* June 9, 2010, p. B1; T. Shifrin, "Grocery Giant Tesco Is Creating a Storm in the US Market with Its Tesco in a Box Set of Systems," www.computerworlduk.com, January 14, 2008; P. Olson, "Tesco's Landing," *Forbes,* June 4, 2007, pp. 116–118; and P. M. Senge, *The Fifth Discipline: The Art and Practice of Learning Organizations* (New York: Doubleday, 1990).

43. J. J. Salopek, "Keeping Learning Well-Oiled," *T&D,* October 2011, pp. 32–35.

44. A. C. Edmondson, "The Competitive Imperative of Learning," *Harvard Business Review,* July–August 2008, pp. 60–67.

45. S. A. Sackmann, P. M. Eggenhofer-Rehart, and M. Friesl, "Long-Term Efforts Toward Developing a Learning Organization," *Journal of Applied Behavioral Science,* December 2009, pp. 521–549; D. A. Garvin, A. C. Edmondson, and F. Gino, "Is Yours a Learning Organization?" *Harvard Business Review,* March 2008, pp. 109–116; A. N. K. Chen and T. M. Edgington, "Assessing Value in Organizational Knowledge Creation: Considerations for Knowledge Workers," *MIS Quarterly,* June 2005, pp. 279–309; K. G. Smith, C. J. Collins, and K. D. Clark, "Existing Knowledge, Knowledge Creation Capability, and The Rate of New Product Introduction in High-Technology Firms," *Academy of Management Journal,* April 2005, pp. 346–357; R. Cross, A. Parker, L. Prusak, and S. P. Borgati, "Supporting Knowledge Creation and Sharing in Social Networks," *Organizational Dynamics,* Fall, 2001, pp. 100–120; M. Schulz, "The Uncertain Relevance of Newness: Organizational Learning and Knowledge Flows," *Academy of Management Journal,* August 2001, pp. 661–681; G. Szulanski, "Exploring Internal Stickiness: Impediments to the Transfer of Best Practice within the Firm," *Strategic Management Journal,* Winter Special Issue, 1996, pp. 27–43; and J. M. Liedtka, "Collaborating across Lines of Business for Competitive Advantage," *Academy of Management Executive*, April 1996, pp. 20–37.

46. J. Liedtka and T. Ogilvie, *Designing for Growth: A Design Thinking Tool Kit for Managers,* (New York: Columbia Business School Press), 2011.

47. R. E. Silverman, "Companies Change Their Way of Thinking," *Wall Street Journal,* June 7, 2012, p. B8; and R. L. Martin, "The Innovation Catalysts," *Harvard Business Review,* June 2011, pp. 82–87.

48. J. Useem, "Jim McNerney Thinks He Can Turn 3M from a Good Company into a Great One—With a Little Help from His Former Employer, General Electric," *Fortune*, August 12, 2002, pp. 127–132; and C. Hymowitz, "How Leader at 3M Got His Employees to Back Big Changes," *Wall Street Journal*, April 23, 2002, p. B1.

49. See T. H. Fitzgerald, "Can Change in Organizational Culture Really Be Managed?" *Organizational Dynamics*, Autumn 1988, pp. 5–15; B. Dumaine, "Creating a New Company Culture," *Fortune*, January 15, 1990, pp. 127–131; P. F. Drucker, "Don't Change Corporate Culture—Use It!" *Wall Street Journal*, March 28, 1991, p. A14; J. Martin, *Cultures in Organizations: Three Perspectives* (New York: Oxford University Press, 1992); D. C. Pheysey, *Organizational Cultures: Types and Transformations* (London: Routledge, 1993); C. G. Smith and R. P. Vecchio, "Organizational Culture and Strategic Management: Issues in the Strategic Management of Change," *Journal of Managerial Issues*,

Spring 1993, pp. 53–70; P. Bate, *Strategies for Cultural Change* (Boston: Butterworth-Heinemann, 1994); and P. Anthony, *Managing Culture* (Philadelphia: Open University Press, 1994).

50. M. L. Wald and J. Schwartz, "Shuttle Inquiry Uncovers Flaws in Communication," *New York Times*, August 4, 2003, http://nytimes .com.

51. M. L. Wald and J. Schwartz, "Shuttle Inquiry Uncovers Flaws in Communication." *New York Times*, August 4, 2003, http://nytimes.com.

52. See, for example, R. H. Kilmann, M. J. Saxton, and R. Serpa, eds., *Gaining Control of the Corporate Culture* (San Francisco: Jossey-Bass, 1985); and D. C. Hambrick and S. Finkelstein, "Managerial Discretion: A Bridge between Polar Views of Organizational Outcomes," in *Research in Organizational Behavior*, vol. 9, ed. B. M. Staw and L. L. Cummings (Greenwich, CT: JAI Press, 1987), p. 384.

53. P. A. McLagan, "Change Leadership Today," *Training & Development*, November 2002, p. 29.

54. W. Pietersen, "The Mark Twain Dilemma: The Theory and Practice for Change Leadership," *Journal of Business Strategy*, September–October 2002, pp. 32–37; C. Hymowitz, "To Maintain Success, Managers Must Learn How to Direct Change," *Wall Street Journal*, August 13, 2002, p. B1; and J. E. Dutton, S. Ashford, K. O'Neill, and K. Lawrence, "Moves That Matter: Issue Selling and Organizational Change," *Academy of Management Journal*, August 2001, pp. 716–736.

55. P. A. McLagan, "The Change-Capable Organization," *Training & Development*, January 2003, pp. 50–58.

56. Based on J. P. Kotter and L. A. Schlesinger, "Choosing Strategies for Change," *Harvard Business Review*, March–April 1979, pp. 106–114; and T. A. Stewart, "Rate Your Readiness to Change," *Fortune*, February 7, 1994, pp. 106–110.

57. B. Horovitz, "In Search of Next Big Thing," *USA Today,* July 9, 2012, pp. 1B+; press release, "Under Armour Reports Fourth Quarter Net Revenues Growth of 34% and Fourth Quarter EPS Growth of 40%," investor.underarmour.com, January 26, 2012; D. Roberts, "Under Armour Gets Serious," *Fortune,* November 7, 2011, pp. 153–162; E. Olson, "Under Armour Applies Its Muscle to Shoes," *New York Times Online,* August 8, 2011; M. Townsend, "Under Armour's Daring Half-Court Shot," *Bloomberg BusinessWeek,* November 1–November 7, 2010, pp. 24–25; and E. Olson, "Under Armour Wants to Dress Athletic Young Women," *New York Times Online,* August 31, 2010.

58. A. Hill, "How to Conform to Creative Deviance," *Financial Times Online,* April 30, 2012; A. Lashinsky, "Inside Apple," May 23, 2011, pp. 125–134; and C. Mainemelis, "Stealing Fire: Creative Deviance in the Evolution of New Ideas," *Academy of Management Review,* December 2010, pp. 558–578.

Chapter 7

1. Based on Jad Mouawad, "Bone-Chilling Cold a Crippling Blow to Air Travel," *New York Times*, January 6, 2014, http://www.nytimes .com/2014/01/07/business/frigid-weather-cripples-air-travel-system .html (accessed May 25, 2014).

2. L. Artani, "January flight disruptions cost passengers $2,5 billion," *Washington Post*, February 3, 2014, http://www.washingtonpost .com/blogs/dr-gridlock/wp/2014/02/03/january-flight-disruptions-cost-passengers-2-5-billion/ (accessed May 25, 2014).

3. D. A. Garvin and M. A. Roberto, "What You Don't Know about Making Decisions," *Harvard Business Review*, September 2001, pp. 108–116.

4. E. Frauenheim, "Managers Don't Matter," *Workforce Management Online*, April 2010; and K. A. Tucker and V. Allman, "Don't Be a Cat-and-Mouse Manager," The Gallup Organization, www.brain.gallup .com, September 9, 2004.

5. "Work USA 2008/2009 Report: Driving Business Results through Continuous Engagement," Watson Wyatt Worldwide, Washington, DC.

6. R.J. Volkema, "Problem Formulation: Its Portrayal in the Texts," *Organizational Behavior Teaching Review* 11, no. 3 (1986–1987), pp. 113–126.

7. P. C. Nutt, *Why Decisions Fail: Avoiding the Blunders and Traps That Lead to Debacles* (San Francisco, CA: Berrett-Koehler, 2002).

8. "Toronto Pearson (Deplaned, enplaned) Passengers," Jan 31, 2014, http://www.torontopearson.com/uploadedFiles/GTAA/Content/About_GTAA/Statistics/12-DecPax(1).pdf (accessed May 25, 2014).

9. Statistics Canada, "Total aircraft movements by class of operation — NAV CANADA," June 4, 2014, http://www.statcan.gc.ca/pub/51-209-x/2013001/t002-eng.htm (accessed May 25, 2014).

10. T. A. Stewart, "Did You Ever Have to Make Up Your Mind?" *Harvard Business Review*, January 2006, p. 12; J. Pfeffer and R. I. Sutton, "Why Managing by Facts Works," *Strategy+Business*, Spring 2006, pp. 9–12; and E. Pooley, "Editor's Desk," *Fortune*, June 27, 2005, p. 16.

11. See H. A. Simon, "Rationality in Psychology and Economics," *Journal of Business*, October 1986, pp. 209–224; and A. Langley, "In Search of Rationality: The Purposes Behind the Use of Formal Analysis in Organizations," *Administrative Science Quarterly*, December 1989, pp. 598–631.

12. See, for example, J. G. March, *A Primer on Decision Making* (New York: Free Press, 1994), pp. 8–25; and A. Langley, H. Mintzberg, P. Pitcher, E. Posada, and J. Saint-Macary, "Opening Up Decision Making: The View from the Black Stool," *Organization Science*, May–June 1995, pp. 260–279.

13. J. G. March, "Decision-Making Perspective: Decisions in Organizations and Theories of Choice," in A. H. Van de Ven and W.F. Joyce (eds.), *Perspectives on Organization Design and Behavior* (New York: Wiley-Interscience, 1981), pp. 232–233.

14. See N. McK. Agnew and J. L. Brown, "Bounded Rationality: Fallible Decisions in Unbounded Decision Space," *Behavioral Science*, July 1986, pp. 148–161; B. E. Kaufman, "A New Theory of Satisficing," *Journal of Behavioral Economics*, Spring 1990, pp. 35–51; and D. R. A. Skidd, "Revisiting Bounded Rationality," *Journal of Management Inquiry*, December 1992, pp. 343–347.

15. See, for example, G. McNamara, H. Moon, and P. Bromiley, "Banking on Commitment: Intended and Unintended Consequences of an Organization's Attempt to Attenuate Escalation of Commitment," *Academy of Management Journal,* April 2002, pp. 443–452; V. S. Rao and A. Monk, "The Effects of Individual Differences and Anonymity on Commitment to Decisions," *Journal of Social Psychology*, August 1999, pp. 496–515; C. F. Camerer and R. A. Weber, "The Econometrics and Behavioral Economics of Escalation of Commitment: A Re-examination of Staw's Theory," *Journal of Economic Behavior and Organization*, May 1999, pp. 59–82; D. R. Bobocel and J. P. Meyer, "Escalating Commitment to a Failing Course of Action: Separating the Roles of Choice and Justification," *Journal of Applied Psychology*, June 1994, pp. 360–363; and B. M. Staw, "The Escalation of Commitment to a Course of Action," *Academy of Management Review*, October 1981, pp. 577–587.

16. W. Cole, "The Stapler Wars," *Time* Inside Business, April 2005, p. A5.

17. See K. R. Hammond, R. M. Hamm, J. Grassia, and T. Pearson, "Direct Comparison of the Efficacy of Intuitive and Analytical Cognition in Expert Judgment," in *IEEE Transactions on Systems, Man, and Cybernetics* SMC-17, no. 5 (1987), pp. 753–770; W. H. Agor, ed., *Intuition in Organizations* (Newbury Park, CA: Sage, 1989); O. Behling and N. L. Eckel, "Making Sense Out of Intuition," *The Executive*, February 1991, pp. 46–47; L. A. Burke and M. K. Miller, "Taking the

Mystery Out of Intuitive Decision Making," *Academy of Management Executive*, October 1999, pp. 91–99; A. L. Tesolin, "How to Develop the Habit of Intuition," *Training & Development*, March 2000, p. 76; and T. A. Stewart, "How to Think with Your Gut," *Business 2.0*, November 2002, pp. 98–104.

18. See M. H. Bazerman and D. Chugh, "Decisions without Blinders," *Harvard Business Review*, January 2006, pp. 88–97; C. C. Miller and R. D. Ireland, "Intuition in Strategic Decision Making: Friend or Foe in the Fast-Paced 21st Century," *Academy of Management Executive*, February 2005, pp. 19–30; E. Sadler-Smith and E. Shefy, "The Intuitive Executive: Understanding and Applying 'Gut Feel' in Decision-Making," *Academy of Management Executive*, November 2004, pp. 76–91; T. A. Stewart, "How to Think with Your Gut," *Business 2.0*, November 2002, pp. 98–104; A. L. Tesolin, "How to Develop the Habit of Intuition," *Training & Development*, March 2000, p. 76; L. A. Burke and M. K. Miller, "Taking the Mystery Out of Intuitive Decision Making," *Academy of Management Executive*, October 1999, pp. 91–99; O. Behling and N. L. Eckel, "Making Sense Out of Intuition," *The Executive*, February 1991, pp. 46–47; W. H. Agor, ed., *Intuition in Organizations* (Newbury Park, CA: Sage, 1989); and K. R. Hammond, R. M. Hamm, J. Grassia, and T. Pearson, "Direct Comparison of the Efficacy of Intuitive and Analytical Cognition in Expert Judgment," *IEEE Transactions on Systems, Man, and Cybernetics* SMC-17, no. 5 (1987), pp. 753–770.

19. C. C. Miller and R. D. Ireland, "Intuition in Strategic Decision Making: Friend or Foe," p. 20.

20. E. Sadler-Smith and E. Shefy, "Developing Intuitive Awareness in Management Education," *Academy of Management Learning & Education,* June 2007, pp. 186–205.

21. M. G. Seo and L. Feldman Barrett, "Being Emotional During Decision Making—Good or Bad? An Empirical Investigation," *Academy of Management Journal,* August 2007, pp. 923–940.

22. B. Roberts, "Hire Intelligence," *HR Magazine,* May 2011, p. 63.

23. R. B. Briner, D. Denyer, and D. M. Rousseau, "Evidence-Based Management: Concept Cleanup Time?" *Academy of Management Perspective,* November 2009, p. 22.

24. J. Pfeffer and R. Sutton, "Trust the Evidence, Not Your Instincts," *New York Times Online,* September 3, 2011; and T. Reay, W. Berta, and M. K. Kohn, "What's the Evidence on Evidence-Based Management?" *Academy of Management Perspectives,* November 2009, p. 5.

25. K. R. Brousseau, M. J. Driver, G. Hourihan, and R. Larsson, "The Seasoned Executive's Decision-Making Style," *Harvard Business Review*, February 2006, pp. 111–121.

26. "Giant Pool of Money," *This American Life,* National Public Radio, September 5, 2008, www.thisamericanlife.org/radio-archives/episode/355/the-giant-pool-of-money (accessed July 20, 2010).

27. Future Vision box based on A. Alter, "Your E-Book Is Reading You," *Wall Street Journal,* June 29, 2012, pp. D1+; R. Kurzweil, "Man or Machine?" *Wall Street Journal,* June 29, 2012, p. C12; D. Jones and A. Shaw, "Slowing Momentum: Why BPM Isn't Keeping Pace with Its Potential," *BPM Magazine,* February 2006, pp. 4–12; B. Violino, "IT Directions," *CFO,* January 2006, pp. 68–72; D. Weinberger, "Sorting Data to Suit Yourself," *Harvard Business Review,* March 2005, pp. 16–18; and C. Winkler, "Getting a Grip on Performance," *CFO-IT,* Winter 2004, pp. 38–48.

28. *Greater Toronto Airport Authority,* "Meet our Executive Team," GTAA About Page, http://www.torontopearson.com/en/gtaa/management/## (accessed May 25, 2014).

29. Striving to be your global front door, GTAA About Page, http://www.torontopearson.com/en/gtaa/strategy//## (accessed May 25, 2014).

30. A. J. Rowe and R. O. Mason, *Managing with Style* (San Francisco: Jossey-Bass, 1987); and A. J. Rowe, J. D. Boulgarides, and M. R. McGrath, *Managerial Decision Making, Modules in Management Series* (Chicago: SRA, 1984), pp. 18–22.

31. S. Holmes, "Inside the Coup at Nike," *BusinessWeek,* February 6, 2006, pp. 34–37; and M. Barbaro, "Slightly Testy Nike Divorce Came Down to Data vs. Feel," *New York Times Online,* www.nytimes.com, January 28, 2006.

32. C. M. Vance, K. S. Groves, Y. Paik, and H. Kindler, "Understanding and Measuring Linear–NonLinear Thinking Style for Enhanced Management Education and Professional Practice," *Academy of Management Learning & Education,* June 2007, pp. 167–185.

33. D. Kahneman and A. Tversky, "Judgment under Uncertainty: Heuristics and Biases," *Science* 185 (1974), pp. 1124–1131.

34. Information for this section is taken from S. P. Robbins, *Decide and Conquer* (Upper Saddle River, NJ: Financial Times/Prentice Hall, 2004).

35. data points box based on D. Kahneman, D. Lovallo, and O. Siboney, "Before You Make That Big Decision," *Harvard Business Review,* June 2011, pp. 50–60; N. Tasler, "Prime Your Mind for Action," *BusinessWeek Online,* November 3, 2009; B. Dumaine, "The Trouble with Teams," *Fortune,* September 5, 1994, pp. 86–92; A. S. Wellner, "A Perfect Brainstorm," *Inc.,* October 2003, pp. 31–35; "Hurry Up and Decide," *BusinessWeek,* May 14, 2001, p. 16; J. MacIntyre, "Bosses and Bureaucracy," *Springfield, Missouri Business Journal,* August 1–7, 2005, p. 29; J. Crick, "Hand Jive," *Fortune,* June 13, 2005, pp. 40–41; and "On the Road to Invention," *Fast Company,* February 2005, p. 16.

36. L. Margonelli, "How IKEA Designs Its Sexy Price Tags," *Business 2.0,* October 2002, p. 108.

37. P. C. Chu, E. E. Spires, and T. Sueyoshi, "Cross-Cultural Differences in Choice Behavior and Use of Decision Aids: A Comparison of Japan and the United States," *Organizational Behavior & Human Decision Processes,* vol. 77, no. 2 (1999), pp. 147–170.

38. D. Ariely, "Good Decisions. Bad Outcomes," *Harvard Business Review,* December 2010, p. 40.

39. S. Thurm, "Seldom-Used Executive Power: Reconsidering," *Wall Street Journal,* February 6, 2006, p. B3.

40. J. S. Hammond, R. L. Keeney, and H. Raiffa, *Smart Choices: A Practical Guide to Making Better Decisions* (Boston, MA: Harvard Business School Press, 1999), p. 4.

41. This discussion is based on E. W. Ford, W. J. Duncan, A. G. Bedeian, P. M. Ginter, M. D. Rousculp, and A. M. Adams, "Mitigating Risks, Visible Hands, Inevitable Disasters, and Soft Variables: Management Research That Matters," *Academy of Management Executive,* November 2005, pp. 24–38; K. H. Hammonds, "5 Habits of Highly Reliable Organizations: An Interview with Karl Weick," *Fast Company,* May 2002, pp. 124–128; and K. E. Weick, "Drop Your Tools: An Allegory for Organizational Studies," *Administrative Science Quarterly,* vol. 41, no. 2 (1996), pp. 301–313.

42. D. Dunne and R. Martin, "Design Thinking and How It Will Change Management Education: An Interview and Discussion," *Academy of Management Learning & Education,* December 2006, p. 512.

43. M. Korn and R. E. Silverman, "Forget B-School, D-School Is Hot," *Wall Street Journal,* June 7, 2012, pp. B1+; R. Martin and J. Euchner, "Design Thinking," *Research Technology Management,* May/June 2012, pp. 10–14; T. Larsen and T. Fisher, "Design Thinking: A Solution to Fracture-Critical Systems," *DMI News & Views,* May 2012, p. 31; T. Berno, "Design Thinking versus Creative Intelligence," *DMI News & Views,* May 2012, p. 28; J. Liedtka and Tim Ogilvie, "Helping Business Managers Discover Their Appetite for Design Thinking,"

Design Management Review, Issue 1, 2012, pp. 6–13; and T. Brown, "Strategy By Design," *Fast Company,* June 2005, pp. 52–54.

44. C. Guglielmo, "Apple Loop: The Week in Review," Forbes.com, May 25, 2012, p. 2.

45. D. Dunne and R. Martin, "Design Thinking and How It Will Change Management Education: An Interview and Discussion," p. 514.

46. "Toronto Pearson (Deplaned, enplaned) Passengers," Jan 31, 2014, http://www.torontopearson.com/uploadedFiles/GTAA/Content/About_GTAA/Statistics/12-DecPax(1).pdf (accessed May 25, 2014).

47. Statistics Canada, "Total aircraft movements by class of operation—NAV CANADA," June 4, 2014, http://www.statcan.gc.ca/pub/51-209-x/2013001/t002-eng.htm (accessed May 25, 2014).

48. Situation adapted from information in N. Weinberg, "Holier Than Whom?" *Forbes,* June 23, 2003, p. 711; and E. Baum, "Schwab Campaign Bundles Controversy, Consistency," *Fund Marketing Alert,* March 10, 2003, p. 10.

49. Based on J. Calano and J. Salzman, "Ten Ways to Fire Up Your Creativity," *Working Woman,* July 1989, p. 94; J. V. Anderson, "Mind Mapping: A Tool for Creative Thinking," *Business Horizons,* January–February 1993, pp. 42–46; M. Loeb, "Ten Commandments for Managing Creative People," *Fortune,* January 16, 1995, pp. 135–136; and M. Henricks, "Good Thinking," *Entrepreneur,* May 1996, pp. 70–73.

50. "Eurotunnel Boosts Capacity," *Rail Business Intelligence,* May 31, 2012, p. 2; "Eurostar Trains Disrupted by French Power Cable Fault," *BBCNews Online,* March 6, 2012; N. Clark, "Eurostar Criticized for Winter Breakdowns," *New York Times Online,* February 13, 2010; B. Mellor and S. Rothwell, "Eurostar Cuts Service Amid Cold Snap," *BusinessWeek,* January 11, 2010, p. 10; D. Jolly, "Eurostar Service Disrupted as Train Stalls in Channel Tunnel," *New York Times Online,* January 8, 2010; and G. Corkindale, "Does Your Company's Reputation Matter?" *BusinessWeek Online,* December 29, 2009.

Chapter 8

1. Based on R. Ouzounian, "Down the Tube," *Toronto Star,* January 7, 2007, p. C6; S. Sperounes, "A Sensation Rises from Out of the Blue," *Edmonton Journal,* September 30, 2003, p. C1; "Masters of Splatter May Turn Your Mood Indigo," *People Weekly,* June 8, 1992, pp. 108–110; and Blue Man Group website, www.blueman.com (accessed July 20, 2007).

2. V. Pilieci, "The Lost Generation of Business Talent," *Vancouver Sun,* May 2, 2001, pp. D1, D9.

3. See, for example, D. K. Sinha, "The Contribution of Formal Planning to Decisions," *Strategic Management Journal,* October 1990, pp. 479–492; N. Capon, J. U. Farley, and J. M. Hulbert, "Strategic Planning and Financial Performance: More Evidence," *Journal of Management Studies,* January 1994, pp. 22–38; C. C. Miller and L. B. Cardinal, "Strategic Planning and Firm Performance: A Synthesis of More Than Two Decades of Research," *Academy of Management Journal,* March 1994, pp. 1649–1685; P. J. Brews and M. R. Hunt, "Learning to Plan and Planning to Learn: Resolving the Planning School/Learning School Debate," *Strategic Management Journal,* December 1999, pp. 889–913; and R. Wiltbank, N. Dew, S. Read, and S. D. Sarasvathy, "What to Do Next? The Case for Non-Predictive Strategy," *Strategic Management Journal* 27, no. 10 (October 2006), pp. 981–998.

4. S. Sperounes, "A Sensation Rises from Out of the Blue," *Edmonton Journal,* September 30, 2003, p. C1; K. Powers, "Blue Coup," *Forbes,* March 19, 2001, p. 136; and S. Hampson, "Blue Cogs in a Corporate Wheel," *Globe and Mail,* July 12, 2003, p. R3.

5. R. Molz, "How Leaders Use Goals," *Long Range Planning*, October 1987, p. 91.

6. C. Hymowitz, "When Meeting Targets Becomes the Strategy, CEO Is on Wrong Path," *Wall Street Journal*, March 8, 2005, p. B1.

7. McDonald's 2010 Proxy Statement, www.mcdonalds.com, May 24, 2010; and McDonald's Annual Report 2007, www.mcdonalds.com, April 21, 2008.

8. Royal Bank of Canada, "Vision and Values," http://www.rbc.com/aboutus/visionandvalues.html (accessed May 13, 2014).

9. Nike, www.nikebiz.com/crreport/; Deutsche Bank, www.db.com/en/content/company/mission_and_brand.htm; and EnCana Corporate Constitution (2010), www.encana.com.

10. See, for instance, J. Pfeffer, *Organizational Design* (Arlington Heights, IL: AHM Publishing, 1978), pp. 5–12; and C. K. Warriner, "The Problem of Organizational Purpose," Sociological Quarterly, Spring 1965, pp. 139–146.

11. J. D. Hunger and T. L. Wheelen, *Strategic Management and Business Policy,* 10th ed. (Upper Saddle River, NJ: Prentice Hall, 2006).

12. J. L. Roberts, "Signed. Sealed. Delivered?" *Newsweek,* June 20, 2005, pp. 44–46.

13. J. K. Nestruck, "Blue Man Scoop: Founding Members Reveal How It All Began," *National Post*, June 8, 2005, p. AL1; S. Sperounes, "A Sensation Rises from Out of the Blue," *Edmonton Journal*, September 30, 2003, p. C1; K. Powers, "Blue Coup," *Forbes*, March 19, 2001, p. 136; and S. Hampson, "Blue Cogs in a Corporate Wheel," *Globe and Mail*, July 12, 2003, p. R3.

14. Based on R. L. Brandt, "Birth of a Salesman," *Wall Street Journal,* October 15–16, 2012, pp. C1+; D. Lyons, "Jeff Bezos," *Newsweek,* December 28, 2009/January 4, 2010, pp. 85–86; B. Stone, "Can Amazon Be Wal-Mart of the Web?" *New York Times Online,* September 20, 2009; and K. Kelleher, "Why Amazon Is Bucking the Trend," CNNMoney.com, March 2, 2009.

15. J. Jusko, "Unwavering Focus," *Industry Week,* January 2010, p. 26.

16. P. N. Romani, "MBO By Any Other Name is Still MBO," *Supervision,* December 1997, pp. 6–8; and A. W. Schrader and G. T. Seward, "MBO Makes Dollar Sense," *Personnel Journal*, July 1989, pp. 32–37.

17. R. Rodgers and J. E. Hunter, "Impact of Management by Objectives on Organizational Productivity," *Journal of Applied Psychology*, April 1991, pp. 322–336.

18. E. A. Locke and G. P. Latham, "Has Goal Setting Gone Wild, or Have Its Attackers Abandoned Good Scholarship?" *Academy of Management Perspectives,* February 2009, pp. 17–23; and G. P. Latham, "The Motivational Benefits of Goal-Setting," *Academy of Management Executive,* November 2004, pp. 126–129.

19. L. Wayne, "P&G Sees the World as Its Client," *New York Times Online,* December 12, 2009.

20. For additional information on goals, see, for instance, P. Drucker, *The Executive in Action* (New York: HarperCollins Books, 1996), pp. 207–214; and E. A. Locke and G. P. Latham, *A Theory of Goal Setting and Task Performance* (Upper Saddle River, NJ: Prentice Hall, 1990).

21. data points box based on American Management Association, "Mercer Study Shows Workforce Priorities for 2010," www.amanet.org, October 21, 2009; M. Weinstein, "Coming Up Short? Join the Club," *Training,* April 2006, p. 14; G. Kranz, "Workers Unprepared," *Workforce Management Online,* March 13, 2008; J. Yang, "Disaster Recovery Plan," *USA Today,* November 13, 2005, p. 1B; and American Management Association, "2003 Survey on Leadership Challenges," www.amanet.org, April 24, 2004.

22. Several of these factors were suggested by R. K. Bresser and R. C. Bishop, "Dysfunctional Effects of Formal Planning: Two Theoretical Explanations," *Academy of Management Review*, October 1983, pp. 588–599; and J. S. Armstrong, "The Value of Formal Planning for Strategic Decisions: Review of Empirical Research," *Strategic Management Journal*, July–September 1982, pp. 197–211.

23. Brews and Hunt, "Learning to Plan and Planning to Learn: Resolving the Planning School/Learning School Debate."

24. D. Rowinski, "As Apple Dominates U.S. Sales, Smartphone Focus Shifts Overseas," http://www.readwriteweb.com/mobile/2012/04/as-apple-dominates-us-sales-smartphone-focus-shifts-overseas.php, April 26, 2012.

25. R. Farzad, "AT&T's iMess," *Bloomberg BusinessWeek,* February 15, 2010, pp. 34–40.

26. A. Campbell, "Tailored, Not Benchmarked: A Fresh Look at Corporate Planning," *Harvard Business Review*, March–April 1999, pp. 41–50.

27. J. H. Sheridan, "Focused on Flow," *IW*, October 18, 1999, pp. 46–51.

28. J. Vance, "Ten Cloud Computing Leaders," *IT Management Online,* May 26, 2010; A. Rocadela, "Amazon Looks to Widen Lead in Cloud Computing," *Bloomberg BusinessWeek Online,* April 28, 2010; and S. Lawson, "Cloud Computing Could Be a Boon for Flash Storage," *Bloomberg Business Week Online,* August 24, 2009.

29. J. Ribeiro, "Wipro Sees Drop in Outsourcing Revenue," *Bloomberg BusinessWeek Online,* July 22, 2009; S. N. Mehta, "Schooled by China and India," *CNNMoney Online,* May 5, 2009; R. J. Newman, "Coming and Going," *US News and World Report,* January 23, 2006, pp. 50–52; T. Atlas, "Bangalore's Big Dreams," *US News and World Report,* May 2, 2005, pp. 50–52; and K. H. Hammonds, "Smart, Determined, Ambitious, Cheap: The New Face of Global Competition," *Fast Company,* February 2003, pp. 90–97.

30. G. Fairclough and V. Bauerlein, "Pepsi CEO Tours China to Get a Feel for Market," *Wall Street Journal,* July 1, 2009, p. B5.

31. See, for example, P. Tarraf and R. Molz, "Competitive Intelligence," *SAM Advanced Management Journal*, Autumn 2006, pp. 24–34; W. M. Fitzpatrick, "Uncovering Trade Secrets: The Legal and Ethical Conundrum of Creative Competitive Intelligence," *SAM Advanced Management Journal*, Summer 2003, pp. 4–12; L. Lavelle, "The Case of the Corporate Spy," *BusinessWeek*, November 26, 2001, pp. 56–58; C. Britton, "Deconstructing Advertising: What Your Competitor's Advertising Can Tell You About Their Strategy," *Competitive Intelligence*, January/February 2002, pp. 15–19; and L. Smith, "Business Intelligence Progress in Jeopardy," *Information Week*, March 4, 2002, p. 74.

32. S. Greenbard, "New Heights in Business Intelligence," *Business Finance*, March 2002, pp. 41–46; K. A. Zimmermann, "The Democratization of Business Intelligence," *KN World*, May 2002, pp. 20–21; and C. Britton, "Deconstructing Advertising: What Your Competitor's Advertising Can Tell You About Their Strategy," *Competitive Intelligence*, January/February 2002, pp. 15–19.

33. L. Weathersby, "Take This Job and ***** It," *Fortune*, January 7, 2002, p. 122.

34. D. Leonard, "The Corporate Side of Snooping," *New York Times Online,* March 5, 2010; B. Acohido, "Corporate Espionage Surges in Tough Times," *USA Today,* July 29, 2009, pp. 1B+; and B. Rosner, "HR Should Get a Clue: Corporate Spying is Real," *Workforce,* April 2001, pp. 72–75.

35. P. Lattman, "Hotel Feud Prompts Probe by Grand Jury," *Wall Street Journal,* October 7, 2009, p. A1+; "Starwood vs. Hilton," *Hotels' Investment Outlook,* June 2009, p. 14; R. Kidder, "Hotel Industry Roiled by Corporate Espionage Claim," *Ethics Newsline,*

www.globalethicslorg/newsline; Reuters, "Hilton Hotels Is Subpoenaed in Espionage Case," *New York Times Online,* April 22, 2009; T. Audi, "U.S. Probes Hilton Over Theft Claims," *Wall Street Journal,* April 22, 2009, p. B1; and T. Audi, "Hilton Is Sued Over Luxury Chain," *Wall Street Journal,* April 17, 2009, p. B1.

36. S. Bergsman, "Corporate Spying Goes Mainstream," *CFO,* December 1997, p. 24; and K. Western, "Ethical Spying," *Business Ethics,* September–October 1995, pp. 22–23.

37. "Wayward At Safeway," *Workforce.com,* November 8, 2011; S. Halzack, "Safeway Sandwich Theft Allegation: Charges Dropped; What Do You Think?" Washingtonpost.com, November 2, 2011; and "Couple Jailed, Lose Custody of Daughter, over Stolen Sandwiches," Reuters.com, October 30, 2011.

38. S. Jones, J. Insley, H. Osborne, "Iceland volcano eruption leaves holiday plans in ashes," *The Guardian*, April 15, 2010, http://www.theguardian.com/world/2010/apr/15/iceland-volcano-ash-flights-cancelled; http://en.wikipedia.org/wiki/Air_travel_disruption_after_the_2010_Eyjafjallaj%C3%B6kull_eruption.

39. "Garmin Finds Route Higher," Forbes.com, May 2, 2012; "Come on Baby, Drive My Car," *Tech Talk,* April 2012, pp. 24–28; E. Rhey, "A GPS Maker Shifts Gears," *Fortune,* March 19, 2012, p. 62; "Garmin® Arrives at a Milestone: 100 Million Products Sold," Garmin.com, May 2, 2012; and B. Charny, "Garmin's Positioning Comes Under Scrutiny," *Wall Street Journal,* April 2, 2008, p. A5.

Chapter 9

1. Based on H. Shaw, "Indigo Pens Next Chapter," *Financial Post (National Post)*, June 22, 2007, www.canada.com/nationalpost/financialpost/story.html?id=d1bc522d-712c-42f4-b2e4-fe71c0c5d0ba&k=68292 (accessed July 27, 2007); and Indigo Books & Music website, www.chapters.indigo.ca (accessed July 27, 2007).

2. Based on *Indigo Annual Report for the 52 Week Period Ended March 31, 2013*, http://static.indigoimages.ca/2013/corporate/Indigo2013_AnnualReport.pdf (accessed May 15, 2014).

3. S. Martin, "Tablet Wars Heat Up With Mini iPad," *USA Today,* July 6-8, 2012, p. 1A; D. Michaels, J. Ostrower, and D. Pearson, "Airbus's New Push: Made in the U.S.A." *Wall Street Journal,* July 3, 2012, p. A1+; "Applebee's Gets Fresh," *USA Today,* July 2, 2012, pp. 1B+; and A. Sharma and J. Hansegard, "IKEA Says It Is Ready to Give India a Try," *Wall Street Journal,* June 25, 2012, p. B1.

4. J. W. Dean Jr. and M. P. Sharfman, "Does Decision Process Matter? A Study of Strategic Decision-Making Effectiveness," *Academy of Management Journal,* April 1996, pp. 368–396.

5. Based on A. A. Thompson Jr., A. J. Strickland III, and J. E. Gamble, *Crafting and Executing Strategy,* 14th ed. (New York: McGraw-Hill Irwin, 2005).

6. J. Magretta, "Why Business Models Matter," *Harvard Business Review,* May 2002, pp. 86–92.

7. B. Carter, "'American Idol' and Its Owner to Undergo a Retooling," *New York Times Online,* May 30, 2012; B. Keveney, "'Idol' May be Down, But It's Not Out," *USA Today,* May 22, 2012, p. 1D; G. Levin and B. Keveney, "NBC Upstart 'The Voice' Calls Out 'American Idol'," *USA Today,* February 16, 2012, pp. 1B+; S. Schechner, "Fewer Viewers Tune in for Cowell's 'Idol' Finale," *Wall Street Journal,* May 28, 2010, p. B7; B. Keveny, "Idol Ratings Take A Tumble," *USA Today,* May 4, 2010, p. 1D; R. Bianco, "Time for Producers to Fix 'Idol' Franchise," *USA Today,* May 4, 2010, p. 7D; and D. J. Lang, Associated Press *Springfield News-Leader* (Missouri), May 3, 2008, p. 4C.

8. E. H. Bowman and C. E. Helfat, "Does Corporate Strategy Matter?" *Strategic Management Journal* 22 (2001), pp. 1–23; P. J. Brews and M. R. Hunt, "Learning to Plan and Planning to Learn: Resolving the Planning School/Learning School Debate," *Strategic Management*

Journal, December 1999, pp. 889–913; D. J. Ketchen Jr., J. B. Thomas, and R. R. McDaniel Jr., "Process, Content and Context; Synergistic Effects on Performance," *Journal of Management* 22, no. 2 (1996), pp. 231–257; C. C. Miller and L. B. Cardinal, "Strategic Planning and Firm Performance: A Synthesis of More Than Two Decades of Research," *Academy of Management Journal,* December 1994, pp. 1649–1665; and N. Capon, J. U. Farley, and J. M. Hulbert, "Strategic Planning and Financial Performance: More Evidence," *Journal of Management Studies*, January 1994, pp. 105–110.

9. "A Solid Strategy Helps Companies' Growth," *Nation's Business*, October 1990, p. 10.

10. See, for example, H. Mintzberg, *The Rise and Fall of Strategic Planning* (New York: Free Press, 1994); S. J. Wall and S. R. Wall, "The Evolution (Not the Death) of Strategy," *Organizational Dynamics*, Autumn 1995, pp. 7–19; J. A. Byrne, "Strategic Planning: It's Back!" *BusinessWeek*, August 26, 1996, pp. 46–52; and R. M. Grant, "Strategic Planning in a Turbulent Environment: Evidence from the Oil Majors," *Strategic Management Journal* 24, no. 6 (June 2003), pp. 491–517.

11. See *Indigo Annual Report for the 52 Week Period Ended March 31, 2013*, http://static.indigoimages.ca/2013/corporate/Indigo2013_AnnualReport.pdf (accessed May 15, 2014).

12. "About Our Company," Indigo Books & Music website, www.chapters.indigo.ca/About-Indigo-Books-Music-Inc/chaptersinc-art.html (accessed July 23, 2007).

13. "About Us," WorkSafeBC website, www.worksafebc.com/about_us/default.asp (accessed July 23, 2007).

14. "Company Overview," eBay, http://pages.ebay.ca/aboutebay/the-company/companyoverview.html (accessed July 23, 2007).

15. C. K. Prahalad and G. Hamel, "The Core Competence of the Corporation," *Harvard Business Review*, May–June 1990, pp. 79–91.

16. A. Taylor, "How Toyota Does It," *Fortune*, March 6, 2006, pp. 107–124; C. Woodyard, "Slow and Steady Drives Toyota's Growth," *USA Today*, December 21, 2005, pp. 1B+; I. M. Kunii, C. Dawson, and C. Palmeri, "Toyota Is Way Ahead of the Hybrid Pack," *BusinessWeek*, May 5, 2003, p. 48; and S. Spear and H. K. Bowen, "Decoding the DNA of the Toyota Production System," *Harvard Business Review*, September–October 1999, pp. 96–106.

17. See, for example, H. J. Cho and V. Pucik, "Relationship between Innovativeness, Quality, Growth, Profitability, and Market Value," *Strategic Management Journal* 26, no. 6 (2005), pp. 555–575; W. F. Joyce, "Building the 4+2 Organization," *Organizational Dynamics*, May 2005, pp. 118–129; R. S. Kaplan and D. P. Norton, "Measuring the Strategic Readiness of Intangible Assets," *Harvard Business Review*, February 2004, pp. 52–63; C. M. Fiol, "Managing Culture as a Competitive Resource: An Identity-Based View of Sustainable Competitive Advantage," *Journal of Management*, March 1991, pp. 191–211; T. Kono, "Corporate Culture and Long-Range Planning," *Long Range Planning*, August 1990, pp. 9–19; S. Green, "Understanding Corporate Culture and Its Relation to Strategy," *International Studies of Management and Organization*, Summer 1988, pp. 6–28; C. Scholz, "Corporate Culture and Strategy—The Problem of Strategic Fit," *Long Range Planning*, August 1987, pp. 78–87; and J. B. Barney, "Organizational Culture: Can It Be a Source of Sustained Competitive Advantage?" *Academy of Management Review*, July 1986, pp. 656–665.

18. J. P. Kotter and J. L. Heskett, *Corporate Culture and Performance* (New York: Free Press, 1992).

19. K. E. Klein, "Slogans That Are the Real Thing," *BusinessWeek*, August 4, 2005, www.businessweek.com/smallbiz/content/aug2005/sb20050804_867552.htm (accessed July 27, 2007); and T. Mucha, "The Payoff for Trying Harder," *Business 2.0*, July 2002, pp. 84–85.

20. A. Carmeli and A. Tischler, "The Relationships between Intangible Organizational Elements and Organizational Performance," *Strategic Management Journal* 25 (2004), pp. 1257–1278; P. W. Roberts and G. R. Dowling, "Corporate Reputation and Sustained Financial Performance," *Strategic Management Journal*, December 2002, pp. 1077–1093; and C. J. Fombrun, "Corporate Reputations as Economic Assets," in *Handbook of Strategic Management*, ed. M. A. Hitt, R. E. Freeman, and J. S. Harrison, pp. 289–312 (Malden, MA: Blackwell, 2001).

21. Harris Interactive, "Johnson & Johnson Ranks No. 1 in National Corporate Reputation Survey for Seventh Consecutive Year," news release, December 7, 2005.

22. Based on H. Shaw, "Indigo Pens Next Chapter," *Financial Post (National Post)*, June 22, 2007, www.canada.com/nationalpost/financialpost/story.html?id=d1bc522d-712c-42f4-b2e4-fe71c0c5d0ba&k=68292 (accessed July 27, 2007); and Indigo Books & Music website, www.chapters.indigo.ca.

23. See *Indigo Annual Report for the 52 Week Period Ended March 31, 2013*, http://static.indigoimages.ca/2013/corporate/Indigo2013_AnnualReport.pdf (accessed May 15, 2014).

24. See http://www.timhortons.com/ca/pdf/TH_Investor_Conference_For_Website_(02-26-2014).pdf (accessed October 30, 2010).

25. J. A. Pearce, II, "Retrenchment Remains the Foundation of Business Turnaround," *Strategic Management Journal* 15 (1994), pp. 407–417.

26. *Best Buy Fiscal 2014 Annual Report*, http://phx.corporate-ir.net/phoenix.zhtml?c=83192&p=irol-reportsannual (accessed June 5, 2014).

27. *Target 2013 Annual Report*, https://corporate.target.com/annual-reports/2013/financials/financial-summary (accessed June 5, 2014).

28. H. Quarls, T. Pernsteiner, and K. Rangan, "Love Your Dogs," *Strategy+Business*, Spring 2006, pp. 58–65; and P. Haspeslagh, "Portfolio Planning: Uses and Limits," *Harvard Business Review*, January–February 1982, pp. 58–73.

29. Boston Consulting Group, *Perspective on Experience* (Boston: Boston Consulting Group, 1970).

30. *Indigo Annual Report for the 52 Week Period Ended March 31, 2013*, http://static.indigoimages.ca/2013/corporate/Indigo2013_AnnualReport.pdf (accessed May 15, 2014).

31. R. Rumelt, "Towards a Strategic Theory of the Firm," in *Competitive Strategic Management*, ed. R. Lamb, pp. 556–570 (Upper Saddle River, NJ: Prentice Hall, 1984); M. E. Porter, *Competitive Advantage: Creating and Sustaining Superior Performance* (New York: Free Press, 1985); J. Barney, "Firm Resources and Sustained Competitive Advantage," *Journal of Management* 17, no. 1 (1991), pp. 99–120; M. A. Peteraf, "The Cornerstones of Competitive Advantage: A Resource-Based View," *Strategic Management Journal*, March 1993, pp. 179–191; and J. B. Barney, "Looking Inside for Competitive Advantage," *Academy of Management Executive*, November 1995, pp. 49–61.

32. T. C. Powell, "Total Quality Management as Competitive Advantage: A Review and Empirical Study," *Strategic Management Journal*, January 1995, pp. 15–37.

33. Based on W. Hanley, "Mowat's Lefty Ways Pay Big Dividends," National Post, February 28, 2004, p. IN01.

34. See http://www.peicreditunions.com/news/article.php?ID=594 (accessed September 26, 2007).

35. D. Dunne and R. Martin, "Design Thinking and How It Will Change Management Education: An Interview and Discussion," *Academy of Management Learning & Education*, December 2006, pp. 512–523.

36. See, for example, M. E. Porter, *Competitive Strategy: Techniques for Analyzing Industries and Competitors* (New York: Free Press, 1980); M. E. Porter, *Competitive Advantage: Creating and Sustaining Superior Performance* (New York: Free Press, 1985); G. G. Dess and P. S. Davis, "Porter's (1980) Generic Strategies as Determinants of Strategic Group Membership and Organizational Performance," *Academy of Management Journal*, September 1984, pp. 467–488; G. G. Dess and P. S. Davis, "Porter's (1980) Generic Strategies and Performance: An Empirical Examination with American Data—Part I: Testing Porter," *Organization Studies*, no. 1 (1986), pp. 37–55; G. G. Dess and P. S. Davis, "Porter's (1980) Generic Strategies and Performance: An Empirical Examination with American Data—Part II: Performance Implications," *Organization Studies*, no. 3 (1986), pp. 255–261; M. E. Porter, "From Competitive Advantage to Corporate Strategy," *Harvard Business Review*, May–June 1987, pp. 43–59; A. I. Murray, "A Contingency View of Porter's 'Generic Strategies,'" *Academy of Management Review*, July 1988, pp. 390–400; C. W. L. Hill, "Differentiation versus Low Cost or Differentiation and Low Cost: A Contingency Framework," *Academy of Management Review*, July 1988, pp. 401–412; I. Bamberger, "Developing Competitive Advantage in Small and Medium-Sized Firms," *Long Range Planning*, October 1989, pp. 80–88; D. F. Jennings and J. R. Lumpkin, "Insights between Environmental Scanning Activities and Porter's Generic Strategies: An Empirical Analysis," *Strategic Management Journal* 18, no. 4 (1992), pp. 791–803; N. Argyres and A. M. McGahan, "An Interview with Michael Porter," *Academy of Management Executive*, May 2002, pp. 43–52; and A. Brandenburger, "Porter's Added Value: High Indeed!" *Academy of Management Executive*, May 2002, pp. 58–60.

37. data points box based on M. E. Mangelsdorf, "Interview with Dr. Peter Weill: Getting an Edge from IT," *Wall Street Journal*, November 30, 2009, p. R2; M. E. Raynor, M. Ahmed, and A. D. Henderson, "Are 'Great' Companies Just Lucky?" *Harvard Business Review*, April 2009, pp. 18–19; J. Yang and M. E. Mullins, "Employee's Concerns in Mergers and Acquisitions," *USA Today*, June 6, 2007, p. 1B; and J. Choi, D. Lovallo, and A. Tarasova, "Better Strategy for Business Units: A McKinsey Global Survey," *The McKinsey Quarterly Online*, www.mckinseyquarterly.com, July 2007.

38. See www.peicreditunions.com/news/article.php?ID=594 (accessed September 26, 2007).

39. J. W. Bachmann, "Competitive Strategy: It's O.K. to Be Different," *Academy of Management Executive*, May 2002, pp. 61–65; S. Cappel, P. Wright, M. Kroll, and D. Wyld, "Competitive Strategies and Business Performance: An Empirical Study of Select Service Businesses," *International Journal of Management*, March 1992, pp. 1–11; D. Miller, "The Generic Strategy Trap," *Journal of Business Strategy*, January–February 1991, pp. 37–41; R. E. White, "Organizing to Make Business Unit Strategies Work," in H. E. Glass (ed.), *Handbook of Business Strategy*, 2nd ed. (Boston: Warren Gorham and Lamont, 1991), pp. 1–24; and Hill, "Differentiation versus Low Cost or Differentiation and Low Cost: A Contingency Framework."

40. B. Sisario, "Out to Shake Up Music, Often with Sharp Words," *New York Times Online*, May 6, 2012; and J. Plambeck, "As CD Sales Wane, Music Retailers Diversify," *New York Times Online*, May 30, 2010.

41. S. Clifford, "Amazon Leaps into High End of the Fashion Pool," *New York Times Online*, May 7, 2012 and "Can Amazon Be a Fashion Player?" *Women's Wear Daily*, May 4, 2012, p. 1.

42. S. Ghoshal and C. A. Bartlett, "Changing the Role of Top Management: Beyond Structure to Process," *Harvard Business Review*, January–February 1995, pp. 86–96.

43. R. Calori, G. Johnson, and P. Sarnin, "CEO's Cognitive Maps and the Scope of the Organization," *Strategic Management Journal*, July 1994, pp. 437–457.

44. R. D. Ireland and M. A. Hitt, "Achieving and Maintaining Strategic Competitiveness in the 21st Century: The Role of Strategic Leadership," *Academy of Management Executive*, February 1999, pp. 43–57.

45. J. P. Wallman, "Strategic Transactions and Managing the Future: A Druckerian Perspective," *Management Decision,* vol. 48, no. 4, 2010, pp. 485–499; D. E. Zand, "Drucker's Strategic Thinking Process: Three Key Techniques," *Strategy & Leadership,* vol. 38, no. 3, 2010, pp. 23–28; and R. D. Ireland and M. A. Hitt, "Achieving and Maintaining Strategic Competitiveness in the 21st Century: The Role of Strategic Leadership."

46. K. Shimizu and M. A. Hitt, "Strategic Flexibility: Organizational Preparedness to Reverse Ineffective Decisions," *Academy of Management Executive,* November 2004, p. 44.

47. E. Kim, D. Nam, and J. L. Stimpert, "The Applicability of Porter's Generic Strategies in the Digital Age: Assumptions, Conjectures, and Suggestions," *Journal of Management,* 30, no. 5 (2004), pp. 569–589; and G. T. Lumpkin, S. B. Droege, and G. G. Dess, "E-Commerce Strategies: Achieving Sustainable Competitive Advantage and Avoiding Pitfalls," *Organizational Dynamics,* Spring 2002, pp. 325–340.

48. E. Kim, D. Nam, and J. L. Stimpert, "The Applicability of Porter's Generic Strategies in the Digital Age: Assumptions, Conjectures, and Suggestions," *Journal of Management*, 30, no. 5 (2004), pp. 569–589.

49. S. Clifford, "Luring Online Shoppers Offline," *New York Times Online,* July 4, 2012.

50. J. Gaffney, "Shoe Fetish," *Business 2.0*, March 2002, pp. 98–99.

51. D. Fickling, "The Singapore Girls Aren't Smiling Anymore," *Bloomberg BusinessWeek,* May 21–May 27, 2012, pp. 25–26; L. Heracleous and J. Wirtz, "Singapore Airlines' Balancing Act," *Harvard Business Review,* July-August 2010, pp. 145–149; and J. Doebele, "The Engineer," *Forbes,* January 9, 2006, pp. 122–124.

52. S. Ellison, "P&G to Unleash Dental Adult-Pet Food," *Wall Street Journal*, December 12, 2002, p. B4.

53. A. O'Leary, "Tech Companies Leave Phone Calls Behind," *New York Times Online,* July 6, 2012.

54. Materials for developing a business plan can be found at Small Business Administration, *The Business Plan Workbook* (Washington, DC, May 17, 2001); and on the Small Business Administration website, www.sba.gov. In addition, readers may find software such as Business Plan Pro Software, available at www.businessplanpro.com, useful.

55. D. Roman and W. Kemble-Diaz, "Owner of Fast-Fashion Retailer Zara Keeps Up Emerging-Markets Push," *Wall Street Journal,* June 14, 2012, p. B3; Press Releases, "Inditex Achieves Net Sales of 9,709 Million Euros, An Increase of 10 percent," www.inditex.com, February 22, 2012; C. Bjork, "'Cheap Chic' Apparel Sellers Heat Up U.S. Rivalry on Web," *Wall Street Journal,* September 6, 2011, pp. B1+; A. Kenna, "Zara Plays Catch-up with Online Shoppers," *Bloomberg BusinessWeek,* August 29–September 4, 2011, pp. 24–25; K. Girotra and S. Netessine, "How to Build Risk into Your Business Model," *Harvard Business Review,* May 2011, pp. 100–105; M. Dart and R. Lewis, "Break the Rules the Way Zappos and Amazon Do," *Bloomberg BusinessWeek Online,* April 29, 2011; K. Cappell, "Zara Thrives by Breaking All the Rules," *BusinessWeek,* October 20, 2008, p. 66; and C. Rohwedder and K. Johnson, "Pace-Setting Zara Seeks More Speed to Fight Its Rising Cheap-Chic Rivals," *Wall Street Journal,* February 20, 2008, pp. B1+.

56. D. Reisinger, "Dark Days Ahead for Netflix?" Fortune.com, July 12, 2012; S. Woo and I. Sherr, "Netflix's Growth Disappoints," *Wall Street Journal,* April 24, 2012, pp. B1+; S. Woo and I. Sherr, "Netflix Recovers Subscribers," *Wall Street Journal,* January 26, 2012,

pp. B1+; J. Pepitone, "Netflix CEO: We Got Overconfident," CNNMoney.com, December 6, 2011; D. McDonald, "Netflix: Down, But Not Out," *CNN.com,* November 23, 2011; H. W. Jenkins, Jr., "Netflix Isn't Doomed," *Wall Street Journal,* October 26, 2011, p. A13; C. Edwards, "Netflix Drops Most Since 2004 After Losing 800,000 Customers," BusinessWeek.com, October 25, 2011; N. Wingfield and B. Stelter, "How Netflix Lost 800,000 Members and Good Will," *New York Times Online,* October 24, 2011; C. Edwards and R. Grover, "Can Netflix Regain Lost Ground?" BusinessWeek.com, October 19, 2011; and R. Grover, C. Edwards, and A. Fixmer, "Can Netflix Find Its Future By Abandoning the Past?" *Bloomberg BusinessWeek,* September 26–October 2, 2011, pp. 29–30.

Module 2

1. J. Brustein, "Star Pitchers in a Duel? Tickets Will Cost More," *New York Times Online,* June 27, 2010; and A. Satariano, "Innovator: Barry Kahn," *Bloomberg BusinessWeek,* May 24–May 30, 2010, p. 39. See also http://senators.nhl.com/club/page.htm?id=65616

2. F. Vogelstein, "Search and Destroy," *Fortune,* May 2, 2005, pp. 73–82.

3. S. C. Jain, "Environmental Scanning in U.S. Corporations," *Long Range Planning*, April 1984, pp. 117–128; see also L. M. Fuld, *Monitoring the Competition* (New York: John Wiley & Sons, 1988); E. H. Burack and N. J. Mathys, "Environmental Scanning Improves Strategic Planning," *Personnel Administrator*, April 1989, pp. 82–87; R. Subramanian, N. Fernandes, and E. Harper, "Environmental Scanning in U.S. Companies: Their Nature and Their Relationship to Performance," *Management International Review,* July 1993, pp. 271–286; B. K. Boyd and J. Fulk, "Executive Scanning and Perceived Uncertainty: A Multidimensional Model," *Journal of Management*, 22, no. 1, 1996, pp. 1–21; D. S. Elkenov, "Strategic Uncertainty and Environmental Scanning: The Case for Institutional Influences on Scanning Behavior," *Strategic Management Journal*, vol. 18, 1997, pp. 287–302; K. Kumar, R. Subramanian, and K. Strandholm, "Competitive Strategy, Environmental Scanning and Performance: A Context Specific Analysis of Their Relationship," *International Journal of Commerce and Management,* Spring 2001, pp. 1–18; C. G. Wagner, "Top 10 Reasons to Watch Trends," *The Futurist,* March–April 2002, pp. 68–69; and V. K. Garg, B. A. Walters, and R. L. Priem, "Chief Executive Scanning Emphases, Environmental Dynamism, and Manufacturing Firm Performance," *Strategic Management Journal,* August 2003, pp. 725–744.

4. B. Gilad, "The Role of Organized Competitive Intelligence in Corporate Strategy," *Columbia Journal of World Business*, Winter 1989, pp. 29–35; L. Fuld, "A Recipe for Business Intelligence," *Journal of Business Strategy*, January–February 1991, pp. 12–17; J. P. Herring, "The Role of Intelligence in Formulating Strategy," *Journal of Business Strategy*, September–October 1992, pp. 54–60; K. Western, "Ethical Spying," *Business Ethics*, September–October 1995, pp. 22–23; D. Kinard, "Raising Your Competitive IQ: The Payoff of Paying Attention to Potential Competitors," *Association Management*, February 2003, pp. 40–44; K. Girard, "Snooping on a Shoestring," *Business 2.0,* May 2003, pp. 64–66; and "Know Your Enemy," *Business 2.0,* June 2004, p. 89.

5. C. Davis, "Get Smart," *Executive Edge,* October–November 1999, pp. 46–50.

6. B. Ettore, "Managing Competitive Intelligence," *Management Review*, October 1995, pp. 15–19.

7. A. Serwer, "P&G's Covert Operation," *Fortune,* September 17, 2001, pp. 42–44.

8. Security of Information Act (R.S.C., 1985, c. O-5).

9. Western, "Ethical Spying."

10. W. H. Davidson, "The Role of Global Scanning in Business Planning," *Organizational Dynamics,* Winter 1991, pp. 5–16.

11. T. Smart, "Air Supply," *US News & World Report,* February 28, 2005, p. EE10.

12. "Is Supply Chain Collaboration Really Happening?" *ERI Journal,* www.eri.com, January–February 2006; L. Denend and H. Lee, "West Marine: Driving Growth T=through Shipshape Supply Chain Management, A Case Study," *Stanford Graduate School of Business,* www.vics.org, April 7, 2005; N. Nix, A. G. Zacharia, R. F. Lusch, W. R. Bridges, and A. Thomas, "Keys to Effective Supply Chain Collaboration: A Special Report from the Collaborative Practices Research Program," *Neeley School of Business, Texas Christian University,* www.vics.org, November 15, 2004; Collaborative, Planning, Forecasting, and Replenishment Committee, www.cpfr.org, May 20, 2003; and J. W. Verity, "Clearing the Cobwebs from the Stockroom," *BusinessWeek,* October 21, 1996, p. 140.

13. See A. B. Fisher, "Is Long-Range Planning Worth It?" *Fortune,* April 23, 1990, pp. 281–284; J. A. Fraser, "On Target," *Inc.,* April 1991, pp. 113–114; P. Schwartz, *The Art of the Long View* (New York: Doubleday/Currency, 1991); G. Hamel and C. K. Prahalad, "Competing for the Future," *Harvard Business Review,* July–August 1994, pp. 122–128; F. Elikai and W. Hall, Jr., "Managing and Improving the Forecasting Process," *Journal of Business Forecasting Methods & Systems,* Spring 1999, pp. 15–19; L. Lapide, "New Developments in Business Forecasting," *Journal of Business Forecasting Methods & Systems,* Summer 1999, pp. 13–14; and T. Leahy, "Building Better Forecasts," *Business Finance,* December 1999, pp. 10–12.

14. J. Goff, "Start with Demand," *CFO,* January 2005, pp. 53–57.

15. L. Brannen, "Upfront: Global Planning Perspectives," *Business Finance,* March 2006, pp. 12+.

16. V. Ryan, "Future Tense," *CFO,* December 2008, pp. 37–42.

17. R. Durand, "Predicting a Firm's Forecasting Ability: The Roles of Organizational Illusion of Control and Organizational Attention," *Strategic Management Journal,* September 2003, pp. 821–838.

18. J. Katz, "Forecasts Demand Change," *Industry Week,* May 2010, pp. 26–29; A. Stuart, "Imperfect Futures," *CFO,* July–August 2009, pp. 48–53; C. L. Jain and M. Covas, "Thinking About Tomorrow," *Wall Street Journal,* July 7, 2008, p. R10+; T. Leahy, "Turning Managers into Forecasters," *Business Finance,* August 2002, pp. 37–40; M. A. Giullian, M. D. Odom, and M. W. Totaro, "Developing Essential Skills for Success in the Business World: A Look at Forecasting," *Journal of Applied Business Research,* Summer 2000, pp. 51–65; F. Elikai and W. Hall, Jr., "Managing and Improving the Forecasting Process;" and N. Pant and W. H. Starbuck, "Innocents in the Forest: Forecasting and Research Methods," *Journal of Management,* June 1990, pp. 433–460.

19. T. Leahy, "Turning Managers into Forecasters," *Business Finance,* August 2002, pp. 37–40.

20. J. Hope, "Use a Rolling Forecast to Spot Trends," *Harvard Business School Working Knowledge,* hbswk.hbs.edu, March 13, 2006.

21. This section is based on Y. K. Shetty, "Benchmarking for Superior Performance," *Long Range Planning* vol. 1, April 1993, pp. 39–44; G. H. Watson, "How Process Benchmarking Supports Corporate Strategy," *Planning Review,* January–February 1993, pp. 12–15; S. Greengard, "Discover Best Practices," *Personnel Journal,* November 1995, pp. 62–73; J. Martin, "Are You as Good as You Think You Are?" *Fortune,* September 30, 1996, pp. 142–152; R. L. Ackoff, "The Trouble with Benchmarking," *Across the Board,* January 2000, p. 13; V. Prabhu, D. Yarrow, and G. Gordon-Hart, "Best Practice and Performance Within Northeast Manufacturing," *Total Quality Management,* January 2000, pp. 113–121; "E-Benchmarking: The Latest E-Trend," *CFO,* March 2000, p. 7; E. Krell, "Now Read This," *Business Finance,* May 2000, pp. 97–103;

and H. Johnson, "All in Favor Say Benchmark!" *Training,* August 2004, pp. 30–34.

22. "Newswatch," *CFO,* July 2002, p. 26.

23. Benchmarking examples from the following: S. Carey, "Racing to Improve," *Wall Street Journal,* March 24, 2006, pp. B1+; D. Waller, "NASCAR: The Army's Unlikely Adviser," *Time,* July 4, 2005, p. 19; A. Taylor, III, "Double Duty," *Fortune,* March 7, 2005, p. 108; P. Gogoi, "Thinking Outside the Cereal Box," *BusinessWeek,* July 28, 2003, pp. 74–75; "Benchmarkers Make Strange Bedfellows," *Industry Week,* November 15, 1993, p. 8; G. Fuchsberg, "Here's Help in Finding Corporate Role Models," *Wall Street Journal,* June 1, 1993, p. B1; and A. Tanzer, "Studying at the Feet of the Masters," *Forbes,* May 10, 1993, pp. 43–44.

24. E. Krell, "The Case against Budgeting," *Business Finance,* July 2003, pp. 20–25; J. Hope and R. Fraser, "Who Needs Budgets?" *Harvard Business Review,* February 2003, pp. 108–115; T. Leahy, "The Top 10 Traps of Budgeting," *Business Finance,* November 2001, pp. 20–26; T. Leahy, "Necessary Evil," *Business Finance,* November 1999, pp. 41–45; J. Fanning, "Businesses Languishing in a Budget Comfort Zone?" *Management Accounting,* July/August 1999, p. 8; "Budgeting Processes: Inefficiency or Inadequate?" *Management Accounting,* February 1999, p. 5; A. Kennedy and D. Dugdale, "Getting the Most from Budgeting," *Management Accounting,* February 1999, pp. 22–24; G. J. Nolan, "The End of Traditional Budgeting," *Bank Accounting & Finance,* Summer 1998, pp. 29–36; and J. Mariotti, "Surviving the Dreaded Budget Process," *IW,* August 17, 1998, p. 150.

25. See, for example, S. Stiansen, "Breaking Even," *Success,* November 1988, p. 16.

26. S. E. Barndt and D. W. Carvey, *Essentials of Operations Management* (Upper Saddle River, NJ: Prentice Hall, 1982), p. 134.

27. E. E. Adam Jr. and R. J. Ebert, *Production and Operations Management,* 5th ed. (Upper Saddle River, NJ: Prentice Hall, 1992), p. 333.

28. See, for instance, C. Benko and F. W. McFarlan, *Connecting the Dots: Aligning Projects with Objectives in Unpredictable Times* (Boston, MA: Harvard Business School Press, 2003); M. W. Lewis, M. A. Welsh, G. E. Dehler, and S. G. Green, "Product Development Tensions: Exploring Contrasting Styles of Project Management," *Academy of Management Journal,* June 2002, pp. 546–564; C. E. Gray and E. W. Larsen, *Project Management: The Managerial Process* (Columbus, OH: McGraw-Hill Higher Education, 2000); J. Davidson Frame, *Project Management Competence: Building Key Skills for Individuals, Teams, and Organizations* (San Francisco, CA: Jossey-Bass, 1999).

29. For more information, see Project Management Software Directory, www.infogoal.com/pmc/pmcswr.htm.

30. D. Zielinski, "Soft Skills, Hard Truth," *Training,* July 2005, pp. 19–23.

31. H. Collingwood, "Best Kept Secrets of the World's Best Companies: Secret 05, Bad News Folders," *Business 2.0,* April 2006, p. 84.

32. G. Colvin, "An Executive Risk Handbook," *Fortune,* October 3, 2005, pp. 69–70; A. Long and A. Weiss, "Using Scenario Planning to Manage Short-Term Uncertainty," *Outward Insights,* www.outwardinsights.com, 2005; B. Fiora, "Use Early Warning to Strengthen Scenario Planning," *Outward Insights,* www.outwardinsights.com, 2003; L. Fahey, "Scenario Learning," *Management Review,* March 2000, pp. 29–34; S. Caudron, "Frontview Mirror," *Business Finance,* December 1999, pp. 24–30; and J. R. Garber, "What if…?," *Forbes,* November 2, 1998, pp. 76–79.

33. S. Caudron, "Frontview Mirror," *Business Finance,* December 1999, p. 30.

34. L. Ramsay, "Lessons Learned from SARS Crisis," *Globe and Mail*, May 22, 2003, p. B16.

35. L. Ramsay, "Lessons Learned from SARS Crisis," *Globe and Mail*, May 22, 2003, p. B16.

Chapter 10

1. See http://www.mlse.com/inside_mlse/leadersatmlse.aspx, (accessed August 29, 2014); and http://www.theglobeandmail.com/report-on-business/rob-magazine/regrets-richard-peddie-has-a-few/article4096724/ (accessed August 29, 2014).

2. J. Nickerson, C. J. Yen, and J. T. Mahoney, "Exploring the Problem-Finding and Problem-Solving Approach for Designing Organizations," *Academy of Management Perspectives,* February 2012, pp. 52–72; R. Greenwood and D. Miller, "Tackling Design Anew: Getting Back to the Heart of Organizational Theory," *Academy of Management Perspectives*, November 2010, pp. 78–89.

3. See, for example, R. L. Daft, *Organization Theory and Design*, 6th ed. (St. Paul, MN: West Publishing, 1998).

4. C. Dougherty, "Workforce Productivity Falls," *Wall Street Journal*, May 4, 2012, p. A5; and S. E. Humphrey, J. D. Nahrgang, and F. P. Morgeson, "Integrating Motivational, Social, and Contextual Work Design Features: A Meta-Analytic Summary and Theoretical Expansion of the Work Design Literature," *Journal of Applied Psychology*, September 2007, pp. 1332–1356.

5. S. Melamed, I. Ben-Avi, and M. S. Green, "Objective and Subjective Work Monotony: Effects on Job Satisfaction, Psychological Distress, and Absenteeism in Blue-Collar Workers," *Journal of Applied Psychology*, February 1995, pp. 29–42.

6. W. Hillier, "BC Forest Fires: A Time of Need," *Canadian Underwriter* 71, no. 1 (January 2004), pp. 22–23.

7. For a discussion of authority, see W. A. Kahn and K. E. Kram, "Authority at Work: Internal Models and Their Organizational Consequences," *Academy of Management Review*, January 1994, pp. 17–50.

8. B. Arthur, "Peddie Gives New GM 'Autonomy' for Change," *National Post*, June 8, 2004, p. S2.

9. See www.fan590.com/columnists/columnist1article.jsp?content=20060327_113940_4056 (accessed September 24, 2006).

10. C. I. Barnard, *The Functions of the Executive,* 30th Anniversary Edition (Cambridge, MA: Harvard University Press, 1968), pp. 165–166.

11. R. Ashkenas, "Simplicity-Minded Management," *Harvard Business Review,* December 2007, pp. 101–109; and P. Glader, "It's Not Easy Being Lean," *Wall Street Journal,* June 19, 2006, pp. B1+.

12. R. C. Morais, "The Old Lady Is Burning Rubber," *Forbes,* November 26, 2007, pp. 146–150.

13. G. L. Neilson and J. Wulf, "How Many Direct Reports?" *Harvard Business Review,* April 2012, pp. 112–119; and D. Van Fleet, "Span of Management Research and Issues," *Academy of Management Journal*, September 1983, pp. 546–552.

14. G. Anders, "Overseeing More Employees—With Fewer Managers," *Wall Street Journal,* March 24, 2008, p. B6.

15. H. Fayol, *General and Industrial Management*, trans. C. Storrs (London: Pitman Publishing, 1949), pp. 19–42.

16. J. Zabojnik, "Centralized and Decentralized Decision Making in Organizations," *Journal of Labor Economics,* January 2002, pp. 1–22.

17. See, for example, H. Mintzberg, *Power In and Around Organizations* (Upper Saddle River, NJ: Prentice Hall, 1983); and J. Child, *Organization: A Guide to Problems and Practices* (London: Kaiser & Row, 1984).

18. A. Ross, "BMO's Big Bang," *Canadian Business*, January 1994, pp. 58–63; and information on the company from Hoover's Online, www.hoovers.com (accessed May 25, 2003).

19. E. W. Morrison, "Doing the Job Well: An Investigation of Pro-Social Rule Breaking," *Journal of Management*, February 2006, pp. 5–28.

20. E. W. Morrison, "Doing the Job Well: An Investigation of Pro-Social Rule Breaking," *Journal of Management*, February 2006, pp. 5–28.

21. See http://www.mlse.com/inside_mlse/our_company.aspx.

22. data points box based on J. Yang and P. Trap, "What Size Company Do You Prefer?" *USA Today*, March 19,2012, p. 1 B; F. Hassan, "The Frontline Advantage," *Harvard Business Review*, May 2011, p. 109; P. Dvorak, "Firms Shift Underused Workers," *Wall Street Journal*, June 22, 2009, p. B2; M. Weinstein, "It's A Balancing Act," *Training*, May 2009, p. 10; J. Yang and A. Lewis, "Is Teleworking a Good Idea?" *USA Today*, October 28, 2008, p. 1 B; "Drive Time: More Employees Get to Work Remotely," *Workforce Management Online,* www.workforce.com, September 23, 2008; J. Yang and K. Gelles, "Working Remotely vs. In the Office," *USA Today*, April 24, 2008, p. 1 B; A. R. Carey and S. Parker, "Workers Take Home Their Offices," *USA Today*, October 7, 2008, p. 1 A.

23. T. Burns and G. M. Stalker, *The Management of Innovation* (London: Tavistock, 1961); and D. A. Morand, "The Role of Behavioral Formality and Informality in the Enactment of Bureaucratic versus Organic Organizations," *Academy of Management Review*, October 1995, pp. 831–872.

24. J. Dee, "All the News That's Fit to Print Out," *New York Times Magazine*, July 1, 2007, pp. 34–39; and wikipedia.com.

25. R. D. Hof, "Yahoo's Bartz Shows Who's Boss," *BusinessWeek Online,* February 27, 2009; and J. E. Vascellaro, "Yahoo CEO Set to Install Top-Down Management," *Wall Street Journal,* February 23, 2009, p. B1.

26. A. D. Chandler Jr., *Strategy and Structure: Chapters in the History of the Industrial Enterprise* (Cambridge, MA: MIT Press, 1962).

27. See, for instance, L. L. Bryan and C. I. Joyce, "Better Strategy Through Organizational Design," *The McKinsey Quarterly* no. 2 (2007), pp. 21–29; D. Jennings and S. Seaman, "High and Low Levels of Organizational Adaptation: An Empirical Analysis of Strategy, Structure, and Performance," *Strategic Management Journal*, July 1994, pp. 459–475; D. C. Galunic and K. M. Eisenhardt, "Renewing the Strategy–Structure–Performance Paradigm," in B. M. Staw and L. L. Cummings (eds.), *Research in Organizational Behavior*, vol. 16 (Greenwich, CT: JAI Press, 1994), pp. 215–255; R. Parthasarthy and S. P. Sethi, "Relating Strategy and Structure to Flexible Automation: A Test of Fit and Performance Implications," *Strategic Management Journal* 14, no. 6 (1993), pp. 529–549; H. A. Simon, "Strategy and Organizational Evolution," *Strategic Management Journal*, January 1993, pp. 131–142; H. L. Boschken, "Strategy and Structure: Re-conceiving the Relationship," *Journal of Management*, March 1990, pp. 135–150; D. Miller, "The Structural and Environmental Correlates of Business Strategy," *Strategic Management Journal*, January–February 1987, pp. 55–76; and R. E. Miles and C. C. Snow, *Organizational Strategy, Structure, and Process* (New York: McGraw-Hill, 1978).

28. See, for instance, P. M. Blau and R. A. Schoenherr, *The Structure of Organizations* (New York: Basic Books, 1971); D. S. Pugh, "The Aston Program of Research: Retrospect and Prospect," in *Perspectives on Organization Design and Behavior*, ed. A. H. Van de Ven and W. F. Joyce, pp. 135–166 (New York: John Wiley, 1981); and R. Z. Gooding and J. A. Wagner III, "A Meta-Analytic Review of the Relationship between Size and Performance: The Productivity and

Efficiency of Organizations and Their Subunits," *Administrative Science Quarterly*, December 1985, pp. 462–481.

29. J. Woodward, *Industrial Organization: Theory and Practice* (London: Oxford University Press, 1965).

30. See, for instance, C. Perrow, "A Framework for the Comparative Analysis of Organizations," *American Sociological Review*, April 1967, pp. 194–208; J. D. Thompson, *Organizations in Action* (New York: McGraw-Hill, 1967); J. Hage and M. Aiken, "Routine Technology, Social Structure, and Organizational Goals," *Administrative Science Quarterly*, September 1969, pp. 366–377; and C. C. Miller, W. H. Glick, Y. D. Wang, and G. P. Huber, "Understanding Technology-Structure Relationships: Theory Development and Meta-Analytic Theory Testing," *Academy of Management Journal*, June 1991, pp. 370–399.

31. D. Gerwin, "Relationships between Structure and Technology," in *Handbook of Organizational Design*, vol. 2, ed. P. C. Nystrom and W. H. Starbuck, pp. 3–38 (New York: Oxford University Press, 1981); and D. M. Rousseau and R. A. Cooke, "Technology and Structure: The Concrete, Abstract, and Activity Systems of Organizations," *Journal of Management*, Fall–Winter 1984, pp. 345–361.

32. See, for instance, J. Zhang and C. Baden-Fuller, "The Influence of Technological Knowledge Base and Organizational Structure on Technology Collaboration," *Journal of Management Studies,* June 2010, pp. 679–704; C. C. Miller, W. H. Glick, Y. D. Wang, and G. Huber, "Understanding Technology-Structure Relationships: Theory Development and Meta-Analytic Theory Testing," *Academy of Management Journal,* June 1991, pp. 370–399; J. Hage and M. Aiken, "Routine Technology, Social Structure, and Organizational Goals," *Administrative Science Quarterly*, September 1969, pp. 366–377; J. D. Thompson, *Organizations in Action* (New York: McGraw-Hill, 1967); and C. Perrow, "A Framework for the Comparative Analysis of Organizations," *American Sociological Review*, April 1967, pp. 194–208.

33. D. M. Rousseau and R. A. Cooke, "Technology and Structure: The Concrete, Abstract, and Activity Systems of Organizations," *Journal of Management*, Fall–Winter 1984, pp. 345–361; and D. Gerwin, "Relationships between Structure and Technology," in P. C. Nystrom and W. H. Starbuck (eds.), *Handbook of Organizational Design*, vol. 2 (New York: Oxford University Press, 1981), pp. 3–38.

34. F. E. Emery and E. Trist, "The Causal Texture of Organizational Environments," *Human Relations*, February 1965, pp. 21–32; P. Lawrence and J. W. Lorsch, *Organization and Environment: Managing Differentiation and Integration* (Boston: Harvard Business School, Division of Research, 1967); and M. Yasai-Ardekani, "Structural Adaptations to Environments," *Academy of Management Review*, January 1986, pp. 9–21.

35. Based on www.nba.com/raptors/news/mlsel_management.html; www.mapleleafs.com/team/Management.asp; http://mapleleafs.nhl.com/team/app/?service=page&page=NHLPage&id=12839; www.torontomarlies.com/news/News.asp?story_id=14; and www.toronto-marlies.com/news/news.asp?story_id=433.

36. H. Mintzberg, *Structure in Fives: Designing Effective Organizations* (Upper Saddle River, NJ: Prentice Hall, 1983), p. 157.

37. R. J. Williams, J. J. Hoffman, and B. T. Lamont, "The Influence of Top Management Team Characteristics on M-Form Implementation Time," *Journal of Managerial Issues*, Winter 1995, pp. 466–480.

38. N. Wingfield, "To Rebuild Windows, Microsoft Razed Walls," *Wall Street Journal,* October 20, 2009, p. B9.

39. Q. Hardy, "Google Thinks Small," *Forbes,* November 14, 2005, pp. 198–202.

40. See, for example, A. C. Edmondson, "Teamwork On the Fly," *Harvard Business Review,* April 2012, pp. 72–80; D. R. Denison,

S. L. Hart, and J. A. Kahn, "From Chimneys to Cross-Functional Teams: Developing and Validating a Diagnostic Model," *Academy of Management Journal*, December 1996, pp. 1005–1023; D. Ray and H. Bronstein, *Teaming Up: Making the Transition to a Self-Directed Team-Based Organization* (New York: McGraw Hill, 1995); J. R. Katzenbach and D. K. Smith, *The Wisdom of Teams* (Boston: Harvard Business School Press, 1993); J. A. Byrne, "The Horizontal Corporation," *BusinessWeek,* December 20, 1993, pp. 76–81; B. Dumaine, "Payoff from the New Management," *Fortune,* December 13, 1993, pp. 103–110; and H. Rothman, "The Power of Empowerment," *Nation's Business*, June 1993, pp. 49–52.

41. E. Krell, "Managing the Matrix," *HR Magazine,* April 2011, pp. 69–71.

42. J. Hyatt, "Engineering Inspiration," *Newsweek,* June 14, 2010, p. 44; T. McKeough, "Blowing Hot and Cold," *Fast Company,* December 2009–January 2010, p. 66; H. Walters, "Inside the Design Thinking Process," *BusinessWeek Online,* December 15, 2009; P. Kaihla, "Best-Kept Secrets of the World's Best Companies," *Business 2.0,* April 2006, p. 83; C. Taylor, "School of Bright Ideas," *Time Inside Business,* April 2005, pp. A8–A12; and B. Nussbaum, "The Power of Design," *BusinessWeek,* May 17, 2004, pp. 86–94.

43. R. L. Hotz, "More Scientists Treat Experiments as a Team Sport," *Wall Street Journal,* November 20, 2009, p. A23.

44. See, for example, G. G. Dess, A. M. A. Rasheed, K. J. McLaughlin, and R. L. Priem, "The New Corporate Architecture," *Academy of Management Executive*, August 1995, pp. 7–20.

45. For additional readings on boundaryless organizations, see Rausch and Birkinshaw, June 2008; M. F. R. Kets de Vries, "Leadership Group Coaching in Action: The Zen of Creating High-Performance Teams," *Academy of Management Executive,* February 2005, pp. 61–76; J. Child and R. G. McGrath, "Organizations Unfettered: Organizational Form in an Information-Intensive Economy," *Academy of Management Journal,* December 2001, pp. 1135–1148; M. Hammer and S. Stanton, "How Process Enterprises Really Work," *Harvard Business Review*, November–December 1999, pp. 108–118; T. Zenger and W. Hesterly, "The Disaggregation of Corporations: Selective Intervention, High-Powered Incentives, and Modular Units," *Organization Science,* 1997, vol. 8, pp. 209–222; R. Ashkenas, D. Ulrich, T. Jick, and S. Kerr, *The Boundaryless Organization: Breaking the Chains of Organizational Structure* (San Francisco: Jossey-Bass, 1997); R. M. Hodgetts, "A Conversation with Steve Kerr," *Organizational Dynamics*, Spring 1996, pp. 68–79; and J. Gebhardt, "The Boundaryless Organization," *Sloan Management Review*, Winter 1996, pp. 117–119. For another view of boundaryless organizations, see B. Victor, "The Dark Side of the New Organizational Forms: An Editorial Essay," *Organization Science*, November 1994, pp. 479–482.

46. J. Marte, "An Internship from Your Couch," *Wall Street Journal,* September 9, 2009, pp. D1+.

47. See, for instance, R. J. King, "It's a Virtual World," *Strategy+Business,* www.strategy-business.com, April 21, 2009; Y. Shin, "A Person-Environment Fit Model for Virtual Organizations," *Journal of Management,* December 2004, pp. 725–743; D. Lyons, "Smart and Smarter," *Forbes,* March 18, 2002, pp. 40–41; W. F. Cascio, "Managing a Virtual Workplace," *Academy of Management Executive,* August 2000, pp. 81–90; G. G. Dess, A. M. A. Rasheed, K. J. McLaughlin, and R. L. Priem, "The New Corporate Architecture"; H. Chesbrough and D. Teece, "When Is Virtual Virtuous: Organizing for Innovation," *Harvard Business Review,* January–February 1996, pp. 65–73; and W. H. Davidow and M. S. Malone, *The Virtual Corporation* (New York: Harper Collins, 1992).

48. Q. Hardy, "Bit by Bit, Work Exchange Site Aims to Get Jobs Done," *New York Times Online,* November 6, 2011.

49. M. V. Rafter, "Cultivating A Virtual Culture," *Workforce Management Online,* April 5, 2012.

50. R. Reisner, "A Smart Balance of Staff and Contractors," *BusinessWeek Online,* June 16, 2009; and J. S. Lublin, "Smart Balance Keeps Tight Focus on Creativity," *Wall Street Journal,* June 8, 2009, p. B4.

51. R. Merrifield, J. Calhoun, and D. Stevens, "The Next Revolution in Productivity," *Harvard Business Review,* June 2008, pp. 73–80; R. E. Miles et al., "Organizing in the Knowledge Age: Anticipating the Cellular Form," *Academy of Management Executive,* November 1997, pp. 7–24; C. Jones, W. Hesterly, and S. Borgatti, "A General Theory of Network Governance: Exchange Conditions and Social Mechanisms," *Academy of Management Review,* October 1997, pp. 911–945; R. E. Miles and C. C. Snow, "The New Network Firm: A Spherical Structure Built on Human Investment Philosophy," *Organizational Dynamics,* Spring 1995, pp. 5–18; and R. E. Miles and C. C. Snow, "Causes of Failures in Network Organizations," *California Management Review,* 1992, vol. 34, no. 4, pp. 53–72.

52. G. Hoetker, "Do Modular Products Lead to Modular Organizations?" *Strategic Management Journal,* June 2006, pp. 501–518; C. H. Fine, "Are You Modular or Integral?" *Strategy & Business,* Summer 2005, pp. 44–51; D. A. Ketchen, Jr. and G. T. M. Hult, "To Be Modular or Not to Be? Some Answers to the Question," *Academy of Management Executive,* May 2002, pp. 166–167; M. A. Schilling, "The Use of Modular Organizational Forms: An Industry-Level Analysis," *Academy of Management Journal,* December 2001, pp. 1149–1168; D. Lei, M. A. Hitt, and J. D. Goldhar, "Advanced Manufacturing Technology: Organizational Design and Strategic Flexibility," *Organization Studies,* 1996, vol. 17, pp. 501–523; R. Sanchez and J. Mahoney, "Modularity Flexibility and Knowledge Management in Product and Organization Design," *Strategic Management Journal,* 1996, vol. 17, pp. 63–76; and R. Sanchez, "Strategic Flexibility in Product Competition," *Strategic Management Journal,* 1995, vol. 16, pp. 135–159.

53. J. Fortt, "The Chip Company That Dares to Battle Intel," *Fortune,* July 20, 2009, pp. 51–56.

54. C. Hymowitz, "Have Advice, Will Travel," *Wall Street Journal,* June 5, 2006, pp. B1+.

55. S. Reed, A. Reinhardt, and A. Sains, "Saving Ericsson," *BusinessWeek,* November 11, 2002, pp. 64–68.

56. P. Engardio, "The Future of Outsourcing," *BusinessWeek,* January 30, 2006, pp. 50–58.

57. P. Sonne, "Tesco's CEO-to-Be Unfolds Map for Global Expansion," *Wall Street Journal,* June 9, 2010, p. B1; T. Shifrin, "Grocery Giant Tesco Is Creating a Storm in the US Market with Its Tesco in a Box Set of Systems," www.computerworlduk.com, January 14, 2008; P. Olson, "Tesco's Landing," *Forbes,* June 4, 2007, pp. 116–118; and P. M. Senge, *The Fifth Discipline: The Art and Practice of Learning Organizations* (New York: Doubleday, 1990).

58. J. J. Salopek, "Keeping Learning Well-Oiled," *T&D,* October 2011, pp. 32–35.

59. A. C. Edmondson, "The Competitive Imperative of Learning," *Harvard Business Review,* July–August 2008, pp. 60–67.

60. S. A. Sackmann, P. M. Eggenhofer-Rehart, and M. Friesl, "Long-Term Efforts Toward Developing a Learning Organization," *Journal of Applied Behavioral Science,* December 2009, pp. 521–549; D. A. Garvin, A. C. Edmondson, and F. Gino, "Is Yours a Learning Organization?" *Harvard Business Review,* March 2008, pp. 109–116; A. N. K. Chen and T. M. Edgington, "Assessing Value in Organizational Knowledge Creation: Considerations for Knowledge Workers," *MIS Quarterly,* June 2005, pp. 279–309; K. G. Smith, C. J. Collins, and K. D. Clark, "Existing Knowledge, Knowledge Creation Capability, and The Rate of New Product Introduction in High-Technology Firms," *Academy of Management Journal,* April 2005, pp. 346–357; R. Cross, A. Parker, L. Prusak, and S. P. Borgati, "Supporting Knowledge Creation and Sharing in Social Networks," *Organizational Dynamics,* Fall, 2001, pp. 100–120; M. Schulz, "The Uncertain Relevance of Newness: Organizational Learning and Knowledge Flows," *Academy of Management Journal,* August 2001, pp. 661–681; G. Szulanski, "Exploring Internal Stickiness: Impediments to the Transfer of Best Practice within the Firm," *Strategic Management Journal,* Winter Special Issue, 1996, pp. 27–43; and J. M. Liedtka, "Collaborating across Lines of Business for Competitive Advantage," *Academy of Management Executive,* April 1996, pp. 20–37.

61. C. Hausman, "Lifeguard Fired for Leaving Patrol Zone to Save Drowning Man," *Ethics Newsline Online,* July 9, 2012; S. Grossman, "Lifeguard Who Got Fired for Saving Drowning Swimmer Declines Offer to Return," *newsfeed.time.com,* July 6, 2012; E. Illades and C. Teproff, "Fired Lifeguard Says 'No Thanks' When He's Re-offered Job," *MiamiHerald.com,* July 5, 2012; and W. Lee, "Florida Lifeguard Helps Save Life, Gets Fired," *USA Today Online,* July 4, 2012.

62. Based on P. L. Hunsaker, *Training in Management Skills* (Upper Saddle River, NJ: Prentice Hall, 2001), pp. 135–136 and 430–432; R. T. Noel, "What You Say to Your Employees When You Delegate," *Supervisory Management,* December 1993, p. 13; and S. Caudron, "Delegate for Results," *IndustryWeek,* February 6, 1995, pp. 27–30.

63. S. Silbermann, "How Culture and Regulation Demand New Ways to Sell," *Harvard Business Review,* July/August 2012, pp. 104–105; P. Miller and T. Wedell-Wedellsborg, "How to Make an Offer That Managers Can't Refuse?" *IESE Insight,* 2011 (second quarter), issue 9, pp. 66–67; S. Hernández, "Prove Its Worth," *IESE Insight,* 2011 (second quarter), issue 9, p. 68; T. Koulopoulos, "Know Thyself," *IESE Insight,* 2011 (second quarter), issue 9, p. 69; M. Weinstein, "Retrain and Restructure Your Organization," *Training,* May 2009, p. 36; J. McGregor, "The Chore Goes Offshore," *BusinessWeek,* March 23 & 30, 2009, pp. 50–51; "Pfizer: Making It 'Leaner, Meaner, More Efficient,'" *BusinessWeek Online,* March 2, 2009; and A. Cohen, "Scuttling Scut Work," *Fast Company,* February 2008, pp. 42–43.

64. B. Philbin, "Schwab's Net Drops 20%," *Wall Street Journal,* April 17, 2012, p. C9; M. Tian, "Charles Schwab—An Unnoticed Transformation," *Morningstar Opportunistic Investor,* March 2012, pp. 6–9; B. Morris, "Chuck Schwab Is Worried About the Small Investor," *Bloomberg BusinessWeek,* May 31– June 6, 2010, pp. 58–64; L. Gibbs, "Chuck Would Like a Word With You," *Money,* January/February 2010, pp. 98–103; R. Markey, F. Reichheld, and A. Dullweber, "Closing the Customer Feedback Loop," *Harvard Business Review,* December 2009, pp. 43–47; and R. Farzad and C. Palmeri, "Can Schwab Seize the Day?" *Bloomberg BusinessWeek,* July 27, 2009, pp. 36–39.

Chapter 11

1. M. Lopresti, "Elimination by Twitter," *USA Today,* July 26, 2012, p. 1C; K. Paulson, "College Athlete Tweet Ban? Free Speech Sacks That Idea," *USA Today,* April 16, 2012, p. 9A; L. East, "Les Miles' Tweets Entertain CWS Fans," theadvocate.com/sports; July 12, 2012; P. Thamel, "Tracking Twitter, Raising Red Flags," *New York Times Online,* March 30, 2012; L. Dugan, "Twitter To Surpass 500 Million Registered Users on Wednesday," www.mediabistro.com, February 21, 2012; C. Ho, "Companies Tracking College Athletes' Tweets, Facebook Posts Go After Local Universities," *Washington Post Online,* October 16, 2011; D. Rovell, "Coaches Ban of Twitter Proves College Sports Isn't About Education," *CNBC Sports Business Online,* August 8, 2011; Staff of Corporate Executive Board, "Corporate Confidential: How Twitter Changes Everything," *BusinessWeek Online,* September 4, 2009; S. Johnson, "How Twitter Will Change the Way We Live," *Time,* June 15, 2009, pp. 30–37; J. Swartz, "A World That's All a-Twitter," *USA Today,* May 26, 2009, pp. 1B+; and K. Whiteside, "College Coaches Are Chirping About Twitter!" *USA Today,* April 29, 2009, pp. 1C+.

2. P. G. Clampitt, *Communicating for Managerial Effectiveness*, 3rd ed. (Thousand Oaks, CA: Sage, 2005); T. Dixon, *Communication, Organization, and Performance* (Norwood, NJ: Ablex, 1996), p. 281; P. G. Clampitt, *Communicating for Managerial Effectiveness* (Newbury Park, CA: Sage, 1991); and L. E. Penley, E. R. Alexander, I. E. Jernigan, and C. I. Henwood, "Communication Abilities of Managers: The Relationship to Performance," *Journal of Management*, March 1991, pp. 57–76.

3. S. Carey, "Southwest Grounds Pilot after Obscene Radio Rant," *Wall Street Journal,* June 23, 2011, p. B1; and "Southwest Pilot Grounded after Radio Rant," www.wctv.tv, June 23, 2011.

4. C. O. Kursh, "The Benefits of Poor Communication," *Psychoanalytic Review*, Summer–Fall 1971, pp. 189–208.

5. "Irene Lewis, CEO of SAIT Polytechnic, to Receive IABC's 2012 EXCEL Award," www.iabc.com/awards, July 29, 2012.

6. W. G. Scott and T. R. Mitchell, *Organization Theory: A Structural and Behavioral Analysis* (Homewood, IL: Richard D. Irwin, 1976).

7. M. W. DiStaso and T. M. McCorkindale, "A Benchmark Analysis of the Strategic Use of Social Media for Fortune's Most Admired U. S. Companies on Facebook, Twitter and Youtube," *Public Relations Journal*, 7(1), pp. 1–33, http://www.instituteforpr.org/scienceofsocialmedia/a-benchmark-analysis-of-the-strategic-use-of-social-media-for-fortunes-most-admired-u-s-companies-on-facebook-twitter-and-youtube/ (accessed June 30, 2014).

8. D. K. Berlo, *The Process of Communication* (New York: Holt, Rinehart & Winston, 1960), pp. 30–32.

9. P. G. Clampitt, *Communicating for Managerial Effectiveness* (Newbury Park, CA: Sage, 1991).

10. A. Warfield, "Do You Speak Body Language?" *Training & Development*, April 2001, pp. 60–61; D. Zielinski, "Body Language Myths," *Presentations*, April 2001, pp. 36–42; and "Visual Cues Speak Loudly in Workplace," *Springfield News-Leader*, January 21, 2001, p. 8B.

11. J. Levine, "Conversations on Culture," *DMI News & Views,* June 2012, p. 31; "Keeping It Creative," *Fast Company*, June 2012, pp. 22–24; E. Florian, "Tony Hsieh," *Fortune,* April 30, 2012, p. 19; M. Stettner, "Zappos Chief Treasures the Company's Culture," *Investors Business Daily,* April 30, 2012, p. A07; R. E. Silverman, "Firms Share Spaces, Ideas," *Wall Street Journal,* March 21, 2012, p. B8; T. Hsieh and R. Ten Pas, *Delivering Happiness: A Path to Profits, Passion, and Purpose* (Writers of the Round Table Press), 2012; and B. Stone, "What Starts Up in Vegas Stays in Vegas," *Bloomberg BusinessWeek,* February 6, 2012, pp. 37–39.

12. T. R. Kurtzberg, C. E. Naquin, and L. Y. Belkin, "Electronic Performance Appraisals: The Effects of E-Mail Communication on Peer Ratings in Actual and Simulated Environments," *Organizational Behavior and Human Decision Processes* 98, no. 2 (2005), pp. 216–226.

13. J. Kruger, N. Epley, J. Parker, and Z.-W. Ng, "Egocentrism over E-Mail: Can We Communicate as Well as We Think?" *Journal of Personality and Social Psychology* 89, no. 6 (2005), pp. 925–936.

14. Thanks to an anonymous reviewer for providing this elaboration.

15. C. Cavanagh, *Managing Your E-Mail: Thinking Outside the Inbox* (Hoboken, NJ: John Wiley & Sons, 2003).

16. S. Radicati, ed. *Email Statistics Report 2010*, www.radicati.com/wp/wp-content/uploads/2010/04/Email-Statistics-Report-2010-2014-Executive-Summary2.pdf (accessed January 22, 2011).

17. K. Macklem, "You've Got Too Much Mail," *Maclean's*, January 30, 2006, pp. 20–21.

18. D. K. Berlo, *The Process of Communication* (New York: Holt, Rinehart & Winston, 1960), p. 103.

19. L. Haggerman, "Strong, Efficient Leadership Minimizes Employee Problems," *Springfield Business Journal*, December 9–15, 2002, p. 23.

20. See, for instance, S. P. Robbins and P. L. Hunsaker, *Training in InterPersonal Skills*, 4th ed. (Upper Saddle River, NJ: Prentice Hall, 2006); M. Young and J. E. Post, "Managing to Communicate, Communicating to Manage: How Leading Companies Communicate with Employees," *Organizational Dynamics*, Summer 1993, pp. 31–43; J. A. DeVito, *The Interpersonal Communication Book*, 6th ed. (New York: HarperCollins, 1992); and A. G. Athos and J. J. Gabarro, *Interpersonal Behavior* (Upper Saddle River, NJ: Prentice Hall, 1978).

21. C. O'Donnell, "New study quantifies use of social media in Arab Spring," *University of Washington*, September 12, 2011, http://www.washington.edu/news/2011/09/12/new-study-quantifies-use-of-social-media-in-arab-spring/ (accessed June 30, 2014).

22. O. Thomas, "Best-Kept Secrets of the World's Best Companies: The Three Minute Huddle," *Business 2.0*, April 2006, p. 94.

23. V. Galt, "Top-Down Feedback," *Vancouver Sun*, February 15, 2003, pp. E1, E2.

24. Cited in "Heard It through the Grapevine," *Forbes*, February 10, 1997, p. 22.

25. See, for instance, A. Bruzzese, "What to Do about Toxic Gossip," *USA Today*, March 14, 2001, www.usatoday.com; N. B. Kurland and L. H. Pelled, "Passing the Word: Toward a Model of Gossip and Power in the Workplace," *Academy of Management Review*, April 2000, pp. 428–438; N. DiFonzo, P. Bordia, and R. L. Rosnow, "Reining in Rumors," *Organizational Dynamics*, Summer 1994, pp. 47–62; M. Noon and R. Delbridge, "News from Behind My Hand: Gossip in Organizations," *Organization Studies* 14, no. 1 (1993), pp. 23–26; and J. G. March and G. Sevon, "Gossip, Information and Decision Making," in *Decisions and Organizations*, ed. G. March, pp. 429–442 (Oxford: Blackwell, 1988).

26. Gensler, "The U.S. Workplace Survey, 2008," www.gensler.com, July 11, 2010.

27. Gensler, "The U.S. Workplace Survey, 2008," www.gensler.com, July 11, 2010,, p. 11.

28. C. C. Sullivan and B. Horwitz-Bennett, "High-Performance Workplaces," *Building Design + Construction,* January 2010, pp. 22–26.

29. J. B. Stryker, "In Open Workplaces, Traffic and Head Count Matter," *Harvard Business Review,* December 2009, p. 24.

30. K. D. Elsbach and M. G. Pratt, "The Physical Environment in Organizations," in *The Academy of Management Annals,* vol. 1, 2007, J. P. Walsh and A. P. Brief (eds.), pp. 181–114.

31. S. Shellenbarger, "Indecent Exposure: The Downsides of Working in a Glass Office," *Wall Street Journal,* January 4, 2012, p. D1+.

32. J. B. Stryker, "In Open Workplaces, Traffic and Head Count Matter;" and K. D. Elsbach and M. G. Pratt, "The Physical Environment in Organizations."

33. S. E. Needleman, "Office Personal Space Is Crowded Out," *Wall Street Journal,* December 7, 2009, p. B7.

34. These examples taken from A. Dizik, "Chefs Solve a Modern Kitchen Crisis: Recipe Clutter," *Wall Street Journal,* June 30, 2011, p. D1+; T. Henneman, "At Lockheed Martin, Social Networking Fills Key Workforce Needs while Improving Efficiency and Lowering Costs," *Workforce Management Online,* March 2010; S. Kirsner, "Being There," *Fast Company,* January–February 2006, pp. 90–91; R. Breeden, "More Employees Are Using the Web at Work," *Wall Street Journal,* May 10, 2005, p. B4; C. Woodward, "Some Offices Opt for Cellphones Only," *USA Today,* January 25, 2005, p. 1B; and

J. Rohwer, "Today, Tokyo. Tomorrow, the World," *Fortune*, September 18, 2000, pp. 140–152.

35. G. Colvin, "Brave New Work: The Office of Tomorrow," *Fortune,* January 16, 2012, pp. 49+.

36. J. Karaian, "Where Wireless Works," *CFO,* May 2003, pp. 81–83.

37. S. Srivastava, "Doing More on the Go," *Wall Street Journal,* June 12, 2007, p. B3.

38. B. White, "Firms Take a Cue from YouTube," *Wall Street Journal,* January 2, 2007, p. B3.

39. K. Hafner, "For the Well Connected, All the World's an Office," *New York Times*, March 30, 2000, p. D11.

40. See "Fact Sheets," *Office of the Privacy Commissioner of Canada*, http://www.priv.gc.ca/resource/fs-fi/02_05_d_15_e.asp (accessed June 30, 2014).

41. " Personal Information Protection and the Electronic Documents Act (PIPEDA)—Part 1," Treasury Board of Canada Secretariat, www.tbs-sct.gc.ca/pgol-pged/piatp-pfefvp/course1/mod2/mod2-3-eng.asp (accessed September 30, 2010).

42. "About the Law," *Canada's Anti-Spam Legislation (CASL),* http://fightspam.gc.ca/eic/site/030.nsf/eng/home (accessed July 1, 2014).

43. S. Shellenbager, "Backlash against E-Mail Builds," *Wall Street Journal,* April 29, 2010, p. D6.

44. H. Green, "The Water Cooler Is Now on the Web," *BusinessWeek,* October 1, 2007, pp. 78–79.

45. The Associated Press, "Whole Foods Chief Apologizes for Posts," *New York Times Online,* July 18, 2007; E. White, J. S. Lublin, and D. Kesmodel, "Executives Get the Blogging Bug," *Wall Street Journal,* July 13, 2007, pp. B1+; C. Alldred, "U.K. Libel Case Slows E-Mail Delivery," *Business Insurance,* August 4, 1997, pp. 51–53; and T. Lewin, "Chevron Settles Sexual Harassment Charges," *New York Times Online,* February 22, 1995.

46. J. Eckberg, "E-Mail: Messages Are Evidence," *Cincinnati Enquirer,* www.enquirer.com, July 27, 2004.

47. M. Scott, "Worker E-Mail and Blog Misuse Seen as Growing Risk for Companies," *Workforce Management,* www.workforce.com, July 20, 2007.

48. K. Byron, "Carrying Too Heavy a Load? The Communication and Miscommunication of Emotion by E-Mail," *Academy of Management Review,* April 2008, pp. 309–327.

49. J. Marquez, "Virtual Work Spaces Ease Collaboration, Debate among Scattered Employees," *Workforce Management,* May 22, 2006, p. 38; and M. Conlin, "E-Mail Is So Five Minutes Ago," *BusinessWeek,* November 28, 2005, pp. 111–112.

50. H. Green, "The Water Cooler Is Now on the Web"; E. Frauenheim, "Starbucks Employees Carve Out Own 'Space,'" *Workforce Management,* October 22, 2007, p. 32; and S. H. Wildstrom, "Harnessing Social Networks," *BusinessWeek,* April 23, 2007, p. 20.

51. J. Scanlon, "Woman of Substance," *Wired*, July 2002, p. 27.

52. E. Wenger, R. McDermott, and W. Snyder, *Cultivating Communities of Practice: A Guide to Managing Knowledge* (Boston: Harvard Business School Press, 2002), p. 4.

53. E. Wenger, R. McDermott, and W. Snyder, *Cultivating Communities of Practice: A Guide to Managing Knowledge*(Boston: Harvard Business School Press, 2002), p. 39.

54. data points box based on "What's Your Social IQ?" *CFO,* May 2012, p. 12; J. Yang and V. Bravo, "Average Office Space per Worker," *USA Today,* February 27, 2012, p. 1B; "Technology," *HR Magazine,* HR Trendbook 2011, p. 70; L. Kwoh, "When Face Time Counts,"

Wall Street Journal, April 25, 2012, p. B8; A. R. Carey and P. Trap, "When North American Workers Use Mobile Devices to Work Outside the Office," *USA Today,* September 28, 2011, p. 1A; J. Yang and K. Gelles, "Do You Have a Negative View of Workers with a Messy Desk?" *USA Today,* September 14, 2011, p. 1B; J. Yang and K. O'Callaghan, "What Would You Say to Your Boss if There Were No Consequences?" *USA Today,* August 9, 2011, p. 1B; "Common Workplace Distraction by Activity," *T&D,* July 2011, p. 23; T. Neeley and P. Leonardi, "Effective Managers Say the Same Thing Twice (or More)," *Harvard Business Review,* May 2011, p. 38; A. Smith, "E-Mail Training Needed to Avoid Cyber Battles," www.shrm.org/legal_issues, May 6, 2011; and "Smart Women, Dumb E-mails," *Women's Health,* January/February 2011, p. 118.

55. B. A. Gutek, M. Groth, and B. Cherry, "Achieving Service Success through Relationship and Enhanced Encounters," *Academy of Management Executive*, November 2002, pp. 132–144.

56. R. C. Ford and C. P. Heaton, "Lessons from Hospitality That Can Serve Anyone," *Organizational Dynamics*, Summer 2001, pp. 30–47.

57. M. J. Bitner, B. H. Booms, and L. A. Mohr, "Critical Service Encounters: The Employee's Viewpoint," *Journal of Marketing*, October 1994, pp. 95–106.

58. S. D. Pugh, J. Dietz, J. W. Wiley, and S. M. Brooks, "Driving Service Effectiveness through Employee-Customer Linkages," *Academy of Management Executive*, November 2002, pp. 73–84.

59. J. Ewing, "Nokia: Bring on the Employee Rants," *BusinessWeek,* June 22, 2009, p. 50.

60. J. V. Thill and C. L. Bovee, *Excellence in Business Communication,* 9th ed. (Upper Saddle River, NJ: Prentice Hall, 2011), pp. 24–25.

61. J. V. Thill and C. L. Bovee, *Excellence in Business Communication,* 9th ed. (Upper Saddle River, NJ: Prentice Hall, 2011), pp. 24–25.

62. J. V. Thill and C. L. Bovee, *Excellence in Business Communication,* 9th ed. (Upper Saddle River, NJ: Prentice Hall, 2011), pp. 24–25.

63. J. V. Thill and C. L. Bovee, *Excellence in Business Communication,* 9th ed. (Upper Saddle River, NJ: Prentice Hall, 2011), pp. 24–25.

64. J. V. Thill and C. L. Bovee, *Excellence in Business Communication,* 9th ed. (Upper Saddle River, NJ: Prentice Hall, 2011), pp. 24–25.

65. M. Villano, "The Online Divide between Work and Play," *New York Times Online,* April 26, 2009.

66. J. Fortt and M. V. Copeland, "The Great Debate," *Fortune,* May 3, 2010, p. 32.

67. M. V. Rafter, "Too Much Email on the Menu? Here Are Five Tips to Curb Company Consumption," *Workforce Management Online,* April 24, 2012; M.V. Rafter, "If Tim Fry Has His Way, He'll Eradicate Email for Good," *Workforce Management Online,* April 24, 2012; M. A. Field, "Turning Off Email, Turning Up Productivity," *Workforce Management Online,* February 29, 2012; "Internet 2011 in Numbers," royalpingdom.com, January 17, 2012; "Should Workplaces Curtail Email?" *New York Times Online,* December 7, 2011; W. Powers, "The Phony 'Zero Email' Alarm," *New York Times Online,* December 6, 2011; L. Suarez, "What We Would Miss," *New York Times Online,* December 5, 2011; P. Duncan, "Break Bad Habits," *New York Times Online,* December 5, 2011; N. Carr, "Put the Cost Back in Communication," *New York Times Online,* December 5, 2011; P. Allen, "One of the Biggest Information Technology Companies in the World to Abolish E-mails," www.dailymail.com, November 30, 2011; and R. Z. Arndt, "25th Anniversary of Listserv," *Fastcompany.com,* June 2011, p. 32.

68. B. Levisohn and E. Gibson, "An Unwelcome Delivery," *BusinessWeek,* May 4, 2009, p. 15; S. Clifford, "Video Prank at Domino's Taints Brand," *New York Times Online,* April 16, 2009; B. Horovitz, "Domino's Nightmare Holds Lessons for Marketers," *USA Today,* April 16, 2009, p. 3B; and E. Bryson York, "Employee

Misconduct and Internet Video Create PR Disaster for Domino's Pizza," *Workforce Management Online,* April 15, 2009.

Chapter 12

1. Based on Hoover's Online, www.hoovers.com (accessed March 9, 2014); R. Waugh, "Getting More Leaders Is Hard Enough, but the Job Skills Needed Are Changing, Too," *Canadian HR Reporter*, January 26, 2004, p. 18; J. Kirby, "In the Vault," *Canadian Business*, March 1–14, 2004, pp. 68–72; S. Greengard, "Brett Ellison," *IQ Magazine*, November–December 2002, p. 52; www.scotiabank.com/cda/content/0,1608,CID821_LIDen,00.html; http://cgi.scotiabank.com/annrep2006/en/pdf/ScotiaAR06_ConsolidatedFinancialStatements.pdf; and www.scotiabank.com/cda/content/0,1608,CID11095_LIDen,00.html.

2. *2013 Scotiabank Annual Report*, http://www.scotiabank.com/ca/en/files/13/12/BNS_2013_Annual_Report.pdf (accessed May 31, 2014).

3. A. Carmeli and J. Shaubroeck, "How Leveraging Human Resource Capital with Its Competitive Distinctiveness Enhances the Performance of Commercial and Public Organizations," *Human Resource Management,* Winter 2005, pp. 391–412; L. Bassi and D. McMurrer, "How's Your Return on People?" *Harvard Business Review,* March 2004, p. 18; C. J. Collins and K. D. Clark, "Strategic Human Resource Practices, Top Management Team Social Networks, and Firm Performance: The Role of Human Resource Practices in Creating Organizational Competitive Advantage," *Academy of Management Journal,* December 2003, pp. 740–751; J. Pfeffer, *The Human Equation* (Boston: Harvard Business School Press, 1998); J. Pfeffer, *Competitive Advantage Through People* (Boston: Harvard Business School Press, 1994); A. A. Lado and M. C. Wilson, "Human Resource Systems and Sustained Competitive Advantage," *Academy of Management Review,* October 1994, pp. 699–727; and P. M. Wright and G. C. McMahan, "Theoretical Perspectives for Strategic Human Resource Management," *Journal of Management* 18, no. 1 (1992), pp. 295–320.

4. "Maximizing the Return on Your Human Capital Investment: The 2005 Watson Wyatt Human Capital Index® Report;" "WorkAsia 2004/2005: A Study of Employee Attitudes in Asia;" and "European Human Capital Index 2002," Watson Wyatt Worldwide (Washington, DC).

5. See, for example, C. H. Chuang and H. Liao, "Strategic Human Resource Management in Service Context: Taking Care of Business by Taking Care of Employees and Customers," *Personnel Psychology,* Spring 2010, pp. 153–196; M. Subramony, "A Meta-Analytic Investigation of the Relationship Between HRM Bundles and Firm Performance," *Human Resource Management,* September–October 2009, pp. 745–768; M. M. Butts et al., "Individual Reactions to High Involvement Work Practices: Investigating the Role of Empowerment and Perceived Organizational Support," *Journal of Occupational Health Psychology,* April 2009, pp. 122–136; L. Sun, S. Aryee, and K. S. Law, "High-Performance Human Resource Practices, Citizenship Behavior, and Organizational Performance: A Relational Perspective," *Academy of Management Journal,* June 2007, pp. 558–577; A. Carmeli and J. Shaubroeck, "How Leveraging Human Resource Capital with Its Competitive Distinctiveness Enhances the Performance of Commercial and Public Organizations," 2005; Y. Y. Kor and H. Leblebici, "How Do Interdependencies among Human-Capital Deployment, Development, and Diversification Strategies Affect Firms' Financial Performance?" *Strategic Management Journal,* October 2005, pp. 967–985; D. E. Bowen and C. Ostroff, "Understanding HRM–Firm Performance Linkages: The Role of the 'Strength' of the HRM System," *Academy of Management Review,* April 2004, pp. 203–221; A. S. Tsui, J. L. Pearce, L. W. Porter, and A. M. Tripoli, "Alternative Approaches to the Employee-Organization Relationship: Does Investment in Employees Pay Off?" *Academy of Management Journal,* October 1997,

pp. 1089–1121; M. A. Huselid, S. E. Jackson, and R. S. Schuler, "Technical and Strategic Human Resource Management Effectiveness as Determinants of Firm Performance," *Academy of Management Journal,* January 1997, pp. 171–188; J. T. Delaney and M. A. Huselid, "The Impact of Human Resource Management Practices on Perceptions of Organizational Performance," *Academy of Management Journal,* August 1996, pp. 949–969; B. Becker and B. Gerhart, "The Impact of Human Resource Management on Organizational Performance: Progress and Prospects," *Academy of Management Journal,* August 1996, pp. 779–801; M. J. Koch and R. G. McGrath, "Improving Labor Productivity: Human Resource Management Policies Do Matter," *Strategic Management Journal,* May 1996, pp. 335–354; and M. A. Huselid, "The Impact of Human Resource Management Practices on Turnover, Productivity, and Corporate Financial Performance," *Academy of Management Journal,* June 1995, pp. 635–672.

6. "Human Capital a Key to Higher Market Value," *Business Finance,* December 1999, p. 15.

7. M. Boyle, "Happy People, Happy Returns," *Fortune,* January 11, 2006, p. 100.

8. data points box based on "Find the Sharpest Needle in the Stack," *HR Magazine,* June 2012, p. 16; J. Yang and P. Trap, "If You Started a Job and You Didn't Like It, How Long Would You Stay?" *USA Today,* June 11, 2012, p. 1B; J. Yang and P. Trap, "Do You Use Social Networking Sites to Research Candidates?" *USA Today,* June 5, 2012, p. 1B; J. Yang and A. Gonzalez, "Top Actions Workers Feel Are Grounds for Termination," *USA Today,* May 7, 2012, p. 1B; L. Weber," Little Time for Resumes," *Wall Street Journal,* March 21, 2012, p. B8; J. Yang and V. Bravo, "How Often Are You Late for Work?" *USA Today,* February 8, 2012, p. 1B; K. Madden, "Playing Hooky From the Office," Careerbuilder, *Springfield News-Leader* (Missouri), November 6, 2011, p. 1G; J. Yang and P. Trap, "Top Reasons Why Someone Hired Would Not Work Out in the Position," *USA Today,* October 26, 2011, p. 1B; J. Yang and V. Salazar, "Are Annual Performance Reviews an Accurate Appraisal for Employees' Work?" *USA Today,* September 27, 2011, p. 1B; J. Yang and S. Ward, "What Are the Most Common Mistakes Candidates Make During Job Interviews?" *USA Today,* August 15, 2011, p. 1B; and P. Kujawa, "For Some Workers, the Piggy Bank Is Fat for Retirement," *Workforce Management Online,* July 16, 2012.

9. J. Clenfield, "A Tear in Japan's Safety Net," *Bloomberg BusinessWeek,* April 12, 2010, pp. 60–61.

10. CIA World Factbook, https://www.cia.gov/library/publications/the-world-factbook/geos/ee.html, 2012; and "EU: Not Working," *Business Europe,* March 1, 2010, p. 1.

11. A. Kohpaiboon et al., "Global Recession: Labour Market Adjustment and International Production Networks," *ASEAN Economic Bulletin,* April 2010, pp. 98–120.

12. J. Schramm, "Tomorrow's Workforce," *HR Magazine,* March 2012, p. 112; C. Isidore, "Say Goodbye to Full-Time Jobs with Benefits," CNNMoney.com, June 1, 2010; C. Rampell, "In a Job Market Realignment, Some Left Behind," *New York Times Online,* May 12, 2010; and P. Izzo, "Economists Expect Shifting Work Force," *Wall Street Journal Online,* February 11, 2010.

13. F. Hansen, "Jobless Recovery Is Leaving a Trail of Recession-Weary Employees in Its Wake," *Compensation & Benefits Review,* May/June 2010, pp. 135–136; J. Hollon, "Worker 'Deal' Is Off," *Workforce Management,* April 2010, p. 42; and "The New Employment Deal: How Far, How Fast, and How Enduring? The 2010 Global Workforce Study," *Towers Watson,* www.towerswatson.com, April 2010.

14. "Indicators of Well-Being in Canada: Work—Unionization Rates," Human Resources and Skills Development Canada, www4.hrsdc.gc.ca/.3ndic.1t.4r@-eng.jsp?iid=17 (accessed June 9, 2014).

15. "Trade Union Density," *OECD Stats Extracts,* http://stats.oecd.org/Index.aspx?DataSetCode=UN_DEN (accessed June 9 2014).

16. S. Premack and J. E. Hunter, "Individual Unionization Decisions," *Psychological Bulletin* 103, no. 2 (1988), pp. 223–234.

17. Based on "Just Us! Coffee Shop Says It's First to Unionize in Canada," *CBC,* December 23, 2013, http://www.cbc.ca/news/canada/nova-scotia/just-us-coffee-shop-says-it-s-first-to-unionize-in-canada-1.2474999 (accessed June 9, 2014).

18. S. Armour, "Lawsuits Pin Target on Managers," *USA Today,* October 1, 2002, www.usatoday.com.

19. Canadian Human Rights Act, http://laws-lois.justice.gc.ca/eng/acts/h-6/.

20. See http://laws-lois.justice.gc.ca/eng/regulations/sor-86-1082/page-1.html.

21. "Indicators of Well-Being in Canada: Canadians in Context—Aging Population," Human Resources and Skills Development Canada, www4.hrsdc.gc.ca/.3ndic.1t.4r@-eng.jsp?iid=33 (accessed June 9, 2014).

22. R. Waugh, "Getting More Leaders Is Hard Enough, But the Job Skills Needed Are Changing, Too," *Canadian HR Reporter,* January 26, 2004, p. 18.

23. J. Sullivan, "Workforce Planning: Why to Start Now," *Workforce,* September 2002, pp. 46–50.

24. T. J. Bergmann and M. S. Taylor, "College Recruitment: What Attracts Students to Organizations?" *Personnel,* May–June 1984, pp. 34–46; and A. S. Bargerstock and G. Swanson, "Four Ways to Build Cooperative Recruitment Alliances," *HR Magazine,* March 1991, p. 49.

25. J. R. Gordon, *Human Resource Management*: A Practical Approach (Boston: Allyn and Bacon, 1986), p. 170.

26. S. Burton and D. Warner, "The Future of Hiring—Top 5 Sources for Recruitment Today," *Workforce* Vendor Directory, 2002, p. 75.

27. C. Reynolds, "McDonald's Hiring Day Draws Crowds, High Hopes," AP Business Writer, *Springfield News-Leader* (Missouri), April 20, 2011, p. 6A; and A. Gasparro, "Fast-Food Chain Aims to Alter 'McJob' Image," *Wall Street Journal,* April 5, 2011, p. B9.

28. J. Walker, "Firms Invest Big in Career Sites," *Wall Street Journal Online,* June 8, 2010.

29. L. Petrecca, "With 3,000 Applications a Day, Google Can Be Picky," *USA Today,* May 19, 2010, p. 2B; and M. Helft, "In Fierce Competition, Google Finds Novel Ways to Feed Hiring Machine," *New York Times Online,* May 28, 2007.

30. K. Plourd, "Lights, Camera, Audits!" *CFO,* November 2007, p. 18.

31. G. Shaw, "An Offer That's Hard to Refuse," *Vancouver Sun,* November 12, 2003, p. D5.

32. See, for example, J. P. Kirnan, J. E. Farley, and K. F. Geisinger, "The Relationship between Recruiting Source, Applicant Quality, and Hire Performance: An Analysis by Sex, Ethnicity, and Age," *Personnel Psychology,* Summer 1989, pp. 293–308; and R. W. Griffeth, P. Hom, L. Fink, and D. Cohen, "Comparative Tests of Multivariate Models of Recruiting Sources Effects," *Journal of Management* 23, no. 1 (1997), pp. 19–36.

33. A. Douzet, "Quality of Fill an Emerging Recruitment Metric," *Workforce Management Online,* June 24, 2010; and "Quality of Hire Metrics Help Staffing Unit Show Its Contribution to Bottom Line," *Society for Human Resource Management Online,* January 25, 2009.

34. G. W. England, *Development and Use of Weighted Application Blanks*, rev. ed. (Minneapolis: Industrial Relations Center, University

of Minnesota, 1971); J. J. Asher, "The Biographical Item: Can It Be Improved?" *Personnel Psychology,* Summer 1972, p. 266; G. Grimsley and H. F. Jarrett, "The Relation of Managerial Achievement to Test Measures Obtained in the Employment Situation: Methodology and Results," *Personnel Psychology,* Spring 1973, pp. 31–48; E. E. Ghiselli, "The Validity of Aptitude Tests in Personnel Selection," *Personnel Psychology,* Winter 1973, p. 475; I. T. Robertson and R. S. Kandola, "Work Sample Tests: Validity, Adverse Impact, and Applicant Reaction," *Journal of Occupational Psychology* 55, no. 3 (1982), pp. 171–183; A. K. Korman, "The Prediction of Managerial Performance: A Review," *Personnel Psychology,* Summer 1986, pp. 295–322; G. C. Thornton, *Assessment Centers in Human Resource Management* (Reading, MA: Addison-Wesley, 1992); C. Fernandez-Araoz, "Hiring without Firing," *Harvard Business Review,* July–August, 1999, pp. 108–120; and A. M. Ryan and R. E. Ployhart, "Applicants' Perceptions of Selection Procedures and Decisions: A Critical Review and Agenda for the Future," *Journal of Management* 26, no. 3 (2000), pp. 565–606.

35. See, for example, Y. Ganzach, A. Pazy, Y. Ohayun, and E. Brainin, "Social Exchange and Organizational Commitment: Decision-Making Training for Job Choice as an Alternative to the Realistic Job Preview," *Personnel Psychology,* Autumn 2002, pp. 613–637; B. M. Meglino, E. C. Ravlin, and A. S. DeNisi, "A Meta-Analytic Examination of Realistic Job Preview Effectiveness: A Test of Three Counter Intuitive Propositions," *Human Resource Management Review* 10, no. 4 (2000), pp. 407–434; J. A. Breaugh and M. Starke, "Research on Employee Recruitment: So Many Studies, So Many Remaining Questions," *Journal of Management* 26, no. 3 (2000), pp. 405–434; and S. L. Premack and J. P. Wanous, "A Meta-Analysis of Realistic Job Preview Experiments," *Journal of Applied Psychology,* November 1985, pp. 706–720.

36. A. Wahl, "People Power," *Canadian Business,* March 29–April 11, 2004, p. 58.

37. D. G. Allen, "Do Organizational Socialization Tactics Influence Newcomer Embeddedness and Turnover?" *Journal of Management,* April 2006, pp. 237–256; C. L. Cooper, "The Changing Psychological Contract at Work: Revisiting the Job Demands–Control Model," *Occupational and Environmental Medicine,* June 2002, p. 355; D. M. Rousseau and S. A. Tijoriwala, "Assessing Psychological Contracts: Issues, Alternatives and Measures," *Journal of Organizational Behavior* 19 (1998), pp. 679–695; and S. L. Robinson, M. S. Kraatz, and D. M. Rousseau, "Changing Obligations and the Psychological Contract: A Longitudinal Study," *Academy of Management Journal,* February 1994, pp. 137–152.

38. See, for instance, E. G. Tripp, "Aging Aircraft and Coming Regulations: Political and Media Pressures Have Encouraged the FAA to Expand Its Pursuit of Real and Perceived Problems of Older Aircraft and Their Systems. Operators Will Pay," *Business and Commercial Aviation,* March 2001, pp. 68–75.

39. "A&S Interview: Sully's Tale," *Air & Space Magazine,* www.airspacemag.com, February 18, 2009; A. Altman, "Chesley B. Sullenberger III," *Time,* www.time.com, January 16, 2009; and K. Burke, Pete Donohue, and C. Siemaszko, "US Airways Airplane Crashes in Hudson River—Hero Pilot Chesley Sullenberger III Saves All Aboard," *New York Daily News,* www.nydailynews.com, January 16, 2009.

40. "2006 Industry Report," *Training,* December 2006, www.trainingmag.com/managesmarter/images/pdfs/IndRep06.pdf (accessed September 6, 2007).

41. D. Sankey, "Canadian Companies Skimp on Training," Canada.com, June 27, 2007, www.canada.com/working/feeds/resources/atwork/story.html?id=30a5d031-8f8b-4f64-b607-2bcf11bead9d (accessed September 6, 2007); and "2006 Industry Report," *Training,* December 2006, www.trainingmag.com/managesmarter/images/pdfs/IndRep06.pdf (accessed September 6, 2007).

42. B. Hall, "The Top Training Priorities for 2003," *Training*, February 2003, p. 40; and T. Galvin, "2002 Industry Report," *Training*, October 2002, pp. 24–33.

43. H. Dolezalek, "2005 Industry Report," *Training*, December 2005, pp. 14–28.

44. B. Hall, "The Top Training Priorities for 2003," *Training*, February 2003, p. 40.

45. Based on K. Harding, "Once and Future Kings," *Globe and Mail*, April 9, 2003, pp. C1, C6.

46. L. Fowlie, "Online Training Takes the Slow Train: 'Next Big Thing' Fails to Live Up to Initial Hype," *Daily Townsman*, March 5, 2004, p. 11.

47. Technology, Media & Telecommunications Predictions 2014, Deloitte, http://www.deloitte.com/view/en_CA/ca/industries/tmt/ tmt-predictions-2014/index.htm?utm_content=buffer59eed&utm_ medium=social&utm_source=twitter.com&utm_campaign=buffer (accessed May 31, 2014).

48. Our Employee Population, About Scotiabank, http://www.scotia-bank.com/ca/en/0,,420,00.html#turnover (accessed May 31, 2014).

49. A. Pace, "The Performance Management Dilemma," *T&D,* July 2011, p. 22.

50. K. Sulkowicz, "Straight Talk at Review Time," *BusinessWeek*, September 10, 2007, p. 16.

51. This section is based on R. I. Henderson, *Compensation Management in a Knowledge-Based World*, 9th ed. (Upper Saddle River, NJ: Prentice Hall, 2003).

52. L. R. Gomez-Mejia, "Structure and Process of Diversification, Compensation Strategy, and Firm Performance," *Strategic Management Journal* 13 (1992), pp. 381–397; and E. Montemayor, "Congruence between Pay Policy and Competitive Strategy in High-Performing Firms," *Journal of Management* 22, no. 6 (1996), pp. 889–908.

53. J. D. Shaw, N. Gupta, A. Mitra, and G. E. Ledford Jr., "Success and Survival of Skill-Based Pay Plans," *Journal of Management*, February 2005, pp. 28–49; C. Lee, K. S. Law, and P. Bobko, "The Importance of Justice Perceptions on Pay Effectiveness: A Two-Year Study of a Skill-Based Pay Plan," *Journal of Management* 26, no. 6 (1999), pp. 851–873; G. E. Ledford, "Paying for the Skills, Knowledge and Competencies of Knowledge Workers," *Compensation and Benefits Review*, July–August 1995, pp. 55–62; and E. E. Lawler III, G. E. Ledford Jr., and L. Chang, "Who Uses Skill-Based Pay and Why," *Compensation and Benefits Review*, March–April 1993, p. 22.

54. J. D. Shaw, N. Gupta, A. Mitra, and G. E. Ledford Jr., "Success and Survival of Skill-Based Pay Plans," *Journal of Management*, February 2005, pp. 28–49.

55. M. Rowland, "It's What You Can Do That Counts," *New York Times*, June 6, 1993, p. F17.

56. Information from Hewitt Associates Studies, "Hewitt Study Shows Pay-for-Performance Plans Replacing Holiday Bonuses," December 6, 2005; "Salaries Continue to Rise in Asia Pacific," *Hewitt Annual Study Reports*, November 23, 2005; and "Hewitt Study Shows Base Pay Increases Flat for 2006 with Variable Pay Plans Picking Up the Slack," *Hewitt Associates*, August 31, 2005, www.hewitt.com.

57. D. E. Super and D. T. Hall, "Career Development: Exploration and Planning," in *Annual Review of Psychology*, vol. 29, ed. M. R. Rosenzweig and L. W. Porter (Palo Alto, CA: Annual Reviews, 1978), p. 334.

58. A. K. Smith, "Charting Your Own Course," *U.S. News & World Report*, November 6, 2000, pp. 56–65; S. E. Sullivan, "The Changing Nature of Careers: A Review and Research Agenda," *Journal of Management* 25, no. 3 (1999), pp. 457–484; D. T. Hall, "Protean Careers of the 21st Century," *Academy of Management Executive*, November 1996, pp. 8–16; M. B. Arthur and D. M. Rousseau, "A Career Lexicon for the 21st Century," *Academy of Management Executive*, November 1996, pp. 28–39; N. Nicholson, "Career Systems in Crisis: Change and Opportunity in the Information Age," *Academy of Management Executive*, November 1996, pp. 40–51; and K. R. Brousseau, M. J. Driver, K. Eneroth, and R. Larsson, "Career Pandemonium: Realigning Organizations and Individuals," *Academy of Management Executive*, November 1996, pp. 52–66.

59. M. B. Arthur and D. M. Rousseau, *The Boundaryless Career: A New Employment Principle for a New Organizational Era* (New York: Oxford University Press, 1996).

60. M. Cianni and D. Wnuck, "Individual Growth and Team Enhancement: Moving toward a New Model of Career Development," *Academy of Management Executive*, February 1997, pp. 105–115.

61. L. K. Trevino, M. Brown, and L. P. Hartman, "A Qualitative Investigation of Perceived Executive Ethical Leadership: Perceptions from Inside and Outside the Executive Suite," *Human Relations*, January 2003, pp. 5–37.

62. Based on C. Petten, "Progressive Aboriginal Relations Important to Scotiabank," *Windspeaker*, March 2002, p. B7.

63. L. Crawford, "Motivation, Not a Degree Key at IKEA," *Financial Post (National Post)*, February 24, 2004, p. FP12; and interview with André de Wit, general manager of IKEA Ibérica, S.A., *Interes*, www.interes.org/icex/cda/controller/inte res/0,5464,5322992_5325168_39745871_519802_0,00.html (accessed September 7, 2007).

64. T. J. Erickson, "The Leaders We Need Now," *Harvard Business Review,* May 2010, pp. 63–66.

65. S. Thurm, "Recalculating the Cost of Big Layoffs," *Wall Street Journal,* May 5, 2010, pp. B1+; and J. Pfeffer, "Lay Off the Layoffs," *Newsweek,* February 15, 2010, pp. 32–37.

66. W. F. Cascio, "Use and Management of Downsizing as a Corporate Strategy," *HR Magazine,* June 2010, special insert; D. K. Datta, J. P. Guthrie, D. Basuil, and A. Pandey, "Causes and Effects of Employee Downsizing: A Review and Synthesis," *Journal of Management,* January 2010, pp. 281–348; B. Conaty, "Cutbacks: Don't Neglect the Survivors," *Bloomberg BusinessWeek,* January 11, 2010, p. 68; and P. Korkki, "Accentuating the Positive After a Layoff," *New York Times Online,* August 16, 2009.

67. "Employers Underestimate Extent of Sexual Harassment, Report Says," *Vancouver Sun*, March 8, 2001, p. D6.

68. J. Monchuk, "Female Mounties Allege Sex Harassment Not Investigated to Protect RCMP," *Canadian Press* Newswire, September 26, 2003.

69. D. Spears, "Is a Well Drafted Harassment Policy Enough?" *Ottawa Business Journal*, February 20, 2006, www.ottawabusinessjournal. com/293617634517614.php (accessed October 14, 2007).

70. "Employers Underestimate Extent of Sexual Harassment, Report Says," *Vancouver Sun*, March 8, 2001, p. D6.

71. "Sexual Harassment Charges: FY 1992—FY 2005," U.S. Equal Employment Opportunity Commission, www.eeoc.gov.

72. "U.S. Leads Way in Sex Harassment Laws, Study Says," *Evening Sun*, November 30, 1992, p. A11; and W. Hardman and J. Heidelberg, "When Sexual Harassment Is a Foreign Affair," *Personnel*, April 1996, pp. 91–97.

73. *Janzen v. Platy Enterprises Ltd.* (1989), 10 C.H.R.R. D/6205 (S.C.C.).

74. "Facts About Sexual Harassment," U.S. Equal Employment Opportunity Commission, www.eeoc.gov (accessed June 1, 2003).

75. A. Fisher, "After All This Time, Why Don't People Know What Sexual Harassment Means?" *Fortune*, January 12, 1998, p. 68; and A. R. Karr, "Companies Crack Down on the Increasing Sexual Harassment by E-Mail," *Wall Street Journal*, September 21, 1999, p. A1.

76. See T. S. Bland and S. S. Stalcup, "Managing Harassment," *Human Resource Management*, Spring 2001, pp. 51–61; K. A. Hess and D. R. M. Ehrens, "Sexual Harassment—Affirmative Defense to Employer Liability," *Benefits Quarterly*, Second Quarter 1999, p. 57; J. A. Segal, "The Catch-22s of Remedying Sexual Harassment Complaints," *HR Magazine*, October 1997, pp. 111–117; S. C. Bahls and J. E. Bahls, "Hands-Off Policy," *Entrepreneur*, July 1997, pp. 74–76; J. A. Segal, "Where Are We Now?" *HR Magazine*, October 1996, pp. 69–73; B. McAfee and D. L. Deadrick, "Teach Employees to Just Say No," *HR Magazine*, February 1996, pp. 86–89; G. D. Block, "Avoiding Liability for Sexual Harassment," *HR Magazine*, April 1995, pp. 91–97; and J. A. Segal, "Stop Making Plaintiffs' Lawyers Rich," *HR Magazine*, April 1995, pp. 31–35.

77. S. Jayson, "Workplace Romance No Longer Gets the Kiss-Off," *USA Today*, February 9, 2006, p. 9D.

78. R. Mano and Y. Gabriel, "Workplace Romances in Cold and Hot Organizational Climates: The Experience of Israel and Taiwan," *Human Relations*, January 2006, pp. 7–35; J. A. Segal, "Dangerous Liaisons," *HR Magazine*, December 2005, pp. 104–108; "Workplace Romance Can Create Unforeseen Issues for Employers," *HR Focus*, October 2005, p. 2; C. A. Pierce and H. Aguinis, "Legal Standards, Ethical Standards, and Responses to Social-Sexual Conduct at Work," *Journal of Organizational Behavior*, September 2005, pp. 727–732; and C. A. Pierce, B. J. Broberg, J. R. McClure, and H. Aguinis, "Responding to Sexual Harassment Complaints: Effects of a Dissolved Workplace Romance on Decision-Making Standards," *Organizational Behavior and Human Decision Processes*, September 2004, pp. 66–82.

79. J. A. Segal, "Dangerous Liaisons," *HR Magazine*, December 2005, pp. 104–108.

80. E. Zimmerman, "When Cupid Strikes at the Cubicle," *New York Times Online*, April 9, 2010.

81. I. Towers, L. Duxbury, C. Higgins, and J. Thomas, "Time Thieves and Space Invaders: Technology, Work and the Organization," *Journal of Organizational Change Management* 19, no. 5 (2006), pp. 593–618; and L. Duxbury and C. Higgins, "Work–Life Conflict in Canada in the New Millennium: A Status Report," *Australian Canadian Studies* 21, no. 2 (2003), pp. 41–72.

82. C. Oglesby, "More Options for Moms Seeking Work-Family Balance," *CNN.com*, May 10, 2001, www.cnn.com.

83. J. Miller and M. Miller, "Get A Life!" *Fortune*, November 28, 2005, pp. 108–124.

84. M. Elias, "The Family-First Generation," *USA Today*, December 13, 2004, p. 5D.

85. F. Hansen, "Truths and Myths about Work/Life Balance," *Workforce*, December 2002, pp. 34–39.

86. J. H. Greenhaus and G. N. Powell, "When Work and Family Are Allies: A Theory of Work–Family Enrichment," *Academy of Management Review*, January 2006, pp. 72–92; L. Duxbury, C. Higgins, and D. Coghill, "Voices of Canadians: Seeking Work–Life Balance," HRSDC, January 2003, www.hrsdc.gc.ca; and S. D. Friedman and J. H. Greenhaus, *Work and Family—Allies or Enemies?* (New York: Oxford University Press, 2000).

87. J. H. Greenhaus and G. N. Powell, "When Work and Family Are Allies: A Theory of Work–Family Enrichment," *Academy of Management Review*, January 2006, pp. 72–92.

88. L. B. Hammer, M. B. Neal, J. T. Newsom, K. J. Brockwood, and C. L. Colton, "A Longitudinal Study of the Effects of Dual-Earner Couples' Utilization of Family-Friendly Workplace Supports on Work and Family Outcomes," *Journal of Applied Psychology*, July 2005, pp. 799–810.

89. M. M. Arthur, "Share Price Reactions to Work–Family Initiatives: An Institutional Perspective," *Academy of Management Journal*, August 2003, pp. 497–505.

90. N. P. Rothbard, T. L. Dumas, and K. W. Phillips, "The Long Arm of the Organization: Work–Family Policies and Employee Preferences for Segmentation" (paper presented at the 61st Annual Academy of Management meeting, Washington, DC, August 2001).

91. Based on J. Gerson, "Veteran RCMP officer stripped of his uniform for publicly smoking medical marijuana hands in his red serge," *The National Post*, November 28, 2013, http://news.nationalpost.com/2013/11/28/veteran-rcmp-officer-stripped-of-his-uniform-for-publicly-smoking-medical-marijuana-in-his-red-serge/ (accessed June 8, 2014); R. Pyrillis, "Workers Using Medical Marijuana Hold Their Breath, but Employers Worry They'll Take a Hit," *Workforce Management Online*, April 2011; "Puffing Up Over Pot in Workplace," *Workforce Management*, March 2011, p. 41; D. Cadrain, "The Marijuana Exception," *HR Magazine*, November 2010, pp. 40–42; D. Cadrain, "Do Medical Marijuana Laws Protect Usage by Employees?" *HR Magazine*, November 2010, p. 12; A. K. Wiwi and N. P. Crifo, "The Unintended Impact of New Jersey's New Medical Marijuana Law on the Workplace," *Employee Relations Law Journal*, Summer 2010, pp. 33–37; S. Simon, "At Work, A Drug Dilemma," *Wall Street Journal*, August 3, 2010, p. D1; and J. Greenwald, "Medical Marijuana Laws Create Dilemma for Firms," *Business Insurance*, February 15, 2010, pp. 1–20.

92. D. S. Urban, "What to Do About 'Body Art' at Work?" *Workforce Management Online*, March 2010.

93. T. Bingham and P. Galagan, "Delivering 'On-Time, Every Time' Knowledge and Skills to a World of Employees," *T&D*, July 2012, pp. 32–37; J. Levitz, "UPS Thinks Outside the Box on Driver Training," *Wall Street Journal*, April 6, 2010, pp. B1+; and K. Kingsbury, "Road to Recovery," *Time*, March 8, 2010, pp. Global 14–Global 16.

94. "Digital Report: Tug-of-War for Digital Talent," *Campaign Asia-Pacific*, June 2012, p. 12; N. Blacksmith and Y. Yang, "Executives: Your Company Isn't Attracting the Best Talent," *Gallup Management Journal Online*, May 29, 2012, p. 1; J. Cullen, "Stop Searching for the Elusive Purple Squirrel," *Computerworld*, April 9, 2012, p. 25; G. Anders, "The Rare Find," *Bloomberg BusinessWeek*, October 17–October 23, 2011, pp. 106–112; and J. Light, "At Mature Techs, A Young Vibe," *Wall Street Journal*, June 13, 2011, p. B7.

Chapter 13

1. Based on B. McRae, *The Seven Strategies of Master Leaders* (Toronto: Northbridge, 2009).

2. B. McRae, *The Seven Strategies of Master Leaders* (Toronto: Northbridge, 2009).

3. Most leadership research has focused on the actions and responsibilities of managers and extrapolated the results to leaders and leadership in general.

4. RBC appoints Phil Fontaine as Special Advisor, September 2, 2009, RBC Media Newsroom, http://www.rbc.com/newsroom/2009/0902-fontaine.html (accessed May 31, 2014).

5. "B. McRae, *The Seven Strategies of Master Leaders* (Toronto: Northbridge, 2009).

6. P. Bacon Jr. and M. Calabresi, "The Up-and-Comers," *Time Canada*, April 24, 2006, p. 28; P. Bacon Jr., "The Exquisite Dilemma of Being Obama," *Time*, February 20, 2006, pp. 24–28; A. Stephen, "10 People Who Will Change the World," *New Statesman*, October 17, 2005, pp. 18–20; "Ten to Watch," *Fortune*, September 9, 2005, p. 282; P. Bacon Jr., "Barack Obama," *Time*, April 18, 2005, pp. 60–61; and A. Ripley, D. E. Thigpen, and J. McCabe, "Obama's Ascent," *Time*, November 11, 2004, pp. 74–78.

7. See S. A. Kirkpatrick and E. A. Locke, "Leadership: Do Traits Matter?" *Academy of Management Executive*, May 1991, pp. 48–60; and T. A. Judge, J. E. Bono, R. Ilies, and M. W. Gerhardt, "Personality and Leadership: A Qualitative and Quantitative Review," *Journal of Applied Psychology*, August 2002, pp. 765–780.

8. J. Kirby, "In the Vault," *Canadian Business*, March 1–March 14, 2004, pp. 68–72.

9. J. Kirby, "In the Vault," *Canadian Business*, March 1–March 14, 2004, pp. 68–72.

10. K. Lewin and R. Lippitt, "An Experimental Approach to the Study of Autocracy and Democracy: A Preliminary Note," *Sociometry* 1 (1938), pp. 292–300; K. Lewin, "Field Theory and Experiment in Social Psychology: Concepts and Methods," *American Journal of Sociology* 44 (1939), pp. 868–896; K. Lewin, R. Lippitt, and R. K. White, "Patterns of Aggressive Behavior in Experimentally Created Social Climates," *Journal of Social Psychology* 10 (1939), pp. 271–301; and R. Lippitt, "An Experimental Study of the Effect of Democratic and Authoritarian Group Atmospheres," *University of Iowa Studies in Child Welfare* 16 (1940), pp. 43–95.

11. B. M. Bass, *Stogdill's Handbook of Leadership* (New York: The Free Press, 1981), pp. 289–299.

12. R. M. Stogdill and A. E. Coons, eds., *Leader Behavior: Its Description and Measurement*, Research Monograph No. 88 (Columbus: Ohio State University, Bureau of Business Research, 1951). For an updated literature review of Ohio State research, see S. Kerr, C. A. Schriesheim, C. J. Murphy, and R. M. Stogdill, "Toward a Contingency Theory of Leadership Based upon the Consideration and Initiating Structure Literature," *Organizational Behavior and Human Performance*, August 1974, pp. 62–82; and B. M. Fisher, "Consideration and Initiating Structure and Their Relationships with Leader Effectiveness: A Meta-Analysis," in *Proceedings of the 48th Annual Academy of Management Conference*, ed. F. Hoy, pp. 201–205 (Anaheim, CA, 1988).

13. R. Kahn and D. Katz, "Leadership Practices in Relation to Productivity and Morale," in *Group Dynamics: Research and Theory*, 2nd ed., D. Cartwright and A. Zander (Elmsford, NY: Row, Paterson, 1960).

14. R. R. Blake and J. S. Mouton, *The Managerial Grid III* (Houston: Gulf Publishing, 1984).

15. L. L. Larson, J. G. Hunt, and R. N. Osborn, "The Great Hi-Hi Leader Behavior Myth: A Lesson from Occam's Razor," *Academy of Management Journal*, December 1976, pp. 628–641; and P. C. Nystrom, "Managers and the Hi-Hi Leader Myth," *Academy of Management Journal*, June 1978, pp. 325–331.

16. B. McRae, *The Seven Strategies of Master Leaders* (Toronto: Northbridge, 2009).

17. "*Financial Times* and ArcelorMittal Award Boldest Business Leaders in 2014," March 21, 2014, ft.com/About us, http://aboutus.ft.com/2014/03/21/financial-times-and-arcelormittal-award-boldest-business-leaders-in-2014/#axzz33K5ylL30 (accessed May 31, 2014).

18. W. G. Bennis, "The Seven Ages of the Leader," *Harvard Business Review*, January 2004, p. 52.

19. F. Fiedler, *A Theory of Leadership Effectiveness* (New York: McGraw-Hill, 1967).

20. R. Ayman, M. M. Chemers, and F. Fiedler, "The Contingency Model of Leadership Effectiveness: Its Levels of Analysis," *Leadership Quarterly*, Summer 1995, pp. 147–167; C. A. Schriesheim, B. J. Tepper, and L. A. Tetrault, "Least Preferred Co-worker Score, Situational Control, and Leadership Effectiveness: A Meta-Analysis of Contingency Model Performance Predictions," *Journal of Applied Psychology*, August 1994, pp. 561–573; and L. H. Peters, D. D. Hartke, and J. T. Pholmann, "Fiedler's Contingency Theory of Leadership: An Application of the Meta-Analysis Procedures of Schmidt and Hunter," *Psychological Bulletin*, March 1985, pp. 274–285.

21. See E. H. Schein, *Organizational Psychology*, 3rd ed. (Upper Saddle River, NJ: Prentice Hall, 1980), pp. 116–117; and B. Kabanoff, "A Critique of Leader Match and Its Implications for Leadership Research," *Personnel Psychology*, Winter 1981, pp. 749–764.

22. P. Hersey and K. Blanchard, "So You Want to Know Your Leadership Style?" *Training and Development Journal*, February 1974, pp. 1–15; and P. Hersey and K. H. Blanchard, *Management of Organizational Behavior: Leading Human Resources*, 8th ed. (Upper Saddle River, NJ: Prentice Hall, 2001).

23. See, for instance, E. G. Ralph, "Developing Managers' Effectiveness: A Model with Potential," *Journal of Management Inquiry*, June 2004, pp. 152–163; C. L. Graeff, "Evolution of Situational Leadership Theory: A Critical Review," *Leadership Quarterly* 8, no. 2 (1997), pp. 153–170; and C. F. Fernandez and R. P. Vecchio, "Situational Leadership Theory Revisited: A Test of an Across-Jobs Perspective," *Leadership Quarterly* 8, no. 1 (1997), pp. 67–84.

24. R. J. House, "A Path–Goal Theory of Leader Effectiveness," *Administrative Science Quarterly*, September 1971, pp. 321–338; R. J. House and T. R. Mitchell, "Path–Goal Theory of Leadership," *Journal of Contemporary Business*, Autumn 1974, p. 86; and R. J. House, "Path–Goal Theory of Leadership: Lessons, Legacy, and a Reformulated Theory," *Leadership Quarterly*, Fall 1996, pp. 323–352.

25. M. L. Dixon and L. K. Hart, "The Impact of Path-Goal Leadership Styles on Work Group Effectiveness and Turnover Intention," *Journal of Managerial Issues*, Spring 2010, pp. 52–69; J. C. Wofford and L. Z. Liska, "Path-Goal Theories of Leadership: A Meta-Analysis," *Journal of Management*, Winter 1993, pp. 857–876; and A. Sagie and M. Koslowsky, "Organizational Attitudes and Behaviors as a Function of Participation in Strategic and Tactical Change Decisions: An Application of Path-Goal Theory," *Journal of Organizational Behavior*, January 1994, pp. 37–47.

26. B. McRae, *The Seven Strategies of Master Leaders* (Toronto: Northbridge, 2009).

27. "Walmart Highlights Progress in 2014 Global Responsibility Report," *Walmart News*, http://news.walmart.com/news-archive/2014/04/23/walmart-highlights-progress-in-2014-global-responsibility-report (accessed June 11, 2014).

28. David Cheeswright, Our Story – David Cheeswritght, http://corporate.walmart.com/our-story/leadership/executive-management/david-cheesewright/ (accessed May 31, 2014).

29. B. M. Bass and R. E. Riggio, *Transformational Leadership*, 2nd ed. (Mahwah, NJ: Lawrence Erlbaum Associates, 2006), p. 3.

30. R. M. Dienesch and R. C. Liden, "Leader–Member Exchange Model of Leadership: A Critique and Further Development," *Academy of Management Review*, July 1986, pp. 618–634; G. B. Graen and M. Uhl-Bien, "Relationship-Based Approach to Leadership: Development of Leader–Member Exchange (LMX) Theory of Leadership Over 25 Years: Applying a Multi-Domain Perspective," *Leadership Quarterly*, Summer 1995, pp. 219–247; R. C. Liden, R. T. Sparrowe, and S. J. Wayne, "Leader–Member Exchange Theory: The Past and Potential for the Future," in G. R. Ferris (ed.), *Research in Personnel and Human*

Resource Management, vol. 15 (Greenwich, CT: JAI Press, 1997), pp. 47–119; and C. P. Schriesheim, S. L. Castro, X. Zhou, and F. J. Yammarino, "The Folly of Theorizing 'A' but Testing 'B': A Selective Level-of-Analysis Review of the Field and a Detailed Leader–Member Exchange Illustration," *Leadership Quarterly,* Winter 2001, pp. 515–551.

31. R. C. Liden and G. Graen, "Generalizability of the Vertical Dyad Linkage Model of Leadership," *Academy of Management Journal,* September 1980, pp. 451–465; R. C. Liden, S. J. Wayne, and D. Stilwell, "A Longitudinal Study of the Early Development of Leader–Member Exchanges," *Journal of Applied Psychology,* August 1993, pp. 662–674; S. J. Wayne, L. J. Shore, W. H. Bommer, and L. E. Tetrick, "The Role of Fair Treatment and Rewards in Perceptions of Organizational Support and Leader–Member Exchange," *Journal of Applied Psychology,* June 2002, pp. 590–598; and S. S. Masterson, K. Lewis, and B. M. Goldman, "Integrating Justice and Social Exchange: The Differing Effects of Fair Procedures and Treatment on Work Relationships," *Academy of Management Journal,* August 2000, pp. 738–748.

32. D. Duchon, S. G. Green, and T. D. Taber, "Vertical Dyad Linkage: A Longitudinal Assessment of Antecedents, Measures, and Consequences," *Journal of Applied Psychology,* February 1986, pp. 56–60; R. C. Liden, S. J. Wayne, and D. Stilwell, "A Longitudinal Study of the Early Development of Leader–Member Exchanges"; M. Uhl-Bien, "Relationship Development as a Key Ingredient for Leadership Development," in S. E. Murphy and R. E. Riggio (eds.), *Future of Leadership Development* (Mahwah, NJ: Lawrence Erlbaum, 2003), pp. 129–147; R. Vecchio and D. M. Brazil, "Leadership and Sex-Similarity: A Comparison in a Military Setting," *Personnel Psychology,* vol. 60, 2007, pp. 303–335; and V. L. Goodwin, W. M. Bowler, and J. L. Whittington, "A Social Network Perspective on LMX Relationships: Accounting for the Instrumental Value of Leader and Follower Networks," *Journal of Management,* August 2009, pp. 954–980.

33. See, for instance, C. R. Gerstner and D. V. Day, "Meta-analytic Review of Leader–Member Exchange Theory: Correlates and Construct Issues," *Journal of Applied Psychology,* December 1997, pp. 827–844; R. Ilies, J. D. Nahrgang, and F. P. Morgerson, "Leader–Member Exchange and Citizenship Behaviors: A Meta-analysis," *Journal of Applied Psychology,* January 2007, pp. 269–277; Z. Chen, W. Lam, and J. A. Zhong, "Leader–Member Exchange and Member Performance: A New Look at Individual-Level Negative Feedback-Seeking Behavior and Team-Level Empowerment Culture," *Journal of Applied Psychology,* January 2007, pp. 202–212; and Z. Zhang, M. Wang, and J. Shi, "Leader-Follower Congruence in Proactive Personality and Work Outcomes: The Mediating Role of Leader-Member Exchange," *Academy of Management Journal,* February 2012, pp. 111–130.

34. B. M. Bass and R. E. Riggio, *Transformational Leadership*, 2nd ed. (Mahwah, NJ: Lawrence Erlbaum Associates, 2006), p. 3.

35. B. M. Bass, "Leadership: Good, Better, Best," *Organizational Dynamics,* Winter 1985, pp. 26–40; and J. Seltzer and B. M. Bass, "Transformational Leadership: Beyond Initiation and Consideration," *Journal of Management*, December 1990, pp. 693–703.

36. B. J. Avolio and B. M. Bass, "Transformational Leadership, Charisma, and Beyond." Working paper, School of Management, State University of New York, Binghamton, 1985, p. 14.

37. R. S. Rubin, D. C. Munz, and W. H. Bommer, "Leading from Within: The Effects of Emotion Recognition and Personality on Transformational Leadership Behavior," *Academy of Management Journal*, October 2005, pp. 845–858; T. A. Judge and J. E. Bono, "Five-Factor Model of Personality and Transformational Leadership," *Journal of Applied Psychology*, October 2000, pp. 751–765; B. M. Bass and B. J. Avolio, "Developing Transformational Leadership: 1992 and Beyond," *Journal of European Industrial Training*, January 1990, p. 23; and J. J. Hater and B. M. Bass, "Supervisors' Evaluation and Subordinates' Perceptions of Transformational and Transactional Leadership," *Journal of Applied Psychology*, November 1988, pp. 695–702.

38. A. E. Colbert, A. L. Kristof-Brown, B. H. Bradley, and M. R. Barrick, "CEO Transformational Leadership: The Role of Goal Importance Congruence in Top Management Teams," *Academy of Management Journal*, February 2008, pp. 81–96; R. F. Piccolo and J. A. Colquitt, "Transformational Leadership and Job Behaviors: The Mediating Role of Core Job Characteristics," *Academy of Management Journal*, April 2006, pp. 327–340; O. Epitropaki and R. Martin, "From Ideal to Real: A Longitudinal Study of the Role of Implicit Leadership Theories on Leader-Member Exchanges and Employee Outcomes," *Journal of Applied Psychology*, July 2005, pp. 659–676; J. E. Bono and T. A. Judge, "Self-Concordance at Work: Toward Understanding the Motivational Effects of Transformational Leaders," *Academy of Management Journal*, October 2003, pp. 554–571; T. Dvir, D. Eden, B. J. Avolio, and B. Shamir, "Impact of Transformational Leadership on Follower Development and Performance: A Field Experiment," *Academy of Management Journal*, August 2002, pp. 735–744; N. Sivasubramaniam, W. D. Murry, B. J. Avolio, and D. I. Jung, "A Longitudinal Model of the Effects of Team Leadership and Group Potency on Group Performance," *Group and Organization Management*, March 2002, pp. 66–96; J. M. Howell and B. J. Avolio, "Transformational Leadership, Transactional Leadership, Locus of Control, and Support for Innovation: Key Predictors of Consolidated-Business-Unit Performance," *Journal of Applied Psychology*, December 1993, pp. 891–911; R. T. Keller, "Transformational Leadership and the Performance of Research and Development Project Groups," *Journal of Management*, September 1992, pp. 489–501; and B. M. Bass and B. J. Avolio, "Developing Transformational Leadership: 1992 and Beyond," *Journal of European Industrial Training*, January 1990, p. 23.

39. F. Vogelstein, "Mighty Amazon," *Fortune*, May 26, 2003, pp. 60–74.

40. J. M. Crant and T. S. Bateman, "Charismatic Leadership Viewed from Above: The Impact of Proactive Personality," *Journal of Organizational Behavior*, February 2000, pp. 63–75; G. Yukl and J. M. Howell, "Organizational and Contextual Influences on the Emergence and Effectiveness of Charismatic Leadership," *Leadership Quarterly*, Summer 1999, pp. 257–283; and J. A. Conger and R. N. Kanungo, "Behavioral Dimensions of Charismatic Leadership," in *Charismatic Leadership*, J. A. Conger, et al., pp. 78–97 (San Francisco: Jossey-Bass, 1988).

41. J. A. Conger and R. N. Kanungo, *Charismatic Leadership in Organizations* (Thousand Oaks, CA: Sage, 1998).

42. K. S. Groves, "Linking Leader Skills, Follower Attitudes, and Contextual Variables via an Integrated Model of Charismatic Leadership," *Journal of Management*, April 2005, pp. 255–277; J. J. Sosik, "The Role of Personal Values in the Charismatic Leadership of Corporate Managers: A Model and Preliminary Field Study," *Leadership Quarterly*, April 2005, pp. 221–244; A. H. B. deHoogh, et al., "Leader Motives, Charismatic Leadership, and Subordinates' Work Attitudes in the Profit and Voluntary Sector," *Leadership Quarterly*, February 2005, pp. 17–38; J. M. Howell and B. Shamir, "The Role of Followers in the Charismatic Leadership Process: Relationships and Their Consequences," *Academy of Management Review*, January 2005, pp. 96–112; J. Paul, et al., "The Effects of Charismatic Leadership on Followers' Self-Concept Accessibility," *Journal of Applied Social Psychology*, September 2001, pp. 1821–1844; J. A. Conger, R. N. Kanungo, and S. T. Menon, "Charismatic Leadership and Follower Effects," *Journal of Organizational Behavior* 21 (2000), pp. 747–767; R. W. Rowden, "The Relationship between Charismatic Leadership Behaviors and Organizational Commitment," *Leadership & Organization Development Journal*, January 2000, pp. 30–35; G. P. Shea and C. M. Howell, "Charismatic Leadership and Task Feedback: A Laboratory Study of Their Effects on Self-Efficacy," *Leadership Quarterly*, Fall 1999, pp. 375–396; S. A. Kirkpatrick and E. A. Locke, "Direct and Indirect Effects of Three Core Charismatic Leadership Components on Performance and Attitudes," *Journal of Applied Psychology*, February 1996, pp. 36–51; D. A. Waldman,

B. M. Bass, and F. J. Yammarino, "Adding to Contingent–Reward Behavior: The Augmenting Effect of Charismatic Leadership," *Group & Organization Studies*, December 1990, pp. 381–394; and R. J. House, J. Woycke, and E. M. Fodor, "Charismatic and Noncharismatic Leaders: Differences in Behavior and Effectiveness," in *Charismatic Leadership*, J. A. Conger, et al., pp. 103–104 (San Francisco: Jossey-Bass, 1988).

43. B. R. Agle, N. J. Nagarajan, J. A. Sonnenfeld, and D. Srinivasan, "Does CEO Charisma Matter? An Empirical Analysis of the Relationships among Organizational Performance, Environmental Uncertainty, and Top Management Team Perceptions of CEO Charisma," *Academy of Management Journal*, February 2006, pp. 161–174.

44. R. Birchfield, "Creating Charismatic Leaders," *Management*, June 2000, pp. 30–31; S. Caudron, "Growing Charisma," *IndustryWeek*, May 4, 1998, pp. 54–55; and J. A. Conger and R. N. Kanungo, "Training Charismatic Leadership: A Risky and Critical Task," in *Charismatic Leadership*, J. A. Conger, et al., pp. 309–323 (San Francisco: Jossey-Bass, 1988).

45. J. G. Hunt, K. B. Boal, and G. E. Dodge, "The Effects of Visionary and Crisis-Responsive Charisma on Followers: An Experimental Examination," *Leadership Quarterly*, Fall 1999, pp. 423–448; R. J. House and R. N. Aditya, "The Social Scientific Study of Leadership: Quo Vadis?" *Journal of Management* 23, no. 3 (1997), pp. 316–323; and R. J. House, "A 1976 Theory of Charismatic Leadership," in *Leadership: The Cutting Edge*, ed. J. G. Hunt and L. Larson, pp. 189–207 (Carbondale, Illinois: Southern Illinois University Press), 1977.

46. This definition is based on M. Sashkin, "The Visionary Leader," in *Charismatic Leadership*, J. A. Conger, et al., pp. 124–125 (San Francisco: Jossey-Bass, 1988); B. Nanus, *Visionary Leadership* (New York: The Free Press, 1992), p. 8; N. H. Snyder and M. Graves, "Leadership and Vision," *Business Horizons*, January–February 1994, p. 1; and J. R. Lucas, "Anatomy of a Vision Statement," *Management Review*, February 1998, pp. 22–26.

47. B. Nanus, *Visionary Leadership* (New York: The Free Press, 1992), p. 8.

48. D. Archer and A. Cameron, "Collaborative Leadership," www.trainingjournal.com, June 2012, pp. 35–38; J. Katzenbach, "The Steve Jobs Way," *Strategy+Business Online*, April 23, 2012; W. Isaacson, "The Real Leadership Lessons of Steve Jobs," *Harvard Business Review*, April 2012, pp. 93–102; R. Williams, "Why Steve Jobs Was Not A Leader," www.psychologytoday.com, April 7, 2012; R. Foroohar, "The Leadership Lessons of Steve Jobs," business.time.com, February 16, 2012; R. Foroohar, "What Would Steve Do?" www.time.com, February 27, 2012; F. E. Allen, "Steve Jobs Broke Every Leadership Rule. Don't Try It," www.forbes.com, August 27, 2011; J. Nocera, "What Makes Steve Jobs Great," *New York Times Online*, August 26, 2011; A. Sharma and D. Grant, "The Stagecraft of Steve Jobs," *Strategy+Business Online*, June 10, 2011; and A. Lashinsky, "How Apple Works: Inside the World's Biggest Startup," tech.fortune.com, May 9, 2011.

49. S. Caminiti, "What Team Leaders Need to Know," *Fortune*, February 20, 1995, pp. 93–100.

50. S. Caminiti, "What Team Leaders Need to Know," *Fortune*, February 20, 1995, p. 93.

51. S. Caminiti, "What Team Leaders Need to Know," *Fortune*, February 20, 1995, p. 100.

52. data points box based on D. Meinert, "Executive Briefing," *HRMagazine,* May 2012, p. 18; J. Yang and S. Ward, "Is Involvement in Office Politics Necessary to Get Ahead?" *USA Today*, May 2, 2012, p. 1B; "The Simple List," Realsimple.com, October 2011, p. 10; J. Yang and P. Trap, "I'm Concerned Most about My Manager," *USA Today,* April 25, 2011, p. 1B; and J. Yang and A. Gonzalez, "Bossy Bosses," *USA Today,* November 3, 2010, p. 1B.

53. N. Steckler and N. Fondas, "Building Team Leader Effectiveness: A Diagnostic Tool," *Organizational Dynamics*, Winter 1995, p. 20.

54. R. S. Wellins, W. C. Byham, and G. R. Dixon, *Inside Teams* (San Francisco: Jossey-Bass, 1994), p. 318.

55. N. Steckler and N. Fondas, "Building Team Leader Effectiveness: A Diagnostic Tool," *Organizational Dynamics*, Winter 1995, p. 21.

56. B. McRae, *The Seven Strategies of Master Leaders* (Toronto: Northbridge, 2009).

57. Anetter Verschuren, NRSTOR Management, http://www.nrstor.com/#!management (accessed May 31, 2014).

58. G. Colvin, "The FedEx Edge," *Fortune*, April 3, 2006, pp. 77–84.

59. See J. R. P. French Jr. and B. Raven, "The Bases of Social Power," in *Group Dynamics: Research and Theory*, ed. D. Cartwright and A. F. Zander, pp. 607–623 (New York: Harper & Row, 1960); P. M. Podsakoff and C. A. Schriesheim, "Field Studies of French and Raven's Bases of Power: Critique, Reanalysis, and Suggestions for Future Research," *Psychological Bulletin*, May 1985, pp. 387–411; R. K. Shukla, "Influence of Power Bases in Organizational Decision Making: A Contingency Model," *Decision Sciences*, July 1982, pp. 450–470; D. E. Frost and A. J. Stahelski, "The Systematic Measurement of French and Raven's Bases of Social Power in Workgroups," *Journal of Applied Social Psychology*, April 1988, pp. 375–389; and T. R. Hinkin and C. A. Schriesheim, "Development and Application of New Scales to Measure the French and Raven (1959) Bases of Social Power," *Journal of Applied Psychology*, August 1989, pp. 561–567.

60. See the Royal Australian Navy website, www.navy.gov.au.

61. J. M. Kouzes and B. Z. Posner, *Credibility: How Leaders Gain and Lose It, and Why People Demand It* (San Francisco: Jossey-Bass, 1993), p. 14.

62. Based on F. D. Schoorman, R. C. Mayer, and J. H. Davis, "An Integrative Model of Organizational Trust: Past, Present, and Future," *Academy of Management Review*, April 2007, pp. 344–354; G. M. Spreitzer and A. K. Mishra, "Giving Up Control without Losing Control," *Group & Organization Management*, June 1999, pp. 155–187; R. C. Mayer, J. H. Davis, and F. D. Schoorman, "An Integrative Model of Organizational Trust," *Academy of Management Review*, July 1995, p. 712; and L. T. Hosmer, "Trust: The Connecting Link between Organizational Theory and Philosophical Ethics," *Academy of Management Review*, April 1995, p. 393.

63. P. L. Schindler and C. C. Thomas, "The Structure of Interpersonal Trust in the Workplace," *Psychological Reports*, October 1993, pp. 563–573.

64. H. H. Tan and C. S. F. Tan, "Toward the Differentiation of Trust in Supervisor and Trust in Organization," *Genetic, Social, and General Psychology Monographs*, May 2000, pp. 241–260.

65. R. C. Mayer and M. B. Gavin, "Trust in Management and Performance: Who Minds the Shop While the Employees Watch the Boss?" *Academy of Management Journal*, October 2005, pp. 874–888; and K. T. Dirks and D. L. Ferrin, "Trust in Leadership: Meta-Analytic Findings and Implications for Research and Practice," *Journal of Applied Psychology*, August 2002, pp. 611–628.

66. R. Zemke, "The Confidence Crisis," *Training*, June 2004, pp. 22–30; J. A. Byrne, "Restoring Trust in Corporate America," *BusinessWeek*, June 24, 2002, pp. 30–35; S. Armour, "Employees' New Motto: Trust No One," *USA Today*, February 5, 2002, p. 1B; J. Scott, "Once Bitten, Twice Shy: A World of Eroding Trust," *New York Times*, April 21, 2002, p. WK5; J. Brockner, et al., "When Trust Matters: The Moderating Effect of Outcome Favorability," *Administrative Science Quarterly*, September 1997, p. 558; and J. Brockner, et al., "When Trust Matters: The Moderating Effect of

Outcome Favorability," *Administrative Science Quarterly*, September 1997, p. 558.

67. Watson Wyatt, "Weathering the Storm: A Study of Employee Attitudes and Opinions," *WorkUSA 2002 Study*, www.watsonwyatt .com.

68. This section is based on R. B. Morgan, "Self- and Co-Worker Perceptions of Ethics and Their Relationships to Leadership and Salary," *Academy of Management Journal*, February 1993, pp. 200–214; E. P. Hollander, "Ethical Challenges in the Leader–Follower Relationship," *Business Ethics* Quarterly, January 1995, pp. 55–65; J. C. Rost, "Leadership: A Discussion about Ethics," *Business Ethics Quarterly*, January 1995, pp. 129–142; R. N. Kanungo and M. Mendonca, *Ethical Dimensions of Leadership* (Thousand Oaks, CA: Sage, 1996); J. B. Ciulla, ed., *Ethics: The Heart of Leadership* (New York: Praeger, 1998); J. D. Costa, *The Ethical Imperative: Why Moral Leadership Is Good Business* (Cambridge, MA: Perseus Press, 1999); and N. M. Tichy and A. McGill, eds., *The Ethical Challenge: How to Build Honest Business Leaders* (New York: John Wiley & Sons, 2003).

69. J. M. Burns, *Leadership* (New York: Harper & Row, 1978).

70. J. M. Avolio, S. Kahai, and G. E. Dodge, "The Ethics of Charismatic Leadership: Submission or Liberation?" *Academy of Management Executive*, May 1992, pp. 43–55.

71. L. K. Trevino, M. Brown, and L. P. Hartman, "A Qualitative Investigation of Perceived Executive Ethical Leadership: Perceptions from Inside and Outside the Executive Suite," *Human Relations*, January 2003, pp. 5–37.

72. W. A. Randolph, "Navigating the Journey to Empowerment," *Organizational Dynamics*, Spring 1995, pp. 19–32; R. C. Ford and M. D. Fottler, "Empowerment: A Matter of Degree," *Academy of Management Executive*, August 1995, pp. 21–31; R. C. Herrenkohl, G. T. Judson, and J. A. Heffner, "Defining and Measuring Employee Empowerment," *Journal of Applied Behavioral Science*, September 1999, p. 373; C. Robert and T. M. Probst, "Empowerment and Continuous Improvement in the United States, Mexico, Poland, and India," *Journal of Applied Psychology*, October 2000, pp. 643–658; C. Gomez and B. Rosen, "The Leader-Member Link between Managerial Trust and Employee Empowerment," *Group & Organization Management*, March 2001, pp. 53–69; W. Alan Rudolph and M. Sashkin, "Can Organizational Empowerment Work in Multinational Settings?" *Academy of Management Executive*, February 2002, pp. 102–115; and P. K. Mills and G. R. Ungson, "Reassessing the Limits of Structural Empowerment: Organizational Constitution and Trust as Controls," *Academy of Management Review*, January 2003, pp. 143–153.

73. J. Schaubroeck, J. R. Jones, and J. L. Xie, "Individual Differences in Utilizing Control to Cope with Job Demands: Effects on Susceptibility to Infectious Disease," *Journal of Applied Psychology* 86, no. 2 (2001), pp. 265–278; and A. M. Owens, "Empowerment Can Make You Ill, Study Says," *National Post*, April 30, 2001, pp. A1, A8.

74. "Delta Promotes Empowerment," *Globe and Mail*, May 31, 1999, Advertising Supplement, p. C5.

75. M. Elliott, "Who Needs Charisma?" *Time*, July 20, 2009, pp. 35–38.

76. F. W. Swierczek, "Leadership and Culture: Comparing Asian Managers," *Leadership & Organization Development Journal*, December 1991, pp. 3–10.

77. R. J. House, "Leadership in the Twenty-First Century," in *Culture and Leadership Across the World*, ed. J. S. Chhokar, F. C. Brodbeck, and R. J. House (Mahwah, NJ: Lawrence Erlbaum Associates, 2007); M. F. Peterson and J. G. Hunt, "International Perspectives on International Leadership," *Leadership Quarterly*, Fall 1997, pp. 203–231; and J. R. Schermerhorn and M. H. Bond, "Cross-Cultural Leadership in Collectivism and High Power Distance Settings," *Leadership & Organization Development Journal* 18, no. 4/5 (1997), pp. 187–193.

78. R. J. House, et al., "Culture Specific and Cross-Culturally Generalizable Implicit Leadership Theories: Are the Attributes of Charismatic/Transformational Leadership Universally Endorsed?" *Leadership Quarterly*, Summer 1999, pp. 219–256; and D. E. Carl and M. Javidan, "Universality of Charismatic Leadership: A Multi-Nation Study" (paper presented at the National Academy of Management Conference, Washington, DC, August 2001).

79. D. E. Carl and M. Javidan, "Universality of Charismatic Leadership: A Multi-Nation Study," (paper presented at the National Academy of Management Conference, Washington, DC, August 2001), p. 29.

80. See, for instance, R. Lofthouse, "Herding the Cats," *EuroBusiness*, February 2001, pp. 64–65; and M. Delahoussaye, "Leadership in the 21st Century," *Training*, September 2001, pp. 60–72.

81. See, for instance, A. A. Vicere, "Executive Education: The Leading Edge," *Organizational Dynamics*, Autumn 1996, pp. 67–81; J. Barling, T. Weber, and E. K. Kelloway, "Effects of Transformational Leadership Training on Attitudinal and Financial Outcomes: A Field Experiment," *Journal of Applied Psychology*, December 1996, pp. 827–832; and D. V. Day, "Leadership Development: A Review in Context," *Leadership Quarterly*, Winter 2000, pp. 581–613.

82. K. Y. Chan and F. Drasgow, "Toward a Theory of Individual Differences and Leadership: Understanding the Motivation to Lead," *Journal of Applied Psychology*, June 2001, pp. 481–498.

83. M. Sashkin, "The Visionary Leader," in *Charismatic Leadership*, J. A. Congeret al., p. 150 (San Francisco: Jossey-Bass, 1988).

84. S. Kerr and J. M. Jermier, "Substitutes for Leadership: Their Meaning and Measurement," *Organizational Behavior and Human Performance*, December 1978, pp. 375–403; J. P. Howell, P. W. Dorfman, and S. Kerr, "Leadership and Substitutes for Leadership," *Journal of Applied Behavioral Science* 22, no. 1 (1986), pp. 29–46; J. P. Howell, et al., "Substitutes for Leadership: Effective Alternatives to Ineffective Leadership," *Organizational Dynamics*, Summer 1990, pp. 21–38; and P. M. Podsakoff, B. P. Niehoff, S. B. MacKenzie, and M. L. Williams, "Do Substitutes for Leadership Really Substitute for Leadership? An Empirical Examination of Kerr and Jermier's Situational Leadership Model," *Organizational Behavior and Human Decision Processes*, February 1993, pp. 1–44.

85. Adapted with permission from T. Sergiovanni, R. Metzcus, and L. Burden, "Toward a Particularistic Approach to Leadership Style: Some Findings," *American Educational Research Journal* 6, no. 1 (January 1969), American Educational Research Association, Washington, DC.

86. S. Adams, "The World's Best Companies for Leadership," Forbes.com, May 2, 2012; J. R. Hagerty and J. S. Lublin, "3M Taps 33-Year Veteran and Operating Chief as CEO," *Wall Street Journal*, February 9, 2012, p. B3; R. M. Murphy, "How Do Great Companies Groom Talent?" management.fortune.cnn.com, November 3, 2011; J. R. Hagerty and B. Tita, "3M Works on Succession Plan," *Wall Street Journal*, December 21, 2010, p. B2; A. Bernasek, "World's Most Admired Companies," *Fortune*, March 22, 2010, pp. 121+; "Selected Results from Best Companies for Leadership Survey," *Bloomberg BusinessWeek Online*, February 16, 2010; J. Kerr and R. Albright, "Finding and Cultivating Finishers," *Leadership Excellence*, July 2009, p. 20; D. Jones, "3M CEO Emphasizes Importance of Leaders," *USA Today*, May 18, 2009, p. 4B; G. Colvin, "World's Most Admired Companies 2009," *Fortune*, March 16, 2009, pp. 75+; and M. C. Mankins and R. Steele, "Turning Great Strategy into Great Performance," *Harvard Business Review*, July–August 2005, pp. 64–72.

87. Bharat Vaid, "Book Review: Maverick!" *Global Management Review*, August 2011, pp. 96–97; R. Spitzer, "Take Responsibility: How the Best Organizations in the World Survive in a Down Economy and

Thrive When Times Are Good," *The Journal for Quality & Participation,* October 2010, p. 16; M. Skapinker, "The American Global Dream," *Foreign Policy,* September/October 2010, pp. 157–159; J. Krohe, Jr., "If You Love Your People, Set Them Free," *Conference Board Review,* Summer 2010, pp. 28–37; L. M. Fisher, "Ricardo Semler Won't Take Control," *Strategy and Business,* Winter 2005 pp. 78–88; R. Semler, *Maverick: The Success Story Behind the World's Most Unusual Workplace* (New York: Grand Central Publishing, 2005); R. Semler, *The Seven-Day Weekend: Changing the Way Work Works* (New York: Penguin Group, 2004); A. J. Vogl, "The Anti-CEO," *Across the Board,* May/June 2004, pp. 30–36; G. Colvin, "The Anti-Control Freak," *Fortune,* November 26, 2001, p. 22; and R. Semler, "Managing Without Managers," *Harvard Business Review,* September/October 1989, pp. 76–84.

Chapter 14

1. Based on Hoover's Online, www.hoover.com; S. Butcher, "Relentless Rise in Pleasure Seekers," *Financial Times*, July 6, 2003, http://news.ft.com (accessed July 7, 2003); C. Blackhurst, "The Chris Blackhurst Interview: Sir Terry Leahy," *Management Today,* February 2004, pp. 32–34; "Tesco at a Glance," and Tesco, www.tescocorporate.com/page.aspx?pointerid=A8E0E60508F94A8DBA909E2ABB5F2CC7 (accessed September 20, 2007); and *Tesco: Preliminary Results 2009/10,* www.tescoplc.com/plc/ir/pres_results/analyst_packs/ap2010/prelim10/prelim10.pdf (accessed February 14, 2011).

2. G. A. Fowler, "In the Search for a Hot Job Title, Enter the Ninja," *Wall Street Journal,* April 7, 2010, pp. A1+.

3. A. Carmeli, B. Ben-Hador, D. A. Waldman, and D. E. Rupp, "How Leaders Cultivate Social Capital and Nurture Employee Vigor: Implications for Job Performance," *Journal of Applied Psychology,* November 2009, pp. 1533–1561.

4. R. M. Steers, R. T. Mowday, and D. L. Shapiro, "The Future of Work Motivation Theory," *Academy of Management Review,* July 2004, pp. 379–387.

5. N. Ellemers, D. De Gilder, and S. A. Haslam, "Motivating Individuals and Groups at Work: A Social Identity Perspective on Leadership and Group Performance," *Academy of Management Review,* July 2004, pp. 459–478.

6. "U.S. workers generally like their jobs, but believe there is room for improvement," *Business Wire,* November 18, 2013, http://www.businesswire.com/news/home/20131117005081/en/Monster-GfK-Survey-Reveals-International-Work-Attitude-Gap#.U57Cc_IdV8E (accessed June 14, 2014).

7. Based on S. Butcher, "Relentless Rise in Pleasure Seekers" *Financial Times,* July 6, 2003, http://news.ft.com (accessed July 7, 2003).

8. A. Maslow, *Motivation and Personality* (New York: McGraw-Hill, 1954); A. Maslow, D. C. Stephens, and G. Heil, *Maslow on Management* (New York: John Wiley & Sons, 1998); M. L. Ambrose and C. T. Kulik, "Old Friends, New Faces: Motivation Research in the 1990s," *Journal of Management* 25, no. 3 (1999), pp. 231–292; and "Dialogue," *Academy of Management Review,* October 2000, pp. 696–701.

9. See, for example, D. T. Hall and K. E. Nongaim, "An Examination of Maslow's Need Hierarchy in an Organizational Setting," *Organizational Behavior and Human Performance,* February 1968, pp. 12–35; E. E. Lawler III and J. L. Suttle, "A Causal Correlational Test of the Need Hierarchy Concept," *Organizational Behavior and Human Performance,* April 1972, pp. 265–287; R. M. Creech, "Employee Motivation," *Management Quarterly,* Summer 1995, pp. 33–39; J. Rowan, "Maslow Amended," *Journal of Humanistic Psychology,* Winter 1998, pp. 81–92; J. Rowan, "Ascent and Descent in Maslow's Theory," *Journal of Humanistic Psychology,* Summer 1999, pp. 125–133; and M. L. Ambrose and C. T. Kulik, "Old Friends, New Faces:

Motivation Research in the 1990s," *Journal of Management* 25, no. 3 (1999), pp. 231–292.

10. E. McGirt, "Intel Risks It All … Again," *Fast Company,* November 2009, pp. 88+.

11. D. McGregor, *The Human Side of Enterprise* (New York: McGraw-Hill, 1960). For an updated description of Theories X and Y, see an annotated edition with commentary of *The Human Side of Enterprise* (McGraw-Hill, 2006); and G. Heil, W. Bennis, and D. C. Stephens, *Douglas McGregor, Revisited: Managing the Human Side of Enterprise* (New York: Wiley, 2000).

12. J. M. O'Brien, "The Next Intel," *Wired,* July 2002, pp. 100–107.

13. F. Herzberg, B. Mausner, and B. Snyderman, *The Motivation to Work* (New York: John Wiley, 1959); F. Herzberg, *The Managerial Choice: To Be Effective or to Be Human,* rev. ed. (Salt Lake City, Olympus, 1982); R. M. Creech, "Employee Motivation"; and M. L. Ambrose and C. T. Kulik, "Old Friends, New Faces: Motivation Research in the 1990s."

14. D. C. McClelland, *The Achieving Society* (New York: Van Nostrand Reinhold, 1961); J. W. Atkinson and J. O. Raynor, *Motivation and Achievement* (Washington, DC: Winston, 1974); D. C. McClelland, *Power: The Inner Experience* (New York: Irvington, 1975); and M. J. Stahl, *Managerial and Technical Motivation: Assessing Needs for Achievement, Power, and Affiliation* (New York: Praeger, 1986).

15. D. C. McClelland, *The Achieving Society* (New York: Van Nostrand Reinhold, 1961).

16. D. C. McClelland, *Power: The Inner Experience* (New York: Irvington, 1975); and D. C. McClelland and D. H. Burnham, "Power Is the Great Motivator," *Harvard Business Review,* March–April 1976, pp. 100–110.

17. D. Miron and D. C. McClelland, "The Impact of Achievement Motivation Training on Small Businesses," *California Management Review,* Summer 1979, pp. 13–28.

18. "McClelland: An Advocate of Power," *International Management,* July 1975, pp. 27–29.

19. Based on S. Butcher, "Relentless Rise in Pleasure Seekers" *Financial Times,* July 6, 2003, http://news.ft.com (accessed July 7, 2003); A. Nottage, "Tesco," *Human Resources,* May 2003, p. 10; and C. Blackhurst, "The Chris Blackhurst Interview: Sir Terry Leahy," *Management Today,* February 2004, pp. 32–34.

20. R. M. Steers, R. T. Mowday, and D. L. Shapiro, "The Future of Work Motivation Theory," *Academy of Management Review,* July 2004, pp. 379–387; E. A. Locke and G. P. Latham, "What Should We Do About Motivation Theory? Six Recommendations for the Twenty-First Century," *Academy of Management Review,* July 2004, pp. 388–403; and M. L. Ambrose and C. T. Kulik, "Old Friends, New Faces: Motivation Research in the 1990s," *Journal of Management* 25, no. 3 (1999), pp. 231–292.

21. M. L. Ambrose and C. T. Kulik, "Old Friends, New Faces: Motivation Research in the 1990s," *Journal of Management* 25, no. 3 (1999), pp. 231–292.

22. J. C. Naylor and D. R. Ilgen, "Goal Setting: A Theoretical Analysis of a Motivational Technique," in *Research in Organizational Behavior*, vol. 6, ed. B. M. Staw and L. L. Cummings, pp. 95–140 (Greenwich, CT: JAI Press, 1984); A. R. Pell, "Energize Your People," *Managers Magazine,* December 1992, pp. 28–29; E. A. Locke, "Facts and Fallacies About Goal Theory: Reply to Deci," *Psychological Science,* January 1993, pp. 63–64; M. E. Tubbs, "Commitment as a Moderator of the Goal–Performance Relation: A Case for Clearer Construct Definition," *Journal of Applied Psychology,* February 1993, pp. 86–97; M. P. Collingwood, "Why Don't You Use the Research?" *Management Decision,* May 1993, pp. 48–54; M. E. Tubbs, D. M. Boehne, and J. S. Dahl, "Expectancy, Valence, and Motivational Force Functions in Goal-

Setting Research: An Empirical Test," *Journal of Applied Psychology*, June 1993, pp. 361–373; E. A. Locke, "Motivation Through Conscious Goal Setting," *Applied and Preventive Psychology* 5 (1996), pp. 117–124; M. L. Ambrose and C. T. Kulik, "Old Friends, New Faces: Motivation Research in the 1990s," *Journal of Management* 25, no. 3 (1999), pp. 231–292; E. A. Locke and G. P. Latham, "Building a Practically Useful Theory of Goal Setting and Task Motivation: A 35-Year Odyssey," *American Psychologist*, September 2002, pp. 705–717; Y. Fried and L. H. Slowik, "Enriching Goal-Setting Theory with Time: An Integrated Approach," *Academy of Management Review*, July 2004, pp. 404–422; and G. P. Latham, "The Motivational Benefits of Goal-Setting," *Academy of Management Executive*, November 2004, pp. 126–129.

23. J. B. Miner, *Theories of Organizational Behavior* (Hinsdale, IL: Dryden Press, 1980), p. 65.

24. J. A. Wagner III, "Participation's Effects on Performance and Satisfaction: A Reconsideration of Research and Evidence," *Academy of Management Review*, April 1994, pp. 312–330; J. George-Falvey, "Effects of Task Complexity and Learning Stage on the Relationship between Participation in Goal Setting and Task Performance," *Academy of Management Proceedings*, on disk, 1996; T. D. Ludwig and E. S. Geller, "Assigned Versus Participative Goal Setting and Response Generalization: Managing Injury Control among Professional Pizza Deliverers," *Journal of Applied Psychology*, April 1997, pp. 253–261; and S. G. Harkins and M. D. Lowe, "The Effects of Self-Set Goals on Task Performance," *Journal of Applied Social Psychology*, January 2000, pp. 1–40.

25. J. M. Ivancevich and J. T. McMahon, "The Effects of Goal Setting, External Feedback, and Self-Generated Feedback on Outcome Variables: A Field Experiment," *Academy of Management Journal*, June 1982, pp. 359–372; and E. A. Locke, "Motivation Through Conscious Goal Setting," *Applied and Preventive Psychology* 5 (1996), pp. 117–124.

26. J. R. Hollenbeck, C. R. Williams, and H. J. Klein, "An Empirical Examination of the Antecedents of Commitment to Difficult Goals," *Journal of Applied Psychology*, February 1989, pp. 18–23; see also J. C. Wofford, V. L. Goodwin, and S. Premack, "Meta-Analysis of the Antecedents of Personal Goal Level and of the Antecedents and Consequences of Goal Commitment," *Journal of Management*, September 1992, pp. 595–615; M. E. Tubbs, "Commitment as a Moderator of the Goal–Performance Relation": A Case for Clearer Construct Definition," *Journal of Applied Psychology*, February 1993, pp. 86–97; J. W. Smither, M. London, and R. R. Reilly, "Does Performance Improve Following Multisource Feedback? A Theoretical Model, Meta-Analysis, and Review of Empirical Findings," *Personnel Psychology*, Spring 2005, pp. 171–203.

27. M. E. Gist, "Self-Efficacy: Implications for Organizational Behavior and Human Resource Management," *Academy of Management Review*, July 1987, pp. 472–485; and A. Bandura, *Self-Efficacy: The Exercise of Control* (New York: Freeman, 1997).

28. E. A. Locke, E. Frederick, C. Lee, and P. Bobko, "Effect of Self-Efficacy, Goals, and Task Strategies on Task Performance," *Journal of Applied Psychology*, May 1984, pp. 241–251; M. E. Gist and T. R. Mitchell, "Self-Efficacy: A Theoretical Analysis of Its Determinants and Malleability," *Academy of Management Review*, April 1992, pp. 183–211; A. D. Stajkovic and F. Luthans, "Self-Efficacy and Work-Related Performance: A Meta-Analysis," *Psychological Bulletin*, September 1998, pp. 240–261; and A. Bandura, "Cultivate Self-Efficacy for Personal and Organizational Effectiveness," in E. Locke (ed.), *Handbook of Principles of Organizational Behavior* (Malden, MA: Blackwell, 2004), pp. 120–136.

29. A. Bandura and D. Cervone, "Differential Engagement in Self-Reactive Influences in Cognitively-Based Motivation," *Organizational Behavior and Human Decision Processes*, August 1986, pp. 92–113; and R. Ilies and T. A. Judge, "Goal Regulation Across Time: The

Effects of Feedback and Affect," *Journal of Applied Psychology*, May 2005, pp. 453–467.

30. See J. C. Anderson and C. A. O'Reilly, "Effects of an Organizational Control System on Managerial Satisfaction and Performance," *Human Relations*, June 1981, pp. 491–501; and J. P. Meyer, B. Schacht-Cole, and I. R. Gellatly, "An Examination of the Cognitive Mechanisms by Which Assigned Goals Affect Task Performance and Reactions to Performance," *Journal of Applied Social Psychology* 18, no. 5 (1988), pp. 390–408.

31. K. Maher and K. Hudson, "Wal-Mart to Sweeten Bonus Plans for Staff," *Wall Street Journal*, March 22, 2007, p. A11; and Reuters, "Wal-Mart Workers to Get New Bonus Plan," CNNMoney.com, March 22, 2007.

32. B. F. Skinner, *Science and Human Behavior* (New York: The Free Press, 1953); and B. F. Skinner, *Beyond Freedom and Dignity* (New York: Knopf, 1972).

33. The same data, for instance, can be interpreted in either goal-setting or reinforcement terms, as shown in E. A. Locke, "Latham vs. Komaki: A Tale of Two Paradigms," *Journal of Applied Psychology*, February 1980, pp. 16–23. Also see M. L. Ambrose and C. T. Kulik, "Old Friends, New Faces: Motivation Research in the 1990s," *Journal of Management* 25, no. 3 (1999), pp. 231–292.

34. J. Katz, "Cozy Up to Customers," *Industry Week,* February 2010, p. 16.

35. See, for example, R. W. Griffin, "Toward an Integrated Theory of Task Design," in *Research in Organizational Behavior*, vol. 9, ed. B. Staw and L. L. Cummings, pp. 79–120 (Greenwich, CT: JAI Press, 1987); and M. Campion, "Interdisciplinary Approaches to Job Design: A Constructive Replication with Extensions," *Journal of Applied Psychology*, August 1988, pp. 467–481.

36. S. Caudron, "The De-Jobbing of America," *IndustryWeek*, September 5, 1994, pp. 31–36; W. Bridges, "The End of the Job," *Fortune*, September 19, 1994, pp. 62–74; and K. H. Hammonds, K. Kelly, and K. Thurston, "Rethinking Work," *BusinessWeek*, October 12, 1994, pp. 75–87.

37. M. A. Campion and C. L. McClelland, "Follow-Up and Extension of the Interdisciplinary Costs and Benefits of Enlarged Jobs," *Journal of Applied Psychology*, June 1993, pp. 339–351; M. L. Ambrose and C. T. Kulik, "Old Friends, New Faces: Motivation Research in the 1990s," *Journal of Management* 25, no. 3 (1999), pp. 231–292.

38. See, for example, J. R. Hackman and G. R. Oldham, *Work Redesign* (Reading, MA: Addison-Wesley, 1980); J. B. Miner, *Theories of Organizational Behavior* (Hinsdale, IL: Dryden Press, 1980), pp. 231–266; R. W. Griffin, "Effects of Work Redesign on Employee Perceptions, Attitudes, and Behaviors: A Long-Term Investigation," *Academy of Management Journal*, June 1991, pp. 425–435; J. L. Cotton, *Employee Involvement* (Newbury Park, CA: Sage, 1993), pp. 141–172; and M. L. Ambrose and C. T. Kulik, "Old Friends, New Faces: Motivation Research in the 1990s," *Journal of Management* 25, no. 3 (1999), pp. 231–292.

39. J. R. Hackman and G. R. Oldham, "Development of the Job Diagnostic Survey," *Journal of Applied Psychology*, April 1975, pp. 159–170; and J. R. Hackman and G. R. Oldham, "Motivation through the Design of Work: Test of a Theory," *Organizational Behavior and Human Performance*, August 1976, pp. 250–279.

40. J. R. Hackman, "Work Design," in *Improving Life at Work*, ed. J. R. Hackman and J. L. Suttle (Glenview, IL: Scott, Foresman, 1977), p. 129; M. L. Ambrose and C. T. Kulik, "Old Friends, New Faces: Motivation Research in the 1990s," *Journal of Management* 25, no. 3 (1999), pp. 231–292.

41. D. J. Holman, C. M. Axtell, C. A. Sprigg, P. Totterdell, and T. D. Wall, "The Mediating Role of Job Characteristics in Job Redesign

Interventions: A Serendipitous Quasi-Experiment," *Journal of Organizational Behavior*, January 2010, pp. 84–105.

42. P. S. Goodman, "An Examination of Referents Used in the Evaluation of Pay," *Organizational Behavior and Human Performance*, October 1974, pp. 170–195; S. Ronen, "Equity Perception in Multiple Comparisons: A Field Study," *Human Relations*, April 1986, pp. 333–346; R. W. Scholl, E. A. Cooper, and J. F. McKenna, "Referent Selection in Determining Equity Perception: Differential Effects on Behavioral and Attitudinal Outcomes," *Personnel Psychology*, Spring 1987, pp. 113–127; and C. T. Kulik and M. L. Ambrose, "Personal and Situational Determinants of Referent Choice," *Academy of Management Review*, April 1992, pp. 212–237.

43. A. Wahl, "Canada's Best Workplaces: Overview," *Canadian Business*, April 26, 2007, www.canadianbusiness.com/managing/career/article.jsp?content=20070425_85420_85420 (accessed September 20, 2007).

44. J. Camps and R. Luna-Arocas, "High Involvement Work Practices and Firm Performance," *The International Journal of Human Resource Management,* May 2009, pp. 1056–1077; M. M. Butts, R. J. Vandenberg, D. M. DeJoy, B. S. Schaffer, and M. G. Wilson, "Individual Reactions to High Involvement Work Practices: Investigating the Role of Empowerment and Perceived Organizational Support," *Journal of Occupational Health Psychology,* April 2009, pp. 122–136; P. Boxall and K. Macky, "Research and Theory on High-Performance Work Systems: Progressing the High-Involvement Stream," *Human Resource Management Journal,* vol. 19, no. 1, 2009, pp. 3–23; R. D. Mohr and C. Zoghi, "High-Involvement Work Design and Job Satisfaction," *Industrial and Labor Relations Review,* April 2008, pp. 275–296; and C. D. Zatzick and R. D. Iverson, "High-Involvement Management and Workforce Reduction: Competitive Advantage or Disadvantage?" *Academy of Management Journal,* October 2006, pp. 999–1015.

45. "Entrepreneur Profile," *National Post,* www.canada.com/nationalpost/entrepreneur/ail.html (accessed September 20, 2007).

46. J. S. Adams, "Inequity in Social Exchanges," in *Advances in Experimental Social Psychology*, vol. 2, ed. L. Berkowitz, pp. 267–300 (New York: Academic Press, 1965); and M. L. Ambrose and C. T. Kulik, "Old Friends, New Faces: Motivation Research in the 1990s," *Journal of Management* 25, no. 3 (1999), pp. 231–292.

47. See, for example, P. S. Goodman and A. Friedman, "An Examination of Adams' Theory of Inequity," *Administrative Science Quarterly*, September 1971, pp. 271–288; M. R. Carrell, "A Longitudinal Field Assessment of Employee Perceptions of Equitable Treatment," *Organizational Behavior and Human Performance*, February 1978, pp. 108–118; E. Walster, G. W. Walster, and W. G. Scott, *Equity: Theory and Research* (Boston: Allyn & Bacon, 1978); R. G. Lord and J. A. Hohenfeld, "Longitudinal Field Assessment of Equity Effects on the Performance of Major League Baseball Players," *Journal of Applied Psychology*, February 1979, pp. 19–26; J. E. Dittrich and M. R. Carrell, "Organizational Equity Perceptions, Employee Job Satisfaction, and Departmental Absence and Turnover Rates," *Organizational Behavior and Human Performance*, August 1979, pp. 29–40; and J. Greenberg, "Cognitive Reevaluation of Outcomes in Response to Underpayment Inequity," *Academy of Management Journal,* March 1989, pp. 174–184.

48. P. S. Goodman, "An Examination of Referents Used in the Evaluation of Pay," *Organizational Behavior and Human Performance*, October 1974, pp. 170–195; S. Ronen, "Equity Perception in Multiple Comparisons: A FieldStudy," *Human Relations*, April 1986, pp. 333–346; R. W. Scholl, E. A. Cooper, and J. F. McKenna, "Referent Selection in Determining Equity Perception: Differential Effects on Behavioral and Attitudinal Outcomes," *Personnel Psychology*, Spring 1987, pp. 113–127; and C. T. Kulik and M. L. Ambrose, "Personal and Situational Determinants of Referent Choice," *Academy of Management Review*, April 1992, pp. 212–237.

49. Based on "Councillors Approve Own Pay Hike," cbc.ca, July 28, 2006; and Z. Ruryk, "Most T.O. Residents Against Council Raise," TorontoSun.com, September 9, 2007.

50. See, for example, J. Brockner, "Why It's So Hard to Be Fair," *Harvard Business Review*, March 2006, pp. 122–129; J. A. Colquitt, "Does the Justice of One Interact with the Justice of Many? Reactions to Procedural Justice in Teams," *Journal of Applied Psychology*, August 2004, pp. 633–646; M. A. Konovsky, "Understanding Procedural Justice and Its Impact on Business Organizations," *Journal of Management* 26, no. 3 (2000), pp. 489–511; R. C. Dailey and D. J. Kirk, "Distributive and Procedural Justice as Antecedents of Job Dissatisfaction and Intent to Turnover," *Human Relations*, March 1992, pp. 305–316; and D. B. McFarlin and P. D. Sweeney, "Distributive and Procedural Justice as Predictors of Satisfaction with Personal and Organizational Outcomes," *Academy of Management Journal*, August 1992, pp. 626–637.

51. G. P. Latham and C. C. Pinder, "Work Motivation Theory and Research at the Dawn of the Twenty-First Century," *Annual Review of Psychology* 56, 2005, pp. 485–516; P. S. Goodman, "Social Comparison Process in Organizations," in *New Directions in Organizational Behavior*, ed. B. M. Staw and G. R. Salancik, pp. 97–132 (Chicago: St. Clair, 1977); and J. Greenberg, "A Taxonomy of Organizational Justice Theories," *Academy of Management Review*, January 1987, pp. 9–22.

52. V. H. Vroom, *Work and Motivation* (New York: John Wiley, 1964).

53. See, for example, H. G. Heneman III and D. P. Schwab, "Evaluation of Research on Expectancy Theory Prediction of Employee Performance," *Psychological Bulletin*, July 1972, pp. 1–9; and L. Reinharth and M. Wahba, "Expectancy Theory as a Predictor of Work Motivation, Effort Expenditure, and Job Performance," *Academy of Management Journal*, September 1975, pp. 502–537.

54. See, for example, V. H. Vroom, "Organizational Choice: A Study of Pre- and Postdecision Processes," *Organizational Behavior and Human Performance*, April 1966, pp. 212–225; L. W. Porter and E. E. Lawler III, *Managerial Attitudes and Performance* (Homewood, IL: Richard D. Irwin, 1968); W. Van Eerde and H. Thierry, "Vroom's Expectancy Models and Work-Related Criteria: A Meta-Analysis," *Journal of Applied Psychology*, October 1996, pp. 575–586; and M. L. Ambrose and C. T. Kulik, "Old Friends, New Faces: Motivation Research in the 1990s," *Journal of Management* 25, no. 3 (1999), pp. 231–292.

55. See, for instance, M. Siegall, "The Simplistic Five: An Integrative Framework for Teaching Motivation," *Organizational Behavior Teaching Review* 12, no. 4 (1987–1988), pp. 141–143.

56. S. Butcher, "Relentless Rise in Pleasure Seekers," *Financial Times*, July 6, 2003, http://news.ft.com (accessed July 7, 2003); "Tesco Pilots Student Benefits," *Employee Benefits*, November 7, 2003, p. P12; and www.tescocorporate.com/annualreview07/01_tescostory/tescostory3.html (accessed October 14, 2007).

57. J. M. O'Brien, "Zappos Know How to Kick It," *Fortune,* February 2, 2009, pp. 54–60.

58. T. Barber, "Inspire Your Employees Now," *Bloomberg BusinessWeek Online,* May 18, 2010; D. Mattioli, "CEOs Welcome Recovery to Look After Staff," *Wall Street Journal,* April 5, 2010, p. B5; J. Sullivan, "How Do We Keep People Motivated Following Layoffs?" *Workforce Management Online,* March 2010; S. Crabtree, "How to Bolster Employees' Confidence," *The Gallup Management Journal Online,* February 25, 2010; S. E. Needleman, "Business Owners Try to Motivate Employees," *Wall Street Journal,* January 14, 2010, p. B5; H. Mintzberg, "Rebuilding Companies as Communities," *Harvard Business Review,* July–August 2009, pp. 140–143; and R. Luss, "Engaging Employees Through Periods of Layoffs," *Towers Watson,* www.towerswatson.com, March 3, 2009.

59. J. W. Miller and D. Kesmodel, "Drinking on the Job Comes to a Head at Carlsberg," *Wall Street Journal,* April 10–11, 2010, pp. A1+; and Associated Press, "Carlsberg Workers Balk At Loss of On-the-Job Beer," *Wall Street Journal,* April 9, 2010, p. B2.

60. N. J. Adler with A. Gundersen, *International Dimensions of Organizational Behavior*, 5th ed. (Cincinnati, OH: South-Western College Pub., 2008).

61. data points box based on K. Tyler, "Undeserved Promotions," *HR Magazine,* June 2012, p. 79; R. R. Hastings, "Survey Suggests Room for Improvement in Employee Recognition," www.shrm.org, April 13, 2012; S. Castellano, "The Trust Differentiator," *T&D,* March 2012, p. 20; R. Huggins and K. Gelles, "How Do Americans Think Rewards in the Workplace Are Distributed Today vs. Five Years Ago?" *USA Today,* January 10, 2012, p. 1A; S. Miller, "Salary Increases to Stay Consistent in 2012, with Focus on Variable Pay," www.shrm.org, September 6, 2011; C. Jones and R. Yu, "Incentive Travel Bounces Back," *USA Today,* September 6, 2011, p. 3B; J. Yang and P. Trap, "Does Your Manager Acknowledge and Appreciate You At Work?" *USA Today,* March 24, 2011, p. 1B; and A. R. Carey and K. Gelles, "Which of These Is Most Important about Your Job?" *USA Today,* January 31, 2011, p. 1A.

62. G. Hofstede, "Motivation, Leadership and Organization: Do American Theories Apply Abroad?" *Organizational Dynamics,* Summer 1980, p. 55.

63. G. Hofstede, "Motivation, Leadership and Organization: Do American Theories Apply Abroad?" *Organizational Dynamics,* Summer 1980, p. 55.

64. J. K. Giacobbe-Miller, D. J. Miller, and V. I. Victorov, "A Comparison of Russian and U.S. Pay Allocation Decisions, Distributive Justice Judgments and Productivity under Different Payment Conditions," *Personnel Psychology,* Spring 1998, pp. 137–163.

65. S. L. Mueller and L. D. Clarke, "Political-Economic Context and Sensitivity to Equity: Differences between the United States and the Transition Economies of Central and Eastern Europe," *Academy of Management Journal,* June 1998, pp. 319–329.

66. S. D. Sidle, "Building a Committed Global Workforce: Does What Employees Want Depend on Culture?" *Academy of Management Perspective,* February 2009, pp. 79–80; and G. A. Gelade, P. Dobson, and K. Auer, "Individualism, Masculinity, and the Sources of Organizational Commitment," *Journal of Cross-Cultural Psychology,* vol. 39, no. 5, 2008, pp. 599–617.

67. P. Brotherton, "Employee Loyalty Slipping Worldwide; Respect, Work-Life Balance Are Top Engagers," *T&D,* February 2012, p. 24.

68. I. Harpaz, "The Importance of Work Goals: An International Perspective," *Journal of International Business Studies,* First Quarter 1990, pp. 75–93.

69. G. E. Popp, H. J. Davis, and T. T. Herbert, "An International Study of Intrinsic Motivation Composition," *Management International Review,* January 1986, pp. 28–35.

70. R. W. Brislin, B. MacNab, R. Worthley, F. Kabigting Jr., and B. Zukis, "Evolving Perceptions of Japanese Workplace Motivation: An Employee-Manager Comparison," *International Journal of Cross-Cultural Management,* April 2005, pp. 87–104.

71. J. T. Marquez, "Tailor-Made Careers," *Workforce Management Online,* January 2010.

72. J. R. Billings and D. L. Sharpe, "Factors Influencing Flextime Usage among Employed Married Women," *Consumer Interests Annual,* vol. 45 (Ames, IA: American Council on Consumer Interests, 1999), pp. 89–94; and I. Harpaz, "The Importance of Work Goals: An International Perspective," *Journal of International Business Studies,* First Quarter 1990, pp. 75–93.

73. N. Ramachandran, "New Paths at Work," *U.S. News & World Report*, March 20, 2006, p. 47; S. Armour, "Generation Y: They've Arrived at Work with a New Attitude," *USA Today*, November 6, 2005, pp. B1+; R. Kanfer and P. L. Ackerman, "Aging, Adult Development, and Work Motivation," *Academy of Management Review*, July 2004, pp. 440–458; and R. Bernard, D. Cosgrave, and J. Welsh, *Chips and Pop: Decoding the Nexus Generation* (Toronto: Malcolm Lester Books, 1998).

74. See, for instance, M. Alpert, "The Care and Feeding of Engineers," *Fortune*, September 21, 1992, pp. 86–95; G. Poole, "How to Manage Your Nerds," *Forbes ASAP*, December 1994, pp. 132–136; T. J. Allen and R. Katz, "Managing Technical Professionals and Organizations: Improving and Sustaining the Performance of Organizations, Project Teams, and Individual Contributors," *Sloan Management Review,* Summer 2002, pp. S4–S5; and S. R. Barley and G. Kunda, "Contracting: A New Form of Professional Practice," *Academy of Management Perspectives,* February 2006, pp. 45–66.

75. S. D. Sidle, "Building a Committed Global Workforce: Does What Employees Want Depend on Culture?" *Academy of Management Perspective,* February 2009, pp. 79–80; and G. A. Gelade, P. Dobson, and K. Auer, "Individualism, Masculinity, and the Sources of Organizational Commitment," *Journal of Cross-Cultural Psychology,* vol. 39, no. 5, 2008, pp. 599–617.

76. P. Brotherton, "Employee Loyalty Slipping Worldwide; Respect, Work-Life Balance Are Top Engagers," *T&D,* February 2012, p. 24.

77. I. Harpaz, "The Importance of Work Goals: An International Perspective," *Journal of International Business Studies,* First Quarter 1990, pp. 75–93.

78. P. Falcone, "Motivating Staff without Money," *HR Magazine*, August 2002, pp. 105–108.

79. K. E. Culp, "Playing Field Widens for Stack's Great Game," *Springfield News-Leader* (Missouri), January 9, 2005, pp. 1A+.

80. K. Berman and J. Knight, "What Your Employees Don't Know Will Hurt You," *Wall Street Journal,* February 27, 2012, p. R4; J. Case, "The Open-Book Revolution," *Inc.*, June 1995, pp. 26–50; J. P. Schuster, J. Carpenter, and M. P. Kane, *The Power of Open-Book Management* (New York: John Wiley, 1996); J. Case, "Opening the Books," *Harvard Business Review*, March–April 1997, pp. 118–127; and D. Drickhamer, "Open Books to Elevate Performance," *Industry Week,* November 2002, p. 16.

81. J. Ruhlman and C. Siegman, "Boosting Engagement While Cutting Costs," *The Gallup Management Journal Online,* June 18, 2009.

82. D. McCann, "No Employee Left Behind," *CFO,* April 2012, p. 29.

83. F. Luthans and A. D. Stajkovic, "Provide Recognition for Performance Improvement," in *Principles of Organizational Behavior*, ed. E. A. Locke, pp. 166–180 (Oxford, UK: Blackwell, 2000).

84. K. J. Dunham, "Amid Sinking Workplace Morale, Employers Turn to Recognition," *Wall Street Journal,* November 19, 2002, p. B8.

85. Cited in S. Caudron, "The Top 20 Ways to Motivate Employees," *Industry Week,* April 3, 1995, pp. 15–16. See also B. Nelson, "Try Praise," *Inc.,* September 1996, p. 115; and J. Wiscombe, "Rewards Get Results," *Workforce,* April 2002, pp. 42–48.

86. R. Flandez, "Vegetable Gardens Help Morale Grow," *Wall Street Journal Online,* August 18, 2009; "Pay Raise Alternatives = Motivated Employees," *Training,* July/August 2009, p. 11; D. Koeppel, "Strange Brew: Beer and Office Democracy," CNNMoney.com, June 9, 2009; and B. Brim and T. Simon, "Strengths on the Factory Floor," *The Gallup Management Journal Online,* March 10, 2009.

87. V. M. Barret, "Fight the Jerks," *Forbes,* July 2, 2007, pp. 52–54.

88. E. White, "The Best vs. the Rest," *Wall Street Journal,* January 30, 2006, pp. B1+.

89. R. K. Abbott, "Performance-Based Flex: A Tool for Managing Total Compensation Costs," *Compensation and Benefits Review*, March–April 1993, pp. 18–21; J. R. Schuster and P. K. Zingheim, "The New Variable Pay: Key Design Issues," *Compensation and Benefits Review*, March–April 1993, pp. 27–34; C. R. Williams and L. P. Livingstone, "Another Look at the Relationship between Performance and Voluntary Turnover," *Academy of Management Journal*, April 1994, pp. 269–298; A. M. Dickinson and K. L. Gillette, "A Comparison of the Effects of Two Individual Monetary Incentive Systems on Productivity: Piece Rate Pay versus Base Pay Plus Incentives," *Journal of Organizational Behavior Management*, Spring 1994, pp. 3–82; and C. B. Cadsby, F. Song, and F. Tapon, "Sorting and Incentive Effects of Pay for Performance: An Experimental Investigation," *Academy of Management Journal*, April 2007, pp. 387–405.

90. M. Spector and D. Mattioli, "Bonuses Sought for Kodak Brass," *Wall Street Journal,* July 12, 2012, p. B3; and M. J. De La Merced, "Eastman Kodak Files for Bankruptcy," *New York Times Online,* January 19, 2012.

91. "Patagonia CEO & President Casey Sheahan Talks Business, Conservation & Compassion," offyonder.com, February 13, 2012; T. Henneman, "Patagonia Fills Payroll with People Who Are Passionate," www.workforce.com, November 4, 2011; M. Hanel, "Surf's Up at Patagonia," *Bloomberg BusinessWeek,* September 5–September 11, 2011, pp. 88–89; J. Wang, "Patagonia, From the Ground Up," *Entrepreneur,* June 2010, pp. 26–32; and J. Laabs, "Mixing Business with Pleasure," *Workforce,* March 2000, pp. 80–85.

92. S. Miller, "Study: Flexible Schedule Reduce Conflict, Lower Turnover," www.shrm.org, April 13, 2011; K. M. Butler, "We Can ROWE Our Way to a Better Work Environment," EBN.BenefitNews.com, April 1, 2011, p. 8; P. Moen, E. L. Kelly, and R. Hill, "Does Enhancing Work-Time Control and Flexibility Reduce Turnover? A Naturally Occurring Experiment," *Social Problems,* February 2011, pp. 69–98; M. Conlin, "Is Optimism a Competitive Advantage?" *BusinessWeek,* August 24 & 31, 2009, pp. 52–53; "New ROLE," *Training,* June 2009, p. 4; C. Ressler and J. Thompson, *Why Work Sucks and How to Fix It* (New York: Penguin Group, 2008); J. Marquez, "Changing A Company's Culture, Not Just Its Schedules, Pays Off," *Workforce Management Online,* November 17, 2008; S. Brown, "Results Should Matter, Not Just Working Late," *USA Today,* June 16, 2008, p. 4B; and J. Thottam, "Reworking Work," *Time,* July 25, 2005, pp. 50–55.

Chapter 15

1. Based on D. Cox, "Team Canada Has It All: Depth, Experience and, Oh Yes, Talent," *Toronto Star*, December 22, 2005, p. A1; M. MacDonald, "Teamwork Key to Gold—On and Off the Ice," *Nanaimo Daily News*, January 27, 2003, p. A9; S. Burnside and B. Beacon, "Lafleur Says Team Canada Well Chosen, Even if There's No Canadiens," *Canadian Press*, May 18, 2004; and "Primeau Looks Like Conn Man," *Star Phoenix*, May 17, 2004, p. C2.

2. Wendy Gillis, "Canada's Hat Trick: Sidney Crosby's Golden Goal at Vancouver Olympics the Biggest in a Generation," *Toronto Star*, September 21, 2012.

3. R. MacGrgeor, "Naming of Team Canada Unites Hockey-Mad Nation," *Globe and Mail*, January 7, 2014, http://www.theglobeand-mail.com/sports/olympics/"acgregor-naming-of-team-canada-unites-hockey-mad-nation/article16239693/ (accessed September 14, 2014).

4. D. Shoalts, "Speed and Smarts Were Prerequisites for Roster Spot on Team Canada," *Globe and Mail*, January 7, 2014, http://www.theglobeandmail.com/sports/olympics/shoalts-speed-and-smarts-were-prerequisites-for-roster-spot-on-team-canada/article16239838/ (accessed September 14, 2014).

5. Rosie DiManno, "Picking Team Canada Makes Steve Yzerman All Business Now," *Toronto Star*, January 8, 2014.

6. B. W. Tuckman and M. C. Jensen, "Stages of Small-Group Development Revisited," *Group and Organizational Studies*, December 1977, pp. 419–427; and M. F. Maples, "Group Development: Extending Tuckman's Theory," *Journal for Specialists in Group Work*, Fall 1988, pp. 17–23.

7. L. N. Jewell and H. J. Reitz, *Group Effectiveness in Organizations* (Glenview, IL: Scott Foresman, 1981); and M. Kaeter, "Repotting Mature Work Teams," *Training*, April 1994, pp. 54–56.

8. A. Robinson, "Canada Left to Lick Its Wounds," *Pittsburgh Post Gazette*, February, 26, 2006.

9. L. Fox, "31 Days to Sochi: 25 Lessons from Team Canada," Retreieved June 18, 2014 from http://www.sportsnet.ca/olympics/25-things-we-learned-from-team-canadas-brain-trust.

10. A. Sobel, "The Beatles Principles," *Strategy+Business*, Spring 2006, p. 42.

11. This model is based on the work of P. S. Goodman, E. Ravlin, and M. Schminke, "Understanding Groups in Organizations," in *Research in Organizational Behavior*, vol. 9, ed. L. L. Cummings and B. M. Staw, pp. 124–128 (Greenwich, CT: JAI Press, 1987); J. R. Hackman, "The Design of Work Teams," in *Handbook of Organizational Behavior*, ed. J. W. Lorsch, pp. 315–342 (Upper Saddle River, NJ: Prentice Hall, 1987); G. R. Bushe and A. L. Johnson, "Contextual and Internal Variables Affecting Task Group Outcomes in Organizations," *Group and Organization Studies*, December 1989, pp. 462–482; M. A. Campion, C. J. Medsker, and A. C. Higgs, "Relations Between Work Group Characteristics and Effectiveness: Implications for Designing Effective Work Groups," *Personnel Psychology*, Winter 1993, pp. 823–850; D. E. Hyatt and T. M. Ruddy, "An Examination of the Relationship Between Work Group Characteristics, and Performance: Once More into the Breach," *Personnel Psychology*, Autumn 1997, pp. 553–585; and P. E. Tesluk and J. E. Mathieu, "Overcoming Roadblocks to Effectiveness: Incorporating Management of Performance Barriers into Models of Work Group Effectiveness," *Journal of Applied Psychology*, April 1999, pp. 200–217.

12. G. L. Stewart, "A Meta-Analytic Review of Relationships Between Team Design Features and Team Performance," *Journal of Management*, February 2006, pp. 29–54; T. Butler and J. Waldroop, "Understanding 'People' People," *Harvard Business Review*, June 2004, pp. 78–86; J. S. Bunderson, "Team Member Functional Background and Involvement in Management Teams: Direct Effects and the Moderating Role of Power Centralization," *Academy of Management Journal*, August 2003, pp. 458–474; and M. J. Stevens and M. A. Campion, "The Knowledge, Skill, and Ability Requirements for Teamwork: Implications for Human Resource Management," *Journal of Management*, Summer 1994, pp. 503–530.

13. V. U. Druskat and S. B. Wolff, "The Link between Emotions and Team Effectiveness: How Teams Engage Members and Build Effective Task Processes," *Academy of Management Proceedings*, on CD-ROM, 1999; D. C. Kinlaw, *Developing Superior Work Teams: Building Quality and the Competitive Edge* (San Diego: Lexington, 1991); and M. E. Shaw, *Contemporary Topics in Social Psychology* (Morristown, NJ: General Learning Press, 1976), pp. 350–351.

14. McMurry, Inc., "The Roles Your People Play," *Managing People at Work*, October 2005, p. 4; G. Prince, "Recognizing Genuine Teamwork," *Supervisory Management*, April 1989, pp. 25–36; R. F. Bales, *SYMOLOG Case Study Kit* (New York: The Free Press, 1980); and K. D. Benne and P. Sheats, "Functional Roles of Group Members," *Journal of Social Issues* 4 (1948), pp. 41–49.

15. data points box based on J. Yang and S. Ward, "Would You Report a Colleague Who's Seriously Underperforming?" *USA Today,* September 21, 2011, p. 1B; M. B. O'Leary, M. Mortensen, and A. W. Woolley, "Multiple Team Membership: A Theoretical Model of Its Effects on Productivity and Learning for Individuals and Teams," *Academy of Management Review,* July 2011,

p. 461; J. Yang and P. Trap, "As a Manager, It's Most Challenging To…," *USA Today,* April 19, 2011, p. 1B; J. Yang and K. Gelles, "Workplace Friendships," *USA Today,* April 13, 2010, p. 1B; K. Merriman, "Low-Trust Teams Prefer Individualized Pay," *Harvard Business Review,* November 2008, p. 32; M. Weinstein, "Coming Up Short? Join the Club," *Training,* April 2006, p. 14; B. J. West, J. L. Patera, and M. K. Carsten, "Team Level Positivity: Investigating Positive Psychological Capacities and Team Level Outcomes"; L. G. Boiney, "Gender Impacts Virtual Work Teams," *The Graziadio Business Report,* Fall 2001, Pepperdine University; and J. Yang and K. Simmons, "Traits of Good Team Players," *USA Today,* November 21, 2007, p. 1B.

16. A. Erez, H. Elms, and E. Fong, "Lying, Cheating, Stealing: Groups and the Ring of Gyges" (paper presented at the Academy of Management Annual meeting, Honolulu, HI, August 8, 2005).

17. S. E. Asch, "Effects of Group Pressure upon the Modification and Distortion of Judgments," in *Groups, Leadership and Men,* ed. H. Guetzkow, pp. 177–190 (Pittsburgh: Carnegie Press, 1951); and S. E. Asch, "Studies of Independence and Conformity: A Minority of One Against a Unanimous Majority," *Psychological Monographs: General and Applied* 70, no. 9 (1956), pp. 1–70.

18. R. Bond and P. B. Smith, "Culture and Conformity: A Meta-Analysis of Studies Using Asch's [1952, 1956] Line Judgment Task," *Psychological Bulletin,* January 1996, pp. 111–137.

19. M. E. Turner and A. R. Pratkanis, "Mitigating Groupthink by Stimulating Constructive Conflict," in *Using Conflict in Organizations,* ed. C. DeDreu and E. Van deVliert, pp. 53–71 (London: Sage, 1997).

20. A. Deutschman, "Inside the Mind of Jeff Bezos," *Fast Company,* August 2004, pp. 50–58.

21. See, for instance, E. J. Thomas and C. F. Fink, "Effects of Group Size," *Psychological Bulletin,* July 1963, pp. 371–384; and M. E. Shaw, *Group Dynamics: The Psychology of Small Group Behavior,* 3rd ed. (New York: McGraw-Hill, 1981).

22. R. C. Liden, S. J. Wayne, R. A. Jaworski, and N. Bennett, "Social Loafing: A Field Investigation," *Journal of Management,* April 2004, pp. 285–304; and D. R. Comer, "A Model of Social Loafing in Real Work Groups," *Human Relations,* June 1995, pp. 647–667.

23. S. G. Harkins and K. Szymanski, "Social Loafing and Group Evaluation," *Journal of Personality and Social Psychology,* December 1989, pp. 934–941.

24. C. R. Evans and K. L. Dion, "Group Cohesion and Performance: A Meta-Analysis," *Small Group Research,* May 1991, pp. 175–186; B. Mullen and C. Copper, "The Relation Between Group Cohesiveness and Performance: An Integration," *Psychological Bulletin,* March 1994, pp. 210–227; and P. M. Podsakoff, S. B. MacKenzie, and M. Ahearne, "Moderating Effects of Goal Acceptance on the Relationship Between Group Cohesiveness and Productivity," *Journal of Applied Psychology,* December 1997, pp. 974–983.

25. See, for example, L. Berkowitz, "Group Standards, Cohesiveness, and Productivity," *Human Relations,* November 1954, pp. 509–519; and B. Mullen and C. Copper, "The Relation Between Group Cohesiveness and Performance: An Integration," *Psychological Bulletin,* March 1994, pp. 210–227.

26. S. E. Seashore, *Group Cohesiveness in the Industrial Work Group* (Ann Arbor: University of Michigan, Survey Research Center, 1954).

27. M. Basadur and M. Head, "Team Performance and Satisfaction: A Link to Cognitive Style within a Process Framework," *Journal of Creative Behaviour* 35, no. 4 (2001), pp. 227–248.

28. C. Shaffran, "Mind Your Meeting: How to Become the Catalyst for Culture Change," *Communication World,* February–March 2003, pp. 26–29.

29. I. L. Janis, *Victims of Groupthink* (Boston: Houghton Mifflin, 1972); R. J. Aldag and S. Riggs Fuller, "Beyond Fiasco: A Reappraisal of the Groupthink Phenomenon and a New Model of Group Decision Processes," *Psychological Bulletin,* May 1993, pp. 533–552; and T. Kameda and S. Sugimori, "Psychological Entrapment in Group Decision Making: An Assigned Decision Rule and a Groupthink Phenomenon," *Journal of Personality and Social Psychology,* August 1993, pp. 282–292.

30. See, for example, L. K. Michaelson, W. E. Watson, and R. H. Black, "A Realistic Test of Individual vs. Group Consensus Decision Making," *Journal of Applied Psychology* 74, no. 5 (1989), pp. 834–839; R. A. Henry, "Group Judgment Accuracy: Reliability and Validity of Postdiscussion Confidence Judgments," *Organizational Behavior and Human Decision Processes,* October 1993, pp. 11–27; P. W. Paese, M. Bieser, and M. E. Tubbs, "Framing Effects and Choice Shifts in Group Decision Making," *Organizational Behavior and Human Decision Processes,* October 1993, pp. 149–165; N. J. Castellan Jr., ed., *Individual and Group Decision Making* (Hillsdale, NJ: Lawrence Erlbaum Associates, 1993); and S. G. Straus and J. E. McGrath, "Does the Medium Matter? The Interaction of Task Type and Technology on Group Performance and Member Reactions," *Journal of Applied Psychology,* February 1994, pp. 87–97.

31. E. J. Thomas and C. F. Fink, "Effects of Group Size," *Psychological Bulletin,* July 1963, pp. 371–384; F. A. Shull, A. L. Delbecq, and L. L. Cummings, *Organizational Decision Making* (New York: McGraw-Hill, 1970), p. 151; A. P. Hare, *Handbook of Small Group Research* (New York: The Free Press, 1976); M. E. Shaw, *Group Dynamics: The Psychology of Small Group Behavior,* 3rd ed. (New York: McGraw-Hill, 1981); and P. Yetton and P. Bottger, "The Relationships Among Group Size, Member Ability, Social Decision Schemes, and Performance," *Organizational Behavior and Human Performance,* October 1983, pp. 145–159.

32. This section is adapted from S. P. Robbins, *Managing Organizational Conflict: A Nontraditional Approach* (Upper Saddle River, NJ: Prentice Hall, 1974), pp. 11–14. Also see D. Wagner-Johnson, "Managing Work Team Conflict: Assessment and Preventative Strategies," Center for the Study of Work Teams, University of North Texas, November 3, 2000, www.workteams.unt.edu/reports; and M. Kennedy, "Managing Conflict in Work Teams," Center for the Study of Work Teams, University of North Texas, November 3, 2000, www.workteams.unt.edu/reports.

33. See K. A. Jehn, "A Multimethod Examination of the Benefits and Detriments of Intragroup Conflict," *Administrative Science Quarterly,* June 1995, pp. 256–282; K. A. Jehn, "A Qualitative Analysis of Conflict Type and Dimensions in Organizational Groups," *Administrative Science Quarterly,* September 1997, pp. 530–557; K. A. Jehn, "Affective and Cognitive Conflict in Work Groups: Increasing Performance through Value-Based Intragroup Conflict," in *Using Conflict in Organizations,* ed. C. DeDreu and E. Van deVliert, pp. 87–100 (London: Sage, 1997); K. A. Jehn and E. A. Mannix, "The Dynamic Nature of Conflict: A Longitudinal Study of Intragroup Conflict and Group Performance," *Academy of Management Journal,* April 2001, pp. 238–251; C. K. W. DeDreu and A. E. M. Van Vianen, "Managing Relationship Conflict and the Effectiveness of Organizational Teams," *Journal of Organizational Behavior,* May 2001, pp. 309–328; and J. Weiss and J. Hughes, "Want Collaboration? Accept—And Actively Manage—Conflict," *Harvard Business Review,* March 2005, pp. 92–101.

34. C. K. W. DeDreu, "When Too Little or Too Much Hurts: Evidence for a Curvilinear Relationship Between Task Conflict and Innovation in Teams," *Journal of Management,* February 2006, pp. 83–107.

35. K. W. Thomas, "Conflict and Negotiation Processes in Organizations," in *Handbook of Industrial and Organizational Psychology,* 2nd ed., vol. 3, ed. M. D. Dunnette and L. M. Hough, pp. 651–717 (Palo Alto, CA: Consulting Psychologists Press, 1992).

36. A. Li and R. Cropanzano, "Fairness at the Group Level: Justice Climate and Intraunit Justice Climate," *Journal of Management,* June 2009, pp. 564–599.

37. See, for example, J. R. Hackman and C. G. Morris, "Group Tasks, Group Interaction Process, and Group Performance Effectiveness: A Review and Proposed Integration," in *Advances in Experimental Social Psychology*, ed. L. Berkowitz, pp. 45–99 (New York: Academic Press, 1975); R. Saavedra, P. C. Earley, and L. Van Dyne, "Complex Interdependence in Task-Performing Groups," *Journal of Applied Psychology*, February 1993, pp. 61–72; M. J. Waller, "Multiple-Task Performance in Groups," *Academy of Management Proceedings*, on disk, 1996; and K. A. Jehn, G. B. Northcraft, and M. A. Neale, "Why Differences Make a Difference: A Field Study of Diversity, Conflict, and Performance in Workgroups," *Administrative Science Quarterly*, December 1999, pp. 741–763.

38. R. MacGregor, "Naming of Team Canada Unites Hockey-Mad Nation," *Globe and Mail*, January 7, 2014, http://www.theglobeandmail.com/sports/olympics/macgregor-naming-of-team-canada-unites-hockey-mad-nation/article16239693/ (accessed September 14, 2014); D. Shoalts, "Speed and Smarts Were Prerequisites for Roster Spot on Team Canada," *Globe and Mail*, January 7, 2014, http://www.theglobeandmail.com/sports/olympics/shoalts-speed-and-smarts-were-prerequisites-for-roster-spot-on-team-canada/article16239838/ (accessed September 14, 2014); E. Duhatschek, "Canadian Men's Olympic Hockey Team Unveiled," *Globe and Mail,* January 7, 2014, http://www.theglobeandmail.com/sports/olympics/canadas-mens-olympic-hockey-team-to-be-unveiled-in-toronto/article16228127/?page=all (accessed September 14, 2014).

39. Cited in T. Purdum, "Teaming, Take 2," *Industry-Week*, May 2005, p. 43; and C. Joinson, "Teams at Work," *HRMagazine*, May 1999, p. 30.

40. See, for example, S. A. Mohrman, S. G. Cohen, and A. M. Mohrman Jr., *Designing Team-Based Organizations* (San Francisco: Jossey-Bass, 1995); P. MacMillan, *The Performance Factor: Unlocking the Secrets of Teamwork* (Nashville, TN: Broadman & Holman, 2001); and E. Salas, C. A. Bowers, and E. Eden, eds., *Improving Teamwork in Organizations: Applications of Resource Management Training* (Mahwah, NJ: Lawrence Erlbaum, 2002).

41. See, for instance, E. Sunstrom, DeMeuse, and D. Futrell, "Work Teams: Applications and Effectiveness," *American Psychologist*, February 1990, pp. 120–133.

42. J. S. McClenahen, "Bearing Necessities," *IndustryWeek*, October 2004, pp. 63–65; P. J. Kiger, "Acxiom Rebuilds from Scratch," *Workforce*, December 2002, pp. 52–55; and T. Boles, "Viewpoint— Leadership Lessons from NASCAR," *IndustryWeek* online, May 21, 2002, www.industryweek.com.

43. M. Cianni and D. Wanuck, "Individual Growth and Team Enhancement: Moving Toward a New Model of Career Development," *Academy of Management Executive*, February 1997, pp. 105–115.

44. "Teams," *Training*, October 1996, p. 69; and C. Joinson "Teams at Work," *HRMagazine*, May 1999, p. 30.

45. G. M. Spreitzer, S. G. Cohen, and G. E. Ledford Jr., "Developing Effective Self-Managing Work Teams in Service Organizations," *Group & Organization Management*, September 1999, pp. 340–366.

46. "Meet the New Steel," *Fortune*, October 1, 2007, pp. 68–71.

47. J. Appleby and R. Davis, "Teamwork Used to Save Money; Now It Saves Lives," *USA Today* online, March 1, 2001, www.usatoday.com.

48. A. Malhotra, A. Majchrzak, R. Carman, and V. Lott, "Radical Innovation without Collocation: A Case Study at Boeing-Rocketdyne," *MIS Quarterly*, June 2001, pp. 229–249.

49. A. Stuart, "Virtual Agreement," *CFO*, November 2007, p. 24.

50. A. Malhotra, A. Majchrzak, and B. Rosen, "Leading Virtual Teams," *Academy of Management Perspectives*, February 2007, pp. 60–70; B. L. Kirkman and J. E. Mathieu, "The Dimensions and Antecedents of Team Virtuality," *Journal of Management*, October 2005, pp. 700–718; J. Gordon, "Do Your Virtual Teams Deliver Only Virtual Performance?" *Training*, June 2005, pp. 20–25; L. L. Martins, L. L. Gilson, and M. T. Maynard, "Virtual Teams: What Do We Know and Where Do We Go from Here?" *Journal of Management*, December 2004, pp. 805–835; S. A. Furst, M. Reeves, B. Rosen, and R. S. Blackburn, "Managing the Life Cycle of Virtual Teams," *Academy of Management Executive*, May 2004, pp. 6–20; B. L. Kirkman, B. Rosen, P. E. Tesluk, and C. B. Gibson, "The Impact of Team Empowerment on Virtual Team Performance: The Moderating Role of Face-to-Face Interaction," *Academy of Management Journal*, April 2004, pp. 175–192; F. Keenan and S. E. Ante, "The New Teamwork," *BusinessWeek* e.biz, February 18, 2002, pp. EB12–EB16; and G. Imperato, "Real Tools for Virtual Teams," *Fast Company*, July 2000, pp. 378–387.

51. J. Mathieu, M. T. Maynard, T. Rapp, and L. Gilson, "Team Effectiveness 1997–2007: A Review of Recent Advancements and a Glimpse into the Future," *Journal of Management*, June 2008, pp. 410–476; S. W. Lester, B. W. Meglino, and M. A. Korsgaard, "The Antecedents and Consequences of Group Potency: A Longitudinal Investigation of Newly Formed Work Groups," *Academy of Management Journal*, April 2002, pp. 352–368; M. A. Marks, M. J. Sabella, C. S. Burke, and S. J. Zaccaro, "The Impact of Cross-Training on Team Effectiveness," *Journal of Applied Psychology*, February 2002, pp. 3–13; J. A. Colquitt, R. A. Noe, and C. L. Jackson, "Justice in Teams: Antecedents and Consequences of Procedural Justice Climate," *Personnel Psychology* 55 (2002), pp. 83–100; J. M. Phillips and E. A. Douthitt, "The Role of Justice in Team Member Satisfaction with the Leader and Attachment to the Team," *Journal of Applied Psychology*, April 2001, pp. 316–325; J. E. Mathieu, et al., "The Influence of Shared Mental Models on Team Process and Performance," *Journal of Applied Psychology*, April 2000, pp. 273–283; G. L. Stewart and M. R. Barrick, "Team Structure and Performance: Assessing the Mediating Role of Intrateam Process and the Moderating Role of Task Type," *Academy of Management Journal*, April 2000, pp. 135–148; J. D. Shaw, M. K. Duffy, and E. M. Stark, "Interdependence and Preference for Group Work: Main and Congruence Effects on the Satisfaction and Performance of Group Members," *Journal of Management* 26, no. 2 (2000), pp. 259–279; V. U. Druskat and S. B. Wolff, "The Link Between Emotions and Team Effectiveness: How Teams Engage Members and Build Effective Task Processes," *Academy of Management Proceedings*, on CD-ROM, 1999; R. Forrester and A. B. Drexler, "A Model for Team-Based Organization Performance," *Academy of Management Executive*, August 1999, pp. 36–49; A. R. Jassawalla and H. C. Sashittal, "Building Collaborative Cross-Functional New Product Teams," *Academy of Management Executive*, August 1999, pp. 50–63; and G. R. Jones and G. M. George, "The Experience and Evolution of Trust: Implications for Cooperation and Teamwork," *Academy of Management Review*, July 1998, pp. 531–546.

52. D. Coutou, interview with J. R. Hackman, "Why Teams Don't Work."

53. A. Bruce, " Golden Generation Leads Canadian Men to Olympic Gold, Again in Sochi," *National Post*, Februrary 23, 2013.

54. B. L. Kirkman, C. B. Gibson, and D. L. Shapiro, "Exporting Teams: Enhancing the Implementation and Effectiveness of Work Teams in Global Affiliates," *Organizational Dynamics*, Summer 2001, pp. 12–29; J. W. Bing and C. M. Bing, "Helping Global Teams Compete," *Training & Development*, March 2001, pp. 70–71; C. G. Andrews, "Factors That Impact Multi-Cultural Team Performance," Center for the Study of Work Teams, University of North Texas, November 3, 2000, www.workteams.unt.edu/reports/; P. Christopher Earley and E. Mosakowski, "Creating Hybrid Team Cultures: An Empirical Test of Transnational Team Functioning," *Academy of Management Journal*, February 2000, pp. 26–49; J. Tata, "The

Cultural Context of Teams: An Integrative Model of National Culture, Work Team Characteristics, and Team Effectiveness," *Academy of Management Proceedings*, on CD-ROM, 1999; D. I. Jung, K. B. Baik, and J. J. Sosik, "A Longitudinal Investigation of Group Characteristics and Work Group Performance: A Cross-Cultural Comparison," *Academy of Management Proceedings*, on CD-ROM, 1999; and C. B. Gibson, "They Do What They Believe They Can? Group-Efficacy Beliefs and Group Performance Across Tasks and Cultures," *Academy of Management Proceedings*, on CD-ROM, 1996.

55. R. Bond and P. B. Smith, "Culture and Conformity: A Meta-Analysis of Studies Using Asch's [1952, 1956] Line Judgment Task," *Psychological Bulletin*, January 1996, pp. 111–137.

56. I. L. Janis, *Groupthink*, 2nd ed. (New York: Houghton Mifflin, 1982), p. 175.

57. See P. C. Earley, "Social Loafing and Collectivism: A Comparison of the United States and the People's Republic of China," *Administrative Science Quarterly*, December 1989, pp. 565–581; and P. C. Earley, "East Meets West Meets Mideast: Further Explorations of Collectivistic and Individualistic Work Groups," *Academy of Management Journal*, April 1993, pp. 319–348.

58. N. J. Adler, *International Dimensions of Organizational Behavior*, 4th ed. (Cincinnati, OH: South-Western, 2002), p. 142.

59. K. B. Dahlin, L. R. Weingart, and P. J. Hinds, "Team Diversity and Information Use," *Academy of Management Journal*, December 2005, pp. 1107–1123.

60. N. J. Adler, *International Dimensions of Organizational Behavior*, 4th ed. (Cincinnati, OH: South-Western, 2002), p. 142.

61. S. Paul, I. M. Samarah, P. Seetharaman, and P. P. Mykytyn, "An Empirical Investigation of Collaborative Conflict Management Style in Group Support System-Based Global Virtual Teams," *Journal of Management Information Systems*, Winter 2005, pp. 185–222.

62. S. Chang and P. Tharenou, "Competencies Needed for Managing a Multicultural Workgroup," *Asia Pacific Journal of Human Resources* 42, no. 1 (2004), pp. 57–74; and N. J. Adler, *International Dimensions of Organizational Behavior*, 4th ed. (Cincinnati, OH: South-Western, 2002), p. 142.

63. C. E. Nicholls, H. W. Lane, and M. Brehm Brechu, "Taking Self-Managed Teams to Mexico," *Academy of Management Executive*, August 1999, pp. 15–27.

64. M. O'Neil, "Leading the Team," *Supervision,* April 2011, pp. 8–10; and A. Gilley, J. W. Gilley, C. W. McConnell, and A. Veliquette, "The Competencies Used by Effective Managers to Build Teams: An Empirical Study," *Advances in Developing Human Resources,* February 2010, pp. 29–45.

65. B. V. Krishnamurthy, "Use Downtime to Enhance Skills," *Harvard Business Review,* December 2008, pp. 29–30.

66. J. Reingold and J. L. Yang, "The Hidden Workplace: What's Your OQ?" *Fortune*, July 23, 2007, pp. 98–106; and P. Balkundi and D. A. Harrison, "Ties, Leaders, and Time in Teams: Strong Inference About Network Structures' Effects on Team Viability and Performance," *Academy of Management Journal*, February 2006, pp. 49–68.

67. T. Casciaro and M. S. Lobo, "Competent Jerks, Lovable Fools, and the Formation of Social Networks," *Harvard Business Review*, June 2005, pp. 92–99.

68. P. Balkundi and D. A. Harrison, "Ties, Leaders, and Time in Teams: Strong Inference About Network Structures' Effects on Team Viability and Performance," *Academy of Management Journal*, February 2006, pp. 49–68.

69. J. McGregor, "The Office Chart That Really Counts," *BusinessWeek*, February 27, 2006, pp. 48–49.

70. P. Klaus, "Thank You for Sharing. But Why at the Office? *New York Times Online*, August 18, 2012; and E. Bernstein, "You Did What? Spare the Office the Details," *Wall Street Journal*, April 6, 2010, pp. D1+.

71. N. Byrnes, "Pepsi Brings in the Health Police," *Bloomberg BusinessWeek*, January 25, 2010, pp. 50–51.

72. A. Schein, "Lonely Planet Publications," Hoovers.com, July 25, 2012; J. Koppisch, "2012 Australian Philanthropists," Forbes.com, June 20, 2012, p. 1; N. Denny, "Digital and the Bookshop," *Bookseller,* June 8, 2012, p. 3; M. Costa, "Travel Guru Explores New Routes," *Marketing Week*, April 12, 2012, p. 20; and K. Cuthbertson and R. Haynes, "Duo Came With 27 cents and left with $100 million," *The Herald Sun,* October 2, 2007, p. 11.

73. D. Michaels and J. Ostrower, "Airbus, Boeing Walk a Fine Line on Jetliner Production," *Wall Street Journal,* July 16, 2012, p. B3; D. Kesmodel, "Boeing Teams Speed Up 737 Output," *Wall Street Journal,* February 7, 2012, p. B10; and A. Cohen, "Boeing Sees Demand for Existing, Re-engined 737s," blog on *Seattle Post-Intelligencer Online,* October 26, 2011.

Chapter 16

1. Based on "Energy Roughneck," *Canadian Business*, August 1996, pp. 20+; Hoover's Online, www.hoovers.com; and C. Cattaneo, "Husky CEO Lau Reveals Intention to Retire," *National Post (Financial Post)*, April 23, 2004, p. FP4.

2. Based on B. Hagenbauh, "State Quarter's Extra Leaf Grew Out of Lunch Break," *USA Today*, January 20, 2006, p. 1B.

3. K. A. Merchant, "The Control Function of Management," *Sloan Management Review*, Summer 1982, pp. 43–55.

4. E. Flamholtz, "Organizational Control Systems as a Managerial Tool," *California Management Review*, Winter 1979, p. 55.

5. P. Magnusson, "Your Jitters Are Their Lifeblood," *BusinessWeek*, April 14, 2003, p. 41; S. Williams, "Company Crisis: CEO Under Fire," *Hispanic Business*, March 2003, pp. 54–56; T. Purdum, "Preparing for the Worst," *IndustryWeek*, January 2003, pp. 53–55; and S. Leibs, "Lesson from 9/11: It's Not About Data," *CFO*, September 2002, pp. 31–32.

6. S. Kerr, "On the Folly of Rewarding A, While Hoping for B," *Academy of Management Journal*, December 1975, pp. 769–783.

7. C. Cattaneo, "Li May Usher in Sea Change at Air Canada," *National Post (Financial Post)*, November 24, 2003, p. FP03; C. Cattaneo, "Stranger in a Strange Land," *National Post (Financial Post)*, December 13, 2003, p. FP1F; Husky Energy, *Annual Report 2006*, p. 6, www.huskyenergy.ca/downloads/InvestorRelations/2006/ HSE_Annual2006. pdf (accessed September 22, 2007); and "Husky Energy [The Investor 500]," *Canadian Business*, www.canadianbusiness.com/rankings/investor500/index. jsp?pageID=profile&profile=16&year=2007&type=profile (accessed September 22, 2007).

8. M. Lewis, *Moneyball: The Art of Winning an Unfair Game* (New York: W.W. Norton & Company, 2004).

9. "The Top 1000: Canada's Power Book," *Globe and Mail*, www.glo-beinvestor.com/series/top1000.

10. S. Brearton and J. Daly, "50 Best Employers in Canada," *Globe and Mail*, December 29, 2003, p. 33; and "Study Guidelines," *Best Employers in Canada*, http://was7.hewitt.com/bestemployers/canada/study_guidelines.htm (accessed September 21, 2007).

11. See http://list.canadianbusiness.com/rankings/profit100/2008/intro/Default.aspx?sp2=1&d1=d&sc1=9 (accessed March 27, 2011).

12. A. H. Jordan and P. G. Audia, "Self-Enhancement and Learning from Performance Feedback," *Academy of Management Review*,

April 2012, pp. 211–231; D. Busser, "Delivering Effective Performance Feedback," *T&D*, April 2012, pp. 32–34; and "U.S. Employees Desire More Sources of Feedback for Performance Reviews," *T&D*, February 2012, p. 18.

13. D. Busser, "Delivering Effective Performance Feedback," *T&D*, April 2012, pp. 32–34.

14. Based on C. Cattaneo, "Li May Usher in Sea Change at Air Canada," *National Post (Financial Post)*, November 24, 2003, p. FP03.

15. H. Koontz and R. W. Bradspies, "Managing through Feedforward Control," *Business Horizons*, June 1972, pp. 25–36.

16. M. Helft, "The Human Hands Behind the Google Money Machine," *New York Times Online*, June 2, 2008, www.nytimes.com.

17. "An Open Letter to McDonald's Customers," *Wall Street Journal*, August 22, 2001, p. A5.

18. W. H. Newman, *Constructive Control: Design and Use of Control Systems* (Upper Saddle River, NJ: Prentice Hall, 1975), p. 33.

19. R. Ilies and T. A. Judge, "Goal Regulation across Time: The Effects of Feedback and Affect," *Journal of Applied Psychology* 90, no. 3 (May 2005), pp. 453–467.

20. J. H. Cushman, Jr., "U.S. Tightens Security for Economic Data," *New York Times Online*, July 16, 2012; B. Worthen, "Private Sector Keeps Mum on Cyber Attacks," *Wall Street Journal*, January 19, 2010, p. B4; G. Bowley, "Ex-Worker Said to Steal Goldman Code," *New York Times Online*, July 7, 2009; and R. King, "Lessons from the Data Breach at Heartland," *BusinessWeek Online*, July 6, 2009.

21. Deloitte & Touche and the Ponemon Institute, "Research Report: Reportable and Multiple Privacy Breaches Rising at Alarming Rate," *Ethics Newsline*, www.ethicsnewsline.wordpress.com, January 1, 2008.

22. B. Grow, K. Epstein, and C-C. Tschang, "The New E-Spionage Threat," *BusinessWeek*, April 21, 2008, pp. 32–41; S. Leibs, "Firewall of Silence," *CFO*, April 2008, pp. 31–35; J. Pereira, "How Credit-Card Data Went Out Wireless Door," *Wall Street Journal*, May 4, 2007, pp. A1+; and B. Stone, "Firms Fret as Office E-Mail Jumps Security Walls," *New York Times Online*, January 11, 2007.

23. D. Whelan, "Google Me Not," *Forbes*, August 16, 2004, pp. 102–104.

24. K. Hendricks, M. Hora, L. Menor, and C. Wiedman, "Adoption of the Balanced Scorecard: A Contingency Variables Analysis," *Canadian Journal of Administrative Sciences*, June 2012, pp. 124–138; E. R. Iselin, J. Sands, and L. Mia, "Multi-Perspective Performance Reporting Systems, Continuous Improvement Systems, and Organizational Performance," *Journal of General Management*, Spring 2011, pp. 19–36; T. L. Albright, C. M. Burgess, A. R. Hibbets, and M. L. Roberts, "Four Steps to Simplify Multimeasure Performance Evaluations Using the Balanced Scorecard," *Journal of Corporate Accounting & Finance*, July–August 2010, pp. 63–68; H. Sundin, M. Granlund, and D. A. Brown, "Balancing Multiple Competing Objectives with a Balanced Scorecard," *European Accounting Review*, vol. 19, no. 2, 2010, pp. 203–246; R. S. Kaplan and D. P. Norton, "How to Implement a New Strategy without Disrupting Your Organization," *Harvard Business Review*, March 2006, pp. 100–109; L. Bassi and D. McMurrer, "Developing Measurement Systems for Managers in the Knowledge Era," *Organizational Dynamics*, May 2005, pp. 185–196; G. M. J. DeKoning, "Making the Balanced Scorecard Work (Part 2)," *Gallup Brain*, brain.gallup.com, August 12, 2004; G. J. J. DeKoning, "Making the Balanced Scorecard Work (Part 1)," *Gallup Brain*, brain. gallup.com, July 8, 2004; K. Graham, "Balanced Scorecard," *New Zealand Management*, March 2003, pp. 32–34; K. Ellis, "A Ticket to Ride: Balanced Scorecard," *Training*, April 2001, p. 50; and T. Leahy, "Tailoring the Balanced Scorecard," *Business Finance*, August 2000, pp. 53–56.

25. T. Leahy, "Tailoring the Balanced Scorecard," *Business Finance*, August 2000, pp. 53–56.

26. T. Leahy, "Tailoring the Balanced Scorecard," *Business Finance*, August 2000, pp. 53–56.

27. V. Fuhrmans, "Replicating Cleveland Clinic's Success Poses Major Challenges," *Wall Street Journal*, July 23, 2009, p. A4.

28. R. Pear, "A.M.A. to Develop Measure of Quality of Medical Care," *New York Times Online*, February 21, 2006; and A. Taylor III, "Double Duty," *Fortune*, March 7, 2005, pp. 104–110.

29. S. Minter, "How Good Is Your Benchmarking?" *Industry Week*, October 2009, pp. 24–26; and T. Leahy, "Extracting Diamonds in the Rough," *Business Finance*, August 2000, pp. 33–37.

30. B. Bruzina, B. Jessop, R. Plourde, B. Whitlock, and L. Rubin, "Ameren Embraces Benchmarking As a Core Business Strategy," *Power Engineering*, November 2002, pp. 121–124.

31. Based on P. Fitzpatrick, "Wacky WestJet's Winning Ways: Passengers Respond to Stunts That Include Races to Determine Who Leaves the Airplane First," *National Post*, October 16, 2000, p. C1.

32. Based on "Corporate Governance," Husky Energy, www.huskyenergy.ca/abouthusky/corporategovernance/ (accessed June 23, 2014).

33. J. Yaukey and C. L. Romero, "Arizona Firm Pays Big for Workers' Digital Downloads," *Springfield News-Leader*, May 6, 2002, p. 6B.

34. A. Taylor, "Enterprise Asks What Customer's Thinking and Acts," *USA Today*, May 22, 2006, p. 6B; and A. Taylor, "Driving Customer Satisfaction," *Harvard Business Review*, July 2002, pp. 24–25.

35. S. D. Pugh, J. Dietz, J. W. Wiley, and S. M. Brooks, "Driving Service Effectiveness Through Employee–Customer Linkages," *Academy of Management Executive*, November 2002, pp. 73–84; J. L. Heskett, W. E. Sasser, and L. A. Schlesinger, *The Service Profit Chain* (New York: Free Press, 1997); and J. L. Heskett, T. O. Jones, G. W. Loveman, W. E. Sasser, Jr., and L. A. Schlesinger, "Putting the Service Profit Chain to Work," *Harvard Business Review*, March–April 1994, pp. 164–170.

36. "A Revolution Where Everyone Wins: Worldwide Movement to Improve Corporate-Governance Standards," *BusinessWeek*, May 19, 2003, p. 72.

37. J. S. McClenahen, "Executives Expect More Board Input," *IndustryWeek*, October 2002, p. 12.

38. See Institute of Corporate Directors website, http://www.icd.ca/ Home.aspx (accessed June 20, 2014); D. Salierno, "Boards Face Increased Responsibility," *Internal Auditor*, June 2003, pp. 14–15.

39. E. O'Connor, "Pulling the Plug on Cyberslackers," *StarPhoenix*, May 24, 2003, p. F22.

40. S. Armour, "Companies Keep an Eye on Workers' Internet Use," *USA Today*, February 21, 2006, p. 2B.

41. B. White, "The New Workplace Rules: No Video-Watching," *Wall Street Journal*, March 4, 2008, pp. B1+.

42. D. Hawkins, "Lawsuits Spur Rise in Employee Monitoring," *U.S. News & World Report*, August 13, 2001, p. 53; L. Guernsey, "You've Got Inappropriate Mail," *New York Times*, April 5, 2000, p. C11; and R. Karaim, "Setting E-Privacy Rules," *Cnnfn Online*, December 15, 1999, www.cnnfn.com.

43. E. Bott, "Are You Safe? Privacy Special Report," *PC Computing*, March 2000, pp. 87–88.

44. E. O'Connor, "Pulling the Plug on Cyberslackers," *StarPhoenix*, May 24, 2003, p. F22.

45. B. Acohido, "An Invitation to Crime," *USA Today*, March 4, 2010, pp. A1+; W. P. Smith and F. Tabak, "Monitoring Employee E-mails: Is There Any Room for Privacy?" *Academy of Management Perspectives*, November 2009, pp. 33–38; and S. Boehle, "They're Watching You," *Training*, September 2008, pp. 23–29.

46. J. Divon, "Why more employees are stealing from you," *Globe and Mail*, November 26, 2012, http://www.theglobeandmail.com/report-on-business/small-business/sb-managing/human-resources/why-more-employees-are-stealing-from-you/article5609168/.

47. A. Perry, "Back-to-School Brings Pilfering: Some Employees Raid Office for Kids," *Toronto Star*, August 30, 2003, p. B01.

48. See PricewaterhouseCoopers Canada, "Canadian Retailers Lose Over $3 Billion Annually to Crime: Retail Council of Canada, PricewaterhouseCoopers Survey," September 16, 2009, www.pwc.com/ca/en/media/release/2009-09-16-canadian-retailers-crime.jhtml (accessed March 30, 2011).

49. J. Greenberg, "The STEAL Motive: Managing the Social Determinants of Employee Theft," in *Antisocial Behavior in Organizations*, ed. R. Giacalone and J. Greenberg), pp. 85–108 (Newbury Park, CA: Sage, 1997.

50. "Crime Spree," *BusinessWeek*, September 9, 2002, p. 8; B. P. Niehoff and R. J. Paul, "Causes of Employee Theft and Strategies That HR Managers Can Use for Prevention," *Human Resource Management*, Spring 2000, pp. 51–64; and G. Winter, "Taking at the Office Reaches New Heights: Employee Larceny Is Bigger and Bolder," *New York Times*, July 12, 2000, p. C11.

51. This section is based on J. Greenberg, *Behavior in Organizations: Understanding and Managing the Human Side of Work*, 8th ed. (Upper Saddle River, NJ: Prentice Hall, 2003), pp. 329–330.

52. A. H. Bell and D. M. Smith, "Why Some Employees Bite the Hand That Feeds Them," *Workforce*, May 16, 2000, www.workforce.com (accessed December 3, 2000).

53. A. H. Bell and D. M. Smith, "Protecting the Company against Theft and Fraud," *Workforce*, May 18, 2000, www.workforce.com (accessed December 3, 2000); J. D. Hansen, "To Catch a Thief," *Journal of Accountancy*, March 2000, pp. 43–46; and J. Greenberg, "The Cognitive Geometry of Employee Theft," in *Dysfunctional Behavior in Organizations: Nonviolent and Deviant Behavior*, ed. S. B. Bacharach, A. O'Leary-Kelly, J. M. Collins, and R. W. Griffin, pp. 147–193 (Stamford, CT: JAI Press, 1998).

54. *#Fail: The Power of Analytics and Social Media*, Personal Communication with John Weigelt, April 9, 2013.

55. S. D. Pugh, J. Dietz, J. W. Wiley, and S. M. Brooks, "Driving Service Effectiveness through Employee-Customer Linkages," *Academy of Management Executive*, November 2002, pp. 73–84.

56. Situation adapted from information in K. Cushing, "E-Mail Policy," *Computer Weekly*, June 24, 2003, p. 8; and "Spam Leads to Lawsuit Fears, Lost Time," *InternetWeek*, June 23, 2003, www.internetweek.com.

57. D. Kirka, "Heathrow Handles Record Numbers for Olympics," www.aviationpros.com, July 17, 2012; E. Lawrie, "London Heathrow Olympic Surge Spurs Record Traffic Plan," www.bloomberg.com, July 16, 2012; K. Kühn, "How Has T5 Taken Off?" *Caterer & Hotelkeeper*, March 12, 2010, pp. 22–25; C. Dosh, "Debunking T5 Terror," *Successful Meetings*, April 2009, p. 99; M. Frary, "A Tale of Two Terminals," *Business Travel World*, August 2008, pp. 16–19; K. Capell, "British Airways Hit by Heathrow Fiasco," *BusinessWeek*, April 3, 2008, p. 6; The Associated Press, "Problems Continue at Heathrow's Terminal 5," *International Herald Tribune*, www.iht.com, March 31, 2008; M. Scott, "New Heathrow Hub: Slick, but No Savior," *BusinessWeek*, March 28, 2008, p. 11; and G. Katz, "Flights Are Canceled, Baggage Stranded, as London's New Heathrow Terminal Opens," *The Seattle Times Online*, www.seattletimes.nwsource.com, March 27, 2008.

58. T. Fowler, "U.S. Nears BP Settlement," *Wall Street Journal*, June 29, 2012, p. A3; T. Tracy, "BP, Contractors Cited," *Wall Street Journal*, October 13, 2011, p. B3; J. M. Broder, "Companies, Crews and Regulators Share Blame in Coast Guard Report on Oil Spill," *New York Times Online*, April 22, 2011; R. Brown, "Oil Rig's Siren Was Kept Silent, Technician Says," *New York Times Online*, July 23, 2010; I. Urbina, "Workers on Doomed Rig Voiced Concern about Safety," *New York Times Online*, July 21, 2010; R. Gold, "Rig's Final Hours Probed," *Wall Street Journal*, July 19, 2010, pp. A1+; S. Lyall, "In BP's Record, a History of Boldness and Costly Blunders," *New York Times Online*, July 12, 2010; B. Casselman and R. Gold, "Unusual Decisions Set Stage for BP Disaster," *Wall Street Journal*, May 27, 2010, pp. A1+; H. Fountain and T. Zeller, Jr., "Panel Suggests Signs of Trouble Before Rig Explosion," *New York Times Online*, May 25, 2010; and R. Gold and N. King Jr., "The Gulf Oil Spill: Red Flags Were Ignored Aboard Doomed Rig," *Wall Street Journal*, May 13, 2010, p. A6.

Module 3

1. Based on Eldis Group home page, http://eldisgroup.com (accessed June 23, 2014).

2. Data from the Compete website, www.compete.com/ (accessed June 24, 2014).

3. D. Clark, "Inside Intel, It's All Copying," *Wall Street Journal*, October 28, 2002, pp. B1+.

4. D. McGinn, "Faster Food," *Newsweek*, April 19, 2004, pp. E20–E22.

5. D. McGinn, "Faster Food," *Newsweek*, April 19, 2004, pp. E20–E22; and *World Fact Book 2006*, www.odci.gov/cia/publications.

6. D. Michaels and J. L. Lunsford, "Streamlined Plane Making," *Wall Street Journal*, April 1, 2005, pp. B1+.

7. J. Ordonez, "McDonald's to Cut the Cooking Time of Its French Fries," *Wall Street Journal*, May 19, 2000, p. B2.

8. C. Fredman, "The Devil in the Details," *Executive Edge*, April–May 1999, pp. 36–39.

9. Information from Škoda website, www.skoda-auto.com (accessed May 30, 2006); and T. Mudd, "The Last Laugh," *IndustryWeek*, September 18, 2000, pp. 38–44.

10. W. E. Deming, "Improvement of Quality and Productivity Through Action by Management," *National Productivity Review*, Winter 1981–1982, pp. 12–22.

11. T. Vinas, "Little Things Mean a Lot," *IndustryWeek*, November 2002, p. 55.

12. S. Levy, "The Connected Company," *Newsweek*, April 28, 2003, pp. 40–48; and J. Teresko, "Plant Floor Strategy," *IndustryWeek*, July 2002, pp. 26–32.

13. T. Laseter, K. Ramdas, and D. Swerdlow, "The Supply Side of Design and Development," *Strategy+Business*, Summer 2003, p. 23; J. Jusko, "Not All Dollars and Cents," *IndustryWeek*, April 2002, p. 58; and D. Drickhamer, "Medical Marvel," *IndustryWeek*, March 2002, pp. 47–49.

14. J. H. Sheridan, "Managing the Value Chain," *IndustryWeek*, September 6, 1999, pp. 1–4.

15. J. H. Sheridan, "Managing the Value Chain," *IndustryWeek*, September 6, 1999, p. 3.

16. . Teresko, "Forward, March!" *IndustryWeek*, July 2004, pp. 43–48; D. Sharma, C. Lucier, and R. Molloy, "From Solutions to Symbiosis: Blending with Your Customers," *Strategy+Business*, Second Quarter 2002, pp. 38–48; and S. Leibs, "Getting Ready: Your Suppliers," *IndustryWeek*, September 6, 1999.

17. D. Bartholomew, "The Infrastructure," *IndustryWeek*, September 6, 1999, p. 1.

18. T. Stevens, "Integrated Product Development," *IndustryWeek*, June 2002, pp. 21–28.

19. T. Vinas, "A Map of the World: IW Value-Chain Survey," *IndustryWeek*, September 2005, pp. 27–34.

20. C. Burritt, C. Wolf, and M. Boyle, "Why Wal-Mart Wants to Take the Driver's Seat," *Bloomberg BusinessWeek,* May 31–June 6, 2010, pp. 17–18.

21. R. Normann and R. Ramirez, "From Value Chain to Value Constellation," *Harvard Business Review* on Managing the Value Chain (Boston: Harvard Business School Press, 2000), pp. 185–219.

22. J. Teresko, "The Tough Get Going," *IndustryWeek*, March 2005, pp. 25–32; D. M. Lambert and A. M. Knemeyer, "We're in This Together," *Harvard Business Review*, December 2004, pp. 114–122; and V. G. Narayanan and A. Raman, "Aligning Incentives in Supply Chains," *Harvard Business Review*, November 2004, pp. 94–102.

23. D. Drickhamer, "Looking for Value," *IndustryWeek*, December 2002, pp. 41–43.

24. J. L. Yang, "Veggie Tales," *Fortune,* June 8, 2009, pp. 25–30.

25. J. H. Sheridan, "Managing the Value Chain," *IndustryWeek*, September 6, 1999, p. 3.

26. S. Leibs, "Getting Ready: Your Customers," *IndustryWeek*, September 6, 1999, p. 1.

27. G. Taninecz, "Forging the Chain," *IndustryWeek*, May 15, 2000, pp. 40–46.

28. S. Leibs, "Getting Ready: Your Customers," *IndustryWeek*, September 6, 1999, p. 1.

29. N. Zubko, "Mindful of the Surroundings," *IndustryWeek,* January 2009, p. 38.

30. ASIS International and Pinkerton, *Top Security Threats and Management Issues Facing Corporate America: 2003 Survey of Fortune 1000 Companies*, www.asisonline.org/newsroom/surveys/pinkerton.pdf.

31. J. H. Sheridan, "Managing the Value Chain," *IndustryWeek*, September 6, 1999, p. 4.

32. D. Joseph, "The GPS Revolution: Location, Location, Location," *BusinessWeek Online,* May 27, 2009.

33. S. Anderson, "Restaurants Gear Up for Window Wars," *Springfield News-Leader* (Missouri), January 27, 2006, p. 5B.

34. S. McCartney, "A Radical Cockpit Upgrade Southwest Fliers Will Feel," *Wall Street Journal,* April 1, 2010, p. D1.

35. D. Bartholomew, "Quality Takes a Beating," *IndustryWeek*, March 2006, pp. 46–54; J. Carey and M. Arndt, "Making Pills the Smart

Way," *BusinessWeek*, May 3, 2004, pp. 102–103; and A. Barrett, "Schering's Dr. Feelbetter?" *BusinessWeek*, June 23, 2003, pp. 55–56.

36. T. Vinas, "Six Sigma Rescue," *IndustryWeek*, March 2004, p. 12.

37. J. S. McClenahen, "Prairie Home Companion," *IndustryWeek*, October 2005, pp. 45–46.

38. T. Vinas, "Zeroing In on the Customer," *IndustryWeek*, October 2004, pp. 61–62.

39. W. Royal, "Spotlight Shines on Maquiladora," *IndustryWeek*, October 16, 2000, pp. 91–92.

40. See B. Whitford and R. Andrew, eds., *The Pursuit of Quality* (Perth, UK: Beaumont, 1994).

41. D. Drickhamer, "Road to Excellence," *IndustryWeek*, October 16, 2000, pp. 117–118.

42. Information from International Organization for Standardization, The ISO Survey—*2006*, www.iso.org/iso/survey2006.pdf.

43. "ISO 14000 Essentials," www.iso.org/iso/iso_catalogue/management_and_leadership_standards/environmental_management/iso_14000_essentials.htm (accessed October 7, 2010).

44. "ISO 26000—Social Responsibility," www.iso.org/iso/iso_catalogue/management_and_leadership_standards/social_responsibility.htm (accessed October 7, 2010).

45. G. Hasek, "Merger Marries Quality Efforts," *IndustryWeek*, August 21, 2000, pp. 89–92.

46. M. Arndt, "Quality Isn't Just for Widgets," *BusinessWeek*, July 22, 2002, pp. 72–73.

47. E. White, "Rethinking the Quality Improvement Program," *Wall Street Journal*, September 19, 2005, p. B3.

48. M. Arndt, "Quality Isn't Just for Widgets," *BusinessWeek*, July 22, 2002, pp. 72–73.

49. S. McMurray, "Ford's F-150: Have It Your Way," *Business 2.0*, March 2004, pp. 53–55; "Made-to-Fit Clothes Are on the Way," *USA Today*, July 2002, pp. 8–9; and L. Elliott, "Mass Customization Comes a Step Closer," *Design News*, February 18, 2002, p. 21.

50. E. Schonfeld, "The Customized, Digitized, Have-It-Your-Way Economy," *Fortune*, October 28, 1998, pp. 114–120.

51. Heizer and Render, *Operations Management*, p. 636; and S. Minter, "Measuring the Success of Lean," *Industry Week,* February 2010, pp. 32–35.

52. Heizer and Render, *Operations Management,* p. 636.

Prince Edward Island

Quebec

Saskatchewan

"learning-and-discovery" culture, 94

learning organization. An organization that has developed the capacity to continuously learn, adapt, and change. 265f, **268**

least-preferred co-worker (LPC) questionnaire. A questionnaire that measured whether a leader was task or relationship oriented. **338**

legal-political conditions, 51–52

legal-political environment, 75

legitimate power. The power a leader has as a result of his or her position in an organization. **348**

leverage ratios, 424

licensing. An approach to going global in which a manufacturer gives another organization the right to use its brand name, technology, or product specifications. **73**

line authority. Authority that entitles a manager to direct the work of an employee. **254**–255, 255f, 256f

linear-nonlinear thinking style profile, 176–177

linear programming. A mathematical technique that solves resource allocation problems. **243**–245, 247f

linear thinking style. Decision style characterized by a person's preference for using external data and facts and processing this information through rational, logical thinking. **176**

liquidity ratios, 424

Lisbon Treaty, 66

listening skills, 47

load chart. A modified Gantt chart that schedules capacity by entire departments or specific resources, 239, 240f, 246

locus of control. A personality attribute that reflects the degree to which people believe they control their own fate. **123**

long-term orientation, 78

long-term plans. Plans with a time frame beyond three years. **192**

low external controls, 151

loyalty, 349

M

Malaysia, 79, 352f

the Maldives, 69

management. Coordinating work activities with and through other people so the activities are completed efficiently and effectively. **5**

effectiveness, 5, 5f

efficiency, 5, 5f

functions, 5–7, 6f, 7–8

in a global environment, 74–81

global management. See global environment

history of. See management history

major approaches to, 25f

omnipotent view of management, 36

principles of management, 27, 27t

roles, 7–8, 8f

skills, 8–9, 9f

study of, 15–17

symbolic view of management, 36–37

universality of management, 16, 16f

management by objectives (MBO). A process of setting mutually agreed-upon goals and using those goals to evaluate employee performance. **195**, 195f, 318f

management by walking around. A term used to describe a manager being out in the work area, interacting directly with employees. 415f, **423**

management functions. Planning, organizing, leading, and controlling. 5–7, **6**, 6f

see also specific management functions

controlling, 7

decisions in, 167f

leading, 6

organizing, 6

planning, 6

vs. roles, 7–8

management history

behavioural approach, 29–30

classical approach, 25–28

contemporary approaches, 32–34

early management, 24–25

general administrative theory, 27–28

organizational behaviour (OB), 29, 29f

parameters of managerial discretion, 38f

quantitative approach, 30–32

scientific management, 25–27, 26f

total quality management (TQM), 31, 31f

management information system (MIS). A system used to provide management with needed information on a regular basis. **425**

management roles. Specific categories of managerial behaviour. **7**–8, 7–9, 8f

decisional roles, 7

vs. functions, 7–8

informational roles, 7

interpersonal roles, 7

management science, 30

management skills, 8–9, 9f

manager. Someone who coordinates and oversees the work of other people so organizational goals can be accomplished. **3**

changing job of managers, 12–15

as decision maker, 167–171

entrepreneurial managers, 89

first-line managers, 3

functions of managers, 4, 5–7, 6f, 7–8

and global teams, 404

importance of managers, 2–3

managerial levels, 4f

middle managers, 3

vs. nonmanagerial employee, 3

organizational culture, effect of, 44–45

organizational environment, effect of, 54–56

project manager, 246

top managers, 3

traditional manager, 181

types of managers, 3–4

managerial ethics. See ethics

managerial grid. A two-dimensional grid of leadership behaviours-concern for people and

concern for production-that results in five different leadership styles. 336f, **337**

manager's job

adaptability, importance of, 14

changes in, 12–15

customers, importance of, 12–13

innovation, importance of, 14

social media, importance of, 13–14

sustainability, 14–15

manuals, 317f

manufacturing organizations. Organizations that produce physical goods. **440**–441

Marine Stewardship Council (MSC) certification, 117

market growth, 217

market share, 217

marketplace, 139

Marshall Plan, 70

masculinity, 377

Maslow's hierarchy of needs theory, 362, 362f

mass customization. Providing customers with a product when, where, and how they want it. **451**

mass production. The production of items in large batches. **262**

material artifacts and symbols, 44

matrix structure. An organizational structure that assigns specialists from different functional departments to work on one or more projects. 265f, **266**, 266f

maximax choice, 174

maximin choice, 174

MCC. See multinational corporation (MNC)

McGregor's Theory X and Theory Y, 363

means-ends chain. An integrated network of goals in which the accomplishment of goals at one level serves as the means for achieving the goals, or ends, at the next level. **195**

mechanistic organization. An organizational design that is rigid and tightly controlled. **259**, 260f

mechanistic structures, 259–261

mentoring, 317f

Mercosur, 68

message. A purpose to be conveyed. **278**, 280

Mexico, 67, 79, 305, 377

microchronometer, 27

middle managers. Managers between the first-line level and the top level of the organization who manage the work of first-line managers. **3**

Millennials, 53

minimax choice, 174, 175

minimum-wage employees, 380

Mintzberg's management roles, 7–8, 8f

mission. The purpose of an organization; a statement of an organization's purpose, **196**, 210, 211f

mobile workers, 291

moderately challenging goals, 366

Moneyball, 420

monolingualism, 63

scientific management. An approach that involves using the scientific method to find the "one best way" for a job to be done. 25–27, **26**, 26f

selection
  decision outcomes, 311f
  and ethics, 127
  meaning of, 311–312
  reliability of selection device, 312
  selection devices, 313–314, 313f, 314f
  selection process, 310–311
  validity of selection device, 312

selection devices, 313–314, 313f, 314f

selection process. The process of screening job applicants to ensure that the most appropriate candidates are hired. **310–311**

selective perception, 282

selective perception bias, 177

self-actualization needs. A person's need to grow and become what he or she is capable of becoming. **362**

self-efficacy. An individual's belief that he or she is capable of performing a task. **366**

self-employment, 17

self-managed work teams. A type of work team that operates without a manager and is responsible for a complete work process or segment. 388f, **400**

self-serving bias, 178

selling, 340

sender, 280

Serbia, 66

service jobs, 13

service organizations. Organizations that produce nonphysical outputs in the form of services. **440–441**

service-oriented organizations, 47–48

service profit chain. The service sequence from employees to customers to profit, **428**, **433**

sexual harassment. Any unwelcome behaviour of a sexual nature in the workplace that negatively affects the work environment or leads to adverse job-related consequences for the employee. 322–324, **323**

shared culture, 39

shared values, 120–121, 120f, 149

short-term orientation, 78

short-term plans. Plans covering one year or less. **192**

Silent Spring (Carson), 115

simple structure. An organizational structure with low departmentalization, wide spans of control, authority centralized in a single person, and little formalization. **263**, 264f

Singapore, 79, 125, 378

single-use plan. A one-time plan specifically designed to meet the needs of a unique situation. **192**

situational factors, and cultural change, 153–154

Situational Leadership® theory (SLT). A leadership contingency theory that focuses on followers' readiness. **340–341**, 341f

Six Sigma. A quality standard that establishes a goal of no more than 3.4 defects per million units or procedures. **450–451**

size, and organizational structure, 261–262

skill-based pay. A pay system that rewards employees for the job skills and competencies they can demonstrate. **319**

skill variety. The degree to which a job requires a variety of activities so that an employee can use a number of different skills and talents. **368**, **369**

skilled workers, 251

slack time. The amount of time an individual activity can be delayed without delaying the whole project. **240**

Slovakia, 377

Slovenia, 79

small business. An organization that is independently owned, operated, and financed; has fewer than 100 employees; doesn't necessarily engage in any new or innovative practices; and has relatively little impact on its industry. **89**

social audits, 129–130

social capital, 81f

social enterprises/ventures. Organizations that are started in response to needs within the community. **88**

social groups, 388

social inequality, 52

social loafing. The tendency for individuals to expend less effort when working collectively than when working individually. **394**, 404

social media. Forms of electronic communication through which users create online communities to share ideas, information, personal messages, and other content. **13**
  manager's job, importance to, 13–14
  as marketing tool, 290
  and personal interaction, 294
  role in communication, 285

social need. A need of a segment of society caused by factors such as physical and mental disabilities; language barriers; and cultural, social, or geographical isolation. **111**

social needs. A person's need for affection, belongingness, acceptance, and friendship. **362**

social network structure. The patterns of informal connections among individuals within a group. **405**

social networking sites, 199

social obligation. A firm's engaging in social actions because of its obligation to meet certain economic and legal responsibilities. **110**

social responsibility. A need of a segment of society caused by factors such as physical and mental disabilities; language barriers; and cultural, social, or geographical isolation. 92, 110, **111–113**
  and economic performance, 114–115
  vs. social responsiveness, 112f, 113

social responsiveness. A firm's engaging in social actions in response to some popular social need. **111**, 112f, 113

social return on investment (SROI), 89

social screening. Applying social criteria (screens) to investment decisions. **114**

socialization. The process that helps employees adapt to the organization's culture. **42**, 289

socially responsible management
  see also corporate social responsibility
  classical view, 110
  economic performance, 114–115
  evolution of, 113
  meaning of, 110–113
  social obligation, 110
  social responsibility, 111–113, 112f, 114–115
  social responsiveness, 111, 112f, 113
  socio-economic view, 111–113
  sustainable management practices, 115–118
  values-based management, 119–121

socio-cultural conditions, 52–54

socio-economic view. The view that management's social responsibility goes beyond making profits and includes protecting and improving society's welfare. **111–113**

solidarity, 67

Somalia, 75

South Africa, 79

South Asian Association for Regional Cooperation (SAARC), 69

South Korea, 68, 79

South Sudan, 75

Southern Common Market, 68

Spain, 79, 80

spam, 292

span of control. The number of employees a manager can efficiently and effectively manage. **256–257**, 257f

special-interest groups, 51

specialized terminology, 283

specific environment. The part of the external environment that is directly relevant to the achievement of an organization's goals. **49–51**

specific plans. Plans that are clearly defined and leave no room for interpretation. **192**

Spirit, 152

Sri Lanka, 69

stability strategy. A strategy characterized by an absence of significant change in what the organization is currently doing. **216**

stable environment, 54

staff authority. Positions with some authority that have been created to support, assist, and advise those holding line authority. **255**, 256f

stages of moral development, 122–123, 122f

stakeholders. Any constituencies in the organization's external environment that are affected by the organization's decisions and actions. **55–56**, 56f

standing plans. Ongoing plans that provide guidance for activities performed repeatedly. **192–193**

stars, 217

start-up issues, 93–97

and organizational structure, 262–263

routineness of task technology, 33f

technology-based training methods, 317f

teleconferencing, 317f

telling, 340

temporary employees, 379–380

Thailand, 79, 125

Theory X. The assumption that employees dislike work, are lazy, avoid responsibility, and must be coerced to perform. **363**

Theory Y. The assumption that employees are creative, enjoy work, seek responsibility, and can exercise self-direction. **363**

therbligs. A classification scheme for labelling basic hand motions. **27**

threat of new entrants, 220

threat of substitutes, 220

threats. Negative trends in external environmental factors. **212**

360-degree feedback, 318f

three-needs theory. McClelland's motivation theory, which says that three acquired (not innate) needs-achievement, power, and affiliation-are major motives in work. **364–365**

time of consumption, 279

time series analysis, 235f

time-space constraint, 279

Timmons model of entrepreneurial process, 91, 91f

tolerance of the impractical, 151

top managers. Managers at or near the top level of the organization who are responsible for making organization-wide decisions and establishing the plans and goals that affect the entire organization. **3**

total quality management (TQM). A philosophy of management that is driven by continuous improvement and responsiveness to customer needs and expectations. **31,** 31f, 152

tough economic times, 376

town hall meetings. Informal public meetings whereby information can be relayed, issues can be discussed, or employees can gather to celebrate accomplishments. **286**

TQM. See total quality management (TQM)

traditional goal-setting. An approach to setting goals in which top managers set goals that then flow down through the organization and become subgoals for each organizational area. **194,** 194f

traditional manager, 181

traditional organization, 11f

traditional training methods, 317f

traditional view of conflict. The view that all conflict is bad and must be avoided. **396**

training

employees, 315–317, 316f, 317f

leaders, 353

training methods, 316–317, 317f

trait theories, 334–335

Trans-Pacific Partnership (TPP), 68

transactional leaders. Leaders who lead primarily by using social exchanges (or transactions). **344**

transformational leaders. Leaders who stimulate and inspire (transform) followers to achieve extraordinary outcomes. **344**

transnational or borderless organization. An MNC in which artificial geographical barriers are eliminated. **72**

triple bottom line (TBL), 118

trust. The belief in the integrity, character, and ability of a leader. 47, **349**–350, 350f, 401

Turkey, 65

turnaround strategy. A renewal strategy for situations in which the organization's performance problems are more serious. **217**

turnover, 251, 314, 317

tweets, 275

two-factor theory. Herzberg's theory that intrinsic factors are related to job satisfaction and motivation, whereas extrinsic factors are related to job dissatisfaction. **363**–364, 364f

U

Uganda, 69

uncertainty. A condition in which a decision maker is not certain about the outcomes and cannot even make reasonable probability estimates. **174,** 189

see also environmental uncertainty

uncertainty avoidance, 78, 79

unfreezing, 141

unified commitment, 401

unionization, 305

unit production. The production of items in units or small batches. **262**

United Kingdom, 66, 80

United Nations, 125

United Nations Global Compact, 125, 126f, 127

United States, 66, 67, 76, 79, 80, 90, 305, 377, 378, 403, 404, 429

unity of command. The management principle that each person should report to only one manager. **255,** 256

universality of management. The reality that management is needed in all types and sizes of organizations, at all organizational levels, in all organizational work areas, and in organizations in all countries around the globe. **16,** 16f

universities, 332

University of Iowa studies, 336, 336f

University of Michigan studies, 336f, 337

unrelated diversification. When a company grows by combining with firms in different and unrelated industries. **216**

unskilled workers, 251

unstructured problems. Problems that are new or unusual and for which information is ambiguous or incomplete. **172**

upward communication. Communication that flows upward from employees to managers. **286**–287

US-Central America Free Trade Agreement (CAFTA), 67

US Equal Employment Opportunity Commission (EEOC), 323

V

valence, 373

validity. The proven relationship that exists between the selection device and some relevant job criterion. **312**

value. The performance characteristics, features, and attributes, as well as any other aspects of goods and services for which customers are willing to give up resources. **442**

value chain. The entire series of organizational work activities that add value at each step from raw materials to finished product. **442**

value chain management. The process of managing the sequence of activities and information along the entire value chain. **442**

benefits of, 443

collaboration, 444

coordination, 444

cultural attitudes, 447

employees/human resources, 445–446

goal of, 442–443

importance of, 441–443

leadership, 445

obstacles to, 446–447, 446f

and operations management, 443–447

organizational barriers, 446

organizational culture and attitudes, 446

organizational processes, 444–445

people, 447

required capabilities, 447

requirements of, 443–446, 444f

technology investment, 444

value proposition. . An analysis of the benefits, costs, and value that an organization can deliver to customers and other groups within and outside of the organization, **96**

values. Basic convictions about what is right and wrong. **123**

core values, 42

cultural values, 146

shared values, 120–121, 120f, 149

values-based management. An approach to managing in which managers establish and uphold an organization's shared values. **119**–121

variable costs, 242

variables

cultural variables, 151

human resource variables, 152

innovation variables, 150–152, 150f

structural variables, 150–151

Venezuela, 75

Venice, 24

verbal intonation. An emphasis given to words or phrases that conveys meaning. **279**–280

vertical integration, 215

videoconferencing, 317f